The World Economy

John Williamson and Chris Milner

The World Economy

A Textbook in International Economics

NEW YORK UNIVERSITY PRESS
Washington Square, New York

First published in the USA in 1991 by
NEW YORK UNIVERSITY PRESS
Washington Square,
New York, NY 10003

Library of Congress Cataloging-in-Publication Data

Williamson, John 1937–
　　The world economy : a textbook in international economics / John
Williamson : Chris Milner.
　　　　p.　cm.
　　Includes bibliographical references and index.
　　ISBN 0-8147-9245-6 (cloth)　ISBN 0-8147-9246-4 (pbk)
　　1. International economic relations.　2. Commercial policy.
3. Macroeconomics.　I. Milner, Chris.　II. Title.
HF1359.W55　1991
337—dc20　　　　　　　　　　　　　　　　　91-24958
　　　　　　　　　　　　　　　　　　　　　　　　CIP

Printed and bound in Great Britain

To
Denise, André, Daniel and Theresa

and
Ruth, James and Elizabeth

Contents

III
TRADE POLICY

IV
OPEN-ECONOMY MACROECONOMICS

VI
WORLD ECONOMY

Preface

This book is an adaptation and extension of *The Open Economy and the World Economy*. It is something more than a second edition and something less than a totally original work. The additions and changes are substantial; on the other hand, where there seemed no good reason for changing what one of us had written almost a decade ago, the previous material has been retained with most of its eccentricities intact.

The coverage of the present work has been substantially expanded, primarily by the addition of considerable material on those parts of trade theory that had passed the senior author by. Chris Milner has taken responsibility for venturing into higher-dimensional trade theory, intermediate goods, the product cycle and intra-industry trade, as well as expanding the treatment of commercial policy and revising the chapters on trade and development and the world trading system.

We have also corrected (where necessary), revised and updated the rest of the book. This has involved a sketch of recent developments in how exchange markets work (a new section called 'News, bubbles and chaos'), and a separate appendix on the algebra of the Mundell–Fleming model, in the chapter on flexible exchange rates. The material on real capital flows has been incorporated into the chapter on factor accumulation in the open economy. There are also new treatments of the debt crisis, the European Monetary System, the post-Plaza efforts to build a more structured international monetary system, the payments imbalances of the 1980s and the emerging debate on the international economics of preserving the global environment.

In several other respects the approach of the earlier edition has been consciously maintained.

Small-economy assumption. We retain a major simplification adopted in the previous work that has a minimal cost in terms of relevance for most students: namely, abandonment of the traditional two-country model in favour of the simpler case of the small country that trades with an outside world large enough to be treated as parametric. Since most countries are indeed small in the relevant technical sense for most purposes, students from most countries will find the simpler model to be the one that they will normally need to use. Occasionally, notably where dealing with intra-industry trade, we resort to two-country models, which are appropriate in that context since even small countries mutually adapt their production patterns. In addition, a number of chapters contain short addenda which deal with the large-country case, partly to provide a link to the literature and partly to help students from large countries (by which one means primarily the United States) understand the extra complications that are relevant in understanding the position of their own country in the world economy.

World economy section. A potential trouble with the small-economy approach is that it avoids treating those issues of interdependence that determine what drives the world economy as a whole. To circumvent that danger, a substantial final section is devoted to analysis of the operation of the world economy. This two-stage approach – first analyzing how the individual unit reacts to the parametric whole, then considering what the sum total of those individual reactions implies for the operation of the system – is familiar enough to economists from microeconomic theory.

Simple models. There are various criteria for selecting models, depending on the purpose for which they are to be used: for example, a model to be used for econometric estimation or for projection and simulation needs qualities like realism and comprehensiveness. But models in textbooks are there to help students gain an understanding of how the world works, not to provide blueprints of what to estimate in a Master's thesis. For the former purpose, simplicity is a virtue: a 2×2 model is better than an $n \times n$ model because one can understand what is going on in it. Not only should models be simple, but there is virtue in familiarity: production possibility curves or IS/LM are to be preferred to weird concoctions that have never made it outside the trade literature. Even familiar models have been explained from first principles when introduced, although in a sufficiently succinct way as to be more suitable for the student who has already met them and merely needs the memory jogging than for the student to whom they are completely new.

An applied economics approach. One of us once heard a distinguished economist lament the fact that we have lots of models instead of only one. What rubbish! The world is a complicated place, and hence any one model would be either totally unwieldy or ridiculously inadequate. What the applied economist needs is not a single model but a rich choice, with a sense of the relationship between different models and of the considerations that are relevant in deciding which one should be applied in a particular context. In order to help students develop this feeling, we have included frequent discussion of the circumstances which make one model more applicable than another, of the real-world implications of models, of how worldly events can be interpreted in terms of models, and of stylized facts[1] about model parameters – all based on a conviction that models are there to be used, not to provide aesthetic pleasure or to compete against Latin as a source of mental gymnastics. A theoretical construct whose real-world counterpart one cannot recognize when reading the newspaper is of no more interest than a set of facts undisciplined by a theoretical perspective.

A hint of history. While neither of us claims to be a historian, we believe it important to try and place the analysis within some historical perspective. Hence there is an introductory sketch of how the world economy came to be where it is today. We have also tried to give some idea of how economic theory has evolved, and of the pressures that influenced its evolution, rather than just plucking models out of thin air.

The book is organized in six parts. The first, which is restricted to a single chapter, provides the historical background. The second part covers trade theory, and the third turns to trade policy. The fourth part deals with balance of payments theory and policy, or the macroeconomics of the open economy. The fifth part explores the international dimensions of economic development. The final part studies the world economy.

The primary audience to whom the book is addressed is the one-year advanced undergraduate course in international economics, plus half-year courses in either trade or international monetary economics. We also hope that it may find a role in graduate-level courses, especially where – as in courses on international political economy – the professional pressures to work with highly mathematical models are absent or muted.

Note

1. By a 'stylized fact' economists mean a characterization of what they perceive to be the essential factual aspects of the normal case. For example, it is a stylized fact that import propensities are bigger for small countries than for large ones. That does not mean that the proposition would hold in every pair-wise comparison, but it does imply that it is a strong regularity with important implications.

I

Introduction

This introductory part of the book contains only one chapter, the aim of which is to provide a minimal historical background for the study of international economics. The material is sufficiently non-technical to be read with profit even by students whose professor prefers to plunge straight into theory.

1

A historical perspective

Gross world product (GWP), measured properly on the basis of purchasing power comparisons,[1] amounted to about \$26,000,000,000,000 in 1990. When the modern economic world started to emerge something over 200 years ago, real GWP was perhaps 3 per cent of that. World population has multiplied in the interim more than six times, from some 800 million to around 5.2 billion, while on average output per head has increased almost as much. That average conceals a range from stagnation or worse in some traditional societies to increases of over 2,500 per cent in extreme cases like Sweden or (prior to its invasion by Iraq) Kuwait. The variation in income per head among countries is enormously larger than it was before economic development got under way – which was, in historical terms, not long ago.

About a fifth of world expenditure is now directed at goods (or services) produced abroad – certainly a much higher proportion than 200 years ago. Income earned abroad, migration, tourism and international investment, let alone the international flow of technical knowledge or the production of multinational companies, have all exploded over the last two centuries. Economic interdependence, like development, is a historically recent phenomenon.

The purpose of this book is to enhance understanding of the causes and consequences of that interdependence. We start our study by a sketch of the joint evolution of interdependence and development.

1.1 The industrial revolution, 1760–1850

The modern world started to emerge with the 'industrial revolution', which has traditionally been dated from about 1760. British workers were increasingly concentrated into factories, coal mines and iron works where the technical advances in cotton manufacturing, coal mining and iron smelting could be exploited, in due course by the harnessing of steam. New towns – largely distinct from the medieval cities with their traditional crafts regulated by the guilds – grew up around these workplaces, linked by a growing network of canals. Growth accelerated from perhaps 0.3 per cent per annum before 1750 to around 1.3 per cent by the first half of the nineteenth century.

This was by no means the first time in history that a society had experienced

3

widespread growth sustained for several decades or even centuries. The French economic historian Fernand Braudel (1902–85) tells of a great age of invention in Alexandria between 100 and 50 BC, which even exploited steam as a source of power (Braudel 1984, vol. III, p. 543). The British economic historian Eric Jones (b. 1936) compares the advances in pre-modern Europe with earlier economic progress achieved by the Islamic world united under the Ottoman Empire (which peaked in the early sixteenth century) and with the achievements of China between the eleventh and fourteenth centuries. Europe itself had undergone previous growth spurts, rather widely spread between the eleventh and thirteenth centuries, along an axis from Holland through Germany to Italy from about 1470 to 1535, and in England from 1560 to 1640.

Nor did the industrial revolution strike contemporary observers as particularly revolutionary, let alone as benign. Those familiar with European history had no particular reason to imagine that this growth spurt would go further than its pre-decessors. The term 'industrial revolution' was not coined until about 1840 and did not become standard until as late as 1884 (Braudel 1984, vol. III, p. 537).[2] Real wages declined from about 1750 to 1810. Even when they started to rise, after the end of the Napoleonic wars, it is doubtful whether living standards rose with them, for the new industrial towns imposed an utterly wretched life devoid of even such community support and environmental benefits as the traditional village had offered. According to the measure, real wages surpassed their previous (fifteenth-century) peak only at the end of the nineteenth century.

Perhaps the most interesting question in economic history is why industrialization should have started when and where it did. Some have tended to regard the series of inventions that launched large-scale industry as more or less an accident, which happened to give British capitalists the chance to dominate foreign competition and accumulate capital. Others have placed primary emphasis on the human capital factor, the availability of engineers and entrepreneurs: the German economist-sociologist Max Weber (1864–1920) linked the emergence of the entrepreneurial spirit to the Protestant ethic. Others again have pointed to external factors, such as the riches made from the slave trade or plundered from Bengal in the Seven Years War (1756–63) and the foreign markets ripe for exploitation by whoever first pulled together the capital to exploit the technical advances that would have been feasible anywhere. Sir Arthur Lewis (b. 1915), the West Indian economist and economic historian who won the Nobel prize in 1979, has argued that the decisive factor was the progress of British agriculture, which both released manpower for the factories and created a demand for their production. The Peruvian economist Hernando de Soto (b. 1943) points to a legal framework which opened opportunities to those not born into the aristocracy or a guild, thus allowing the birth of an impersonal, competitive market economy. Eric Jones, while at pains to eschew the simple explanations that attract economists, places much emphasis on the emergence of a political system providing reasonable personal security and open to innovation, with sufficient dispersion of power to permit a competitive economy to develop.

Whatever the combination of reasons that nurtured the industrial revolution, it is clear that by the beginning of the nineteenth century Britain was securely on the way to becoming the world's first industrial country. It was in fact not until well into the century that the proportion of the labour force in agriculture was surpassed by that in industry, but the pace of technical advance and industrial expansion was sustained and built up a cumulative force that Walter Rostow (b. 1916) christened the 'take-off' into self-sustaining growth. Eventually the demand for labour by the modern sector became strong enough to support rising real wages. This contributed to a fall in the birth rate, and, with the demographic transition in train, the road was open for the gradual evolution of a developed society in the sense that we now use the term.

Industrialization started to spread from its British birthplace soon after the beginning of the century of near-peace that was ushered in by the conclusion of the Napoleonic wars in 1815. Before 1850 it was already well under way in Belgium, France and the United States. Canals began to give way to railways. New sectors were mechanized. New products, such as gas, appeared. Growth had become the rule, not the exception.

1.2 The age of capitalism, 1850–1914

The Great Exhibition of 1851 marked the zenith of British industrial pre-eminence. But for the remainder of the nineteenth century, and indeed until the First World War, London remained the centre of a capitalist economic system whose geographical domain constantly expanded.

In the second half of the nineteenth century, industrialization spread to Germany, Italy, Japan, Scandinavia, Austria-Hungary and even, to a limited extent, Russia – a list that includes virtually all the countries presently classified as 'industrialized'. Development with little industrialization, based on the export of primary products to satisfy the growing needs of the industrial 'centre' countries, took off in what became known as the 'countries of recent settlement': Canada, Australia, New Zealand, South Africa and the Southern Cone (Argentina, Chile, Uruguay). Growth without much development, involving the export of primary products but on a scale too small and with too few repercussions on the rest of the economy to overcome Malthusian forces and lead to take-off, occurred at widely scattered places throughout the tropics. Views differ on whether the failure of export growth to stimulate general development in the tropical countries should be attributed to imperialism ('dependency theory') or to the limited scale of the export growth and the shortage of complementary human capital.

International trade has often been called the engine of nineteenth-century growth. Foreign markets were important destinations for the expanding output of British industry: by 1854 Britain was exporting over 20 per cent of its gross national product (GNP) and the British share of world exports of manufactures was more than 40 per cent (Deane and Cole, 1969, p. 33). Exports were important also in sustaining demand in the newly industrializing countries of mid-century – Belgium, France and the United States. They were central to the expansion of the areas of recent settlement in the second half of the century. Without a measure of *laissez-faire* in the industrial centre and the dramatic fall in transport costs following the spread of railways after 1860 and the large-scale introduction of steamships after 1870, the export-led growth that occurred would have been impossible.

There were, however, some countries in which protection to promote import substitution played a role complementary to or more important than that of export expansion. Germany provides the best-known and clearest case, but infant-industry protection was important also in the United States, Japan, Italy, Austria-Hungary and Russia. Where development was based on industrialization, it was typically associated in the early stages with a degree of protection.

Trade was by no means the only way in which international conditions impinged on national growth rates. Unprecedented numbers of migrants moved from Europe to the United States and the lands of recent settlement and also, sometimes less voluntarily, from China and India to tropical countries with low population densities and exploitable natural resources, like Malaya, Mauritius and Kenya. On the other hand, the flow of slaves from Africa to the Americas finally ceased. Capital, overwhelmingly in the form of long-term fixed-interest bonds, moved in vast quantities from the older industrial countries of Western Europe, Britain and France, to the developing countries of the periphery, like the United States, Russia, the areas of recent settlement and the tropics. After the turn of the century Britain was exporting some half of its savings, or 7 per cent of its GNP – an equivalent flow from Japan today would be of the order of $200 billion per annum!

For the last third of the nineteenth century, the world was also increasingly integrated by virtue of its monetary system. Gold had long been used to provide the basis of the coinage in certain countries, but it was only after about 1870 that gold triumphed over silver and the gold standard became the international norm. The gold standard involved countries defining their currencies in gold (thus maintaining fixed exchange rates against one another), holding gold reserves with which to settle deficits with one another, and often using gold coins as well. This system made it easy to settle international debts and thus facilitated the growth of international trade. Orthodoxy also held that the system ensured balance of payments adjustment, since a country losing gold would contract its money supply and this would create pressures of progressively greater intensity towards the restoration of balance (see section 12.1). The gold base of the monetary system meant that extensive gold discoveries (Colorado and California in the 1840s, South Africa in the 1890s) tended to produce periods of inflation, while other periods witnessed downward pressure on prices and considerable distress in trade, but countries sticking to a fixed gold parity were spared major, substantial inflations. The gold base prevented governments doing much to combat crises, which were often quite sharp but at least were rarely prolonged.

It is worth asking why industrialization did not spread even more rapidly during this Golden Age and, in particular, why it barely affected the tropical countries. One reason is certainly the prevalence of colonialism: India, for example, which was industrially quite advanced at the start of the nineteenth century, could not protect its industries because of British control. The textile industry survived on the basis of cheap labour, but other industries were slow to develop. However, even at the height of colonialism there were many countries that were not constrained as India was and most made even less progress. Explanations tend to come back to that same set of factors invoked to explain why Britain was the first country to industrialize: the primitive state of tropical agriculture, which denied a local market to aspiring industrialists; the retention of political power in the hands of landowners with a vested interest in buying cheap imports rather than promoting industrialization; the failure to develop a legal framework that would nurture a competitive economy; political instability; and the lack of technical education and entrepreneurial drive.

1.3 The age of crises, 1914–45

The confident, if still not universal, economic progress of the nineteenth century was rudely shattered by the outbreak of the First World War in 1914. Free trade, free movement of persons, free mobility of capital and the gold standard were progressively replaced in the combatant countries by whatever controls and restrictions were judged expedient to the pursuit of total war.

The war wrought unprecedented physical, as well as human, destruction on the European continent. It led to the downfall of the Tsarist regime and its replacement by the world's first Communist government in the Soviet Union. This new government renounced Russian debts, thus annihilating a large part of France's accumulated foreign wealth. Britain realized a large part of its stock of foreign assets and contracted large debts to finance the war. Countries outside Europe suffered a shortage of imported manufactures and coal from their traditional European suppliers; while this created hardship at the time, it also provided a boost to import-substituting industrialization in a whole range of peripheral countries.

When the carnage was finally over and the world went back to making peace in 1919, the dominant economic aim was that of restoring pre-war normality. Exporters sought their old export markets, but found in many cases that they no longer existed. Capital mobility was restored; however, capital no longer flowed from Britain and France to capital-poor developing countries, but from the new dominant world power, the United States, to (above all) war-ravaged Germany. An attempt was made to restore the gold standard, even with unchanged parities on the part of the United States and Britain, despite the intervening – and differential – inflation; thus condemning Britain to high unemployment throughout the 1920s. Countries like Germany and some of the new states of Eastern Europe (Poland, Austria, Hungary) suffered the world's first experiences of unambiguous hyperinflation. But when they finally stabilized, at least they pegged their exchange rates at competitive levels, thus getting the chance to share in the fleeting prosperity of the late 1920s.

The whole unrealistic attempt to restore the status quo ante was finally shattered in the economic whirlwind of the depression into which the world plunged after 1929. Unemployment mounted to unprecedented levels of 20 or 30 per cent or even more as banks failed, debts were renounced, capital markets dried up, the gold standard was abandoned, competitive devaluation became a vogue and protectionism prevailed. The countries that did least badly out of the 1930s were those (Germany, Britain, Brazil) that jumped most quickly on to the bandwagon of economic nationalism and renounced most decisively the old orthodoxy of the gold standard, combining depreciation and protectionism with the sort of expansionary measures subsequently rationalized by Keynes. Their gains were in part at the expense of those who stuck longest to the gentlemanly rules of a bygone age and gamely imported the unemployment being exported by the beggar-my-neighbour policies of the more ruthless (to use the phrase of the English economist Joan Robinson, 1903–83).

Nationalism and economic collapse fanned the flames that led once more to total war in 1939. To all participants except infantry soldiers, the Second World War proved even more devastating than the first. But even while the fighting was at its peak, there was this time a determination to plan a post-war world conducive to prosperity and development which would give peace a chance. Almost a year before the war ended, a historic conference met at Bretton Woods, New Hampshire, and agreed to establish two international institutions designed to nurture the emergence of a liberal international economic order: the International Monetary Fund (IMF) (see Chapter 19), intended to deal with monetary questions, and the International Bank for Reconstruction and Development, or World Bank (see Chapter 18), whose purpose was to promote a flow of long-term loans for reconstruction and development to replace the international capital market that had vanished in the Great Depression. Plans were also in hand to create an International Trade Organization to prevent a recurrence of the commercial warfare that had occurred in the 1930s (see Chapter 17). The Soviet Union participated in the Bretton Woods conference, and there were hopes that after the war it would not retreat into virtual isolation from the world economy as it had during the inter-war period.

1.4 The great boom, 1945–73

Those hopes were quickly dashed. The Soviet Union did not join the Bretton Woods organizations but instead set about creating Communist governments in Eastern Europe under the umbrella of the Red Army. Relations between East and West quickly deteriorated into the cold war, to the point where the victory of the Chinese Communists in 1949 was interpreted in the West simply as an extension of Russian power. Post-war reconstruction proved even more painful and took much longer than had been expected, and would no doubt have been more difficult still had not the cold war goaded the United States into an unprecedentedly generous aid programme for Western Europe – the European Recovery Programme, or the Marshall Plan as it is more popularly known. The cold war looked like escalating into a third world war with the Berlin blockade of 1949 and the Korean War of 1950–3. At the time it seemed like an extension of the age of crises.

In retrospect 1950 was the darkest hour before the dawn. Political confrontation began to ease almost imperceptibly until the death of Stalin in 1953. As relaxation occurred, it became apparent that the hard years of reconstruction had been well spent in preparing a solid base for future growth. Liberalization of intra-European trade under the auspices of the Organization for European Economic Co-operation (OEEC) and with the stimulus of the European Payments Union (EPU) yielded major benefits in terms of increased efficiency, growth and welfare. By the mid-1950s the period of post-war reconstruction was over and the biggest boom in world history was recognizably under way. The recovery was formalized by the declaration of currency convertibility made jointly by the leading European countries at the end of 1958, and by the subsequent transformation of the OEEC into the Organization for Economic Co-operation and Development (OECD).

Between 1960 and 1973, when the boom ended under the twin pressures of accelerating inflation and the first major oil price increase, GWP grew by something like 5.5 per cent per annum. This may be compared with the estimated growth of British output of 2.5 per cent per *decade* in the early eighteenth century or with a growth of probably something over 1.5 per cent per annum in GWP in the previous great period of world expansion from the 1860s to 1914.[3] The spurs to this growth may be found in unprecedented technological dynamism, cheap energy, expansion of education, rather successful application of Keynesian concepts of economic management and increasing interdependence. Costs of this growth subsequently became evident in the form of increasing pollution and environmental destruction, as well as accelerating inflation in the later stages. Nevertheless, the general view was that such ills were curable with enough attention (and resources), and that the main causes for concern were the danger that expansion might some day be halted by resource constraints and the inadequate participation of some countries in the fruits of growth.

In fact, while many countries fretted about being left behind – from the United States worrying about Sputnik to the developing countries (LDCs) who complained of an ever-widening gap – the growth was extraordinarily generally dispersed. As the technologically leading country with the fewest opportunities for shifting resources out of low-productivity traditional sectors to high-productivity modern sectors, it was not at all surprising that the United States should grow more slowly than most other countries; but it grew more rapidly than before. Europe, stimulated by the formation of the European Economic Community (EEC) in 1958, continued right into the early 1970s to grow at rates that were initially regarded as a freak maintainable only while making up ground lost during the war. Japanese growth was without historical precedent, over 10 per cent per annum from 1960 to 1973 and still accelerating in the late 1960s, thus taking the country from the stage of semi-industrialization to affluence in a mere quarter-century. The Communist countries experienced growth that, even if not quite as rapid as the outpacing of capitalism suggested by the official statistics, was undoubtedly fast, especially in the 1950s. Nor were the developing countries as a group left behind. Their growth got under way more slowly, partly because there was little leeway to catch up as in the war-torn industrialized countries, partly because they lacked an educated labour force waiting to be deployed, partly because economic development rarely became a priority until political independence had been achieved, and perhaps partly because too many developing countries pursued an import substitution strategy appropriate for the economic warfare of the 1930s rather than the export promotion strategy possible in a world boom (see Chapter 15). But get under way it did, so that their average growth rate overtook that of the developed countries in the late 1960s, and even per capita growth was more rapid in the 1970s. Of course, this growth was unequally distributed, with the oil exporters enjoying a privileged position even before 1973 and East Asia and Latin America doing substantially better than South Asia and Africa. Nevertheless, for the first time in history, growth became the global norm.

Trade became once more, as it had been in the nineteenth century but had ceased to be during the age of crises, an engine of growth. Obviously, increased export demand cannot explain the growth of the system as a whole, since the world is a closed economy; but for individual countries the stimulus provided by external demand was typically central to their being caught up in the general expansion. The volume of world trade multiplied almost four times between 1955 and 1973. The most dynamic components were interchange of manufactures *among* the developed countries, stimulated by regional trade liberalization, especially within the EEC, and general tariff reduction under the auspices of the General Agreement on Tariffs and Trade (GATT) (see Chapter 17); the export of oil by those countries blessed with abundant supplies; and, in the later years, exports of relatively unsophisticated manufactures by some of the developing countries to the developed countries. Exports of primary products other than oil continued to suffer cyclical fluctuations in price, and demand was relatively stagnant between the Korean boom in 1950–1 and 1973.

Capital mobility also played an important role in generating growth. Initially the major forms of international capital flows were foreign aid and World Bank lending to the developing countries, and direct foreign investment by multinationals (mainly with a United States base) in both developed and developing countries. This last form of lending first emerged in the late nineteenth century, became important with the development of differentiated products incorporating technical and managerial know-how in the inter-war period, and boomed in the 1950s. The distinctive characteristic of direct investment is that the investor retains managerial control and thus makes available on an equity basis intangible capital (patents, know-how, trademarks, etc.) rather than just cash. It is because of this that the share of output controlled by multinationals continued growing in the 1970s despite rather stagnant flows of finance: much direct investment is now financed by retained earnings or local borrowing, but the decisive advantage provided by transnationality, the ability to draw upon a pool of intangible capital generated by other companies of the group in the outside world, is still present. Foreign borrowing, on the other hand, increasingly took the form of bank credits, typically from the Eurodollar market that, to general surprise, started to emerge in the late 1950s (see section 18.1). For ten years or so the borrowers from this new international capital market were overwhelmingly from the developed countries, but LDC borrowing also began on a significant scale in the late 1960s.

As the European boom ran up against labour constraints in the late 1960s, it was sustained by an influx of *Gästarbeiter* (guest workers) from the Mediterranean area. Emigrants' remittances suddenly became a major source of foreign exchange for an increasing number of countries. Nor was this temporary migration the only form of international mobility of persons to assume economic importance: increasing affluence led to a boom in tourist expenditures.

Throughout these years of unprecedented and almost uninterrupted prosperity, there were voices warning of the fragility of the good times. The reasons given varied, from the insidious effects of inflation to the danger of a new depression, from strangulation by pollution to the exhaustion of key natural resources or the inadequacy of food production, from the breakdown of the international monetary system to revolutionary explosion – not to mention the threat of nuclear war. The prophets of doom could not all be right about the precise shock that would bring the boom to an end, but they were correct in warning that it would not go on forever. One can identify two or possibly three factors that in the event contributed to the decisive slowdown which started in 1974.

1. A marked acceleration in inflation. This gathered pace slowly through the 1960s as inflationary wage expectations became entrenched, and received renewed impetus from the deficit financing of the Vietnam War in the United States and, to a lesser extent, from French appeasement of the 1968 quasi-revolution and from increased expenditures on such worthy aims as pollution control. Inflation was generalized by the attempt to hold together the pegged exchange-rate system inherited from Bretton Woods and finally got out of hand during the massive simultaneous world boom of 1973 with its rocketing primary product prices. To combat the inflation, policy had already turned severely restrictive in the major industrial countries before the end of 1973.

2. Following the Arab–Israeli War of October 1973, the Organization of Petroleum Exporting Countries (OPEC) quadrupled the oil price and thereby transferred something like 2 per cent of GWP from the consumers to the producers of oil. The immediate effect was to intensify both inflation and recession, as well as to create balance of payments disequilibria of unprecedented size which added to the general uncertainty (see Chapter 20).

3. More controversially, some would add the long-predicted breakdown of the Bretton Woods system. This occurred in stages: the two-tier gold market in 1968, United States' renunciation of gold convertibility of the dollar in 1971, and finally the abandonment of pegged in favour of floating exchange rates in early 1973. In that year it also became apparent that the attempt to agree on a successor system to that designed at Bretton Woods was going to fail.

1.5 The triumph of the market economy, 1974–89

The end of the world boom in 1973 ushered in a troubled era. World growth slowed down from its average 5.5 per cent per annum prior to 1974 to around 3 per cent. Given that world population continued to grow at around 2 per cent, this implied a drastic cut in the average rate of growth of per capita income.

The immediate cause of this deceleration was a combination of the deflationary policies introduced to combat the accelerating inflation of the early 1970s and the oil price increase of late 1973. These induced the most severe global recession since the Second World War, in 1975. This did not last long, but policy-makers realized only slowly that they could not return to the status quo ante. In the developed countries, inflation stabilized on a much higher plateau in the second half of the 1970s while growth never returned to previous levels, principally because the opportunities for easy growth in Western Europe and Japan were exhausted as they caught up with the technological level of North America. Initially the developing countries did rather better in terms of maintaining growth, but only at the cost of a rapidly increasing level of debt: the whole of the 'oil deficit' – the counterpart of OPEC's surplus – was passed on to the middle-income developing countries as the world emerged from the 1975 recession.

When the oil price lurched up again in 1979, the developed countries decided that they were not prepared to permit the rate of inflation to be ratcheted up again. Instead, led by the newly appointed Chairman of the US Federal Reserve Board, Paul Volcker (b. 1927), they decided to pay whatever price was needed to wind inflation down again. That price proved to be heavy. Europe and North America, and the world as a whole, suffered in 1980–2 the most severe recession since the Great Depression, and Europe recovered only slowly (talk of 'Eurosclerosis' was heard at least until 1987). The middle-income developing countries initially tried to borrow their way through the 1980–2 recession as they had done in 1975, but their higher debt levels interacted with a recession-induced cut in their debt-servicing capacity to produce the debt crisis that started in August 1982.

Performance differed dramatically across regions in the 1980s. Japan largely avoided recession and continued to grow more rapidly than the other industrial countries (with essentially zero inflation) even as it surpassed US levels of productivity in a number of industries. The United States recovered from recession quickly, but at the cost of a massive current account deficit that raised questions about the sustainability of its recovery. Europe was much slower in resuming robust growth, which came only in 1988 after agreement to 'complete the internal market' of the European Community by 1992.

Differences were even starker among the developing countries. East and South-East Asia boomed. South Asia also improved, if modestly, on its past performance. But west of the Pakistan–Iran border the picture was sombre. The Middle East's prosperity dimmed as oil prices fell, first modestly in 1981 and then precipitously in 1986. Latin America suffered a 'lost decade' following the outbreak of the debt crisis: per capita income fell almost 10 per cent during the 1980s, a stunning setback compared to the gains of about 30 per cent in the 1960s and 40 per cent in the 1970s. Africa was the saddest case of all: per capita income was already declining in the 1970s, and by 1990 it was about back to where it had been at the time of independence some three decades earlier.

The other major development of the 1980s was the collapse of the centrally planned economies. Back in the 1950s the claim of communism to be the wave of the future looked entirely plausible, as those economies grew faster than the market economies. Defenders of free markets typically argued the case for their system as a support for individual liberty rather than on account of its superior efficiency. In the 1960s the two systems delivered roughly equal growth. In the 1970s growth declined more in the East than in the West, despite significant borrowing. In the 1980s, growth collapsed. China was the exception that proved the rule: its strong growth performance up to 1989 was clearly linked to the liberalization undertaken at the start of the decade.

The collapse of Communist rule in Eastern Europe in 1989, and the determination of the successor governments to embrace market economics as well as political democracy, was the culmination of a decade that had been marked by an increasing conviction that economic growth was primarily the result of institutions and policies supportive of individual initiative responding to market forces. At the start of the decade the cause of the competitive market economy was still sullied by its association with the military dictatorships in Argentina and Chile. Then Margaret Thatcher launched the first drive for privatization, soon after she took office in 1979. In 1981 President Reagan came to office, embracing 'the magic of the market'. The Bretton Woods institutions exploited this change in the political climate to propagate market economics more actively. Before long left-of-centre governments – in Australia, New Zealand and Spain – were also liberalizing their economies.

By the end of the decade it seemed overwhelmingly clear that the key to progress lay in devolving both opportunities and responsibilities to individuals, giving them the education to enable them to respond and ensuring that they confront price incentives that give them a personal interest in actions that also contribute to the social good. Hernando de Soto argued powerfully that Peru impoverished itself by regulating vast numbers of entrepreneurs into the informal sector where they neither could compete effectively nor were expected to share the burden of supporting the state. Economists found massive evidence of the wastes generated by the diversion of talent from productive to rent-seeking activities. The countries that prospered most were not the resource-rich oil exporters but the resource-poor East Asian new industrial countries (NICs).[4] Africa's plight was linked to the existence of myriad tiny states seeking semi-autarchy and spurning market forces, with performance not varying perceptibly depending on whether that rejection was motivated by paternalism or greed. Above all, the market-oriented West had clearly outperformed the Communist East, to the point where the latter decided to emulate rather than compete. Adam Smith had, at least for the time being, triumphed over Karl Marx.

1.6 The future

Even if 'history has ended', in the strictly limited sense of Fukuyama (1989) – who thus described what he interpreted as the definitive victory of liberalism over the various totalitarian ideologies with which it had wrestled for two centuries – it seems most unlikely that mankind will suffer from a shortage of challenges in future years. Three or four issues seem likely to dominate the 1990s.

  1. A number of former centrally planned economies are attempting to convert

themselves into market economies. Paradoxically, there had never been any intellectual effort to think through what would be implied in such an exercise comparable to the treatises on the transition to socialism that turn out to have been wasted effort. Many developing countries, in Latin America and perhaps elsewhere as well, may make a similar effort to transform their traditional ('mercantilistic', according to Hernando de Soto) economic systems into a more competitive model.

2. The end of the cold war will make the world even less hegemonic than in the past. If a coherent international order is to survive, and it would seem more necessary than ever in the light of the globalization of production and finance, it will have to be on the basis of shared leadership. The emergence of economic summits and the Group of 7 may be seen as initial attempts to respond to this need, but they have not yet resulted in a robust system of global economic management.

3. The late 1980s witnessed the emergence of widespread concern about the global environment. This had already become a major new area of international negotiation by 1989, when it dominated discussion at the summit meeting. But much remains to be done to put in place the international mechanisms needed to deflect the dangers now perceived.

4. Although there is not much sign of it in 1990, one may hope that at some stage the world will resolve that it can no longer tolerate mass poverty and will initiate an effort to reinvigorate development.

1.7 Summary

Economic development and increasing economic interdependence have evolved simultaneously since Adam Smith first explained the benefits of a market economy and the modern economic world started to emerge in the late eighteenth century. This is not entirely coincidental: development is fostered by interdependence in a range of ways, involving trade (export-led growth, allocative efficiency, competition), capital flows, migration and the transfer of technology. Both the periods of great world prosperity, in the late nineteenth century and after the Second World War, were marked by a functioning international system that enabled individual countries to grow by integrating themselves into the world economy. By contrast, a sick international system such as that of the 1930s makes it far more difficult for the component nations to prosper. In 1990 the world seems to be more committed than ever before to the concept of the market economy, but it remains to be seen whether this will be embodied in an international regime that will allow markets to function to best advantage.

1.8 Bibliography

Any student who has not taken a course dealing with the economic history of his or her own country should make it a priority to find and read a book that deals with the topic.

Stimulating discussions of why some countries developed while others did not can be found in Jones (1981, 1988) and Lewis (1978). Hartwell (1971) also touches on this theme. The three volumes of Braudel (1984) provide a massive amount of information on the four centuries that led up to the emergence of the modern economy, and Crafts (1985) gives a careful account of the industrial revolution. Gerschenkron (1962) provided the classic statement of the 'convergence thesis' (that backward countries can be expected to catch up once they adopt appropriate institutions and policies), which implicitly underlies much that is argued in the text; see Landes (1990) for the contention that this is over-optimistic.

The classic treatment of the role of trade as the engine of growth in the late nineteenth century is to be found in Ragnar Nurkse's 1959 Wiksell lectures (Nurkse 1959). Rostow (1958) has been much criticized for his zeal in attempting to force diverse historical experiences into a common mould of five stages of economic growth, but the idea of take-off into self-sustaining growth is nevertheless worthwhile. Ashworth (1962) provides a general history of the international economy since 1850. Hernando de Soto (1989) deals mainly with the informal sector in Peru, but he touches on the displacement of mercantilism by the market economy in Europe.

Notes

1. The most common method of adding up GDP figures to form an international aggregate is to multiply each country's GDP expressed in its national currency by its exchange rate against some common currency (in practice the US dollar). This procedure suggests a 1990 GWP of about $22 trillion. However, this method yields a severe and systematic underestimate of the income of the poorer countries, for reasons explained in section 14.2. The alternative involves making detailed comparisons of purchasing power in different countries, as has now been done by the UN and World Bank-sponsored International Comparisons Project headed by Irving Kravis at the University of Pennsylvania. The estimate quoted in the text is based on an extrapolation of the results yielded by that project (Summers and Heston 1988).
2. It now seems to be going out of fashion again.
3. This very rough estimate is based on a combination of the growth rates for the main progressive countries cited by Kuznets (1956, p. 13), together with guesstimates for the remainder.
4. Hong Kong, Korea, Singapore and Taiwan: also variously known as the new industrial economies (NIEs), the Gang of Four, the four tigers and the four dragons.

II

Trade theory

This part of the book deals with trade theory, sometimes called barter theory or real trade theory. The analysis is microeconomic, and is conducted according to the customary rules of the game of micro theory, namely that macroeconomic equilibrium (full employment and payments equilibrium) is maintained.

Some professors prefer to teach macro theory before micro on the ground that the more apparent relevance of the analysis to real-world problems makes it easier to motivate students. Our view is that this is outweighed by the greater importance that micro foundations have in permitting an appreciation of macro analysis, as opposed to the need to appreciate macro assumptions in order to understand micro. For those who disagree, Part IV can be studied before Part II without undue difficulty. The problem of irrelevance is best tackled by counter-example, by discussing the implications of supposed abstractions like the Stolper-Samuelson or Rybczynski theorems.

2

Comparative advantage

The science of economics, like the phenomenon of economic growth, took off in the second half of the eighteenth century. At that time the conventional wisdom on foreign trade was derived from the writings of the mercantilist school. Although economists nowadays tend to hurl the epithet 'mercantilist' at their opponents as a term of abuse, it is worth devoting a little time to understanding the doctrines of the school, as is done in the first section of the chapter. The second section develops a model that represents the idea of *absolute advantage* as providing the basis for trade, in accordance with the ideas of the founding father of modern economics, the great Scottish economist Adam Smith (1723–90). The third section then shows that this model needs only minor reinterpretation in order to represent the far weaker condition that a country have a *comparative advantage* in production – an insight originally due to the English economist David Ricardo (1772–1823), usually counted as the founder of modern trade theory. Finally the fourth section considers why differences in comparative advantage may arise, and how different sources of specialization can be used to explain modern trade flows.

2.1 Mercantilism

Mercantilists argued that the attraction of trade lay in the opportunity that it offered of earning a surplus in the balance of payments. Exports are a blessing since they stimulate industry and lead to an import of the precious metals, gold and silver (which mercantilists identified with true wealth, as real estate agents in the old gold mining area of Colorado still do). Imports are a burden since they reduce the demand for the products of domestic industry and drain away bullion. The policy advice offered by mercantilists was that exports and production should be encouraged by state support and subsidies, while imports should be discouraged by protectionist restrictions especially in industries of strategic importance.

These views are not wholly absurd. There are times when demand does fall short of the capacity to produce and hence when higher demand stemming from more exports or fewer imports is to be welcomed. There are times when a country is having difficulty balancing its overseas accounts and hence welcomes a surplus in foreign trade. Even when a country has no immediate need for the funds earned by a surplus, it may like to accumulate them with an eye to the future flexibility this gives. This was a potent consideration in the eighteenth century when a good stock of bullion enhanced a country's ability to finance foreign wars, which were a more agreeable pastime for princes than having to defend their native soil. Again, protecting industries of strategic importance is not absurd so long as there is a probability of war. Finally, while the mercantilists erred analytically in associating a high *level* of the money supply – caused by past imports of bullion – with prosperity, the error is one shared with naive Keynesianism; both the mercantilist and the Keynesian position can be given an element of respectability by recognizing that it is the *increase* in the money supply that has stimulating effects on business.

One can therefore find situations and senses in which most of the mercantilist positions are defensible. The problem with mercantilism is that it missed the main point of what trade is about and thereby failed to recognize that its conclusions were valid only in certain cases rather than in general. As with so many other areas of economics, the main point was established once and for all by Adam Smith in his opus *The Wealth of Nations* (1776). He showed that voluntary exchange between countries brings benefits to both, without the need for one to have a surplus (or the other a deficit). This demonstration did not banish mercantilist sentiments from the world, but it did draw a sharp dividing line between the populist politicians and their like who have continued to talk in such terms to the present day and professional economists who learned to discriminate between the situations in which a surplus is a national blessing and those in which it is not.

2.2 Absolute advantage

Adam Smith presented a very simple and intuitive theory to explain how trade could benefit both participants. He supposed that one country could produce a certain good – let us call it M and think of it as machines or manufactures – better than another country, while that second country could produce some other product X – think of it as a primary product extracted from nature – better than the first. Obviously, if both countries concentrate their production on the good in which they enjoy an absolute advantage and then export that good to their trading partner, they can both consume more than if they refuse to trade. To increase consumption is the fundamental object of trading.

While it is very simple to understand Smith's argument intuitively without any formal analysis, further developments demand mastery of the analytical tools of the trade. We therefore proceed to construct a formal model that embodies the assumption of absolute advantage, using the tools of modern theory rather than the arithmetical examples that classical authors used.

Postulate two countries, U and W, with U as *us* (our country) and W the rest of the *world*. Clearly this means that country W is going to be very large relative to U. In fact, like the individual firm or consumer in a perfectly competitive market, U will be able to trade as much as it likes at the parametric prices determined by competition in W.[1]

Suppose that W has an absolute advantage in the production of M. This means that the input requirement per unit of output in the M industry is less in W than in U. Suppose also that there is only one scarce factor of production, labour, and that there are constant returns to scale. This means that it is possible to summarize the production technology in a single parameter, the quantity of labour required to produce a unit of output (an input–output coefficient). Call this parameter l_m in the home country U and l_m* in the foreign country W. Then the assumption that W has an absolute advantage in the production of M implies that $l_m* < l_m$.

Similarly, U having an absolute advantage in the production of X implies that $l_x <$ l_x*, where l_x and l_x* are respectively the home and foreign labour inputs per unit of output of X, with labour the only scarce input and constant returns to scale.

Denote the size of the labour force available in the home country U by L. Then if the whole labour force were to be devoted to the production of X, it would be possible to produce L/l_x. Similarly, if country U concentrated all its resources on the production of M, it could produce L/l_m of M. Because of the linear technology (only one scarce factor and constant returns to scale), deployment of half the labour force in X and the other half in M would result in a production level of half the maximum possible production of X *and* half the maximum possible production of M. In other words, that point would lie midway on the straight line connecting L/l_x and L/l_m. Reflection will show that any other division of the total labour force L between the X and M industries would also yield a point on the straight line connecting L/l_x and L/l_m. In other words, the production possibility curve, or transformation curve, is in the linear model a straight line, as shown in Figure 2.1

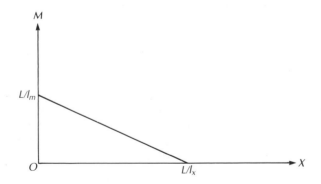

Figure 2.1 Transformation curve in the home country (U)

What would the equilibrium in such an economy look like if the economy were closed (that is, if there were no trade)? As usual in microeconomics, equilibrium is determined by the interaction between demand and supply factors, the latter represented by the transformation curve already constructed. We shall assume that the demand side can be represented by a community or social indifference curve (I)

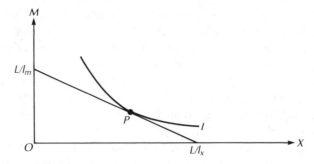

Figure 2.2 Equilbrium in the closed economy (U)

with all the usual properties of indifference curves.[2] Such a curve is introduced in Figure 2.2

Obviously equilibrium would occur at point P, the point of production and consumption. Furthermore, the relative price of X has to be equal to the relative cost of production: $p_x/p_m = l_x/l_m$. Graphically, this relative price is represented by the slope of the transformation curve.[3]

So much for equilibrium in economy U in autarchy. Consider next the situation in the large country W. It also will have a straight-line transformation curve, with a slope equal to l_x^*/l_m^*. Since by the pattern of absolute advantage we have postulated $l_x^* > l_x$ and $l_m^* < l_m$, it is certainly true that $l_x^*/l_m^* > l_x/l_m$: that is, the transformation curve in country W is steeper than that in U. Furthermore, the slope of the transformation curve in W will represent the relative price prevailing there. But, assuming that there is free trade and zero transport costs,[4] competition will ensure that the same price prevails in both U and W. Since W is by assumption large relative to U, the price that will prevail in both countries is that determined by W's costs of production. This means that U gets the opportunity of trading with W at W's prices.

The relative price at which a country trades is called the *terms of trade*, sometimes referred to as the *commodity terms of trade*. It is measured by the price of exports divided by the price of imports. In the example analyzed here, country U will export the primary product X and import the manufactured good M, so that the terms of trade will be represented by p_x/p_m. It may be easier to remember that X is the exportable and M is the importable good.

Figure 2.2 has to be modified to reflect trading possibilities to see what happens when country U is opened up to foreign trade. This is done in Figure 2.3. Given that country U can buy or sell as much as it likes at the fixed terms of trade determined by production costs in the large country W, this is very simple. The terms of trade are represented by a (negative) slope, with steeper slopes representing more favourable terms of trade (that is, higher relative prices for exports). The country can trade along any line with the slope that represents the terms of trade. In particular, it can trade along PC, which is exactly what it will do. Since the economy is open to foreign trade, production and consumption do not have to coincide as they did in the closed economy. Given the terms of trade, the optimal point for production is P, since this

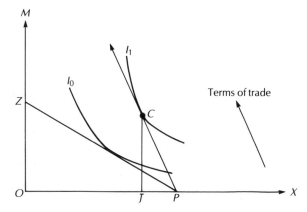

Figure 2.3 Equibrium in the open economy (U)

enables the economy to reach higher consumption levels by trading up PC than would be attainable by producing at any other point on the transformation curve (let alone at any point within the production possibility frontier). U will therefore specialize in production of the good X in which it has an absolute advantage.[5]

Consumers also face prices equal to the terms of trade. Their utility is maximized where the indifference curve is tangential to the trading line, so that C represents the point of consumption. Since U is no longer producing any M, its entire consumption, equal to CJ, has to be imported. The country pays for these imports by exporting a part of its production of X equal to JP, the remainder (OJ) being consumed at home.[6]

It is clear that country U has unequivocally benefited from the opening of the economy and its consequent specialization in production of the good in which it has an absolute advantage. This can be seen by noting that the consumption point C lies on an indifference curve I_1 that is higher than I_0, the highest that is attainable under autarchy. Note also two important implications of this result. First, country U's gains from trade are not at the expense of country W, indeed, mutually beneficial trade is possible given suitable terms of trade. Second, welfare-improving trade is compatible with balanced trade: there is a motive to specialize and trade to where the value of imports is equal to the value of exports.

2.3 Comparative advantage

Was it really worth all that trouble to establish formally that a country able to produce one type of good with fewer resources than another can gain by concentrating on the production of that good and then exporting part of its output to buy a good that another country can make with fewer resources than would be required for domestic production?

If that case, of absolute advantage, were the only one for which the analysis held good, the answer would surely be no. But in fact it is now very easy to see that this is not true. In constructing Figure 2.3 we made use of the fact that $l_x^*/l_m^* > l_x/l_m$ so that *PC* is steeper than *PZ*. We argued that $l_x^*/l_m^* > l_x/l_m$ because $l_x^* > l_x$ and $l_m^* < l_m$. But these conditions are by no means necessary. It would be possible for $l_x^* > l_x$ and $l_m^* > l_m$: that is, for our country to have an absolute advantage in the production of *both* goods, but for l_x^*/l_m^* still to exceed l_x/l_m. In that case we would get exactly the same diagram as Figure 2.3, and hence the whole analysis would remain valid: our country's producers would still have an incentive to specialize in the production of X, the exportation of part of which would still permit the country to buy enough M to make consumers better off. Or it would be equally possible for $l_x^* < l_x$ and $l_m^* < l_m$: that is, for our country to have an absolute *dis*advantage in the production of both goods, but as long as l_x^*/l_m^* still exceeded l_x/l_m, the diagram, the analysis and the conclusions would all remain valid.

What the argument in the preceding paragraph shows is that it is not *absolute* advantage that determines the direction of and the possibility of benefiting from trade but rather *comparative* advantage. Our country has a comparative advantage in the production of X so long as $l_x^*/l_m^* > l_x/l_m$. Whenever that condition holds, our country has to give up less M to produce an extra unit of X than does country W. In other words, the *opportunity cost* of producing X is less in country U than in country W. That is enough to give U an incentive to produce and export X in return for M, whether it be absolutely more productive or less productive in all goods than W – as well as in Adam Smith's case where each country has an absolute advantage in the production of one good.

On the other hand, suppose that l_x^*/l_m^* were equal to l_x/l_m. Then the trade opportunity line *PC* in Figure 2.3 would coincide with the transformation curve *PZ* and trade would be pointless since it would not enable consumers to achieve any higher indifference curve. That is, of course, the case in which a country has no comparative advantage to exploit. But the worst thing that can happen is that the country lacks any comparative advantage – it cannot suffer a comparative disadvantage in everything, as is sometimes implied by the economically illiterate.

There is also the possibility of $l_x^*/l_m^* < l_x/l_m$. In that case U would have a comparative advantage in the production of M, and Figure 2.3 would need modifying to show a set of trade possibility lines flatter than the transformation curve. It is important to figure out what the equilibrium would then look like.

The addition to the argument made in this section looks very simple when the model has been set up. But of course Adam Smith and his successors did not have the benefit of modern analytical techniques – they were still arguing in verbal terms or at most with the help of arithmetical examples. It was some forty years after the publication of Adam Smith's *Wealth of Nations* before Ricardo pointed out that mutually beneficial trade required only the weak condition of *comparative* advantage rather than the strong condition that each country have an absolute advantage in something.

2.4 Sources of comparative advantage

The immediate cause of international exchange of goods and services is the existence (pre-trade) of inter-country differences in the price or quality of competing goods. There are a large number of demand and supply factors which may account for these inter-country differences. In later chapters the resulting diversity of models of trade will be illustrated. Various models emphasize different sources of comparative advantage. Countries will tend to specialize in the products of specific industries, or of a certain product range or of a certain stage of production, and export those products which in advance of trade have the lowest relative cost of production. Differences of relative costs between countries are in turn the product of differences in the production or supply characteristics of countries. In other words, 'dissimilarity' of supply or production conditions between countries is a source of comparative advantage and therefore of trade.

Of course, given the complexities of the real world, there are likely to be a large range of inter-country differences in supply conditions that simultaneously influence relative costs of production. Empirical studies (e.g. Hufbauer 1970; Leamer 1974) demonstrate that the commodity composition of the exports of developed and developing countries is significantly correlated with a range of national attributes such as resource endowments and technological factors. Indeed, this evidence might be interpreted as supporting the view that actual international flows are 'explained' by an amalgam of theories. Specific theories tend to concentrate, however, on a single source of 'dissimilarity' or comparative advantage.

Classical theory, including the Ricardian model, isolated differences in technology or labour productivities between countries as the source of trade. Recall that in Figure 2.3 country U has a comparative advantage in the production of X if the condition $l_x^*/l_m^* > l_x/l_m$ is satsified, i.e. the *relative* amount of labour required to produce a unit of X in U is less than in the other country. Alternatively, we may express this condition in relative productivity terms. A difference in technology between the countries means that the output of good X from a unit of labour in country U is *relatively* higher than from a unit of labour in the other country. The condition has in effect been stated in terms of the reciprocals of the technical coefficients (l_i). If all costs are accounted for by labour, commodities exchange for each other in a ratio that reflects labour inputs or productivity characteristics. If twice as many person-hours are needed to produce a unit of M as to produce a unit of X in one economy, then prior to trade the price of M under competitive conditions is double that of X. Indeed, given the assumption of constant returns – the number of person-hours required per unit of output remains constant as output expands – the (relative) supply curve $(S_{x/m})$ is horizontal in the Ricardian trade model.

Consider Figure 2.4. Pre-trade (relative) price differentials between countries are wholly determined by supply or technological factors. (Demand plays no role in influencing relative prices.) Competitive equilibrium requires for each good (i) that $l_i.w = p_i$, and therefore the relative price of X (p_x/p_m) in Figure 2.4 is determined by relative costs of production $(l_x w/l_m w)$. The pattern of trade is determined by these technologically determined differences between countries in relative costs of production. Country U is an exporter of X when its *relative* supply curve ($S_{x/m}$) is lower than that of country W ($^*S_{x/m}$). (The diagram also means that W will be an exporter of M.) Indeed, in this simple formulation of the model, and with zero transport costs, there is an incentive for complete specialization of production with the opening of trade.

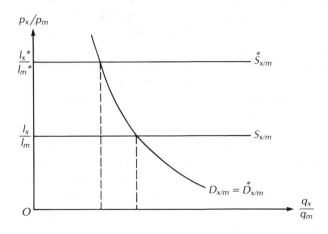

Figure 2.4 Relative costs and prices in the Ricardian model

Ricardian theory, in its original formulation, was based on 'the labour theory of value'. In its more modern presentation (here) we capture the principles in production function terms, where labour is the only input or factor of production. We would be reluctant, however, to attempt to operationalize a model where (homogeneous) labour is the only factor of production. But therein lies a fundamental problem of testing the Ricardian hypothesis: namely, that export patterns (the direction and commodity composition) are deterministically related to labour productivities. Consider the first serious empirical testing of the Ricardian model by MacDougall (1951, 1952). MacDougall identified a clear tendency for the USA and UK to capture a larger share of (third) export markets as labour productivity increased relative to wage costs. (Similar correlations between export shares and labour productivities have been identified in later studies.)[7] But, given that there are many factors of production and that endowment of factors varies between countries, the cause of these labour productivity differences internationally is ambiguous. Labour productivity may differ between two countries with similar endowments of factors of production because techniques of production or technology differ. But it may also differ because there are differences in the endowments of the factors of production used with labour (e.g. capital) to produce a given commodity. Labour productivity differences internationally may be consistent with other models of trade – in this case the factor endowments model of trade that is examined in detail in Chapter 3.

In the ensuing chapters it will become evident that trade theory, like many areas of economics, is composed of a range of competing and complementary models or explanations of trade. One skill an economist must learn is that of selecting the model or models that best suit the purpose in hand. Technological factors are a source of comparative advantage in trade between certain types of economy and in particular types of commodity. Geographical proximity and the rapid diffusion of technological know-how mean that technological differences are unlikely to be relevant for trade in relatively standardized products between countries within the EC, for example. With increased distance, increased dissimilarity between the characteristics of economies and differing stages of economic development and barriers to the transfer of knowledge, the Ricardian model may come into its own – for example, when explaining trade between the United States and South America in technologically sophisticated products.

It is not necessary, therefore, to reject one model because it does not fit all or most circumstances. It is certainly the case that it is the neo-classical, rather than the classical Ricardian, model of trade that is the dominant paradigm in trade theory. But in turning to the neo-classical or factor endowments model, as we do in Chapter 3 we are seeking to add greater richness and generality to the analysis of international trade rather than to reject the Ricardian explanation. Note in particular that the principle of comparative advantage does *not* depend upon the Ricardian model of trade. Comparative advantage is a universal condition for the potential existence of mutually beneficial trade, which does not rely upon technological differences between countries.

2.5 Summary

Before the advent of modern economics the mercantalists argued that trade was good when it led to an export surplus. There are circumstances where countries may wish to increase their net exports and may gain from increasing their surplus (or reducing their deficit). But this misses the main point: the exchange of products a country is good at producing for those it is not good at producing can permit given productive resources to satisfy human needs better, through higher consumption. Thus balanced exchange of goods can be mutually beneficial. Such beneficial exchanges are possible whenever the relative ability to produce goods differs between countries: that is, whenever a country has a *comparative advantage* – even if it is *absolutely* more or less productive than some other country in the production of all goods. In the Ricardian model of the direction and commodity composition of trade, the relative ability to produce varies between countries as the technique of production and therefore labour productivity varies internationally. But technology is only one of a range of influences that may fashion the pattern of comparative advantage.

2.6 Addendum: the large economy

The purpose of this addendum is to provide a brief sketch of the consequences of relaxing the assumption that our economy is small relative to that of the rest of the world. Suppose, therefore, that we have two countries of comparable size, and that U has the comparative advantage in the production of X so that its transformation curve is flatter than W's.

The assumption of comparable size allows us to add together the two production possibility curves to construct a world transformation curve as shown by *GEH* in Figure 2.5. The point *G* represents the maximum possible production of X if all resources in both countries are devoted to X production; it is the sum of *OP* in Figure 2.3 and the analogous maximum possible production of X in country W. Analogously, *H* represents the maximum possible production of M. Point *E* represents the situation in which each country specializes in production of the good in which it has a comparative advantage, so its horizontal ordinate corresponds to *OP* in Figure 2.3 and its vertical ordinate to the maximum possible production of M in country W. The

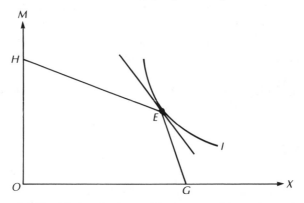

Figure 2.5 Equilibrium in the world economy with two large countries

segment *EG* represents positions where U is specializing in the production of X while W produces a mixture of M and X, so it has the slope of W's transformation curve. Analogously, the segment *EH* has the slope of U's transformation curve and shows situations where W is specializing in the production of M while U produces both goods. The world transformation curve is necessarily concave[8] to the origin because, for example, when the world first starts to produce some X – that is, to move right and down from point *H*, it first transfers productive capacity in U into X production. Since U has a comparative advantage in X, its opportunity cost – the amount of M that has to be sacrificed to produce an extra unit of X – is relatively low. Only when all U's capacity has already been absorbed in X production – that is, after point *E* – does the world economy have to switch W's resources into producing X and so incur the higher opportunity cost represented by the steeper transformation curve in W.

Suppose that it is possible to represent the sum of world consumer preferences by a well-behaved social indifference curve (I) as drawn in Figure 2.5. (This would, for example, be possible if consumer tastes were identical and homothetic not merely within but also between countries.) It is clear that there are five qualitatively different possibilities as to the form of the tangency between the highest indifference curve attainable and the world transformation curve: (1) at point E, as shown; (2) along the segment EG; (3) along the segment EH; (4) at point G; and (5) at point H.

In case 1, both countries specialize and the relative price of good X, which also happens to be country U's terms of trade, lies between the relative costs of U and W. Exactly where in that range it falls depends on consumer demand: that is, on the slope of the social indifference curve at point E. This is the classical case considered by Ricardo. When it holds, the situation in country U can still be represented by a diagram like Figure 2.3, but with the important difference that the trade possibility line is now endogenous rather than exogenous: that is, the terms of trade open to U depend upon the distribution of its demand.

Consider the next case 2, the segment EG, where U specializes but W does not. It is easy to see that this is identical to the small-economy case: U can trade with W at the fixed terms of trade determined by W's relative costs.

In case 3, the segment EH, W specializes but U does not. This produces a radical change in conclusions. As Figure 2.6 shows, U modifies its production and starts to trade as a result of opening up the economy. But consumption stays at C, exactly where it was in the closed economy. All the benefits of trade go to W. But the conclusion that specialization is *necessary* to derive gains from trade is critically dependent upon the linear technology embodied in the present model, as Chapter 3 will show.

Cases 4 and 5 are degenerate cases where there is no trade, and hence introducing the possibility of trade alters nothing.

Finally, the smaller country U is relative to W, the closer will be the peak E of the world transformation curve (Figure 2.5) to H. This increases the probability of case 2, equilibrium on the segment EG, arising. But case 2 was exactly the same as the small-country case previously analyzed (see p. 22), where it is the small country that

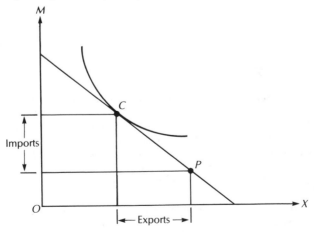

Figure 2.6 Trade with non-specialization in economy U

draws all the benefit from trade, while the large country finds itself in the situation that U did in case 3. The conclusion that the large country would not benefit from trade is dependent upon the special assumptions embodied in the model. But the converse conclusion, that small countries are particularly likely to benefit from trade, is a very robust one.[9] At a pinch, large countries like the United States or Brazil could survive a blockade. For a small country like Luxembourg or Singapore, the end of trade would quickly mean a return to the Stone Age.

2.7 Bibliography

It is well worth delving into the classical writings on absolute and comparative advantage: see Smith (1776) and Ricardo (1817). Ricardo, in fact, constructed a dynamic model of trade and growth, with analytical richness far beyond that explored in this chapter. For a review of that strand of the literature, see Findlay (1984).

It is also helpful to read the pioneering works on the modern economic analysis of trade theory: Haberler (1937) and Ellis and Metzler (1949). This work is surveyed in Chipman (1965).

The ambitious student who would like to gain a flavour at least of 'higher-dimensional' issues in recent trade theory should see Ethier (1984).

For a consideration of the methodological problems of setting up testable hypotheses that distinguish between alternative models of trade, see Deardorff (1984). Greenaway and Milner (1987) examine how alternative trade theories can be employed to explain the trade flows of developing countries.

Notes

1.   This assumption cannot in general be *exactly* correct, except in the special case treated in this chapter where prices are determined by the 'Ricardian technology' of the large country. We shall, however, continue to use the assumption in future chapters where that justification is absent. In that context, each country must have *some* influence on price – otherwise there would be no way in which price could vary in a world composed entirely of small countries! What we are essentially doing is making the empirical assumption that the national influence on world prices is sufficiently modest to be ignored as a first approximation – which appears to be a quiet acceptable approximation to reality for most countries.

2.   This convenient assumption will be used throughout, but the reader should be aware that the assumption that preferences can be represented by a set of well-behaved social indifference curves is uncomfortably strong. The basic problem is that the quantity of additional X needed to maintain the utility of each consumer constant when the quantity of M declines by one unit will in general depend on the distribution of income between consumers. To rule this out one has to make some set of very special assumptions. For example, one may assume that tastes are both identical and 'homothetic' (which means that each indifference curve is a blown-up version of each other one: that is, that the marginal rate of substitution is independent of the level of consumption). Casual observation indicates that in the real world preferences are far from identical, while the stylized fact of Engels' law suggests that they are not homothetic. Alternatively, one may

assume that the income distribution remains constant, or that it is adjusted optimally – for example, by a set of lump-sum taxes and transfers. Since many of the changes we wish to study involve changes in the distribution of income, while in general there is little reason to believe income distribution to be optimal, the alternative approaches are not very satisfactory either. The fact is that any attempt to deal with the ambiguities resulting from endogeneity of the income distribution would at this level impose costs in terms of obscuring the main points of the analysis that far outweighed the benefits in terms of more precise understanding. The serious student should, however, pursue the subject further, by consulting the references in the bibliography.

3. The equation of the transformation curve is $l_m M + l_x X = L$. Since L is a constant, total differentiation gives $l_m dM + l_x dX = 0$, or $dM/dX = -l_x/l_m = -p_x/p_m$.

4. This assumption provides the polar case of complete integration of the country into the international economy, in contrast with the other polar case of complete autarchy. The intermediate case of partial integration resulting from a policy of protection provides the subject matter of Chapter 8.

5. It is easy to see that individual profit-maximizing producers would find it in their interest to concentrate on producing X. The value of production at the relative price given by the terms of trade will be the same at any point on a given trading line and will be greater the further that trading line is from the origin. Thus the maximum revenue that producers can earn, given that they are restricted to the triangle OPZ, is yielded by producing at the point P.

6. The value of exports is $p_x(JP)$ and that of imports is $p_m(CJ)$, while the terms of trade p_x/p_m is the slope of the trading line: that is, CJ/JP.

7. See, for example, Balassa (1963) and Stern (1962). But less supportive evidence is also available from direct testing of the model on bilateral trade flows within the EC – see Agarwal, Askari and Corson (1975).

8. Concave but not strictly concave. The definition of strict concavity is that any chord joining two points in the feasible production set lies wholly in the interior of the production set. The definition of concavity is that any chord joining two points in the feasible production set lies wholly in the production set, including its frontier. In common language, a concave transformation curve is 'bowed out' from the origin.

9. A proposition is said to be 'robust' if it remains valid under a wide range of circumstances. Economists often assess the robustness of a conclusion by examining whether it holds under a variety of different plausible models.

3

Heckscher–Ohlin model

David Ricardo reasoned in terms of a one-factor model in which the product of his single factor, labour, happened to be different between countries. But it is natural to ask *why* the productivity of labour should vary. There are answers consistent with Ricardo's one-factor model – for example, such differences might be due to climatic conditions or to different levels of technology, as analyzed in Chapter 2. However, an alternative explanation was suggested in the 1920s by the Swedish economists Eli Heckscher (1879–1952) and Bertil Ohlin (1899–1979), and has since become the orthodox explanation of the source of comparative advantage. The basic idea is that countries differ in their relative stocks of the different factors of production, and that these differential factor supplies influence the costs of producing particular goods. For example, a country with an abundant supply of capital finds it relatively cheap to produce goods whose production requires much capital and little labour, and therefore has a comparative advantage in – and exports – such *capital-intensive* goods.

This basic idea has been much refined and explored in the past half-century, in particular in a most famous series of papers by Paul Samuelson (b. 1915), the 1970 winner of the Nobel prize for economics. This chapter presents the theory and discusses its principal implications. The analysis is largely conducted in terms of what is called the 2 × 2 × 2 framework: with two factors of production, labour (L) and capital (K); two goods, still M and X; and two countries, still U (our small country) and W (the large country representing the rest of the world). As a preliminary, the first section of the chapter reviews the basic microeconomic theory of a 2 × 2 closed economy.

3.1 Equilibrium in the closed economy

The starting point for analysis of production is the isoquant diagram (see Figure 3.1). An isoquant is the locus of combinations of factors of production that can efficiently produce a given level of output of a certain good – for example, X. It is the production-side analogue of the indifference curve, which shows the locus of combinations of two consumer goods that will induce a given level of satisfaction for a certain consumer. The isoquant diagram thus has input of the two factors, L and K,

32

on the two axes. With a neo-classical technology of continuous substitution between L and K, each isoquant is smooth and convex to the origin as in Figure 3.1(a). With Leontief-type fixed coefficients, each isoquant has the right-angled form shown in Figure 3.1(b). With two Leontief-type fixed coefficient production processes available for the same good, each isoquant would have three linear segments as shown in Figure 3.1(c): the sloping segment represents combinations of the two production processes represented by the two corners. Obviously, with more processes available one would get more segments on the isoquant, ultimately tending to approach the neo-classical formulation with many processes.

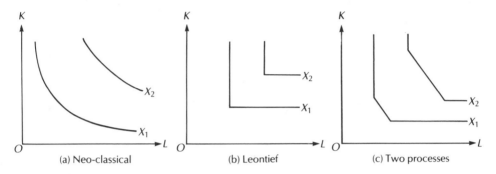

Figure 3.1 Isoquant diagram

In the case of constant returns to scale, or a linear homogeneous production function, a single isoquant tells us everything we need to know about the production side of the economy. Once the isoquant is known for some output level X_1, the isoquant for any other output level X_2 can be calculated by seeking points (X_2/X_1) as far from the origin as those on the isoquant X_1. Figure 3.1 shows a second isoquant, $X_2 = 2X_1$, which implies that the input of both factors is always double that on the X_1 isoquant. The assumption of constant returns to scale will be made throughout this chapter. How reasonable an assumption is it? For parts of manufacturing industry, it is quite acceptable. Existing plants can normally be duplicated or expanded at approximately constant costs, at least beyond some minimum size. But in resource-based industries, including agriculture, it is not uncommon to find decreasing returns to scale. And in quite a few manufacturing industries, most notably aircraft production (where learning by doing is important), large parts of engineering (those using batch production methods) and the chemical and other process industries (where it matters that the volume of containers expands more rapidly than their surface area as size increases), evidence indicates that normal-sized plants have unexhausted economies of scale. Nevertheless, the case of constant returns to scale provides a natural benchmark; it is easier to learn the analysis by studying this case and subsequently to modify it when there is reason to believe that returns to scale are either increasing or decreasing.

It is possible to study the production equilibrium of an economy (with two goods and two factors) by bringing together the two isoquant diagrams for the two goods in a diagram called the Edgeworth box, named after its inventor, the English neo-classical economist Francis Edgeworth (1845–1926). The sides of the box represent the quantities of the two factors of production available to the economy in question. Figure 3.2 shows the length of the box representing the quantity of labour L available to U and its height representing the quantity of capital K. Now insert the isoquant diagram of export good X starting from the bottom left-hand corner: that is, from the origin O_x. The diagram is simply reproduced from Figure 3.1(a). Industry M also has an isoquant diagram, which can also be inserted in the Edgeworth box. In this case, however, it must be flipped over and placed with its origin at O_m in the top right-hand corner. An isoquant representing a higher level of production of M lies further from O_m, which of course means that it is closer to O_x.

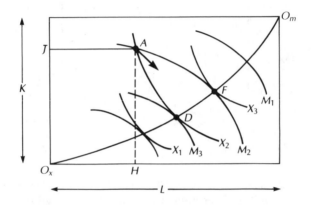

Figure 3.2 Edgeworth box

Consider a typical point in the Edgeworth box, such as point A. That point represents a certain allocation of the given supplies of the two factors of production between the two industries: O_xH of L to industry X and the remainder of L to industry M; and O_xJ of K to industry X with the remainder to industry M. Looking at industry X's isoquants, we can see that the quantities O_xH of L and O_xJ of K are sufficient to produce an output of X_2. Similarly, the remaining quantities of L and K have to be looked at from the standpoint of M's isoquant map with the origin at O_m. It can be seen that they would permit production of M_2. In general, then, any point in the Edgeworth box represents a specific division of the available factor supplies between the two industries and, hence, specific output levels of the two goods. It is assumed that the supplies of both factors are fully utilized: that is, that full employment prevails.

Does point A represent an 'efficient' division of the factors of production, in the sense of a division that cannot allow a higher output of one type of good without sacrificing output of the other? No, since by reallocating K from industry X to industry M and L from industry M to industry X, we can move down in the direction indicated by the arrow and reach higher isoquants for *both* goods. This process can continue until the point where the isoquants are tangential to one another. After that point any further progress towards the lower right-hand corner would involve moving to lower isoquants of both goods. Hence the set of efficient production points in the diagram are those like D and F. These points of tangency can be joined up to form the *contract curve* running from O_x to O_m.

As drawn, the contract curve is convex towards the lower right-hand corner. This is not an accident, but represents an important assumption about technology: that the X industry is intensive in L. The meaning of X being L-intensive is shown in Figure 3.3(a). This diagram shows representative isoquants for both the X and M industries. It is not true that the X industry *must* employ more L (per unit of K) than the M industry: at point D the M industry's labour–capital ratio (measured by the

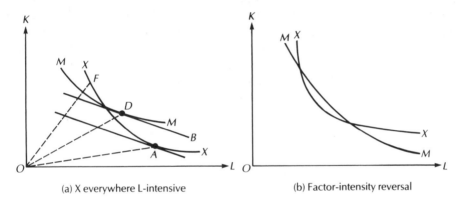

(a) X everywhere L-intensive (b) Factor-intensity reversal

Figure 3.3 Factor intensity

flatness of the ray from the origin to point D) is higher than that of the X industry at point F. But comparing points D and F is not comparing like with like. If relative factor prices, which are represented by the slope of the isocost line BD, were to give the M industry an incentive to pick the factor combination represented by D, they would give the X industry an incentive to pick the factor combination represented by A rather than F. That is, X being intensive in L means that *for given factor prices* X will always have an incentive to produce with a higher L/K ratio than will M. Now it can be seen why X being intensive in L implies that the contract curve in Figure 3.2 must lie below the diagonal. For any given factor prices, the L/K ratio is higher in X than in M, which is precisely what is implied by lying below the diagonal.

If isoquants never cross more than once, the same industry is everywhere L-intensive (and the other is everywhere K-intensive). However, one cannot rule out *a priori* the possibility shown in Figure 3.3(b) where the isoquants cross twice – that one industry is L-intensive at one set of factor prices and the other L-intensive at a different set of factor prices. In the case shown, X is L-intensive when the price of labour relative to capital is high and K-intensive when the price of labour relative to capital is low. In fact, it seems that factor-intensity reversals do sometimes occur: for example, the production of rice is labour-intensive in Thailand but capital-intensive in Texas. For the moment we shall simply assume away factor-intensity reversals, but it will be necessary to return later and explore some of their implications.

The next step in the analysis is to derive the production possibility curve – a construct first introduced into trade theory in 1930 by the Austrian-born economist Gottfried Haberler (b. 1900). In the one-factor model (see Figure 2.1) studied in the previous chapter, this was a straight line. In the neo-classical two-factor model used in this chapter, with possibilities of substitution in production, the curve is downward sloping and concave to the origin, as shown in Figure 3.4. This can be seen by recognizing that, since the production possibility curve is defined as the curve showing the maximum possible output of one good for given levels of production of the other, it represents all those combinations of outputs found along the contract curve in the Edgeworth box (see Figure 3.2). Thus the point X_{max} in Figure 3.4 shows the maximum possible output of X, which occurs when all resources are devoted to X production, which is represented by the point O_m in Figure 3.2; X_{max} is in fact the value of the X isoquant at the upper right-hand corner of the Edgeworth box. Similarly, M_{max} represents the value of the M isoquant at the point O_x in the Edgeworth box, where all resources are devoted to M production. The point Y corresponds to a point like D on the contract curve of the Edgeworth box. It definitely lies outside the straight line joining X_{max} and M_{max} because a point like Z

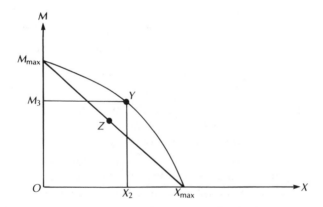

Figure 3.4 Neo-classical production possibility curve

on that line corresponds in the Edgeworth box to a point on the diagonal joining O_x and O_m, and we know that when the two industries have different factor intensities, the contract curve does not coincide with the diagonal. Hence it is possible to produce more of both commodities than at Z by reallocating K to M production and L to X production to yield a point Y consistent with a concave production possibility curve (ppc). This argument can be repeated to show that the ppc is everywhere concave, as shown. The argument can be used, for example, to show that the point on the ppc corresponding to point F in the Edgeworth box must lie outside the straight line connecting Y and X_{max} in Figure 3.4.

Naturally, different assumptions about the nature of technology lead to different shapes of the ppc. Two interesting special cases are shown in Figures 3.5 and 3.6. In the former, technology is assumed to have the form $X = f(L)$, $M = g(K)$; the production of X uses only labour and that of M uses only capital. The X isoquants are

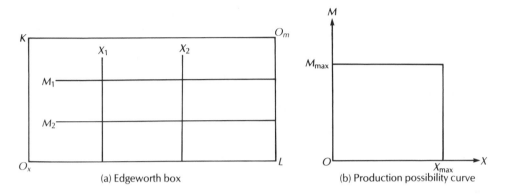

Figure 3.5 One-factor production functions

therefore vertical lines and the M isoquants horizontal lines in the Edgeworth box, and the contract curve is O_xLO_m. Obviously the corresponding ppc is a rectangle; it is possible to produce up to X_{max} of X (whose isoquant is LO_m) and up to M_{max} of M (whose isoquant is O_xL) with no cost in terms of lost output of the other good.

The second interesting case is that of two Leontief-type fixed-coefficient production functions. With X having the more labour-intensive fixed coefficients, the Edgeworth box appears as in Figure 3.6(a). The X isoquants are the L-shaped constructions along the ray O_xY, and the M isoquants are the inverted Ls along the ray from O_m to Z. Those two rays represent the technologically determined

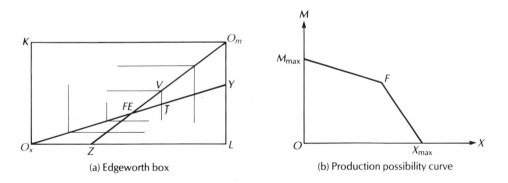

Figure 3.6 Fixed coefficients production functions

combinations of L and K in the production of X and M, respectively. Since input coefficients are fixed, there need not be full employment of both factors of production. For example, if production of X is at point J, there will only be enough labour left over to permit production of M at V, and VJ of capital will remain unutilized. This means that there is no well-defined contract curve in this model. In fact, the only point where both factors will be fully employed and the contract curve well defined is where the two production rays intersect, marked FE. However, the ppc is still perfectly definitely specified. It has two linear segments, one from X_{max} (equivalent to point Y in the Edgeworth box) to F where X production is being contracted along $Y.FE$ while M production expands along $O_m.FE$, and the other from F to M_{max} where X production contracts along $FE.O_x$ while M production expands along $FE.Z$. The reason that the opportunity cost of X is higher in the second segment is that the scarce factor of production switches from being K to being L after the point of full employment (FE in the Edgeworth box and the kink F in the ppc diagram) is passed, and X is, of course, the good intensive in L.

Finally, general equilibrium in the closed economy is determined by the interaction between the supply side, which is represented by the production possibility curve, and the demand side, which is represented by a set of community indifference curves (as introduced in Chapter 2). This is shown by the point of tangency E in Figure 3.7. The competitive relative price of X (that is, p_x/p_m), which

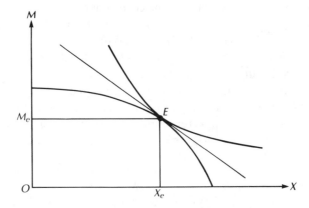

Figure 3.7 General equilibrium in the closed economy

will induce consumers to demand those same quantities X_e and M_e of the two goods that it will persuade producers to supply, is shown by the (negative of the) slope of the tangent (to *both* curves). A higher relative price of X is shown by a steeper set of price lines and would result in producers wishing to produce more X than X_e and consumers wishing to purchase less X than X_e, with resulting excess supply of X (and excess demand for M). Only at point E is there equilibrium.

The equalization of slopes at tangency point E is sometimes expressed in terms of marginal conditions: namely, that the rate of consumer substitution (at the margin) between X and M equals the rate of producer transformation (at the margin) between X and M, which in turn equals the price ratio of the goods.

3.2 Heckscher–Ohlin model

The Heckscher–Ohlin model is concerned with balanced trade between two neo-classical economies. The basic idea is that the country in which labour, for example, is relatively abundant will find itself able to produce the labour-intensive good relatively cheaply; thus, it will have a comparative advantage in production of that good. As in Chapter 2, we assume that our country, U, has a comparative advantage in production of the L-intensive good X. This means that the relative price of good X would be higher in country W than in the country U in the absence of trade. The assumption is that country U is a small economy able to trade at will at the prices set in the large country W. It is therefore merely necessary to introduce a line – or rather a set of parallel lines – representing the exogenous terms of trade into Figure 3.7. The result is shown in Figure 3.8, with *CP* being the terms-of-trade line along which trade occurs.

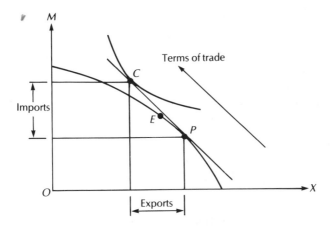

Figure 3.8 Small economy in equilibrium with free trade

The international price of X is higher than the autarchy price shown in Figure 3.7. As a consequence, producers adjust their output from *E* to *P*, the production point where the new price line is tangential to the ppc. Output of X increases, at the expense of the production of M. Real income is now sufficient to permit consumers to reach any point on *PC*, so in accordance with their preferences as represented by the social indifference curves, they pick the point of tangency *C*. Trade equilibrium (*P*, *C*) has the following properties in comparison with autarchy equilibrium (E, E):[1]

1. X is more expensive and M is cheaper (in terms of each other).
2. Production of X increases and that of M decreases.

3. Real income is higher at P than at E, measured at free trade prices.
4. Consumption of M increases because of both a positive income effect (unless M is an inferior good) and a positive substitution effect (M is now cheaper to consumers), while that of X may either increase (if the positive income effect is strong enough) or decrease (if the negative substituton effect is strong enough).
5. The excess of the production over the consumption of X consists of exports, while the excess of the consumption over the production of M consists of imports (both shown on Figure 3.8).
6. Since the slope of the line CP represents the terms of trade – that is, the price of exports in terms of imports – the value of exports is equal to that of imports.
7. Consumers are on a higher indifference curve at C than they were at E. In fact, free trade – trade along the terms-of-trade line CP – enables consumers to reach the highest position consistent with the technological limits on production represented by the ppc and the exogenous terms of trade represented by the slope of PC.

Underlying this important set of conclusions are three sets of assumptions. First, there are the assumptions about *technology* that were outlined in the previous section:

— That the production function is homogeneous of the first degree (linear homogeneous): that is, production processes exhibit constant returns to scale.
— That the factors K and L are substitutes in production: that is, the production function is well behaved.
— That there are no factor-intensity reversals.
— That adjustment is instantaneous so that the economy is always in equilibrium.

Second, there is a set of assumptions which jointly guarantee that after trade the same price will prevail in our country as rules in the rest of the world:

— No transport costs.
— Free trade.
— Perfect competition in all markets (including factor markets).

Finally, there are assumptions made for the sake of reducing the size of the problem to something manageable:

— That there are two goods, two factors of production and two countries, one of which is small.
— That the factors of production are available in fixed quantities (referred to as 'endowments') and fully used.
— That consumer preferences can be represented by a set of conventionally shaped (that is, convex to the origin) social indifference curves.

It is important not to fall into the trap of dismissing a conclusion that runs against some personal predilection just because the proof used to establish that conclusion adopted some unrealistic assumption. For example, the seventh proposition above concluded that free trade is a good thing. There *are* grounds on which that conclusion can be challenged (discussed in Chapter 1). But it *cannot* be dismissed by pointing out that the assumption of no transport costs is unrealistic. Positive transport costs would simply mean that the internal price line would not be quite as steep as the external price line (by an amount representing the costs of transport), but welfare would still be maximized by letting producers maximize profits and consumers maximize utility and reconciling the differences between production and consumption through free trade.

Of course, it is not always as obvious as this whether a conclusion will remain valid when one of the supporting assumptions is relaxed. For example, if preferences cannot be represented by a set of social indifference curves, because income distribution varies and tastes differ, then there is not much that one can conclude with any rigour. However, many economists are willing to take the position that, in the absence of any specific evidence to the contrary, it is reasonable to draw conclusions as though a set of social indifference curves existed. This amounts to adopting the view of the agnostic – if one does not know who will benefit or how to weigh their gains against the losers' losses, just count an extra peso of income as the same to everyone.[2]

While often difficult to do, it is important to develop a sense of the extent to which the conclusions depend on the assumptions being strictly satisfied. An assumption critical to a particular conclusion will often be indicated in the text, but it is simply not possible to do this in a comprehensive way, at least without making the book unreadable. In addition, it would still not be adequate, for new contexts will constantly arise. There is absolutely no substitute for individual, independent consideration of the implications of assumptions by the reader. For example, consider whether the *laissez-faire* proposition is dependent upon the assumption of substitution in production (see Figures 3.5 and 3.6). How about constant returns to scale (see sections 5.1)? How about many goods and factors (see section 3.6)?

3.3 Hecksher–Ohlin theorem

The Heckscher–Ohlin theorem is a famous proposition about the pattern of trade between two economies each of which has the characteristics described in the previous section. It may be stated as follows: each country will export the good that is intensive in its abundant factor. In our example the abundant factor of production in country U is labour, L, the theorem therefore predicts that the country will export X, the labour-intensive good.

Most of the assumptions needed to prove the theorem have already been made in the previous section. What remains is merely to ensure that the two countries are equal in various respects: (1) that Country W also has all the characteristics previously attributed to U (this is not necessary when we are merely characterizing the impact on U of its interaction with a parametric rest of the world, but it is necessary when, as now, we wish to compare the situation in U with that in W): (2) that both countries have identical technology; and (3) that tastes are identical and homothetic in the two countries.[3] These assumptions mean that the two countries differ in only two respects: with regard to their size and with respect to the ratio K/L in which they are endowed with capital and labour. In other words, the two countries differ only with regard to the dimensions of the Edgeworth boxes.

The proof of the theorem starts by noting that with equal tastes in both countries and with prices of goods equalized through free, competitive and costless trade, the pattern of consumption must be identical in the two countries. Suppose that both countries also produced the two goods in the same ratio in which they were consumed, so that there was no trade. This situation is shown by points C and D in Figure 3.9, which displays the Edgeworth box of our small labour abundant country U at the bottom left-hand corner of the box for the large and relatively capital-abundant

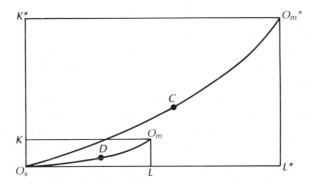

Figure 3.9 Two Edgeworth boxes

country W, whose variables are denoted by asterisks.[4] It is clear that, when C and D represent the same ratio of X to M production in the two countries, the slope of the ray from O_x to C must be greater than the slope of the ray from O_x to D. But this implies that the K/L ratio in the production of X in W (shown by the slope of the ray from O_x to C) must be greater than that in U. It is also true that the K/L ratio will be greater in W than in U in the production of M (to see this geometrically, redraw the two Edgeworth boxes with U's box now sharing the top right-hand origin O_m with O_m^*). In other words, with equal production ratios the capital intensity of production would be greater in both industries in the capital-abundant country (which is re-assuringly unsurprising).

But greater capital intensity implies that the capital-intensive good will have a lower opportunity cost – it will be necessary to give up less of the labour-intensive good in order to secure a marginal increase in the output of the capital-intensive good. Conversely, the labour-intensive good will have a higher opportunity cost where capital intensity K/L is greater. So the opportunity cost of M must be lower in W, and that of X must be lower in U, when production ratios are similar: that is, along any ray in the production possibility curve diagram (see Figure 3.10). A lower opportunity cost of M is shown by a steeper ppc (along any ray such as OR), since

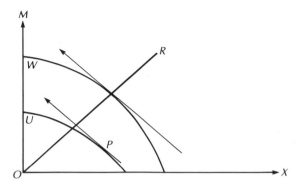

Figure 3.10 Two production possibility curves

that represents a situation in which a given sacrifice of X allows a greater increase in M. Thus W's ppc is steeper along every ray than is U's, as shown. In particular, if *OR* is the ray that represents equilibrium in the large country W, where the social indifference curve is tangential to the ppc, then U's production point *P* must lie to the right of *OR*. However, U's consumption point must lie on *OR* (as already established by virtue of equal tastes and prices), so U must be producing more of the L-intensive good X than it consumes, and exporting the excess. Correspondingly, W must be producing more of the K-intensive good M than it consumes (although the diagram does not show this difference by virtue of the assumption that W is so much larger relative to U as to make the displacement from *OR* along W's ppc insignificant), and exporting the excess.

3.4 Factor price equalization theorem

Heckscher and Ohlin argued that trade would produce a tendency towards the equalization of factor prices, on the intuitive grounds that, since a country would export goods intensive in its abundant factor of production and import goods intensive in its scarce factor, the effect of trade would be to increase the derived demand for the abundant factor and thereby reduce the relative scarcity of the other factor. The outcome would be a reduction in the difference in factor prices between countries.

Samuelson (1948, 1949) proved that the logic of the technological assumptions embodied in the Heckscher–Ohlin model, in conjunction with those of perfect competition, *laissez-faire* and zero transport costs so as to guarantee equal commodity prices, permitted a much stronger result: that factor prices would be *completely* equalized by trade in goods alone, without any factor movements. The logic of the argument is as follows. Trade equalizes commodity prices between the two countries. With a given neo-classical technology, factor prices determine commodity prices uniquely, since the factor prices determine the cost-minimizing point on the isoquant and with perfect competition and constant returns to scale price is equal to

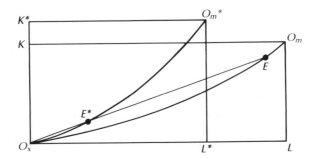

Figure 3.11 Factor price equalization

cost $wL + p_kK$. Hence both countries produce along the same ray from O_x and parallel rays from O_m and $O_m{}^*$ as shown in Figure 3.11.

The interest lies in establishing the set of assumptions that are necessary for this argument to hold. First, there are the technological assumptions of constant returns to scale, substitutability in production, an absence of factor intensity reversals and identical technology in both countries. The last two of these assumptions are of particular interest, inasmuch as it can be shown that factor intensity reversals can actually cause trade to widen factor price differentials and the assumption that two countries have identical technology is much stronger than the assumption that each individual country has a neo-classical technology. Second, there are the relatively innocuous assumptions of no transport costs, free trade and perfect competition needed to guarantee commodity price equalization. Relaxing these would simply mean that trade could not completely equalize factor prices, but the tendency would remain. Third, there are the simplifying assumptions of two goods and two factors in fixed supply. These can be generalized to some extent, by allowing factor supplies to vary and by increasing the number of goods and factors, provided that the number of goods remains equal to or greater than the number of factors. But this may be a big proviso: we do not have very satisfactory ways of deciding how goods or factors should be defined, given that they are not in reality homogeneous. Finally, there is an assumption specific to the factor price equalization theorem: that the factor endowments not be so different as to drive one or other of the countries to specialization. Figure 3.12 shows that the small economy would indeed specialize, unless total world demand for the good X intensive in its abundant factor were negligible.

We know from reading newspapers, looking at statistics or keeping our eyes open when we travel that in reality factor prices are not equal between countries or, for that matter, within countries. It is also abundantly clear that some factor prices are a lot more equal than others: specifically, that the returns to internationally mobile factors like capital or skilled labour are far less unequal than those to the factors with minimal mobility, like land and unskilled labour. In other words, the empirical evidence suggests that commodity trade alone does not equalize factor prices, contrary to the conclusion suggested by the factor price equalization theorem. The

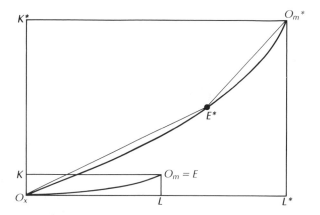

Figure 3.12 Specialization and non-equalization of factor prices in the small economy

questions that arise are why that is so and whether this dictates a rejection of the Heckscher–Ohlin model *in toto*.

There is no question but that the factor price equalization theorem does involve some very strong assumptions: in particular, those on identical technologies, the number of goods and factors, and an economy sufficiently large to avoid specialization. Presumably the technologies actually available to countries do differ drastically, given the vast differences in the supply of technically trained workers. As noted above, we have no idea whether the condition on the relative number of goods and factors is satisfied. Similarly, do countries specialize? Obviously, none of them produces only one good, but there are lots of small countries which produce only a small part of the total range of goods that they consume. So perhaps it is not surprising to find so little evidence of factor price equalization in the real world. However, this discussion leaves intact the commonsense argument with which we started: that trade can be expected to raise the derived demand for abundant factors and relieve the shortage of scarce factors, and in that way to have a (partial) equalizing impact on factor prices. Empirical studies in countries like Brazil have provided reinforcement to the belief that a greater opening of the economy to foreign trade would have this effect.

Can one set aside the factor price equalization theorem without simultaneously rejecting the rest of the Heckscher–Ohlin approach? The answer is yes. One does not need all of the above assumptions to support the Heckscher–Ohlin theorem or the conclusion regarding the benefits of free trade. For example, the Heckscher–Ohlin theorem does not require non-specialization, and it would presumably survive if technologies were similar though not identical. And the free-trade conclusion relies on none of the three questionable assumptions. In other words, it is a mistake to suppose that the Heckscher–Ohlin model is something that either has to be accepted as an all-embracing explanation of trade or else totally rejected as reactionary orthodoxy. Like all models, it is a way of representing reality that picks out certain features as crucial and enables us to understand their implications. In those contexts where the features modelled are in fact the crucial ones, the model can be useful. Application of the model in other contexts can be misleading and mischievous. The job of an applied economist involves deciding what model is appropriate to the particular problem under analysis. The Heckscher–Ohlin model should always be considered when the question concerns trade and will often be found useful provided that it is interpreted with appropriate care for the problem of dimension (see section 3.6).

3.5 Leontief paradox

In 1953 the Russian-born Nobel laureate Wassily Leontief (b. 1906) published an article in which he described an attempt to verify empirically the Heckscher–Ohlin theorem. His earlier work, for which he was awarded the Nobel prize in 1973, had involved the development of input–output theory. In response to his work, statistical efforts to construct input–output tables began. The first table to be published was for the United States in 1947. Leontief recognized that this provided the opportunity to make empirical estimates of the total factor content of United States trade and thus to see whether its exports were capital intensive and its imports labour intensive as the Heckscher–Ohlin theorem predicts. (In 1947 the United States unquestionably had far more capital per head than virtually all of its trading partners, so there seemed no question which was the relatively abundant factor.)

Leontief encountered no difficulty in using the input–output tables plus data on the commodity composition of exports in order to construct an estimate of the quantities of capital and labour embodied in a representative $1 million of exports. However, he could not do the same for *imports* because he had an input–output table only for the United States and not for the countries from which the United States was buying its imports. Instead he calculated from United States data the factor intensity of the *import substitutes* that would have been bought from United States sources had a representative $1 million of imports not been available.

The results of this exercise (Leontief 1953) showed that exports were more *labour intensive* than were import substitutes, contrary to the prediction of the Heckscher–Ohlin model. Paradoxically, the world's most capital-abundant country appeared to be exporting goods more labour intensive than it was importing. There are several ways to explain, or explain away, this paradox.

Statistical error. One possible explanation might be that Leontief's sums were wrong, or he happened to pick data that were in some ways unrepresentative. There is, however, no strong evidence to support this conjecture. On the contrary, many subsequent investigations (see section 3.6) have repeated the type of test pioneered by Leontief, and his results have often, though by no means always, been replicated. There is not much reason to doubt that capital-abundant countries on balance do sometimes export goods that are labour-intensive and import relatively capital-intensive goods especially when capital and labour are treated as homogenous inputs and industries are finely delineated.

Factor intensity reversal. Ronald Jones (b. 1931) argued that the Leontief paradox might be due to a factor-intensity reversal as shown in Figure 3.3(b). In fact, it was the attempt to resolve the Leontief paradox that prompted the search for empirical instances of factor-intensity reversal, which yielded the example cited earlier of rice growing being labour intensive in Thailand and capital intensive in Texas. This explanation implies that, while United States import substitutes would be more capital intensive than United States exports, United States *imports* would be more labour intensive, as predicted by the Heckscher–Ohlin model. While theoretically interesting, there does not seem to be evidence that factor-intensity reversals are so commonplace as to be the sole explanation of the general tendency of the United States to export more labour-intensive goods than its import substitutes.

Demand conditions. Another theoretical possibility is that the paradox could be due to Americans having such strong preferences for capital-intensive goods as to outweigh the greater abundance of capital in the United States. There is not the slightest doubt that in reality tastes do vary from one country to another, rather than being identical as we have been assuming. There also seems to be a pretty systematic tendency for people to have an exceptionally pronounced taste for the goods that their own country is good at producing: Brazilians drink vast quantities of coffee and the French large quantities of wine. But the evidence also suggests that these differences on the demand side are dwarfed by those on the supply side. There is, therefore, not much basis for using differences in tastes to explain the Leontief paradox.

Protection. Our model assumes free trade, whereas in fact the United States (like all other countries) had very high levels of protection in 1947. Suppose United States tariffs were directed principally at excluding labour-intensive goods from their home market (as they were, for reasons that are explained in Chapter 8). Then possibly, the only goods other countries had the chance of exporting to the United States *were* rather capital intensive. A problem with this explanation is that it is not clear why other countries would have wanted to trade with the United States if they could only export goods they were bad at making in exchange for goods in which they had a comparative advantage. However, if the model is extended to include natural resources, as suggested below, then this difficulty is overcome, and it may well be that in reality the structure of United States tariffs did partly explain the Leontief paradox.

Better United States workers. Leontief's own explanation was that United States workers were so much more efficient than their foreign counterparts that the country was really a labour-abundant and not a capital-abundant country. He was *not* saying that each worker produced three times (that was his figure) as much because he or she had much more capital, but that with a *given* capital stock a United States worker would produce three times as much because he or she worked that much better. Some economists (no doubt mainly those without close ties to the United States) have a certain emotional resistance to this explanation, but that does not constitute a scientific ground for rejecting it. Rejected it nevertheless should be, on the eminently scientific ground that empirical testing of theories would be a complete farce if any finding at odds with *a priori* expectations could be explained away by changing the unit of measurement by three without rigorous demonstration that such a change was empirically justified on the basis of evidence other than the finding to be explained away.

More factors of production. To be more charitable to Leontief's original explanation, one might interpret him as groping for what is probably accepted as the leading explanation at the present time: the contention that human capital is important. The charge is that putting only the two factors labour and capital in the Heckscher–Ohlin model has oversimplified to the point of obscuring what is central. Specifically, it is argued that an understanding of the determination of comparative advantage and the pattern of trade demands a model with at least four factors of production: capital, unskilled labour, professionally trained labour and land. The latter represents all natural resources, and it is in fact again a gross simplification to aggregate all of these into a single factor – land suitable for growing coffee is not the same as that suitable for growing tea, let alone for growing rice or mining copper. For some purposes it would obviously be essential to recognize the heterogeneity of natural resources: indeed, it is exactly the possession of some scare natural resource that provides the basis for the bulk of the exports of many developing countries. For present purposes we can note that many United States exports were (and are) intensive in some of the many natural resources with which the United States is abundantly endowed, and it may well be that production of resource-intensive goods is more labour-intensive than capital-intensive. Research of the past twenty years has also amply confirmed the economic importance of the human capital embodied in technically trained and professional labour. The argument is that the most abundant factor in the United States was *not* the physical capital captured by Leontief's measure but the human capital whose reward was included by Leontief among labour costs. Discrimination between human capital, which is relatively abundant in the United States, and unskilled labour, which is the scarce factor (relative to other countries), has shown that it is indeed the former and not the latter that is embodied in United States exports.

Heckscher–Ohlin is wrong. An obvious possible explanation that has received rather little attention in the literature (perhaps reflecting the low regard in which empirical evidence is held by too many economists) is that the Heckscher–Ohlin theorem is wrong: not logically wrong, of course, but wrong in the sense that it directs attention to something – factor endowment – that is in practice not very important in determining the pattern of trade. This heretical thought will be discussed in the following chapters.

3.6 Higher dimensions

The $2 \times 2 \times 2$ model that we have examined so far in this chapter is theoretically elegant. But in this form its predictions about the sources of comparative advantage and the commodity composition and direction of trade appear to be strongly rejected by some studies. Since Leontief's classic study there have been a number of other studies, in particular relating to US multilateral trade, that confirm the apparent paradox.[5]

However, most of these studies employ a restrictive test. A complete test of the Heckscher–Ohlin theorem would measure the country's factor endowments and compare them with the factor intensities of the commodities it exports and imports. The above tests fall short of this in two ways. First, the nature of a country's factor abundance is assumed, not empirically identified. Countries are expected to export the services of their *assumed* abundant factor, embodied as factor content in the goods exported (hence the tests are sometimes described as 'factor content' tests). Second, the assumed factor abundance or scarcity invariably relates to a very limited number of factors of production. The Leontief test assumed not only that the United States was physical-capital abundant, but also that inputs into the production process need only be broken down into one form of capital and labour. Not only is this an unrealistic assumption, but it is methodologically unsatisfactory to employ it in an empirical setting where there are many, not two, countries and many, again not two, commodities. Robust empirical testing of the Heckscher–Ohlin model is better based on a more general formulation of the model, not on the highly specific $2 \times 2 \times 2$ version.

If the model is extended and tested in a fairly piecemeal fashion, there is evidence which is more supportive of factor endowment explanations of trade. Studies have shown, for instance, that Brazil's *imports* of manufactures are human-capital intensive, India's exports are labour intensive and British exports to developing countries are skill and R & D intensive.[6] These results are compatible with the factor proportions principle – if Brazil is relatively deficient in human capital, if India is relatively labour abundant and if Britain is relatively better endowed with skills and technical know-how than developing countries. Everyone believes these propositions to be true, but they are again factor content tests of *ad hoc* extensions of the simple model, and we have not established yet whether the Heckscher–Ohlin theorem still holds with this type of expansion of the number of factors.

Adding to only one of the dimensions of the model in isolation and as currently formulated (i.e. adding a third country to two commodities and two factors, or a third commodity to two factors and countries, etc.) tends in fact to cause difficulties. With an additional country it is possible to predict the trade patterns of the countries at the extremes of the rank order of relative factor endowments – the most capital abundant will export capital-intensive goods, and the most labour abundant will export labour-intensive goods – but the trade pattern of the intermediate country is indeterminate. Alternatively, if we add a third commodity by itself, the pattern of production becomes ambiguous, and therefore the detailed pattern of trade cannot be predicted. In this case, however, it is possible to predict something about the average content of a country's trade. On average, the capital (labour)-abundant country will export capital (labour)-intensive goods. The final possibility, adding a third factor, is particularly problematic. Indeed, the model tends to break down since it is impossible to identify the abundant factor for each country and therefore to predict the trade pattern.

Rather than extending the dimensions of the model one dimension at a time, we could more realistically consider increasing all the dimensions simultaneously. The theoretically convenient extension is the 'even' expansion of the model's dimensions. As with the even $2 \times 2 \times 2$ model, the $n \times n \times n$ model (where $n > 2$) will have a unique and determinate solution, in which each country produces a subset of the n commodities determined by the country's factor endowments. But it will be difficult to make predictions about the pattern of trade in this context, since in a multi-factor world it is difficult to define the factor intensity of commodities. 'Even' extension of the dimensions of the model is not, however, the most fruitful area of investigation from a practical point of view. Empirical observation suggests that there are many more commodities (n) than countries (m) and probably more countries than meaningfully separable factors of production (u): i.e. $n > m > u$.

Chains of comparative advantage

The easiest 'non-even' extension of the Heckscher–Ohlin model is n commodities, m countries and two factors ($n > m > 2$). With more commodities than factors of production the fundamental indeterminacy of production and trading patterns remains, if all the assumptions of the model are maintained. However, it will again be the case that a country exports a combination of commodities which embody (on average) relatively more of its abundant factor than those that are imported. We can overcome this indeterminacy problem by relaxing specific assumptions of the model.

For example, when factor prices are not equalized between countries, each country tends to produce a range of commodities in the chain of comparative advantage.[7] Consider Figure 3.13. Isoquants for some of the n commodities ($1 \ldots n$)

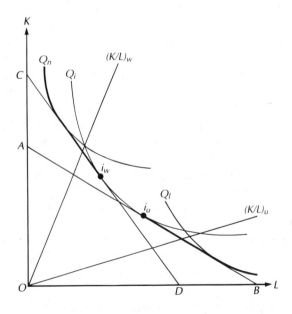

Figure 3.13 Chains of comparative advantage without factor price equalization

are ranked in order of increasing capital intensity, from commodity 1, the least capital intensive, to n, the most. If relative factor prices for the extreme countries are shown by AB (the most labour-abundant country) and CD (the most capital-abundant country), and if factor endowments for these two countries are shown by $(K/L)_u$ and $(K/L)_w$ respectively, then commodity i is the only intermediate commodity that will be produced in both countries. The capital-abundant country W produces this commodity with a higher capital–labour ratio than country U because of the factor price differences. (Compare factor intensities at tangency points i_w and i_u.) By extension, any other commodities produced by country W will have higher K/L ratios than that at i_w, and by country U will have lower K/L ratios than that at i_U. Thus commodities can be ranked by factor intensities and the Heckscher–Ohlin theorem holds for a chain of comparative advantage. For intermediate countries, the point at which they enter the chain of comparative advantage will be dependent on their factor endowment ratio.

It is more difficult to generalize the model in the above manner where more than two factors are considered, since factor-intensity characteristics cannot be ranked in a simple manner. One possible restriction is to rank each commodity consistently according to (only) one factor (j). Once factor-intensities of commodities have been defined, then the commodity form of the Heckscher–Ohlin theorem holds as an average relationship: a relatively j-abundant country will export a set of commodities that on average embody relatively more of factor j than those which are imported.

Indeed, it is this aspect of the theoretical literature that has provided the focus for the recent, more sophisticated, testing of the Heckscher–Ohlin model. Edward Leamer (1984), for instance, sets up a carefully specified multi-factor, multi-product and multi-country Heckscher–Ohlin model. He then tests it with data from 60 countries (20 industrial, 40 developing), distinguishing between ten aggregates of goods (including four aggregates of manufactures) and eleven factors (listed in Table 3.1). Table 3.1 reports the effect of factor endowment on net exports of four groups of manufactures. Although there are measurement and econometric concerns that call for caution in the interpretation of the results, the results do give support for the role of factor endowments in explaining broad trade flows. Leamer's model explains quite a large proportion of the export patterns, and the type of factors and their signs are those that we would expect in the case of comparative advantage in manufactured goods.

Note that the model is being applied to broad aggregates of goods, not specific industries (as in the case of Leontief's study), and certainly not to specific products. Once we disaggregate, it is likely that there will be other important influences on trade flows: characteristics of production processes (e.g. scale economies), characteristics of demand (e.g. demand for differentiated products), characteristics of markets (e.g. imperfect competition and oligopolistic conditions) and policy interventions (e.g. tariff and non-tariff barriers). We will consider these factors in later chapters. But note that the later models of trade we examine do not necessarily need to be viewed as competing theories. It is quite legitimate to employ the Heckscher–Ohlin model to explain the broad patterns of comparative advantage,

Table 3.1 Factor endowment sources[1] of comparative advantage in manufactures

Types of manufactured goods	Factor endowments									
	Labour			Land type[2]				Natural resources		
	Non-professional		Professional and technical	A	B	C	D	Coal	Minerals	Oil
	(1) Illiterate	(2) Literate								
Labour intensive	−	+					−			(−)
Capital intensive	+	−	+	(+)						
Machinery	+	(−)								(+)
Chemicals	+	(+)	−			−	(−)			(−)

[1] Robust statistical support for a positive relationship is shown by a + sign and for an inverse relationship by a − sign. A sign in brackets indicates weak statistical support for a relationship.
[2] Land area respectively in tropical, arid, two temperate climate zones.
Source: Leamer (1984), table 6.6 (1975 data).

i.e. the balance of comparative advantage between manufactured and agricultural goods or between labour- and capital-intensive goods, and to employ alternative models to explain patterns of specialization and trade within sectors of an economy.

3.7 Specific factors model

An older model, used by Haberler in the 1930s, was revived by Jones (1971) and Samuelson (1971). Instead of assuming perfect intersectoral mobility of factors, it is assumed that at least one factor is specific to a particular industry. In the two-sector case, the natural assumption would be that capital is specific to a particular industry, while the other factor (labour) is drawn from a common pool.

The properties of this model contrast markedly with those of the Heckscher–Ohlin model. The pattern of trade can no longer be inferred from knowledge of aggregate factor endowments and factor intensities alone: relative supply elasticities and elasticities of substitution now play a role. Naturally, a country with greater relative abundance of the factor specific to a particular industry is likely to export the products of that industry. Specificity of a factor to a particular industry gives that factor a much stronger interest in trade policy than a mobile factor has – either in seeking protection if the industry is threatened by imports, or in lobbying for greater export opportunities if it is a potential export industry.

Such a model is useful for thinking about the trading opportunities of countries with particular natural resource endowments, in particular, perhaps, with minerals. It may also be a useful way of thinking of the short run. In the long run even capital goods depreciate and have to be renewed, and as that happens capital can be redeployed from one industry to another. We shall return to examine a model where capital is sector specific in the short run but mobile between sectors in the long run in discussing adjustment problems in section 7.4.

3.8 Summary

Orthodox trade theory has for the past fifty years been based on the idea that the fundamental determinant of the pattern of trade is the relative endowment of the factors of production that a country has at a given time. A country with an abundant supply of labour relative to capital will export labour-intensive goods, and vice versa – a proposition known as the Heckscher–Ohlin theorem. Leontief's empirical study, intended to confirm the Heckscher–Ohlin theorem as derived from a $2 \times 2 \times 2$ formulation, yielded instead the paradoxical result that the United States tended to import capital-intensive goods and export labour-intensive goods. While there are a number of possible explanations of the paradox, one that appears to be empirically important and consistent with the spirit of the Heckscher–Ohlin model involves recognizing the existence of more factors of production than homogeneous capital and homogeneous labour. Specifically, trade patterns appear to be importantly influenced by supplies of other factors, such as skilled labour and natural resources. The United States may export 'labour-intensive' goods because the high salaries that accrue to its abundant supply of skilled labour, which should from an analytic point of view be considered a return to human capital, are computed statistically as labour income. Similarly, the exports of many countries reflect their exploitation of particular natural resource endowments.

Indeed, there is now a substantial literature concerned with examining the theoretical robustness of the Heckscher–Ohlin theorem when the dimensions of the model are increased. The multi-factor, multi-product and multi-country framework does pose difficulties for the generalization of the theorem. But some specific restrictions or relaxations of the assumptions of the model that are empirically credible do allow us to make predictions about a chain of comparative advantage. When empirically tested in higher dimensions, the Heckscher–Ohlin model appears to be more robust than the earlier 'paradoxical' results suggested. But these recent applied studies suggest that we should view factor endowments as explaining broad sectoral patterns of trade and specialization. Additional factors may be important in explaining trade patterns at a more disaggregated level.

Reality inevitably diverges from the convenient assumptions of the basic Heckscher–Ohlin model. Some of the theoretical elegance and simplicity is lost by relaxation of these assumptions or by extending the dimensions of the model, but the richness of the model is increased as a result. The specific factors approach offers an alternative model that may be particularly useful in analyzing the short run.

3.9 Bibliography

The classic work introducing the Heckscher–Ohlin model is Ohlin (1933). The main work of formalizing the model was undertaken in a series of papers by Paul Samuelson, now conveniently available in Stiglitz (1966).

The outstanding contemporary exponent of the Heckscher–Ohlin model is Ronald Jones. A collection of his most important papers is in Jones (1979). Important surveys of trade theory which give substantial attention to factor endowment explanations of trade are Bhagwati (1964), Chipman (1965, 1966) and Jones and Neary (1984). A factor content form of the Heckscher–Ohlin theorem was formally elaborated by Vanek (1968).

Leontief first published the results that became known as the Leontief paradox in 1953; the paper is reprinted in Caves and Johnson (1968). Surveys of subsequent empirical work can be found in Baldwin (1971), Stern (1975), Deardorff (1984) and Tharakan (1985). A major recent test of a factor endowments model of trade is Leamer (1984).

Important papers on the specific factors model include Jones (1971) and Neary (1978). The determinants of comparative advantage in the context of specific factors models are also examined by Amano (1977).

A new and difficult area of trade theory not treated in the text concerns the introduction of uncertainty into trade models. The authoritative work on this topic is Helpman and Razin (1978). A survey of this and subsequent work is to be found in Pomery (1984).

Notes

1. The first term in parentheses indicates the point of production, and the second that of consumption.
2. Where economists do differ quite sharply is in their willingness to modify the agnostic position. On one side are those who argue that, since any departure from this position requires the application of subjective weights, there should be no such departures. On the other side are those who argue that the agnostic position itself implies a particular (and morally questionable) set of distributional weights, in which the marginal social utility of income is treated as the same regardless of whether the income accrues to a millionaire or a pauper. Those who take this position are relatively willing to attach subjective distributional weights to gains and losses and to use slender evidence as to who is gaining and who is losing in order to justify and guide government intervention.
3. The treatment in the text defines relative factor abundance in physical terms, so that L is the abundant factor in U when $L/K > L^*/K^*$. When this definition is used, it is necessary to add the assumption of identical (and homothetic) preferences in order to prove the theorem. There is, however, an alternative approach, which is to define L as being the abundant factor in U when $p_l/p_k < p_l^*/p_k^*$ in the absence of trade. That is, the abundant factor is defined as the one that would be relatively cheap if the economies were closed. This definition has the advantage of avoiding the need to make an additional assumption about consumer tastes, since if a greater physical abundance of labour were to be outweighed by a greater consumer preference for the labour-intensive good, this would already be reflected in a higher relative price of labour in autarchy. The drawback with this alternative definition is that since we do not observe countries in autarchy, we cannot even in principle know which factor is the abundant one. In our view this criticism is decisive, which is why the alternative approach has been relegated to a footnote.
4. Note that, while U's Edgeworth box has been drawn smaller than W's to remind us of the small-economy assumption, its scale is nevertheless much enlarged as compared to that of

W. (The small-economy assumption implies that U is negligibly small relative to W, but there would be no point in drawing a negligibly small Edgeworth box for U since then we could not see what was happening there.)

5. Stern and Maskus (1981), for instance, confirm the paradox for 1958, but not for 1972. This may be due to the declining importance of US imports of natural resources (imports of which tend to require high levels of capital in production/extraction). These researchers also find some support for the Heckscher–Ohlin model when tested in a multi-factor context.

6. Studies by Lowinger (1971) and Tyler (1972) on Brazil, by Bhagwati and Bharadwaj (1967) on India and by Cable and Rebelo (1980) on the UK.

7. Deardorff (1982) has demonstrated that the factor content form of the Heckscher–Ohlin model generalizes without factor price equalization, with different technologies in each country, or with differences in consumer preferences between countries.

4

Extending the neo-classical model

The $2 \times 2 \times 2$ Heckscher–Ohlin model set out in Chapter 3 is theoretically elegant, but not empirically robust. We have also seen how some of the manageability of the model is lost as its dimensions are increased. But one should not really expect to be able to explain all trade flows in terms of factor endowment influences, let alone with a model that assumes factor endowments to be fixed and all markets to be perfectly competitive.

This chapter makes a start in relaxing these assumptions. It retains the technological assumptions of the Heckscher–Ohlin model, and explores the implications of monopoly, changing factor endowments, the existence of intermediate goods and differences in demand conditions across countries.

4.1 Monopoly

Perfect competition prevails in the markets for a number of goods, primarily homogeneous commodities, but most industrial products are sold in markets in which competition is imperfect. The analysis of most alternative market structures is postponed to the next two chapters, where the technological assumptions employed are those that are naturally conducive to imperfect competition. But the implications of the extreme case of non-competitive conditions, namely a national monopoly, can be illustrated easily in the standard model.

Consider Figure 4.1. If our small economy (U) is closed and both industries are competitive, production and consumption will be at point E. Suppose, however, that industry M is monopolized; profits are now maximized in M by reducing output below the competitive level and raising the price above the marginal cost of production. This means that the economy's production mix shifts to a point such as F, with more resources being shifted into the production of X than would be the case in the absence of this distortion. (The relative price of X falls from DD to dd.)

Suppose now that the economy is opened to trade. Given the small-country assumption, the domestic monopolist is unable to influence world prices, and so the relative price of M (the assumed importable good under non-distorted conditions) will be driven down by the exposure to international competition. What this means for the production pattern depends, of course, upon the terms of trade. Consider the

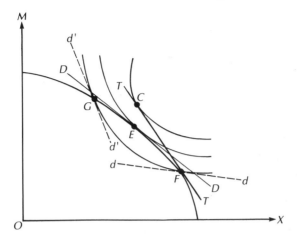

Figure 4.1 Effect of monopoly on specialization and trade

case shown in the diagram with terms of trade shown by TT; there is in this case no production effect, although trade takes place with M imported in exchange for X. Note that the economy gains more in this case from the opening of trade than if there had been no monopoly-induced distortion: compare the move from F to C in the monopoly case with that from E to C in the undistorted case. (The gains from trade are discussed in detail in Chapter 7.)

When it is the importable-producing industry that is monopolized, specialization is in line with genuine comparative advantage. However, the production effect of the opening of trade *may* be in the opposite direction to the perfect competition case: if the slope of TT were close to that of dd in Figure 4.1, then trade would result in output of the importable *expanding*.

Monopoly may therefore cause either over- or under-specialization in the activity of comparative advantage. This is not, however, the case where the monopolized sector produces the exportable product (X). Thus with autarchic production at G rather than at the competitive equilibrium E, the opening of trade might result in either a higher or lower relative price of X. But given the inability of the monopolist to exploit monopoly power on the home market once unrestricted re-import of X is possible, the industry will adjust its output to the competitive, free-trade equilibrium at F. The expansion of trade and welfare is again larger than would occur when starting from a competitive situation. This is a very general result and an extremely important conclusion: one of the benefits of international trade is its ability to break down national monopolies and introduce competition where it would not otherwise exist.

4.2 Changing factor endowments

We argued in Chapter 3 that factor endowments go furthest towards explaining the pattern of trade at a high level of product aggregation. Even for this purpose, however, we can go beyond the traditional static analysis developed in Chapter 3, to analyze the implications of changing factor endowments. We introduce this topic by presenting a classic theorem (the Rybczynski theorem) that deals with the impact of a one-off change in factor endowment, and then consider a stylized representation of a generalized development process (the stages approach to comparative advantage).

Rybczynski theorem

The theorem is due to T. Rybczynski (b. 1923), a Pole by birth and a British banker since his graduate student days when, in 1955, he published the paper introducing the theorem that bears his name. This theorem may be stated as follows: an increase in the endowment of one factor will reduce the production of the goods intensive in the *other* factor. In our example, this says that an increase in the quantity of labour (for example) would reduce output of M. At first this may seem surprising, inasmuch as an increase in the supplies of the factors of production is the basis of economic growth, and one associates growth with increases rather than decreases in the output of goods.

The assumptions on which this theorem is based are once more the 2×2 neo-classical technology, perfect factor mobility and, in this case, that the country accepts parametrically the commodity prices determined on the world market (the small-country assumption). The relative commodity price given by the world market dictates that a particular point, for example E in Figure 4.2, should be the equilibrium point on the contract curve (not shown) that runs from O_x to O_m^0 when the labour supply is $O_x L_0$. Suppose, however, that the labour supply expands to $O_x L_1$ because of an influx of migrant workers forced to return home when recession

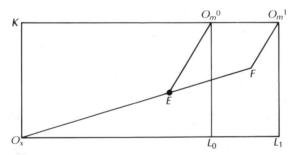

Figure 4.2 Effect of a population influx

strikes the former host country. What can be said about the new optimum point on the new contract curve (again not shown) that runs from O_x to O_m^1? Since commodity prices (and technology) are by assumption unchanged, factor prices must also remain unchanged. But in that case, given that the production functions are linear homogeneous, production of X and M must still take place with the same factor proportions as before. This means that production of X must take place on the ray $O_x E$ extended, while that of M must lie on a ray $O_m^1 F$ from O_m^1 parallel to $O_m^0 E$: that is, the new production point must be F in Figure 4.2. (Point F must lie on the new contract curve because the slopes of both X and M isoquants are – by virtue of the linear homogeneity of the production functions – the same at F as at E and are therefore equal to one another at F as they were by assumption at E.) But at F the output of M is lower than at E, as the theorem says.

The stages approach

Economic growth typically involves relative growth in the stock of capital, rather than the isolated growth of the labour force considered in the above example. The Rybczynski theorem tells us that countries enjoying such growth should expect to see the size of their labour-intensive industries contract. Unfortunately for both countries trying to industrialize and consumers in developed countries, most members of the parliaments of the industrialized countries are not acquainted with the Rybczynski theorem, and consequently many of them attempt to sustain their labour-intensive industries through protection. Those who have grasped the implications of the Rybczynski theorem realize that comparative advantage is not something given once and for all, to be clung to obstinately as factor supplies change, any more than it is to be spurned as something that condemns a country to the role of hewer of wood and drawer of water; rather it should be exploited at any moment while striving to expand supplies of capital and qualified workers. To the extent that those endeavours succeed, the comparative advantage of the country will move up to more sophisticated products, while economic pressures make for a withdrawal from yesterday's more basic and labour-intensive goods, in the process making way for newcomers to develop manufactured exports and take their first steps up the ladder of economic progress. Such is, at least, the optimistic story of how an export-oriented strategy can harness dynamic comparative advantage in the cause of development (see Chapter 15).

In fact, barriers to trade imposed by industrial countries against labour-intensive imports from developing countries in the post-war period (for example, in the case of textiles under the Multi-fibre Arrangement) have hindered this process. Nonetheless a significant number of developing countries have increased their exports of manufactured goods and have made steps up the ladder of economic development, in a way that is consistent with the dynamics of comparative advantage as represented by the Rybczynski theorem. Consider Table 4.1, which compares the nature of the trade balance on labour and capital goods of a number of countries in 1958 with that in 1958. Several industrializing countries, from Spain to Yugoslavia in the table, were already net exporters of labour-intensive goods by 1975. But to this group of most industrially developed exporters has been added a large number of newly industrializing countries (NICs) that by 1975 were also net exporters of labour-intensive goods: Brazil to Turkey of the countries listed in Table 4.1. In the same way that these countries have taken the first step on the development ladder, a few countries have gone further: thus Korea and Spain had achieved a surplus on (physical) capital-intensive exports by 1975. The corollary of this shift of comparative advantage and production towards newcomers is a shift away from some existing producers. Thus

Table 4.1 Comparative advantage and the ladder of development

Country	Sign[1] on trade balance for:			
	Labour-intensive[2] goods		Capital-intensive[2] goods	
	1958	1975	1958	1975
France	+	+	+	+
Germany	+	−	+	+
UK	+	−	+	+
USA	+	−	+	−
Korea	−	+	−	+
Spain	+	+	−	+
Hong Kong	+	+	−	−
Israel	+	+	−	−
Portugal	+	+	−	−
Yugoslavia	+	+	−	−
Brazil	−	+	−	−
Colombia	−	+	−	−
Cyprus	−	+	−	−
Egypt	−	+	−	−
Greece	−	+	−	−
Malta	−	+	−	−
Philippines	−	+	−	−
Thailand	−	+	−	−
Turkey	−	+	−	−

[1] Trade surplus (+) and deficit (−).
[2] Aggregates of two-digit categories of trade in the Standard International Trade
Classification. Machinery and chemicals are treated as two further aggregates but not
reported here.
Source: Leamer (1984).

the table shows how countries such as Germany and the UK have become net
importers of labour-intensive goods, and the United States of both labour- and
capital-intensive goods. These countries' comparative advantage has shifted further
towards the production of human capital- and technology-intensive goods, such as
machinery and chemicals.

Since 1975 there appears to have been further progress up the development ladder
at many points. The Asian NICs have been very successful in expanding and
diversifying their exports further. Similarly, at the 'bottom of the ladder' there have
been a significant number of new entrants, such as Mauritius, Malaysia, Tunisia and
Morocco.

This evidence of a changing pattern of comparative advantage, with the structure
of exports developing in line with changing relative factor endowments, has prompted
what has been referred to as a 'stages approach' to comparative advantage. It would
be unwise to view trade and development as precisely and generally following some
predetermined pattern. But it is helpful to view comparative advantage in a dynamic
setting in which some common and recurring characteristics of development fashion

the evolution, at least in broad outline, of the commodity composition of a country's trade.

4.3 Footloose industries and intermediate goods

The previous section has shown how the Heckscher–Ohlin theorem, when extended to allow for factor accumulation, is able to explain why and which production processes have tended to be drawn towards the NICs. Typically, the NICs have established a comparative advantage in the production of labour-intensive, final goods, or rather in the final stage of processing of finished goods (initially textiles and footwear and subsequently electrical consumer goods). Their comparative advantage has been in the standardized assembly of imported raw materials and intermediate inputs, where highly specialized capital and labour skills are not required. The simple nature of the technologies and the ability of firms, often foreign multinationals, to 'import' and maintain the necessary machinery has meant that such activities have expanded rapidly where labour is cheap and government policy is supportive. It is also true that these activities can be contracted quickly as the relative profitability of alternative locations changes. Thus the basic Heckscher–Ohlin model of trade needs to be further extended to allow for trade in intermediate goods and 'footloose industries'. We must recognize that factors of production are not the only inputs into production, and that international exchange of final goods is not the only form of international exchange.

Intermediate goods

The production of most final goods involves a series of intermediate stages of production: skins become hides, hides are transformed into leather and then leather is an input into numerous final products (footwear, furniture, clothing). Often different stages of the transformation are performed by different industries, with different factor input requirements. Comparative advantage may therefore dictate that the location of the various processes should be in different countries, exploiting different factor endowments. A country with a cost advantage in hides or leather may be inappropriately endowed in terms of factor inputs to produce furniture or clothing. Thus the Heckscher–Ohlin model must be related to processes rather than to products, and intermediate goods as well as final goods may enter into international trade. The outputs of one country can be inputs in production processes in other countries. The patterns of international production and trade may in these circumstances differ from those predicted by the 'classical paradigm' of trade in final goods only.

A simple extension of our basic model illustrates this. Suppose that the goods M and X are final consumer goods, and that they are produced with (non-traded) capital and labour *and* each with an intermediate input (m_i and x_i respectively) (for simplicity we assume that m_i and x_i are available in fixed amounts and require no further factors to acquire when not imported). If m_i and x_i cannot be traded on world markets then our economy's production possibility curve is shown in Figure 4.3 by the curve PP; m_i is assumed to be relatively abundant domestically. Suppose, however, that both x_i and m_i can be traded on world markets at world prices which reflect a relative abundance internationally of x_i. If some of our country's m_i can be exchanged for x_i at world prices, this will cause a shift in the production possibility frontier, say to $P'P'$. In fact an infinite number of PP frontiers are possible (including the original one) as the composition of the bundle of inputs (of a given value) changes. The frontier $P''P''$ represents the envelope of all the possible curves and is the production possibility

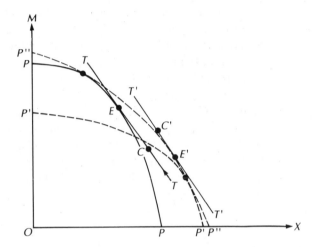

Figure 4.3 Trade in intermediate inputs and patterns of trade and specialization

schedule for our country with balanced trade in intermediate inputs (and constant world prices). With the international terms of trade for final goods represented by TT (or $T'T'$), production and consumption without trade in inputs are at E and C respectively (assuming conventionally shaped indifference curves that have been omitted for presentational convenience). But with (balanced) trade in inputs equilibrium is at E' and C'. Thus our country shifts from exporting M to exporting X. Our country's pattern of production and trade in final goods, and the commodity composition of trade, have been dramatically affected by the ability to trade in intermediate goods. The reason is the ability that trade provides to overcome the mismatch between the relative supply of intermediate inputs (which favours the importable) and the factor endowment for production of final goods (which favours the exportable).

It is evident from the construction of this revised model that the scope for gains is enhanced by the possibility of trade in inputs. (C' is on a higher indifference curve than C in Figure 4.3.) The case presented involves balanced trade in intermediates. But this is an arbitrary constraint and there may be a possibility of increasing these gains further by having unbalanced trade in intermediates. Thus a country like Japan is a net importer of intermediates and raw materials, and is able as a result to take advantage of its comparative advantage in the export of a wide range of final goods; net export of these final goods finances net import of intermediates. The story is reversed in the case of countries abundant in natural resources, such as Canada or Saudi Arabia.

Footloose production processes

This analysis of trade in intermediate goods is clearly relevant to the explanation of the NICs' success in expanding exports of final consumer goods. But we also need to recognize that factors of production may move internationally. In particular, capital may move from high-wage industrial countries to developing countries, in order to take advantage of lower wages for more labour-intensive stages of production. Such fragmentation of industrial processes and geographical spread of activities is profitable where the specialization and wage cost advantages exceed the additional transport costs incurred, provided product quality is maintained. It can, as shown earlier, be consistent with unfettered and efficient allocation of global resources.

Economic policies are also an important influence. For instance, developing countries often create what are termed 'export-processing zones' (EPZs); manufacturers in these zones are eligible for a set of policy incentives. These incentives typically include duty exemptions on imported intermediate inputs, exemption from national wages and employment legislation, subsidized provision of factories and other infrastructure support, and 'tax holidays' which grant exemption from profits taxes for specified periods. EPZ firms typically employ low-skilled labour and sell all or most of their output abroad. Given the competitive bidding that takes place between countries to attract the processing activities of multinational firms, the firms have a strong incentive to be highly flexible about where they locate a particular process. However, given the costs of the incentives provided to foreign-owned firms and the possibility of distorting the host country's pattern of production, the allocation of global resources associated with this type of processing activity is not necessarily optimal, and the host countries are not necessarily net gainers.

We return to the issues of gains from trade and the welfare effects of trade policies in subsequent chapters. The discussion in this section has been concerned with demonstrating some important ways in which the Heckscher–Ohlin model needs to be extended if it is to be operationally useful. There are other dimensions that could be explored: for example, the implication of differences in national income tax treatment where factor inputs are footloose. But we will leave the reader to explore this issue with the aid of the analysis in this section.

4.4 Demand differences

All the preceding discussion of the determinants of trade has abstracted from demand-side differences between countries. The neo-classical theory of trade, like earlier classical theories, focuses predominantly on supply-side differences between countries as the major determinant of international trade. Thus the Heckscher–Ohlin theorem holds when, amongst other things, preferences are identical between countries. Of course, it is not surprising that there should be this emphasis on supply, rather than demand, differences: systematic differences in tastes between industrialized countries were not perceived to exist, and resource endowment differences between industrial and developing countries offered a plausible explanation of trade between these countries. But differences in demand conditions between countries do influence trade patterns at the detailed product level.

It is possible to construct a model in the neo-classical tradition in which there are no (relative) factor endowment differences between countries, and trade as a result takes place merely as a result of demand differences between countries. Consider Figure 4.4. If all the (supply-side) assumptions of the Heckscher–Ohlin model are retained and we now assume also that relative factor endowments are identical between our country and the rest of the world, then the production possibility frontier (PP) is identical for all countries (except for scale). With identical

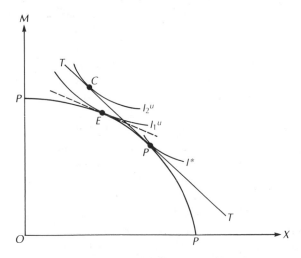

Figure 4.4 Demand differences and trade

preferences between countries there would be no incentive to trade. However, if our country has a distinct set of preferences represented by the I^u indifference curves, then there will be a pre-trade relative price difference between our country and the rest of the world. At the autarchic equilibrium, good M is relatively expensive in our country and is relatively cheap in the rest of the world, given the world's preference for X (represented by the indifference curve I^*). The opening of trade lowers the relative price of M to the international terms of trade (TT). The result is less specialization in our country in the production of the preferred good M (a shift from E to P) and more specialization in consumption (a shift from E to C); our country exports X in order to acquire more of M through importing than it could acquire without trade.

In specific products and in trade between countries with similar factor endowments it may be appropriate to focus on demand factors as a source of trade. There are traditional and cultural differences that generate demand dissimilarities at the product level between countries, even though they may have similar levels of average capita income. But as a theory of trade in general, demand dissimilarity is not very appealing. In the post-war period international trade has been dominated by trade between industrialized countries with increasingly similar per capita incomes. This, combined with increased openness and increased international communications and travel, suggests that dissimilarity of demand is likely to have declined over time. Supply similarity has presumably increased as well, as a result of factor mobility and technology transfer. Yet these developments have been associated with *increasing* trade, which is highly paradoxical from a neo-classical standpoint. It was this paradox, as well as the Leontief paradox, which induced a search from the mid-1950s onwards for alternative models of trade in manufactures between industrial countries. It is to a consideration of these alternative explanations of trade that we turn next.

4.5 Summary

The Heckscher–Ohlin model can be extended beyond the restrictive assumptions that were adopted to introduce it in Chapter 3. The model can show how trade can break down the power of a national monopoly, in the process altering the volume and perhaps even the composition of trade from that which would have occurred starting from a position of perfect competition. Relaxation of the assumption that factor endowments are fixed can help to illuminate the emergence of newly industrializing countries as exporters of manufactured goods. Multinational firms can move capital, for example, to the best production location according to the factor input requirements of alternative stages of the production process. Indeed, once we relate the Heckscher–Ohlin model to processes or stages of activity rather than products (in particular, final products), then we need to recognize that intermediate goods are likely to be exchanged internationally and that comparative advantage in higher-stage products may be different from that applying in the absence of trade in inputs. In recent years a remote developing country, Mauritius, has had considerable success in exporting knitted woollen garments to European markets. The wool is not acquired from sheep reared on the island! Foreign garment producers have taken advantage of Mauritius' export-processing zone and relatively cheap labour. Thus relative factor endowment differences between countries play a central role in explaining trade between developed and developing countries.

However, most trade in manufactured goods is between industrial countries, whose relative factor endowments are similar. Demand dissimilarity may play a role in generating trade in specific cases. But overall demand and supply characteristics in industrialized countries have become more similar over time, and the Heckscher–Ohlin model would predict diminishing specialization and trade. The evidence is at odds with this prediction. We need, therefore, to explore alternative explanations of trade.

4.6 Bibliography

There is a very recent literature on the role of imperfect competition in international trade where there are no factor endowment differences between countries. These new theories of trade are examined in Chapter 6. In the context of neo-classical trade theory there are important contributions on imperfect competition by Melvin and Warne (1973) and Caves (1979). The survey article by Jones and Neary (1984) also includes some useful material in this area.

The Rybczynski theorem appeared in Rybczynski (1955) and is reprinted in Caves and Johnson (1968). The 'stages approach' to comparative advantage was formalized by Balassa (1979). There is also an important literature on formally modelling the effects of growth on trade, which has not been considered in the text: see, for example, Johnson (1955) and Findlay (1984).

Sanyal and Jones (1982) develop a model of trade in intermediate goods and processed raw materials. An evaluation of the benefits and costs of export-processing zones is provided by Warr (1989). Hufbauer and Chilas (1974) show the potential losses from competitive efforts to attract foreign manufacturers.

5

Beyond factor endowments

In Chapters 3 and 4 on factor endowment explanations of trade, two apparent paradoxes were identified. One was the Leontief paradox; the other was the existence of intense and rapidly expanding trade between industrial countries with similar factor endowments. One explanation, of course, of why the United States might export relatively labour-intensive goods and why trade is not most intense between countries with very different supply characteristics (such as between industrialized and primary-producing countries) is that the Heckscher–Ohlin model is mistaken in identifying differences in resource endowment as the major source of trade. This possibility has in fact received considerable attention in the last decade in the new theoretical literature on trade in differentiated goods, in which the possibility of simultaneous import and export by the same country of very similar products has been recognized. These new theories of two-way (intra-industry) exchange, which were predominantly a response to the second paradox and to a search for an understanding of why the enormous growth of trade among industrial countries during the post-war period had not been associated with substantial adjustment problems, are considered in detail in Chapter 6.

The search for alternative explanations of trade in fact began shortly after identification of the Leontief paradox, and had yielded a number of important insights before the modelling of intra-industry trade got under way. This chapter deals with these contributions, all of which involve departures from the technological assumptions of the Heckscher–Ohlin model.

5.1 Economies of scale

In the one case that can be analyzed using the same techniques as those developed in the previous chapters, there are two distinct (as opposed to differentiated) products both subject to increasing returns to scale. Consider first the implications of economies of scale (alias increasing return to scale or a production function homogeneous of degree greater than 1) for the production possibility curve of a single country. In a world with only one factor of production, it is clear that increasing returns would imply a production possibility frontier *convex* to the origin, as shown in Figure 5.1(a). (To emphasize that we believe these models to be relevant to trade in manufactures rather than to all trade, we call the two goods M_1 and M_2.) With all the single factor devoted to the production of M_1 it would be possible to produce M_1^{max}, and with it all devoted to the production of M_2 it would be possible to produce M_2^{max}, but with half devoted to the production of each it would not be possible to produce as much as $\frac{1}{2}M_1^{max}$ and $\frac{1}{2}M_2^{max}$, but only $\overline{M}_1$ and $\overline{M}_2$. Because a doubling of input permits more than a doubling of output, from $\overline{M}_1$ to M_1^{max}, and from $\overline{M}_2$ to M_2^{max}, the centrepoint of the ppc must lie *inside* the straight line from M_1^{max} to M_2^{max}. That is, the ppc is convex to the origin as shown.

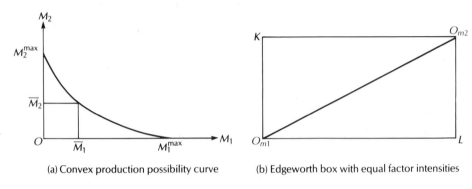

(a) Convex production possibility curve   (b) Edgeworth box with equal factor intensities

Figure 5.1 Production possibilities under increasing returns to scale

Consider next the situation with two factors of production, but where the factor intensities of the two goods happen to be equal. Then the Edgeworth box has the diagonal as contract curve, as shown in Figure 5.1(b). The midpoint of that contract curve corresponds to the isoquants of $\overline{M}_1$ and $\overline{M}_2$ in Figure 5.1(a), while the corners correspond to M_1^{max} (at O_{m2}) and M_2^{max} (at O_{m1}). Because of increasing returns, M_1^{max} would be more than $2\overline{M}_1$ and M_2^{max} would be more than $2\overline{M}_2$. Once again, therefore, we would get a convex ppc as in Figure 5.1(a).

In general, of course, factor intensities are not equal. Changes in the scale of production of the two goods therefore require changes in the factor intensity in each industry in order to maintain full utilization of both factors, and so the contract curve lies below (or above) the diagonal. With constant returns to scale these differing factor intensities imply a concave ppc (see Chapter 3). With increasing returns to scale and different factor intensities we therefore have two effects at work and operating in opposite directions: increasing returns making for convexity of the ppc, differing factor intensities making for concavity. Where the second factor dominates, we have the same analysis as in the previous chapters.[1] Where the two factors just counterbalance one another, we would be back to the straight-line ppc of Chapter 2. And where increasing returns outweigh differing factor intensities, we get a convex ppc. This case is more probable the greater are increasing returns and the less are the differences in factor intensities.

Consider next what would happen in a world with two countries each possessing a convex ppc. To clarify the central point, let us suppose that these two countries are identical in every respect: not only with respect to technology and tastes as assumed in Chapter 3, but also with respect to size and relative factor endowments. It follows that their ppcs, as well as their social indifference curves, would be identical. Suppose that they both have the form shown in Figure 5.2(a), in which increasing returns to scale outweigh the effect of differing factor intensities. This would give rise to a *world* ppc with the form shown by the bold curve in Figure 5.2(b). The reason for this strange shape is as follows. If they both specialized in the production of M_1, it would be possible to achieve a world output of $2M_1^{max}$ (and zero M_2). Similarly, if both produced only M_2, total world production of M_2 would be $2M_2^{max}$. It would also be possible to achieve the point E, with production at M_1^{max} and M_2^{max}, by having one (either one) country specialize in the production of M_1 and the other specialize in the production of M_2. If each country divided its factors between the two industries

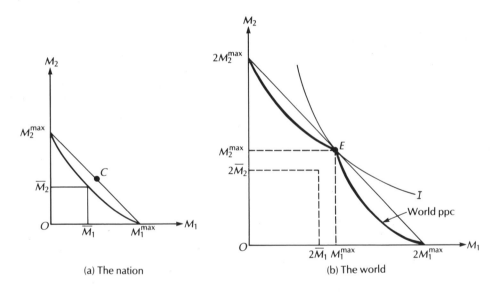

(a) The nation   (b) The world

Figure 5.2 National and world production possibilities with increasing returns

rather than specializing, world production would reach only $2\overline{M}_1$, $2\overline{M}_2$, because neither of them would be exploiting the available economies of scale. Between E and $2M_1^{max}$, the world ppc would follow the form of the national ppc in Figure 5.2(a), since one country would specialize in M_1 while the other would divide its factors between M_1 and M_2. The world ppc would follow an identical form between E and $2M_2^{max}$, with one country specializing (producing M_2) and the other producing both goods.

Suppose that world conditions of demand happened to be as portrayed by the social indifference curve I in Figure 5.2(b), which not only touches the world ppc at E but also is tangential to the straight line from $2M_1^{max}$ to $2M_2^{max}$ through E. In this case both countries can gain by agreeing to specialize – it does not matter on which product – and then trading along the world price line to consume at C in Figure 5.2(a), which lies outside the national ppc. The point is that increasing returns to scale provide an *additional* source of gain from trade: countries that are identical with respect to factor endowments and tastes can *still* gain from mutual exchange.

However, there is no reason to suppose that world demand would be such as to lead to the symmetrical outcome portrayed in Figure 5.2. It is easy to imagine a situation where demand is much stronger for M_2, for example, than for M_1, as shown in Figure 5.3.[2] It can be seen from Figure 5.3(b) that the world can still reach the highest possible indifference curve by both countries specializing, but, as seen in Figure 5.3(a), the country that specializes in the product M_1 in lesser demand will end up at point C with much lower real income than the one that specializes in M_2 and can

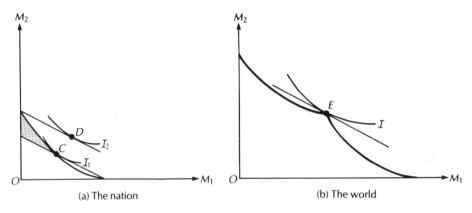

(a) The nation   (b) The world

Figure 5.3 Problems of world equilibrium with increasing returns

trade down to point D. The country producing M_1 might well rue the historical accident that resulted in its specializing in M_1 rather than M_2, but nevertheless conclude that the cost of trying to displace an established foreign monopoly in the production of M_2 would be prohibitive. The economists of the so-called dependency school, led by the Egyptian Samir Amin (b. 1931), tend to view the world division of labour between Northern producers of manufactures and Southern producers of primary products somewhat in these terms.

There is another problem with the equilibrium portrayed in Figure 5.3: it is not clear that it *is* an equilibrium. The equilibria encountered in the previous chapters had all points preferred by consumers to the equilibrium point *above* the price line (which is still true here) and the whole of the production set below the price line (which is not true of the shaded area in Figure 5.3(a)). This means that at the prevailing prices producers could make more money if they were to switch their resources from the production of M_1 to M_2. If they did this, they would not *in fact* make more money, since the price of M_2 would decline; but no individual *competitive* producer would recognize this. In other words, perfect competition could not sustain the equilibrium shown in Figure 5.3. This should not occasion surprise, since increasing returns is one of the classic causes of the breakdown of perfect competition. But it is useful to have this reminder that trade in manufactures is generally not conducted under market conditions approximating perfect competition. The norm, especially for consumer goods, is for the firm to list a price and sell all that is demanded at that price. The British economist Sir John Hicks (b. 1904), winner of the Nobel prize in 1972, called markets where this occurs *fixprice* markets. (With capital goods, prices are often individually negotiated.) Among manufactures, it is only intermediate goods where market conditions at all often approach the *flexprice* markets[3] which provide the basis for the competitive abstraction beloved of economic theory.

Thus increasing returns to scale provide an *additional* factor motivating trade, which may lead to both countries benefiting from trade even when they are *identical* with respect to technology and tastes. However, such trade cannot be carried on in conditions of perfect competition, and equilibrium will require that the firms involved have some degree of market power. Moreover, it is by no means guaranteed that the benefits of trade will be distributed symmetrically, and it is entirely possible that those who gain relatively less will regard such an asymmetrical distribution of the benefits as inequitable, even though they too are better off with trade than without it.

5.2 Technological change

The Heckscher–Ohlin model takes technology to be both exogenous and fixed. The best technology is costlessly available to all countries. Needless to say, this is a caricature of technological conditions in such industries as chemicals or electronics. Differences in technology underlie at least a substantial part of the trade in such products.

Technology-gap theorem

This theorem proposes that 'temporary' differences in industry-specific knowledge determine trade. A country will export the goods of those industries in which it has a technology-gap advantage over other countries, even though both exporting and importing countries may have similar factor endowments.

There are two basic premises which underpin the informal model first developed by the English economist Michael Posner (b. 1931). First, there are systematic and endogenous factors which influence the initial location of technological advance. At the particular time when Posner was writing, the United States was the clear technological leader in the world. The United States was the largest and richest country, which created both demand and supply conditions conducive to investment in the process of technological progress (that is, in pure research, process or product development and innovation). With high per capita incomes there is likely to be a demand for new, more technologically sophisticated products and on a scale sufficient to allow firms to reduce average fixed costs to levels that make mass marketing feasible. A highly skilled labour force provides the opportunity for innovations, while high wages create the incentive for adopting them, including labour-saving process innovations.

The second of Posner's premises is that technology is not a free input and it is not transferred instantaneously from one country to another. Since technological progress is the outcome of a process that absorbs real resources, there are strong incentives to protect one's investment in the technological lead (e.g. by patents) and reap the rents (including royalties) that result from a monopoly position. Even where not protected by legal or administrative action, transfer of technology may only take place through expenditure on new capital equipment that embodies the latest vintage of technical know-how, or the marketing of new technology-intensive products may require investment.

Given these two premises, it is easy to understand why Posner felt that firms in the United States were more likely to supply risk capital for reseach and development than firms in other countries, and more likely to produce technologically sophisticated goods initially for and in the United States. Once the process of innovation is complete in the country with a technological lead, its implications for the pattern of trade in subsequent time periods depend upon the time lags involved: specifically, in the response of foreign consumers (the 'demand' lag) versus producers (the 'imitation' lag). Where the demand lag is shorter than the imitation lag, technology-gap trade is generated once a demand for the new product emerges in the technologically lagging countries.

An infinite number of possibilities could be rehearsed about the duration and pattern of technology-gap trade, depending upon the length of the imitation lag and the frequency of technological advances. Let us illustrate one feasible scenario, with the aid of Figure 5.4. Up to time t_1 the research and development process is undertaken, with either no production or production for domestic consumption only (i.e. autarchy). At t_1 the new product is made available for export. The extent of the demand lag overseas will determine how quickly exports grow: the slower the demand response, the flatter the shape of the export curve (i.e. the smaller the tangent of α in the figure). It is the imitation lag, however, that will determine how large exports grow (i.e. the maximum level of exports, X_{max}, per time period): the longer the imitation lag, the higher will be X_{max}, provided the exporter's capacity constraint is not reached. Once imitation does take place, exports will tend to decline, with the rate of decline depending upon the speed of imitation and the extent of scale advantages of existing over new entrants to the market. Of course, exports of products associated with the initial technological lead could fall to zero, if all markets can sustain a local producer. However, since there were endogenous factors that gave one country a technological lead in one product or product range, these are likely to result in a recurring pattern of 'temporary' technology gaps. In Figure 5.4 the initiation of exports of a more advanced product at t_3 occurs before exports from the first innovation have fallen back to zero.

Although the model lacks the theoretical precision of the models that we have examined previously, it does draw attention to important considerations omitted by other models. The model was developed at a time when one country, the United

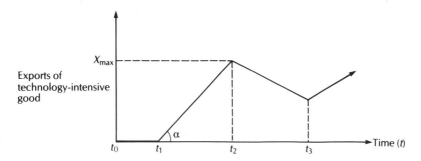

Figure 5.4 Technology gaps and trade

States, had an obvious technological lead. There is now more competition between the major industrial countries or country blocks in technology-intensive products. Thus we are unlikely to be able to use the model to make clear predictions about the commodity content of trade of this nature. But there is a considerable amount of empirical evidence which is consistent, at least, with the technology-gap theorem: namely, of a correlation between export performance and industries' research and development effort.

The model expounded by Posner provides an explanation of why technology gaps emerge and how they might disappear. But it offers little explanation for the duration of the gap and for what factors will determine the location of production, i.e. of comparative advantage, of a particular product once technological diffusion has taken place. The product-cycle model seeks to fill this gap.

Product cycles

The product-cycle theory, developed principally by Raymond Vernon (b. 1913), seeks to incorporate technology-gap principles into a framework in which there are factor endowment differences between countries and in which multinational production is possible. It is a model that might therefore be considered in the context either of trade theory or of the theory of international investment.

The product cycle, like the technology-gap model, starts with an innovation that affects production costs or product characteristics and occurs in a specific type of economy in a world where some countries are relatively labour abundant, some relatively land abundant and some relatively capital abundant. Vernon argued that innovation and new products are more likely to occur in a high-wage, capital-abundant country (in Vernon's exposition this was again the United States).

In the early stages of development, new products will be manufactured close to the market. As the product matures, however, and a certain amount of standardization takes place, an increasing amount of total production is likely to be exported. At this stage of the product's life, however, relative production costs become increasingly important. As the product becomes standardized and knowledge becomes more freely available, potential competition may threaten in export markets. Where the original producer obtains patents for export markets, this threat may be delayed. But at some point the potential competition is most likely to be translated into actual competition in other capital-rich countries. If in these countries unit labour costs are lower than in the innovating country, comparative advantage and the optimal production location will shift. Whether the original innovating firm sets up production facilities in the importing countries or whether production comes predominantly from a local producer, the impliction for trade is the same: exports from the innovating country decline.

The final stage of the product cycle occurs when full standardization is achieved. It is conceivable that the location of production could shift yet again, in this case to labour-abundant economies where unit labour costs are relatively low. Production could be by local, indigenous producers or by multinational firms, with the parent company setting up a production facility in the low-wage economy. Imports into the low-wage economy will decrease and production will increase to such an extent that some output is exported. Thus exports from the high-wage and medium-wage economies decline, and may indeed even be converted into imports.

Figure 5.5 summarizes this interrelationship between product stage and economy type over a product cycle. The segments show a possible stylized representation of the pattern of production and consumption over time for each of the country types. In the case of the innovating, capital-rich/high-wage economy (top segment) the product is exported until the standardized stage. For the other two countries domestic production of the product is initiated later and as a result it is not until after the start of the standardized product stage is reached that these countries may become exporters. Ultimately, comparative advantage is located in the capital-poor/low-wage economy, and the original innovator becomes an importer of the standardized product.

Again this model of technological change as the basis of trade provides some interesting insights into the dynamics of the way in which comparative advantage can shift through time. Clearly, it is more appropriate for certain types of product, e.g. electrical goods and electronics where research and development are important inputs into the production process, than for the many products where the scope for product and process innovation is limited. The criteria for distinguishing product type and therefore for establishing the duration of particular stages of product cycle cannot be precisely and consistently defined for all products. Again the model was easier to apply when the United States was the obvious and sole initial location of comparative advantage in technologically intensive goods. There is impressionistic and some case-study support for the idea that there are product cycles for individual products that cause trade patterns to change over time, but it is difficult to identify the importance at any one moment in time of this source of trade relative to other sources.

The empirical evidence does give support for the view that technological know-how is, among other factors, significant in explaining cross-country variations in export performance. But this evidence may be consistent with an extended version of the Heckscher–Ohlin model in which we recognize more factors of production.

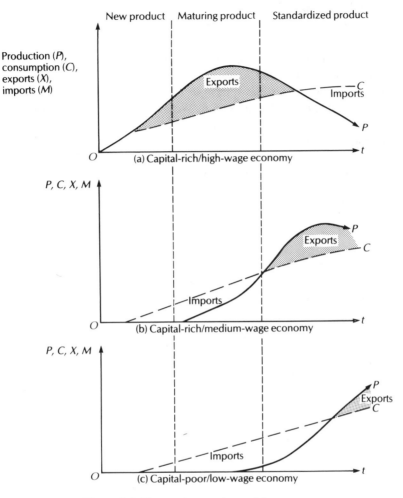

Figure 5.5 The product-cycle model

The absence of robust statistical support, the restricted applicability and the lack of theoretical precision of these models does not mean that we should dismiss the additional insights provided.

5.3 Linder thesis

A more comprehensive attempt to explain the pattern of trade in manufactures was made by the Swedish economist and politician Staffan Linder (b. 1931). In Linder (1961) he drew a sharp distinction between trade in primary products, which he argued would be determined on the basis of factor endowments, especially of natural resources, as in the traditional Heckscher–Ohlin model, and trade in manufactures. In the case of the latter, he argued that factor intensities were much the same and that the principal determinant of the pattern of trade was to be found in the structure of demand, especially in trade between high-income countries.

Linder regarded the structure of demand as the *qualities* of differentiated products demanded in a country. He argued that the principal determinant of the demand structure would be the level of per capita income: countries with high average real income would not just tend to consume *more* cars, for example, but also *better quality* cars. The idea is illustrated in Figure 5.6. We have to suppose that it is possible to array the quality of the various makes of a product – cars provide a good example – in an unambiguous way from the worst below Q_1 to the best above Q_6. On Linder's supposition that the quality of product a consumer wants is rigidly linked to his or her income level, a consumer with income Y_A would demand a product of quality Q_4.

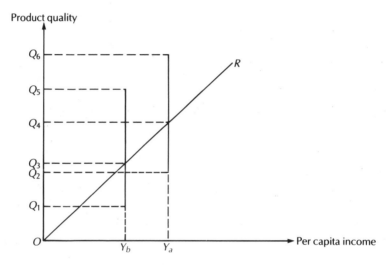

Figure 5.6 Per capita income, product quality and trade

However, because in any country incomes are unequal, a country with *average* income level Y_A will demand a *range* of product qualities between Q_2 and Q_6. Similarly, a country with average per capita income Y_B, whose representative consumer would demand a product of quality Q_3, would have demands for a range of products spread from Q_1 to Q_5. Obviously, this general picture of a range of demands spread around a mean determined by mean (or perhaps median or modal) per capita income would not be essentially affected if we admitted, as surely we must, that the world contains many people who choose not to consume the particular product quality that is typical at their income level. Recognition of this simply provides an additional reason for expecting a demand for a range of product qualities of any good.

Linder argued that each country would confine its production to goods within the range of product quality *consumed* domestically. In the example in the figure, a country with average income Y_A would produce products within the quality range from Q_2 to Q_6, and a country with average income Y_B would produce products within the range between Q_1 and Q_5. He cited three reasons for believing that countries would not initiate production outside those ranges: that is, for the export market. First, the limited information of entrepreneurs would prevent their discerning the existence of demand for a good that was not being consumed locally. Second, even if the need for a good with certain qualities in potential demand abroad were to be correctly perceived, lack of familiarity would impede development of a product with the right characteristics. Third, even if a basically appropriate product were to be conceived, the distance from the market would make it difficult and expensive to make those continuous adaptations to the quality of the product that are necessary for commercial success. For these reasons, production is *initiated* to serve the domestic market, and only *afterwards* do some of those products start being exported. This account also helps to show why trade in primary products is so different: there is normally no question of inventing or even adapting the quality of the product, but just the need to perceive the external market. Linder argued that situations where the necessary natural resources exist but are not being exploited by local entrepreneurs because of the failure to perceive the external market are exactly those where multinationals are attracted into extractive industry.

The last question to consider is which of the various products a country will tend to export. Linder's answer is that, again in terms of Figure 5.6, the countries will exchange products in the quality range from Q_2 to Q_5, where their consumption patterns overlap. From this he derives one of his basic conclusions: that the potential for trade in manufactures is greatest between countries at *similar* income levels. This is, of course, the reverse of the conclusion suggested by the Heckscher–Ohlin model, where differences in per capita income signify different capital-labour ratios and therefore a *greater* potential for trade. Linder also suggests that countries will tend to produce products designed to satisfy the representative demands in their own countries, like Q_4 in the country with mean income Y_A and Q_3 in the country with mean income Y_B, and export those goods that satisfy typical demands at home in order to satisfy minority tastes in other countries. Although he does not provide a completely satisfactory rationale as to why this would be likely to happen, it is not difficult to fill the gap. If there are economies of scale and transport costs, firms will have a competitive advantage in producing those products with greatest sales levels at home and exploiting the scale economies realized by high production volumes in order to export to satisfy minority tastes abroad. The converse strategy, producing to satisfy local minority tastes and exporting the bulk of output, could still realize the scale economies but would involve a larger bill for transportation and therefore be uneconomic without some differences in factor endowment or technology that more than compensated.

In the decades since Linder wrote his paper, there has been an explosive growth in international travel and communication. It stands to reason that this has reduced the barriers to perceiving foreign markets, to understanding the type of product needed to cater to them, and to modifying product characteristics in the light of market reactions. These factors nonetheless remain important, and some limitations on producer horizons when combined with overlapping but similar tastes and economies of scale provide a rationale for bilateral or two-way trade flows between similar economies where factor endowment differences do not exist.

The Linder thesis is not a universal theory of trade, nor a model of a specific type of trade. It is a loosely sketched framework, which offers a plausible explanation for the observed higher volume of trade between high-income countries with similar demand patterns. It combines demand and supply considerations, by recognizing roles both for the demand for product variety and for economies of scale. Consider Figure 5.7. We assume a common production possibility frontier (PP) for the two similar countries which is convex to the origin; this allows us to represent scale economies in the production of M_1 and M_2. We represent a 'majority' preference for M_2 in country U by indifference curve I_u and for M_1 in country W by I_w. Under free-trade conditions (the international terms of trade are given by the broken line PP)

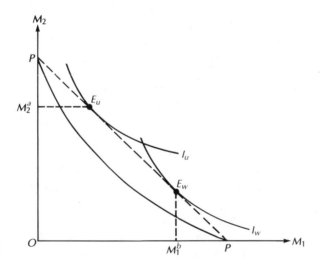

Figure 5.7 Demand similarity, scale economies and trade

country U specializes completely in the production of M_2 and consumes at E_u. Country W produces only M_1 and consumes at E_w. The outcome is two-way trade, with country U exporting M_2 and importing M_1 and country W exporting M_1 and importing M_2.

What type of two-way trade is involved? If manufactured good M_1 is the product of one industry and M_2 is from a different industry, then the two-way trade is of an *inter*-industry nature: specialization between industries resulting in the import and export of the products of different industries. On the other hand, it may well be that M_1 and M_2 are different varieties of the same good and produced or producable within the same industry. In this latter case the bilateral trade is of an *intra*-industry nature:

specialization within an industry resulting in the simultaneous import and export of similar but differentiated goods of that one industry. In the former case, importables and exportables are the products of distinct industries; while in the latter case, a single industry is involved in the production of both importable and exportable varieties.

The Linder thesis is often viewed as being predominantly concerned with intra-industry trade. The thesis was certainly a precursor of many of the models of intra-industry trade, concerned with imperfect competition and differentiated products, that have emerged in recent years, but it was not intended to be exclusively a model of intra-industry trade. Indeed, the pioneering work on the specific phenomenon of intra-industry trade substantially post-dates Linder's contribution to trade theory. Linder's thesis competes with the neo-classical paradigm by providing a rationale for trade between similar economies. It is true that trade between similar economies tends to be of an intra-industry nature, while trade between dissimilar economies where factor endowment explanations are more appropriate tends to be predominantly of an inter-industry nature.[4] But factor proportion considerations may also be of relevance in understanding intra-industry trade. If different varieties, especially different qualities, of a given product require different factor intensities, then differences in countries' factor endowments may push a country's comparative advantage towards a specific variety or range of varieties. It may export those varieties that incorporate its most abundant factor most intensively and import the varieties that are intensive in the country's relatively scarce factor.

5.4 Summary

The Leontief paradox induced a search for alternative sources of trade to those offered by the basic Heckscher–Ohlin model or by the extensions considered in Chapter 4. In particular, attention focused on explanations for the growth of trade in manufactured goods between similar high-income industrial countries. Although the alternative 'models' of trade that emerged from this search are less general and less formal, they do offer new insights. Economies of scale of some form are important in the case of manufacturing activities, and we have shown that the presence of such economies can alone provide a motive for trade. The problem for empirical work is that the location of production and in turn therefore the direction and commodity composition of trade is indeterminate where scale economies alone drive trade. In some industries it is clear also that technological change and its geographical location will fashion the dynamic pattern of comparative advantage. The technology-gap and product-cycle models offer a stylized representation of the location of innovation and its subsequent international transfer. Again the dynamics are product or industry specific and indeterminate on a priori grounds. It is difficult therefore to investigate the empirical robustness of these models. As originally formulated, these models of endogenous technological change are unlikely to be as valid now as they were in the 1960s, when the United States was the clear technological leader. Nonetheless there are strong reasons for believing that the essential elements of the model are relevant to an understanding of trade in technology-intensive goods. In fact the product-cycle model integrates considerations of scale economies, technological change and factor endowments.

The Linder thesis contends that trade results from overlapping tastes, or demand similarity. The underlying structure of the 'model' is not well articulated, but it does provide an analytical framework that does not rely on differences in factor proportions. We will construct more specific and formally structured models of trade in similar goods between similar economies in Chapter 6. But it is important to emphasize that acceptance of these alternative models does not require one to reject the Heckscher–Ohlin model as redundant. It can complement the alternative models examined in this chapter, which apply to different types of trade and at different levels of product aggregation. We have a range of models to explain trade between similar and dissimilar economies, and in similar and dissimilar products. Inter-industry trade between dissimilar economies is probably best viewed within a Heckscher–Ohlin framework, while intra-industry trade between similar economies is better explained by a Linder-type framework, or by one of the models analyzed in Chapter 6. The choice of models will increase yet further!

5.5 Bibliography

The influence of increasing returns on the incentive to specialize can be identified as early as Young (1928). Other important theoretical contributions on increasing returns are Lerner (1932), Melvin (1969) and Chacholiades (1970).

The seminal works on technology-gap and product-cycle trade are respectively Posner (1961) and Vernon (1966). Hufbauer (1966) developed a similar model of trade to that of Posner. Tharakan (1985) reviews the evidence on technology-gap trade. Empirical support for the importance of technological know-how in explaining export performance is presented in Hirsch (1975) and Aquino (1981).

Grubel and Lloyd (1975) is regarded as the seminal work that identified the importance of intra-industry specialization, although the phenomenon had already been identified in empirical studies of the 1960s on formation of the European Community – and is even mentioned in the theoretical literature of the 1930s.

The demand similarity thesis was presented by Linder (1961). Although there is some case-study evidence (e.g. Hocking 1980) on European trade in cars, there is not strong support for the thesis from cross-sectional empirical studies; Deardorff (1984) summarizes several of these studies.

Notes

1. There is an important qualification to this statement. Even though the ppc is concave, the existence of increasing returns makes the perpetuation of perfect competition impossible. Thus the analysis should really be modified to incorporate imperfect rather than perfect competition.
2. The argument developed below would be even stronger if the point of tangency between the world indifference curve and the world ppc occurred at a point other than E.

3. An alternative terminology is 'customer markets' for fixprice markets and 'auction markets' for flexprice markets.
4. Clearly there is an empirical problem in separating activities or products into industries, but the distinction in conceptual terms is less problematic.

6

Models of intra-industry trade

Some non-factor proportion explanations of trade flows, especially trade in manufactures, were identified in Chapter 5. We argued there, however, that the existence of increasing returns to scale or of a demand for variety may be present under conditions of either inter-industry trade (exchanges of the products of distinct industries) or intra-industry trade (exchanges of similar products of a given industry). The Linder thesis, for instance, is not a model specifically of intra-industry trade, although it should be viewed as an important precursor to the 'new' theories of trade.

Although there are earlier references in the literature to trade within industries,[1] sustained interest in intra-industry trade is of much more recent vintage. Early empirical studies on the effects of intra-European trade liberalization (Verdoorn 1960) discovered, contrary to expectation, evidence of increasing intra-industry specialization. Here was a phenomenon which appeared to be inexplicable by reference to the dominant paradigm of trade theory, namely the Heckscher–Ohlin model. Admittedly, there were those who were sceptical about the extent to which the phenomenon was an economic fact rather than a statistical artefact (Finger 1975; Pomfret 1979). Increasing specialization and fragmentation of industrial processes may mean that the number of 'industries' tends to increase through time, and that two-way trade at a constant level of product aggregation may be recorded as a result of the idiosyncrasies of the trade classifications: that is, by error. The pioneering work by Grubel and Lloyd, in systematically documenting and analyzing possible sources of intra-industry trade, meant that the 'statistical artefact' explanation never became widely accepted. Rather Grubel and Lloyd's book became a catalyst in the decade after its publication in 1975 for the modelling of intra-industry trade for a variety of market structures and of types of product differentiation. Unlike the theory of inter-industry trade, with its single and dominant Heckscher–Ohlin model, the theory of intra-industry trade comprises a range of models specific to particular conditions. The aim of this chapter is to illustrate the rich diversity of these 'new' theories of intra-industry trade.

6.1 Oligopoly and homogeneous goods

Neo-classical trade theory emphasizes the role of factor endowment differences between countries, where tastes are identical across countries, markets are perfectly competitive, goods are homogeneous (i.e. there is no product differentiation) and there are constant unit costs of production. The theory of intra-industry trade, by contrast, abstracts from the role of inter-country differences in factor endowments and concentrates on the role of influences such as non-competitive market structures, product differentiation and decreasing costs. In this section we examine the link between market structure and trade, and show that the former can be an independent source of trade (intra-industry in nature). In the extreme case, two identical countries of the same size, with the same taste patterns and access to technology may still engage in trade when trade takes place under duopoly conditions.

Consider a world consisting of two identical countries, with one producer of a given, identical (homogeneous) commodity in each country. The domestic and foreign firm may produce for the foreign (W) as well as home (U) market. We denote output produced by firm i for market j by Q_{ij}. The total supply in the home market equals Q_{uu} plus Q_{fu} and in the foreign market Q_{uf} plus Q_{ff}. The production cost function of both producers is of the form:

$$C_i = C_0 + cQ_i \tag{6.1}$$

where Q_i = total production of firm i.

Thus although the cost function is linear, i.e. there is a constant marginal cost of production c, the presence of a fixed cost element (C_0) means that average cost (C_i/Q_i) falls as the firm's total production increases. For the sake of simplicity the demand functions in each country are assumed to be linear and identical, i.e.

$$P_j = a - bQ_j \tag{6.2}$$

where Q_j = total production for market j.

While delivery of the good to the local market is assumed to require no transportation costs, such costs have to be incurred when products are sold in the foreign market. Transport costs can be incorporated into the model by assuming that some proportion $(1 - g)$ of exports is absorbed or melts away before reaching the export market: that is, that production for a foreign market has to be $(1/g)$ times sales.

Thus the profit (π) function of each firm can be specified as follows:

$$\pi_u = [a - bQ_u]Q_{uu} + [a - bQ_w]Q_{uw} - c[Q_{uu} + Q_{uw}/g] - C_0 \tag{6.3}$$
$$\pi_w = [a - bQ_w]Q_{ww} + [a - bQ_u]Q_{wu} - c[Q_{ww} + Q_{wu}/g] - C_0 \tag{6.4}$$

where $Q_u = Q_{uu} + Q_{wu}$
and $Q_w = Q_{uw} + Q_{ww}$.

The feature of this type of oligopolistic market which makes it difficult to handle theoretically is the presence of strategic interdependence between the firms. Each firm is sufficiently large relative to the total market to recognize that it should make decisions on its own price or output with a view to the strategic reaction of the other firm. In other words, in the absence of collusion each firm has to guess at its competitor's reaction or conjectural variation. We assume the simplest model of oligopolistic rivalry, that due to Cournot. That is, the strategic variable is assumed to be the setting of output and the conjectural variation is zero (each firm sets its output on the assumption that the other firm will not alter its production). The first-order profit maximization conditions can then be stated as follows:

$$\frac{\delta \pi_u}{\delta Q_{uu}} = -2bQ_{uu} - bQ_{wu} + a - c = 0 \qquad (6.5)$$

$$\frac{\delta \pi_u}{\delta Q_{uw}} = -2bQ_{uw} - bQ_{ww} + a - c/g = 0 \qquad (6.6)$$

$$\frac{\delta \pi_w}{\delta Q_{wu}} = -2bQ_{wu} - bQ_{uu} + a - c/g = 0 \qquad (6.7)$$

$$\frac{\delta \pi_w}{\delta Q_{ww}} = -2bQ_{ww} - bQ_{uw} + a - c = 0 \qquad (6.8)$$

Let us isolate equations 6.5 and 6.7, which can be solved for the equilibrium values Q_{uu}^* and Q_{wu}^* independently of the other equations. (Indeed, given the identical demand and cost conditions between countries there would be symmetry between the results, i.e. $Q_{uu}^* = Q_{ww}^*$ and $Q_{wu}^* = Q_{uw}^*$. But note that, because of transport costs, $Q_{uu}^* > Q_{wu}^*$ and $Q_{ww}^* > Q_{uw}^*$.) Equation 6.5 constitutes the home firm's best-reply or reaction function: it specifies how much the home producer will sell on the home market given the production for the home market by the foreign producer. It is represented in Figure 6.1 by the locus *UU*. Similarly, equation 6.7 is the reaction function of the foreign firm for (export) sales to the home market, and is represented in Figure 6.1 by the locus *WW*. The reaction functions are downward sloping because each firm's marginal revenue declines when the other firm's output increases. Furthermore, *UU* is assumed to be steeper than *WW* because 'own' effects are stronger than 'cross' effects.

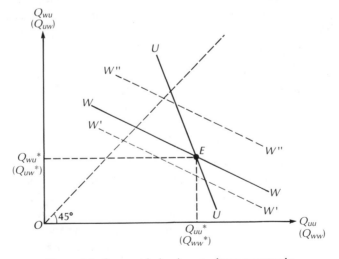

Figure 6.1 Cournot behaviour and two-way trade

The point of intersection E in Figure 6.1 represents equilibrium[2] in the home market. But given the symmetry characteristics of the model we can conceive of Figure 6.1 as representing the situation in both markets. In equilibrium both firms produce for their own market, but also supply the overseas market; Q_{wu}^* are exports from country F to country U, and Q_{uw}^* are exports of the identical good from U to F. With a very simple model of duopoly we are able to generate two-way (balanced) trade between identical economies in identical products: that is, within- or intra-industry trade. Each producer is acting in a profit-maximizing manner, relating perceived or expected marginal revenue to marginal cost in each market. Although both producers find the marginal cost of exported production higher (given transport costs) than production for the local market, the perceived marginal revenue in export sales is greater than in local sales. The net price received by each producer will be lower, however, from export than from local sales as a result of the absorption of transport costs. This type of behaviour is a form of price discrimination between local and export markets, resulting from perceived differences between the price elasticities in different markets.

This model of two-way trade is sometimes referred to as a 'reciprocal dumping' model, since each producer receives a lower net price for export sales. This term may suggest that such cross-hauling of identical products is socially wasteful. Certainly resources are used up in transporting goods from abroad that could be supplied locally. But it must be recognized also that there is an offsetting social gain resulting from increased competition: consumers face lower prices after trade than they would with a monopolistic, domestic supplier. The social value of such trade depends, therefore, on the net effect of these transport costs and competitive effects.

It is the case, as one would expect, that increasing transport costs will reduce the volume of trade: WW shifts towards $W'W'$ as transport costs increase and Q_{wu}^* (or Q_{uw}^*) declines. But note that the reverse of this argument means that as WW shifts towards $W''W''$, and Q_{uu}^* tends towards Q_{wu}^*. As transport costs decline, the share of exports in total local sales increases, and in the extreme where there are no transport costs the local market is equally shared by the local and foreign producer. Thus intra-industry trade is not dependent in this extreme case on price discrimination (permitted by the absorption of transport costs). Two-way trade between identical countries can be the outcome of oligopolistic rivalry alone. Indeed, the result is quite robust; it holds for alternative demand and cost functions.

The Cournot assumption turns out to be more significant. If we relax the zero conjectural variation assumption, then the existence and amount of intra-industry trade depends on the type of conjectural assumption adopted. Similarly, if we make price, rather than quantity, the key strategic variable of the firm, then the results of the duopoly model alter quite radically. Nevertheless, it has been shown that the Cournot assumption is not a necessary condition for the existence of two-way trade in duopoly models with homogeneous goods.

6.2 Oligopoly and product differentiation

In the previous section we investigated the possibility of intra-industry trade in homogeneous goods. Product heterogeneity or differentiation resulting from a demand for variety may be an additional source of two-way trade. Indeed, casual observation suggests that intra-industry trade typically involves the exchange of similar, but not identical products. What is needed is an explanation of trade in differentiated products. This inevitably involves representing product differentiation and modelling demand for differentiated goods.

In broad terms we can distinguish between *vertical product differentiation*, or quality variation between products, and *horizontal product differentiation*, or attribute variation between products of a similar quality. Of course, in practice products may differ in both characteristics and quality, but for analytical reasons it is useful to distinguish between the two polar forms. Clearly the type of factors accounting for the simultaneous import of fashion clothes and export of mass-market clothes may be quite different to those explaining the simultaneous import and export of motor cars of a given quality range, of similar size, engine capacity and performance. Although the analytical distinction is quite clear, the manner in which we model the distinction is more problematic. In this and later sections a number of alternative approaches used by trade theorists are described.

In a series of papers Shaked and Sutton examined the case of 'natural oligopoly' and trade in vertically differentiated goods. They focused on situations where the number of firms that can enter a market with new, higher-quality varieties is 'bounded' by the demand and supply characteristics of the market. We would expect large numbers of qualities to be available if the income range is wide, fixed costs associated with quality improvements are low, and average variable costs rise sharply as a result of quality improvements. By contrast, where there are high fixed costs (e.g. research and development expenditure) associated with quality improvement but average variable costs are little affected by this improvement, then there is likely to be a small numbers solution: that is, 'natural oligopoly'. The pharmaceutical industry is one where there are high fixed costs associated with quality improvement but (variable) production costs are not particularly different for higher-quality varieties than for existing varieties.

Let us consider a case where under autarchy only two home firms producing distinct qualities can survive, given the country's income distribution. The reason for this is that competition on quality drives all firms to produce the highest quality possible, but (Bertrand) price competition between similar products or qualities drives price to marginal cost, zero profit and the exit of firms. What then will be the implications for the number of firms, the level of product quality and the nature of trade if there is a move from autarchy to trade? If the two economies are identical in all respects, their combined market will still support only two firms. Given the competition in quality and price referred to above, the number of firms that can be supported is independent of market size. When trade opens, therefore, two of the firms will exit and two will remain to serve the joint market. A priori it is impossible to predict the direction and type of trade involved. But in the event that one firm

from each country exists, the result would be intra-industry trade in vertically differentiated goods. The opening of two-way trade will also raise welfare, since
competition will drive down prices, while market expansion will induce overall
quality improvement.

Of course, in this simple case of identical economies one-way trade is also possible,
if both home or both foreign producers are the ones that are driven from the market.
But the nature and direction of trade may be pinned down if we relax, for instance,
the assumption of identical income distributions. Differences in income distribution
would facilitate a larger number of firms in the post-trade equilibrium, with the
higher (average)-income country specializing in a range of higher-quality products
and the lower (average)-income country specializing in lower-quality products. Note
that since trade drives down prices in general and consumers prefer higher quality, it
is lowest-quality firms that tend to be driven from the market. Thus, other things
being equal, intra-industry trade is more likely the greater the degree of taste overlap
between economies. Thus this result, which seemed so paradoxical when we first
encountered it in connection with the Linder thesis, emerges also in these models of
trade in differentiated goods under oligopoly. The direction of trade is, however,
very sensitive to the assumptions in these new models.

6.3 Monopolistic competition

Can we identify motives for two-way trade under other market structures? The
robustness of the intra-industry trade paradigm would be severely challenged if two-
way trade were dependent on the existence of oligopolistic rivalry. What we shall
discover is that in fact the demand for variety and the relaxation of the constant costs
assumption provide sufficient conditions for intra-industry trade, and that these can
be modelled under all kinds of market structures.

When products are vertically differentiated consumers presumably rank alternatives according to product quality. With horizontal differentiation, in contrast,
preferences for alternative varieties of a given general quality will typically differ
between consumers and no unique ranking would be agreed by all. On the supply
side, product differentiation can be modelled by means of single-product firms
producing different varieties. Thus a large number of firms implies a large number of
varieties, and the analysis can be organized along the lines of the Chamberlinian
model of imperfect or monopolistic competition.

On the demand side, we might model the demand for variety in alternative ways.
For instance, we might apply a form of spatial analysis to the modelling of the
demand for mixes of attributes. According to this 'ideal-variety approach', individuals have different most preferred 'locations', i.e. mixes of attributes, and each
individual consumes only his or her most preferred variety, or the 'nearest' available.
This is the natural way to model demand for cars or other consumer durables. The
alternative, Chamberlinian, 'love of variety' approach is to postulate that all varieties
enter the individual's utility function in a symmetrical fashion. Individuals gain utility
from greater variety, i.e. from being able to consume *more* varieties, rather than

from being able to consume a *preferable* variety. Within limits, at least, this seems a natural way to model the demand for wine. Both sources of gain can co-exist, and indeed we might build a model that incorporates both influences. For the present purpose, however, we will focus on a neo-Chamberlinian approach since it is analytically more convenient. It yields conclusions about the possibility and determinants of intra-industry trade that are similar to those of the alternative tradition.

The essential elements of the approach in an open-economy setting can be brought out with a very simple model, based on work by Paul Krugman (b.1953) (Krugman, 1980). We assume that all consumers are alike and that the representative consumer has the following utility (U_t) function:

$$U_t = \sum_i v(c_i) \qquad [v' > 0; v'' < 0] \tag{6.9}$$

where c_i denotes consumption of the ith good. Equation 6.9 has the property that all goods enter the utility function symmetrically and that the level of utility increases as the number of varieties consumed increases, even if money income and the prices of goods are unaltered. Following increased availability of variety, the individual consumes less of each variety but consumes more varieties.

Turning to the supply side of this (single-sector) economy, we may assume for simplicity that there is one factor (labour) which can produce some combination of a large number of goods (i). We can express the common production function for all goods as follows:

$$l_i = a + bq_i \qquad [a, b > 0] \tag{6.10}$$

where l_i equals the number of labour units required to produce q_i of good i. The coefficients a and b refer to the fixed and marginal costs respectively. Given that the coefficient a is assumed to be positive, i.e. that there are positive fixed costs, then there are economies of scale in production – or, more strictly, there are continuously declining average (total) costs as output increases. Thus there will be only a single producer of any particular product or variety, and as many varieties available as can be sustained by the size of the total market.

This type of model yields the standard monopolistic competition solution. Each producer tries to exploit its monopoly control over the supply of a specific variety, but no (abnormal) profits can be made in equilibrium since new firms are free to enter the market. In equilibrium the output of each variety (q_i) has to sum to the total consumption by all individuals of the variety $(\sum c_i)$, and the common price of each variety (P_i) – given identical production functions across varieties – must be such that total income is fully absorbed by the n available varieties. The number of varieties is in fact technologically determined under full employment conditions by the size of the labour force (L) and the amount of labour required (l_i) to produce a representative variety:

$$n = \frac{L}{l_i} = \frac{L}{a + bq_i} \ . \tag{6.11}$$

We are now in a position to show how this model of imperfect competition and horizontal product differentiation can be applied to open economies and used to explain intra-industry trade. We simply assume the existence of a second economy which is identical in every respect to the home economy. Assuming zero transport costs, two-way trade in differentiated goods will take place even if an identical range of varieties was produced in each country pre-trade. This follows because there can only be a single producer of each variety. Thus further product differentiation will occur once trade opens: competition forces a producer from one of the two countries to exit the industry or produce a new variety. Where exit occurs, a supply-side opportunity is created for a new entrant.

The characteristics of the post-trade equilibrium will be similar to those of the pre-trade equilibrium: prices and outputs of all varieties will be identical. No country has a comparative advantage in any subset of products and yet there is a basis for trade: namely, increased variety. The total number of varieties available to all consumers (n^*) will now be increased to:

$$n^* = \frac{L_u + L_w}{l_i} \tag{6.12}$$

where $n^* = n_u + n_w$. Thus, although the opening up of trade has no effect on the level of output or the number of firms producing in either country, consumers have twice the number of products available. Given their preference for diversity, they consume some of all varieties. If n^* varieties are consumed by everyone at home (U) and in the other country (W), but only $n_u = n_w$ are produced in each country, then there must be two-way trade between the two countries through the exchange of varieties.

Note, however, that in this very simple one-sector framework, where there are no differences in factor endowments or country size, the direction of trade is indeterminate. We cannot say anything about what type of varieties each country will produce and export. It may be that future theoretical work will increasingly seek to integrate factor proportion differences and demand for variety into multi-sector models with both differentiated and homogeneous goods sectors, and as a result offer predictions about the commodity composition of trade and the relative importance of intra- and inter-industry trade. Such elaboration of trade models will no doubt improve their empirical relevance. But the simple one-sector model set out in this section suffices to demonstrate the possibility of two-way trade in horizontally differentiated goods between identical economies.

We return to the issue of the gains from trade in some depth in Chapter 7. But we can note at this stage that the gains in this particular model derive wholly from increased variety. This is a consequence of the special form of the utility function adopted. If per unit costs decrease as the scale of production increases, gains could come simultaneously from increased variety and from reduced prices of domestic and foreign-produced differentiated goods following the enlargement of markets which results from the opening of trade.

6.4 Neo-factor proportions

Thus far in this chapter our models of intra-industry trade have been concerned with trade between similar economies. This may be viewed as the modal type of intra-industry trade, but some two-way trade in similar goods takes place between developed and developing countries (just as some trade among industrial countries is doubtless explained by factor endowments). The export of denim by developing countries and the simultaneous import by them of high-quality textiles from industrial countries is a good example. Clearly there is an element of both the 'new' approach, namely the demand for variety (in this case of differing qualities), and the 'traditional' approach, involving differences in factor endowments affecting comparative advantage in different quality ranges of a given product. Such considerations have been captured by the so-called neo-factor proportions model of trade.

Consider again a two-country, two-factor framework, where each country has different endowments of capital and labour. Our country (U) is relatively capital abundant and therefore capital is relatively cheap, while labour is relatively cheap in the other country (W). The model differs from the standard Heckscher–Ohlin model in two important respects. First, although there are two industries, one of them can produce a range of vertically differentiated goods (M_i), i.e. a range of qualities of the same product, while the other produces a homogeneous good (X). Second, labour is mobile within and between industries, but capital is industry specific: that is, transferable between firms in the industry, but not between industries. The amount of the industry-specific capital incorporated in the differentiated good determines its quality: more capital relative to labour means higher quality. Both the differentiated and the homogeneous good are consumed by all individuals in both countries. Consumers prefer a higher- to a lower-quality variety, but their choice is income constrained. Given some variation in incomes across consumers in both countries, there can be a demand for a range of qualities in both countries. The utility (U_t) function of any individual can be written as:

$$U_t = U(M, \alpha, X) \tag{6.13}$$

where α = quality, i.e. the capital intensity of the differentiated variety consumed.

It is assumed that the homogeneous good is produced with a Ricardian production function, requiring only labour in a fixed proportion (l_x) per unit of output. In the case of the differentiated product, we assume that all varieties require one unit of labour per unit of output plus varying amounts of capital. Under competitive conditions the prices (P) of the two goods will be equal to their unit cost of production, i.e.:

$$P_x = l_x w \tag{6.14}$$

$$P_m = w + \alpha r \tag{6.15}$$

where w and r are the competitive factor prices of labour and capital respectively.

If our home country has a technological advantage in the production of X, i.e. l_x is smaller at home than in the foreign country, then the home country will have a competitive advantage in the homogeneous good, which it will export to the other country with the opening of trade. The equalization of P_x across countries after the opening of trade means that wages must be higher in the home country than the foreign country. Given also the relative factor endowments of the two countries, which means that capital is relatively cheap at home but relatively expensive in the foreign country, the home country will have a comparative advantage in high-quality varieties of good M, as well as in the homogeneous good. For low values of α the price of M is dominated by wage costs (equation 6.15). However, as quality increases, it is capital costs that begin to dominate, and our home country has a competitive advantage over the capital-poor, foreign country in the upper part of the quality spectrum. With a range of incomes in both countries such that the homogeneous good and all qualities are consumed in both countries, there is a basis for both inter-industry and intra-industry trade. Only our country exports X and only the foreign country imports X: inter-industry trade takes place. In addition, however, our country specializes in the production of high-quality varieties of M and exports them to the foreign country, where they are consumed by high-income consumers. The foreign country, by contrast, specializes on the lower part of the quality spectrum, exporting those varieties to our country, where they are consumed by low-income consumers. Thus intra-industry trade is also generated, in the context of a model containing both Ricardian and Heckscher–Ohlin features.

It is possible, therefore, to construct models where inter- and intra-industry trade occur simultaneously, in this case with perfectly competitive markets.

6.5 Summary

Previous chapters identified a series of factors that can create incentives for international trade. It may be useful at this point to provide a systematic list of these factors:

1. Technical differences in the relative productivity of labour in different industries, e.g. due to differing climatic conditions (Ricardo).
2. Differences in relative factor endowments (Heckscher–Ohlin).
3. Differences in demand patterns across countries.
4. Economies of scale.
5. A technology gap.
6. The product cycle.
7. Demand in any one country for a variety of products, some of which, typically those catering to minority tastes, are more efficiently produced abroad, especially when they cater there to majority tastes (the Linder thesis).

To this list the present chapter has added the following:

8. Oligopolistic rivalry: (a) 'reciprocal dumping' of homogeneous products; or (b) competition between different varieties of differentiated products.

Table 6.1 What trade flows different theories hope to explain[1]

	'Dissimilar' countries	'Similar' countries[2]
Homogeneous goods	1, 2, 3[3]	4, 8(a)
Differentiated products	5, 6	7, 8(b), 9

[1] Numbers in the table refer to the factors explaining trade flows listed on p. 91 and below.
[2] 'Similar' countries have similar factor endowments (and therefore income levels).
[3] Dissimilar with respect to tastes (demand patterns) rather than factor endowments.

9. The demand for variety, either because consumers differ in their evaluation of the ideal variety, or because each consumer prefers consuming a wide variety of similar products.

10. Quality variations between countries in similar goods resulting from factors endowment differences, where tastes overlap between countries.

The 'new' theories presented in this chapter have been criticized as excessively simple (e.g. single sector) or based on naive assumptions (e.g. Cournot behaviour) or as suffering from a lack of generality. But recent years have seen a rapid proliferation of models with alternative and sometimes more realistic assumptions, ones that extend the analysis of imperfect competition and strategic behaviour in oligopolistic competition to an open-economy setting. What emerges is that market structure, economies of scale and product differentiation can generate trade, including two-way trade, independently of the classic sources of trade. With increased sophistication and model-specific analysis comes diminished generality, but this can be viewed as a strength, not a weakness, of the analysis. The neat and uniform theoretical elegance of the Heckscher–Ohlin model has been sacrificed, but the reward is access to a wide range of new insights.

As we have stressed before, acceptance of these 'new' models of intra-industry trade does not require one to reject the earlier models of inter-industry trade as wrong or redundant. On the contrary, the various models should be viewed as complementary. Table 6.1 illustrates how the ten different motivations for trade listed above can explain trade in different types of goods (homogeneous versus differentiated products) and between different types of country (similar and dissimilar). This gives the applied economist a range of models with which to analyze different situations. As the neo-factor proportions model presented at the end of the chapter demonstrated, different sources of trade can be integrated within the same general equilibrium model.

6.6 Bibliography

The first systematic analysis of intra-industry trade was Grubel and Lloyd (1975). The proliferation of 'new' models of trade in differentiated goods under imperfectly competitive conditions started in the late 1970s with papers by Krugman (1979, 1980) and Lancaster (1980). Much of this work has been rigorously synthesized in Helpman and Krugman (1985) and thoroughly surveyed in Greenaway and Milner (1986), who compare and contrast the neo-Hotelling and neo-Chamberlinian approaches. The characterization as 'ideal variety' and 'love-of-variety' approaches is due to Helpman (1990).

Monopolistic competition in general equilibrium is rigorously treated by Dixit and Norman (1980). Oligopolistic rivalry has been modelled under a variety of demand and cost conditions: see, for example, Brander and Krugman (1983) and Eaton and Kierzkowski (1984). Shaked and Sutton (1983) examine trade in vertically differentiated products under conditions of 'natural oligopoly'.

There is now some theoretical work on general equilibrium models that simultaneously incorporate factor endowment influences, scale economies and the demand for variety: see, for example, Lawrence and Spiller (1983) and Helpman and Krugman (1985).

The work on neo-factor proportions models was pioneered by Falvey (1981).

Other useful surveys of the literature include Helpman (1984) and Greenaway and Milner (1987a). A particularly accessible introduction to the theoretical demands of these 'new' models is provided by Kierzkowski (1985).

Notes

1. Ohlin (1933) himself suggested its possibility and offered some possible explanations for its existence.
2. The equilibrium depicted in Figure 6.1 is stable since any departure from it will trigger off an adjustment which will move the system back to E.

III

Trade policy

This part of the book is concerned with the theory of trade or commercial policy. It applies many of the tools of analysis developed in Part II to the analysis of the effects of government interventions on trade flows and economic welfare. The impact and desirability of a variety of policy measures are investigated from the viewpoint of individual countries. Trade policy issues from the perspective of developing countries (Chapter 15) and of the global trading system (Chapter 17) are considered later.

7

Gains from trade

Almost all of the discussion in the trade section has been concerned with explaining trade: that is, with identifying sources of inter- and intra-industry trade. In developing the alternative models, the immediate motivation for and effects of trade have been identified. Thus, we have seen how inter-country pre-trade differences in (relative) costs and prices or in product characteristics provide motives for residents of one country to purchase goods from other countries. Similarly, the analysis has identified potential trade-induced changes in costs and prices, when, for instance, there are specialization benefits associated with drawing additional resources into activities of comparative advantage, or efficiency improvements which result from the increased scale of production. We have not sought to identify systematically the nature and extent of those gains, to consider what factors determine the incidence and magnitude of those gains, or to investigate how gains from trade are distributed within and between countries. The aim of this chapter is to make the welfare implications of trade and specialization more explicit. This should help to reinforce the reader's understanding of the motivation for international trade. But it will also serve as a prerequisite to discussion of trade policy. In order to understand why and if governments might or should seek to intervene so as to alter international trade flows, it is necessary to understand what conditions need to be satisfied to obtain mutually beneficial trade, and what adjustment problems and income redistributions might result from unrestricted opportunities for international exchange.

7.1 Inter-industry specialization

Consider again the Heckscher–Ohlin model of trade, from which we can identify the standard gains from specialization in distinct activities according to comparative advantage. The movement from autarchy to free trade for *a small economy* unable to influence the terms of trade and characterized by full-employment conditions was illustrated by Figure 3.8. (See section 3.2 for a full elaboration of the assumptions underpinning the model.) In Figure 7.1 the earlier diagram is elaborated in order to illustrate the precise nature of the welfare effects associated with trade-induced specialization.

In moving from a pre-trade production and consumption equilibrium at E to a post-trade consumption equilibrium at C and production equilibrium at P (which results from the change in relative prices from autarchy represented by DD to free trade at international terms of trade TT) the country moves from community indifference curve I_a to indifference level I_t'. From the country's point of view this represents an aggregate improvement in welfare ($I_t' > I_a$).

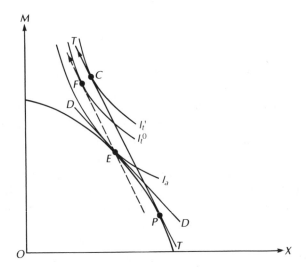

Figure 7.1 Gains from trade for a small economy

The movement from I_a to I_t' can also be broken down into two conceptually distinct components. First, the country has been able to take advantage of a more favourable relative price ratio. The shift from autarchic terms of exchange (DD) to the international terms of trade raises (lowers) the relative price of the exportable X (importable M): namely, the country's activity of comparative advantage (disadvantage). Even with the pre-trade level of production of exportables associated with point E, at the international terms of trade it would be possible to exchange exports for imports so as to consume at point F. Thus the movement from E to F and the rise in utility associated with the shift from I_a to I_t^0 can be viewed as a pure *gain from exchange*.

The opening of trade also allows the country to shift resources towards production of the exportable, the activity of comparative advantage. Thus with greater production of exportables (X) at free-trade equilibrium P than at E (and with the higher relative price of exportables) it is possible to increase consumption (of both goods) further from F to C, and to raise welfare further from I_t^0 to I_t'. Thus the welfare gain from the reallocation of resources from importables to exportables production is the pure *gain from specialization*.

An alternative way of representing these gains is demonstrated in Figure 7.2. In each segment the demand and supply schedules for importables (Figure 7.2(a)) and for exportables (Figure 7.2(b)) are plotted against relative prices (P_m/P_x).[1] The autarchy relative price is P_a and both markets are cleared: that is, local production satisfies consumption. With the opening of trade the relative price of importables (exportables) falls (rises) to P_t. The production of importables (exportables) contracts (expands) and the consumption of importables (exportables) expands (contracts); exports equal excess production of exportables $(P_x - C_x)$ and imports equal excess consumption of importables $(C_m - P_m)$.

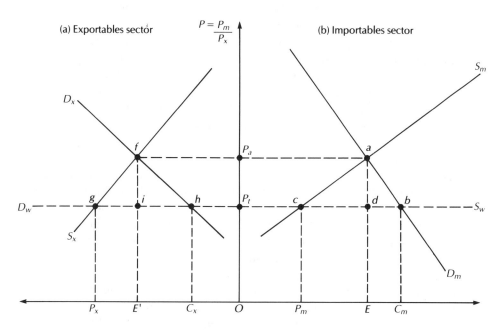

Figure 7.2 Trade-induced changes in consumer and producer surplus: the small-country case

If we assume full employment throughout, then the equilibria at P_a and P_t correspond with the pre- and post-trade equilibria in Figure 7.1. The net welfare comparison in Figure 7.1 is an ordinal one based on aggregate welfare. With Figure 7.2 we are able to identify welfare effects in a cardinal manner using consumer and producer surplus measures of welfare, and to break down those welfare effects between sectors and between producers and consumers. In the importables sector, consumer surplus increases by an amount equivalent to P_aabP_t. Producer surplus in this sector, by contrast, falls by P_aacP_t. The net welfare benefit to the economy is therefore the area abc. This area can be further decomposed into a production gain (analogous to the gain from specialization) resulting from the replacement of less efficient local producers by imports from more efficient foreign producers (the area adc), and a consumption gain (analogous to the gain from exchange) as cheaper imports induce demand expansion (the area adb). These net gains can also be represented in the exportables sector. But the redistribution this time is from consumers to producers. Producer surplus rises by the amount $P_d fgP_t$ as the *relative* price of exportables *rises* and production of exportables increases. Consumer surplus falls, however, as relative prices rise, by the amount $P_d fhP_t$. The net gain is therefore represented by *fgh*, and again this can be decomposed into the gain from exchange (*fhi*) and the gain from specialization (*fgi*).

We can draw a number of conclusions from this analysis:

1. The opening of trade is net welfare improving if the international terms of trade raise the relative price of a country's exportable.
2. The extent of that net gain depends on the extent of the divergence between autarchic and international relative prices, and on the pattern of domestic preferences. The more important are importables in the domestic consumption basket, the greater are the net benefits: the gross consumer gains in the importables sector will be larger and gross consumer losses in the exportables sector will be smaller as the consumption share of importables increases relative to that of exportables.
3. In order that the net gains of trade are fully realized, full adjustment must occur: resources displaced in the importables sector must be fully re-employed in the exportables sector. In the short run, the supply functions S_m and S_x may be relatively inelastic (i.e. tend towards being vertical). In that case the full specialization gains *adc* or *fgi* may not accrue. We return to the adjustment issue later, but suffice it to say that to the extent that adjustment is frustrated the gains from trade will be lower than they otherwise would be. Even with zero adjustment, however, there are potential gains from exchange.
4. There are likely to be both gainers and losers from trade. In the increasing cost case represented, exportables producers gain and importables producers lose, while consumers of importables gain and consumers of exportables lose. Thus the argument that trade increases welfare is an aggregative or net one: advocacy of free trade on efficiency grounds requires that we are willing to apply the criterion of potential compensation of losers by gainers.[2]

Besides the redistributions between types of producer and consumer, changes in the relative price of final goods (exportables and importables) will in this neoclassical framework alter relative prices of factor inputs. Trade is likely, therefore, to have significant distributional as well as efficiency implications. We return to this issue in section 7.3. (Before proceeding to the next section the reader might wish to consider how sensitive the conclusions about the extent of the (net) gains from trade are to the assumption that the country is small and unable to influence the terms of trade. This is considered in the addendum to this chapter, section 7.6.)

7.2 Intra-industry specialization

It is still possible to identify gains from exchange and gains from specialization in the case of intra-industry trade. The nature of these gains may be different, however. As was shown in Chapter 5, product variety in particular is an important source of gain in many models of intra-industry trade and its role must be recognized in any evaluation of gains from trade. Furthermore, when specialization produces intra-industry trade the gains which result may be static resource reallocation gains, as in the Heckscher–Ohlin model; there may also however, be gains associated with the realization of scale economies. Finally, the nature and relative importance of these sources of gain can vary from model to model.

As shown earlier, there are a considerable variety of models that predict intra-industry trade. We shall illustrate the analysis with a simple horizontal product differentiation model developed by Greenaway (1982). Several assumptions underpin the analysis:

1. Two commodities can be produced in the economy or economies under consideration, agriculture and manufactures. The former is homogeneous, while the latter can be differentiated. Our interest lies only in examining the market for manufactures.
2. Initially we will assume that we are dealing with horizontal or attribute product differentiation.
3. For the commodity in question consumer preferences are uniformly distributed across characteristics (or attribute) space, such that a potential demand exists for all possible specifications.
4. There is an equal intensity of preferences. Thus two individuals consuming their 'ideal' varieties will reach the same level of welfare.
5. Consumption technologies are fixed. Consumers are therefore constrained either to consume those varieties which are offered, or not to consume at all. Given preference diversity, those consumers who are provided with their ideal variety will be better off than those who consume a variety that is less than ideal.
6. Production functions for all varieties exhibit decreasing costs as a result of overheads of production or development, thereby ensuring that the actual number of varieties produced is less than the number that would enable each individual to consume his or her ideal variety.
7. Even where monopoly supply exists, price discrimination is ruled out. Thus a producer cannot offer a given variety to one consumer for whom it is 'ideal' at a higher price than to a consumer for whom it was less than ideal.
8. Entry into the market is limited and will occur when the surplus available to an entrant from introducing a new specification exceeds development costs.
9. Changes in welfare can be measured by changes in producer and consumer surplus.

The basis for the methodology developed can be outlined by reference to Figure 7.3(a). The attribute characteristics (a_1 and a_2) vary along the line CD. The variety specification (i.e. the relative proportions of a_1 and a_2 which the product embodies) determines the point on this line at which any particular variety is located. Defining the variety specification V, as:

$$V_i = \left[\dfrac{a_1}{a_2} \right]$$
(7.1)

it follows that varieties located further to the left of the plane have a higher relative proportion of a_1 than those located further to the right. Although product differentiation often involves a mixture of quality and attribute variation, this framework seeks to represent the type of variation in specification associated with final consumer goods of a similar quality. Thus cars of given price range and engine capacity may vary in terms of the proportion of the car's space devoted to boot capacity (a_1) and leg room (a_2) for passengers.

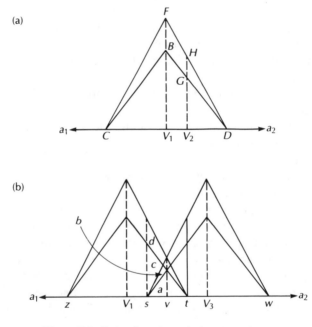

Figure 7.3 Gains from intra-industry trade

Since consumer preferences are uniformly distributed across characteristics space, it follows that a potential demand can exist for every conceivable variety. To illustrate the welfare implications of less than the maximum number of varieties being produced, consider the situation where only one variety (V_1) is *initially* marketed *at a given price*. Consumers either purchase some amount of V_1 or nothing at all. Given a uniform distribution and intensity of preferences and perfect divisibility, a consumer whose ideal variety is V_1 will unequivocally consume more of V_1 than a consumer whose ideal varieties are unavailable. In Figure 7.3(a) the amount of consumer and producer surplus is 'measured'[3] in terms of vertical distance from the line CD. For that consumer whose preferences are uniquely located at V_1, both consumer and producer surplus will be at a maximum (i.e. the distances V_1B and BF

respectively); he or she consumes her most preferred variety, consumes more of this variety than consumers for which this is not the most preferred variety, and thereby generates more surplus for herself and the producer of this variety. Consumers located either side of V_1 consume less and as a result consumer and producer surplus falls until boundary points such as C and D are reached. Thus, for consumers whose most preferred variety is located at V_1, the producer surplus associated with those consumers' consumption of the good will be V_1B; for a consumer located at V_2 the associated producer surplus would be V_2G; and so on. A separate function could be shown for consumer surplus. For expository convenience, however, consumer surplus is simply added vertically to producer surplus. Thus, for the consumer with preferences at V_1 consumer surplus is BF; for the individual at V_2, consumer surplus is GH. Thus the areas CBD and $CFDB$ are equivalent to the total producer and consumer surplus respectively associated with the production and consumption of variety V_1.

Consider now two countries with identical factor endowments, both of which are also identical in terms of market size, number of consumers and income distribution, and both of which are self-sufficient in agriculture. Suppose that although good V, the manufactured good, is produced in both countries in autarchy, different varieties of V are produced in response to different preference distributions. Since only one variety was initially produced in both countries, its supply was monopolized. If both monopolists are profit-maximizers, a uniform distribution of preferences will result in each producing a variety which combines a_1 and a_2 in such a way as best to suit the consumer in the middle of the market.

In Figure 7.3(b) country U's market is represented by the horizontal distance zt, while country F is represented by sw. In autarchy varieties V_1 and V_3 are produced by countries U and F respectively. There is, therefore, an area of taste overlap of st. Given the assumed uniform distribution and intensity of preferences, both varieties sell for the same price, which ensures that the peaks in the surplus functions above V_1 and V_3 are of the same height. At the initial relative prices, gains can be made from the exchange of *existing* varieties. Given access to overseas markets, consumers in country U (F) whose preferences lie in the area of characteristics space vt (sv) would switch consumption from V_1 (V_3) to V_3 (V_1).

A number of welfare changes follow from the exchange. For those consumers in U whose preferences are located in the range vt, variety V_3 more closely resembles their ideal variety than V_1. Consequently, consumption of V_3 will exceed consumption of V_1 and consumer surplus will be higher. This assumes that the prices of V_3 and V_1 remain unchanged, so that the gain in consumer surplus is the outcome simply of increased consumption at unchanged prices. Consumers whose preferences are located in vt would gain by an increase in surplus of $(d - b)$ associated with the switch in consumption to the other variety. (Given the symmetry of the model, consumers in F who switch consumption from V_3 to V_1 will gain an equivalent amount.)

The gross change in producer surplus in country U as a consequence of the exchange amounts to $a + b + c$. Area a is offset by the surplus which is transferred to the overseas producer when exchange takes place, area b is a transfer from overseas consumers and area c results from market expansion: that is, overseas consumers who enter the market are purchasing more of the variety than did domestic consumers who have left the market. (Given the symmetry of the model, these gains apply to both producers.) From the producers' point of view, the exchange will take place as long as $b + c$ exceeds any additional costs associated with transportation. The net social gains from exchange in country U amount to $c + d$.

What we have identified are pure gains from exchanges which result from the ability of international trade to permit some consumers to locate closer to their ideal variety than in autarchy. So far we have ruled out any potential for gains from 'specialization' by assuming that pre- and post-trade relative prices are identical. This is unlikely to be the case. As the producer in each country increases output of its 'majority' variety, the relative price of differentiated manufactures will fall for one (or both) of two possible reasons. First, there may be a competitive cutting of prices as a result of introducing a new supplier to each market. Whether this happens will depend on the strategic interaction between the two firms: that is, on whether they collude and seek the joint profit-maximizing price, or whether they compete. Second, this may be reinforced by the effects of market expansion in reducing unit costs. This depends on the characteristics of the production function.

Several factors will therefore affect the magnitude of the gains from trade in this setting, even if there are no transport costs to absorb the potential gains from trade. For example, the number of varieties which exist prior to the opening of trade, and the number which exist in the post-trade equilibrium, have an important bearing on potential gains in consumer surplus. Other things being equal, the greater the number of autarchic varieties, the smaller the potential gains in consumer surplus. The introduction of a new variety not only provides one more consumer with his or her ideal variety; it also permits other consumers to move closer to their ideal. Since the average distance between varieties is reduced, consumers in general gain from the introduction of new varieties even if the new varieties are not located exactly at their ideal point on the product spectrum. It follows, therefore, that the larger the number of varieties prior to trade, the lower the average distance between varieties and, other things being equal, the smaller the potential gains in consumer surplus. Besides increased variety there may also be gains resulting from reduced prices to consumers. The extent of these gains will depend on the slope of the average cost or scale curve over the relevant range and the extent to which reductions in unit costs induced by market expansion are passed on to consumers in the form of lower prices. Clearly, other things being equal, the steeper the scale curve, the greater the potential gain from two-way trade. If product markets are competitive, such gains are more likely to be passed on. If they are made *more* competitive by the entry of foreign producers, there will be an additional source of gain to consumers, though it will represent a transfer from producers rather than a net social gain. But if product markets are concentrated and remain so even after trade is opened, then the gains from scale economies may accrue as rents to domestic or foreign firms. In the latter case they would still be regarded as a source of gain from a global perspective, but as a form of redistribution from a local or national perspective.

This distinction between the global and national gains from trade is an important one, since affecting the distribution of rents between countries through strategic policy interventions may raise national welfare but not global welfare. The corollary of this is the possibility that unrestricted trade raises welfare in global but not in national terms. We return to this issue when discussing commercial policies in Chapter 10.

7.3 Income distribution

As has been shown in this and earlier chapters, trade permits a country to increase its real income. In the Ricardian model there is only one factor of production, namely labour. The corollary of the labour theory of value is that all value accrues to labour and that the opening of trade increases real wages for all labour. Thus until the classic article 'Protection and real wages' by Wolfgang Stolper and Paul Samuelson in 1941, it had been taken for granted that the opening of trade or the expansion of trade would – at least after transitional adjustments were complete – result in higher incomes for everyone. Stolper and Samuelson proved – a result known as the Stolper–Samuelson theorem – that in the Heckscher–Ohlin model this is not true. They showed that those who supply the scarce factor of production gain higher returns (in absolute terms) through protection that restricts imports, even though society as a whole loses. The corollary of this theorem is that those who supply the abundant factor of production gain as a result of the opening of trade (or the liberalization of trade). As we shall see in later discussions of protection, these income distributional implications are an important consideration in the conduct of commercial policy. Political economy considerations undoubtedly matter in determining governments' responses in capital-abundant, industrialized countries to growing imports of (unskilled) labour-intensive imports. Unskilled labour, which is scarce relative to developing countries but may be electorally significant, has a strong incentive to lobby for protection. Hence it is important to examine these income distribution effects in more detail.

Consider again the Edgeworth box which represents the assumed neo-classical technology for our small, labour-abundant country (U) shown in Figure 7.4. Country U is a relatively labour-abundant economy and the exportable (importable) is intensive in the use of labour (capital). Suppose that the autarchic equilibrium occurs at point E on the contract curve. The effect of the opening of trade, as we have shown earlier, is to raise the relative (product) price of X and to provide an incentive to produce more X and less M. Hence the post-trade equilibrium is at some point like C on the contract curve.

What adjustments in factor rewards are required to bring about this adjustment in production? The expansion of X production in response to the change in relative product prices requires that its demand for additional factors (K, L) must be satisfied by the release of resources from the importables (M) sector. But K and L are released from M in different proportions to those currently employed in X, since importables are relatively capital intensive and exportables are relatively labour intensive. Thus

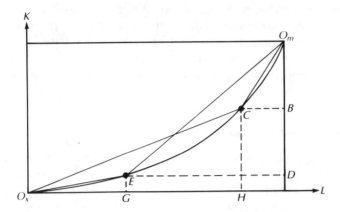

Figure 7.4 Trade and factor rewards

there is an excess demand for labour and excess supply of capital at the initial pre-trade factor intensities. This will tend to raise the price of labour and depress the price of capital. This change in factor prices, of course, provides an incentive for factor substitution. Thus at the post-trade equilibrium (C) both activities are more capital intensive (K/L) than at the autarchic equilibrium (E):

$$\frac{CH}{O_xH} > \frac{EG}{O_xG} \text{ and } \frac{O_mB}{BC} > \frac{O_mD}{ED}$$

The initial changes in relative factor prices are therefore sustained in the new equilibrium situation (point C in Figure 7.4) by the changes in factor intensities. As a result of the increase in capital intensities, the marginal product of labour (which equals the real wage under the assumed competitive conditions) increases in both industries. Similarly, the marginal physical product of capital (i.e. the return to the factor used intensively in the import commodity) falls in both the importables and exportables sectors as a result of trade. (The argument can be repeated to show that in the context of the Heckscher–Ohlin model the real wage (profit) would fall (rise) in a capital-abundant economy as a result of the opening of trade.)

   The corollary of this result is that in the typical developing country, where un-skilled labour is certainly the abundant factor of production, a policy of protection (the restricting of trade) will reduce real wages. This may seem surprising: will the urban working class not gain from the increased demand for their services to increase output of the protected industrial goods? That depends on whether, or how nearly, the critical assumption of perfect factor mobility is satisfied. Where it is satisfied completely, the reduced demand for labour in the labour-intensive export sector, usually agriculture or similar primary-sector activities, will outweigh the increased demand for labour in the capital-intensive industrial sector. With complete im-mobility of labour, on the other hand, the commonsense reasoning is correct (though labour in the unprotected sector continues to suffer from protection). In the real world, labour is typically partially mobile, and it is an empirical question as to which effect will dominate. But even if prevailing factor immobility is such as to reverse the distributional effects of creating or restricting trade, the appropriate policy may be to use adjustment-support measures to increase factor mobility or to use means of achieving distributional goals other than trade restriction. (Adjustment problems are examined in greater depth in the next section of this chapter, and the issue of optimal government intervention is considered in section 9.2.)

The distributional effects of *intra*-industry trade, i.e. trade arising in a framework other than Heckscher–Ohlin, have not been widely explored. However, as in the Heckscher–Ohlin case, they will depend on the effects of trade on relative factor rewards and on consumption possibilities. As we argued in Chapter 6, the theory of intra-industry trade lacks the generality of the Heckscher–Ohlin paradigm, and fairly general implications of intra-industry trade for the distribution of the resulting gains are difficult to draw. Let us briefly illustrate one particular case, using a model developed by Krugman (1981). It is a model of two-way trade in the context of monopolistic competition. (The model is similar to the model described in section 6.3.) Firms produce different varieties of a given commodity and all these varieties enter symmetrically into every consumer's utility function. In order to investigate distributional issues Krugman assumes there to be two industries in each country, each of which produces a differentiated commodity. To simplify matters further he assumes that labour is immobile between industries (i.e. labour is sector specific) and that the two countries are differentially endowed with the two types of labour. Krugman shows that rewards to both factors increase following the opening of two-way trade in differentiated goods, and thus consumption possibilities are increased by increased access to differentiated products. Indeed, Krugman demonstrates that *both* factors (in this case different types of labour) are more likely to gain, the more similar are initial factor endowments between countries. Krugman uses this finding to explain the observation of Hufbauer and Chilas (1974) that much of trade expansion between industrial countries in the post-war period has been relatively free of adjustment problems, because it has been predominantly of an intra-industry nature. Clearly the more similar are (pre-trade) factor endowments, the smaller are adjustments in factor prices induced by trade; if those adjustments are more likely to be in an upward direction and trade also increases consumption possibilities for increased variety, then resistance to trade expansion is likely to be lower.

It must be recognized that this result is dependent on the specific model used by Krugman. Nevertheless, although the generality of the result is not firmly established, it is widely believed that intra-industry trade is more likely to produce a situation in which everyone can gain than does inter-industry trade. Clearly the effect of trade expansion (or contraction) on income distribution is not a trivial matter to be settled by appeal to some handed-down formula as an eternal truth. Economists can hope to say useful things on the subject, but only if theories are understood and the evidence has been examined.

7.4 Adjustment problems

In section 7.1 we described the nature of the gains from trade for a small economy as it shifts from autarchy to facing world prices, and as it reallocates resources (capital and labour) from importables to exportables production. We assumed in that case that there was full employment throughout. We were implicitly assuming either that instantaneous (frictionless and costless) reallocation of factors was possible or that we were only interested in the long-run effects of trade. In practice, of course, there will be frictions and costs associated with the process of market clearing, and policy-makers and economic agents alike will be interested in more than the long run. As economists we too need to consider the nature of the adjustment process towards the economy's new equilibrium.

In associating adjustment problems with imperfect market clearing, one must have in mind some time scale, as well as the nature of the 'imperfection' or rigidity which frustrates the adjustment process. The idea that economic agents permanently fail to respond fully to price change is implausible and empirically unsupportable. Adjustment problems are therefore associated with the short run (when only one factor, typically labour, is at all mobile between sectors) and the medium term (when there is greater elasticity in the supply of all factors of production).

The nature of the adjustment problem can be illustrated by referring back to Figure 7.1. With autarchic relative prices (represented by the line DD) production and consumption are at point E. The opening of trade and the rise in the relative price of exportables provides an incentive for greater consumption of importables (M) and greater domestic production of exportables (X). The new, post-trade equilibrium is achieved with production at point P on the production possibility frontier. But the movement from E to P conceals a great deal of what is going on in the economy: capital and labour are released from sector M and re-employed in sector X. But given that M is a more capital-intensive activity than X, and that some of the factors released by M may not be identical to those required by X, then factor market disequilibrium and adjustment problems are likely to occur.

We can be more specific about the nature of these problems by referring to Figure 7.5, which is based on the specific factors model. We assume that each sector uses labour which is not sector specific: that is, it can be used by all sectors. In addition, each sector uses another factor (e.g. capital) which is specific to it. In other words, there is specific machinery or equipment (or managerial skills) that cannot be transferred, in the short term at least, to the other sector or industry. In Figure 7.5(a), $O^x_l O^m_l$ represents the total stock of labour available to both sectors. L_x represents the demand for labour in X; the law of diminishing returns means that, as more labour is applied to the specific capital, labour's marginal product (MP) declines, so that this schedule is downward sloping. L_m, the demand for labour in M, is analogously constructed by reference to the origin O^m_l. The labour market clears at a wage w_0 with the initial labour demand curves L_x^0 and L_m^0. This labour market equilibrium situation corresponds to the initial allocation of resources and pattern of production associated with autarchic relative

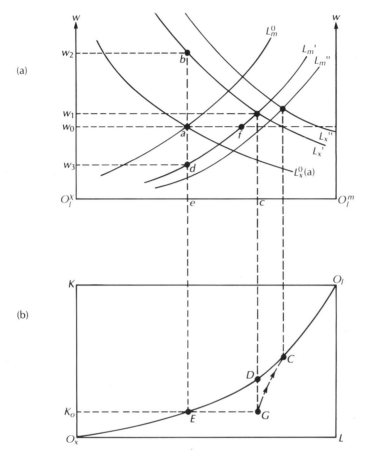

Figure 7.5 Adjustment and factor immobility

prices of exportables and importables. It is represented in the Edgeworth box in Figure 7.5(b) by point E.

Suppose now that the economy has the opportunity to trade. This means in our example that the price of labour-intensive exportables (P_x) increases. Since the value of the marginal product of labour in exportables ($P_x.MP_l$) increases, this shifts L_x to the right. The opposite influences shift L_m inward (also to the right) in Figure 7.5(a). If adjustment were full and instantaneous, this might be represented by the shifts to L_x' and L_m' with a market-clearing higher real wage of w_1 and redistribution of labour from importables to exportables (shown by the move from e to c along the $O^x_lO^m_l$ axis). In Figure 7.5(b) the economy moves instantly along the contract curve from E to D.

But let us now suppose that there is not instantaneous adjustment. There might be no mobility of either factor in the short term: capital is sector specific and the mobility of labour might be constrained by the geographical concentration of industries. Maintenance of equilibrium in the segmented labour markets (i.e. with fixed supplies of labour) following the opening of trade would require a rise in (money) wages to w_2 in the exportables sector ($a \rightarrow b$) and a fall in wages to w_3 in the importables sector ($a \rightarrow d$). There would be no change in the pattern of production. Indeed, if there was resistance to downward movement in money wages in the importables sector with this segmented labour market, unemployment would be created in this sector as the demand for labour at the fixed wage $\overline{w}_0$ contracted by the amount af. Thus rather than moving along the contract curve, there would be a tendency for domestic production of importables to fall without any corresponding increase in output of exportables. Of course, unemployment in the import-substitute sector would create a downward pressure on wages in that sector, and in turn would provide a greater incentive for labour to relocate to the exportables sector in order to gain employment and higher wages.

An alternative possibility is that in the short run capital is immobile but labour is not. Consider again the opening of trade starting from point E in Figure 7.5(b). The shifts in the demand for labour are as described above and the new equilibrium wage is w_1. This corresponds to a move from E to G. The allocation of capital between the sectors is fixed in the short run, and so G lies on the same horizontal line as E. Clearly this is not a long-run equilibrium since it lies off the contract curve. The rise in employment in exportables with a fixed amount of capital will increase the return to capital in that sector, whereas the fall in employment with a fixed stock of capital will reduce the return on capital in the importables sector. There is, as a result, an incentive for capital to move out of importables into exportables production. But the transfer of capital will in turn influence the marginal product of labour and wages. With fixed goods prices, the shift of capital towards (away from) exportables (importables) tends to increase (decrease) the marginal product of labour in exportables (importables). Thus L_x (demand for labour in exportables) shifts further outward (L_x' to L_x'') and L_m shifts further inward (L_m' to L_m''). To ensure continued labour market clearing, the real wage in this case must rise further. The expansion of the relatively labour-intensive (exportables) sector (at the expense of the capital-intensive, importables sector) increases the aggregate demand for labour in the economy and hence puts upward pressure on wage rates.[4] The economy moves along a path, shown in Figure 7.5(b), from G to a long-run equilibrium at C.

The above analysis has demonstrated that the production or inter-industry specialization benefits of trade and the nature of the factor reward effects of trade are more complex than is suggested by the instantaneous adjustment model of trade. Adjustment to a change in relative prices may be protracted if there is wage inflexibility, labour market segmentation, industry-specific capital and/or capital immobility. It is therefore easy to see why proposals for trade liberalization may encounter resistance, where there are anxieties about falling factor prices (even if they are only transitory) and unemployment of resources (of uncertain duration).

Recognition of the potential adjustment problems associated with inter-industry or sectoral specialization has induced speculation about whether intra-industry specialization involves smaller adjustment problems and induces as a result less resistance to trade expansion. The fundamental question is whether wages can be expected to exhibit greater flexibility in a setting of intra-industry trade or, more likely, whether factors can be more easily reallocated from contracting to expanding activities. The question is ultimately an empirical one, but there are indeed grounds for expecting smoother adjustment in the intra-industry trade case.

If technologies and factor intensities between sectors are similar, we should expect labour to transfer from one sector to another with comparative ease. The skills acquired during employment in the import-substitute sector are required (and in similar amount) in the export sector. In the extreme case, where adjustment takes place within the firm, the worker could simply be transferred from one production line to another. By contrast, if labour intensities and skills are very different between sectors, transfer may not be possible without complete retraining and large wage adjustments. It is this contrast which commentators have in mind when discussing adjustment, and it does have a certain intuitive plausibility. After all, intra-industry trade refers to the simultaneous exchange of similar products.

It is, however, a view that requires some qualification. Skill requirements may alter with the process of vertical specialization. An obvious example here is the contrast between the skill inputs in 'low-quality' imports and 'high-quality' exports of clothing in many developed market economies. Differences in capital–labour ratios may therefore be as great or greater within industry groups as between them. It could be argued, however, that adjustment is likely to be smoother in a setting of intra-industry specialization because the expanding and contracting activities are more likely to be based in a given region or even firm than with inter-industry specialization. With the latter, individuals may be required not only to retrain but also to relocate geographically. In so far as there is geographical resistance to mobility, adjustment would be more protracted. As with the issue of occupational mobility, the argument has a certain plausibility. After all, industries frequently are geographically concentrated for a variety of reasons, and if simultaneous expansion and contraction does occur within an industry and within a region, then the need for geographical mobility will be less. Again this is ultimately an empirical issue.

7.5 Summary

Every model that has been examined so far in this part of the book has shown that opening an economy to international trade brings benefits. In the classical Heckscher–Ohlin model, these can be decomposed into the gain from exchange and the gain from specialization. Intra-industry trade offers the possibility of a qualitatively different form of benefit from exchange: namely, increased product variety, which may enable consumers better to satisfy either their individual preferences or their thirst for variety.

Trade liberalization may nonetheless pose problems, of two forms. One concerns income distribution: certain groups may lose, even if society as a whole gains. The Stolper–Samuelson theorem proved that in the Heckscher–Ohlin model the scarce factor of production would lose from the opening of trade. The second problem concerns adjustment: factors may not be mobile in the short run, or labour may become unemployed rather than take a wage cut. There is a widespread presumption, but no certainty, that both the possibility of some groups being net losers and adjustment problems are less with intra-industry than with inter-industry trade.

7.6 Addendum: the large economy

The analysis in section 7.1 is constructed on the assumption that our country (U) is small and hence that the prices at which it trades (i.e. the terms of trade) are given. Thus whatever our country (U) supplies of commodity X to the world market, that supply has no effect on world prices of X. Likewise U's purchases of good M have no influence on the (relative) price of M. In terms of Figure 7.2 this amounts to assuming that the country faces an infinitely elastic demand curve (D_w) for its exports, and an infinitely elastic foreign supply (S_w) curve for imports. Such an assumption is highly plausible for many countries (with relatively small and diversified consumption and production patterns) and for trade in many products, e.g. mass-produced consumer goods (for which there are many locations of production and market outlets). Few countries supply such a large share of the total world market in particular goods that they can influence price by varying their supply. Similarly, few countries consume a sufficiently large share of the total supply of a particular commodity as to be able to influence price through variations in demand.

Although this may be generally true for finished manufactures, one can think of certain markets for commodities where the small-country assumption is inapplicable. There are certainly individual countries that are 'large' suppliers of specific commodities (e.g. copper from Chile), though there are not many except the United States that are 'large' buyers of commodities. There are also instances of bilateral exchanges where country size differences may affect the terms of trade. Many primary-producing developing countries often argue that expansion of their traditional exports is accompanied by a decline in their terms of trade, which may well be true if many of them try to export more simultaneously, even though this is not strictly a 'large-country' effect, since each individual supplier is small. There may also be common influences on output (e.g. weather conditions on crops) such that an increase in one country's output is associated with increased output by many other countries, in which case increased exports may not bring a constant price. Hence there certainly exist circumstances where the extent of the gains from trade is influenced by varying terms of trade.

It is evident from Figure 7.1 that the extent of the gains from trade depend, for a given preference map, on the extent of the difference between the domestic and international terms of trade. Trade is beneficial to our country U because it raises the price of the exportable (X) relative to the importable (M). The more favourable are the international to the domestic terms of trade, the steeper is price line TT compared to DD in Figure 7.1. With constant terms of trade at TT, the expansion of trade (from autarchic equilibrium at E to the post-trade equilibrium) raises welfare from I_a to I_t'. If that expansion of exports of one country alone (the genuine large-country case), or in conjunction with export expansion of the same good from other

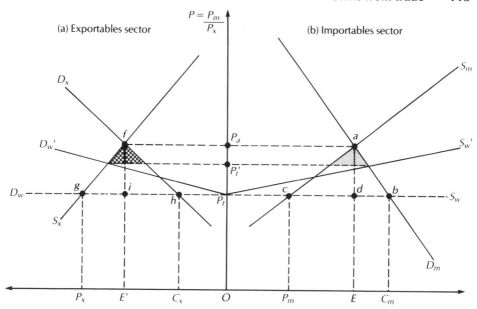

Figure 7.6 Trade-induced changes in consumer and producer surplus: the large-
country case

countries, tends to create excess supply in world markets and to depress the price of
the exportable, then *TT* will tend to shift back towards *DD*. This will reduce the net
gain from trade to below the level $(I_t' - I_a)$. Thus the gains from unrestricted trade
can be expected to be lower (but not negative) for a large country than for a small
country, and for countries subject to decline in their terms of trade.

The genuine large-country case can in fact be illustrated in greater detail with the
aid of Figure 7.6. Domestic demand (D_x and D_m) and supply (S_x and S_m) conditions
are unaltered, but 'foreign' demand (D_w) and supply (S_w) are changed if country U
can affect prices. In the export market D_w becomes D_w': an upward-sloping foreign
demand curve for the exportable implies that U has some monopoly power in the
supply of X (restricting the supply would raise P_x and reduce P_m/P_x in Figure 7.6).
In the import-substitute market the possession of monopsony (buyer) power means
that the price of importables (P_m) can be driven down by U restricting its demand;
S_w' is therefore upward sloping. If either of these conditions of market power
prevails, then *ceteris paribus* the gains from trade are lower than in the small-country
case (where the net gains were represented by the areas of the triangles *abc* or *gfh*).
With S_w' and D_w' the expansion of exports and imports is smaller than in the small-
country case. Thus the net gains from trade are shown by a smaller triangle (the
cross-hatched or shaded areas in Figure 7.6). The existence of market power for the
large country means that the difference between pre- and post-trade relative prices
or terms of trade ($P_a - P_t'$) is smaller than in the small-country case ($P_a - P_t$). The
extent of the gains from trade is dependent on the change in the terms of trade, and
the change in the terms of trade is in turn dependent on country size.

Except possibly for the United States, no country is likely to have both monopoly and monopsony power, or to have market power over a wide range of products. Nevertheless the conclusion of this analysis is that the gains from unrestricted trade are greater in the case of small countries without any market power. Such countries are likely to have a greater interest, therefore, in the creation of global conditions (e.g. commercial policies) that foster trade. If large countries can influence world prices by engaging in international trade, they can also influence world prices by restricting trade. If they can do so to their own advantage, they may have a rather different view about 'optimal' trade or commercial policies from small countries. We return to this issue in Chapter 10, which deals with the theory of protection.

7.7 Bibliography

The gains from trade in the context of the Heckscher–Ohlin model are thoroughly investigated in the classical references on the model (see section 3.9). An additional important reference is Baldwin (1952). Empirical evidence on the traditional gains from trade is usefully summarized by Corden (1975) and Milner (1985).

Similarly, the major references on intra-industry trade offered in the bibliography to Chapter 6 provide discussions of the gains from trade. The model of Greenaway (1982) presented in the text uses the approach first developed by Lancaster (1980). The conditions which determine the continuity, linearity and symmetry characteristics of the model, and the distribution of total welfare between producer and consumer surplus, are described more fully in Greenaway (1982) or Greenaway and Milner (1986). There is a limited literature as yet on measuring the additional gains resulting from trade where there is product differentiation and scope for scale economies. The study by Cox and Harris (1985) is, however, an important contribution in this area.

Chapter 66 of Stiglitz (1966) sets out the Stolper–Samuelson theorem, and the references above on the gains from trade also deal with income distribution issues.

The specific factors model presented is based on Jones (1971) and Neary (1978, 1982). Additional references on adjustment problems in an inter-industry setting are Corden (1974, 1984) and Neary (1985). Adjustment problems in an intra-industry trade setting are discussed in chapter 11 of Greenaway and Milner (1986).

Notes

1. Note that the relative price of M increases as P rises, while the relative price of X increases as P falls. Thus with quantities increasingly from right to left in the exportables sector D_x is positively sloped and S_x is negatively sloped.
2. The compensation principle declares a change desirable if losers *could* compensate gainers, irrespective of whether they do. To *require* compensation would be to insist that only changes to Pareto-preferred situations were desirable, even if the compensation required were from poor to rich. The commonsense compromise view is that an overruling of the efficiency criterion provided by the compensation principle requires a presumption that income distribution would be worsened so much by the change as to imply a loss of

social welfare despite the gain in efficiency. In that event the change should be made only if compensation *is* paid.

3. This could be measured in an ordinal sense or in a cardinal sense if each individual demand curve were integrated to obtain a value of total surplus for all varieties. For our present purposes ordinal ranking is sufficient.

4. The reader may wish to work through the implications of adjustment processes in the case of the opening of trade for a capital-abundant economy; or where the normal price effects of the opening of trade are altered by policy interventions, e.g. by a tariff on imports.

8

Trade interventions and the 'old protectionism'

The models studied in earlier chapters have shown how countries can benefit through engaging in trade. Adam Smith showed the gain possible when each country has an absolute advantage. Ricardo showed that the gain requires only the existence of comparative advantage, which (unlike an absolute advantage) is almost certain to be present. Heckscher and Ohlin showed how comparative advantage is based on differences in factor endowments and how a country can benefit by exporting goods intensive in its abundant factor of production. The models of trade in manufactures, including intra-industry trade, showed how trade based on the exploitation of scale economies and product differentiation could satisfy tastes for diversity, raise real income and benefit both parties even if factor proportions and tastes are identical.

These models suggest not only that some trade is a good thing, but that *free* trade is a good thing. Yet protection did not die out with the mercantilists; governments continue to protect their domestic industries to a greater or lesser extent in most countries, and popular opinion takes it as virtually axiomatic that it is irrational to import something that could be made at home. Is this simple ignorance, or are there qualifications to the case for free trade suggested by economic theory?

In order to be able to answer that question we need to understand the effects of trade interventions. This chapter and the next deal mainly with positive aspects of the theory of commercial policy, while in Chapter 10 we return to the normative questions.

8.1 Forms of intervention and protection

It is important to appreciate that the volume, direction and commodity composition of international trade flows, especially at the detailed product level, may be affected by a vast array of policy interventions. Some of those interventions are aimed directly and overtly at influencing the volume of goods that are traded. Thus import tariffs i.e. *ad valorem* or specific taxes on imports, which alter directly the price of imported goods and as a consequence import volumes, are a typical and immediately recognized form of trade intervention. But many other government policies may not sound like trade interventions. In many developing countries, for example, other border taxes in addition to import tariffs or duties are applied. Stamp duties may apply

116

only against imported goods, or consumption taxes may apply with higher rates on imported than locally produced goods. The operative rate of border taxation may well be higher, therefore, than the rate recorded in the customs schedule. Another example of the ambiguity caused by the labelling of measures arises from multiple exchange rates: these do not sound like an instrument of trade intervention, but if the rate at which export earnings can be exchanged for domestic currency is different from that for import transactions, then the measure amounts to a form of export subsidization or taxation (depending on how the exchange rates are set).

In other cases a measure may not be directly aimed at regulating the volume of traded goods, but it may nonetheless indirectly affect the volume or composition of trade flows. Thus foreign exchange controls may be employed by countries in order to manage the overall balance of payments and international reserves position. But it is possible for central banks to use restrictions on permission to buy foreign exchange in order to regulate the volume and composition of imports. However, fluctuations in foreign exchange earnings are likely to mean that the trade and protective effects of the controls are not necessarily consistent with other measures used to control imports.

It is not always obvious how one can distinguish between trade policy and non-trade policy measures. Industrial or regional policy in industrial countries may be aimed at satisfying objectives that are not trade related. Government support for a domestic coal industry for strategic or regional policy reasons may also affect the international competitiveness of other industries: cheaper electricity from coal-fired generating plant may act as an implicit production or export subsidy to the domestic steel industry. But it may also be that measures of trade intervention are deliberately hidden or obscured by policy-makers. Recent decades have witnessed the growth of deliberate trade interventions with a protective motive, that are deliberately 'hidden' in order to reduce the threat of retaliatory action by other countries and to avoid overtly breaking the international rules of the trading system. (The operation of the General Agreement on Tariffs and Trade is described in Chapter 17.) These hidden measures may involve the use of new, imaginative ways of imposing quantitative restrictions on imports, such as foreign producers in specific countries and of specific 'sensitive' products agreeing 'voluntarily' to restrict their exports.

Import restrictions may also result from the ways in which countries administer normal, bureaucratic procedures that relate to imports. Health and safety requirements may, unintentionally or deliberately, restrict imports. For example, there may be legitimate tests of safety standards for cars before a model can be sold on the domestic market. It may be unavoidable that it is more difficult and expensive for foreign cars to pass the tests because of greater cultural and physical distance from the export market: the exporter's technicians may not speak the bureaucrat's language very well, for example. The bureaucrat may, of course, make this barrier to trade more costly than it has to be merely to satisfy standard requirements. In some cases the bureaucrat may independently exercise his or her power: bribery and corruption are not unknown at international frontiers! In other cases administrative procedures can be used as systematic instruments of trade restriction. The problem is that it is difficult to establish whether a protective effect is intended or not: who can say whether a bureaucrat's willingness to buy a more expensive local product is due to his belief that it is of a superior quality, rather than to a surge of patriotism when he is spending the taxpayer's money? Negotiators in recent rounds of trade negotiations (see Chapter 17) have spent years just trying to define the nature of non-tariff barriers as a necessary precondition to the establishment of any international control.

Even where publicity and international controls 'expose' extra-legal and hidden forms of protection, it does not mean that protection is removed even if the 'exposed' instrument is discarded. Innovation in policy intervention is part of the bureaucrat's skill. In Chapter 17 we will return to this issue, when we consider some of the recent changes in the US and EC fair trade and anti-dumping legislation that increase these countries' ability to protect domestic producers. At this stage it is important to emphasize two points.

First, each form of intervention in the traded goods sector has some distinctive economic effects. It would be tedious and potentially misleading to develop a taxonomy of interventions. The important principles can be grasped by considering examples of the dominant forms of intervention: namely, trade taxes, subsidies and quantitative restrictions. The consequences of specific instruments not considered here can then be deduced as an exercise in applied economics.

Second, a distinction can be drawn between the instruments of the 'old protectionism' and the 'new protectionism'. The former relates to the use of overt interventions, especially import tariffs which were not highly discriminatory between different sources of import supply. The latter involves the use of hidden forms of discriminatory and non-tariff intervention that have emerged as the barriers associated with the 'old protectionism' have been dismantled. Between 1947 and 1979 there were seven GATT rounds of multilateral trade negotiation, which produced substantial reductions in tariff barriers. Average tariffs on manufactured goods in industrialized countries have fallen dramatically: in the United States from around 50 per cent to about 5 per cent, and from about 40 per cent to 4 per cent in the case of Britain, for example. By contrast, the 1970s and 1980s have witnessed a significant increase in product- and source-specific non-tariff barriers. World Bank estimates show that 17 per cent of US and nearly 16 per cent of EC imports are subject to non-tariff barriers of some form. Protection remains a central motive for these trade barriers. But there are important differences (in the type of instrument used and their effects) between the 'new' and 'old' protectionism that justify examining each separately. We begin in this chapter with the instruments of the 'old protectionism'.

8.2 Tariff barriers

Consider a tariff at rate t levied on the import of good M. This will raise the domestic price of the importable good, p_m, in equal proportion above the world price, p_m^w, on the assumption that the domestic market for M is competitive, that imports of M continue and that the imported and import-substitute goods are perfect substitutes. Thus:

$$p_m = (1 + t)p_m^{w}$$

Figure 8.1(a) shows the effect of such a rise in the price of good M in country U in terms of the basic, partial equilibrium demand and supply diagram. Without a tariff, the domestic price is equal to the world price, and hence domestic production is q_1 (determined by the domestic supply curve) and domestic consumption (determined by the demand curve) is q_4. At the tariff-distorted price the production rises to q_2 and consumption falls to q_3, and as a result the volume of imports falls from (q_4-q_1) to (q_3-q_2).

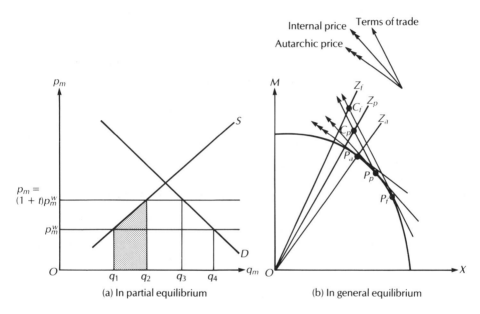

(a) In partial equilibrium   (b) In general equilibrium

Figure 8.1 Displacement of equilibrium by a tariff

There are many purposes for which the partial equilibrium analysis shown in Figure 8.1(a) is appropriate. This is the case whenever one is considering a change in a tariff on an individual good, provided that it accounts for a relatively small share of the economy's total production and consumption. But there are also circumstances where the *ceteris paribus* assumptions that underlie partial equilibrium analysis are seriously violated. This is the case, for example, when one is comparing a general policy of import substitution based on protection with a policy of free trade or export promotion. In such a case one needs to employ a general equilibrium analysis. In practice we resort to the simple two-good general equilibrium analysis developed in Chapter 3.

Figure 8.1(b) shows the effect of a tariff in general equilibrium terms. P_a is the point of production and consumption under autarchy; we know that this occurs where there is a social indifference curve tangential to the production possibility curve. From now on, however, it will be simpler to represent tastes by an income–consumption curve, rather than by the indifference curves themselves. An income–consumption curve consists of the locus of points of tangency between budget line and indifference curve as income is expanded with a fixed relative price; the assumption of identical homothetic tastes implies that each income–consumption curve is a straight line from the origin (that is, a ray). Thus the ray Z_a in Figure 8.1(b) shows the consumption of X and M at various income levels when p_m/p_x is the autarchic price, such as to be tangential to the ppc at P_a. In particular, with the income generated by production at PA, consumers will choose to buy the combination of goods represented by P_a, so that the autarchic economy would indeed be in equilibrium with the price that generates Z_a.

The world relative price of M is lower than the autarchic price (since our country imports M). This lower price of M is represented in Figure 8.1(b) by the terms-of-trade lines which are steeper than the autarchic price lines, since more M exchanges for a given quantity of X. At the lower price of M, consumers substitute M for X, so the income–consumption curve is steeper than the autarchic one, as shown by Z_f. Equilibrium under free trade is shown by production at P_f and consumption at C_f, both of which lie on the same budget line when the relative price is equal to the terms of trade. This is identical to the equilibrium in Figure 3.8, except that preferences have been represented by income–consumption lines instead of by social indifference curves. It involves country U producing more (less) X (M) than it consumes and exporting (importing) the differences, while trade remains balanced in value.

Next we have to consider the effect of the imposition of a non-prohibitive tariff: that is, a tariff that does not choke off imports completely. This has an effect on internal relative prices which is parallel to that in partial equilibrium analysis:

$$p_m/p_x = (1 + t) (p_m^*/p_x^*) = (1 + t) [1/(\text{terms of trade})]$$

This means that the internal relative prices in U are represented by a set of price lines that are flatter than the terms of trade but steeper than the autarchic price, as shown by the set of price lines with double arrows in Figure 8.1(b). This price gives rise to an income–consumption line with intermediate slope, as shown by Z_p (P for *protection*, to match F for *free trade* and A for *autarchy*). Equilibrium consumption must lie on the line Z_p with the tariff t. And, of course, equilibrium production must occur at the point P_p where the with-tariff price line is tangential to the ppc. But the country trades along the terms of trade line P_pC_p, not along the internal price line from P_p.[1] The point is that consumers and producers are motivated by the internal with-tariff prices, but traders are nonetheless able to trade with foreigners at world prices. The country exports the excess of its X production at P_p over its X consumption at C_p, in exchange for the excess of its M consumption at C_p over its M production at P_p.

Nominal and effective tariffs

Before turning to a thorough examination of the effects of a tariff, we should consider a complication that we ignored at the outset of this section. In using Figure 8.1(a) to identify both the production and consumption effects of a tariff, we were assuming that there were no intermediate inputs used in the production of good M. The vertical axis of the diagram measures prices of the imported good in gross terms, and the tariff at rate *t* was similarly expressed in gross terms, i.e. rate *t* on the gross value of imports at the border. Now clearly it is these gross final prices that determine consumers' decisions about how much to consume (Figure 8.1(a) is therefore complete in this regard). In the case of producers, however, the gross price only includes sufficient information on which to base production decisions if there are no intermediate inputs in the production process: that is, if the gross price is the same as the net or effective price. But, as we have suggested in earlier chapters, production often involves (in the manufacturing sector in particular) the processing of or adding value to purchased intermediate inputs which are transformed into higher-stage or final goods. In these circumstances examination of the nominal tariff, i.e. the tariff that applies on the imports competing with the final product, may not accurately represent how the activity is *effectively* protected by tariffs affecting the whole of the production process.

Suppose that our country has a 20 per cent import tariff on footwear, while the tariff on clothes is only 10 per cent. At first glance it might appear that the producers of footwear are being more heavily protected than clothing manufacturers. But this does not necessarily follow. *Ceteris paribus*, a higher nominal tariff on and higher percentage increase in the gross price of the final goods means a higher percentage increase in the net or effective price. But other things are not necessarily equal, and the nominal tariff on the final goods that compete with the industry's output tells only part of the story about how much effective protection the industry is receiving as a result of tariffs. The other element is the tariff the industry must pay on the *inputs* that it buys. The 'output' tariff is a subsidy to the domestic producer, while an 'input' tariff is a tax on local production.

To see why this is important, let us assume that 50 per cent of the costs of both industries consisted of imported materials and that the tariff on leather was 40 per cent while that on textiles was zero. The footwear industry would then find that its 20 per cent tariff on shoes was all used to pay for the 40 per cent addition to the cost of the leather it has to buy, leaving it with zero effective protection. In contrast, the clothing industry does not have to pay tariffs on its inputs, so its apparently modest protection of 10 per cent survives to give real – or effective – protection to the value added in the clothes-making industry. The industry with the lower nominal tariff therefore receives the higher effective protection.

The concept of effective protection was developed primarily by the Australian economist Max Corden (b. 1927) and the Canadian Harry Johnson (1923–77). The rate of effective protection is defined as the proportionate increase in value added in an industry that is possible as a result of the whole structure of protection, on both the output and the input of the industry. The basic formula for measuring the rate of effective protection (e_j) in the single-input case is:

$$e_j = (t_j - a_{ij}t_i)/(1 - a_{ij}) \tag{8.1}$$

where t_j = tariff rate on output of final good j
$\quad\quad t_i$ = tariff rate on input i
$\quad\quad a_{ij}$ = proportion of total price accounted for by inputs.

While the formula looks simple enough, the problems of actually measuring effective protection are formidable. A first problem is that any given industry will usually face a variety of tariff rates on its output and certainly on the several inputs that it buys, so that both t_j and t_i must be measured as weighted averages rather than simply looked up in the tariff regulations. A second difficulty is that, where an input is also supplied locally, its price need not rise by the full amount of the tariff if domestic supply increases to the point where imports are eliminated. But it would be wrong then to reduce a_{ij} to reflect the fall in the import component, since domestic input supplies are also more expensive as a result of the tariff. What is needed is an estimate of the extent to which the cost of inputs rises as a result of the tariff. A third difficulty is that the calculations should also include implicit protection given by quotas and the effects of taxes and subsidies.

Despite the difficulties, a lot of serious work has gone into the measurement of effective protection. Three important general conclusions have emerged. The first is that the differences between nominal and effective rates of protection are substantial: use of the former to measure the protection given to an industry is likely to be highly misleading. This results from the fact that only where input and output tariff rates are uniform are nominal and effective protection rates identical.[2] That is:

$$e_j = t_j \text{ when } t_j = t_i$$

Otherwise:

$$e_j > t_j \text{ when } t_j > t_i$$
$$\text{or} \quad e_j < t_j \text{ when } t_j < t_i$$

But the extent to which effective and nominal tariff rates diverge depends on technological characteristics (i.e. the a_{ij} coefficient in equation 8.1 above), which may well not be evident to the policy-maker. Indeed, it may well be difficult to 'plan' the tariff structure in order to avoid arbitrary variations in rates of effective protection, since for some producers a good is a final output while for others it is an input.

Although there is some evidence of a positive correlation between nominal and effective protection in many countries, the second general conclusion of the empirical work is that effective rates of protection are often highly uneven. This is especially the case in developing countries where tariff and non-tariff barriers are in general higher in nominal terms than in industrialized countries. Since resource allocation is determined by the relative rates of effective protection, resources may be drawn systematically away from certain types of activity. Export industries are often subject to negative ratcᵉ of effective protection, where their inputs are subject to import taxes while their output is unprotected by import tariffs since it is sold predominantly on world rather than domestic markets. The matching resource pull caused by high effective rates is likely to be towards final consumer goods promoted by import substitution measures.

Indeed, the third finding of the empirical work is that for developing and industrial countries alike there is a general tendency to what is known as tariff escalation: that is, higher nominal protection on final than intermediate stages of production. In other words, the tariff on leather is typically less than that on shoes, implying that the domestic footwear industry receives more effective protection than the nominal tariff would suggest. Since the final stages of production in industrial countries tend to be those involving the more advanced technology, this may constrain developing countries that would otherwise be able to diversify their manufactured exports, especially into technologically more sophisticated products. On the other hand, the developing countries may constrain their export potential by giving negative effective protection to exportables and lower effective protection to intermediate goods production than final goods production irrespective of where comparative advantage lies. We return to the issue of the choice of trade strategy in developing countries in Chapter 15.

For presentational convenience we will henceforth ignore the complication of effective protection, and assume that there are no intermediate inputs.

8.3 Effects of a tariff

In his famous textbook, *International Economics* (1968), Charles Kindleberger (b. 1910) distinguished seven effects of a tariff that apply in the case of a small economy.

Production effect

As can be seen from both parts of Figure 8.1, a tariff increases the output of the good M that receives protection. Figure 8.1(b) also shows explicitly that this increase in output of the protected good comes at the cost of a cut in the output of the non-protected good X. This must be true so long as we are comparing full-employment efficient-factor-combination equilibria, which is exactly what are compared along the production possibility curve. In fact the same thing can be inferred from Figure 8.1(a), since the area under the supply curve represents the opportunity cost of the factors of production absorbed in M production. The shaded area represents the value of the factors withdrawn from the X industry (or, in general, from the rest of the economy), whose output must therefore fall on the full-employment assumption.

Other things being equal, the production effect reduces economic welfare. This can be seen most clearly in Figure 8.1(b): the set of consumption possibilities that are feasible with production at P_p is less extensive than the set that are attainable with production at P_f, given the terms of trade that are tangential to the ppc at that point.

Hence it is proper to regard the change in production as a distortion – as something that prevents the marginal conditions for an optimum from being satisfied.[3] The distorting nature of the production change can also be seen in Figure 8.1(a), from the fact that the value of the resources absorbed in additional M production, represented by the shaded area, exceeds the value at world prices – and therefore at the social opportunity cost – of the additional output, which is the rectangular part of the shaded area, $p_m^*(q_2 - q_1)$. The triangular part of the shaded area, which with a linear supply curve is equal to $\frac{1}{2}tp_m^w(q_2 - q_1)$, represents the inefficiency induced by a tariff.

Consumption effect

Figure 8.1(a) (or 8.2(a)) shows that the tariff will reduce consumption of the protected good, from q_4 to q_3. Figure 8.1(b) also shows that consumption of M must decline, due to two reinforcing effects: the income effect[4] (real income declines from the level represented by P_fC_f to that represented by P_pC_p), and the substitution effect of M becoming more expensive relative to X. Conversely, what happens to consumption of X is ambiguous: the income effect tending to reduce consumption will work in the opposite direction to the substitution effect, since X will be cheaper. In an n-good model the income effect would be rather unimportant, but ambiguity about the sign of the effect on the consumption of products other than that on which the tariff was imposed would remain, the effect depending on whether goods were substitutes or complements to the good with the tariff.

Figure 8.2(b) provides an enlarged view of the critical part of Figure 8.1(b), showing the consumption possibility line P_pC_p (with slope determined by the terms of trade) from the production point P_p as before. We showed that consumers would select the point C_p on that line, on the income–consumption curve Z_p which holds when consumers confront the internal prices represented by the double-arrowed lines. But suppose that consumers confronted the world prices that represent social opportunity costs rather than internal prices: they would then choose a consumption point on the income–consumption curve Z_f (which holds with free-trade prices). They would therefore choose the point C_j. It is easy to see that C_j lies on a higher indifference curve than C_p, since the indifference curve at C_j is tangential to P_pC_j, while that at C_p cuts P_pC_j (and is tangential to the internal price line). The difference between the indifference curves at C_j and C_p represents the cost of the consumption distortion. Once again, it can also be measured in the partial equilibrium diagram (see Figure 8.2(a)). The utility value of consumption is represented by the area under the demand curve, so the reduction in that value is represented by the area of the quadrilateral JHq_4q_3. Of this, the rectangle GHq_4q_3 represents the social value of the resources released by this reduction in consumption, while the triangle JGH represents the social waste stemming from the consumption distortion.

It is difficult to think of a reason why a government would welcome a consumption distortion. If it believes that consumption of a good is too high because of social costs in excess of private costs (the costs of publicly provided medical care for cancer

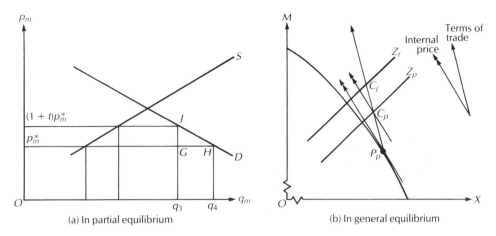

Figure 8.2 Consumption distortion

caused by cigarette smoking, for example), the appropriate remedy is a tax on *all* consumption, not just on consumption of imports. It is true that governments sometimes act in a way which looks as though they think consumption of imports deserves to be discouraged: wine-growing countries tend to tax whisky more heavily than wine, for example. But what they are probably seeking is the production effect on wine, to placate their wine lobby, rather than the consumption effect on whisky.

Revenue effect

Imposition of a non-prohibitive tariff yields revenue to the government. The amount of this revenue can be seen very easily in the partial equilibrium diagram, as the value of the tariff multiplied by the volume of imports, $tp_m^*(q_3 - q_2)$ in Figure 8.1(a). (In the general equilibrium diagram of Figure 8.1(b), the effect of the tariff revenue would be to restrict consumers to a budget line equal to the internal price line tangential to the ppc at P_p, but the question then arises as to what the government does with the tariff revenues. As stated in note 1 above, the theory makes the rather artificial assumption that the government gives it all back to consumers in a non-distortionary way so that their budget line is P_pC_p. Thus the general equilibrium analysis abstracts from the revenue effect.)

Governments need to raise revenue somehow, and any method of doing so involves collection costs. These include the costs of tax administration to the government and also the costs imposed on the taxpayers in complying with the tax law while minimizing their tax burdens. In addition, virtually any tax imposes distortions. Taxes on particular products create a consumption distortion exactly like that analyzed in the previous section. Even income taxes distort the choice between income and leisure. There is still an unfortunate tradition in international economics of glibly supposing that governments have unlimited powers to raise lump-sum taxes and give lump-sum subsidies at zero cost, which suppresses these considerations. The correct procedure is to compare the collection costs and distortions involved in raising revenue through a tariff with those involved in raising revenue in alternative possible ways. (We will return to the issue of optimal taxation and trade taxes in Chapter 10.)

Income distribution effect

We alluded in Chapter 7, on the gains from trade, to the effects of a tariff on the distribution of income between factors. In the case of the two-factor Heckscher–Ohlin model, the Stolper–Samuelson theorem reveals that a tariff benefits a country's scarce factor of production and penalizes its abundant factor. The intuition behind this is that exports augment the derived demand for the abundant factor and imports relieve the relative scarcity of the other factor. Given this theorem, import protection in a labour-abundant, developing country benefits capital at the expense of labour, while the result is reversed in the case of a capital-rich, industrialized country. It is thus not surprising that labour in import-substitute sectors in capital-rich industrialized countries often opposes the removal of protection.

In practice, it is often difficult to predict how tariffs will affect the distribution of income between factors. Even where the effects are predictable, it is certainly not the case that they will necessarily be desirable. If, for example, tariffs in a developing country redistribute income towards capital, this typically benefits the higher-income and wealth-owning classes. Note also that a tariff tends to redistribute away from consumers of the tariff-protected consumer goods and towards the government (in the form of increased tax revenue) and producers (in the form of increased producer surplus). In terms of Figure 8.2(a) the net consumer loss was shown to be the area JGH, but the gross loss experienced by consumers resulting from the increased price of importables is the decline in consumer surplus: that is, the area under the demand curve between $p_m{}^*$ and $(1 + t)p_m{}^*$. The difference between these net and gross consumer losses is accounted for by the redistributions identified above. The equity or otherwise of these redistributions is impossible to establish on a priori grounds. It will depend on the nature of the protected good and the consumption basket of different income groups. But it is not uncommon to find that the real income of low-income consumers is being reduced by tariffs on items such as clothing, footwear and foodstuffs.

Competitive effect

It was possible to demonstrate all the preceding four effects in terms of the Heckscher–Ohlin model (although none of them is specific to that model). This is not possible in the present case, since the Heckscher–Ohlin model assumes perfect competition with or without a tariff. But in reality perfect competition is pretty much confined to agriculture and the financial markets, while the markets for most industrial products and most services are oligopolistic or monopolistically competitive. In such markets the degree of competition can be drastically reduced by the effective exclusion of imports from the domestic market through high protection. This effect is most important in small economies, where the domestic market is large enough to support at most one or two producers at an efficient scale of operations. If competition from imports is effectively excluded by very high tariffs (or in other ways), the domestic producers face little incentive to keep down prices or to pursue efficiency in production.

It is rather difficult to think of reasons why society as a whole might be expected to benefit by shielding domestic producers against foreign competition. But the producers themselves can be expected to favour such shielding and to wield their political influence (and in some cases other instruments, varying from personal friendships to bribery) to establish, enhance or perpetuate it.

Income effect and balance of payments effect

We come finally to two effects that arise when we relax the assumption on which the preceding model building has been based, and which can conveniently be treated together. The first is the effect on the level of *income* and employment. This has been excluded from the analysis up to now by the assumption that the economy is always on the production possibility curve, but of course this is not always true: unemployment occurs in the real world and is represented in the model by production at a point inside the ppc. A tariff is one of a number of ways in which income and output can be stimulated (as will be discussed in the balance of payments theory in Chapter 12). The second is the effect on the *balance of payments*. This has been excluded from the analysis up to now by the assumption that trade is always balanced (which is represented in the general equilibrium diagram by the fact that the country always exchanges exports for imports along its terms-of-trade line). The macroeconomic analysis of Chapter 12 will demonstrate that relaxation of this assumption leads to the expectation that imposition of a tariff will improve the balance of payments on current account, at least in the short run.

Net impact in welfare terms

We will delay an overall evaluation of the case for protection until Chapter 10. At this stage, however, it will be useful to summarize the static welfare effects or net costs of a tariff under conditions of full employment and perfect competition. The gross cost to consumers associated with the tariff-induced rise in the price of importables is equal to the sum of the areas $a + b + c + d$ in Figure 8.3. Area a is a redistribution from consumers to producers, for whom this represents an increase in producer surplus. Area c is the amount of tariff revenue paid by consumers to the government. Again this is a domestic redistribution, and does not involve a cost to the economy as a whole, if the government spends the tax in a manner which does not induce further distortions. We are left with the two 'triangles', area b (the production cost associated with the misallocation of domestic resources) plus area d (the consumption loss). The

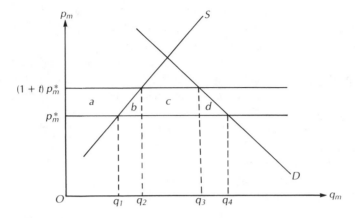

Figure 8.3 Net costs of tariff intervention

sum of these two triangles when aggregated across products represents the net costs of tariff protection to a small economy. The magnitude of these costs depends upon the height of the tariff barriers, domestic demand and supply conditions in the protected sectors, and the relative importance of protected goods in total consumption: *ceteris paribus* the net costs will be higher the higher are the tariffs, the more elastic is demand for and supply of protected goods and the greater is the share of protected goods in total consumption.

8.4 'Equivalent' trade interventions

Import quotas

A second way of providing protection to an import-competing industry is through the imposition of an import quota. An import quota is a *quantitative* restriction of the amount that can be imported: so many thousand tonnes of butter or so many cars or whatever. (Sometimes the quota is expressed in value terms, so many millions of pesos worth of trucks. This is most common where the product is sufficiently heterogeneous that a significant amplification of the value of imports through an upgrading of the quality of the products imported would be possible if the quota were expressed in physical terms.)

In Figure 8.4 the demand and supply curves for some product are illustrated by D and S. Suppose that an import quota equal to $\overline{Q}$ is imposed. Assuming that $\overline{Q}$ is less than the quantity that would be imported under free trade, so that the quota does indeed provide protection, the result will be an equilibrium where the horizontal distance between the demand and supply curves is equal to $\overline{Q}$. The price will therefore rise above the free-trade level p^* to a point p where the joint effect of the increased supply and reduced demand is to cut back imports to $\overline{Q}$ (or $q_4 - q_2$), in contrast to the free-trade level of imports of $(q_6 - q_1)$.

These effects are exactly the same as those that would have resulted from the

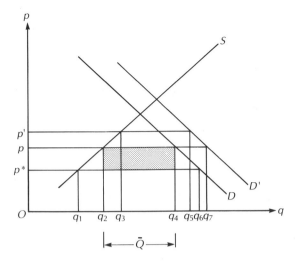

Figure 8.4 Effects of a binding import quota

imposition of a tariff t equal to $(p/p^* - 1)$: that is, a tariff whose value tp^* would be represented by the distance $(p - p^*)$ in Figure 8.4. Both would result in a rise in domestic production from q_1 to q_2, a fall in domestic consumption from q_6 to q_4, a rise in the internal price from p^* to p, and the same volume and value of imports. For this reason the tariff t is said to be *equivalent* to the quota $\bar{Q}$: *ceteris paribus* they have the same effects on prices and quantities, given the assumption of perfect competition. Because of this equivalence, it is unnecessary to examine the general equilibrium effects of a quota. At this level of abstraction they are identical to those of the equivalent tariff.

However, the equivalence of a quota and a tariff is a result that needs to be used with care; a lot hangs on the *ceteris paribus* and perfect competition qualifications noted above. Once one relaxes those restrictions, three major differences between the effects of a tariff and those of a quota emerge.

1. A first difference concerns their implications for *government revenue*. We saw earlier that with a tariff the shaded area in Figure 8.4 accrues to the government as revenue. But with a quota this is not, in general, the case. If the government distributes import licences (the sum of which is, of course, equal to the quota) to importers free, which is the normal practice, then it is the lucky importers who will get the shaded area – for they will be able to buy on the world market at price p^* and sell on the domestic market at price p, pocketing the difference. It is only if the government *sells* import licences for what the market will bear, which under competitive conditions means for the equivalent tariff, that the profits generated by an import quota could be recouped by the government and this difference would be eliminated. Countries have occasionally done just this, by auctioning off import licences: Brazil and Iran in the 1950s are the two leading examples.

2. A second difference concerns the reaction to a *shift in demand or supply*: in

technical jargon, the comparative static implications. Consider the case of a shift in demand from D to D' as shown in Figure 8.4. With a tariff, consumption would expand to q_7 by virtue of an increase in imports of $(q_7 - q_4)$. In contrast, a quota prevents the increase in imports, and hence the price rises instead to p' in order to ration the available supply (which can increase only through a rise in domestic output) in the face of the increase in demand. Thus shifts in demand (or for that matter in supply) provoke changes in the *quantity* of imports with a tariff and changes in the internal *price* with a quota. (After such a shift there is still, of course, a tariff that is equivalent to the quota, but it is a different tariff). Governments with a strong inclination towards central planning tend to regard this difference as an advantage for a system of quotas, since their use ensures that the volume of imports does not depart from the planned level 'just' because demand or supply were forecast incorrectly. Mainstream economists regard this as superficial: they argue that higher or lower levels of demand or supply signify that the good has a higher or lower social value than had been supposed, and thus that the quantity *should* be allowed to adjust, as permitted by the tariff.

3. A third difference concerns secondary distortions introduced through the need to allocate import licences. This is a point whose importance came to be recognized in the 1970s, following an important research project comparing the trade and payments policies of a number of developing countries that was carried out under the joint direction of the Indian economist Jagdish Bhagwati (b. 1934) and Anne Krueger (b. 1934). Unless import licences are auctioned, some bureaucrat has to decide *who* is to receive them. Since import licences are valuable – each one is worth $(p - p^*)$ – it is probable that some importers will seek ways of bribing the bureaucrat into allocating more to them.[5] But suppose that the country has a civil service full of scrupulously honest persons dedicated to the pursuit of social good rather than of private gain, as in the best Fabian fables. They still have to decide how maximizing the social good translates into dividing the import quota between rival claimants. They may be relied on to avoid the obvious error of giving all the licences to one or two firms, which could then collude to import less than permitted and drive the price up to monopolistic levels. Much more likely is that they will seek to make judgements about which industries are socially meritorious, or which types of end use (investment or exports rather than consumption) deserve support, or which regions or types of firm (state rather than private enterprises) are most deserving. Even accepting that such judgements can be made, allocating import licences is not an efficient way of putting them into effect. The reason is that the value of a particular good varies: what may be a crucial input to a consumption goods industry may be a marginal frill to some investment project. The bureaucrat may seek some objective basis for distributing the licences, such as in relation to capacity or to use in some base period (for imports of intermediate goods). The former gives an incentive to expand capacity not where more capacity is socially needed, but in order to qualify for more import licences. This could help explain why India (a country that has relied heavily on quota protection) has such a high ICOR[6] for a country at its stage of development. The latter leads to a freezing of industrial

structure: progressive firms cannot get the input they need to expand more rapidly than others.

In short, no matter how conscientious the bureaucrat, it is virtually impossible for him or her to distribute the licences without creating secondary distortions. And the evidence is that the cost of these distortions is typically much more than marginal.

There are probably few areas of economics where the conclusions are as clear-cut as here: if one is going to protect, a tariff would be better than a quota; and if one insists on using a quota, then the licences should be auctioned.

Export taxes

The idea of the possible equivalence of a tariff and import quota is relatively easy to understand and can be illustrated in terms of partial equilibrium analysis. Less immediately obvious is the idea of an equivalence between an import tariff (an implicit subsidy to local producers of importables) and an export tax (an explicit tax on production of exportables). Although both are border taxes, the immediate motive for import taxes is often a protective one, while it is the need for revenue that often explains the use of export taxes. (In the case of many developing countries a single, traditional export – mineral or agricultural – often offers a large base which is relatively easy and cheap to tax.)

Indeed, in partial equilibrium terms there would at first glance appear to be a clear non-equivalence. The domestic price of a good whose export is taxed would fall: in terms of Figure 8.1(a), the internal price would lie below the world price by a distance representing the export tax (since in the case of an exportable we expect that the world price will be above the autarchic price). There is again a production and consumption effect, but the signs on these are the reverse of those for an import tariff. However, if exportables production is lower than it would otherwise be, in a full-employment world this must involve higher production of non-exportables. In a two-sector model it is importables production that will be increased – as it would be if an equivalent import tariff were imposed instead of an export tax.

This can be demonstrated in terms of the general equilibrium model in Figure 8.1(b). If all exports are taxed at some rate, the internal relative-price line is flatter than the international terms of trade, exactly as in the case of a uniform tariff on all imports. There is indeed a famous theorem, called the Lerner symmetry theorem after the English-born economist Abba Lerner (b. 1903), which asserts that a uniform export tax is equivalent to a uniform import tariff exactly on these grounds. It is important to understand that this is a microeconomic theorem based on a comparison of equilibrium outcomes (the macroeconomic effects on income and the balance of payments are, of course, exactly opposite). It is also worth bearing in mind that *uniform* tariffs and taxes are analytical abstractions rather than realistic policy options.

Some economists would indeed argue that taxing traditional exports is the best way for developing countries to promote new industries and industrial exports. The argument builds on the equivalence theorem. The difference in the macroeconomic effects of an import tariff and an export tax means that the latter instrument tends to depreciate the exchange rate while the former leads to an appreciation. Thus the export tax not only raises revenue, but simultaneously protects import-competing industries and encourages the promotion of non-traditional exports. Thus the symmetry theorem draws attention to the need to consider protection within a general equilibrium framework when considering trade strategy, rather than as policy towards specific tradable goods.

8.5 Customs unions and free trade areas

A large number of regional trading arrangements have been established between developing countries over the last thirty years. There are also signs that regional trading blocs among industrial countries may be becoming more important rather than less. The European Community is likely to widen in membership, the USA and Canada have formed a free trade zone, and integration arrangements in the Pacific basin region are vaguely mooted. Customs unions are, however, overt and GATT-legal forms of commercial policy, so we will analyze them here.

A customs union is a group of countries among which there is free trade and which have a common tariff barrier against the rest of the world. A free trade area shares the feature of internal free trade, but does not involve the members standardizing their tariffs against the rest of the world. The leading historical examples of customs unions are the Zollverein, which was first formed in 1834 and led up to German unification, and in our day the European Economic Community (EEC). Free trade areas have included the European Free Trade Area (EFTA) and the Andean Group. Free trade areas have had a tendency to be partial rather than complete, in regard to both the coverage of products and the extent to which tariffs have been cut.

The theory of customs unions and of free trade areas is almost identical, but the analysis of a free trade area is slightly simpler. To analyze a free trade area one needs to consider at least *three* countries – the two who form the free trade area and the one that is excluded. (Without the first two there is no free trade area, and without the third we would be back to the case of free trade, already studied.) Consider, therefore, the formation of a free trade area between our country U and a neighbouring country V, and let the excluded country be the large country called W.

The central concepts of customs union theory, introduced by the Canadian economist Jacob Viner (1892–1970), are trade creation and trade diversion. *Trade creation* occurs when a country starts to import a good that it previously produced at home, while *trade diversion* occurs when a country starts to import from a partner country a good that it previously imported from the outside world. The concepts can be illustrated in the simplest Ricardian model with constant opportunity costs. Consider U's trade in a particular good with production cost equal to c_u in U, c_v in V and c_w in W. Prior to formation of the free trade area, country U's supply would come from whichever area had the minimum cost to the consumer:

$$c_u; (1 + t)c_v; (1 + t)c_w$$

where t is the non-discriminatory tariff rate. On the formation of the free trade area, the tariff on imports from V is withdrawn, so that imports would come from the minimum of:

$$c_u; c_v; (1 + t)c_w$$

Since the cost of buying from the partner country falls while the costs of buying from the other two areas remain constant,[7] imports from V may be stimulated. Specifically, if:

$$(1 + t)c_v > c_u > c_v$$

and the country previously produced the good itself rather than imported from W, then in the new situation it will cease domestic production and import instead from its partner V. This is trade creation. If, on the other hand:

$$(1 + t)c_w > c_v > c_w$$

and the country previously imported from W rather than producing the good itself, then in the new situation it will buy from V instead of W. This is trade diversion. The concepts are, however, in no way restricted to the Ricardian constant-cost model. Trade expansion with the partner country will still be trade creation so long as it involves an expansion in the total level of trade, and it will still be trade diversion when it involves the redirection of trade from third countries, even if the industries involved face increasing costs due to factor substitution or decreasing costs due to increasing returns to scale, or if they are imperfectly competitive.

Trade creation implies that the country has replaced expensive (domestic) supply by cheaper (partner-country) imports. *Ceteris paribus*, that produces a welfare gain. The magnitude of that gain can be shown in the partial equilibrium tariff diagram (see Figure 8.5), which is drawn for simplicity on the assumption that V as well as W is large relative to U. Prior to formation of the free trade area, U was producing q_2 at the supply price $c_u = (1 + t)c_w$, and consuming q_3. Following trade liberalization, price (equals cost) falls to c_v, production falls to q_1, consumption rises to q_4, and

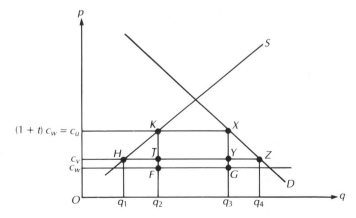

Figure 8.5 Net welfare effect of trade creation and trade diversion

imports rise to $(q_4 - q_1)$. Welfare is given by the area under the demand curve: it rises by q_3q_4ZX, which consists of the cost of extra imports of q_3q_4ZY and a net benefit (consumer's surplus) of the triangle XYZ. The cost of domestic production falls by the reduction of the area under the supply curve, which consists of q_1q_2KH; of this, q_1q_2JH represents the cost of the additional imports, while the triangle HJK is a net social saving. Consumer expenditure also falls by c_uc_vHK and $KJYX$, but these represent transfers rather than pure social benefits: the former are profits forgone by producers of the good in question, while the latter is the tariff revenue lost by the government. Thus the net social gain of trade creation is the two small triangles. On the assumption of linear demand and supply curves, this is equal to half the tariff suppressed multiplied by the volume of trade created – a number that can be sensibly estimated with relative ease.

If the partner country (V) is consistently the lowest-cost producer in the world (i.e. $c_v < c_w$), the union is wholly trade creating, and as a result unambiguously raises net welfare. But formation of the free trade area from U's viewpoint is no different in this case to pursuing a policy of non-discriminatory free trade. Most free trade areas, however, involve some trade creation and some trade diversion. Consider Figure 8.5 again. Before the free trade agreement, U was importing $(q_3 - q_2)$ from W since $c_w < c_v$. After the agreement $c_v < (1 + t)c_w$ and all country U's imports (including $q_3 - q_2$) come from country V; $(q_3 - q_2)$ of imports are diverted from W to V. Thus *trade diversion* implies that the country has replaced cheap imports from outside the free trade area by more expensive imports from its new partner. The additional costs of these diverted imports is $(c_v - c_w)$ per unit, and for a volume $(q_3 - q_2)$ this means that the additional resource cost to U is the area $JYGF$ in Figure 8.5. The free trade area can result, therefore, either in a net welfare increase if HJK plus XYZ exceeds $JYGF$ or in a net welfare loss if the reverse condition applies.

The relative magnitude of trade creation and diversion effects will be influenced by factors such as the size and membership of the union (the larger the union and the more industrialized the countries in the union, the greater the likelihood of trade creation predominating) and the degree of overlap in members' industrial structures (the greater the overlap and the degree of substitutability in production, the lower the possibility of trade diversion). Clearly on a priori grounds one would expect customs unions and regional trading arrangements among industrialized countries to have a greater probability of being welfare improving than those among developing countries. In terms of the analysis represented by Figure 8.5 discriminatory tariff reduction is at best a second-best measure. Indeed, multilateral free trade is unambiguously superior to the formation of a customs union. Even where tariff liberalization is not reciprocated, a non-discriminatory tariff reduction may still be preferable to a discriminatory one. But if tariff reductions are not reciprocated multilaterally and if there are terms-of-trade benefits associated with preferential access of your country's exports into the markets of partner countries, a customs union may be preferable from a *national* viewpoint to unilateral free trade. The fact that countries have been more willing to reciprocate tariff reductions to a restricted number of partners than they have to all countries suggests that these terms-of-trade gains are perceived to be important. Welfare maximization, however, may not be the only factor that has motivated regional trading arrangements.

In the case of integration among developed, industrialized countries the empirical evidence suggests that trade creation has predominated (by as much as 4 to 1 in the case of the EC). Even where trade creation has been overwhelming, however, many economists have argued that integration is of minimal quantitative importance. Trade is typically 20 per cent of GNP; the intra-regional trade being liberalized is perhaps a half of total trade; it may be expected to expand by about 50 per cent;[8] and the tariff removed is at most 10 per cent on average. Therefore, applying the formula for the benefit of trade creation and ignoring the losses for trade diversion, we have a potential gain of the order of 0.25 per cent of GNP. Double any of the estimates and the gain is still derisory. And for integration movements between developing countries the theory indicates losses rather than gains of any size, inasmuch as the empirical estimates have typically suggested a predominance of trade diversion rather than creation.

These estimates are, however, seriously incomplete. First, the above calculations ignore the favourable effect on the terms of trade of increased exports. There is no contradiction between the assumption that the country is small and can sell all it wants to at the world price, and the assumption that it would get a better price if it had tariff-free access to foreign markets. A study (1967) by the Canadians Paul and Ronald Wonnacott (b. 1933, b. 1930) suggested that as much as two-thirds of the benefits to Canada of free trade with the United States would come from this source. Second, Figure 8.5 shows the welfare gain realized from additional trade in increasing-cost Heckscher–Ohlin goods, not in decreasing-cost differentiated products. As we have seen in Chapter 6, some fairly major extensions of the theory are needed to take account of this type of case. It is necessary, for example, to recognize that a country which is able to capture its partners' market will benefit from a *cost-reduction effect*, enabling it to supply its domestic market more cheaply. Because of this, the welfare gain can quite easily exceed the increase in trade multiplied by the size of the tariff removed. Empirical evidence shows that it is mainly this type of trade that has expanded as a result of trade liberalization among industrial countries. This is not to claim that common markets are a magic key to instant wealth, but it is to suggest that their benefits can amount to a useful several per cent of GNP rather than a derisory fraction of 1 per cent.

It is commonly held that attempts at trade integration among developing countries have failed (see Chapter 17). Not only does the statistical evidence suggest that trade diversion may have exceeded trade creation, but members have often squabbled bitterly about the distribution of new industry attracted by the enlarged market. Does that mean that these attempts at integration were misguided? The fact is that countries on the road to industrialization generally want to establish infant industries: their aim in forming a common market or free trade area is to provide a bigger market to permit them to establish and expand infant industries more rapidly, and/or more cheaply, than would otherwise be possible. Thus trade diversion may well be precisely what the union members envisaged was necessary to achieve import-substituting industrialization. The problem is that each member prefers the new industry created by trade diversion to be located in its own country; hence the squabbles about the location of new industry within the region! The wisdom of regional integration for developing countries cannot in any case be judged independently of assessment of the appropriateness of a strategy of import-substituting industrialization, an issue discussed in Chapter 15.

8.6 Summary

There are diverse ways in which governments can influence the size and composition of a country's trade flows and production of tradable goods. This chapter has illustrated the economic effects of a number of dominant and traditional forms of intervention associated with the 'old protectionism'. The analysis of import tariffs provides a framework for considering resource allocation and income distribution effects of a range of other instruments. Often there is a degree of equivalence between different interventions, but invariably the equivalence is incomplete and different measures have distinctive features. Thus the price-raising effects of a quota may be expressed as a tariff-equivalent rate on imports, but the different dynamic and competitive effects of quotas mean that economists would invariably rank a tariff as a less costly means (in welfare terms) of protection or import restriction. Similarly, the equivalence in general equilibrium terms of an import tariff (which subsidizes importables production relative to exportables production) and an export tax (which taxes exportables production relative to importables production) emphasizes the need to consider protection in relative, not absolute terms.

For the small, perfectly competitive economy we explicitly demonstrated that trade interventions impose costs. Implicitly, therefore, we have established what has sometimes been called the central theorem of trade and welfare, which states that *laissez-faire* is Pareto-efficient for a perfectly competitive economy with no monopoly power in trade. We will return to the rationale and motives for intervention and protection in Chapters 9 and 10.

8.7 Bibliography

The literature on protection is vast. The most authoritative treatment of positive aspects of the subject is to be found in Corden (1971). Other valuable general references are Johnson (1971) and Greenaway (1983). For a survey of the literature on trade policies in industrialized countries see Baldwin (1984), and for developing countries see Krueger (1984).

The classic references on effective protection are Corden (1966) and Johnson (1965a). A useful guide to measurement problems and the interpretation of estimated rates of effective protection for a number of industrializing countries is provided by Balassa (1982).

The early developments in customs union theory are the contributions by Viner (1950) and Meade (1955b). A useful collection of readings on the topic can be found in Krauss (1973), while a survey of theoretical and empirical work is provided in chapters 6–8 of Pomfret (1988).

Notes

1. There is an implicit assumption here that the government redistributes the tariff revenue to consumers, and in a way that does not influence their perception of the relative price they are confronting in the market. If the government did not redistribute the revenue yielded by the tariff, or spend it itself, then society would not be able to trade up the terms-of-trade line P_pC_p. And if the government redistributed tariff proceeds according to how much each household had paid (which is a simple rule for preserving distributional neutrality) and households recognized the rule, they would realize that the true relative price confronting them was p_m^*/p_x^* instead of p_m/p_x.

2. The statement assumes that all protection is given by tariffs. Matters are even more complex where other forms of protection are involved.

3. The relevant marginal condition is the requirement that the marginal rate of transformation (the slope of the ppc) be equal to the opportunity cost of one good in terms of the other in trade (the slope of the terms-of-trade line).

4. Assuming that M is not an inferior good.

5. Where these potential rents exist there is an incentive for resources to be devolved to rent-seeking activities; resources that could be used otherwise in productive activities. Thus the net welfare loss associated with a quota may be higher than a tariff as a result of rent-seeking activity. In terms of Figure 8.3 the area c represents the internal redistribution from consumers to government associated with tariff revenue. In the case of all allocated import licences there is an incentive to devote resources up to the value represented by area a to rent-seeking activities. This is a cost to the economy, not an internal redistribution.

6. Incremental capital–output ratio.

7. This is where the analysis of a customs union differs from that of a free trade area. Establishment of a common external tariff implies that in general the tariff on imports from outside the area will change. If it falls, there is the possibility that the country will start importing from W a good that was previously produced at home: this is called 'external trade creation'. If it rises, the country may start to produce what it previously imported from W: this may be termed 'external trade destruction'.

8. That was the estimate officially accepted in the British White Paper of 1971 on the effect of British entry to the EEC (*The United Kingdom and the European Communities*, Cmnd 4715, July 1971).

9

The economics of the 'new protectionism'

It was stated in Chapter 8 that the post-war period has witnessed a fairly dramatic reduction of trade barriers associated with the 'old protectionism'. GATT outlawed the use in general of import quota restrictions and has provided a negotiating framework for the progressive reduction of tariffs. Similarly, it was clearly demonstrated that net costs are imposed when trade is restricted. However, the 1970s and 1980s have witnessed the emergence of a 'new protectionism'. Why have many industrial countries in the last two decades sought to defy or circumvent the rules of the international system and the logic of economic theory?

The new protectionism has been typified by two key features. First, the measures used have tended to be less overt and more subject to administrative discretion than the instruments of the old protectionism (i.e. tariffs and non-discriminatory import quotas). Second, the measures have tended to be applied in a manner which discriminates between products and countries: in other words, they have taken the form of product- and source-specific restrictions.

It is possible to offer some plausible conjectures to explain both the emergence and the form of the new protectionism. The new competitive challenge from the NICs in a relatively narrow range of labour-intensive goods (e.g. textiles, clothing, footwear, electrical goods) is no doubt one factor. The potential adjustment problems were therefore associated with imports from specific sources. General restrictions on trade in these goods, however, were constrained by GATT rules and the threat of retaliation by other industrial countries. Of course, politicians and administrators are not always convinced by the logic of free trade and specialization according to comparative advantage; the mercantilist approach continues to have its appeal. The reciprocity aspect of GATT negotiations has in fact helped to harness the mercantilist tendencies of politicians and administrators, by creating domestic export lobbies with an interest in pressing their own governments to concede some import liberalization, in order for the exporters themselves to acquire larger export markets. The idea of pressure groups lobbying governments for particular policy changes draws attention to another influence on the 'new protectionism': namely, the political, as well as economic, influences on trade policy. Protectionism may be 'endogenously' determined in the political marketplace rather than set independently by benevolent governments aiming to maximize social welfare.

We will return to a consideration of the instruments used to conduct the new protectionism, but first we discuss the wider political economy dimensions of the formulation of trade policy.

9.1 Political economy of protection

We alluded above to the obvious gap between theory and reality in the area of commercial policy: free trade is not a widely pursued policy. It may be that misconception and lack of information account for part of this gap: consumers, for instance, may not always appreciate that import barriers increase the costs of the goods they buy. This type of explanation would appear to be far from complete, however. In the last two decades public choice analysis has been applied to the determination of trade policy.

Even in a world where there was instantaneous adjustment of resources there would be gainers and losers from freer trade. A benign and omniscient government could, in principle, use non-distortionary taxes and subsidies to redistribute income from gainers to losers, so as to leave no one worse off as a result of the (net welfare-raising) reduction of a trade barrier. But this is not how the world works.

One might expect that a democratic system would be well placed to ensure that the majority interest in free trade would prevail. The continuing strength of protectionism, even though consumers represent a majority of voters, is usually ascribed to free-rider and externality problems associated with organizing pressure groups.

Consumers are too numerous and widely dispersed to form effective anti-protection pressure groups. The costs of forming and sustaining the consumer lobby are likely to be large, and since it is impossible to exclude free-riders from the benefits of reduced protection, the required funding for such pressure group formation is unlikely to be forthcoming. Producers, by contrast, are likely to be able to form pressure groups more easily, especially if the producer group is small and geographically concentrated. As a result, the costs of co-ordinating and monitoring the group are lower and free-riders more easily identifiable. Even though any one lobby represents only the interests of a single industry or sector, it may be possible for a coalition of lobbies to trade their voting power to defeat a number of policy reforms, only one of which may be the direct concern of any particular lobby.

Hence the degree and form of protection tend to be endogenously determined in the political marketplace rather than set by a benevolent government seeking to maximize social welfare. Protection may therefore be analyzed in a conflict resolution setting. The market for protection is a political market with both a demand side and a supply side.

The demand for protection

If capitalists and workers in a particular industry lose or expect to lose in real-income terms as a result of unrestricted international trade, as they would in the specific factors model, and if they can organize themselves into an interest group, they will 'demand' or seek protection or some form of assistance from the state. Thus the demand for protection can be modelled as a function of the perceived benefits from protection, minus the costs of obtaining that protection:

$$R = B - C = B - (F + V)$$

where R is the net benefit obtainable from protection, B the gross benefit from protection, F the fixed costs of obtaining protection and V the variable costs of obtaining protection. Consider Figure 9.1. B can be thought of as the increase in producer's surplus resulting from a given level of protection, which will be positive up to the prohibitive trade barrier (b_p).[1] F can be thought of as sunk costs associated with lobbying for protection. These may result from formation of the lobby, or they

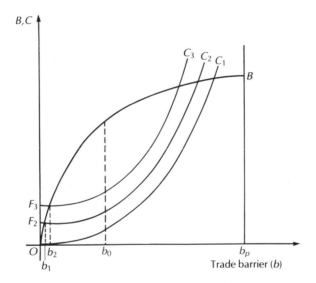

Figure 9.1 An interest-group model of protection

might be a fixed commission paid to a professional lobbyist. V then varies according to how much actual lobbying is undertaken: that is, the marginal cost of obtaining additional protection is positive. This is likely to rise at an increasing rate due to the fact that higher and higher levels of protection are increasingly costly to obtain, as other industry groups and consumer groups become increasingly resistant as protection levels increase.

Clearly there will be an 'optimal' or target level of protection (b_0) from the interest group's standpoint: it will maximize its net gains from lobbying efforts by collecting and spending funds up to the point where the additional cost of protection-seeking activities equals the additional income benefits from further protection. This option can be anywhere between $b_0 = 0$, when F is sufficiently large, and $b_0 = b_p$. The value of b_0 will be determined by the configuration of the B and V functions over the relevant range. B and V will, of course, vary across industries. The benefits of protection will be greater, for instance, for import-competing than for export industries. The costs of lobbying will tend to be lower in industries which are more regionally concentrated and where there are fewer producers. For some industries, the benefit function may be entirely below the cost (C) function so that no protection will be sought. Thus we can expect inter-industry variations in the demand for protection.

The supply of protection

The decision to change trade barriers is ultimately taken by governments (as the outcome of some varying mixture of executive and legislative involvement) and implemented by the public administration (or bureaucracy). Thus whether the demand for protection is conceded by the 'suppliers' of protection is influenced by a number of factors: ideological, electoral and funding considerations are major ones, along with the country's international obligations. A government committed to interventionist economic policies will presumably be more willing to concede to protectionist demands than one of a more liberal persuasion. But even a government committed on ideological grounds to *laissez-faire* policies may be tempted to concede to protectionist demands if its re-election chances are enhanced. This may be because of the geographical location of marginal constituencies in the vote for control of the legislative branch of government: such constituencies may contain more import-competing industries. Alternatively, interest groups lobbying for protection may be able to make contributions to election campaigns: to the extent that more funding increases re-election chances, a 'bargain' may be struck. Similarly, the government's actions may be influenced by the advice given by the administration. To the extent that prestige and power are important elements in a bureaucrat's utility function, and that administrative responsibilities are allocated along sector-specific lines (e.g. a ministry of agriculture being responsible for agriculture), the bureaucrat has an incentive to fight for the interests of his or her sphere of influence and is likely to be influenced by (indeed, some might say 'captured' by)[2] 'his' or 'her' interest group. Thus the bureaucrat may offer advice that supports the demand for protection. He or she may also advocate the use of instruments that allow for administrative discretion rather than ones subject to legislative control, like taxation. This provides power-hungry administrators with an incentive to recommend non-tariff rather than tariff forms of protection.

Endogenous protection?

There is now a vast theoretical and empirical literature, especially for the United States, on the determinants of the structure of protection across industries, and on how the characteristics of political processes influence legislative decisions or administrative action on trade policy. Given measurement problems and difficulties in distinguishing between alternative models, it is not surprising that overwhelming and unambiguous support for the political economy approach is not to be found.

Nonetheless both political and economic factors do seem to influence the pattern of protection in a systematic manner: that is, there is some support for the view that protection is, in part at least, endogenously determined. Certainly the logic of this view is intuitively appealing, and it offers one plausible explanation for the perpetuation of protection and the forms of policy innovation experienced under the 'new protectionism'.

9.2 Quantitative non-tariff barriers

Non-discrimination is one of the central principles underpinning GATT and has been a feature of the dismantling of the 'old protectionism'. Thus if two countries agree on a reduction in their tariffs in a given product line, this tariff concession must be extended to other members of GATT.[3] The most significant early departure from this principle was the arrangement for textiles imposed by the industrial countries on developing countries. Initially, in 1961, this was supposed to be a short-term arrangement outside the GATT framework. It imposed bilateral (i.e. source-specific) quotas on developing countries' exports of specified cotton textiles to the industrial countries. This ultimately became a long-term arrangement covering a wide range of textile and clothing products – the Multi-fibre Arrangement (MFA) – that is still operative. These bilateral quotas in textiles were precursors to the less overt, bilateral restrictions (e.g. voluntary export restraints) on labour-intensive imports from the NICs and also on more technology-intensive imports by the USA and the EC from Japan.

We examined the effects of global or non-discriminatory import quotas in Chapter 8. Bilateral or source-specific quotas have similar effects on domestic production and consumption (see Figure 8.1). There are, however, two important potential differences between global and bilateral quotas, relating to the distribution of quota premiums and the possibility of monopoly supply.

In the case of a general or global quota it was shown how the quota rent associated with restricting the quantity of imports (the shaded area in Figure 8.4) may accrue either to domestic importers (if the quota was administratively distributed, e.g. through the issue of import licences) or to the government (if the quota was auctioned). There is a different income distribution between the alternative methods of allocation, but this is a domestic redistribution. Consider now the case of a bilateral quota. Again the quota may be administratively allocated or auctioned by the government among the producers who export from the country subject to the quantitative restriction. If the quota were auctioned, the quota rent would again constitute a redistribution from consumers to the government of the quota-imposing country, so that the net welfare effect from a national point of view is as in the case of the global quota. But if the quota is allocated to existing exporters in the country subject to the restriction, then the quota rent will accrue to those exporters: the redistribution is from domestic consumers to exporters in the foreign country. The net costs of the restriction are not different in global terms as a result of this, but from a national viewpoint the net welfare loss increases by the amount of the quota rent.

The MFA arrangements for bilateral quotas in textiles and clothing have been based on a system which places responsibility for their distribution on the exporting countries. In some exporting countries (e.g. Hong Kong) there are even well-developed markets for trading licences.[4] The prices or premiums paid for quotas in these markets are a guide to the scale of the rent or the scarcity value of the quota.[5] For the year 1982, for example, it has been estimated (Greenaway and Hindley 1985) that the transfer from British consumers to Hong Kong suppliers alone, resulting from bilateral quotas on clothing, was over £20 million. This increased the combined (net) welfare costs of tariff and quota protection against Hong Kong clothing in this year by about 50 per cent. If the redistribution to all the constrained exporters under the MFA arrangements are combined, it is evident that a series of bilateral import quotas may have very different welfare effects from the national perspective than an equivalent global quota.

Where the quota rent accrues abroad, another aspect of the equivalence between tariffs and quotas breaks down. Reconsider Figure 8.4. With a global quota the world price remains at p^*, although with a quota of $\overline{Q}$ the domestic price rises to p. If the quota rent accrues abroad, it means that the import (or world) price rises to p. In other words, there is a terms-of-trade effect which will not be the same as for an 'equivalent' tariff. With a tariff both the volume and world value of imports fall: in terms of Figure 8.4 the volume falls by q_1q_2 plus q_4q_6 and the value falls by $[(q_2 - q_1) + (q_6 - q_4)]$ multiplied by the world price (p^*). This would also be the case for a global quota. With a bilateral quota where quota rent accrues abroad, the volume effect is the same but the value of imports does not necessarily fall; without a trade intervention the value of imports in Figure 8.4 is $(q_6 - q_1) \times p^*$ and with the bilateral quota $(q_4 - q_3) \times p$. Bilateral quotas are more likely to be used for protective purposes rather than as a means of foreign exchange control, since foreign exchange requirements may actually increase!

The terms-of-trade effect applies even with competitive supply conditions in the exporting country, since the premium is a reflection of scarcity conditions elsewhere: that is, in the importing country. In the case of clothing and textile production in Hong Kong, the size of viable production units and of total exports allows supply conditions to be highly competitive. But where production in the exporting country is concentrated, with only a single firm or a small number, and the restricted export is differentiated from those supplied by other countries, a bilateral quota may allow the exporting producer(s) to take advantage of the monopolization of the export supply of a specific product.[6] This can be illustrated with the aid of Figure 9.2, which for simplicity does not allow for a domestic production capability. With exports competitively supplied the free-trade price is p^* and the quantity of imports is Oq_3. With a bilateral quota ($\overline{Q}$) and competitive supply the price rises to p, which will involve a terms-of-trade deterioration unless the quota is auctioned by the importing country. If the administration of this quota encourages suppliers to exploit collectively their latent market power, the final equilibrium may be at price p' and Oq_1 volume of imports. The profit-maximizing 'monopolist' would equate the marginal cost of production (in this case the competitive supply price p^*) and marginal

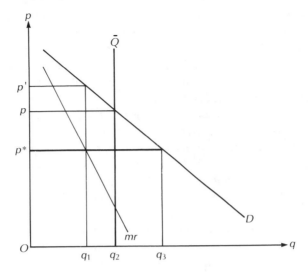

Figure 9.2 Bilateral quotas and monopolization of export supply

revenue (mr); the result is a more restricted output and higher price than occurs where the bilateral quota is applied under competitive conditions. The deterioration in the terms of trade on this product is larger than in the competitive case. As a result the cost to the domestic consumer and to the economy in net terms is larger than in the competitive supply case. Of course, the higher prices mean that there will be an even greater protective effect for any competing domestic producers. Domestic and foreign producers may have a common interest in supporting bilateral quotas under such circumstances!

A further common consequence of bilateral quotas that merits mention is the phenomenon of 'upgrading'. Typically, a bilateral quota is defined in terms of quantities of a particular commodity category that can be imported into the country imposing the restriction. If the quota premium on restricted imports is the same for all units of the category, regardless of grade or quality, sale of a higher grade with a higher price may offer a higher net return on the premium-inclusive costs of production. This means a tendency towards higher quality and more sophisticated exports. Such 'upgrading' helps the restricted exporter circumvent the trade barrier and increase the competitive challenge on a greater range of the industry's products. If only specific products of an industry or commodity category are protected by quantitative restrictions, then 'upgrading' to unrestricted imports may also occur.

Voluntary export restraints

Article XIX of GATT permits (temporary) emergency action against imports to safeguard domestic industry from market disruption, but, in line with the GATT principle of non-discrimination, only global and not bilateral quotas are permitted. (The MFA arrangements are a special case 'negotiated' originally outside of GATT.)

Since bilateral restrictions are 'extra-legal', they have had to be presented in a way which reduces the chance of their detection and obscures their effects. Thus they have been given labels such as 'voluntary export restraints' (VERs) or 'orderly marketing arrangements'. VERs have been applied, for example, by the USA and several EC countries against Japanese passenger car exports, and against the exports of consumer electronics from a number of Asian countries to various industrial countries. They are invariably presented as the outcome of an informal discussion or negotiation between the governments of the countries involved. In fact the agreements are not voluntary inasmuch as the exporting country is explicitly or implicitly threatened by the use of alternative trade barriers. However, the VER has certain attractions for the exporting country. It administers the restriction on supply, and therefore the quota rent accrues to it; this is a 'bribe' for the exporting country to accept the arrangement. Since the VER is applied to a specific commodity category and in volume terms, the exporting country also has the opportunity to 'upgrade'. Finally, the types of product that have been targeted by VERs are ones where numbers of producers tend to be limited, and resulting monopoly supply or cartelization may allow for further price increases.

There are also other interesting possible consequences of VERs for trade patterns that may encourage 'third-party' countries, as well as the voluntarily restricted exporters, to remain passive or silent about the extra-legal nature of the measures.[7] Consider a case where a VER is applied by a member of a free trade area (e.g. Canada–US) or customs union (e.g. EC), and there are other developing countries beside the restricted exporter that are potential exporters to the VER-imposing country. This possibility is modelled in Figure 9.3, where U denotes the importing home country, X the exporting country subject to a VER, C the partner country in a customs union and O other outside, exporting countries. The price of imports to the home country from X, including the customs unions common external tariff, is p_x^t.

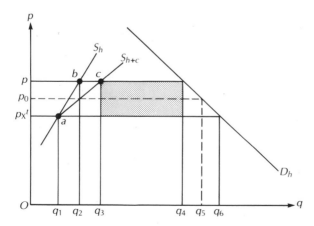

Figure 9.3 Gainers and losers from VERs in importing, exporting and partner
        countries

Imports by U from country X only are initially $(q_6 - q_1)$ and the home country produces Oq_1. Suppose that the home country wishes to protect its domestic producers by means of a VER so as to raise domestic output to Oq_2. A VER set at $(q_4 - q_3)$ will raise the price in U to p, and allow the home country to achieve its production target. But the rise in the price of the import will allow the partner country to increase its exports to the home country; at price $p_x{}^t$ there are no imports from C, but at price p the home country imports $(q_3 - q_2)$ from C. (This is the horizontal distance at price p between country H's supply curve, S_h, and the combined customs union supply curve, S_{h+c}). Thus, in addition to restricting trade, the VER also diverts trade to the customs union partner. Producers in both the home and partner country gain: producer surplus rises (the area of $p_x{}^t abp$ in U and the area of abc in C, as shown in Figure 9.3). The constraint on these gains is, of course, the (tariff-inclusive) price of imports from non-restricted exporters outside the union, p_o. In Figure 9.3 a price for p_o less than p is illustrated. In this case the quota rent (the shaded area in Figure 9.3) will be smaller, as will the production effects in countries U and C. But there is as a result another group of countries with a motive for favouring U's demand for X to impose a VER. At price p_o other exporting countries can capture up to $(q_3 - q_2)$ plus $(q_5 - q_4)$ of U's market.

It is not difficult to understand, therefore, why VERs are attractive instruments of trade intervention to mercantilistically inclined policy-makers. They are administratively flexible, they are not highly overt and they offer compensations to both restricted and non-restricted exporters. On economic or efficiency grounds, however, VERs are inferior, more costly forms of intervention than formal instruments like global quotas and tariffs.

9.3 Fiscal non-tariff barriers

Faced by a budget constraint, governments are likely to prefer trade interventions that either raise revenue (tariffs) or involve no direct revenue use (quotas). Nonetheless governments do use subsidies of various forms to influence trade patterns. In the spirit of the 'new protectionism', and given GATT constraints on the use of subsidies, they may not involve direct payments from the public purse, or may be presented as for purposes other than protection. Regional policy in Britain has relied heavily on a variety of fiscal incentives to stimulate investment and employment in certain regions; the stated purpose is employment stimulation in these regions, but they serve as production subsidies which may have protective effects. The same is true of underwriting the losses of public corporations: in the absence of the intervention, the corporations concerned would have had to charge higher prices. The industries affected by these types of measure have often been traditional ones such as coal, steel and shipbuilding, subject to increasing international competition, where lobbying for protection has been active. In these cases ostensibly non-trade objectives may have been used to justify measures of import substitution.

Production subsidies

We can illustrate the effects of formal or *de facto* production subsidies in the importables sector with the aid of Figure 9.4. For the small-country case where there are no domestic distortions, the free-trade production and consumption levels would again be Oq_1 and Oq_4 respectively. If the aim of the subsidy is to raise domestic production from Oq_1 to Oq_2, then this can be achieved by a production subsidy which rotates the domestic supply function from S to S^s. (A lump-sum subsidy would cause

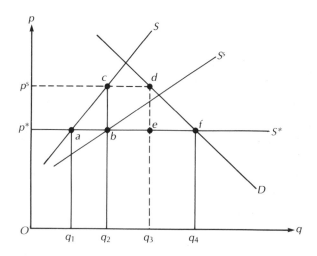

Figure 9.4 Trade and welfare effects of production subsidies

a parallel, rightward shift in the supply function.) Producers now receive the world price, p^*, plus a subsidy in absolute terms equal to the vertical distance bc (i.e. a total price of p^s). However, consumers continue to pay p^* per unit and therefore to consume Oq_4. Thus the production subsidy causes the volume of imports to contract from $(q_4 - q_1)$ to $(q_4 - q_2)$. Note that this import-reducing effect is smaller than under a tariff which gave an equivalent subsidy to producers. If a tariff raised the price of importables to p^s, this would be the price facing both domestic producers and consumers, in which case consumption would contract to Oq_3 and the volume of imports would be $(q_3 - q_2)$. It is this difference between production subsidies and tariffs that causes economists to prefer subsidies to import tariffs: a given level of protection is achieved at lower welfare cost. The subsidy costs the government the area p^*bcp^s; of this payment from the government to producers the area p^*acp^s is an increase in producer surplus, leaving a net cost to the economy of distorted production represented by the triangle abc. (The net cost of the consumption deadweight loss associated with a tariff, i.e. triangle def, is saved in this case.)

There are, however, two caveats to the above analysis and ranking. First, the comparison between a tariff and subsidy has been in terms of a given level of protection. If the aim of the policy intervention were to restrict imports to the volume $(q_3 - q_2)$ in Figure 9.4, then a much larger subsidy would be required, and at greater net cost to the economy than the tariff offering the same level of import restriction. Second, it was assumed that a production subsidy can be financed by the government through non-distorting taxation. In practice this is not the case. The traditional ranking remains if the by-product financing distortion is less than the avoided consumption distortion (*def* in Figure 9.4). But in developing countries tariffs may be preferred to subsidies because other feasible forms of tax collection are highly distortionary. Alternatively, this factor might provide a rationale for using tariffs and production subsidies together, with the tariff revenue being used to finance the subsidy.

Export subsidization

Thus far we have assumed that protection is restricted to importables. It is certainly true that trade interventions have typically concentrated on import restrictions. There are a number of reasons for this. The fact that tariffs raise revenue is one. Another is the emphasis in many developing countries on import-substituting industrialization strategies. It is also the case that the effects of import protection are certain and the gainers from this type of protection easily identifiable: workers threatened with job loss are more likely to be able to influence political decisions than the uncertain gainers of additional jobs that might be created in the export sector.

However, in recent years developing countries have been encouraged to adopt more outward-oriented strategies. Calls for greater production by industries with a comparative advantage rather than a comparative disadvantage seem to have an increasing appeal to policy-makers. In fact it is often the case that, where import protection remains in developing countries, measures of export promotion are used to compensate exporters for the costs imposed upon them by import protection. For many countries, developing and industrial, one of the attractions of export inter-ventions may be the potential for obfuscation. GATT regulations circumscribe the use of export subsidies, but it is often difficult to establish the intent and effects of export interventions. It may be difficult to establish, for instance, whether export credits have been provided at below market rates of interest. The increasing import-ance of intra-industry trade in industrial countries also means that export promotion may be seen as a means of simultaneous protection in both domestic and foreign markets, as a result of increased scale economies.

We investigate next the effects of interventions for the traditional increasing-cost case, where the world price p^* is above the autarchic price and the domestic supply curve is upward sloping. This situation is represented in Figure 9.5. In the absence of interventions Oq_3 is produced and Oq_2 consumed at home. The country exports $(q_3 - q_2)$ of the good. Again we take this to be the optimal situation, and consider the effects of first an export subsidy and second a production subsidy on exportables.

An export subsidy (i.e. a subsidy paid to exporters only for the goods they export)

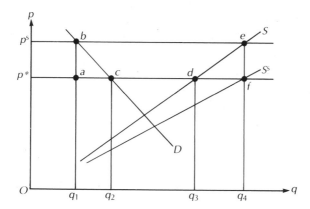

Figure 9.5 Export subsidization measures

has domestic consumption and production effects that are analogous to a tariff. With the export subsidy set equal to $(p^s - p_*)$ a wedge is driven between the domestic (p^s) and the international price (p_*). If producers receive the price p^s for each unit, they will expand production along the supply curve S from d to e. But producers will only receive the price p^s for everything they produce either if they export everything they produce (and thereby receive the subsidy from the government) or if domestic consumers pay the higher price. Indeed, producers will not be willing to produce for the domestic market unless they receive p^s. On the assumption that re-import to the domestic market at the world price (p_*) is not possible,[8] the domestic price will be driven to p^s. Thus, as with a tariff, an export subsidy induces a consumption distortion (consumption falls below the 'optimal' level Oq_2 to Oq_1) and a production distortion (production rises above the 'optimal' level from Oq_3 to Oq_4); the net welfare costs of these distortions is again the sum of the areas of the triangles abc (the consumption loss) and def (the production loss). Domestic producers, of course, gain: producer surplus rises by the area p_*dep^s. This is paid for by domestic consumers in the form of higher prices for the goods consumed at home, and by the government which pays for the subsidy on the actual exports (the area $abef$, which is the quantity of exports $(q_4 - q_1)$ multiplied by the subsidy per unit of $(p^s - P^*)$).

The equivalence with the import tariff continues if we consider the alternative of a production subsidy for exportables. Again it is possible to induce the production effect associated with the direct trade intervention, without imposing a tax on domestic consumption. This is shown in Figure 9.5 by the shift in the supply curve from S to S^s; at output level Oq_4 the vertical distance between S and the subsidy-inclusive function S^s (ef) indicates that the subsidy to producers is the same per unit as in the case of the export subsidy. Thus domestic producers now receive this subsidy payment from the government for every unit of output regardless of whether it is exported or consumed at home. The cost to the exchequer is, of course, larger than for an export subsidy: the exchequer cost is now p^*fep^s. The domestic consumer, however, suffers no direct loss from the intervention: the price remains at

p^* and there is therefore no consumption distortion. The only distortion, assuming that the subsidy can be financed in a non-distortionary manner, is the production distortion: the area *def*, which represents the excess cost of domestic resources over the international value of the additional output.

Subject to the caveat concerning financing, we have again established a preference on efficiency grounds for production subsidies over direct trade interventions that result in different prices to foreign and domestic consumers of tradable goods. This is an important result to which we will return in Chapter 10.

The formal analysis in the last two sections has concentrated on quantitative and fiscal non-tariff barriers whose effects can be demonstrated relatively clearly. But there is a whole gamut of decisions (customs valuation procedures, health and safety regulations, etc.) taken in the process of administering government, where both the intent and effects are less clear. Government procurement policies might be used deliberately in a discriminatory manner in order to offer protection to local producers. On the other hand, there may well be objectives, other than protection as such, for the policy. In the case of defence goods, for instance, strategic considerations may predominate. But even when there is a protective motive it may not be clear how the administrative action affects production and consumption. Discriminatory government procurement may, for example, act as a subsidy to local producers in certain circumstances, while in others differential specification requirements on foreign tenders may fulfil the function of a tax on imports. Although we may find it difficult to judge when administrative and technical requirements constitute an unnecessary barrier to trade, the absence of formal analysis should not be taken to mean that administered protection is less important than other forms of intervention. It may well be a most effective form of restraint on international trade. As other forms of intervention are more fully documented and the GATT increases its surveillance of other forms of hidden protection, administered protection may well become more, rather than less, important.

9.4 Summary

Any analysis of the 'new protectionism' has to explain why non-tariff barriers have increased, while tariff barriers have continued to fall. It must also explain why certain types of non-tariff barrier (namely, country- and source-specific interventions) have been employed by governments. The political economy models of endogenous protection offer an explanation for both the demand and supply of protection. Although international obligations constrain the overt actions of government, policy-makers are likely also to prefer trade interventions that give considerable administrative discretion and flexibility. Measures such as voluntary export restraints and administrative barriers offer the protection 'demanded' by interest groups, but may also offer compensations to both the restricted exporters and third-party countries not directly affected by the bilateral restriction. Thus there may be an unexpected coalition of interests in trade restrictions of this form. The group that invariably loses, consumers, is often the one least able to represent its interest in the political marketplace. Despite the economists' preference on efficiency grounds for overt and non-discriminatory measures such as tariffs, political economy considerations explain why policy-makers have resorted to hidden and discriminatory measures such as voluntary export restraints or subsidies.

9.5 Bibliography

The most authoritative early work on the identification, effects and extent of non-tariff barriers is Baldwin (1970). Krauss (1979) and Greenaway (1983) provide analyses of the economic effects of a range of non-tariff barriers. A very interesting set of essays on many of the trade policy issues raised in this chapter can be found in Baldwin (1988).

The economic theory of politics from which the political economy models of protection have developed is thoroughly expounded by Mueller (1979). Some of the important contributions on the political economy of trade policies are Brock and Magee (1978) and a number of papers in Bhagwati (1982), Frey (1984) and Baldwin (1985).

A very clear analysis of voluntary export restraints is provided by Hamilton (1985). Formal analyses can be found in Takacs (1978) and Murray, Schmidt and Walter (1983). A detailed consideration of the political economy of VERs is Jones (1984).

A detailed review of subsidies can be found in Malmgren (1977).

Notes

1. These marginal benefits are shown in Figure 9.1 to be decreasing over the whole range of the benefits function, but this does not have to be the case.
2. Bribery of officials is one means of capture, but clearly there may be other means, besides corruption, that may be used by sectional interests to gain the support of the bureaucracy.
3. This is referred to as the most favoured nation (MFN) principle: i.e. all signatories to GATT benefit to the same extent as the most favoured nation.
4. Quotas are allocated to exporters on the basis of their past shipments to the market in question over a designated reference period. Exporters are constrained by regulations administered by the Department of Trade in Hong Kong, but they can sell or transfer up to 50 per cent of their quota to other firms.
5. The premiums paid may not be accurate guides to the actual quota rents involved, where information flows are poor and the market is thin.
6. The potential for monopolization of exports in these circumstances applies in the absence of trade interventions. But the administration of the bilateral quota may nevertheless foster conditions in which a number of producers are more likely to act collusively or form a producer cartel.
7. Some of the 'third-party' countries may also use VERs themselves, and so wish to avoid reciprocal criticisms!
8. Transport costs and/or tariffs may mean that this is a reasonable assumption.

10

Normative issues in trade policy

Chapters 8 and 9 have concentrated on positive aspects of trade interventions. The analysis established that economic efficiency and welfare are maximized by an absence of trade intervention. This central tenet of neo-classical trade theory applies to the case of a perfectly competitive economy with no monopoly power in international markets: that is to a small economy faced with no domestic or international market distortions.

But what if there are distortions? If the conditions for Pareto optimality are not satisfied, then the possibility of welfare-raising interventions exists. We should then focus on two considerations. First, the nature of the market imperfection needs to be clearly identified. Arguments for intervention are often based, for example, on the existence of infant industries. But not all new industries are necessarily ones where external economies will be large enough to justify the infant-industry argument. Second, the best policy response to the particular distortion needs to be identified. It is clear from what was said in the previous chapters that the costs of alternative interventions are likely to vary. We should attempt to rank alternative instruments of intervention.

In this chapter, therefore, we move from a first-best to a second-best world. The theory of the second best says that the satisfaction of one marginal condition does not necessarily improve welfare unless all other marginal conditions are already satisfied. Since they rarely are – there are invariably numerous distortions elsewhere in the economy – some theorists argue that one can never legitimately say anything about the desirability of policy changes or interventions. Applied economists, whose job it is to offer advice to policy-makers, perforce have to be more pragmatic. This means trying where possible to quantify distortions, and recommending policy responses that minimize the distortions that arise as a by-product of intervention. This is the approach that will be adopted here.

10.1 Arguments for intervention and protection

Harry Johnson (1965a) once asserted that there are economic, non-economic and non-arguments for intervention. Although the distinction between each set of arguments that Johnson had in mind often gives policy-makers some difficulty, it is one that we as economists should find easier. Economic arguments arise from market imperfections and externalities which cause divergences between social and private costs or benefits, and where therefore production and consumption distortions exist. Employment protection for industries facing increased competition from lower-cost foreign producers does not constitute an economic argument for intervention or protection. It is, according to Johnson's schema, a non-argument unless intervention can be justified in terms of some non-economic objective, such as security or preservation of a 'way of life'.

The classic economic argument for protection is the *infant-industry argument*. Its basis is the contention that it is difficult for industry to establish itself in an under-developed country – such as England was when the argument was used in the reign of Elizabeth I, or Germany was when the argument was popularized by its most famous exponent, Friedrich List (1789–1846) – if it has to face the blast of free competition from established industries elsewhere. Even though domestic production may be relatively inefficient in the short run, it is argued that there is a long-run national advantage in establishing or extending the industrial base as a necessary condition for economic development. Hence it may be desirable to nurture an infant industry that has the potential of becoming viable in time. Most economists accept that this may make sense, although not all new industries will necessarily be profitable in the long run, and some new industries will be potentially profitable to capitalist investors and therefore do not need protection. There are, however, a number of possible externalities associated with infant industries, such as the fact that society can rationally accept a degree of risk that appears prohibitive to an individual entre-preneur because society is in a position to pool a number of such risks, and the argument that a part of the cost of being a pioneer is the cost of training a suit-able labour force which cannot be guaranteed to stay with the firm that provides the training.[1]

'Non-economic' arguments refer to cases where intervention fulfils some essentially political objective. The use of protection to maintain an activity of strategic import-ance is the classic case. Armanents industries are obvious examples. Protection of the agricultural sector is often treated as another. There is a danger that large numbers of industries will claim that their protection satisfies some important political objective and that the 'special cases' are given more protection than is required to satisfy the non-economic objectives. The costs of satisfying political objectives should not be ignored!

Any 'arguments' that do not fall in either of the two preceding categories are non-arguments: that is, arguments grounded in some fallacy or misconception. The 'cheap foreign labour' argument is a good example. It is often argued in industrial-ized countries that competition from low-wage economies is unfair so the domestic industry deserves protection. Since relatively low wages are a reflection of relative factor endowments and unrestricted trade allows the importing country to benefit from this inter-country difference in relative factor endowments, the argument is wholly fallacious.

10.2 Optimal intervention analysis

On a number of occasions in earlier chapters we have identified the characteristics of a general equilibrium solution after the opening of trade. These equilibrium characteristics are also conditions for optimality (in a Paretian sense) where first-best conditions hold, where the economy is perfectly competitive and well functioning. Thus the marginal conditions for optimality are:

$$MRT_{xm} = p_x/p_m = MRS_{xm}$$

In other words, the (private = social) marginal rate of transformation between goods X and M (*MRT* or slope of the production possibility frontier) should equal the international terms of trade ((p_x/p_m) or post-trade relative prices of X and M to both domestic producers and consumers), which in turn should equal the (private = social) marginal rate of substitution in consumption (*MRS* or slope of the social indifference curve). Divergences from an optimum solution can be caused either by market failure or by policy. The former relates to the characteristics of markets, such as market power and externalities, while the latter describes the impact of government interventions, such as taxes and subsidies. Our concern here is with the former, and with the use of government interventions to *remedy* market failure. (Unlike in Chapter 9, we now assume that government is benevolent and concerned with the maximization of social welfare: that is, that there is no 'government failure'.)

Table 10.1 sets out a taxonomy of various possible domestic distortions, which may provide an economic argument for intervention. For example, a production externality means that relative prices do not equal the social MRT, and there is a

Table 10.1 Domestic sources of market failure

Source of domestic distortion	Consequence
Product markets	
Consumption externality	Non-optimal consumption level
Production externality	Non-optimal production level
Monopolized production	Non-optimal production and consumption levels (price in excess of marginal cost)
Factor markets	
Monopolized supply of labour	Employment below optimal level (wage in excess of marginal revenue product)
Non-competitive capital market	Investment at non-optimal level (private interest rates not equal to social discount rate)

production distortion that could in principle be corrected by altering relative prices facing private producers. The government has a wide range of instruments available to alter relative incentives in product and factor markets: taxes which affect consumption patterns (indirect taxes on sales or consumption, import tariffs), taxes which affect production and employment patterns (turnover taxes, income taxes), explicit subsidies on production or implicit ones such as import tariffs, and subsidies on consumption and wages. In addition, the government has the power to regulate the structure and behaviour of markets (e.g. through anti-trust legislation) and to deploy an array of direct controls (e.g. quantitative import restrictions, foreign exchange controls). How should the government decide which is the appropriate instrument to employ?

Consider a specific example. Suppose a new entrant into an industry provides know-how and skills that may be used by subsequent entrants to this activity. Due to this unpriced external benefit the level of output, which happens to be of an importable, is below the socially optimal level. We illustrate this with the aid of a partial equilibrium diagram in Figure 10.1. (In a full-employment world, underproduction of one good implies overproduction of another, and so focusing only on the partial equilibrium production effects at the source of the distortion suffices.) If S^d reflects domestic supply decisions based upon private valuations, then with free trade Oq_4 will be consumed and Oq_1 produced at the world price, p^*. The socially optimal level of domestic production, however, is Oq_2; $(q_2 - q_1)$ represents the level of domestic underproduction and corresponding over-importing. The net cost of this distortion is represented by the area efg, the excess cost of acquiring $(q_2 - q_1)$ through importing rather than through domestic production.

Production could be stimulated through the use of an import tariff which raised the price to $p^*(1 + t)$. This eliminates the production distortion, but at the cost of inducing

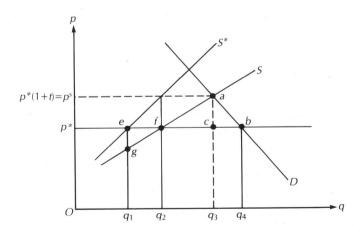

Figure 10.1 Remedying a production distortion

a further by-product distortion to consumption. Prior to the tariff, consumption was at the optimal level of Oq_4, but the effect of the increased price of importables is to cause consumption to contract to Oq_3. The cost of this consumption distortion can be measured by the triangle *abc*, the excess of the social benefit of $(q_4 - q_3)$ imports over their cost to the economy. The tariff may, but only may, be welfare improving in net terms, depending on whether the cost of the by-product consumption distortion is less than the social saving associated with removing the production distortion (i.e. if area *abc* is less than *efg*).

But the production distortion could have been eliminated without inducing a by-product distortion, by a production subsidy which shifts the domestic supply curve from S^d to S, raises the price to domestic producers to p^s and production to Oq_2, but leaves the price to consumers at p^*. Assuming that the subsidy can be financed in a non-distortionary manner, the production subsidy is an unambiguously superior instrument of intervention to a tariff in this particular case.

The above ranking of instruments follows from the fact that interventions have spillover effects which induce by-product distortions. These by-product distortions vary from one instrument to another. It is this insight that led a number of leading trade economists to develop a theory of optimal intervention. There is a hierarchy of policies to deal with each and every externality, with the optimal intervention for a particular case being that which avoids or minimizes by-product distortions. This means using an instrument which treats the distortion at its source. Invariably some kind of subsidy is superior to a tariff or quota unless the objective is to reduce imports *per se* (an objective that cannot be justified on efficiency grounds).

Let us illustrate how optimal intervention analysis might be applied to the argument for infant-industry protection. One version of the argument relates to a capital market distortion: information deficiencies or myopia on the part of private investors deter investment in infant industries. If projects are socially profitable but do not appear privately profitable, then there is an argument for intervention. A first-best policy might be to improve information flows or to reduce interest rates through improved macroeconomic policies. A second-best policy could be an interest-rate subsidy. A tariff or quota comes further down the rank order.

Another group of infant-industry arguments relate to 'first-mover disadvantages'. Suppose, for example, that an initial investor in an infant industry must incur the cost of training labour that a subsequent entrant to the industry could bid away with more attractive wages but at lower cost than the investment in human capital incurred by the first entrant. If all potential entrants perceive scope for this, then no firm may be willing to be first entrant. Some form of training subsidy would be more efficient than trade interventions that restrict international competition.[2] The second-best policy would be to subsidize production; the disadvantage of this is that firms would not have the incentive to provide the optimal level of training. Implicit subsidization of production through tariffs would bring an additional consumption distortion and would be third best as a result.

*N*th best policies, however, may sometimes have to be adopted, where there are constraints on the use of higher-ranking instruments. One constraint is that subsidies may not be financed in a non-distortionary way; lump-sum taxation is not common (at least prior to Mrs Thatcher's poll tax) since it is regressive. Thus where income taxes (which distort the choice between income and leisure) or expenditure taxes (which distort the choice between savings and consumption) are employed to finance subsidies, the ranking of subsidies may need to be revised. If tariffs offer a less distortionary way of raising revenue than other taxes, then a tariff may be preferable to a subsidy alone but inferior to the combined use of both measures. Tariff revenue could be earmarked to finance production subsidies in order to minimize the by-product distortion of the tariff. In order to eliminate the same production distortion in Figure 10.1 (i.e. to raise output from Oq_1 to Oq_2), the tariff-cum-subsidy can be at rates lower than the tariff or subsidy-only cases. Producers still receive the price p^s, but consumers pay a lower price than the previous tariff-inclusive price $p^* (1 + t)$. The consumption loss (area abc) is greater than the subsidy-only case because the import price is greater than p^*, but smaller than the tariff-only case. If the consumption loss (area abc) associated with this combination of policies is less than the by-product distortions associated with distortionary financing of the subsidy-only case, then the combination of policies has a higher position in the hierarchy of policy interventions.

There are two further caveats to the analysis in this section. First, it may be emphasized that the analysis has been concerned with distortions in the domestic economy. Does the argument that zero tariffs are invariably required in both first- and second-best conditions hold when there are distortions in international markets? The answer is no. Once we drop the small-economy assumptions and allow countries to have buyer or seller power in international markets, then the possibility of optimal non-zero trade taxes arises – at least with a nationalistic welfare criterion. We again consider the large-country case in the addendum to this chapter (section 10.6). The second caveat is that our concern in this section has been with the use of tariffs when dealing with *microeconomic* distortions. The fact that tariffs are sometimes, though not widely, advocated as an instrument of *macroeconomic* policy or balance of payments regulation will not delay us at this point. Later sections of the book will show that there are other and preferable means of macroeconomic management.

10.3 Optimal taxation and trade taxes

One argument for tariffs that does merit further examination is the use of tariffs for revenue purposes.

Traditional welfare economics argues that all distortionary taxes must be avoided if an efficient allocation of resources is to be achieved. Hence if the government has a revenue requirement, it must be satisfied through non-distortionary lump-sum taxes. But since lump-sum taxation is not feasible or politically acceptable on equity grounds, there is a more recent literature on optimal taxation that is concerned with how a given amount of revenue should be raised so as to minimize the loss of social welfare. Although the precise tax rules that emerge from this literature are sensitive to the specification of the social welfare function (e.g. to the relative importance given to efficiency and equity considerations), tariffs are not a second-best (after lump-sum taxation) means of raising fiscal revenue. In the small-country case, consumption and production efficiency requires that the marginal rates of substitution in consumption between any two goods be the same for all consumers, and equal to the marginal rate of transformation in trade, given by world prices. Tariffs induce distortions for a variety of reasons, typically including distorting the choice between different imports. Even a uniform tariff on all imports is non-optimal where it makes the marginal rate of transformation between exportables and importables different to that implied by world prices. A superior means of raising revenue is through taxation of all commodity consumption: a tax on sales to final consumers of domestically produced *and* imported goods.

In many developing countries, however, the option of levying widely based expenditure or income taxes may not be available. If per capita income is low and there is a substantial amount of non-monetized, subsistence activity, then the cost–yield ratio of non-trade taxes may be high compared with that of trade taxes. Collection of trade taxes may be relatively cheap, given the limited number of ports of entry for (legally) traded goods. Given the importance of foreign markets for traditional exports and of foreign supplies for the modern industrial sector, trade taxes can be levied on a range of well-defined commodities and collected from a limited number of higher-income economic agents (mineral producers, manufacturing firms, etc.). In these circumstances, therefore, there may be a (second-best) argument for a revenue tariff. Since a tariff on an import competing with local production will raise tax revenue as well as offering protection, it is understandable that tariffs are more widely used than subsidies!

The revenue motive is more important for developing than industrial countries because the constraints on the use of higher-ranking instruments tend to decline as the expansion of a cash-based economy, urbanization and increased administrative expertise result in falling costs of collecting non-trade taxes. This fall in collection costs might be viewed as a type of technical progress which affects the 'productivity' of alternative taxes. Other features of the development process are relevant too. As per capita incomes increase and industrialization proceeds, demand for imported intermediate goods increases. In such circumstances, revenue may have to be raised through higher input tariffs. This will tend to lower effective protection on finished goods, and will be desirable on efficiency grounds. But political economy pressures against reduced protection may encourage a greater reliance on non-trade tax sources of revenue. Moreover, as the potential of developing countries to produce final goods increases (i.e. supply curves for final goods become more elastic) a given tariff will tend to generate less revenue and a greater production distortion, since for a given domestic demand the volume of final imports will decline.

The empirical evidence confirms that developing countries tend to have a high dependence on trade taxes as a source of government revenue, and that this dependence declines with industrialization. For the least developed economies, especially in Africa, trade taxes tend to account for between 40 and 60 per cent of government revenue: the average for the 1976–82 period for Rwanda was 54 per cent, for example.[3] For middle-income developing countries the comparable figures are about 20 to 40 per cent: Tunisia averaged 25 per cent during 1976–82. For semi-industrial countries the average share falls below 20 per cent, while for industrial countries the average is well below 5 per cent.

'Optimal' tariff structures

Having established that there may be a second-best case for the revenue tariff, we need to consider whether there is any advice that economists can give regarding the optimal level and structure of tariffs that may be justified on revenue grounds.

Several notions of optimality are suggested by the earlier analysis. Under first-best conditions, economic 'optimality' requires that all tariff rates be zero. In terms of Figure 10.2, $(q_5 - q_1)$ is imported at price p^*. If revenue maximization is the objective, then there is a tariff t_m somewhere between the zero and prohibitive rate (t_p), at which tariff revenue is at its maximum for given demand and supply functions. But even if all tariffs could be set at their revenue-maximizing rates (which would be an administratively and technically difficult process to undertake and maintain since it requires detailed information on demand and supply elasticities), this would not minimize the welfare costs of collecting a required amount of tax revenue. Assuming that the required revenue is less than the maximum level (area $bcde$ in Figure 10.2), this could be achieved with a tariff rate either above (e.g. t_2) or below (e.g. t_1) rate t_m. But the efficiency losses associated with these two equal-revenue tariff rates (t_1 and t_2) are not identical. The net welfare cost of the revenue-maximizing tariff (t_m) is the triangle abc (the production distortion) plus the triangle def (the consumption distortion). Clearly the sizes of these triangles increase for rates in excess of t_m and decline as the rate falls below t_m. In terms of 'optimal taxation' principles the optimal

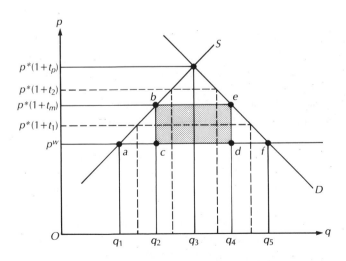

Figure 10.2 'Optimal' tariff rates and tariff revenue

tariff can be no greater than t_m, and will be less than t_m where the revenue requirement is less than the maximum amount that can be raised from tariffs.

Applying the Ramsey rule of optimal taxtion, which aims to minimize the welfare cost of raising a given amount of revenue, the optimal tariff rate would vary between imports depending on demand and supply elasticities. The story becomes even more complicated if 'optimality' is defined in terms of both efficiency and equity: on efficiency grounds optimal taxation principles would suggest higher tariffs on necessities, which are inelastic in demand, but on equity grounds lower tariffs would be called for. Clearly the practical feasibility of setting tariffs in this second-best, optimal manner is very limited. Non-uniform tariff rates provide opportunities for local producers to lobby for higher and more protective rates, and for importers to evade tariffs by misclassifying imports (from higher- to lower-rate import categories). A similar practical argument applies in the case of tariffs on inputs. If non-uniform tariffs on final goods minimize consumption distortions, then it is impossible to set non-uniform input tariffs so as to avoid production distortions where the same input is used to make differently taxed final products. Indeed, what are inputs to one producer may be the final output of another local producer. Although it may in principle be possible to identify an optimal input tariff for one specific producer,[4] it is virtually impossible to conceive that a consistent set of non-uniform, 'optimal' tariffs could be designed. If first-best policies are not feasible and tariffs are used for revenue purposes, then a uniform tariff on all imports (intermediate and final goods) has considerable merit.

10.4 Strategic trade policy

The analysis of trade policy has been conducted thus far in an orthodox framework: that is, one in which there are increasing costs of production. From this we have established a number of robust results. First, free trade is optimal for a small country under first-best conditions. Second, where there are domestic distortions which merit intervention, a tariff *may* raise economic welfare, but a subsidy is invariably superior to a tariff unless there is a large welfare cost in raising the revenue to fund the subsidy. And finally, a single policy instrument can import protect or export promote, but it cannot do both things simultaneously.

As we established in Chapters 5 and 6, however, many traded industrial goods are produced in industries subject to decreasing rather than increasing costs, and imperfect rather than perfect competition. There is now a body of 'new' theories of international trade in which increasing returns are a factor, independent of factor endowment differences, which determines the international division of labour. The question that is inevitably posed by this 'new international economics' is whether the robustness of the traditional conclusions of commercial policy is challenged.

The answer to the above question is yes, but that they are probably not seriously undermined. Let us justify this conclusion.

The new literature identifies circumstances where intervention, including tariff intervention, can raise welfare. Some of these circumstances have been recognized previously in literature on increasing returns. It is not particularly new to recognize the possibility of welfare-raising intervention, in the presence of economies of scale or increasing returns. The analysis of commercial policy in the presence of a 'consumption distortion' induced by divergence between price and marginal cost in industries with increasing returns was extensively researched by authors such as Corden (1967) over twenty years ago. We can illustrate this type of analysis with the aid of Figure 10.3. With the world price at p^* and in the absence of intervention, all the domestic market would be supplied by imports, since at prices below p_1 long-run average costs (LRAC) exceed price. It would be socially desirable to produce the good locally, however, because it is possible to induce entry (raising output to Oq_2) at lower cost than the welfare gains. (Consumers pay p and producers receive the subsidized price p^s, the cost of the subsidy is the area $p^s bcp$, and the consumer surplus gain associated with the fall in price from p^* to p is $p^* acp$; if $p^* acp$ is greater than $p^s bcp$ then there is a net social gain associated with domestic entry.)

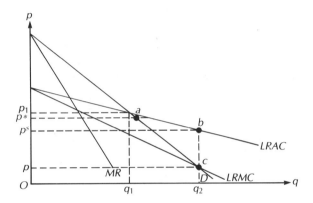

Figure 10.3 Intervention to induce welfare-raising entry of domestic producer

If the 'consumption distortion' argument is not a new argument, is the issue rather that the circumstances where this type of argument applies have become more extensive? It is certainly the case that two-way trade in industrial goods between similar economies has increased, and that scale economies are likely to be important in this type of trade. However, it does not mean necessarily that the number of circumstances where intervention is justified has increased. As Figure 10.3 indicates, the existence of scale economies is not a sufficient condition for welfare-raising intervention. If the world price was low enough, the costs of inducing entry would exceed the gain from removing the consumption distortion. The result is sensitive to both model and parameter specification. What we have seen in recent years is a proliferation of models of alternative market structures where intervention can under specific circumstances be shown to be welfare raising.

Consider again, for example, the duopoly model of intra-industry trade described in section 6.1 and illustrated by Figure 6.1. Assume we start from a free-trade situation without transport costs, where the two Cournot duopolists supply equal amounts to their home and foreign markets. The impact of a tariff introduced by one of the countries (say the home country) has interesting results. The tariff acts as if introducing transport costs on the foreign producer's supply to our market: the foreign producer reduces its supply and the home producer increases its output. Given that economies of scale are available to both producers, the tariff allows the home producer to lower costs and forces the foreign producer up its cost curve. Thus not only does the tariff induce import protection in our economy, but it also allows our producer to increase its share of the foreign market: that is, the tariff also promotes exports! This outcome is dependent, of course, on the foreign country not retaliating. Even ignoring the retaliation issue, it must be doubted whether the simple Cournot model of duopoly is sufficiently representative of actual conditions as to provide an important argument for intervention. There is a genuine danger that, if enough specific models and special cases are created, a general case is falsely established.

Even if the greater practical relevance of the consumption distortion argument is established, the traditional ranking of intervention instruments does not need to be revised. Take the duopoly model again. If a tariff can drive the home producer down its cost curve and the foreign producer in the opposite direction, then a production or an export subsidy could do the same thing. A number of authors in the new intervention literature do not systematically consider the issue of choosing the optimal form of intervention. The comparison of alternative instruments still seems to rank some form of subsidy in advance of tariffs. The intuition behind this conclusion is appealing. A subsidy reduces price to consumers, encourages domestic consumption and as a result reduces the consumption distortion. Consider again Figure 10.3. A tariff which raises the price above p_1 can induce entry of the domestic producer, but the consumption distortion remains (production and consumption will be less than Oq_1). Only the appropriate subsidy can move production and consumption to the socially optimal level (given the world price p^*) of Oq_2.

What, then, is new in the 'new' international economics? The aspect of the recent literature that is distinctive is the possibility of using trade and/or industrial policy strategically to shift or switch rents or profits from other countries. The idea is that if there are economies of scale and limited numbers of producers in international markets, firms can earn excess or abnormal profits. Governments may be able to shift these rents from foreign to domestic firms by deviating from free trade. The deviation may take the form of an import barrier or a subsidy; the optimal measure from one country's viewpoint depends on the structure of the model, the assumed behaviour of the rival firms and the policies of the foreign government.[5] Let us illustrate the idea with a simple model taken from a review by Krugman (1987). Suppose there is room for only one profitable firm in a particular product range of the aircraft industry, such as 50-seat passenger aeroplanes. Because of very high fixed costs of development, there are sharply increasing returns to scale. If Boeing identifies the market opportunities first and starts production, it will make large profits and deter the potential competition, the European Airbus, from entering into production. Assume now that European governments are alert to Boeing's first-entry advantages and commit themselves to subsidize Airbus production so that Airbus will be (privately) profitable irrespective of whether Boeing produces or not. Without reciprocal support in the USA, Boeing will not now produce since they know that Airbus will, and as a result Boeing will lose money. All the monopoly profits will end up going to Airbus, and Europe (though not the world) is better off. Indeed, the European governments may recoup their subsidy by taxing the monopoly profits of Airbus.

The case for strategic trade policy is not, however, as persuasive as it might at first appear. First, there are not many cases in practice where there are only one or two potential producers in the world. Even the international aircraft industry does not fit the example perfectly. Although there are elements of oligopolistic rivalry in a number of industries, most contain far more than two firms. Many other international markets are imperfectly competitive, but with quite large numbers of producers. Second, there is the issue of retaliation. In this game-theory setting where one country acts in a non-cooperative manner, there is a clear incentive for the other country to intervene in similar fashion. With reciprocated interventions, rents will tend to disappear. A co-operative solution invariably results in national interest being served by multilateral liberalization, perhaps accompanied by a global antitrust policy. A third difficulty with the argument is the general equilibrium constraint on successful strategic trade policy. Many of the new theories of trade are one-sector models in which there is no scope for relative incentive effects. But in a more realistic, multi-sector world protection or promotion needs to be viewed as a relative concept. Strategic interventions which promote particular sectors or industries will draw fully employed resources away from other sectors. This imposes substantial information demands on governments, if their strategic interventions are to be consistent and net-welfare raising.

It may be argued that ignorance of which sectors justify intervention, of the optimal form and degree of intervention and of the response of other governments is not a defence for free trade where it is known to be sub-optimal. But retaliation by trade partners to strategic trade policy is almost inevitable. Indeed, it is the prospect of reciprocal action, whether it be to lower or raise protection, that creates coalitions of interest among export industries. Once governments widely concede to pressures for strategic interventions, there must be real danger of excessive and inappropriate interventions. The kinds of intervention that the new trade literature suggests are ones that typically raise the welfare (i.e. profits) of a few firms by a large amount, while allowing the costs of monopoly influence to be borne by diffuse and unorganized consumers. Given these political economy pressures, a general rule of free trade (with exceptions only in very special cases) is the sensible conclusion to draw from the 'new' as well as from the traditional models of trade. Indeed, the presence of economies of scale means that the gains from trade liberalization are greater than in the traditional constant returns case.

10.5 Summary

Free trade maximizes global and national economic efficiency and welfare under first-best (i.e. perfectly competitive) conditions in domestic and international markets. Even where first-best conditions do not apply, free trade may well be an appropriate general policy rule, given the threat of retaliation by other countries and the problems of designing welfare-raising interventions in a general equilibrium setting, and in the face of interest group pressures for self-serving (rather than efficient) interventions. Clearly a lack of perfect competition does not provide a sensible reason for restricting trade: on the contrary, one of the most important social functions served by free trade is that of introducing effective competition where it would not otherwise exist.

The analysis in this chapter has identified some circumstances when intervention may be rational on economic grounds, notably in the case of externalities associated with infant industries and distortions associated with the presence of scale economies. The strategic trade policy literature has added one more case where protection *may* be welfare raising: namely, the rent-snatching case. In some of these cases, including strategic rent snatching, it is not clear that welfare-raising interventions are likely in practice.[6]

Where intervention is, for whatever reason, desired, the question arises of the optimal form that it should take. The theory of optimal intervention recommends the use of measures that minimize by-product distortions. Thus measures that eliminate the distortion, such as competition policies which remove entry barriers and deter monopoly influences, are preferable to fiscal interventions. Where there are constraints on the use of higher-order interventions, theory indicates that policy-makers should consider subsidies before tariffs – especially where revenue considerations can be ignored. If more efficient forms of taxation are not available in developing countries, then the use of tariffs may be justified, not as a means of dealing with distortions, but as a second- or nth-best means of raising revenue. But here again we should give some thought to the appropriate structure and rates of tariff intervention. The optimal-taxation literature indicates that uniform tariffs on all imports are unlikely to be 'optimal' in principle, but there are strong practical grounds for uniform taxation. As the dependence on trade taxes as a source of revenue declines with the progress of development, revenue considerations become less important in the design of trade policies.

10.6 Addendum: the large economy

The most common concept of a large economy in international economics is one that is large enough to be able to influence its terms of trade, rather than acting as a perfect competitor in selling and buying all it wants to at the going price. For such an economy a tariff has a further effect in addition to those identified in Chapter 8: it will improve the country's terms of trade. We have already seen that the effect of a tariff is to reduce the quantity of exports that the country places on the world market and the quantity of imports that it seeks to buy on the world market. These reductions will tend to increase the price of exports (since world *supply* falls by a non-negligible quantity) and to reduce the price of imports (whose *demand* decreases). Since the terms of trade are defined as the ratio of the price of exports to the price of imports, both changes will tend to increase the terms of trade. An increase in the terms of trade is referred to as an improvement, since it means that a given quantity of exports can buy more imports, which is *ceteris paribus* a good thing for the country.

The effect of endogenous terms of trade on the general equilibrium analysis of the chapter is illustrated in Figure 10.4. The point of production under free trade is P_f, and the point of consumption is C_f, reached by trading along the free-trade terms of trade here shown by a single arrow. With a tariff the internal relative price of M must increase, say to the value represented by the lines with double arrows. The equilibrium point of production is thus P_p. So much is unchanged. The novelty is that the country no longer has to trade up from the point P_p at the original free-trade terms of trade. Instead, the terms of trade improve: that is, the relative price of X rises on the world market. This means that the with-tariff terms-of-trade line is *steeper* than the free-trade terms-of-trade line, as shown by the line with the triple arrow in Figure 10.4. It is evident that this terms-of-trade line P_pC_p may cut the free-trade terms-of-trade line P_fC_f and then rise above it. It is evident also that the consumption equilibrium C_p (the point on P_pC_p where an indifference curve is tangential to an *internal price line*) may lie on a higher social indifference curve than does the free-trade equilibrium C_f. That is, the country may be able to improve its level of welfare by imposing a tariff.

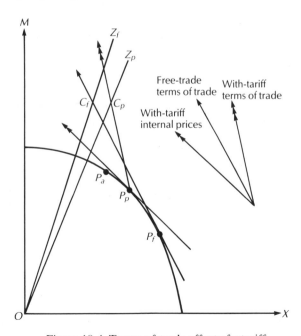

Figure 10.4 Terms-of-trade effect of a tariff

In fact, it can be shown (though we shall not prove it)[7] that a small tariff must always improve the welfare of the country that imposes it, *ceteris paribus*, if that country can influence its terms of trade. On the other hand, a prohibitive tariff eliminates trade altogether and drives the country back to the point of autarchy P_a where consumption is equal to production. So as the tariff is increased from zero to the point at which trade ceases, welfare first rises and then falls. The point where it reaches a maximum is known as the *optimum tariff*, and the desire to increase welfare by improving the terms of trade is known as the *optimum tariff argument for protection*. It has to be added to the list of the infant-industry argument, the strategic argument and the fiscal revenue argument, as a potential rationale for protection.

We saw in Chapter 8 that in the long run a uniform tax on exports has the same effect as a uniform tariff on imports. This suggests that the benefits of an optimum tariff can be secured equally well by imposing a tax on exports, and this is correct. Indeed, since in an n-good world one wishes to restrict the supply of (or demand for) the particular export goods (import goods) with inelastic suppy (demand), it is generally optimal to impose export taxes rather than import tariffs.

How significant a factor is the optimum tariff argument? Quite a lot of countries have some influence over their terms of trade: even countries that would certainly be counted as small in all other respects have some influence over the world price of one or two principal export products – for example, Zambia and Zaire over the price of cobalt and copper. (Very few countries have any market power on the import side.) Furthermore, the optimum tariff argument might be important for a group of countries if they could act jointly even though each individual country acting alone had negligible influence over its export prices (this was discussed in Chapter 7). On the other hand, elasticities of supply of many primary products are much higher in the long run than in the short run, when output may not be able to vary much because new trees take years to grow or new mines take years to develop. This means that a country trying to exploit the optimum tariff argument by restricting the supply of exports might succeed in the short run but find its market position seriously eroded by the emergence of alternative suppliers in the long run – which is what happened to Brazil when it restricted exports of coffee in the 1930s.

Finally, it is important to note that the optimum tariff is an optimum strictly from a national point of view. However, better terms of trade for one country necessarily imply worse terms for its trading partners. Moreover, since the process of achieving the gain in the terms of trade involves introducing distortions in production and consumption that are a deadweight loss for the world as a whole, the losses of the partners exceed the gains of the country imposing protection. Naturally, those countries may resent what they regard as an attempt to exploit them, and they may seek to retaliate by imposing protection too. That is the path to commercial warfare as occurred in the 1930s. Chapter 17 considers how international mechanisms have been created to try to prevent a repetition of that sad chapter in economic history.

10.7 Bibliography

Many of the references given on the positive aspects of commercial policy include discussion of normative issues. The most influential contribution on normative issues in trade policy is Corden (1974). Corden (1984) provides a survey of the vast literature in this area.

The seminal contributions on distortions and optimal intervention are Bhagwati and Ramaswami (1963) and Johnson (1965b). See also Bhagwati (1972).

For a review of the concepts and principles of optimal taxation, see Stern (1984). Bliss (1980) applies the principles of optimal taxation to the setting of a tariff structure. A range of taxation problems in developing countries are covered in a number of essays in Newbery and Stern (1987). The traditional arguments for uniform taxation are set out in Musgrave (1987) and Harberger (1990).

There are a large number of publications associated with strategic trade policy and the new international economics. Some of the most important papers are in the collection edited by Krugman (1986). There is also a useful summary of the arguments in Krugman (1987). Critical analyses of the arguments are to be found in Bhagwati (1989) and Haberler (1990).

Notes

1. The desire to promote manufacturing activity and industrialization has encouraged a belief among policy-makers in developing countries that the circumstances under which infant-industry protection is appropriate are widespread. Certainly economies of scale are pervasive in manufacturing and there may be first-entrant disadvantages. But these are neither necessary nor sufficient conditions for intervention. The evidence of large numbers of 'failed' infant industries (see Bell, Ross-Larson and Westphal 1984) suggests either that policy-makers have been too willing to concede protection or that inappropriate instruments of support have been used.
2. The presence of a potential distortion does not necessarily mean that taxation/subsidy interventions are required. The government can also encourage institutional developments which allow market solutions to be found. Apprenticeships, for example, might be used to protect firms' investments in human capital.
3. In the case of Africa both export and import taxes are important sources of government revenue. For developing countries as a whole, however, import taxes are the major source of revenue from trade taxes.
4. In order to minimize the production distortion on the final good, this input tariff should be zero if local production of final goods is subject to excise duty at the same rate as the tariff on competing imports, but would be greater than the output tariff if there were no local excise duty.
5. The sensitivity of the optimal solution to these types of factor can be seen in papers by Dixit (1984) and Brander and Spencer (1984).
6. The same has been argued in the case of infant-industry protection (Baldwin 1969).
7. The intuition behind this argument is that the first δ of a tariff causes a terms-of-trade improvement that acts on the whole free-trade value of trade, whereas the cost in terms of induced distortions impinges initially on only marginal shifts in production and consumption.

IV

Open-economy macroeconomics

This part of the book is devoted to the study of what has usually been termed international monetary theory or balance of payments theory. The more general expression 'open-economy macroeconomics' has recently gained ground at the expense of those traditional terms, as a result of growing recognition that the balance of payments is determined simultaneously with all other aspects of macroeconomic equilibrium.

11

The accounting framework

In Parts II and III we studied the impact of the openness of an economy on the micro-economic issues of resource allocation and income distribution. As is customary in microeconomic analysis, it was assumed throughout that the economy was in macroeconomic equilibrium: that is, with resources fully employed and payments always in balance. These assumptions were adopted not because of any belief that they are descriptively accurate, but to help analysis by permitting the study of one set of issues at a time. In this part of the book the focus of attention is changed: we abstract from the microeconomic issues by aggregation, taking it for granted that the government is adopting whatever commercial policies it deems desirable on microeconomic grounds, and study the macroeconomic problems of unemployment, inflation and payments deficits and surpluses.

The appropriate tools for this purpose are the macroeconomic models of Keynes and monetary theory. The logical place to start this analysis is with an examination of the accounting relationships that provide the framework of concepts, definitions, classifications and identities into which behavioural hypotheses are fitted in the subsequent chapters in order to provide theories. A preliminary section is devoted to clarifying the relationship between the preceding micro analysis and the macro analysis that follows, by showing how and to what extent macroeconomic disequilibrium can be illustrated in the micro diagrams of Parts II and III, and describing a change in the standard model that seems called for.

11.1 Micro- and macroeconomics

The standard diagram used to illustrate general equilibrium with trade in previous chapters is modified to show the case of a trade deficit in Figure 11.1. In the case studied in previous chapters, production occurs at point P, and consumption at point A_1. Now that the analysis is being extended to recognize the existence of expenditures on investment as well as on consumption, it is no longer appropriate to use the term consumption or its symbol C. That is why the point is labelled A_1, the A standing for absorption – a term that has been used in macroeconomic analysis for some years to signify the total quantity of real resources absorbed in the economy.[1]

The case of a trade deficit is illustrated by absorption at A_2 rather than at A_1. Since

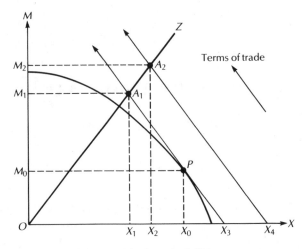

Figure 11.1 A trade deficit

prices remain constant – the terms-of-trade line from X_4 is parallel to that from X_3 – there is no reason for production to change in this model. However, suppose that there is a capital inflow equal to $(X_4 - X_3)$, when its value is measured in terms of the exportable. That enables the country to expand absorption from A_1 to A_2 – with the absorption of X rising from X_1 to X_2 and that of M rising from M_1 to M_2. Hence exports fall from $(X_0 - X_1)$ to $(X_0 - X_2)$, while imports rise from $(M_1 - M_0)$ to $(M_2 - M_0)$, giving a trade deficit measured by the distance between the two budget lines in place of the previous balance. The country is thus a net importer of real resources, which is consistent with the maintenance of overall balance of payments equilibrium because the trade deficit is being financed by the capital inflow. When a capital flow leads to an offsetting adjustment in the current account, it is said to be 'transferred'.

The conclusion that a capital inflow will not change relative prices or, therefore, the production point is specific to the particular model presented above. It would not, for example, remain valid in the case of a large country whose terms of trade changed when it developed a trade deficit. Neither does it remain valid in a small country with exogenous terms of trade but in which some of the goods do not enter into international trade. This can be shown by examining the so-called dependent economy model that was initially developed by Australian economists, notably W. E. G. Salter (1929–63).

Figure 11.2 shows the 'dependent economy'. On the horizontal axis is plotted the non-traded good, N: one thinks of non-traded goods as being mainly services and construction, although some services are also traded and some agricultural or manufactured goods are sufficiently bulky (or sufficiently heavily protected) to qualify as non-traded. On the vertical axis is the composite traded good, for which we retain the nomenclature M; it is legitimate to lump imports and exports together in this way just as long as their relative price (the terms of trade) remains constant. The

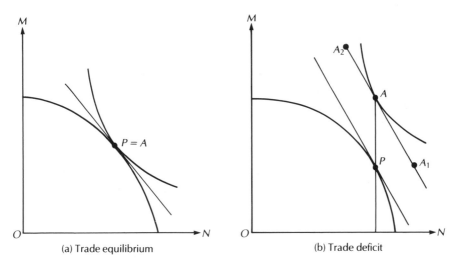

Figure 11.2 Dependent economy model

fact that the terms of trade are exogenous to the small (or dependent) economy provides the justification for treating traded goods as a Hicksian composite. But it must be remembered that exogeneity is *not* the same thing as constancy and, accordingly, that an exogenous shift in the terms of trade changes the basis on which the figure is constructed.

Figure 11.2(a) shows the case of balanced trade, while Figure 11.2(b) shows the case of a trade deficit. In both cases production is equal to absorption of the non-traded good, for one cannot import haircuts (for example). Balanced trade implies that in aggregate production is also equal to absorption of the traded good (although that is perfectly consistent with the simultaneous export and import of different commodities whose relative price remains constant), as is shown in Figure 11.2(a) by the fact that the consumption point lies on the production possibility curve. Conversely, a trade deficit implies that absorption of M exceeds production, so that *A* lies vertically above P, the difference being equal to the trade deficit. In order to move from the situation of equilibrium in Figure 11.2(a) to that of a deficit in Figure 11.2(b) it is necessary for the relative price of N to rise (the budget line to become steeper), so as to induce producers to shift their production towards N and consumers to shift their purchases towards M, the sum of the two effects being sufficient to absorb the additional supply of M that is imported from the outside world.

From now on the dependent economy model rather than the exportable–importable model will be used as the standard frame of reference. In the real world, of course, there are exportables, importables and non-traded goods (not to mention many different kinds of each, as well as marginal cases that might be allocated to two or three of the categories or shift between them depending on relative prices); the point is that even three-good models are too complex to be readily used to gain understanding of particular analytical points, so that it is more fruitful to use a two-good model which is easy to understand. But this procedure requires that the two goods be selected with a view to highlighting whatever happens to be the focus of interest. Up to now the subject matter involved the exchange of goods, and the centre of interest therefore lay in the characteristics of the goods being exported as opposed to those of the goods being imported. But capital flows, and subsequently payments imbalances, involve primarily adjustments between traded goods on the one hand and the domestic economy on the other, so that the traded versus non-traded goods distinction is generally more revealing.

It is often useful to check that both models give the same answer. When they do, one can be fairly certain that the solution is robust, in the sense that it would continue to hold in a more complex model – or in the real world. When they give different answers, one needs to ask which model is more applicable to the particular problem in hand. In the case of the question as to whether the emergence of a trade deficit will generate changes in relative prices and resource allocation, the answer is clear: the existence of non-tradables is a sufficient condition to ensure that the relative price of non-tradables must rise to generate a trade deficit, and the relative price of tradables must rise to generate a trade surplus. But in both models a trade deficit involves an excess of absorption over income while a trade surplus involves an excess of income over absorption; this is a robust property that is independent of the details of the transfer process.

Up to now we have always assumed that production possibilities are fully exploited, so that production always occurs at some point – like P in Figure 11.1 – on the production possibility curve. This position is conventionally described as one of full employment, although it is important to understand that, in most developing countries, production possibilities are constrained by the stock of capital and skilled labour rather than by that of labour in general, so that 'full employment' can be consistent with much disguised or even open unemployment of unskilled labour. A better description would be 'full capacity', but we shall continue to use the conventional terms.

Unemployment, as that term is used in macroeconomics, refers to a point *inside* the production possibility curve. Unfortunately, the idea of excess demand, or overfull employment or excessive demand pressure, cannot be illustrated equally well in the model with exportables and importables shown in Figure 11.1. That is another good reason for switching to the dependent economy model of Figure 11.2 at this stage.

The dependent economy model postulates that the price of M is determined on the world market and its domestic price is simply its world price multiplied by the exchange rate. For the price of N, we may entertain two hypotheses: the first that it is flexible in the short run; the second that it is sticky. When the price is flexible, the production and consumption points must always lie on the same vertical line, like A and P, where the demand for non-traded goods is equal to the supply. The vertical excess of A over P represents the payments deficit – the excess demand for traded goods. If A lay below P, income would exceed expenditure and there would be a corresponding payments surplus. But consumption could not be at a point like A_1

because the excess demand for home goods could not be satisfied through a trade deficit but would instead drive up the price of N, thus steepening the price line and so driving the production mix down the ppc to the right and shifting the consumption mix away from N towards M until demand were equal to supply. With sticky prices, on the other hand, it would be possible for demand to remain at A_1 in the short run. This would still be a situation of excess demand for N and thus of inflationary pressure. Similarly, if consumption were at A_2, there would be excess supply of home goods, and therefore (under sticky prices) unemployment.

However, while it is possible to *illustrate* macroeconomic problems by microeconomic diagrams, it is not possible to get far in *analyzing* them. For that one needs macroeconomic analysis.

11.2 Balance of payments accounts

The balance of payments accounts attempt to record all transactions between the residents of one country and the residents of other countries during a certain period of time (typically a year, though quarterly accounts are also fairly common). The criterion for inclusion is that a transaction be between the residents of different countries, not that it involve a sale or purchase of a foreign currency. The two are, of course, often associated: an importer usually has to buy foreign exchange to pay its foreign supplier. But the import enters the balance of payments even if the importer happens to draw down a foreign-currency bank account to make payments. When you travel or study abroad, your expenditures conceptually enter the balance of payments when you pay your restaurant bills, not when you buy foreign exchange.

Table 11.1 shows the balance of payments for our country U for the year 1990. Our currency is the peso, so all figures are expressed in millions of pesos. (Countries with particularly rapid inflation sometimes choose to present their payments accounts in dollars rather than national currency.) There is a certain amount of choice as to how the balance of payments accounts are presented: for example, it is possible to show all the receipts in one column and all the payments in another, rather than in the form shown. Some observers have found deep significance in the fact that the sum of the two columns must in principle be equal (*in principle*, because in practice this is achieved by putting in an 'errors and omissions' item to *make* them equal). Why? Because any payment to a resident that is not matched by a payment by a resident (including that resident deciding to hold his or her foreign exchange in that form rather than convert it into pesos, which counts as making a foreign investment) is matched instead by the central bank buying the foreign exchange, which shows up in the last line.

The format shown in Table 11.1 is more common than the double column form. Only exports and imports of goods – visible trade – are shown gross. The trade balance is the excess of the value of exports over that of imports; in the example shown, imports exceed exports, so there is a deficit, shown by a minus sign. The minus signifies that residents are paying more than they are receiving. All subsequent entries in the table are shown net: that is, in a form equivalent to the trade balance

Table 11.1 Balance of payments of country U, 1990 (in millions of pesos)

Row			
1	Exports	1,203	
2	Imports	1,304	
3	Trade balance	−101	
4	Balance on non-factor services	− 87	
5	Interest, profits and dividends	−203	
6	Unilateral transfers	+153	
7	Balance on current account		−238
8	Direct investment	+ 96	
9	Medium- and long-term loans	+141	
10	Short-term loans	+ 11	
11	Balance on capital account		+248
12	Errors and omissions		− 22
13	Change in reserves		− 12

Source: Central Statistical Office of country U.

rather than to the gross flows that underlie it. Exports are usually shown f.o.b., free on board (i.e. excluding the cost of transportation beyond the port of export), while imports are usually presented c.i.f. (i.e. with the cost of international insurance and freight included).

The next two items in the table, rows 4 and 5, consist of services, or invisible trade – purchases or sales of anything that cannot be seen and touched. U has a deficit on services of 290.

There is an important analytical distinction between non-factor services, like holidays, ocean freights, insurance or engineering contracting, and factor services, which consist principally of interest, profits and dividends – payments for factors of production employed in a country other than where their owner resides. Non-factor services are in economic respects similar to goods: they are *outputs* whose demand is subject to similar influences, notably income and prices. Factor services, in contrast, are *inputs* (or, in the case of loans, give the power to buy inputs), and the payments made for these are heavily influenced by the stock of factors that has come into, or left, the country in question.

Unilateral transfers refer to unrequited payments across national frontiers. There are two principal elements covered here. First, there are remittances sent by migrant workers to the families back home. This element has become important for quite a large number of countries in the last twenty years – as a debit item for the United States, Northern Europe and the Arab Gulf states, and as a corresponding credit item in the Caribbean, Mediterranean and Muslim non-oil countries respectively. Second, there are grants – pure aid – made by one government to another.

The sum of the above items constitutes the *current account* of the balance of payments.[2] The distinguishing characteristic of current transactions is that they do not involve the participant acquiring or surrendering claims *vis-à-vis* the residents of another country. Such transactions are presented in the *capital account*, in rows 8 to 11.

The most basic distinction within the capital account is between *direct* investment and *portfolio* investment. Direct investment occurs when the investor acquires an ownership claim that involves his or her control of the asset. In its typical form a multinational corporation transfers funds in order to finance the expansion of a foreign subsidiary. But an individual transferring funds in order to buy a holiday home also satisfies the definition.

Portfolio investment can be broken down in a number of ways. The most important are into equity investment and loans, by maturity and by direction of investment. Equity investment involves the acquisition of shares, which are ownership claims on a firm – but without giving control, so that they are effectively financial claims which involve the investor participating in the residual risk of the enterprise. Loans, by contrast, involve the investor having a preferred claim, but a claim limited to a specified rate of interest. The distinction by maturity relates only to loans (since ownership claims are by definition of indefinite maturity). The normal distinctions are short term (under one year); medium term (one to five or ten years); and long term (over five or ten years). These definitions may relate either to the *original life* of the asset, or to the *term to maturity* as from the date the asset is bought (which is economically more meaningful but administratively more complex to record). The direction of investment refers to whether the investor is acquiring an asset in a foreign country, or whether he or she is surrendering one – for example, because the borrowing country is making amortization payments. In the example presented in Table 11.1, U has an inflow of both direct investment and loans; equity investment is negligible and is therefore not recorded separately. The figures are presented broken down by maturity, but amortization is not shown separately.

Line 12 in Table 11.1 is a measure of the statisticians' incompetence and bad luck. In principle, any receipts on lines 1 to 11 that are not matched by payments should generate a receipt of reserves by the central bank: that is, a surplus in line 13. In practice the central bank knows perfectly well whether or not it has been buying reserves, but the statisticians fail to record all the transactions that account for those reserve changes. The 'errors and omissions' item is inserted to make the accounts balance. Current account errors tend to be particularly important for countries with large illegal exports, notably of narcotics, and those with a large stock of flight capital abroad. Many capital flows, especially those of capital flight, are also underestimated.

The last line records whether the central bank has been buying or selling reserves and is equal to the sum of the preceding rows. In the example shown, U had a deficit of 12 million pesos because it bought goods and services on current account worth that much more than the capital inflow. (The difference between the recorded current account deficit and the recorded capital account surplus is actually a surplus of 10, but the errors and omissions item tells us that the current deficit must have been 22 larger or the capital inflow 22 smaller or some combination of the two.) The central bank of U must therefore have drawn on its international reserves to an extent equivalent to 12 million pesos. Typically, it would have sold United States dollars. It might also have sold some SDRs (see Chapter 19), borrowed from the IMF or sold some other currency that it was holding. In principle it might have sold some gold, though this is not very likely nowadays.

11.3 External wealth accounts

Another important, though less familiar and less available, set of accounts shows a country's wealth position *vis-à-vis* the rest of the world. Such accounts have the nature of a balance sheet: they show the stock of a country's assets and liabilities with respect to other countries as of a particular date. U's accounts are shown, again in millions of pesos, in Table 11.2.

The main distinction is once again that between financial claims and real claims. Financial assets are shown in the table disaggregated between equities, loans made by domestic banks to foreigners, deposits of residents in foreign banks (the main constituent of what is often referred to as 'flight capital' and is typically much underestimated) and international reserves. Financial liabilities are disaggregated into foreign holdings of equities (in local stocks), loans made to public- and private-sector entities and (net) trade credit received. The net total of these financial claims constitutes the balance of indebtedness: it can be seen that U has a net debt of 1,115 million pesos, made up of a gross debt of 1,766 million pesos partly offset by assets totalling 651 million pesos. The statistical estimates of debt are typically somewhat worse than those of capital flows, partly because they are sometimes compiled by cumulating the flow figures and include an early period when data collection was less adequate, but mainly because they are influenced over time by capital gains and losses, which are rarely estimated systematically.

In addition to these debts, countries incur assets and liabilities abroad in the form of direct investments. U is shown as a typical capital-importing country in that its own firms have made only modest overseas investments, but the value of direct investments within the country by foreign multinationals is substantial. It should be noted that these statistics of the value of direct investments are usually quite

Table 11.2 External wealth accounts of U, 31 December 1990 (in millions of pesos)

Assets		Liabilities		Net
Equity holdings	23	Equity	42	
Loans by banks	130	Loans to public sector	947	
Deposits in foreign banks	66	Loans to private sector	604	
International reserves	432	Trade credit received (net)	173	
Total financial assets	651	Total financial liabilities	1,766	−1,115
Direct investment	79	Direct investment	864	
Total assets	730	Total liabilities	2,630	−1,900

Source: Central Statistical Office of country U.

unreliable, if indeed they exist at all. The reason is that the current value of a subsidiary is a pretty subjective notion. Even if there is a statistical requirement to report such a figure, which often there is not, accountants can within quite wide limits report whatever figure is most to their client's liking: there is no market test of their choice. The increase in the value of an enterprise is not in general equal to the sum of new investment and retained earnings because reported profits do not include changes in the value of existing assets.

If country U makes no attempt to revalue its assets each year, the changes in the balance sheet positions of Table 11.2 are related to the balance of payments of Table 11.1. In particular, since there was a current account deficit of 238 during 1990, it must be true that the recorded net external wealth position was $-1,662$ a year earlier at the end of 1989. Furthermore, since 96 of the current deficit of 238 was financed by an inflow of direct investment, which does not result in an increase in debt, the balance of international indebtedness at the end of 1989 must have been -973 ($-1,115$ plus $(238 - 96)$).

In principle, in order to track the evolution of net external wealth positions correctly, the conventional balance of payments accounts shown in Table 11.1 would need supplementing by an extra line. This would show changes in the value of existing assets and liabilities. These can be very large: for example, in 1988 Britain had a current account deficit of £14.6 billion, but nonetheless increased the value of its net external assets by an estimated £3.9 billion. This means that the capital gains on its previous assets must have been £18.5 billion.

11.4. National income accounts

A third set of accounts, which are of fundamental importance in macroeconomic model building, are the national income accounts that form the basis for Keynesian analysis. Like the balance of payments accounts, the national income accounts show *flows* during a certain period of time (again typically a year, though some countries publish quarterly figures as well) rather than stocks at a moment of time. The accounts for U in 1990 are shown in Table 11.3.

Total domestic expenditure, or absorption of goods and services, which we shall denote by A, is shown as made up of three components: consumption (C), investment (I), and government expenditure on goods and services (G). In short-term analysis and forecasting it is usual and useful to disaggregate investment into *fixed investment* and *stockbuilding* (or inventory accumulation), since the latter tends to be paticularly volatile and its variations play a large role in determining the state of the business cycle. Gross domestic product (GDP) is the total value of all the goods produced within the economy: in a closed economy it would be equal to the value of total domestic expenditure, since everything produced is either sold or added to inventories (in which case it is counted as stock accumulation in the national income figures even if that accumulation was involuntary, due to a lack of demand). In an open economy, however, there is an additional source of demand in the form of exports (X) and an alternative source of supply in the form of imports (M), so it is

Table 11.3 National income accounts for U, 1990 (in millions of pesos)

1. Private consumption (*C*)	5,428
2. Gross investment (*I*)	1,587
3. Government purchases of goods and services (*G*)	1,336
4. Total domestic expenditure (*A*)	8,351
5. Exports (*X*)	1,431
6. *minus* Imports (*M*)	1,627
7. Gross domestic product (GDP, *Y*)	8,155
8. *minus* Net factor payments abroad	203
9. Gross national product (GNP, *Y*)	7,952

Source: Central Statistical Office of country U.

necessary to add X to A and subtract M to arrive at GDP. Gross national product (GNP) is the value of the income accruing to the factors of production resident in U: in a closed economy it would be equal to GDP, since income would have no one to accrue to *but* domestic residents. In an open economy, however, there are payments of income on foreign capital (corresponding to row 5 in Table 11.1, the balance of payments accounts) to be deducted from GDP to arrive at GNP. (In the case of a creditor country, the receipts of income on capital invested abroad are, of course, added to GDP to give GNP.)

The national income accounts of Table 11.3 are related to the balance of payments accounts of Table 11.1. However, exports and imports are never identical in the two sets of accounts, for two reasons. First, rows 5 and 6 in Table 11.3 show exports and imports of goods and *non-factor services*, so that they include the gross value of line 4 in Table 11.1 as well as lines 1 and 2. Second, there are timing discrepancies between the concepts underlying the two tables. Exports and imports are included in the balance of payments when they cross the frontier (that is, are recorded by customs), whereas in the national income accounts they enter at the moment of production or consumption. But for those timing discrepancies, the difference between GDP and A would be equal to the balance on goods and non-factor services (rows 3 plus 4 of Table 11.1). Row 8 of Table 11.3, net factor payments abroad, corresponds to row 5 in Table 11.1. The difference between GNP and A therefore corresponds to the deficit on current account, row 7 of Table 11.1, plus unilateral transfers, row 6.

In the analysis of the following chapters we shall simplify by ignoring timing discrepancies and assuming that the only current account receipts or payments are those for exports and imports of goods. We thus eliminate rows 4, 5, and 6 of Table 11.1 and row 8 of Table 11.3, which makes the trade balance equal to the current account balance, GNP equal to GDP (hence both can be represented by Y) and the difference between the two equal to the current balance. The complications noted in the preceding paragraph are thus suppressed, and the national income accounts can be expressed by the familiar identity:

$$Y = C + I + G + X - M \qquad (11.1)$$
$$= A + TB.$$

Income Y is equal to domestic expenditure, or absorption, plus the trade balance (TB).

There is another way of arranging equation 11.1 that can be revealing: to put it in a form equivalent to the 'saving equals investment' condition of elementary Keynesian theory. Deduct taxation, which will be denoted by T, from both sides of 11.1, note that private-sector saving $S = Y - C - T$, and rearrange, to get:

$$(S - I) \quad + (T - G) \quad = (X - M) \tag{11.2}$$

| or | Net saving of + Government = Net investment in |
| | private sector saving rest of world |

Or we can turn it around, to say:

$$(M - X) \quad = (I - S) \quad + (G - T)$$

Import surplus $\quad$ = Excess of investment $\quad$ + Government
over saving by private $\quad$ deficit
sector

11.5 Monetary accounts

The final set of accounts that are of fundamental importance in representing the open economy are the monetary accounts. Like the foreign wealth accounts of Table 11.2, these represent a *stock* at a moment of time rather than a flow through time. Table 11.4 presents simplified versions of the balance sheets of the central bank and the commercial banking system of country U.

The central bank is shown as holding two types of asset, international reserves (R) and treasury bills (D_1), and as issuing one type of liability, base money (B). In fact, central banks always have other items in their balance sheets as well, but these are either other forms of government debt or else items of no theoretical significance for present purposes (though they may include loans to banks). The essentials are that a central bank holds *both* international reserves *and* assets issued domestically (hence the notation D, for domestic credit), and that it issues a liability which provides the monetary base (sometimes called 'high-powered money').

With the central bank component of domestic credit (D_1) constant, a decline in reserves (line 13 in Table 11.1) provokes a fall in base money. Why? Because an excess of imports over exports not matched by a capital inflow involves a net drawing by importers on their bank accounts to make payments to foreigners; this payment is made to the foreigners by the central bank out of its reserves, and the accounts of the importers' banks at the central bank are debited accordingly. The quantity of base money would therefore fall. If the central bank did not want this to happen, it could *sterilize* the payments deficit by expanding the central bank component of domestic credit, which in our simplified example necessarily means buying Treasury bills. The concept of sterilization – of neutralizing the monetary impact of payments imbalances – is a very important one.

Table 11.4 Balance sheets of the banking system of U, 31 December 1990 (in millions of pesos)

(a) Central bank			
Assets		Liabilities	
Reserves (R)	432	Base money (B)	639
Treasury bills (D_1)	207		

(b) Commercial banks			
Assets		Liabilities	
Base money (B)	639	Bank deposits (H)	4,210
Treasury bills and Loans to private sector	(D_2) 3,571		

Source: Central Bank of country U.

The simplifications of Table 11.4(b) are more significant than those of Table 11.4(a). In particular, it is assumed that the whole of the base money issued by the central bank is held by the commercial banks as reserves, and that the money supply (denoted by H) consists entirely of bank deposits. In reality a part of base money provides notes and coin, which circulate as the other component of the money supply. This makes the formula for the money multiplier significantly more complex, but it does not alter the essential point, which is that an addition to base money permits the commercial banks to acquire more domestic assets D_2 and thus to expand the volume of bank deposits and the money supply by more than the addition to the monetary base. In the simple case shown, the money multiplier κ is the inverse of the reserve ratio ϕ maintained by the commercial banks. Of course, in order to treat κ as a constant and write:

$$\Delta H = \kappa \Delta B$$

it is necessary that the banks actually do maintain a constant reserve ratio. In fact this is not an overly strong assumption: while banks do have a stronger incentive to lend as much as they legally and prudently can when the interest rate is high, so that the money multiplier κ may increase to some extent when interest rates increase, the fact is that banks *always* have an incentive to lend as much as they can.

The commercial bank component of domestic credit, D_2, is made up of liabilities issued by the government, here represented by Treasury bills, and liabilities of the private sector, represented in the table by bank loans. The fact that these assets may take other forms (government bonds, commercial bills, etc.) is an institutional detail of no great significance. Likewise, commercial banks may issue liabilities (like savings deposits) that are not counted as a part of the money supply, at least on a narrow definition, but this too can be neglected without much harm. For our purposes, the important point is that an unsterilized reserve loss reduces the monetary base and that this sets in train a *multiple* contraction in the money supply. Each individual bank will seek to reduce its bills and loans (D_2) by $(1 - \phi)$ times its loss in deposits, so as to restore its reserve ratio. However, each time a bank does this and re-establishes its own reserve ratio, it reduces the balances of another bank at the central bank and creates a pressure on that bank to reduce the credit that it is extending. The system as a whole is restored to equilibrium only when domestic credit has contracted by $(\kappa - 1)\Delta B$:

$$B + D_2 = H = \kappa B \text{ implies } \Delta D_2 = (\kappa - 1)\Delta B$$

11.6 Summary

Macroeconomic analysis is carried out within a systematic accounting framework. The national income accounts show all income-generating transactions of the residents of our country over a period of time, while the balance of payments accounts show all transactions between the residents of our country and those of the rest of the world over a given period of time. Two other essential sets of accounts are the monetary accounts, which reveal the proximate determinants of the money supply, and the external wealth accounts, which record our country's assets and liabilities with respect to the rest of the world: both of these show stocks at a specific time rather than flows over time. Changes in certain of those stocks may be derived from the flow accounts, for income or the balance of payments, although changes in the external wealth position are also importantly influenced by revaluation of the stock of existing assets and liabilities, which is not at present measured systematically by many countries.

11.7 Bibliography

Reading at length about accounting practices is not most people's idea of fun; browsing through statistical publications to absorb some notion of the factual situation of your country should be much more worthwhile. Memorize how the stylized facts for your country differ from those for our mythical country U in such respects as:

- the average propensity to import, M/Y;
- whether there is normally a surplus on visible trade;
- the importance of service transactions;
- whether there is a surplus or deficit on unilateral transfers;
- whether there is normally a surplus or deficit on current account;
- how the current imbalance is financed;
- how large are errors and omissions;

- how much variability there is in payments flows from one year to the next, and which are the volatile items;
- whether your country is a net creditor or a net debtor (if you cannot find any external wealth accounts, try drawing an inference from the balance of payments or national income statistics);
- whether the counterpart to the current account imbalance is mainly the private sector ($I \neq S$) or the public sector ($G \neq T$);
- the ratio between B and D_1, and the commercial bank reserve ratio ϕ.

You are unlikely to find all these accounts presented together (and may not be able to find any comprehensive external wealth accounts at all) and may have to search through various government publications, central bank reports and commentaries of the conjunctural institute(s). Statistics on the various topics covered by the chapter are published on an internationally comparable basis by various international organizations.

For balance of payments data, see the International Monetary Fund's *International Financial Statistics and World Economic Outlook*, the United Nations' *Monthly Bulletin of Statistics* and the Organization for Economic Co-operation and Development's *Economic Outlook*.

External wealth accounts are improving. The Bank for International Settlements' *Annual Report* gives data on bank assets and liabilities. The World Bank's *World Debt Tables* report the liabilities (though not the assets) of most developing countries. A research project at Kiel, Germany, has assembled data on the external asset positions of 145 countries (Sinn 1990).

For national accounts data the sources are the same as for balance of payments data. In addition, enormous detail, much in arrears, is given by the United Nations' *Yearbook of National Income Statistics*.

Monetary statistics appear in the International Monetary Fund's *International Financial Statistics*.

In the early 1980s, the world recorded by the IMF balance of payments statisticians developed a large current account deficit with itself. The IMF set up a working party to find out what had gone wrong with the statistical records; its report was published as IMF (1987).

Notes

1. See section 12.4 for the historical origin of the term.
2. Aid is sometimes put below the line in the capital account, but this violates the principle of the next sentence in the text.
3. The traditional symbols for money, M and L, have already been preempted by imports and labour. H is an alternative increasingly used, motivated initially by the mnemonic 'high-powered money'; alternatively, one may prefer to remember that in monetary fables the money supply is traditionally increased by *h*elicopter distribution!

12

The current account

Our analysis of balance of payments theory begins by making two simplifying assumptions: that there are no capital movements, and that the exchange rate is fixed by the action of the central bank. Both of these assumptions are relaxed later: capital mobility is introduced in Chapter 13 and flexible exchange rates in Chapter 14.

The chapter is organized around a series of different models, or approaches, that have been developed over the years. These are introduced in the order in which they emerged historically, with a sketch of the circumstances that prompted their evolution. Several of these approaches were presented by their creators as representing a conflict with the preceding approaches, which have indeed been derided by some as erroneous orthodoxy. Our view is that such exclusiveness is unmerited: that any adequate understanding of the macroeconomics of an open economy demands an integration of all the various approaches within the context of a general equilibrium model. Accordingly, the final section of the chapter shows how the various approaches can all be incorporated within the simplest general equilibrium model available: namely, the IS/LM model.

12.1 Hume's price-specie-flow mechanism

Chapter 2 described how the mercantilist preoccupation with achieving a surplus on the balance of payments was faulted by Adam Smith for neglecting the basic source of the gains from trade: the increase in consumption in both countries that is possible by exploitation of their absolute or, more generally, comparative advantage on the basis of balanced trade. But even before Adam Smith's writing, his fellow Scot David Hume (1711–76) had discredited the *macroeconomic* basis of the mercantilist position. In 1752 he showed that a permanent payments surplus was not feasible and therefore made no sense as a policy objective, while a deficit would cure itself, so that it was not necessary to worry about a country losing all its money supply and being reduced to barter in consequence. The basic claim was that the gold standard contained an *automatic* adjustment mechanism, the so-called price-specie-flow mechanism.

In order to understand this mechanism it is necessary to know what a gold standard is. The essential features are that the countries on the gold standard fix the values of their currencies in terms of gold, that they settle their balance of payments surpluses and deficits by transferring gold and that they do not sterilize the effects of those gold flows on their money supplies. These conditions were satisfied in mid-eighteenth-century Europe for those countries, like Britain, that had a monetary unit equal to a defined weight of gold. Clearly each such currency had a value fixed in terms of gold (and therefore their values were also fixed in terms of one another). Gold could be, and was, shipped from one country to another to settle payments deficits; if British importers could not get enough francs from British exporters to France, they sent some gold sovereigns which were melted down and turned into francs. Finally, except occasionally in times of war, governments did not seek to maintain the money supply by printing paper money when gold flowed out: that is, they did not sterilize a payments deficit.

The basic idea of the gold standard adjustment mechanism was that a payments deficit caused a loss of reserves, which reduced the money supply, which lowered the price level, which made the home country's goods more competitive, which stimulated exports and reduced imports, which improved the balance of payments. This process continued until the deficit was eliminated. The converse process operated when a country had a surplus: gold flowed in, the money supply and prices rose, competitiveness declined and in consequence exports fell and imports expanded so that the payments surplus tended to be eliminated. In either case, therefore, a payments imbalance was self-eliminating so long as the automatic mechanisms inherent in the gold standard were allowed to play themselves out. To look at the matter in a slightly different way, a country had a 'natural' quantity of money corresponding to its productive capacity: it could not sustain more than this quantity (any excess would generate a deficit and leak out), and any shortfall would be made up anyway, so the mercantilist preoccupation with the balance of payments was silly.

The steps in the chain of reasoning described verbally above may be summarized schematically as follows:

Payments deficit → Gold outflow → Fall in money supply → Price decline →

Greater competitiveness → More exports, fewer imports → Reduction in payments deficit

It is important to understand exactly what assumptions are necessary to justify each step in this causal chain.

1. An incipient payments deficit can be realized and lead to a loss of reserves (like gold) only if the country has a *fixed exchange rate*. With a flexible exchange rate, the monetary authority is not willing to supply internationally acceptable assets to absorb an excess supply of the currency it issues, so the consequence of such excess supply is a depreciation of the currency rather than a loss of reserves.

2. A reserve loss will lead to a fall in the money supply if the country follows a policy of non-sterilization: that is, does not compensate for the decline in reserves by increasing domestic credit. This became known as following the 'rules of the game'. It seems that central banks did not in fact follow this rule literally even at the apogee of the gold standard in the late nineteenth century. What they typically did was to sterilize partially. With a fractional reserve banking system (which was not a factor in

Hume's day, but became important during the nineteenth century), it is possible for a central bank partially to sterilize a reserve loss but for the money supply to fall by more than the loss in reserves.[1] The essential condition for the second step to operate is therefore the *avoidance of complete sterilization*.

3. The assumption that a fall in the money supply would lead to a price decline was based on the *quantity theory of money*, which held that in the 'equation of exchange':

$$MV = PT$$

V (velocity) and T (volume of transactions) are essentially constants, with the former determined by the technology of exchange and the latter by the condition that full employment prevail, while the money supply M is the independent variable, and the price level P is the dependent variable. The validity of this interpretation of the equation of exchange has always been the chief issue underlying disputes between Keynesians and monetarists (though many on both sides of the disputes have been reluctant to acknowledge this). Hume was in this sense a monetarist. He wrote:

> Suppose that four-fifths of all the money in Great Britain [were] to be annihilated in one night, and the nation reduced to the same condition, with regard to specie, as in the reigns of the Harrys and Edwards, what would be the consequence? Must not the price of all labour and commodities sink in proportion, and everything be sold as cheap as they were in those ages? (Hume 1752, in Cooper 1969, p. 25)

4. A fall in domestic prices will increase international competitiveness provided that it increases the 'real exchange rate', which is defined as ep^*/p. This is, of course, simply the nominal exchange rate e corrected for changes in the general level of prices abroad p^* and at home p. Since we have already assumed e to be constant, a fall in p will certainly increase competitiveness provided that *foreign prices remain constant or rise*. When a small country has a deficit one expects foreign prices to remain constant, while when a large country has a deficit its loss of gold will be sufficient to have a perceptible impact in raising money supplies and hence prices elsewhere.

5. The balance of trade will respond positively to variations in competitiveness provided there is sufficient elasticity in the demand and supply schedules. In the subsequent discussion of the elasticities approach, we shall derive something called the Marshall–Lerner condition, which is a condition on the elasticities that has to be satisfied if an improvement in competitiveness is to improve the balance of trade. Hume assumed (without knowing it) that the *Marshall–Lerner condition is satisfied*.

6. An improvement in the balance of trade must improve the overall balance of payments if trade is the only component of the balance of payments, as we are assuming. In particular, there must be *no capital mobility* to assure this result.

The italicized phrases in the six preceding paragraphs are the assumptions that are needed to ensure that the price-specie-flow mechanism works as described by Hume. There are in fact strong reasons for believing that the gold standard did *not* work like that. One reason is that capital mobility was very important by the late nineteenth century: assumption 6 was not satisfied. A loss of reserves led a central bank to raise its interest rates to attract a capital inflow and stem the fall in the money supply. In a Keynesian version of what happened next, the high interest rates led to a decline in aggregate demand, recession and a fall in imports: the balance of payments on current account indeed improved, but at the cost of a loss of output, since assumption 3 was not satisfied. The Belgian economist Robert Triffin (b. 1911) argued that a rise in the British interest rate forced stock liquidation by the capital-importing peripheral countries which improved the British terms of trade and thus balance of trade: assumptions 4 and 5 failed. There is also a monetarist alternative interpretation in which prices are determined in each country by arbitrage from the world market (contrary to assumption 3), income is determined at the full-employment level by the natural equilibrating forces of the market and the balance of payments is determined by the condition that the demand for money be equal to the supply. (This will be taken up in sections 12.6 and 13.4.)

While the reasons that the gold standard worked differ from one interpretation to another, all of them suggest that there *is* an inherent monetary equilibrating mechanism, albeit one that worked at the cost of output deflation (in the case of the Keynesian interpretation) or crises in the peripheral countries (in Triffin's interpretation). And it is a historical fact that the gold standard did work for the period prior to the First World War, especially the preceding forty-odd years – although interspersed with crises, often sharp but usually fairly short. Then came the war, which brought widespread abandonment of the gold standard and fixed exchange rates.

An attempt was made to restore the gold standard after the war, but in the 1920s there was no evidence of that automatic equilibration that had previously been the essence of the system. Two reasons were advanced to explain this. First, it was said that central banks no longer played by the rules of the game: the newly established Federal Reserve System in the United States, in particular, sterilized the gold inflow so as to avoid fanning inflation. Second, prices did not fall in the deficit countries (notably Britain) in response to tight monetary policies; instead, these suffered deflation and unemployment even amidst the brief spell of world prosperity in the late 1920s. When that prosperity gave way to the Great Depression, the tensions mounted. Britain left the gold standard in the midst of a financial panic in September 1931. From then on it was not sensible to treat Hume's analysis as the centrepiece of payments theory. It was necessary to develop models whose basic hypotheses were in greater accord with the realities of the time.

12.2 Multiplier analysis in an open economy

The major professional response to the Great Depression was, of course, by the famous British economist John Maynard Keynes (1883–1946) in his *General Theory of Employment, Interest and Money*, published in 1936. In this work, he developed a macroeconomic theory of how the levels of income and employment are determined when prices do *not* adjust to clear markets as had traditionally been posited by economists. Although the *General Theory* assumed a closed economy virtually throughout, the basic ideas of Keynesian multiplier analysis were soon applied to balance of payments theory by the British economist Roy Harrod (later Sir Roy Harrod, 1900–78) and the Austrian-born economist Fritz Machlup (1902–83).[2]

The basic assumptions of multiplier analysis are that prices (including the exchange rate) are fixed, that the economy is operating below full employment so that output can respond to variations in demand, and that the money supply adjusts passively to variations in the demand for money (due, for example, to the central bank maintaining the interest rate constant). The starting point of the analysis is the income identity:

$$Y = C + I + G + X - M \tag{12.1}$$

Consumpton can be taken as determined by a conventional consumption function $C = C(Y)$, or in linear form:

$$C = c_0 + cY \tag{12.2}$$

where c is the marginal propensity to consume. Investment (I) and government expenditure (G) are taken as exogenous.

Exports (X) may also be treated as exogenous.[3] Two alternative justifications for this assumption exist. The first is that the country is a small supplier of homogeneous primary products whose price is determined on world markets. It could sell more exports at the going price, but export sales are limited from the *supply* side to the level that is profitable at current prices. The second justification is that the country is selling manufactured goods produced at constant cost; it would like to sell more at current prices, but sales are limited from the *demand* side (given whatever fixprice the suppliers choose to quote).

Imports (M), on the other hand, are endogenous: more domestic income brings in more imports, which the country can buy at a fixed price, given that it is small in the markets for its import goods. An obvious specification for the import function is $M = M(Y)$ or, in linear form:

$$M = m_0 + mY \tag{12.3}$$

where m is the marginal propensity to import. While it seems rather obvious, this specification in fact implies quite a strong assumption about the nature of the goods being imported. Since prices are constant, Y (income) represents output: hence equation 12.3 implies that more *production* requires more imports, as is indeed appropriate when imports consist of intermediate goods. But if imports consist of final goods, then one would expect them to be related to expenditure A rather than to income Y. For example, a fall in autonomous consumption exactly matched by a rise in exports would leave output, and therefore imports, unchanged if imports consisted of intermediate goods (petroleum, for example), while imports would fall (and therefore income would rise) if they consisted of consumer goods. In the real world, of course, imports consist of both intermediate and final goods. It is very important to recognize this when constructing econometric models for forecasting or planning purposes, since the import component of different types of expenditure is in fact very different: typically inventory accumulation has the highest import component, followed by fixed investment, followed by consumption or exports, with government expenditure normally least import intensive. However, alternative specifications of the import function make no difference to the qualitative theorems we shall derive below,[4] and so we shall use the simple form 12.3. Note that m_0 might be negative – domestic production of petroleum, say – without violating accounting conventions so long as $Y > |m_0/m|$.

The basic multiplier formula is derived by substituting 12.2 and 12.3 into 12.1 and manipulating:

$$Y = (c_0 + cY) + I + G + X - (m_0 + mY)$$
$$(1 - c + m)Y = c_0 + I + G + X - m_0$$
$$Y = \frac{1}{s + m}(c_0 + I + G + X - m_0) \tag{12.4}$$

where $s = 1 - c$ is the marginal propensity to save. The term in front of the parenthesis is the multiplier, while that in the parentheses is the multiplicand. As compared to a closed economy, the effect of introducing foreign trade is to *reduce* the value of the multiplier (since m increases the *denominator* of the multiplier formula), and to *increase* the value of the multiplicand by exports less autonomous imports. The intuitive reason that the multiplier declines is that imports, like saving, constitute a leakage from the income stream, which means that a given level of income generates less (domestic) expenditure than it would in a closed economy. This does not imply that the level of equilibrium income is lower in an open economy, because the stimulating effect of exports in increasing the multiplicand also needs to be taken into account. In fact it is easy to see that the foreign sector has a net stimulating effect whenever there is a trade surplus ($X > M$), and leads to a net reduction in the level of income whenever there is a trade deficit.

The formula for the trade balance, TB, is:

$$TB = X - M = X - m_0 - \frac{m}{s + m}(c_0 + I + G + X - m_0) \tag{12.5}$$

We are now in a position to derive the basic multiplier theorems for an open economy. These relate to the effects of changes in the exogenous variables I, G and X on the level of income Y and on the trade balance TB. Since I and G (not to mention the autonomous component of consumption, c_0) enter both 12.4 and 12.5 in an identical form, it suffices to treat one of them, say G. The comparative statics effects of changes in government spending are deduced by differentiating 12.4 and 12.5 with respect to G:

$$dY/dG = 1/(s + m) > 0 \tag{12.6}$$
$$d(TB)/dG = -m/(s + m) < 0 \tag{12.7}$$

Thus an increase in government spending, or any other form of exogenous domestic spending, increases income by a multiplier effect, while it reduces the trade balance by a fraction of the exogenous increase in spending.

It is clear by inspection of 12.4 that an increase in exports would have exactly the same multiplier effect on *income* as an increase in domestic expenditures, but its effect on the balance of trade would differ:

$$d(TB)/dX = 1 - m/(s + m) = s/(s + m) > 0 \qquad (12.8)$$

The effect of the initial increase in exports in improving the trade balance is partially but not wholly offset by the increase in imports induced by the rise in income resulting from the higher exports.[5]

It is possible to develop the preceding analysis in diagrammatic form, using a modified version of the elementary Keynesian savings–investment diagram. Figure 12.1(a) shows the savings and investment schedules. One may either suppose that one is treating a simple model where there is no government, or else interpret the I-schedule to include G and the S-schedule to include T. Figure 12.1(b) shows the export and import schedules. Figure 12.1(c) shows the $(S–I)$ schedule, which is derived from Figure 12.1(a), and the $(X–M)$ schedule, which is derived from Figure 12.1(b). Recalling equation 11.2, we know that a condition for equilibrium income is that total domestic saving must be equal to the balance of trade: this condition is satisfied *ex ante* in Figure 12.1(c) at the income level Y_0 where the two schedules intersect. It happens that the trade balance is negative at that point.

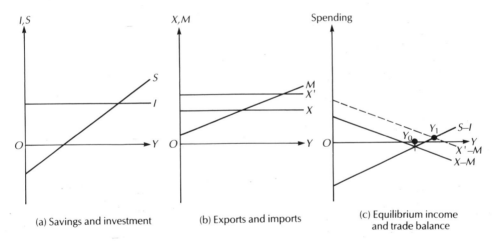

(a) Savings and investment   (b) Exports and imports   (c) Equilibrium income and trade balance

Figure 12.1 Savings, investment and the trade balance

The comparative statics results already established algebraically can now be confirmed in terms of Figure 12.1. The case shown is that of an exogenous increase in exports, which establishes a schedule $(X'–M)$. It can be seen that income rises (to Y_1) and that the trade balance increases (a deficit is replaced by a surplus), as indicated by equations 12.6 and 12.8. However, the increase in the trade balance is less than the increase in exports (which is measured by vertical upward shift in $X–M$), because the $(S–I)$ schedule is positively sloped.

There are two major implications of the foreign trade multiplier analysis. The first is that Keynesian income effects are one of the key elements that have to be incorporated into any model seeking to explain the current account of the balance of payments as a part of the macroeconomic equilibrium of an open economy. The second is that it is possible to explain the international transmission of those economic disturbances known as the business cycle. Exports are exogenous to our country, but they are endogenous with respect to the level of income in our trading partners. Thus a boom there raises their imports and hence our exports, which produces an expansion here as well. In consequence the business cycle is effectively a world rather than a national phenomenon.

12.3 The elasticities approach

The economists who developed the foreign trade multiplier analysis were not under the impression that income effects were the only determinants of trade flows. In fact, one of them, Fritz Machlup, also played a leading role in developing the elasticities approach, which sought to analyze the impact on the trade accounts of the changes in relative prices induced by a devaluation. Analysis of this type was first developed by the great English economist Alfred Marshall (1842–1924) in the heyday of the gold standard, but it became an important part of payments theory only after the Keynesian revolution with the work of Abba Lerner, Joan Robinson, Fritz Machlup, and Gottfried Haberler.

The foreign trade multiplier asks what happens when income changes, with prices constant; the elasticities approach asks what happens when prices change, with income constant. It is simplest to start the analysis if we retain the Keynesian assumption that the general level of internal prices (in both countries) is constant and that changes in relative prices are the result of changes in the nominal exchange rate e. This makes it natural to construct an analysis showing how the demand for and supply of foreign exchange vary with the exchange rate. (However, the exchange rate is still assumed to be determined by an administrative decision rather than by market forces.)

The demand and supply curves are shown, with orthodox shapes, in Figure 12.2. The horizontal axis shows the quantity of country W's currency, the dollar, that is demanded or offered in exchange for country U's currency, the peso. The dollar here represents foreign exchange in general – as it actually does in the foreign exchange markets of most countries, which are almost all conducted overwhelmingly or exclusively in terms of the United States dollar. If an importer in U wishes to pay a British exporter, his or her bank sells pesos to buy dollars and then sells the dollars on the sterling–dollar market to buy the pounds that the British exporter wishes to receive. Thus there is little abstraction from reality in assuming that all U's external payments involve exchanges of pesos for dollars. The vertical axis shows the exchange rate: that is, the price of a dollar in terms of the peso. A higher value of e represents more pesos per dollar: that is, a devaluation of the peso. (This convention varies. Some countries, especially Anglo-Saxon ones, interpret 'a higher exchange rate' to mean a *stronger* domestic currency.)

The demand for dollars is determined by the need of U's importers to make

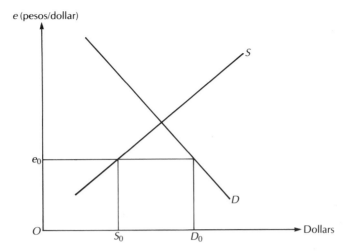

Figure 12.2 Demand and supply in the foreign exchange market

payments to foreigners, who naturally wish to receive dollars rather than pesos. In reality the demand is supplemented by other sources as well as payment for imports: payments for service imports, making loans to other countries, amortizing loans received from abroad, or any other debit item in the balance of payments. The present treatment is limited to visible trade, for simplicity of presentation, so that we shall analyze what lies behind the demand curve for dollars purely in terms of imports.

The volume of imports is determined by demand and supply. The demand curve for imports show how the volume of imports will increase as the *peso* price p_m of imports falls, as in Figure 12.3(a). The supply curve of imports shows that country U can buy as many imports as it wants at the fixed world *dollar* price, p_m^* (the assumption that country U is small), as shown in Figure 12.3(b).

In order to find the demand for dollars, it is necessary to translate the demand at a given *peso* price shown in Figure 12.3(a) into the demand at a given *dollar* price. Since $p_m = ep_m^*$, this can be done for any given exchange rate. The curve $D(e_0)$ in Figure 12.3(c) represents the curve D of Figure 12.3(a) at some exchange rate e_0. The demand for dollars at e_0 is the dollar price of imports p_m^* multiplied by the quantity of imports M_0, say D_0 (which is, of course, the area of the rectangle below the supply curve up to the point M_0 in Figure 12.3(c)). The values e_0 and D_0 represent one point on the demand curve for dollars in Figure 12.2.

Now consider the effect of a devaluation of the peso to some higher exchange rate e_1. This leaves the demand and supply curves of Figures 12.3(a) and 12.3(b) unaffected, since they are both specified in terms of the currency that is relevant to those involved (the peso for buyers, the dollar for sellers). The supply curve in Figure 12.3(c) is similarly unaffected. However, the translation of the peso demand curve of Figure 12.3(a) into the dollar demand curve of Figure 12.3(c) was done at the exchange rate e_0 and has to be revised now that the exchange rate has increased to e_1.

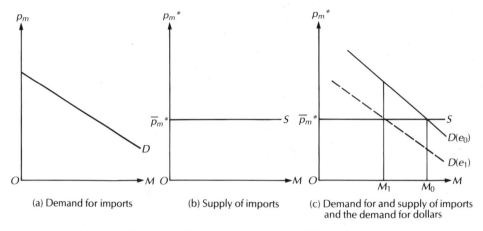

Figure 12.3 Imports and the demand for dollars

The quantity M_0, for example, will now only be bought at a lower dollar price, such that ep_m^*, the peso price, is the same as it was before. At the price $p_m = e_1 p_m^*$, less than M_0 will be bought, say M_1. In other words, the demand curve in Figure 12.3(c) moves down to $D(e_1)$. The new demand for dollars is $p_m^*. M_1$, less than before. Hence at the higher exchange rate e_1 the demand for dollars is less: the demand curve of Figure 12.2 slopes down. Incidentally, the elasticity of the demand curve for dollars in Figure 12.2 depends on the elasticity of the demand for imports in Figure 12.3(a): you can confirm this by considering a very inelastic demand for imports, which implies a very inelastic demand for dollars.

The analogous procedure for determining the supply of dollars is shown in Figure 12.4. The small country is assumed to be able to sell all it wants on the world market at the fixed dollar price $\bar{p}_x^*$ (Figure 12.4(a), carried over directly to Figure 12.4(c)). There is an upward-sloping supply curve of exports as a function of the peso price

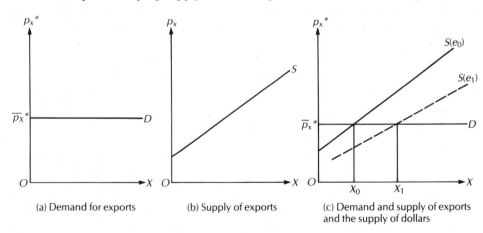

Figure 12.4 Exports and the supply of dollars

(see Figure 12.4(b)), which can be translated into a supply curve as a function of the dollar price for any defined exchange rate (see Figure 12.4(c)). The intersection of the demand and supply curves (given e_0) determines the quantity of exports X_0 and the supply S_0 of dollars $p_x^* X_0$, which can be associated with e_0 to determine a point on the supply curve of dollars in Figure 12.2. The effect of increasing the exchange rate to e_1 is to increase the peso price $p_x = e p_x^*$ corresponding to any dollar price p_x^*, and thus to increase the supply of exports for any p_x^*: in other words, the supply curve in Figure 12.4(c) shifts to the right as shown. The effect is to increase the quantity of exports to X_1 and the value of exports, or supply of dollars, to $\overline{p}_x^* \cdot X_1$. The supply curve in Figure 12.2 is therefore upward sloping.

We have now shown that, for a small country which neutralizes any impact of an exchange-rate change on the level of income, the demand curve for foreign exchange slopes down and the supply curve up. It follows that there is an equilibrium exchange rate e at which demand equals supply. At a lower exchange rate there is an excess demand for dollars, and at a higher exchange rate there is an excess supply. If the country adopts a policy of devaluing when there is excess demand for dollars and revaluing[6] when there is excess supply, it will approach the equilibrium e. In reality, however, implementing this advice is far from being as simple as it may look in Figure 12.2, partly because no real-world equilibrium remains constant over time and even more because trade flows respond to exchange-rate changes with extended lags rather than instantaneously. We shall return to this point subsequently, but it is important to understand that the analysis of demand and supply applies to a specific time period, sufficiently long to allow volumes to respond to price changes.

The conclusion that a devaluation will always improve the trade balance is, as it happens, critically dependent upon the assumption that the country can sell as many exports as it chooses at the going world price. This is, however, a particularly strong assumption. Many countries that would certainly be described as small by any other economic criterion supply a sufficiently large part of the world market with one or two major export products so as not to face an infinitely elastic demand curve: Tanzania is not a small supplier to the world sisal market, nor is Thailand to the world rice or tapioca market.

It is therefore important to examine how the analysis needs to be modified when a country faces a downward-sloping demand curve for its exports. Figure 12.4(c) is transformed to the form shown in Figure 12.5(a). Now it is no longer true that the rightward shift of the supply curve resulting from a devaluation will necessarily increase the country's dollar receipts from exports. In fact, the behaviour of the dollar value of export receipts as e increases depends upon a very simple condition: whether or not the demand curve for exports is elastic. If demand is elastic (that is, if the elasticity of demand exceeds one), export receipts will necessarily increase, and the supply curve of dollars will slope upwards as in Figure 12.2. But if demand is inelastic, the value of export receipts will fall when the exchange rate increases, and hence the supply curve of dollars will bend back as in Figures 12.5(b) and 12.5(c). This may not change the conclusion that devaluation will reduce the excess demand for dollars, as in Figure 12.5(b), where the decline in the demand for dollars induced

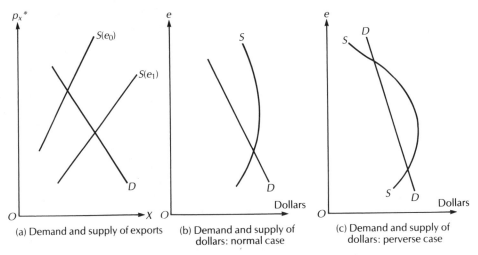

Figure 12.5 Inelastic demand for exports

by devaluation exceeds the decline in supply. But if the demand for imports happens to be very inelastic, it is possible that the demand for dollars declines less than the supply, as at the higher equilibrium exchange rate in Figure 12.5(c). Devaluation then worsens the trade balance because the elasticities are perverse – that is, low.

Whether the perverse case shown in Figure 12.5(c) occurs or not depends on the (price) elasticities of demand and supply for both exports and imports. There is a famous algebraic condition, known as the *Marshall–Lerner condition* (named after the two economists who first derived it), which must be satisfied if a devaluation is to improve the trade balance (under the assumptions listed earlier). On the assumption that trade is initially ballanced,[7] the necessary and sufficient condition for devaluation to improve the balance of trade is that:[8]

$$\frac{\varepsilon_x(\eta_x - 1)}{\varepsilon_x + \eta_x} + \frac{\eta_m(1 + \varepsilon_m)}{\varepsilon_m + \eta_m} > 0 \tag{12.9}$$

where ε_x = price elasticity of supply of exports = $\hat{X}/\hat{p}_x$
η_x = price elasticity of demand for exports = $-\hat{X}/\hat{p}_x^{\,*}$
ε_m = price elasticity of supply of imports = $\hat{M}/\hat{p}_m^{\,*}$
η_m = price elasticity of demand for imports = $-\hat{M}/\hat{p}_m$

Since the elasticities of demand (as well as of supply) have been defined to be positive, it is immediately evident from 12.9 that the perverse case where the Marshall–Lerner condition is not satisfied and devaluation worsens the trade balance can arise only if the demand for exports is inelastic.

There are two special cases of the Marshall–Lerner condition. The first is that of the small country which faces infinitely elastic foreign demand for its exports as well as supply of imports, $\eta_x = \varepsilon_m = \infty$. Our previous finding in this case can be confirmed by taking the limit of (12.9) as those two elasticities go to infinity:

$$\underset{\eta_x,\,\varepsilon_m \to \infty}{\text{Lim.}} \left\{ \frac{\varepsilon_x(\eta_x - 1)}{\not{\varepsilon}_x + \eta_x} + \frac{\eta_m(1 + \varepsilon_m)}{\varepsilon_m + \not{\eta}_m} \right\} = \varepsilon_x + \eta_m > 0$$

(The parameters with a line through them become negligibly small compared to η_x and ε_m, which can then be cancelled.) Thus the balance of payments necessarily improves in the small-country case.

The second special case is the one that has traditionally received a lot of attention, and is indeed sometimes referred to as *the* Marshall–Lerner condition. It is a case that is supposed to be relevant for an industrialized country whose exports consist of manufactures, but most of whose manufactured output is placed on the home market. An addition to export demand will in this case call forth increased output at a constant price: the supply of exports, as well as the supply of imports, is infinitely elastic. Then:

$$\underset{\varepsilon_x\varepsilon_m \to \infty}{\text{Lim.}} \left\{ \frac{\varepsilon_x(\eta_x - 1)}{\varepsilon_x + \eta_x} + \frac{\eta_m(1 + \varepsilon_m)}{\varepsilon_m + \eta_m} \right\} = \eta_x + \eta_m - 1 > 0$$
$$\text{or } \eta_x + \eta_m > 1 \qquad (12.10)$$

Thus devaluation will improve the balance of payments if and only if the sum of the demand elasticities exceeds one.

In fact, with one slight change 12.10 is the condition that is relevant for a small country exporting manufactures, but the model justifying it needs modification. Instead of imagining that cars and television sets are auctioned off in international markets like coffee and tea, and that Ford and Toyota have supply curves with determinate elasticities saying how much they will supply at each price in the London car market, it is more sensible to recognize that the typical manufactured good is sold in a fixprice market. The manufacturer sets the price and is pleased to sell everything that is demanded at that price. This price is typically fixed on a cost-plus basis, with the mark-up coefficient being selected not so much in the light of the level of sales as with a view to the prices being charged by competitors. When competitors' prices rise relative to the firm's own costs, the firm takes the chance of widening its profit margin; when its costs rise relative to competitors' prices, it accepts a squeeze on its profits in order to limit its loss of market share. Devaluation is exactly the sort of shock that increases foreign competitors' prices relative to own costs. Firms typically react by passing through some proportion θ of the exchange-rate change – by adjusting their quoted foreign prices down (up) less than proportionately in response to a devaluation (revaluation). When U devalues, its exporters cut their quoted dollar prices (while allowing their peso profit margins to increase). W's exporters to U raise their quoted peso prices proportionately, given that U is a small country. In the case of initially balanced trade, U's trade balance improves provided that $\theta(\eta_x - 1) + \eta_m > 0$.[9]

When in the 1940s econometricians began estimating elasticities, the estimates of η_x and η_m proved distinctly low. Serious doubt was cast on whether 12.10 was in fact satisfied. Those who held that the condition was likely to fail were dubbed 'elasticity pessimists' – although it is not clear why, since if the condition really failed it would be extremely lucky for the country in question, which would be able to improve its trade balance *and* its terms of trade (not to mention cutting inflation) by *revaluing* its currency. The fact that countries that allowed their real exchange rates to become overvalued have repeatedly encountered payments crises rather than ever-increasing surpluses is one of the factors that eroded the popularity of elasticity pessimism. Another is the realization that the 'small-country assumption' implies that the trade balance *cannot* deteriorate as a result of devaluation.

But perhaps the dominant factor was a revision of what the econometric evidence seemed to be saying: the typical estimates edged up to perhaps 1.5 for η_x and 0.5 to 1 for η_m.[10] In part this may be because the world changed: the early estimates were based on data for the 1930s and 1940s, when widespread controls did tend to make it difficult for trade flows to respond to price changes, while later estimates were based on data for the more liberal period of the 1950s and beyond. In part it is also attributable to the development of econometric technique. In particular, while early estimates regressed *current* trade on current income and prices (or, at best, allowed a single year's lag), it is now routine to allow for the possibility of lengthy lags in response. The evidence is that, while trade responds quickly (within months) to changes in income, responses to price changes are distinctly slow: reasonably complete adjustment may take three or four years. Presumably this is because much trade is conducted with a customary supplier, and changing the source of supply is something that is done only after due consideration and when the benefits promise to continue long enough to make the switch worthwhile. Many econometric estimates made in the 1980s suggested that elasticities have declined again. The most plausible explanation is that the great variability of exchange rates has undermined business confidence that today's exchange rate is a good guide to future exchange rates, leading to a reluctance to change future plans in the light of exchange-rate changes.

The slow adjustment of trade volumes to the price changes induced by devaluation gives rise to the phenomenon known as the 'J-curve' (see Figure 12.6). Suppose that devaluation occurs at some date t_0. Because trade contracts are signed some time before delivery occurs and the transaction enters the trade statistics, there is no immediate effect on the *volume* of trade. But if, as is typically true among industrial countries, exports are predominantly invoiced in the country's own currency while imports are mainly invoiced in the trading partner's currency, the initial effect is to *worsen* the trade balance: the dollar value of exports falls, while the dollar value of imports remains unchanged. If all trade contracts lasted the same time until delivery, this worsening would persist until some date t_1. From that point on, the contracts entering the trade figures would be those signed after t_0, and would thus reflect the higher *peso* prices charged by exporters to take advantage of the devaluation. The trade deficit would thus shrink, though not back to its predevaluation level, until trade *volumes* adjusted in response to the price changes. If we suppose that happens simultaneously in all industries, at time t_2, we would get a path for the trade balance shown by the histograms: the final portion is positive provided the Marshall–Lerner condition is satisfied. But since not all trade contracts have the same time profile, in reality these three phases get muddled up, and the path of the trade balance is shown instead by something like the thick smooth curve. With a good dose of imagination it

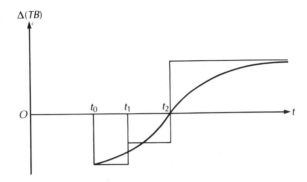

Figure 12.6 J-curve

is possible to turn that into a J shape, hence the name J-curve. (Non-industrial countries denominate their exports in dollars and are less prone to quote prices in their domestic currency, so their J-curves are weaker, if they exist at all.)

The analysis has up to now been conducted on the assumption that the price level in both countries is constant. However, we live in a world where many countries suffer from perennial inflation, and no analysis that cannot be generalized to recognize this fact is much use. In the present instance, we need to generalize in two directions. First, we need to recognize that what determines the degree of competitiveness of U's products on W's market (and vice versa) is not the nominal exchange rate e, but the real exchange rate ep^*/p.[11] One expects a devaluation to stimulate exports and promote import substitutes at the expense of imports only if ep^*/p is increased: a devaluation that leaves that ratio unchanged, because p has increased relative to p^*, will simply prevent the trade balance worsening. Such a devaluation may be said to have the effect of neutralizing excess domestic inflation.[12]

The second generalization that is needed is to recognize that devaluation is liable to increase the domestic price level. There are a variety of channels through which this can occur. Most directly, import prices rise: this pushes up prices of imported final goods and increases the costs of production and thus the prices of domestic goods that use imported materials and intermediates. The prices of exports and import substitutes are likely to rise, either because they are homogeneous goods with prices determined on world markets or because the devaluation lessens competitive pressure and permits the mark-up to be increased. Because workers face increased prices, trade unions are likely to demand higher wages; and because competitive pressures have been eased, employers are likely to concede them. Thus there are ample theoretical reasons for expecting devaluation to produce a spurt of inflation, and there is ample evidence that this does happen in practice. The fear that most or all of a devaluation will be neutralized by induced inflation is the most persuasive reason for questioning the efficacy of devaluation.

12.4 The absorption approach

In 1952 Sidney Alexander (b. 1916), then employed by the IMF, argued that the elasticities approach tended to give an overfacile view of the ease of correcting a deficit by devaluation – not because the elasticities were low or because any devaluation would be neutralized by inflation, but because devaluation cannot be relied on to increase the excess of income over expenditure. From the national income identity, we know that:

$$TB = Y - A, \qquad \text{or} \qquad \Delta(TB) = \Delta Y - \Delta A$$

It follows that, for devaluation to improve the trade balance, it must either increase real income Y or cut real expenditure (absorption) A. The question is why it should be expected to do either of those things.

The change in expenditure can be broken down into two components: that part which comes about as a result of any change in Y, through customary Keynesian 'induced expenditure' effects, and that part which occurs for any other reason. The former component may be written $c\Delta Y$, where c is the marginal propensity to consume, or, more generally, the marginal propensity to absorb. Alexander argued that, since increases in investment, as well as consumption, might be induced by higher output, c could exceed unity, but few economists have subsequently taken this possibility seriously. The second component we shall denote by A_d: Alexander called it the 'direct effect' on absorption, where it is 'direct' in the sense that it includes all effects that are *not* the result of changes in income. Since $\Delta A = c\Delta Y + A_d$:

$$\Delta(TB) = (1 - c)\Delta Y - A_d \tag{12.11}$$

Equation 12.11 says that in order to examine the effect of devaluation on the trade balance it is necessary to examine both its effect on income and its *direct* effect on absorption.

The obvious effect on income arises if the increased demand for exports and import substitutes (whose magnitude is determined by the elasticities) brings forth an increased supply. However, one of Alexander's central points was that this 'idle resources effect' can operate only if the economy has idle capacity that can be brought into operation by an increase in demand. At the time when Alexander was writing, the world economy was in a virtually continuous boom and there was a general presumption that a country in deficit would not have a margin of spare capacity.

A second effect on income to which Alexander drew attention arises from a change in the terms of trade. It is generally assumed that a devaluation tends to worsen the terms of trade, except in the strict small-country case where they are independent of domestic policy. This is not necessarily true: it is possible for a devaluation to improve the terms of trade. There is in fact a very simple algebraic condition that determines whether the terms of trade worsen in the elasticities model of the previous section,[13] namely:

$$\varepsilon_x \varepsilon_m > \eta_x \eta_m$$

that is, that the product of the supply elasticities exceeds the product of the demand elasticities. This condition is satisfied for the simple industrial-country case. More relevant, the fixprice model also discussed in the previous section implies that the terms of trade will deteriorate if exporters cut their dollar prices by more than foreign suppliers cut the dollar prices at which they supply imports; given that the cut in domestic costs is important to exporters while U's market is a drop in the ocean to W's exporters, there is an overwhelming presumption that this condition is satisfied. Thus the general presumption – shared by Alexander – that devaluation would worsen the terms of trade (if it has any effect at all) is well grounded. This means that devaluation tends to *reduce* real income, which for constant real absorption implies a *bigger* trade deficit.[14]

In subsequent debate, Fritz Machlup added a third channel through which devaluation might influence real income, the resource allocation effect. He argued that a devaluation permitted a relaxation of controls and restrictions, which typically produce microeconomic distortions as analyzed in Chapter 8. A programme of simultaneously abolishing such restrictions and devaluing to maintain the same average incentive to export (or produce import substitutes) could be expected to improve allocative efficiency and thus increase real income. Packages of this character have frequently figured in IMF lending programmes – an example of supply-side economics in action long before the term became faddish.

It is next necessary to examine why and how devaluation might be expected to affect absorption directly: that is, other than as a result of changes induced by changes in real income. The basic argument is that this can be expected, at least in certain circumstances and to some degree, as a result of the inflation that is induced by devaluation. For reasons that were discussed at the end of the previous section, prices rise after a devaluation. This *reduces* the competitive gains that persist, but on the other hand it tends to cut absorption. There are two broad channels through which this can occur, monetary and distributional. Assuming that the devaluation-induced inflation is not accompanied by an equivalent rise in the money supply (as, however, may easily happen in countries with 'passive' monetary policies dedicated to maintaining interest rates constant), the real value of the money supply H/P falls. In consequence interest rates rise and choke off investment (according to the traditional Keynesian analysis), while the negative real balance effect also causes consumers to seek to rebuild their liquid assets and thus curtail consumption (according to the wider perspective popularized by the Israeli economist Don Patinkin (b. 1922) and the leading monetarist and 1976 Nobel laureate Milton Friedman (b. 1912)).

The distributional channels through which devaluation may affect absorption involve government versus public and profits versus wages. A country with a progressive tax system tends to reap an increase in tax revenue more than proportional to the increase in the price level when a one-shot inflation occurs, as a result of taxpayers moving into higher tax brackets. If expenditure remains constant in real terms, and thus increases proportionately in nominal terms, it follows that the real budget surplus increases as a result of inflation (a phenomenon known as 'fiscal drag'). In other words, income is redistributed from the private sector to the public sector; since the latter is normally assumed to determine its spending independently of its short-run revenue, it has a marginal propensity to save of unity, and the income redistribution cuts absorption.

While that tends to happen in response to a single surge of inflation resulting from a one-shot devaluation, it should be noted that the *opposite* is more likely to happen when devaluation becomes a habit and inflation accelerates, as the Argentinian economist Julio Olivera (b. 1929) and the Italian-born economist Vito Tanzi (b. 1935) noted. According to the Olivera–Tanzi effect, an acceleration of inflation reduces the real value of tax collections because of the lag in the payment of taxes. Similarly, government expenditures may increase more than proportionately in response to higher inflation: for example, as a result of subsidized credit to favoured sectors being made available at fixed *nominal* interest rates. Income is thus redistributed from the public sector to the private sector. If the government chooses to finance its increased deficit by resort to the printing press, the stage is set for a vicious circle of accelerating inflation.

Another possible, though unreliable, distribution effect involves profits versus wages. Since many prices (especially of traded goods) are pulled up rather directly by devaluation while any impact on wages is indirect and lagged, income may be redistributed from wages to profits. The Marxist savings function, which says that capitalists save a higher proportion of their income than do workers, implies that this redistribution will also cut absorption.

Looking back at equation 12.11 we can now see why Alexander was sceptical as to the potency of devaluation to affect the balance of payments. Even if we rule out the possibility $c > 1$, there is no guarantee that $\Delta(TB)$ will be positive, especially if the country is initially at full employment so that Y cannot increase in response to higher external demand. What remains are the negative terms-of-trade effect and the positive resource-allocation effect on income, whose net effect is ambiguous, and the direct effects on absorption. Alexander argued that these would normally be rather weak. As noted in the preceding paragraph, the redistributive effects – especially that involving the government – can easily be perverse. Even if the monetary effect is dependable, the net result may be rather small or even perverse.

The policy conclusion implied is simple. When undertaken from an initial situation of full employment, devaluation must be accompanied by discretionary policy to reduce demand in order to make room for an improvement in the balance of payments. IMF stabilization programmes designed to deal with a payments deficit typically involve deflationary fiscal and monetary measures, as well as devaluation, with this end in view.

12.5 Meade's synthesis: internal and external balance

A similar conclusion can be drawn from the important work of the 1972 Nobel prize-winning English economist James Meade (b. 1907), whose synthesis of the income and price effects studied in previous sections provides the most authoritative statement of what has been called orthodox balance of payments theory. The central focus of Meade's analysis was on the conditions that had to be satisfied if a country was to succeed in achieving simultaneously internal balance and external balance. The major conclusion was that this requires the use of *two* policy instruments, with differentiated effects on income and the balance of payments. The general idea that achievement of *n* targets requires the use of *n* independent instruments was developed simultaneously by one of the first (1969) winners of the Nobel prize for economics, the Dutch economist Jan Tinbergen (b. 1903), and is known as 'the theory of economic policy'.

The concept of *internal balance* refers to the achievement of as high a level of demand and employment as is consistent with avoidance of the stimulation of unacceptable inflationary pressure. Once upon a time it was customary to refer to this as the achievement of non-inflationary full employment. Then in 1958 came the idea of the Phillips curve, named after the New Zealand economist W. A. Phillips (1912–67), which suggested that there was a continuous trade-off between unemployment and inflation rather than a sharp cut-off; this led to a reformulation of the concept of internal balance to refer to the optimal point on the Phillips curve, where society found that the marginal benefit of any further diminution in unemployment would be outweighed by the marginal cost of the resulting increase in inflation. A decade later came the natural rate hypothesis of Edmund Phelps (b. 1933) and Milton Friedman, which held that there was only one rate of unemployment (the natural rate)[15] that could be sustained in the long run because any lower rate would stimulate more inflation than people were initially expecting, which would shift the Phillips curve up as everyone wrote contracts designed to safeguard their real income against the expected inflation. Similarly, unemployment higher than the natural rate was conceived to initiate a cumulative deceleration of inflation. The implication was that one had to learn to live with the facts of life, however much one might dislike them, and accept an unemployment target high enough to avoid accelerating inflation (or even to reduce inflation, where inherited inflationary expectations are high). Internal balance thus becomes more or less synonymous with the natural rate of unemployment. But whatever one's theory of inflation, internal balance may be defined as the highest level of demand consistent with a prudent control of inflation.

The concept of external balance gives no difficulties in the present context, where there is no capital mobility. It clearly refers to a situation where the balance of payments is in equilibrium, and there is no need to choose whether this refers to equilibrium overall or on current account, since the two amount to the same thing. (The more difficult conceptual issues will be discussed in section 13.2.)

In order to study how policies need to be chosen to permit a country to achieve internal and external balance simultaneously, we shall utilize a diagram (see Figure

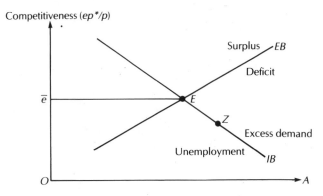

Figure 12.7 Internal and external balance

12.7) developed independently by the Australian economists W. E. G. Salter and Trevor Swan (b. 1918). On the horizontal axis is shown the level of domestic spending, or absorption. On the vertical axis is shown the international competitiveness of our goods, which can *ceteris paribus* be identified with the real exchange rate, ep^*/p.

The main property of the internal balance schedule can be established by the following argument. Suppose we have some combination of A and ep^*/p which produces just that pressure of demand that corresponds to our concept of internal balance. Consider the effect of adopting a policy (for example, cutting taxes) that stimulates absorption. This would tend to push the economy into a state of excess demand. To counter that and preserve internal balance one could appreciate the currency, so as to divert a part of demand away from domestic producers. Thus the locus of points of internal balance (IB) slopes down, as shown, with points of excess demand to the right and of wastefully high unemployment to the left.

A similar argument can be used to establish the slope of the external balance schedule. Suppose absorption increases because of a policy change. We know from the multiplier analysis that that will push the balance of payments into deficit. To preserve external balance, that must be compensated by changing the composition of spending in favour of domestically produced goods, by a real devaluation, as analyzed in the elasticities approach. Thus the external balance (EB) schedule slopes up, with a deficit to the right and a surplus to the left.

The basic theme of Meade's analysis was that in order to achieve internal and external balance simultaneously it is necessary to have one policy to influence the level of expenditure and one to influence its composition. This is clear from Figure 12.7: for example, a country that controlled policy instruments able to influence only A could reach the point E of simultaneous internal and external balance only if competitiveness happened to be $\bar{e}$. If competitiveness were less, the currency would be overvalued and in consequence the country would have to choose between unemployment and a payments deficit (or some of each). Harry Johnson later called policies that influenced the level of expenditure 'expenditure-reducing policies', and those that influenced its composition 'expenditure-switching policies.'

Expenditure-reducing policies – expenditure–changing would be a better term since sometimes the need is to increase rather than reduce absorption – are simple to identify. They consist mainly of the demand management policies identified by Keynesian theory: namely, fiscal and monetary policy.

Expenditure-switching policies are those able to influence international competitiveness. Exchange-rate changes are the leading example – though they will succeed in switching expenditure only to the extent that they lead to changes in the *real* exchange rate rather than being neutralized by induced inflation. However, there are many other policies that may be able to switch expenditure as well: for example, tariffs, export subsidies, quantitative import restrictions, other forms of protection, measures to improve the quality of domestically produced goods, export credit facilities . . . the list is virtually endless. These are the policies held constant in the *ceteris paribus* qualification that was inserted when the concept of competitiveness was equated to the real exchange rate. The argument for assigning pride of place to the real exchange rate is not that these other policies are necessarily unimportant, but that microeconomic efficiency rather than the needs of macroeconomic management should be the criterion that determines what is done in those respects. Macroeconomic management should be prosecuted with a *general* policy, so as to avoid producing microeconomic distortions.

Suppose that the economy were initially at a point such as Z in Figure 12.7, in internal balance but with a payments deficit. It can be seen that re-establishment of payments balance might be accomplished simply by reducing A – by deflating – until one hit the EB schedule. However, the cost would be unemployment. To avoid that cost one must switch expenditure towards domestic goods: for example, by devaluing. But to devalue without deflating would push the economy to a point vertically above Z where the competitive gain from devaluation would soon be eroded by the inflation resulting from excess demand. In other words, a successful devaluation from a point of full employment must be accompanied by a policy of expenditure reduction – the same policy conclusion as emerged from the absorption approach.

This conclusion, and especially the IMF policies based upon it, has been challenged by economists such as Richard Cooper (b. 1934), Paul Krugman and Lance Taylor (b. 1940). They have recalled that devaluation has not just expenditure-switching effects but also direct effects on absorption: that is, expenditure-reducing effects. A rise in e may reduce A as well as increase ep^*/p, with the relative importance of each dependent on the extent to which devaluation provokes inflation. Hence devaluation may push the economy diagonally upward and to the left from Z, not vertically up. It is possible that the economy will be pushed to a point *below IB* even without the reinforcing deflationary measures called for by IMF orthodoxy, in which case application of those orthodox measures will create wasteful unemployment.

One can make some conjectures as to the type of economy in which this is likely to happen. First, if devaluation provokes an offsetting rise in domestic prices – for example, because of the presence of real-wage resistance – then devaluation will not have much effect in improving competitiveness to counter its absorption-reducing effect. Second, where there are few opportunities for substitution between domestically produced and foreign-produced goods, the *IB* curve will be very steep. The second factor suggests that countries like the Persian Gulf oil exporters or plantation-dominated economies are likely to fit the unorthodox case, while any economy suffering a high degree of real-wage resistance may do so as well because of the first factor. Countries with low elasticities will experience an additional deflationary impact if they initially have a trade deficit, since the domestic-currency value of the trade deficit (which constitutes a leakage from the income stream) will increase.

The reason *why* an economy fits the unorthodox case is important in drawing policy implications. For countries with little elasticity in the production structure, the main alternative to a reduction in absorption has to be foreign borrowing, until such time as new investment can come on stream in the export or import-substituting industries. For countries suffering from real-wage resistance, the opportunities may be somewhat broader. When orthodox fiscal–monetary–exchange-rate policies are inadequate to restore simultaneous internal and external balance, the reason is that real-income claims constrain the economy to points on or to the right of the curve *WR* (wage resistance) in Figure 12.8. This curve *WR* might be vertical or it might have a positive slope insofar as workers can be intimidated into accepting lower real wages (requiring lower absorption) by an uncompetitive exchange rate with its threat of bankruptcies. Devaluation from a point like *Z* would produce a neutralizing inflation that would at best leave ep^*/p unchanged and restore the economy to point *Z*. The only ways to restore simultaneous internal and external balance are to operate on the supply side, to the extent that may be feasible, or to develop an incomes policy capable of reconciling the labour force to the harsh facts of life, and thus push the curve *WR* left. Failure to do either guarantees repeated economic crises.

The model underlying the elasticities approach, which together with the multiplier analysis formed the basis for Figure 12.7, is essentially a three-good model with exportables, importables and a large non-traded goods sector. It is worth checking

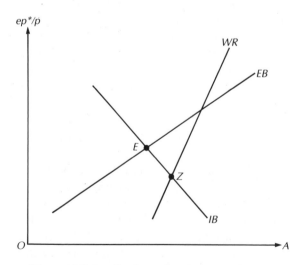

Figure 12.8 Implications of real-wage resistance

that the conclusions of Meade's synthesis are robust, which can be done by examining the dependent economy model introduced in Section 11.1. Consider Figure 12.9. Suppose that the price of the non-traded good N is fixed in domestic currency (or at least sticky), while that of the traded good M is determined by arbitrage from the world market at the level $p_m = e p_m^*$. Suppose that the resulting relative price is represented by budget curves with slope equal to that of A_0. If expenditure is initially in excess of income, at the level represented by the budget line A_0, then consumption will occur at the point C and production at the point P. There is internal balance because the production of home goods is equal to consumption, but an external deficit because the consumption of traded goods M exceeds their production. To achieve external balance by deflation alone would require cutting the value of absorption to A_1, but this would create an excess supply of home goods and thus unemployment. To achieve internal and external balance simultaneously requires a devaluation to raise the relative price of traded goods and thus induce substitution by consumers away from traded goods and by producers towards traded goods, combined with an expenditure-reducing policy to cut absorption to A_2. The combination can achieve the point of internal and external balance at Z.

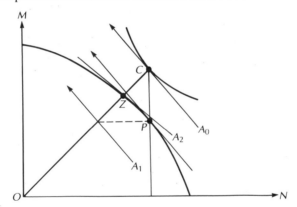

Figure 12.9 Internal and external balance in the dependent economy model

12.6 The monetary approach

The 'orthodox' theory that developed from Keynesian ideas and that was presented in the preceding four sections does not preclude the operation of monetary factors. The money supply is recognized as one of the determinants of aggregate demand. By treating the money supply as a policy variable, it is implicitly assumed that the monetary consequences of payments imbalances are sterilized. It is recognized that a rise in the price level induced by devaluation will reduce real money balances and thus real demand. Money is therefore a part of the picture, but it is not placed at the centre of the stage as it was in Hume's analysis of the gold standard. The monetary approach to the balance of payments was developed by those who believe that giving money anything other than pride of place is misleading.

The monetary approach was developed by two distinct schools. The first was based at the IMF and initiated by the work of the Dutch economist J. J. Polak (b. 1914), the former research director of the Fund. This school was rather undogmatic, the main justification offered for the new approach being to develop models that would be usable to monitor macroeconomic management when only the most rudimentary statistical information – which typically centres on monetary statistics – was available. The second school developed at the University of Chicago in the 1960s under the intellectual leadership of the Canadians Robert Mundell (b. 1932) and Harry Johnson. Many of the writings of this school had a polemical edge, involving some perceived clash with Keynesian orthodoxy.

The consolidated balance sheet of a simplified banking system like that presented in Chapter 11 reveals the identity:

Reserves + Domestic credit = Money supply

or $\quad R + D = H$ $\qquad\qquad\qquad\qquad\qquad\qquad\qquad\qquad$ (12.12)

Since a deficit in the balance of payments implies a loss of reserves, it follows from equation 12.12 that there must be a counterpart to a deficit in the form of either credit creation (sterilization) or dishoarding (a fall in H). Since dishoarding is a temporary or disequilibrium phenomenon, a payments deficit can persist only if it is accompanied by credit creation. To put the matter another way, any additional credit creation will ultimately leak out abroad. This is the central theorem of the monetary approach to the balance of payments.

The monetary approach claims to offer a theory of the balance of payments rather than of the current account. Consequently, our main consideration of it is postponed to Chapter 13, after introduction of the capital account into the analysis. For the present we restrict our attention to those topics where the monetary approach has offered contributions specifically relevant to analysis of the current account. The first is a model of payments adjustment with a fixed exchange rate that was developed by Polak and that became the basis for the stabilization programmes sponsored by the IMF. The second concerns the hypothesis that prices are determined by arbitrage, which was used by the German-born economist Rudiger Dornbusch (b. 1942) to analyze devaluation.

Polak model

The Polak model adopts a number of simplifying assumptions in order to highlight the essence of the monetary adjustment mechanism. In addition to assuming capital immobility and a fixed exchange rate, Polak took exports to be exogenous and domestic credit expansion to be a policy variable and therefore also exogenous. There are two substantive assumptions. The first is that the velocity of circulation is constant, as assumed in the old-fashioned quantity theory. That enables one to normalize velocity to unity, with no loss of generality, and to write:

$Y_t = H_t$ $\qquad\qquad\qquad\qquad\qquad\qquad\qquad\qquad\qquad\qquad$ (12.13)

The second substantive assumption is that imports are always some fixed proportion m of the value of the previous period's nominal income:

$$M_t = mY_{t-1} \qquad (12.14)$$

This implies that the propensity to import is independent of whether a given nominal income is the result of a high price level and low output, or *vice versa*. There is no reason why this should be exactly true, but the approximation simplifies model building enormously. The model is completed by the money supply and balance of payments identities:

$$\Delta H_t = \Delta R_t + \Delta D_t \qquad (12.15)$$

$$\Delta R_t = X_t - M_t \qquad (12.16)$$

Substitution of 12.14 and 12.15 into 12.13 yields:

$$Y_t = H_t = H_{t-1} + \Delta H_t = Y_{t-1} + \Delta R_t + \Delta D_t \qquad (12.17)$$

This gives us the basic monetary theorem already deduced from 12.12. Since $Y_t = Y_{t-1}$ in equilibrium (by definition), a payments deficit ($\Delta R < 0$) can persist only when domestic credit creation (ΔD) is positive.

It is also possible to use the model to tell a story about the time path of imports and income following an exogenous shock: for example, an increase in domestic credit expansion. Suppose that initially, at $t = 0$, the economy is in equilibrium so $\Delta D = 0$ and $M = M_0$, and that this equilibrium is disturbed at $t = 1$ by an expansion of domestic credit of 1, which is maintained each period thereafter. Table 12.1 traces the expansion of imports and income that this would produce. Column (2) calculates 12.14, while column (3) cumulates the difference between current imports and initial imports from column (2). The final column calculates the equation for ΔY derived by substituting 12.16 into 12.17 and recognizing that $X_t = X_0 = M_0$:

$$\Delta Y_t = \Delta D_t + \Delta R_t = \Delta D_t + X_t - M_t = \Delta D_t - (M_t - M_0)$$

The final row shows the limit as $t \to \infty$. Imports and income approach new stationary levels with $\Delta M = \Delta Y = 0$, where imports have increased to match the increase in credit creation, while income has increased by $1 + (1 - m) + (1 - m)^2 \ldots = 1/[1-(1-m)] = 1/m$, a multiple of the credit expansion determined by the import propensity. In this new 'equilibrium' reserves are falling by the amount of credit creation – the whole of the additional credit is leaking out through the balance of payments. Insofar as that cannot persist indefinitely, because ultimately reserves would be exhausted, one cannot consider that to be a long-run equilibrium.

It is also possible to study the impact of a change in exports. The reader should confirm that the long-run impact of a rise in exports will be to increase Y, H and R by $\Delta X/m$ according to the multiplier formula, while imports will gradually rise to match the increase in exports.

The model is a simple one, but its conclusions are quite robust. It suffices to explain the prominent place that the IMF has traditionally given to limiting domestic credit

Table 12.1 Dynamic adjustment in the Polak model

Time (1)	$\Delta M_t = m\Delta Y_{t-1}$ (2)	$M_t - M_0$ (3)	$\Delta Y_t = \Delta D_t - (M_t - M_0)$ (4)
0	0	0	0
1	0	0	1
2	m	m	$1-m$
3	$m(1-m)$	$m[1+(1-m)]$	$1-m(1+1-m) = (1-m)^2$
4	$m(1-m)^2$	$m[1+(1-m)+(1-m)^2]$	$(1-m)^3$
∞	0	1	0

expansion as an element of programmes of balance of payments adjustment. Critics of the Fund claim that it has sometimes paid too little attention to the costs of the decline in income that the model shows will result from credit contraction, tending to assume too readily that falls in nominal income will reflect lower prices rather than lower output.

Arbitrage

The second topic of this section is the role of arbitrage in determining national price levels. The orthodox theory tended to regard price levels as largely fixed by forces internal to each country, whether as constant, being pushed up exogenously by costs, as determined by a Phillips curve, or, in orthodox monetarism, as determined by the quantity of money. In contrast, the global monetarism of the monetary approach argues that price levels are determined by arbitrage from the world market, according to the familiar formula:

$$p = ep^* \tag{12.18}$$

This assumption permits some elegant model building. An interesting example is Dornbusch's analysis of devaluation. Consider a small country whose price level is determined by equation 12.18 – Dornbusch actually assumed a one-good two-money model, to emphasize that devaluation need not necessarily involve relative price changes. Assume away capital flows and credit markets. Suppose that the public has an orthodox demand for money function expressed in real terms so that $H_d = \alpha p$, but that it seeks to adjust any discrepancy between actual and desired money holdings only gradually, at the rate β. Then the rate of hoarding ΔH will be given by:

$$\Delta H = \beta(\alpha p - H) \tag{12.19}$$

which implies that hoarding can be shown as a function of the real value of the money supply as in Figure 12.10. Add the assumption of no credit creation, and the vertical axis also shows the payments surplus or deficit.

Suppose that the economy is in equilibrium at point Z_0, and that the exchange rate is then increased by a sudden devaluation. By equation 12.18, the price level rises proportionally, which implies that H/p falls, for example, to Z_1. The public now

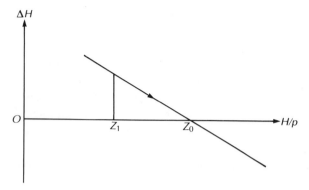

Figure 12.10 Dornbusch model of devaluation

finds itself short of real money balances, so it cuts back on buying goods, which leads to a trade surplus. Real balances climb back slowly towards their equilibrium at Z_0, as shown by the arrow. When they reach Z_0, the payments surplus disappears and the only variables that differ from the initial situation are the price level and the level of reserves. A conclusion much stressed by monetarists is that, while devaluation does indeed cause a surplus, that surplus is temporary.

The mechanism involved here is merely an extreme version of the one responsible for the direct effects on absorption in the absorption approach. From a Meadean perspective, the Dornbusch model implies that devaluation has only expenditure-changing and no expenditure-switching effects. There is very strong empirical evidence that this extreme assumption is not warranted: even traded goods are typically differentiated products, whose prices can differ as between different sources for similar goods, and prices of non-traded goods are even less subject to the influence of arbitrage. The dependent economy model is quite an illuminating way of analyzing the implications of the fact that while arbitrage does have a powerful influence on the prices of traded goods, it nevertheless does not equalize price levels between countries. But one should always remember that in the real world even the assumptions of that model, that the prices of traded goods are equalized by arbitrage, is satisfied only for homogeneous commodities, which do not constitute the bulk of trade.

12.7 General equilibrium: IS/LM/BP

The balance of payments is determined simultaneously with all other macroeconomic variables. The way that economists recognize such interdependence is by constructing general equilibrium models. The simplest general equilibrium model that is reasonably adequate for integrating the analyses presented in preceding sections is the IS/LM model, extended by the addition of a curve representing balance of payments equilibrium. But even this model suffers from three important limitations, which will be noted subsequently.

The analysis is shown in Figure 12.11. The horizontal axis shows real income, and the vertical axis shows the nominal (and real, since we assume away inflationary expectations) interest rate. The IS curve represents the locus of points of (flow) equilibrium in the goods market, which are characterized by the condition that $I = S$ *ex ante*.[16] It slopes down because a lower interest rate stimulates investment, which requires a higher income level to generate a corresponding increase in saving. The LM curve represents the locus of points of (stock) equilibrium in the asset markets: with a model with only two assets, money and bonds, it matters not whether one describes that as equilibrium in the money market or the bond market. It slopes up because an increase in income raises the transactions demand for money and thus requires an increase in the interest rate to induce a corresponding reduction in speculative demand (to use the Keynesian terminology). In the short run (though a short run sufficiently long for the multiplier process to work itself out), the economy goes to an equilibrium at the intersection of the IS and LM curves.

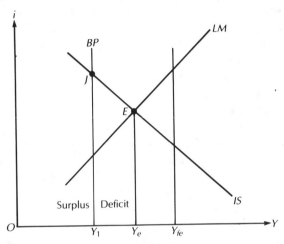

Figure 12.11 IS/LM/BP

The balance of payments can be introduced into this familiar diagram by recalling that the current account balance is lower the higher the level of income (from the multiplier analysis) is. The rate of interest, however, has no direct effect on the balance of payments: it is true that a higher interest rate might improve the current account, but it would do so by cutting income (that is, by inducing a movement along the IS curve) rather than directly. Hence the curve representing balance of payments equilibrium is a vertical line, labelled BP, at some value Y_1. There is a payments deficit to the right of BP and a surplus to the left. In the case shown in Figure 12.11, with income at Y_e, the balance of payments would be in deficit.

The essential ideas of the various approaches analyzed in the preceding sections of this chapter are reflected in this model. First, there is the monetary mechanism of automatic adjustment of Hume and Polak. At the short-run equilibrium shown in Figure 12.11, there is a current account deficit and hence, with no capital mobility, the country is losing reserves. As it does so, with no sterilization, the money supply falls and hence the *LM* curve shifts leftward. The process continues until the *LM* curve intersects the point *J* where *IS* crosses *BP*. At that point the balance of payments is also in equilibrium and so, with downward price rigidity, the economy is in long-run equilibrium. However, the postulated adjustment mechanism involves neither the exclusive price decline of Hume nor even the possibility of a decline in prices as part of the fall in nominal income as in Polak's model, but rather a reduction in real income as in Ohlin's analysis.

Second, consider the multiplier analysis. It has already been pointed out that the position of the *BP* curve reflects this factor. In addition, one needs to consider how the various comparative statics theorems are reflected in this model. An increase in investment pushes *IS* to the right and leaves *BP* unaffected. Since the multiplier analysis presupposes a constant interest rate, the central bank is assumed to accommodate the increase in the demand for money by expansionary open-market operations that push *LM* to the right just far enough to match the shift of *IS*. As the gap between Y_e and Y_1 increases, the balance of payment deteriorates. An increase in exports has the same effect on *IS* and *LM* but also pushes *BP* to the right (by more, though this is not obvious from the diagram), so that income still increases but the balance of payments improves.

Third, consider the elasticities approach. Since prices are not shown in Figure 12.11, the effects of price changes have to be represented by shifts in the curves. A real devaluation definitely pushes *IS* to the right, though the assumption of the algebra is that this effect is neutralized by a contractionary fiscal policy (or by a contractionary monetary policy that pushes *LM* up by enough to maintain *Y* constant). It also pushes *BP* to the right provided the Marshall–Lerner condition is satisfied. However, a nominal devaluation has these effects only to the extent that it leads to a real devaluation rather than being neutralized by price changes. These effects may take several years to work themselves out, and in the interim the balance of payments may deteriorate even if income is held constant rather than being allowed to expand (the J-curve).

Fourth, recall that the absorption approach taught us that a rightward shift of *BP* may not be sufficient to improve the balance of payments. We need to recognize that Figure 12.11 has another important curve, the full-employment benchmark represented by the vertical line above Y_{fe}. If Y_e initially coincides with Y_{fe}, output cannot expand to match an increase in demand, and hence any improvement in the balance of payments is conditional on a cut in absorption. This may come about automatically either because income redistribution has a leftward impact on *IS*, or because the inflation induced by devaluation reduces the real money supply and so pushes *LM* leftward. To the extent that these forces are insufficient to eliminate the inflationary gap, the government needs to take restrictive fiscal–monetary measures to push either *IS* or *LM* (or both) to the left.

Fifth, Meade's analysis is about the combination of policies needed to secure an intersection of all four curves (*IS*, *LM*, *BP* and Y_{fe}) at the same point. Internal balance is represented by *E* being on Y_{fe}, and external balance by *E* being on *BP*.

To make E lie on both simultaneously we need to be able to shift BP and at least one of the two curves IS and LM. Shifting BP requires an expenditure-switching policy, while shifting IS or LM requires an expenditure-changing policy. If devaluation is used as the expenditure-switching policy, it will also shift IS right and LM left. Remember that it has been argued that in some economies with limited substitution possibilities the leftward shift of LM may exceed the righward shift of IS so that it might be appropriate to accompany devaluation by expansionary fiscal or monetary policy even if the economy is initially at full capacity.

Finally, the monetary approach has stressed the impact of devaluation on LM, and even argued that this may be its *only* effect, as well as reviving the idea of the automatic monetary adjustment mechanism. Monetarists tend not to be overconcerned with the possibility that this will provide insufficient instruments to achieve internal and external balance simultaneously, because they assume that price flexibility can be relied on to secure internal balance without any help from government.

The IS/LM/BP model thus provides a simple general equilibrium framework that suffices to show that the various approaches to payments theory are complementary rather than competitive. The main difference in policy conclusions between monetarists and mainstream economists, which is whether or not one needs to worry about internal balance, does not stem from any inability of orthodox theory to incorporate the behavioural relations stressed in the monetary approach, but from their differing degree of faith in the ability of price flexibility to clear markets.

Useful as the IS/LM/BP model is, however, it must be recognized that it suffers from three important limitations. First, it assumes a given price level and does not incorporate a theory of inflation. Second, it assumes static expectations – of a constant future price level, for example, so that it is unnecessary to distinguish the nominal from the real rate of interest. Third, it assumes given stocks of the various assets – money, bonds and physical capital.

These assumptions can, of course, be relaxed. Indeed, we have already noted the effects of varying the stock of money in shifting LM. It is particularly interesting to consider extending the model to include a theory of inflation. Suppose, therefore, that the wage level, instead of being constant, were determined by a Phillips curve (with or without adaptive expectations). It is easy to see that, with this addition, the IS/LM/BP model will generate all the monetarist conclusions as between two positions of long-run equilibrium (with $\hat{w} = 0$). For example, the monetary mechanism of adjustment no longer implies that income would remain at the less than full-employment level Y_1 produced by LM's migration to intersect BP and IS at J. The reason is that at J the unemployment would imply declining wages, which would improve competitiveness and so push both IS and BP right: equilibrium could occur only with full employment (specifically, with unemployment equal to the natural rate). Or, suppose one were to devalue from a position of long-run equilibrium. Unless the direct effects on absorption outweighed the substitution effects induced by the gain in competitiveness, income would increase and unemployment would fall below the natural rate, generating inflation, which would erode the competitive gain from devaluation. Thus the IS/LM/BP model extended by addition of a Phillips curve has long-run comparative statics properties that are essentially monetarist, while its short-run behaviour is eminently Keynesian. This suggests that the relationship between monetarism and Keynesianism is one of the time span judged relevant for policy formation, with monetarists tending to dismiss the short-run and Keynesians to disregard the long-run consequences of policy.

12.8 Summary

The orthodox theory of the current account, incorporating the income effects of the multiplier analysis and the price effects of the elasticities approach as synthesized by Meade, can be summarized in the equation:

$$TB = TB(\overset{-}{Y}, \overset{+}{ep_*/p}) \tag{12.20}$$

The signs over the arguments of the function TB (. . .) represent the direction of the effects of those variables on the trade balance (that is, the signs of the partial derivatives). The negative sign over Y comes from section 12.2, while the positive impact of competitiveness assumes that the Marshall–Lerner condition is satisfied. Thus equation 12.20 should be interpreted in a medium-run rather than short-run sense. This equation is robust to the choice of model and will be used in subsequent chapters to summarize the results of the present chapter.

Even though they do not imply any modification to the current account equation 12.20, the absorption approach and the monetary approach also contribute important perspectives. The absorption approach shows that it will normally be necessary to accompany an expenditure-switching policy like devaluation by an expenditure-reducing policy if devaluation is to improve the balance of payments and the economy is initially at full employment. With capital immobility, the monetary approach shows how monetary factors would dominate the adjustment process in the long run even though the behavioural relations and therefore the short-run properties are impeccably Keynesian.

12.9 Addendum: the large economy

The implication for the price-specie-flow mechanism of assuming the domestic economy to be large was noted in the text. With a large economy, the gold outflow will have a non-negligible effect in expanding foreign reserves, and thus the foreign money supply and price level. This *reinforces* the change in competitiveness and spreads the burden of adjustment.

The changes in domestic income analyzed in the multiplier approach will produce a *foreign repercussion* if the economy is large. For example, an increase in domestic investment raises income and increases imports, which are other countries' exports. Foreign income therefore rises by a non-negligible amount, which raises their imports and, thus, our exports and income. The multiplier is therefore larger.

The large country need not face an infinitely elastic foreign supply of imports, just as it will almost certainly not face an infinitely elastic demand for exports. The implications of assuming a finite elasticity of demand for exports were explored in the text, where it was found that this raised the possibility that a devaluation might worsen the balance of payments, if the Marshall–Lerner condition were not satisfied. A finite elasticity of supply of imports has no such significance, as can be seen by inserting an upward-sloping supply curve in Figure 12.3(c) or looking at the second term in equation 12.9. Another implication is the possibility that a devaluation by one country might provoke devaluation by some others.

The remaining approaches do not require any modifications other than those consequential on the points noted above (for example, a leftward rather than rightward shift of *BP* being induced by devaluation if the Marshall–Lerner condition were to fail), except for the Dornbusch model of devaluation. This was originally presented in a two-country model where prices were continuously equated by arbitrage (but might alter during the adjustment process), while money supplies were slowly redistributed between countries until full equilibrium was achieved.

12.10 Bibliography

The price-specie-flow mechanism was first analyzed by David Hume (1752). The most systematic development of the foreign trade multiplier analysis, Machlup (1943), is now mainly of historical interest. The same might be said of the original writings on the elasticities approach: Machlup (1939), Robinson (1937) and Haberler (1949). The absorption approach was introduced in Alexander (1952); the two most famous contributions to the ensuing controversy were Machlup (1955) and Tsiang (1961). Empirical estimates of income and price elasticities are surveyed by Goldstein and Khan in Chapter 20 of Jones and Kenen (1985, vol. II).

The initial conceptualization of internal and external balance is in *A Tract on Monetary Reform* (Keynes 1923). Meade's synthesis was developed in his careful taxonomic masterpiece (Meade 1951). Its popularization in diagrams like Figure 12.7 was due to the Australians: Swan (1960), first written in 1955; Salter (1959); and Corden (1960). The generalization to expenditure-reducing versus expenditure-switching effects was due to Johnson (1961, ch. 6), reprinted in Caves and Johnson (1968) and Cooper (1969). For the argument that devaluation may be contractionary, see Cooper (1971) and Krugman and Taylor (1978). Gylfason and Risegar (1984) investigate empirically the circumstances under which devaluation will improve the balance of payments (virtually always) and be contractionary (sometimes).

The Polak model was presented in Polak (1957), and reprinted in Heller and Rhomberg (1977), a volume that also contains the other basic papers from the IMF version of the monetary approach. The Dornbusch model of devaluation is in Dornbusch (1973); the gist of that paper, together with an elegant exposition of the theory of the current account (in more mathematical terms than those used above), can be found in Chapters 3–9 of Dornbusch (1980). Most of the principal papers of the Chicago version of the monetary approach are to be found in Frenkel and Johnson (1976). The balance of payments was first incorporated into the IS/LM analysis by Wrightsman (1970).

For further reading on the gold standard, see the bibliography to Chapter 19.

Notes

1. Recall from section 11.5 that the monetary base $B = R + D_1$ and $H = (1/\phi)B$. Define the 'sterilization coefficient' α as that proportion of a change in reserves that is offset by a change in (central bank) domestic credit D_1, so that $\Delta D_1 = -\alpha\Delta R$. A value of α equal to unity signifies total sterilization, while a value of zero signifies zero sterilization. Differencing the first two equations, and substituting, shows that:

$$\Delta H = (1/\phi)(\Delta R + \Delta D_1) = (1/\phi)(1 - \alpha)\Delta R$$

   from which it follows that the money supply will fall as long as sterilization is less than complete ($\alpha < 1$), and will fall by more than R when $(1 - \alpha)/\phi > 1$.

2. It is an often-remarked irony of the intellectual history of the period that Keynes had previously (in a debate in the *Economic Journal* in 1929) combated the efforts of Ohlin to apply what later became regarded as the Keynesian analysis of income effects to analysis of the transfer problem posed by German reparations (see section 13.1 for the nature of the transfer problem).

3. It is sometimes argued that exports are diverted to the home market by a high level of demand, so that $X = X(Y)$, $dX/dY < 0$, and there is empirical evidence supporting this hypothesis from some countries. The student should check that, if such an effect exists, it will reinforce the conclusions of the analysis of this section.

4. It is worth checking this out by working through with the alternative import function $M = m_1 + m_2 A$.

5. Another worthwhile exercise is to analyze the effects on Y and TB of an increase in the domestic production of petroleum.

6. The term 'revalue' is being used, according to current usage, as the opposite of 'devalue', rather than in the old-fashioned (though less ambiguous) way to signify any change in the exchange rate, whether devaluation or 'upvaluation'.

7. This assumption is easily generalized: the first part of the expression in 12.9 must be weighted by the proportion of exports in total trade, and the second part by the proportion that imports constitute. See Note 8.

8. Proof. From the definitions of ε_x and η_x and the identity $\hat{p}_x = \hat{e} + \hat{p}_x{}^*$, derive $\hat{p}_x{}^* = -\hat{X}/\eta_x = -\varepsilon_x\hat{p}_x/\eta_x = -(\varepsilon_x/\eta_x)(\hat{e} + \hat{p}_x{}^*)$, which solves to yield $\hat{p}_x{}^* = -[\varepsilon_x/(\varepsilon_x + \eta_x)]\hat{e}$ and $\hat{p}_x = [\eta_x/(\varepsilon_x + \eta_x)]\hat{e}$. Similarly, the expressions for ε_m and η_m and the equivalent identity can be solved to give $\hat{p}_m{}^* = -[\eta_m/(\varepsilon_m + \eta_m)]\hat{e}$ and $\hat{p}_m = [\varepsilon_m + \eta_m)]\hat{e}$. Since the trade balance in dollars is defined as $TB = p_x{}^*X - p_m{}^*M$, one can take the total differential and substitute:

$$\begin{aligned}
d(TB) &= Xdp_x{}^* + p_x{}^*dX - Mdp_m{}^* - p_m{}^*dM \\
&= Xp_x{}^*\hat{p}_x{}^* + p_x{}^*\varepsilon_x X\hat{p}_x - Mp_m{}^*\hat{p}_m{}^* + p_m{}^*\eta_m M\hat{p}_m \\
&= Xp_x{}^*\frac{[-\varepsilon_x + \varepsilon_x\eta_x]}{\varepsilon_x + \eta_x}\hat{e} + Mp_m{}^*\frac{[\eta_m + \eta_m\varepsilon_m]}{\varepsilon_m + \eta_m}\hat{e} \\
&= Xp_x{}^*\frac{\varepsilon_x(\eta_x - 1)}{\varepsilon_x + \eta_x}\hat{e} + Mp_m{}^*\frac{\eta_m(1 + \varepsilon_m)}{\varepsilon_m + \eta_m}\hat{e}
\end{aligned}$$

   When $Xp_x{}^* = Mp_m{}^*$, it can be seen that devaluation ($\hat{e} > o$) will improve the trade balance TB if and only if the condition 12.9 regarding the elasticities is satisfied.

9. Proof. The pass-through coefficient θ is defined as $-\hat{p}_x{}^*/\hat{e}$, which implies that $\hat{p}_x = [1 - \theta)\hat{e}$ given that $\hat{p}_x = \hat{e} + \hat{p}_x{}^*$. One again uses the formulae for the definition of η_x and η_m. Substitution in the total differential of the formula for TB gives:

$$d(TB) = Xdp_x{}^* + p_x{}^*dX - Mdp_m{}^* - p_m{}^*dM$$
$$= Xp_x{}^*(-\theta\hat{e}) + p_x{}^*X\eta_x\theta\hat{e} + p_m M\eta_m\hat{e}$$
$$= Xp_x{}^*(\eta_x - 1)\theta\hat{e} + Mp_m{}^*\eta_m\hat{e}$$

10. Note that there is no contradiction involved in every country facing a higher elasticity of demand for its exports than its own elasticity of demand for imports, since exports can substitute for the exports of other countries as well as for import substitutes.

11. Note that recognition of the possibility of foreign inflation would require a reinterpretation of the horizontal axis of Figure 12.2 to refer to 'real dollars' ($\$/p^*$), as well as of the vertical axis to refer to the real exchange rate ep^*/p.

12. An alternative definition of the real exchange rate has been adopted by a number of writers in recent years: p_m/p_n, the relative price of traded goods in terms of non-traded goods. Those using this definition usually assume that the price of traded goods is determined by arbitrage from abroad, so that $p_m = ep^*$. If these traded goods include goods produced for export, and the domestic price level p is a weighted average of the prices of traded and non-traded goods so that $p = p_m{}^\alpha p_n{}^{(1-\alpha)}$, then the standard definition $ep^*/p = p_m/p_m{}^\alpha p_n{}^{1-\alpha} = (p_m/p_n)^{1-\alpha}$ is a monotonic transformation of the alternative definition. In practice most measures of the real exchange rate are based on the definition in the text, but the alternative definition is the more relevant measure of the supply-side incentive to produce export goods in a small economy.

13. Proof. Substitute the expressions for $\hat{p}_x$ and $\hat{p}_m$ in n.8 into the formula for the change in the terms of trade:

$$\hat{p}_x - \hat{p}_m = \frac{\eta_x}{\varepsilon_x + \eta_x}\,\hat{e} - \frac{\varepsilon_m}{\varepsilon_m + \eta_m}\,\hat{e}$$
$$= \frac{\eta_x\varepsilon_m + \eta_x\eta_m - \varepsilon_m\varepsilon_x - \varepsilon_m\eta_x}{(\varepsilon_x + \eta_x)(\varepsilon_m + \eta_m)}\,\hat{e}$$
$$= \frac{(\eta_x\eta_m - \varepsilon_m\varepsilon_x)}{(\varepsilon_x + \eta_x)(\varepsilon_m + \eta_m)}\,\hat{e}$$

which is negative so long as $\varepsilon_m\varepsilon_x > \eta_x\eta_m$.

14. Almost every time a country devalues, its newspapers make an analytical error which grossly exaggerates the loss to real income from the terms-of-trade deterioration. They claim that the price for which exports are sold falls, while the price the country has to pay for its imports rises. Of course, there is a sense in which both statements are true: the *dollar* price of exports falls, while the *peso* price of imports rises. But to *compare* those two movements is erroneous: the terms of trade must be measured in a common currency. In dollars, the price of *both* exports and imports fall (if the latter changes at all), while in terms of pesos, they *both* rise.

15. Also known as the 'non-accelerating inflation rate of unemployment' or NAIRU.

16. In the extended model of an open economy with fiscal policy, the condition is, of course, $(I - S) + (G - T) + (X - M) = 0$.

13

Capital flows

This chapter extends balance of payments analysis to include the capital account. This is a vital step under present-day conditions: more than 95 per cent of the value of international transactions are nowadays on capital rather than current account. Many are speculative transactions that are essential to enable a system of floating rates to function at all (see Chapter 14), but that still leaves vast flows of funds on longer maturities, which is the concern of this chapter.

The first section examines the way in which a capital flow induces an adjustment in the current account, so as to transfer real capital – that is, real resources. The rationale of such capital flows is examined in Chapter 16. This is followed by two sections about alternative theories of the determinants of flows of portfolio capital: the flow theory of the late 1950s and early 1960s, and the stock theory that largely supplanted it in the late 1960s. The final section turns to the monetary approach, which is directed at explaining the balance of payments as a whole rather than either the current or capital accounts individually. It is argued that the monetary approach should be treated as a complement rather than a competitor to the other approaches.

13.1 The transfer problem

Suppose that our country has a capital inflow – perhaps because its banks start to raise a stream of loans on the Eurodollar market[1] to expand their domestic lending. It is possible that the country already had a current account deficit that needed financing – indeed, that might well be why the government ordered a tightening of monetary policy that pushed the banks into borrowing abroad. But, in order to see how the transfer process – i.e. the process of creating a transfer of real resources as the counterpart to the capital flow – operates, let us suppose that there was previously a balance on current account. Then the banks start selling the dollars that they have borrowed in order to acquire pesos to expand their loans. That means the central bank starts gaining reserves. The question at issue is: how would a constant stream of capital inflows induce an adjustment to restore payments equilibrium, with a current account deficit equal to the capital account surplus?

The short answer is 'it all depends', but an understanding of Chapter 12 takes one further than this rather unhelpful answer to identify *on what* it depends. For example, if the central bank sterilizes the monetary consequences of the reserve accumulation resulting from the capital inflow, then there will be no further adjustments. The firms that are able to expand their spending by using the resources borrowed abroad will be counterbalanced by those that have to reduce their spending in consequence of the reduction in domestic credit involved in sterilization. When a country is initially in internal balance and the government seeks to perpetuate that by sterilizing the capital inflow, the consequence is to frustrate the transfer. There is a limit to the extent to which sterilization is feasible; it is set by the stock of domestic assets that the central bank can sell and the willingness of the private market to buy such assets at interest rates the authorities are prepared to tolerate. Within that limit, however, which is quite wide in countries with well-developed capital markets, adjustment can be prevented.

Suppose, instead, that the central bank does not sterilize. Then autonomous expenditure will rise, presumably by the amount of the capital inflow. Imports rise, thus transferring at least a part of the capital inflow. Will the whole of the inflow be transferred? Initially no, if there is unemployment. (Why?) Quickly yes, if there is full employment, as inflation reduces competitiveness and brings expenditure switching towards foreign goods. Eventually yes in any event, as the monetary mechanism of adjustment comes into play.

Or suppose that the authorities want to preserve internal balance, including the prevention of inflation, but they wish to secure the inward transfer. What policies would be necessary? The answer is given by the Meade analysis in section 12.5. The inflow on capital account means that payments balance now occurs in the part of Figure 12.7 where the current balance is in deficit: that is, the external balance curve moves to the right. Preservation of internal and external balance therefore requires a combination of an expenditure-increasing policy (such as allowing the capital inflow to increase the money supply) and an expenditure-switching policy (revaluation or tariff reduction) to prevent the reflation creating excess demand for home-produced goods.

It is also worth referring back to Figure 11.2 to see the changes that occur in the dependent economy model between the position of balanced trade in Figure 11.2(a) and that of a trade deficit in Figure 11.2(b). With full employment both before and after the transfer is effected, the two changes needed to secure transfer are an expansion in absorption and an increase in the relative price of non-traded goods. These are precisely the changes that the analysis of the previous paragraph showed to be necessary, when we recognize that expenditure-switching policies are those that change the relative price of non-traded goods. (There will also be a terms-of-trade change in the case of the country with less than infinitely elastic demand for its exports.) And the previous paragraph argued that such expenditure switching would occur automatically as a result of inflation if it were not pursued deliberately by revaluation or equivalent policies.

Ensuring that transfer occurs therefore requires no more than an application of the analysis of Chapter 12. Why then should it have been conceived as a problem? For two general reasons. First, because governments have sometimes willed the ends without willing the means: they have wished to change the trade balance while preserving internal balance and fixed exchange rates. That is just not possible, except by luck (which is, admittedly, the politician's favourite policy weapon). Second, because we have considered the easy case of securing an inward transfer to match a capital inflow, rather than the difficult case of creating a surplus to match a capital outflow (or reparations or debt-service payments). That requires a cut in absorption and a fall in real wages, which is, not surprisingly, usually conceived to be a problem by the country involved.

13.2 The flow theory

As noted in section 11.2, capital flows take various forms – notably direct investment, export credits, amortization and portfolio movements. It is the last of these that are responsive to short-run macroeconomic conditions and which have therefore formed the focus of theoretical interest in attempts to explain the capital account. The transfer of capital resulting from direct investment is incidental to a decision to exploit an investment opportunity; given the long-run time perspective that a firm needs to employ when reaching investment decisions, these are unlikely to be strongly dependent on the current situation. Export credits extended and received depend principally on trade volumes, especially of capital goods. Amortization is largely determined by the pattern of past capital movements. Moreover, to the extent that any of those elements are variable in response to current economic conditions, the variations will tend to move with the flow of portfolio capital. Thus we can restrict our theoretical analysis to the latter case.

In explaining movements of private portfolio capital, economists have typically given pride of place to interest rates. This was already true when economists first began to analyze capital flows seriously in the closing years of the gold standard. They observed that interest rates were normally higher in the peripheral or developing countries of that time (notably the countries of recent settlement) than in the European capital-exporting countries, thus inducing a flow of long-term capital from the centre to the periphery to exploit international differences in thrift and productivity. They also observed that the rules of the game involved countries in deficit raising their interest rates, which quickly drew in funds from abroad and stemmed the gold loss by adjusting the capital account long before the monetary contraction involved in raising interest rates could have had any impact on the current account. That is not to argue that the current account adjustment was an unimportant part of the mechanism: if the high interest rates were maintained for long, they would reduce real income and possibly prices, thus ensuring that the current account would adjust for the reasons studied in Chapter 12. The existence of this backstop presumably helped sustain the general confidence that exchange rates could and would remain constant, which gave high interest rates their power to attract capital inflows and thus obviate the need for costly current account adjustment.

Although the gold standard suffered from occasional financial panics, it functioned blissfully in comparison to the period following the collapse of 1931. Any semblance of an international capital market disappeared, and such international capital flows as occurred took the form of flows of 'hot money' seeking to avoid an impending devaluation or political persecution. When there is no confidence that the exchange rate will be maintained, interest-rate increases are powerless to stem capital flight. (A 10 per cent devaluation one week hence would require an interest rate at an annual rate of about 14,000 per cent for that week[2] to compensate a holder for not selling!) The collapse of a rational international capital market was so complete that when the wartime allies were planning how to reconstruct the post-war world economy they decided to create the World Bank – to provide an official substitute for the private market whose disappearance was taken to be permanent.

There was therefore not much capital mobility to merit great attention or explanation when James Meade was writing his opus *The Balance of Payments* in the late 1940s, which is presumably why he gave his book that title even though its subject matter was largely restricted to an analysis of the current account. In such treatment as capital flows did receive, one can find three ideas:

1. The notion that some capital flows can be treated as exogenous, which, it was argued above, still holds good.
2. The idea that variations in the capital account have a tendency to reinforce those in the current account, as a deterioration in the latter ignites the fear of devaluation and provokes a speculative run (to the extent that this is true, capital flows serve to amplify the payments variations that have to be financed through the reserves).
3. The old idea dating back to the gold standard literature that capital would flow in response to differential interest rates.

When the private international capital market confounded expectations by reviving in the 1950s, that last idea was the natural one (or the only one around) for explaining endogenous, non-crisis capital movements. Without really thinking too much about what they were doing, economists began writing capital flow equations of the form:

$$\dot{F} = f(\overset{+}{i}, \overset{-}{i}^*) \tag{13.1}$$

where F is the stock of net foreign liabilities of the private sector, and $\dot{F}$ is therefore the net inflow of capital.[3] Equation 13.1 says that the inflow of capital depends positively on the domestic interest rate and negatively on the foreign interest rate.[4] This is called the flow theory because it postulates a relationship between the flow of capital and the level of interest rates. One can, of course, add a term representing direct investment and subtract a term representing amortization payments without altering anything fundamental, provided that both are exogenous with respect to the level of short-run endogenous variables like interest and income (as it was previously argued they are).

Consider next what happens when we insert equation 13.1 into an equation for the balance of payments, utilizing the model of the current account developed in the previous chapter:

$$\dot{R} = TB(Y, ep^*/p) + f(i, i^*) \tag{13.2}$$

This has an important consequence in terms of the IS/LM/BP analysis. Instead of being vertical as before, the *BP* curve is now positively sloping as shown in Figure 13.1, assuming that we interpret external balance as a zero change in reserves ($\dot{R} = 0$). The reason is that, while an increase in income will still worsen the current account, this can now be offset by an increase in the domestic interest rate, which will attract a capital inflow and thus preserve balance of payments equilibrium.

Virtually all the properties of the IS/LM/BP model with a positively sloping *BP* curve are the same as those of the model with a vertical *BP* curve studied in section 12.7. For example, Figure 13.1 shows a deficit; this means that reserves would be falling, so unless the central bank is creating credit the *LM* curve will be shifting left, which will continue until it passes through the *IS/BP* intersection.

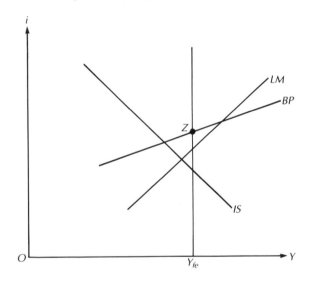

Figure 13.1 IS/LM/BP with capital mobility

When analyzing the IS/LM/BP model without capital mobility, we argued that in order to achieve simultaneous internal and external balance it was essential to have at the disposal of the authorities an instrument for securing expenditure switching. The reason was that both the internal balance curve (Y_{fe}) and the external balance curve (*BP*) were vertical, and hence, unless they happened to coincide, an instrument to shift *BP* to make them coincide was indispensable to satisfactory policy management. However, with *BP* no longer vertical in the case with capital mobility, there is a point (*Z* in Figure 13.1) where it intersects with Y_{fe}. Robert Mundell argued that this implied that it would be possible to attain internal and external balance simultaneously by an appropriate choice of fiscal and monetary policy, without any need for exchange-rate changes or some other expenditure-switching policy. In the case shown in Figure 13.1, one needs an expansionary fiscal policy to push *IS* up till it passes through the point *Z*, combined with a restrictive monetary policy to push *LM* up till it too passes through *Z*. That particular 'mix' of fiscal and monetary policy (two instruments, which now have differential effects on the two objectives) can secure the two targets of internal and external balance.

The same analysis can be presented in a diagram similar to the one that Mundell himself used. Figure 13.2 shows the fiscal surplus, representing fiscal policy, on the horizontal axis, and the interest rate, representing monetary policy, on the vertical axis. Suppose we have a point (like *E*) of internal balance. If the fiscal surplus were increased, this would have a contractionary effect on demand; to preserve internal balance, we would need to counteract this with a more expansionary monetary policy. The internal balance curve therefore slopes down, with points of unemployment (U) above it and excess demand (ED) below it. Now consider a point (again like *E*, by coincidence) of external balance. A tighter fiscal policy would increase the

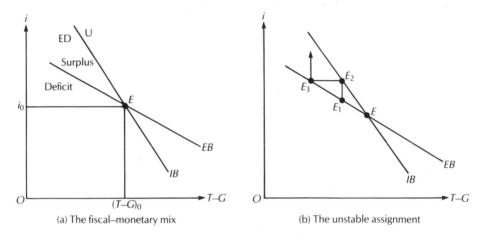

(a) The fiscal–monetary mix   (b) The unstable assignment

Figure 13.2 The fiscal–monetary mix and the assignment problem

current surplus,[5] hence to preserve external balance one would need to loosen monetary policy, which would decrease the current surplus *and* the capital surplus. The external balance curve therefore also slopes down, with a surplus above and a deficit below. Moreover, it is less steep than the internal balance curve. The reason is that income and therefore the current account remain constant along *IB*, while the change in the interest rate means that the capital account and therefore the overall balance of payments alter; specifically, as one goes down *IB* the capital inflow falls, which means that at some point one goes from surplus to deficit (as shown), which is possibly only if *IB* is steeper than *EB*. Given that the two curves have different slopes, a point of intersection *E* exists. The policy mix $(T-G)_0$, i_0 corresponding to *E* is that which would shift *IS* and *LM* to intersect at *Z* in Figure 13.1.

Mundell used his model to analyze what he called the *assignment problem*: whether one should direct, or assign, monetary policy to pursue the internal balance target and fiscal policy to the external balance target, or vice versa. If one assigned monetary policy to internal balance, one would tell the central bank to increase interest rates whenever there was excess demand and cut them whenever unemployment developed. Similarly, assigning fiscal policy to external balance would mean telling the Ministry of Finance to increase the budget deficit whenever the balance of payments was in surplus and to decrease it when there was a payments deficit. Figure 13.2(b) shows what would happen with this assignment. Suppose the economy were initially at E_1. The Ministry of Finance would be happy, but the central bank would be duty bound to fight the inflation caused by excess demand, which it would do by raising the rate of interest till the excess demand was eliminated. That would leave the Ministry of Finance facing the embarrassment of a payments surplus, which it would fight by cutting taxes or increasing government spending till the economy reached E_3. Thereupon the central bank would embark on another round of raising interest rates . . . with the economy moving steadily away from the optimal mix at E. The moral is that one should assign each instrument to the objective over which it has relatively most influence: monetary policy to external balance and fiscal policy to internal balance. That guarantees that uncoordinated policy actions by the central bank and the Ministry of Finance will lead the economy to converge to the point E.

How much sense does this analysis make? Consider first the idea of assigning instruments to targets. If one is going to assign instruments to targets at all, then certainly Mundell's analysis shows how it should be done and the dangers of doing it wrongly. But the idea of assignment is suspect: achieving simultaneous internal and external balance is a general equilibrium problem which demands a general equilibrium solution, in the form of a simultaneous choice of policy instruments. With perfect information, this would enable the authorities to guide the economy straight to E and avoid the zig-zag approach involved in even the stable assignment. The notion that this cannot be done because the two instruments are controlled by different sets of bureaucrats is not very convincing: they can after all call each other. (Even the most undeveloped of countries have telephones between the Ministry of Finance and the central bank.) A more persuasive defence is that the authorities do not have perfect information and therefore cannot lead the economy straight to E. They have to feel their way in that direction, and in doing that they need a rule as to when each policy should be adjusted. But even with imperfect information, one can argue that the authorities should sit down together and seek a strategy that takes account of the moves the other is about to make, which means that an assignment is primarily of public relations rather than of operational significance.

Consider next the idea of determining the mix of fiscal and monetary policy by the desire to secure simultaneous internal and external balance. The fundamental problem with this proposal was long ago identified by Mundell (among others): that it leaves the *composition* of the balance of payments – its division between current and capital accounts – at the mercy of what are essentially arbitrary forces. Suppose that the equilibrium E shown in Figure 13.2 were a position in which there was a capital inflow financing a current account deficit consistent with the forces of thrift and productivity analyzed in Chapter 16, when suddenly the price of a major import good (like oil) increased (with no expectation that it would subsequently fall). The worsening of the terms of trade would push *EB* up and *IB* down, and *E* would in consequence move up and to the left, indicating that the appropriate policy mix would be tighter monetary and easier fiscal policy. The country would maintain its level of output and absorption constant, and would finance rather than seek to adjust away the increase in its current account deficit. It would borrow to sustain consumption (for the higher interest rate would even be tending to reduce investment), and then borrow some more to pay the interest. That is the road to ruin, not the rational intertemporal reallocation of consumption that capital mobility should offer (see Chapter 16). The problem is that the 'mix' involves having the current account (at full employment and the inherited exchange rate) determine the capital account, whereas the classical analysis depends on having capital flows determine the current account balance. The conclusion is inescapable: it is essential to have some mechanism to secure current account adjustment in the medium term, rather than to finance any old deficit or surplus that arises from chance events.

Can one, however, justify the mix as a short-term policy expedient, to finance the current account while longer-term adjustment measures are brought into play? In general, the answer is no. The accumulation and decumulation of reserves over time should enable a country to smooth the path of absorption despite fluctuations in income. Reserves raise welfare by being used, not by being maintained constant. The whole point of holding reserves is to act as a buffer stock that can be allowed to fluctuate to help stabilize some other variables that have some real significance for economic welfare, like output or absorption. In short, the target of external balance should *not* be interpreted as a constant level of reserves, certainly not in a short-run sense.

There is just one case in which the 'mix' analysis comes into its own, and that is when a country cannot afford to run down its reserves any more. In that case it is better to raise interest rates to attract a capital inflow than to allow the waste of unemployment to eliminate the current deficit. But that in no way undermines the need to ensure that there is a mechanism to secure adjustment in the current account over the medium run.

If we are denying ourselves the easy option of defining external balance as a zero change in reserves, how *should* it be defined? The natural choice is to define it as the current account surplus or deficit that is needed to transfer the capital outflow or inflow dictated by the real forces of thrift and productivity (Chapter 16). That means that the payments target in the IS/LM/BP analysis is again vertical, as in Figure 12.11, rather than sloping, as in Figure 13.2, and so attaining payments objectives requires the use of an expenditure-switching policy. This should, however, be interpreted as a medium-run target, with short-run payments variations being accepted and financed through reserve changes.

There is one special (though famous) case that requires separate analysis before we leave the flow theory, since it leads to conclusions that are qualitatively different from those yielded by the case of no capital mobility. This is the case of perfect capital mobility, shown by the horizontal *BP* curve in Figure 13.3. Perfect capital mobility requires that domestic and foreign bonds are considered perfect substitutes by

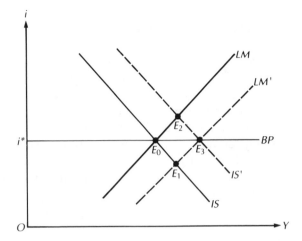

Figure 13.3 IS LM/BP with perfect capital mobility

wealth owners. Consequently, any excess of the domestic interest rate over the foreign interest rate would attract a flood of capital inflows (or any deficiency would provoke a rush to sell domestic assets), implying that *BP* is horizontal.

Suppose that the central bank tried to expand income through an expansionary monetary policy, shifting the *LM* curve to *LM'*. Since *IS* is unchanged, the new equilibrium would be at E_1 with the new higher money supply. But E_1 involves a lower interest rate than i^*, which means that investors would rush to sell domestic bonds, and then domestic money, to buy foreign exchange to buy foreign bonds. This would continue till *LM'* returned to *LM* and i returned to i^*. The conclusion is simple: with perfect capital mobility (and a fixed exchange rate), monetary policy has no power to influence the level of income. But it is an admirable instrument to influence the level of reserves, since it can control them with zero cost in terms of forcing deviations from domestic objectives.

Suppose, on the other hand, that the government attempted to expand income by adopting an expansionary fiscal policy, pushing *IS* to the right to *IS'*. Without capital mobility, the new equilibrium would be at E_2. But E_2 involves an interest rate above i^*, which is not feasible: it would attract a vast capital inflow that would push *LM* to the right, until it reached the point E_3 where *IS'* cuts *BP*. Thus fiscal policy becomes more potent in influencing income: it attracts a capital inflow that increases the money supply and so avoids the rise in the interest rate that otherwise dampens the rise in income.

13.3 The stock theory

The flow theory that we have just studied implies that with a given constellation of interest rates a country can expect to experience a constant rate of inflow (or outflow) of capital period after period. In the second half of the 1960s, economists came to realize that this was inconsistent with the emergent approach of portfolio theory. The stock theory of the capital account incorporates the implications for international capital flows of portfolio theory.

The basic idea of *portfolio theory* is that investors[6] seek to distribute their wealth between the various assets available in such a way as to maximize their utility. Assets, of course, unlike consumer goods, do not yield utility directly but only because of the income that they bring. Why then is it not possible to say that investors buy the assets that will maximize their income? A moment's reflection will reveal why: the income yielded by an asset is rarely certain, and the assets offering to pay the most are usually the most risky. In deciding how to distribute his or her wealth, the rational investor needs to take into account both expected return and risk, and his or her preferences as regards the trade-off between them.

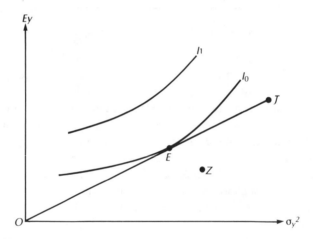

Figure 13.4 Simple case of portfolio choice

Figure 13.4 illustrates the simplest case of the analysis. On the vertical axis we plot the average or expected return, denoted Ey, where E is the expectations operator and y represents income. On the horizontal axis is plotted the variance of income (the variance is the square of the standard deviation), denoted σ_y^2, which is the most common statistical measure of risk. Since risk is a 'bad' to most investors (who are described on this account as being 'risk-averse') while a high level of expected return is a 'good', the indifference curves of a typical investor will be upward sloping and convex from below, as shown by I_0 and I_1 in Figure 13.4. The object of the investor is that of attaining the highest possible indifference curve subject to the wealth he or she has available to invest.

Different assets promise different combinations of expected return and risk. For example, there might be a perfectly safe asset ($\sigma_y^2 = 0$) that paid no return (money, in a country with no inflation and no danger of inflation, if you can imagine such). If his or her entire wealth were placed in that asset, the investor would be at the origin in the diagram. Or imagine that there were also a risky asset, with Ey and σ_y^2 such that, if all wealth were placed in that form, the investor would achieve the combination of expected return and risk represented by the point J. A third asset might yield the point Z. Such an asset would, however, not be bought by our investor, who could instead choose a combination of the first two assets which would yield him the same expected return for less risk, or a greater expected return for the same risk, than the third asset. Combinations of the first two assets could in fact yield the investor any point on the straight line OJ. Given the investor's preferences, it is clear that he or she will choose that combination of the first two assets at point E.

Simple as this model is, we can draw from it a number of conclusions:

1. An investor will not necessarily buy some of every asset on the market, but in order to spread the risks will normally diversify his or her holdings over a number of assets.
2. The demand for a particular asset will depend positively on the expected yield and negatively on its risk as perceived by investors.
3. The demand for all assets will go up as the total wealth available for investment rises.

Portfolio theory imples a fourth conclusion that is of particular significance for international investment, though unfortunately it cannot be illustrated directly in Figure 13.4. This conclusion relates to the significance of the *relationship between the risks* on two different assets. If an asset A always tends to have a high yield at the same time as a second asset B, then one cannot do much to reduce one's risk by diversifying one's portfolio between the two. In technical terms, one says there is a positive covariance between the returns on A and B, $\sigma_{ab} > 0$. But suppose instead that we had two assets A and B, each of which had the same expected return E_z and the same risk σ_z^2 as the asset shown by the point Z in Figure 13.4, but with perfect negative covariance ($\sigma_{ab} = -1$). In non-technical terms, this means that the greater the return to the one, the less the return to the other, as shown in Figure 13.5. Suppose now that one were to make up a compound asset (or mini portfolio) consisting half of A and half of B. Then one would be *guaranteed* a return equal to EZ. This compound asset would therefore fall in Figure 13.4 at the same height as Z but on the vertical axis, thus driving the riskless asset out of the portfolio and raising the investor's utility. It is evident that the covariances between the yields on different assets are very important in portfolio selection: in technical terms, the optimal portfolio depends on the whole variance–covariance matrix and not just the risk of each asset considered in isolation. We may now (somewhat loosely) state the fourth conclusion:

4. The demand for an asset will be greater the more negative is the covariance between its return and the return on alternative assets.

This conclusion is particularly significant for international capital movements because returns in different countries are in fact considerably less closely correlated than those within a single country. This means that investors in each country can

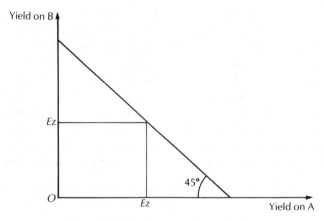

Figure 13.5 Perfect negative covariance

hope to gain by diversifying their holdings over assets drawn from a number of other countries, without this necessarily involving any net flows of capital or therefore net transfers of real resources. Some estimates (Lessard 1981) suggest that the potential welfare gains from this risk diversification are quite substantial, and flows of equity capital – which are the form for which the analysis is most relevant – have become quite significant among the industrial countries. The conclusion is also cheering news for developing countries, since it implies that investors may seek to put a proportion of their assets into the liabilities of developing countries even though they may regard these as relatively risky, provided that they believe that those risks are inversely correlated with the risks of investments in the developed countries. Whether or not what is bad for the rich is actually good for the poor, a belief to that effect will actually be good for the poor.

However, the main implication that has been drawn from the portfolio theory for international capital flows relates more to the second point than to the fourth. Let us assume that our country U is a capital-importing country which does not permit its citizens to make investments abroad, and also that the foreign liabilities F issued by its residents on the world capital market can be considered a homogeneous asset from the standpoint of the rest of the world's investors. Then the demand for F can be written:

$$F_{\text{d}} = \text{f}(\overset{+}{i}, \overset{-}{i}{}^{*}, \overset{+}{creditworthiness}, \overset{+}{wealth})\tag{13.3}$$

It is obviously necessary to include i^{*}, the interest rate on the alternative asset available to investors, as well as i. When we come to apply the portfolio model to the context of international capital flows, the idea of risk can be translated into a country's creditworthiness – roughly speaking, the confidence investors feel that the country will remain able and willing to service its debt. Finally, the relevant wealth variable is the total value of the assets of the lenders and potential lenders.

Suppose for the moment that creditworthiness and wealth remain constant. Then equation 13.3 says that a given pair of interest rates, i and i^{*}, will make investors wish to lend a certain sum F_d, and no more. Suppose they make those loans in period t, and that both interest rates remain constant in period $(t + 1)$. Then the *stock* of loans F_d will remain constant. But since the capital inflow is the difference between the stock of loans at $(t + 1)$ and the stock at t, the capital inflow will be zero. Contrast this with the flow theory, which assumed that a given pair of interest rates maintained through time would sustain a continuing constant capital flow. According to the stock theory, a rise in the domestic interest rate would provoke a one-time capital inflow as portfolios were rearranged to include a larger proportion of the now-more-attractive assets issued by domestic residents. After that, the capital flow would cease – unlike under the flow theory.[7]

Acceptance of the stock theory has important implications for the IS/LM/BP model and the Mundellian fiscal–monetary mix. It implies that one can no longer expect the *BP* curve of Figure 13.1 or the *EB* curve of Figure 13.2 to remain constant through time, since this period's capital inflow depends upon last period's inflow, as well as this period's interest rate. Financing a constant current account deficit through attracting a capital inflow would require a continuing *increase* in the domestic interest rate, rather than merely the maintenance of a constant interest-rate *differential*. This provides yet another reason for rejecting the Mundellian mix as a component of rational economic management.

However, the flow analysis of the preceding section can be partially salvaged by taking account of the final term in equation 13.3. The stock of our liabilities that foreigners wish to hold depends not merely on relative interest rates and credit-worthiness but also on the size of the total portfolios that foreigners have available to invest. Since those are normally growing as a result of savings (that reflect real growth) and inflation, a country which is already a net debtor can expect an increase in the quantity of its liabilities that foreigners are willing to hold even without an increase in its interest rate. If the wealth of investors increases by 10 per cent, then one can expect that *ceteris paribus* there will be a capital inflow equal to 10 per cent of one's existing liabilities. This is known as the *portfolio growth effect*.

Suppose therefore that the domestic interest rate were increased. This would induce a portfolio redistribution effect that would result in a one-time capital inflow as investors rearranged their portfolios to include a larger proportion of our liabilities. After that, things would settle down again, but with a permanently larger capital inflow than before to the extent that our liabilities now constitute a larger proportion of their portfolio, which is still growing at the same rate. The portfolio growth effect would be larger because the same rate of growth would be applied to a bigger base. In consequence the *BP* curve of Figure 13.1 would slope up, in addition to the sudden but temporary jump that it would undergo every time the interest rate changed.

It is also worth noting that there is one case in which the analysis is exactly the same under the stock theory as under the flow theory, and that is in the case of perfect capital mobility. The results that monetary policy is unable to influence income, although having a one-for-one impact on the level of reserves, while the potency of fiscal policy in influencing income is increased, are preserved unchanged.

A useful model for studying the macroeconomic implications of the stock theory has been suggested by the Argentine economist Roberto Frenkel (b. 1943), from whose work the following has been adapted. Instead of analyzing the money market, as has been traditional, the model focuses on the market for credit (or loans, if you prefer). It is assumed that the banks are the only source of loans, and also that they alone have access to the international capital market. (Nothing fundamental depends on these assumptions, which are made for expositional simplicity.) Credit is demanded by the government to finance the sum of its past deficits and by the private sector to finance investment, working capital and even consumption loans. This demand for credit is responsive to the interest rate and may therefore be shown by a downward-sloping demand curve, D_d in Figure 13.6.

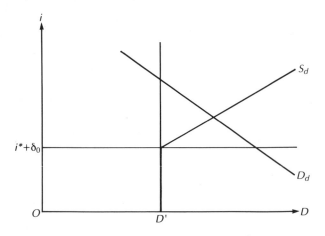

Figure 13.6 Market for credit

The supply of credit is divided into two components. The first, labelled D' in Figure 13.6, is the quantity of loans that the banking system would be able to make even without any resort to foreign borrowing. If the money multiplier is independent of the interest rate, the supply of loans from this source is a vertical line as shown.

The second element of the supply of credit is that which results from foreign borrowing. The bank which contracts a loan abroad and switches it into pesos at the central bank gains additional funds which it can use in order to expand its domestic loans. Naturally, banks will be prepared to do such borrowing only if the interest return they expect to receive exceeds the foreign interest rate i^* by a margin δ large enough to compensate them for their trouble, cost and risk. Furthermore, one might expect that the margin above i^* needed to induce further borrowing will tend to rise with the size of that borrowing, for two reasons. The first is that as the country's international indebtedness rises, its creditworthiness may decline, and to compensate for that foreign lenders may be expected to charge an increasing premium. This does not appear to be a major factor in practice: although spreads may widen by 1 or 2 per cent first, the main consequence of eroded creditworthiness is to make loans unavailable at any price beyond a certain point. The second reason is that the borrowers, in this case the banks, may become concerned about the risk involved in their foreign exchange exposure, in that they would suffer a capital loss if the peso were to be devalued.[8] They require a higher interest differential to compensate them for accepting an increasing amount of this risk.

The slope of the S_d curve to the right of D' therefore depends in part on how rapidly the interest differential required by the banks rises as their foreign exchange exposure increases. The more slowly it rises, the flatter is S_d. In the limit, if the differential needed did not rise, one would have a horizontal line: that is essentially the case of perfect capital mobility. At the other limit, if the banks were unwilling to borrow anything at any differential, the whole of S_d would be a vertical line at D'. In between is the zone of finite capital mobility. In this intermediate zone the slope of S_d depends on a second factor beside the degree of capital mobility: namely, the value of the money multiplier, or the reserve ratio ϕ of the commercial banks. The reason is that when one bank switches in dollars and then makes peso loans, it provides additional base money to the banking system which can form the basis for a multiple expansion of the money supply. The banks whose deposits increase as a result of the customers of the first bank spending their loans are in turn able to expand their loans, and so on, until the banking system is again fully loaned up. Hence, the smaller is ϕ, and the larger is the money multiplier, the flatter will be S_d for any given level of capital mobility.

The model can be used to establish various comparative statics results. The most famous case is that of an expansionary monetary policy. An increase in the central bank component of domestic credit D_1 would increase D'. The diagram shows this would push S_d to the right, lower the interest rate, increase total credit and reduce foreign borrowing.

In an important paper, 'International capital flows and portfolio equilibrium' (1974) the Finnish economist Pentti Kouri (b. 1949) and the Australian economist Michael Porter (b. 1943) focused on that last consequence. They asked: if the central bank increases domestic credit D_1 by a certain sum, how much of that will result in an increase in the monetary base (and thus in the money supply), and how much will be offset by an outflow of capital (a reduction in foreign borrowing in the present instance)? They christened the latter fraction the *offset coefficient*. It varies from zero when capital mobility is zero to unity when capital mobility is perfect, and in fact provides the most satisfactory measure of the degree of capital mobility. Empirical estimates of offset coefficients have typically fallen in the range 0.4 to 0.8, substantially less than the unity that would signify perfect capital mobility.

An expansionary fiscal policy would in time increase the size of government debt to be financed, and so push D_d to the right. The interest rate would increase, foreign borrowing would be pulled in and (the commercial bank component of) domestic credit would rise even without monetary expansion by the central bank, assuming only that it did not sterilize.

A current surplus has to be financed by the central bank issuing pesos in exchange for the dollars it buys, which pushes D' to the right. This would have consequences similar to those of a monetary expansion.

All that is on the assumption that the premium required by the banks to switch in funds would remain constant for any given level of foreign borrowing. But that is not in all circumstances a very reasonable assumption. One expects the required premium to depend not just on the level of foreign borrowing, but also on confidence that the exchange rate will be maintained, which in turn depends on such factors as the level of reserves and expectations as to the evolution of the current account. Clearly a reduction in confidence would mean that larger premiums would be needed to induce a given level of foreign borrowing: the S_d curve would rotate up in its non-vertical section. This provides an explanation of the making of a foreign exchange crisis. Suppose that the current account goes unexpectedly into deficit, thus both reducing D' and causing S_d to rotate up. If the authorities accept the resulting rise in interest rates, they may manage to preserve confidence and avert a crisis. But if they endeavour to limit the rise in interest rates, by credit creation, there is a real danger that their action will make it attractive for the banks to reduce foreign indebtedness still more, which will reduce the reserves, undermine confidence and rotate S_d up yet again in a self-aggravating crisis. A deterioration in the current account sets off a chain of events which leads to an outflow of capital – exactly the pattern that was a part of the conventional wisdom in Meade's 1940s, but had been lost sight of in more recent modelling (although by no means absent from the real world, as witness the experience of Frenkel's own country of Argentina).[9] A virtue of Frenkel's model is that it points one towards studying the forces that can lead to a speculative crisis, as well as helping one see the implications of policy changes under more normal circumstances.

13.4 The monetary approach

Advocates of the monetary approach, especially Michael Mussa (b. 1944), have emphasized that what analysis of the money market can hope to furnish is a theory of the *balance of payments* rather than of the balance of trade or the balance on current account. They have argued that it is a mistaken strategy to try and predict the balance of payments (ΔR) on the basis of an equation like 13.2, as the sum of separately determined current and capital accounts. The overall balance of payments is, they argue (and no one can deny it), an inflow or outflow of money; and if you want to explain that, the natural place to start is in the money market, to see if there is an excess demand or an excess supply there. A typical monetarist model of the balance of payments therefore has the following structure:

$$
\begin{aligned}
& \qquad\qquad\quad \overset{+\ \ +\ \ -}{} \\
H_d &= H(p, Y, i) & (13.4) \\
H_s &= (1/\phi)\,(R + D_1) & (13.5) \\
\therefore\quad R + D_1 &= \phi H(p, Y, i) & (13.6) \\
\therefore\quad dR &= H d\phi + \phi H_1 dp + \phi H_2 dY + \phi H_3 di - dD_1 & (13.7)
\end{aligned}
$$

Equation 13.4 is a demand for money function, with its conventional partial derivatives: higher prices or income increase the demand for money, while a higher interest rate reduces it. Equation 13.5 is the supply of money function: ϕ is the reserve ratio of the commercial banks, $1/\phi$ is therefore the money multiplier, and $(R + D_1)$ is the monetary base. Equation 13.6 equates demand and supply. Equation 13.7 is written to imply that reserve changes are the consequence of changes in the reserve ratio, prices, income, interest rates and (central bank) credit expansion. This is a (or even the) typical monetary approach equation for the balance of payments.

At least some monetarists, most notably Harry Johnson, interpreted equation 13.7 as representing a fundamental challenge to orthodox theories as summarized in equation 13.2. Why? Because equation 13.2 says that an increase in income will pull in imports and so worsen the balance of payments; that an increase in prices will erode competitiveness and so worsen the balance of payments (assuming the Marshall–Lerner condition to be satisfied); and that an increase in the domestic interest rate will improve the balance of payments because it will pull in capital. A look at equation 13.7 and the partial derivatives in 13.4 shows that it says exactly the opposite: an increase in income or prices will increase the demand for money and so pull in reserves, while an increase in the interest rate will decrease the demand for money and so cause a payments deficit. Thus, there is the setting for a great Keynesian–monetarist battle.

Or is there? We have already seen at the end of Chapter 12 that without capital mobility there is no conflict at this level of theory between Keynesian and monetarist approaches when both are cast in a general equilibrium setting. There are certainly policy differences, but these stem from differing judgements on whether changes in income will principally take the form of price changes or output changes, not from theoretically inconsistent systems of equations.

The same is true with capital mobility. The question is whether Y, p and i can be considered exogenous variables: if they can, then 13.2 and 13.7 cannot *both* determine the balance of payments and a choice must be made between them. But if they are not exogenous, then Y, p and i must be determined within a general equilibrium system that may perfectly well accommodate both equations – there is, after all, no contradiction whatever between the underlying behavioural relations embodied in the two equations.

Some monetarists – essentially those that subscribe to the extreme version that has earned the label global monetarism – have indeed argued that Y, p and i are exogeneous. Y is said to be determined at its full-employment level by wage flexibility, while p and i are treated as determined from the world market by perfect arbitrage in goods and securities respectively. Under those conditions the balance of payments would be determined by equation 13.7. In fact, under perfect capital mobility, equation 13.2 is useless for telling one the change in reserves, since the second term on the right-hand side tells one that i must equal i^*, and when it does the change in reserves can be anything at all.

Consider a country where Y, p and i are determined as is assumed in the global monetarist literature:

$$Y = Y_{fe}$$
$$p = ep^*$$
$$i = i^*$$

(13.8)

Suppose we plug these assumptions into our standard version of orthodoxy: namely, the IS/LM/BP model. As in Figure 13.3, the *BP* curve is horizontal because of perfect capital mobility, and the *LM* curve will be shifted as much as is necessary to ensure that the economy is always on the *BP* curve. But now (see Figure 13.7) there is a new element introduced by the assumption of full employment: the economy must lie on Y_{fe} in short-run equilibrium. That means that equilibrium E is determined by the intersection of Y_{fe} and *BP*. But equilibrium also lies at the intersection of *IS* and *LM*. As noted above, *LM* shifts endogenously because of the inflow or outflow of money so that it will cut the point E. The assumption of perfect arbitrage does exactly the same thing for the *IS* curve: any deficiency in domestic demand caused by a higher interest rate can be compensated by selling more on the world market, so the *IS* curve will move endogenously to the point needed to ensure that equilibrium occurs at E.

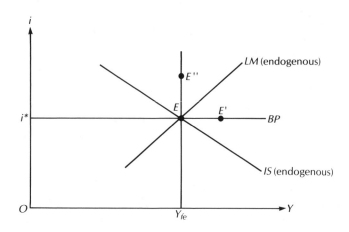

Figure 13.7 IS/LM/BP under global monetarism

Now ask what happens if p, Y or i change in this model:

1. How does an increase in p come about? Only as a result of an increase in e or p^*. Given that ep^*/p remains unchanged by perfect arbitrage, *IS* will remain unchanged, as do *BP* and Y_{fe}. On the other hand, the price increase reduces H/p and pushes *LM* up. To preserve equilibrium at E, the money supply must be re-established in real terms, which requires an *influx* of reserves. Thus the orthodox model with the global monetarist assumptions incorporated gives the monetarist result.

2. How does Y increase? Only by an increase in Y_{fe}. E therefore moves to the right, say to E', which requires that *LM* shift down, which requires an *inflow* of reserves. Once again, therefore, the orthodox model gives the monetarist result after incorporating monetarist assumptions.

3. How does i increase? Only as a result of i^* increasing. That shifts BP up, to give a new equilibrium at, say, E''. To get LM to shift there, it is necessary to reduce H/p, which means to cut H, which requires a reserve *outflow* – once again, the monetarist result.

Hence in the special (global monetarist) case where p, Y and i are exogenous, both models give the same (global monetarist) results. In the general case where p, Y and i are endogenous, it makes no sense to ask questions such as: what is the effect of an increase in i on the balance of payments? The answer is: it all depends. Specifically, it all depends on what causes i to increase. If i increases because i^* increases, then the orthodox model will tell one that capital will flow out – indeed, this is the mechanism that causes i to increase. If, on the other hand, i increases because of a contractionary monetary policy (a fall in D_1), which is the reason for changes in interest rates that Keynesians normally had in mind, then the monetarist equation will also predict a reserve inflow, as the negative coefficient on dD_1 in equation 13.7 suggests. One can reason the same way as regards prices. What should determine whether an observer should predict that the balance of payments will move towards surplus or deficit when p increases is not the observer's ideological position on the Keynesian–monetarist spectrum, but his or her judgement as to whether prices were pushed up by domestic forces (Keynesian case) or pulled up by foreign inflation (monetarist case). The argument is slightly more complex as regards a change in income. An increase in income that results from an increase in supply capacity may even increase the current balance (depending on how prices move and whether imports are essential inputs or substitutes to domestic output). On the other hand, an increase in income that results from an increase in demand will certainly tend to cause a current account deficit, but, depending on the degree of capital mobility and the interest and income elasticities of demand for money, this may be more than offset by an induced capital inflow (always assuming that the increased demand was not the result of lower interest rates produced by monetary expansion).

The conclusion is clear. It is quite wrong to conclude that orthodox and monetarist approaches to the balance of payments imply different conclusions. A general equilibrium model needs to contain both equations. When one recognizes that within such a context p, Y and i cannot be considered exogenous, one cannot ask how changes in them will affect the balance of payments: one needs to go back and ask that question with regard to whatever was the exogenous change that started things off. And to the correct question, the two approaches give the same answers.

That still leaves two important questions. The first is: do the global monetarist assumptions embodied in equation 13.8 represent a useful approximation to the truth?

There is a good deal of empirical evidence on the effectiveness of arbitrage in goods markets. Economists like Irving Kravis (b. 1916), Robert Lipsey (b. 1926) and Peter Isard (b. 1943) have done painstakingly detailed comparisons of changes in prices quoted by sellers from different countries at the most disaggregated levels possible. A whole issue of the *Journal of International Economics* (May 1978) was devoted to reporting the proceedings of a conference that examined the evidence on this question. The results of this careful research support casual observation: it is only the prices of homogeneous primary commodities that are equated internationally by arbitrage, while the prices of manufactures deviate quite widely depending on the source of supply. Exchange-rate changes influence relative prices, certainly in the short run and even persisting into the medium run. The hypothesis that arbitrage quickly equates goods prices internationally has probably been rejected more decisively by empirical evidence than any other hypothesis in the history of economics.

There is also evidence on the effectiveness of arbitrage in securities markets. The results of various econometric estimates of the elasticity of substitution between holdings of domestic and foreign bonds have been surprisingly low. Econometric estimates of the offset coefficient described in section 13.3 have also generally been well below 1, again implying that capital mobility is far from perfect. It would seem that the reason for occasional vast capital flows is not that capital mobility is particularly high but that the *incentive* to shift capital is sometimes enormous. It is again not possible to adopt the monetarist hypothesis of perfect arbitrage equating yields without doing grave violence to the facts.

How about the exogeneity of real income? There is an influential school, known as the new classical macroeconomists, whose basic position is indeed that deviations of Y from full employment are essentially random and cannot be influenced systematically by expansionary or contractionary demand management policies. Only shocks to demand that take the public unaware can have that effect: for example, by deceiving workers into accepting a lower real wage than expected, or by confusing firms into thinking that the *relative* price of their output has risen. This theorem is proved on the basis of two assumptions, rational expectations[10] and ubiquitous flexprice markets. It is the first of these assumptions that is always emphasized in the new classical literature, whereas it is the second that critics believe to be a travesty of the facts. There is still a vigorous debate on what the empirical evidence shows. The new classical macroeconomists point to the substantial evidence that faster trend monetary expansion does not increase employment in order to support their position, while their critics reply that fixprice markets and adaptive expectations are also consistent with that finding. These critics point instead to the evidence that deviations from any concept of full employment are highly serially correlated, whereas the simple version of the new classical theory predicts they would be essentially random. The new classical macroeconomists reply that such serial correlation could be caused by delays in the transmission of the information that enables agents to distinguish between relative and absolute prices or by the costs of adjusting employment to fluctuations in desired output or by delayed effects of capital or inventory accumulation. Most critics, including the authors, probably base their rejection of the new classical story less on formal evidence, important as it is, than on an inability to believe that the extent of unemployment in the OECD area in the early 1980s can possibly be explained away as the result of people being confused into setting false prices.

The empirical evidence therefore indicates that one must reject the global monetarist assumptions of equation 13.8. However, the need to reject this extreme version of monetarism should not lead one to dismiss the whole monetarist contribution: that would be to impute guilt by association. There is in fact an important sense in which the monetary approach is correct and useful. And, as in the case of no capital mobility, it is bound up with the question of the time period of analysis. At the end of Chapter 12 it was argued that the monetary approach gives the correct asymptotic solution to a comprehensive general equilibrium model with properties that are fully Keynesian in the short run – that is, that the monetary approach gets the answer right in the long run but not in the short run. The reason the monetary approach gets the answer right only in the long run is that, with capital immobility, establishment of monetary equilibrium between countries requires current account surpluses and deficits, which, having the dimension of a flow, necessarily require time for the flows to cumulate to a change in the equilibrium stock. But with capital mobility on the stock theory,[11] the situation is reversed. The level of reserves can now change in the short run in such a way as to re-establish monetary equilibrium, even while an underlying portfolio disequilibrium persists and generates current account surpluses or deficits. That being so, the monetarist balance of payments equation becomes a useful tool for predicting the overall balance of payments (reserve change).

This synthesis of Keynesian and monetarist payments theory was first advanced by Kouri and Porter in 1974. What they did was to accept the monetarist payments equation 13.7 and use it, in conjunction with the current balance equation 12.20, in order to predict the capital account:

$$dF = dR(\overset{+}{d\phi}, \overset{+}{dp}, \overset{+}{dY}, \overset{-}{di}, \overset{+}{dD_1}) - TB(\overset{-}{Y}, ep^*/\overset{+}{p})\tag{13.9}$$

where $dR(\ldots)$ is simply a restatement of equation 13.7. Equation 13.9 says that the capital inflow is that part of the shortfall of money supply below money demand that is not made good by a current account surplus, where the latter is determined by the usual Keynesian variables, which can be considered predetermined in the short-run period necessary for adjustment of the financial markets.

Just as we earlier argued that equations 13.2 and 13.7 were mutually consistent, so there is no reason to regard equations 13.3 and 13.9 as mutually exclusive. They are alternatives only in the sense that one may be better adapted than another as a tool for forecasting. And it is as a tool for short-term forecasting of payments flows in countries with a high degree of capital mobility that equation 13.9 and therefore the monetary approach comes into its own. To see why, note that in 13.9 most of the key variables – p, Y, e, p^* and presumably ϕ – can be taken as predetermined in the short run. The same is true of D_1 for countries whose monetary policy is based on the control of domestic credit expansion (as opposed to control of the money supply or the pursuit of an interest-rate target): that is, who do not sterilize.[12] That leaves only the interest rate i as endogenous in equation 13.9. But i also appears in equation 13.3. Indeed, whereas the interest elasticity of the demand for money is generally not so high as to make the capital flow forecast by 13.9 too sensitive to errors in forecasting i, the role of i is critical in 13.3, and a small error in the forecast can make all the difference between a large surplus and a large deficit. In other words, the monetary approach is indispensable to short-run payments forecasting under conditions of high capital mobility.

13.5 Summary

Capital mobility has become one of the dominant facts of international economic life over the past three decades. Initial attempts to explain capital flows centred on the flow theory, which postulated that a given interest differential would induce a permanent inflow or outflow. Portfolio theory showed that this was theoretically implausible; instead one should expect a change in interest rates to stimulate a *temporary* capital flow, although with a possibility of some more permanent effect on flows because of the portfolio growth effect. The resulting stock theory of the capital account is consistent with the monetary approach to the balance of payments, which is in general the best way of forecasting reserve changes for countries with a high degree of capital mobility and a monetary policy based on the control of domestic credit.

13.6 Bibliography

Classic articles on the transfer problem include Keynes (1929), reprinted in volume XVIII of Johnson and Moggridge (various years), Ohlin (1929) and Metzler (1942), all reprinted in Ellis and Metzler (1950); Samuelson (1952), reprinted in volume 2 of Stiglitz (1966); and Johnson (1956), reprinted in Johnson (1961) and Caves and Johnson (1968). A traditional classic on capital movements in general is Iversen (1936).

Mundell's analysis of the fiscal–monetary mix was published as Mundell (1962), reprinted as chapter 16 in Mundell (1968).

Portfolio theory was developed by Markowitz (1952) and Tobin (1958). It was first applied extensively to the study of international capital movements by Branson (1968). A careful technical discussion of the specification of portfolio balance models is provided by Branson and Henderson in volume 2 of Jones and Kenen (1985). Lessard's estimates of the welfare gains from risk diversification are in Lessard (1981). The model of Roberto Frenkel is included in Ffrench–Davis (1983). Dornbusch's treatment of capital mobility with a fixed exchange rate is contained in chapter 10 of Dornbusch (1980).

For the monetary approach one should again consult Frenkel and Johnson (1976), especially the paper of Michael Mussa. A reconciliation of orthodox and monetary approaches, incorporating the flow theory into the orthodox equation and therefore reaching results qualitatively similar to those reached at the end of this chapter, is to be found in Frenkel, Gylfason and Helliwell (1980). The Kouri–Porter synthesis appeared in Kouri and Porter (1974). Both that paper and Herring and Marston (1977) contain estimates of offset coefficients (and also of sterilization coefficients). Evidence against the perfect arbitrage hypothesis is to be found in the *Journal of International Economics*, May 1978 (see especially the paper of Kravis and Lipsey), in Isard (1977) and in Kravis and Lipsey (1978). The main sources for the new classical macroeconomics are Lucas (1981), Sargent and Wallace (1975) and Barro (1976).

Notes

1. See section 18.1 for a discussion of the Eurocurrency markets.
2. $(1.1)^{52} = 142$, or over 14,000 per cent per annum.
3. Note that the nomenclature of Chapter 11 has been reversed: F is now being used to signify foreign *liabilities* rather than *assets*. A dot over a variable signifies its rate of change.
4. This specification is crucially dependent on the assumption that the exchange rate is fixed and expected to remain so. With a flexible exchange rate the relevant comparison is between i and $i^* + E\hat{e}$, where $E\hat{e}$ is the expected rate of depreciation (see section 14.4).
5. Or reduce the current deficit. This symmetry is henceforth taken for granted rather than constantly reiterated. We deliberately avoid the common but pernicious shorthand 'improving the current account' – a larger surplus or smaller deficit is not necessarily better.
6. One is speaking here of investors in financial assets, rather than of the concept of investment in real capital goods that is normal in macroeconomic analysis.
7. A generalization of the stock theory, known as the stock adjustment model, postulates that the process of portfolio reallocation is spread out through time rather than occurring instantaneously. It is typically postulated that the capital flow can be described by an equation of the form $\dot{F} = \alpha(\overline{F} - F)$, where $\overline{F}$ is the equilibrium stock. Such a specification has often been found useful in econometric estimation. This alternative version does not, however, have significantly different theoretical implications from those of the pure stock theory discussed in the text. In particular, while a rise in the domestic interest rate will cause a capital inflow spread out over some period of time, the flow will gradually fall back to zero as F approaches $\overline{F}$.
8. It may be possible for the banks to shift their exchange risk, if a forward market exists, but *someone* will still have to bear the risk and will charge a risk premium for so doing (see appendix B to Chapter 14 for a sketch of the forward market).
9. Perhaps one should remark that Frenkel's paper predated, if not by much, the great Argentine exchange crisis of 1981, which initiated Argentina's decade of almost permanent crisis.
10. See section 14.4 for an explanation and discussion of rational expectations.
11. With capital mobility on the flow theory, the situation is essentially the same as with capital immobility, since correction of monetary disequilibrium through payments flows again necessarily requires time (see Frenkel, Gylfason and Helliwell 1980).
12. Countries that sterilize in a reasonably systematic way can be analyzed by a slight extension of the analysis, involving introduction of the concept of the 'sterilization coefficient' – the proportion of any reserve flow whose effect on the monetary base is neutralized through a change in domestic credit.

14

Flexible exchange rates

The analysis in Chapters 12 and 13 has been conducted on the assumption that the exchange rate is fixed by the central bank. It was not necessarily assumed that the rate of exchange is fixed in the sense of being unalterable: on the contrary, the implications of changes in the exchange rate were often analyzed. Such changes were, however, considered to be exogenous. The main point of the present chapter is to study how the rate of exchange is determined when it is not governed by governmental decision but by market forces. This sets the stage for a discussion of different forms of exchange-rate flexibility, and the factors that should govern a country's choice of exchange-rate policy, in the final section of the chapter.

An exchange rate whose value is not held within certain preannounced limits by official action – to act as the residual buyer or seller of foreign exchange whenever necessary – is said to float. The following sections consider a series of theories of how the value of a floating rate is determined: the current balance model, the purchasing power parity (PPP) model, the Mundell–Fleming model, the asset market view, and recent theories as to why asset markets may be badly behaved. In addition to describing the theories themselves, some of their principal implications, as regards the impact of various policy measures, are studied and compared to the results under a regime of fixed exchange rates.

14.1 The current balance model

If there were no capital mobility, and if the exchange rate were floating freely – meaning that the central bank would not intervene in the foreign exchange market at all – then the current account would have to be in equilibrium if the foreign exchange market were to clear, since there would be no other accounts to balance out any disequilibrium in the current account. What force would make it clear? Just as price theory shows how price flexibility can clear other competitive markets, so the traditional answer is that variations in the price of foreign exchange – that is, in the exchange rate – could ensure that the foreign exchange market clears. This answer provides the basis for one of the oldest theories of what determines the exchange rate under floating: that the rate will adjust to the point where the demand for foreign

242

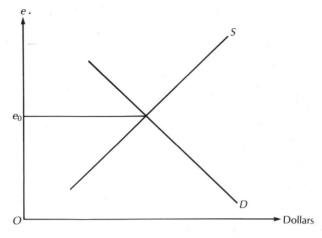

Figure 14.1 Current balance model

exchange to buy imports and make other current payments will equal the supply that is forthcoming from the sale of exports and other current receipts.

In terms of Figure 14.1, the exchange rate would be determined at the value of e_0, where demand for dollars equals the supply. What lies behind the demand and supply curves of Figure 14.1 was examined in the course of the elasticities analysis of Section 12.3. (There is, however, one difference in interpretation. The demand and supply curves were there defined on the assumption that real income was being held constant by compensatory fiscal–monetary policy, but any such assumption would be out of place in the present context.)

There is another technical point that has to be mentioned before proceeeding to the substantive analysis: whether one can reasonably assume that the demand and supply curves have the shapes shown in Figure 14.1. The answer given in Chapter 12 was that when one is considering the demand and supply curves that incorporate the adjustments taking place over several years, this is entirely reasonable: empirical evidence is pretty conclusive that the Marshall–Lerner condition is satisfied in the medium run. But the foreign-exchange market has to clear day by day or even hour by hour, not lumping together all the demands and supplies over a couple of years. The discussion of the J-curve in section 12.3 showed why an increase in the exchange rate can normally be expected (at least for industrial countries) to result in a short-run *decrease* in the trade balance. (The impact effect of depreciation is to reduce the dollar value of exports, which are largely denominated in pesos, relative to that of imports, which are largely denominated in dollars. Even when existing contracts have been fulfilled, the greater reduction in the dollar price of exports relative to the reduction in the dollar price of imports – for countries with some market power at least on the export side – will leave the trade balance in greater deficit or smaller surplus than it would have been without depreciation until volumes have time to adjust.) That means that a depreciation would increase the excess demand for dollars and so increase the pressure towards depreciation. In sum, a freely floating exchange rate of a country with pricing practices typical for an industrial country would be dynamically unstable without capital mobility!

There are two ways around this problem. One is to suppose that the foreign exchange market is exclusively a forward market. That disposes of the denomination problem completely, since traders know the exchange rate they will receive at the time they sign their contracts, and it also opens the possibility of price movements going sufficiently far to kill or kindle the interest of buyers as necessary to ensure short-run stability. The second way around the problem is more realistic, although it does not enable one to tell a story in strict conformity with the assumption of capital immobility. This is to assume that there are well-informed speculators in the market, who are prepared to take short-term positions buying or selling one currency for the other to smooth out excess demands or supplies that may arise, but because they are well informed their interventions cancel out to zero over the course of each year or so, thus leaving the current account in balance over that time. It is, of course, worth remembering that it was necessary to make an assumption like this in order to be able to develop the model: where there are reasons to doubt the realism of the assumption, a floating exchange rate should be expected not to function very efficiently – it would tend to gyrate wildly before enough speculators were drawn in to dampen the natural instability of the current account.

One of the principal theorems to have been drawn from the current balance model is that a floating rate will *insulate* a country against foreign shocks to real income or to prices. The analysis of the foreign trade multiplier in section 12.2 showed how a foreign boom would raise foreign imports and thus our exports and, in turn, our imports. This mechanism cannot work under a floating rate that maintains the current balance in equilibrium, or $X - M = 0$:

$$Y = A(Y,i) + (X - M) = A(Y,i) \tag{14.1}$$

becomes independent of X. Intuitively, the rise in the demand for exports causes the peso to appreciate to whatever extent is necessary to prevent a trade surplus emerging, and thus the domestic economy is insulated from the foreign boom.[1] The theorem is symmetrical: the rest of the world no longer imports our expansions or depressions.

Since the foreign interest rate influences our economy only indirectly via its effect on foreign incomes and thus imports in the current balance model, one may draw the corollary that a floating rate also insulates against changes in the foreign interest rate.

The analysis of Chapters 12 and 13 has also emphasized that, under a fixed exchange rate, shocks to foreign prices will tend to spread to our economy via (imperfect) arbitrage. This mechanism is also ruptured by a floating exchange rate determined by the current balance model. A rise in foreign prices, for example, would tend to increase the real exchange rate and so generate a surplus unless it were offset by an equivalent fall in e, to maintain ep^* constant. Conclusion: e will vary to insulate the domestic economy from variations in p^*. Symmetrically, we can neutralize the external effects of an inflation greater than that in the rest of the world by depreciating at a rate equal to the inflation differential:

$$\hat{e} = \hat{p} - \hat{p}^* \tag{14.2}$$

A second important theorem states that fiscal and monetary policy will both have *more* effect (on the level of real income and thus employment) with a floating rate than with a fixed rate. The analysis assumes fixed prices in the Keynesian tradition. The theorem can be illustrated with a diagram introduced by Mundell (see Figure 14.2). Real income is on the horizontal axis and the exchange rate on the vertical axis. The curve XX shows the locus of points of equilibrium in the goods market. It slopes up because an increase in income implies an equal rise in output, while aggregate demand will rise by less (so long as the marginal propensity to consume is less than 1); a depreciation of the currency is needed to stimulate exports and substitute imports and so close the output gap. There is excess demand for goods (EDG) above XX and excess supply below. The curve FF shows the points of balance

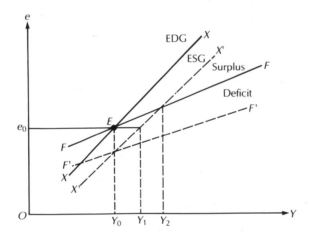

Figure 14.2 Policy changes in the current balance model

of payments equilibrium. It too slopes up because a rise in income pulls in imports which have to be paid for by stimulating more exports, which, in turn, requires a depreciation. FF is less steeply sloped than XX since a given increase in Y requires a larger depreciation to restore goods market equilibrium than to restore payments equilibrium, due to the fact that leakages from the spending stream take the forms of saving and taxes, as well as imports. The balance of payments is in surplus above FF and in deficit below. Given a floating exchange rate that guarantees current account balance, the economy goes to point E.

An expansionary fiscal or monetary policy pushes the XX curve right, to a position such as $X'X'$, which was previously in the area of excess supply of goods. If the exchange rate were fixed, output would expand from Y_0 to Y_1. But given that the current balance must remain in equilibrium, the economy must remain on *FF* and so output must expand to Y_2, which is greater than Y_1. Therefore, expansionary fiscal–monetary policies are more potent under floating rates without capital mobility. Intuitively, the leakage from the expenditure stream represented by an increased current deficit is plugged by floating the exchange rate, thus increasing the multiplier.

The analysis of Chapter 12 showed that another way of expanding income under a fixed exchange rate is by a restrictive commercial policy, such as increasing tariffs on imports. This again has the effect of shifting *XX* to the right, to *X'X'*. However, it also increases the balance of payments surplus corresponding to any combination of *Y* and *e*: that is, it shifts the *FF* curve down. In fact, it must shift *FF* down far enough to intersect *X'X'* at the initial income level Y_0. One can see this by referring back to equation 14.1, which shows that no policy that operates by influencing *M* – when there is a constraint that says *X* − *M* = *0* – can succeed in influencing *Y*.[2] Commercial policy is therefore completely impotent to influence income under floating rates.

The classic article 'Flexible exchange rates and employment policy' (1961) in which Mundell first established the two preceding theorems, was written when his native Canada had a floating exchange rate and a governor of its central bank called James Coyne. Mr Coyne wanted to fight inflation by a restrictive monetary policy (pushing *XX* to the left) and simultaneously to fight unemployment by increasing protection (pushing *XX* back to the right and *FF* down). Mundell's analysis showed once and for all (one hopes) why this was not a very bright idea: however much one may desire supplementary policies to reduce the unemployment cost of fighting inflation through a restrictive monetary policy, a restrictive commercial policy does not fit the bill.

14.2 Purchasing power parity

Another old theory about what determines the exchange rate of a floating currency, first analyzed extensively by the Swedish economist Gustav Cassell (1866–1945) although it has been traced back to 1601, appeals to the concept of purchasing power parity (henceforth PPP). The basic idea is that the exchange rate will adjust to ensure that a dollar will buy as much in our country as it would at home. The strong version of PPP incorporating that idea may be expressed:

$$e = p/p^* \tag{14.3}$$

that is, the exchange rate is the ratio of our price level to the foreign price level. There is also a weak version of PPP, which argues that for various reasons (some of which will be discussed in due course) the exchange rate may differ from p/p^*, but that this divergence will depend on structural characteristics and thus be constant or at least exogenous. This version may be expressed.

$$e = \pi p/p^* \tag{14.4}$$

which, for the case of a constant (rather than merely exogenous) π implies equation 14.2:

$$\hat{e} = \hat{p} - \hat{p}^*$$

The depreciation of the exchange rate will equal the excess of domestic inflation over world inflation.

There are at least three different views of the economic forces that are supposed to underlie equation 14.3 or 14.4. In one view there is something inherent in the nature of money and economic rationality that must lead to PPP and there is no need to specify an adjustment mechanism that ultimately leads to establishment of the PPP condition (we do not pretend to understand this view). A second interpretation appeals to goods arbitrage: if $p > ep^*$, our country would be inundated by foreign goods seeking to take advantage of the better prices available in our market. There are two difficulties with this view. The first is that it does not explain why e rather than p adjusts when $p > ep^*$. The second is that there is abundant empirical evidence[3] that arbitrage is not sufficiently perfect to guarantee that p always remains close to ep^*. But this does not, as has sometimes been assumed, dispose of the usefulness of the PPP concept in explaining exchange rates, for there is a third and much more persuasive interpretation of what lies behind PPP.

The third view is that PPP is a necessary condition for equilibrium. The equation for the current account is $TB(Y, ep^*/p)$. If we require of equilibrium both that $TB(\ldots) = 0$, as in the current balance model of the last section, and that $Y = Y_{fe}$ – that is, full employment – then ep^*/p must have a well-defined value in equilibrium. Call that value π, and we have equation 14.4 as a necessary condition for equilibrium. This interpretation, it is true, works only for the weak version of equation 14.4 and not the strong version of 14.3.

There is in fact strong empirical evidence, not just that π is not necessarily equal to unity, but that it varies in a systematic way with the level of per capita real income or the stage of development of a country. The reason is that the rise in productivity that occurs in the course of development and that is the primary cause of rising per capita income is spread unevenly between sectors. Specifically, productivity tends to rise most rapidly in sectors like manufacturing and agriculture that largely produce traded goods and to grow much less in most services which are predominantly non-traded goods. Assuming that wages are equalized by competition between the two sectors,[4] this means that the relative price of non-traded goods (p_n/p_m) rises in the course of development. In a rich country, haircuts and restaurant meals become expensive relative to radios and cars because they present much less opportunity for raising labour productivity. But p and p^* are indices of the general price level, which consists of the prices of both traded and non-traded goods. Since p_m, the price of traded goods, is more or less equalized by arbitrage, it follows that the general price index (expressed in a common currency) will tend to be higher in the more developed country.[5]

This stylized fact about differential productivity growth explains what at first sight seemed to be a contradiction to PPP. During the 1960s it was observed that the most rapidly growing countries, notably Japan, were experiencing rates of inflation well above those in their more slowly growing trading partners, like the United States. A simple application of the elasticities analysis would have suggested that the current account of the balance of payments would develop a deficit. However, the price index that showed fast Japanese inflation was the consumer price index (CPI), and that fast inflation reflected the rapid rise in the relative price of non-traded goods that was a consequence of the rapid productivity growth in traded goods. If one looked at a price index confined to traded goods, like the unit-value index for exports, one found that Japanese prices were *declining* relative to American prices. Despite the relative behaviour of the CPIs, Japan was in fact gaining competitiveness relative to the United States, a fact that finally resulted in an explosion of the Japanese current account surplus at the end of the decade. The example illustrates just how essential it is to take account of differences in trend productivity growth in making PPP comparisons.

There are two other implications of differential productivity growth that are sufficiently interesting and important to merit a brief discussion, even though they represent diversions from the theme of PPP as a determinant of the exchange rate. The first involves cross-section comparisons between real-income levels in countries at different stages of development. The crude way to make such comparisons is to take figures for GNP per head in terms of the national currency and convert them into dollars at the going exchange rate. The result of this all-too-common procedure is to exaggerate the differences in real income between rich and poor countries, since non-traded goods are counted in the rich country's income at a much higher price (reflecting the differences in productivity in the traded goods industries) than they are in the poor country. That is not for a moment to deny that international differences in real income are large: in fact they are still staggering even when computed correctly, as has now been done for a large number of countries by a research team based at the University of Pennsylvania and headed by Irving Kravis. The correct basis of comparison involves establishing the cost of buying specified quantities of comparable goods in each of numerous expenditure categories for each of the countries to be compared, to yield a PPP for each category of expenditure relative to a numeraire country. Those PPPs are then used to convert expenditure in each category to the numeraire currency unit. The ratio between a country's expenditures and those of the numeraire country then reflects the ratio of the quantities consumed in the two countries.

The second diversion relates to what is known as the Scandinavian model of inflation. The model considers a small country with a fixed exchange rate and a passive monetary policy in which the prices of traded goods are determined by arbitrage, from which it follows that the rate of inflation in traded goods is determined by, and equal to, the world rate of inflation in traded goods ($\hat{p}_m^*$). Wages are assumed to be settled each year at the level that the market will bear but no more, which implies that wage inflation is $\hat{w} = \hat{p}_m^* + \rho$, where ρ is the rate of productivity growth in the traded goods industries. Suppose for simplicity (only) that productivity growth is zero in the non-traded goods industries. Then, assuming that the trade unions or competition in the labour market ensure that wages grow at the same rate in both sectors, inflation in non-traded goods will equal wage growth $\hat{p}_n = \hat{w}$. If non-traded and traded goods have weights of α and $(1 - \alpha)$ respectively in the price index, the overall rate of inflation is given by:

$$\hat{p} = \alpha(\hat{p}_m{}^* + \rho) + (1 - \alpha)\hat{p}_m{}^*$$
$$= \hat{p}_m{}^* + \alpha\rho \tag{14.5}$$

Thus inflation is determined by international inflation plus a fraction of the rate of productivity growth. Two features are worth noting. First, faster productivity growth *raises* inflation – in direct contrast to models based on Phillips curves or real-wage resistance, where higher productivity reduces price increases for any given level of wage inflation or helps to reconcile inconsistent real-income claims. Second, a country that has a rate of productivity growth greater than that abroad can import more inflation than is present in the exporting country! That is, in fact, just what happpened in countries like Germany, Japan and Sweden in the 1960s.

We now return to the main theme of this section, which is the usefulness of the notion of PPP in explaining the level of a floating exchange rate. It has so far been suggested that the relative version of PPP is a necessary condition for equilibrium, but that the value of π can be expected to change systematically over time depending on relative rates of productivity growth. In the simple case considered in the preceding paragraph, where productivity is constant in the non-traded goods industry, it is easy to confirm[6] that

$$\hat{\pi} = \alpha(\rho^* - \rho)$$

The equilibrium rate of depreciation therefore becomes:

$$\hat{e} = \hat{p} - \hat{p}^* - \alpha(\rho - \rho^*) \tag{14.6}$$

Our depreciation can be slower if our productivity growth (in traded goods) is greater than that abroad.[7]

There are certain circumstances under which equation 14.6 will give an exact rule for the depreciation necessary to restore equilibrium: when equilibrium is disturbed by a monetary shock. The classic case is Milton Friedman's helicopter sprinkling fiat money around, which everyone then rushes out to spend, driving prices up. Everyone knows that any well-behaved economy is homogeneous of degree zero in all nominal variables. That means that H, p and e must increase in the same proportion to re-establish equilibrium: equation 14.6 must be exactly satisfied when p rises because of a pure monetary shock.

In reality the money supply is not typically increased by helicopter distribution but rather by government spending programmes that have powerful transitional real effects. Nevertheless, after the monetary expansion has ended, the real effects will tend to die away and what remains is essentially a monetary change. It was in just these circumstances, when the monetary expansions undertaken to finance belligerents' efforts in the First World War had come to an end but had left a legacy of vastly different cumulative inflations since the pre-war fixed exchange rates were abandoned, that Gustav Cassell applied his theory in order to calculate the parities at which rates ought once again to be fixed. Countries like Britain that ignored such calculations and returned to their pre-war parities for the sake of nostalgia paid a high price in terms of unemployment and social strife as the government tried to force wages down. Another good example of the helpful role that a PPP calculation can play in neutralizing an essentially monetary change is provided by the experience of Brazil, which has long followed monetary policies markedly more inflationary than those in its main trading partners but eliminated the damage this would otherwise cause to the balance of payments by depreciating the cruzeiro broadly in accordance with PPP.

There are other circumstances under which equation 14.6 will not give a correct figure for the exchange-rate change necessary to restore equilibrium. These circumstances arise whenever the shock that disturbs equilibrium is essentially a real shock rather than a monetary shock. Suppose, for example, that the price of oil rises, thus worsening the terms of trade, and that it is necessary to adjust this deficit as has been assumed so far in this chapter. That adjustment would require either a fall in real income or a real depreciation. Ruling out the former as involving an irrational waste of real resources, it becomes necessary in this case to depreciate more than is indicated by 14.6. How much more? That cannot be answered by PPP: it requires instead a knowledge of the elasticities. The moral is that PPP should not be applied blindly, but that consideration needs to be given as to whether there are real shocks that create a need for changes in π. The need to exercise such care does not constitute a reason for refusing to exploit such guidance as the theory can give.

14.3 The Mundell–Fleming model

The model that now bears the names of Robert Mundell and the British economist J. Marcus Fleming (1911–76) was introduced more or less simultaneously and apparently independently by the two of them in the early 1960s, shortly after they ceased to be colleagues in the IMF's research department because of Mundell's move to Chicago. It advances on the work so far discussed in this chapter in introducing capital mobility, in the form of the flow theory examined in section 13.2.

The other assumptions are conventional enough. The basic framework is the IS/LM/BP model, with prices (or at least wages) assumed to be fixed. The balance on current account is determined by income and relative prices, ep^*/p. There are no lags: the economy moves to its new equilibrium immediately. The exchange rate floats freely, so that the current deficit is equal to the capital inflow (or vice versa) with no change in reserves. Finally, expectations are static: agents always expect the indefinite perpetuation of the present. The last assumption is crucial in enabling one to treat the interest rates in the two countries as representing the opportunity costs of holding assets in the one country rather than the other, and thus continuing to use a capital flow equation of the form $f(i,i^*)$ introduced in section 13.2. In general, of course, one would expect that investors will be interested in comparing their total expected yields from holding foreign rather than domestic assets, which points to the need for a specification $f(i,i^* + E\hat{e})$. This generalization is introduced in the following section. For the moment, one just has to imagine that investors never have any expectation that the exchange rate is more likely to rise than to fall.

A lot of attention is paid in the literature to the case of perfect capital mobility –

perhaps more than it deserves. With a floating exchange rate, capital mobility could be perfect only if investors had complete confidence in the future maintenance of today's exchange rate, or else if they were completely risk neutral. The former assumption is totally implausible, given that actual floating rates are forever bobbing around. The latter assumption is usually regarded as a very strong one. Accordingly, the case of perfect capital mobility should be treated more as a point of intellectual reference – like the case of perfect immobility, the current balance model of section 14.1 – than as a model to be seriously applied in understanding the real world or giving policy advice. The important case is the intermediate one of finite capital mobility.

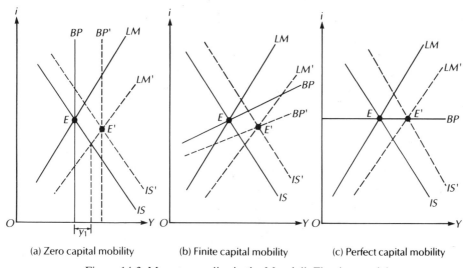

| (a) Zero capital mobility | (b) Finite capital mobility | (c) Perfect capital mobility |

Figure 14.3 Monetary policy in the Mundell–Fleming model

The analysis of monetary policy in the Mundell–Fleming model is illustrated in Figure 14.3 for the three cases of capital mobility. Consider first the case of zero capital mobility (shown in Figure 14.3(a)), which is reflected in a vertical BP curve. Initial equilibrium is at E. The BP curve necessarily cuts the IS/LM intersection at E because of the assumption of a floating exchange rate, which guarantees that the balance of payments be in equilibrium. Now consider the effect of an expansionary monetary policy: that is, an increase in domestic credit. The effect of this is to push the LM curve to the right, to LM'. With a fixed exchange rate that would be the end of the story, at least in the short run:[8] income would expand by y_1 and the balance of payments would go into deficit. But with a floating exchange rate the story cannot end there, even in the short run, because the balance of payments cannot go into deficit. The incipient deficit instead causes the exchange rate to rise (that is, the domestic currency to depreciate), which pushes both IS and BP to the right as analyzed in the elasticities approach analysis of section 12.3. This continues until all three curves intersect at the same point, E'. This point involves a lower interest rate than that which held at E, since monetary policy was expansionary.[9] (We can be sure

Table 14.1 Short-run comparative static effects in the Mundell-Fleming model

	Fixed exchange rate			Floating exchange rate		
Degree of capital mobility	0	+	∞	0	+	∞
Monetary expansion, $\Delta D > 0$	$y_1 > 0$	y_1	0	$> y_1$	$> y_1$	$> y_1$
Fiscal expansion, $\Delta G > 0$	$y_2 > 0$	y_2	$> y_2$	$> y_2$	$+, \lessgtr y_2$	0
Commercial restriction, $\Delta t > 0$	$y_3 > 0$	y_3	$> y_3$	0^1	0^1	0^1

[1] Or negative, if the Laursen–Metzler effect holds (see nn. 1 and 2).

that all three curves will intersect at the same point because we are requiring payments equilibrium, as well as equilibrium in the goods and money markets, and there is a third endogenous variable, e, to add to the pair Y, i of the fixed-rate case.) This necessarily occurs with a Y that has risen by more than y_1, thus showing that monetary expansion is more effective in raising income with a floating exchange rate in the case of zero capital mobility.

Table 14.1 has been designed to summarize the various results that will be established in this section. The results just established are entered in the first row, which shows the effects on Y of a monetary expansion ($\Delta D > 0$). The first column records that with a fixed rate and zero capital mobility the monetary expansion raises Y by an amount $y_1 > 0$ as illustrated in Figure 14.3(a). The fourth column records that with a floating rate the effect on Y is bigger than y_1, which is used as a standard of reference.

The analysis is little changed in the case of finite capital mobility shown by a positively sloping BP curve in Figure 14.3(b). Monetary expansion shifts the LM curve right exactly as before, and the short-run equilibrium with a fixed exchange rate is the same with finite capital mobility as with capital immobility. At the point where IS and LM' intersect there is again an incipient deficit, which implies that the exchange rate must increase. Equilibrium under a floating rate again occurs where the three curves intersect, with an income expansion larger than with fixed rates.

The case of perfect capital mobility differs in that, as already seen in section 13.2, a monetary expansion under fixed rates is immediately reversed through a capital outflow. Thus monetary policy is impotent to influence income with a fixed exchange rate, as reflected in the zero entry in Table 14.1. With a floating rate, however, the monetary expansion causes a depreciation and an increase in income until such point as the demand for money has risen (because of the increased income) to match the rise in supply. At that point the country has developed a current account surplus matched by a capital outflow. It can be seen that income again expands by more than in the reference case.

Consider next the effects of a fiscal expansion (an increase in government spending or cut in taxes), illustrated in Figure 14.4. The impact effect is to shift the IS curve right to IS'. With a fixed exchange rate and zero capital mobility short-run equilibrium would be at E', with a payments deficit. The income expansion of y_2 thus provides our reference case. Since there is a deficit at E', the currency must

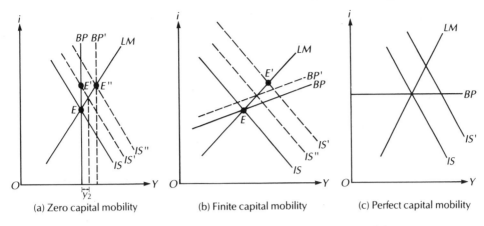

(a) Zero capital mobility   (b) Finite capital mobility   (c) Perfect capital mobility

Figure 14.4 Fiscal policy in the Mundell–Fleming model

depreciate, pushing *IS* and *BP* to the right until their intersection falls on *LM* at *E''*. Thus income expands more than under fixed rates; the potency of fiscal as well as monetary policy is increased by floating, as we found in section 14.1.

This conclusion is critically dependent upon the assumption of zero capital mobility, as Figure 14.4(b) shows. *E'* is now a position of payments *surplus*, not deficit; at least, that is, in the case illustrated, where *LM* is steeper than *BP*. In that case, the exchange rate must fall, pushing *IS* left and *BP* up till an equilibrium occurs somewhere on the segment of *LM* between *E* and *E'*. Income still expands as a result of the expansionary fiscal policy, but by *less* than under fixed rates. Had *BP* been steeper than *LM*, however (reflecting a lower degree of capital mobility), income would have risen more than in the reference case. In either event income rises, but the rise may be greater than, equal to, or less than the rise in the reference case, as the entry in Table 14.1 is intended to indicate.

With perfect capital mobility the situation is different again. With a fixed exchange rate the rightward move of the *IS* curve is matched by a rightward shift of the *LM* curve induced by a capital inflow, as seen in section 13.2; fiscal policy is thus very effective. With a floating rate, however, *LM* cannot move right – the money supply is fixed. Equilibrium therefore has to remain where it was, at the intersection of *LM* and *BP*, since neither moves. The exchange rate makes this happen, by falling to the extent necessary to crowd out a volume of net export expenditures equal to the fiscal stimulus. Thus in this case fiscal policy is impotent to influence income. This provides the final element of a famous set of results: monetary policy is impotent under fixed rates but very effective under floating, while fiscal policy is the exact reverse – all, however, under the assumption of perfect capital mobility.

Consider now the effects of a restrictive commercial policy: for example, an increase in tariffs. The impact effect of this is to push both *IS* and *BP* to the right (Figure 14.5). The intersection of *IS'* and *LM* establishes our reference case, the rise in income that would be induced under a fixed rate, at *E'*. However, *BP* moves to the right by more than does *IS*: the *Y* that equilibrates the balance of payments increases by $(1/m)$ times the reduction in imports due to expenditure switching, while the Y that balances the goods market (for a given level of the interest rate) increases by only $1/(s + m)$ times the initial cut in imports. This means that E' is a point of payments surplus, and so the domestic currency must appreciate to restore equilibrium. In fact, since BP' intersects LM to the right of IS' as long as E' is to the right of IS, equilibrium must lie at point E. Commercial policy cannot increase income (as was already found in section 14.1) under a floating exchange rate with capital immobility.[10]

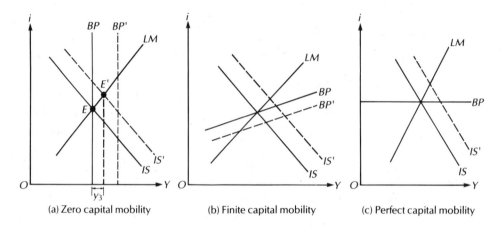

(a) Zero capital mobility   (b) Finite capital mobility   (c) Perfect capital mobility

Figure 14.5 Commercial policy in the Mundell–Fleming model

Figures 14.5(b) and (c) show that the analysis is essentially the same with finite or even perfect capital mobility. In both cases the exchange rate has to fall enough to crowd out completely the expenditure switching induced by the rise in tariffs. Mr Coyne's proposed policy mix cannot be saved by appealing to capital mobility.

Another question that is interesting to ask is whether the conclusion that a flexible exchange rate isolates a country from foreign shocks (to real income, the interest rate or prices) remains valid under capital mobility. Unfortunately, this question cannot be answered by using the graphical analysis that has sufficed up to now, but requires slightly more advanced mathematical techniques. The proofs, which involve elementary matrix algebra, are therefore relegated to an appendix to the chapter.

It is there shown that a floating exchange rate still insulates the domestic economy against changes in foreign income and inflation, under both perfect and imperfect capital mobility. An increase in foreign income still causes an appreciation of the domestic currency sufficient to prevent any increase in domestic income, so the business cycle would be desynchronized internationally. The domestic currency would still appreciate gradually over time to neutralize a foreign inflation and leave domestic inflation unchanged.

In contrast, an increase in the foreign interest rate is transmitted to the domestic economy by incipient interest arbitrage, which causes the domestic currency to depreciate and income to rise by whatever is needed to restore the demand for money (which fell because of the higher interest rate) to equal the unchanged supply. The impact on income is opposite to that under fixed exchange rates, where a rise in the foreign interest rate reduces income.

14.4 The asset market approach

More or less coincidentally with the move of the main industrial countries to floating exchange rates in 1973, economists became gravely dissatisfied with the inadequacies of the Mundell–Fleming model. It embodies a number of assumptions, like the flow theory of the capital account and yield comparisons made purely in terms of interest rates with no consideration of expected changes in the exchange rate, that are clearly unrealistic but are vital to the conclusions that emerge. Furthermore, the conclusion that floating rates would break the international synchronization of the business cycle did not seem to be consistent with the facts, nor was it borne out by the simulation of macroeconometric models like the Canadian RDX–2.

The needed theoretical advance was launched in a series of papers at the Flexible Exchange Rates and Stabilization Policy Conference near Stockholm in 1975. The new generation of models were quickly dubbed the 'asset market approach' because of their emphasis that moneys are assets and that their relative price (the nominal exchange rate) is therefore determined by the willingness to hold the existing stocks of those moneys. Ever since Keynes, economists have recognized that the price of bonds (or, what amounts to the same thing, the rate of interest) is determined by the stocks of money and bonds in conjunction with the portfolio preferences of wealth owners: the asset market approach argues that international capital mobility is sufficiently high to make that same type of force dominant in the foreign exchange market. This is not to deny that over any period of time the flow demand for foreign exchange must equal the flow supply, but to affirm that current account flows are so dwarfed by the flows on capital account that might potentially be generated by portfolio adjustments that one can treat the latter factor as the proximate determinant of the exchange rate. This is in fact an application of the stock theory of the capital account to the context where the exchange rate floats instead of being pegged by the central bank.

It is important at this point to distinguish between two aspects of the concept of perfect capital mobility. One relates to instantaneous adjustment, the other to perfect substitutability between assets. The Mundell–Fleming concept assumes both, but it is quite possible to conceive of either without the other. In fact, the asset market approach always assumes instantaneous adjustment: this is almost tauto-logical, inasmuch as this approach represents the application of the stock theory of the capital account to a regime of floating rates. In contrast, perfect substitutability is sometimes assumed and sometimes not. Since the empirical evidence points strongly against the validity of the perfect substitutability assumption, it would be highly desirable to analyze the more general case. Unfortunately models that do this become very complicated, and so most of this section will assume perfect substitutability between assets (perfect interest arbitrage).

The simplest version of the asset market approach is the monetary approach, introduced at the Stockholm conference by the Israeli economist Jacob Frenkel (b. 1943), who became director of the research department of the IMF in 1987. This postulates that national price levels are determined by the quantity theory, while the strong version of PPP then determines the exchange rate at the level that equates prices internationally. This sort of theory provides a useful first approximation in the circumstances of the German hyperinflation of the 1920s to which Frenkel applied it. But it is not adequate in more normal circumstances, where changes in real exchange rates and interest rates are not necessarily overwhelmed by changes in inflation rates, as Frenkel himself subsequently emphasized.

More general versions of the asset market approach improve on the Mundell–Fleming model in recognizing that investors are not interested in the comparison between nominal interest rates on two different currencies but rather in the comparison between their yields, including the expected rate of appreciation of one in terms of the other. With perfect interest arbitrage, that implies:

$$i = i^* + E\hat{e} \qquad (14.7)$$

The domestic interest rate must be equal to the foreign interest rate plus the expected rate of depreciation.

Equation 14.7 directs attention to another way in which the asset market approach breaks decisively with the models that have been examined up to now: the yields on different assets, and thus the prices that investors will be prepared to pay for them, depend not merely on objective interest rates but also on subjective *expectations*. Expectations can sometimes change rapidly, due to anything from climatic disasters to political assassinations to rumours about what the latest money supply figures signify. Such sudden changes in expectations, it is argued, are what lie behind the sudden price changes that are typical of all asset markets, including the exchange markets.

It is evident that any model that includes expectations as an element that determines yields, and thus asset prices, needs to embody a hypothesis about how expectations are formed. Traditionally, economists tended to minimize the role of such factors as those mentioned in the last paragraph and to concentrate on alternative possible ways in which the actual changes in some variable, say x, may influence expectations as to its own future value, x_{+1}. The four leading simple hypotheses are the following.

1. Static expectations, $Ex_{+1} = x$. Agents expect the present value of x to be maintained in the future. This is the simple hypothesis utilized in the Mundell–Fleming model and implicitly in many other places where expectations were not explicitly mentioned.

2. Adaptive expectations, $Ex_{+1} = E_{-1}x + \alpha(x - E_{-1}x) = \alpha x + (1 - \alpha) E_{-1}x$. Agents have some expectation before the present period starts of the value that x will take; this prior expectation is denoted $E_{-1}x$. When they observe the

value that x actually takes on in this period, they adapt their expectation for the future a part (α) of the way towards what actually happened this period. This is equivalent to taking a weighted average of what actually happened and what was previously expected to happen as one's estimate of what is likely to happen in the next period, as is shown after the second equality sign. This hypothesis became famous in the analysis of inflation, where it formalized the argument that an inflation that exceeded the expected rate would serve to pull up that expected rate, which would in turn shift up the Phillips curve and so ensure that any given unemployment level below the so-called natural rate would result in permanently accelerating inflation. It also implies that any value that is maintained constant long enough will come to be the expected value.

3. Extrapolative expectations, $Ex_{+1} = x + \alpha(x - x_{-1}) = (1 + \alpha)x - \alpha x_{-1}$. Agents extrapolate the change ($x - x_{-1}$) that they have just observed into the future, adding some fraction or multiple of the latest change on to the latest value observed. This is a description of the behaviour that leads to bandwagon effects or speculative runs: the exchange rate starts moving (up or down), which provokes more sales or purchases in the hope of getting out or in before it is too late.

4. Regressive expectations, $Ex_{+1} = \alpha x + (1 - \alpha)\bar{x}$. Agents have some estimate $\bar{x}$ of the normal or equilibrium value of x, and when x deviates from $\bar{x}$ they expect that it will tend to return to $\bar{x}$ over time.

Note that, with the exception of regressive expectations, which provide scope for any sort of information to make an impact on $\bar{x}$, all of these hypotheses amount to using some arbitrary rule of thumb based only on the past behaviour of x in order to forecast future values of x. This, it is now argued, is in general a patently irrational way of forming expectations: if a popular and responsible president is assassinated, that fact is likely to suggest that x will be different from what it would otherwise have been, and one can decide that without waiting to see what starts to happen to x. The now-popular concept of *rational expectations* is based on the idea that agents seek to make the best possible use of the information available to them in forming their expectations. That may seem a pretty obvious idea – so much so that the student might wonder why anyone should ever have entertained any other hypothesis. The reason is that it still leaves the very big question: what is implied by making the best possible use of all available information? It was only after[11] John Muth (b. 1930) had suggested an answer that was both intuitively appealing and amenable to theoretical modelling that rational expectations emerged as the leading expectational hypothesis. Muth's answer was: the best available forecast is the forecast that comes out of using the available information in the analyst's own model. So the modelling strategy is: we assume that the agents know the model and assume it to be true, ask how that implies they make their forecast, and then add that forecasting procedure to the model. The result is to generate forecasts that have the important property of internal consistency: if everyone acts that way, events will tend to ratify the decisions made on the basis of the forecasts (at least if the model is a correct depiction of reality). In fact, when there are no stochastic shocks, this procedure generates exactly the perfect foresight path, along which events indeed unfold as they had been expected to unfold. Rational expectations are the stochastic analogue of perfect foresight.

It is worth noting that rational expectations are not necessarily inconsistent with all of the other hypotheses about expectations formation. In particular, where agents do not know what the economic structure is, but have to learn, adaptive expectations are rational. Or, where there is an equilibrium with some asymptotic adjustment mechanism pushing x towards it, regressive expectations are rational.

Many of the asset market models also break with the Mundell–Fleming model by abandoning the assumption that the domestic price level is fixed. The alternative assumptions incorporated in the models have varied, although they have all been simple: for example, determination by the quantity theory, or sticky prices whose rate of change depends on the level of excess demand (a Phillips-curve type of specification).

The most famous of the asset market models is due to Dornbusch. It assumes perfect interest arbitrage, so 14.7 provides one of the equations:

$$i = i^* + E\hat{e} \tag{14.7}$$

Expectations of exchange-rate changes are assumed to be determined in accordance with the regressive expectations formula: the exchange rate will adjust part way towards its equilibrium value $\bar{e}$. This is, in fact, in accord with rational expectations (for the appropriate value of θ), since the postulated theory of inflation is one where prices adjust depending on the extent of excess demand, which falls towards zero as prices and therefore the exchange rate approach equilibrium:[12]

$$E\hat{e} = \theta(\bar{e} - e) \tag{14.8}$$

Asset market equilibrium requires that the supply of money be equal to the demand:

$$h = p + \xi y - \eta i \tag{14.9}$$

In the simple version of the model, it is assumed that y can be treated as an exogenous variable, whose value is fixed at the full-employment level. Furthermore, prices are assumed sticky, so that p is predetermined at any moment of time. The above three equations therefore determine the values of the three endogenous variables i, e and $E\hat{e}$ as functions of the exogenous variables i^*, $\bar{e}$, h and y and the predetermined variable p. The equations represent the conditions that have to be satisfied if the asset markets are to be in equilibrium: that is, if investors are to be satisfied to hold the existing stocks of money, of domestic bonds with peso yield i, and of foreign bonds with peso yield $i^* + E\hat{e}$.

The above equations can be solved out by substitution from 14.7 and 14.8 into 14.9 and rearrangement to derive a relation between e and p that must be satisfied if the asset markets are to be in equilibrium:

$$e = \bar{e} - (1/\theta\eta)[p - h + \xi y - \eta i^*] \tag{14.10}$$

Equation 14.10 is represented by the curve AA in Figure 14.6, the curve that gives the locus of points consistent with equilibrium in the asset markets. Given a price level p, it reflects what the exchange rate e must be in order to persuade investors to distribute their demands for the various assets in proportion to the available supply.[13] Equation 14.10 shows that it slopes down, since p has a negative coefficient $(-1/\theta\eta)$. The intuitive explanation of this is that when the price level is low, the real stock of money is high, which requires a low interest rate to persuade the public to hold it all; but then to satisfy the interest arbitrage condition and persuade investors to hold domestic bonds, they must expect a future fall in e (appreciation of the peso), which – given regressive expectations – requires that e be above its equilibrium level.

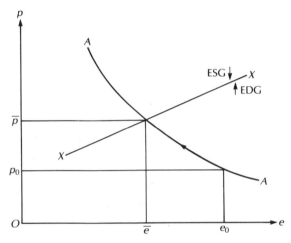

Figure 14.6 The Dornbusch model of the asset market approach

The second component of the model deals with equilibrium in the goods market. Postulate a log-linear specification in which aggregate demand depends positively on foreign demand, a function of the real exchange rate and foreign income, and on a variable g to represent fiscal policy, and negatively on the interest rate. If inflation depends on the excess of demand over the fixed output level $\bar{y}$, according to some rate of adjustment parameter δ, the result is:

$$\hat{p} = \delta[\alpha(e + p^* - p) + \beta y^* - \gamma i + g - \bar{y}] \tag{14.11}$$

One may substitute for i from equation 14.9:

$$\hat{p} = \delta[\alpha(e + p^* - p) + \beta y^* - (\gamma/\eta)(p - h + \xi\bar{y}) + g - \bar{y}] \tag{14.12}$$

Now all the variables in this equation except e and p are exogenous: their role is that of determining the point $(\bar{e}, \bar{p})$ where the goods market equilibrium curve XX cuts AA, but they do not influence the slope of XX. To determine that slope, it suffices to take deviations from equilibrium:

$$\hat{p} = \delta[\alpha(e - \bar{e}) - \alpha(p - \bar{p}) - (\gamma/\eta)(p - \bar{p})]$$
$$= \delta[\alpha(e - \bar{e}) - (\alpha + \gamma/\eta)(p - \bar{p})]$$

Thus the goods market equilibrium curve XX along which $\dot{p} = 0$ implies that:

$$\frac{p - \bar{p}}{e - \bar{e}} = \frac{\alpha}{\alpha + \gamma/\eta}$$

which is positive but less than 1 as shown in Figure 14.6 by a line flatter than a ray to the origin. The intuitive explanation is that a rise in p reduces domestic demand in two ways: it reduces real money balances, raises the interest rate and thus cuts aggregate demand – an expenditure-reducing effect; and it reduces the real exchange rate (cuts competitiveness) – an expenditure-switching effect. The second of these effects can be neutralized by an increase in the exchange rate along the ray from the origin, but that still leaves the expenditure-reducing effect. Thus the ray from the origin must at some point take one from an area of excess demand for goods to an area of excess supply: that is, the XX curve is flatter than the ray to the origin.

Below XX there is excess demand for goods, and prices therefore gradually rise. Above XX there is excess supply, and prices are therefore assumed to fall gradually. Taking the two curves together, the model works as follows. We have a set of exogenous variables that determine $(\bar{e}, \bar{p})$. We also have a particular price level – for example, $p_0 < \bar{p}$ in Figure 14.6 – inherited from the past. Given that price level, the exchange rate adjusts immediately – asset markets are flexprice markets – to the point indicated by the AA curve, e_0. At the point (e_0, p_0), there is excess demand for goods, which exerts upward pressure on the sticky prices in the goods market. As prices rise, the exchange rate falls, this appreciation of the domestic currency compensating investors for the low domestic interest rate caused by the large real money balances. The economy moves along AA towards equilibrium as indicated by the arrow.

Consider now the effects of monetary and fiscal policy in this model. The case of a monetary expansion (an open-market operation to increase the money supply h) is shown in Figure 14.7(a). Inspection of equation 14.12 shows that this will shift the XX curve up to $X'X'$ – this is the normal expansionary effect of an increased money supply. However, a one-time increase in the money supply cannot have any permanent effect on the balance of payments on current account. Thus when the economy achieves its new equilibrium with no excess demand it must also be true that relative prices are restored: that is, that the original PPP once more holds good. Since PPP is represented by a ray from the origin, it follows that the new equilibrium must fall at E', the intersection of $X'X'$ and the PPP ray. But if *we* can deduce this from the model, then so can investors – that is the import of the assumption that expectations are rational in the sense of Muth. And if investors know that equilibrium has shifted from E to E', then the locus of points that will equilibrate the asset markets will shift to cut E': that is, the AA curve will shift to $A'A'$.

Suppose therefore that the economy were initially in equilibrium at E with an exchange rate e_0. There is then a sudden unexpected expansion of the money supply which pushes $X'X'$ up and moves equilibrium to E'. The market knows this and sees not only that the currency must depreciate but also that real balances have suddenly been increased by the monetary expansion and will stay that way until inflation has

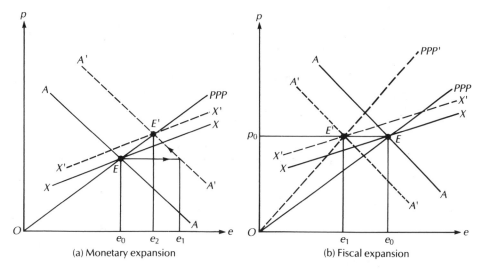

Figure 14.7 Policy changes in the Dornbusch model

reversed the effect of that expansion, implying a period of low domestic interest rates. There is, therefore, a move to sell the domestic currency, which pushes the exchange rate up instantaneously to e_1, the point on the $A'A'$ curve that corresponds to the initial price level. At that point investors can see the prospect of a future appreciation to compensate them for the low interest rate involved in holding domestic bonds, so the depreciation ceases. (Note how crucial the assumption of rational regressive expectations is in generating this orderly move: if the market had no idea what was happening to e and everyone tried to infer the truth from seeing what others were doing, one could easily envision much wilder gyrations of e occurring on the basis of extrapolative expectations.) From then on there is a gradual, simultaneous adjustment of p and e towards the new equilibrium E'.

The model shows that the exchange rate can be expected to *overshoot* in response to changes in monetary policy. Although the monetary expansion requires ultimately only a proportionate depreciation to e_2, the exchange rate first moves up all the way to e_1. This provides an explanation, or at least part of the explanation, as to why floating exchange rates have proved in practice to be so volatile: even credible changes in monetary policy (that is, those accepted as permanent by the market) should be expected to induce exaggerated changes in the exchange rate in the short run. Furthermore, monetary policy seldom is credible: outcomes are constantly inspected by the market to see what they can reveal about the future actions of the authorities. The result is that small changes in policy can sometimes produce large changes in market expectations, with results still more exaggerated than the over-shooting that occurs with full information in the Dornbusch model.

Consider next the case of fiscal expansion shown in Figure 14.7(b). An increase in g also pushes XX up to $X'X'$, as can be seen from equation 14.12. From then on, however, the story is quite different. A permanent fiscal deficit requires offsetting in the new equilibrium by a permanent current account deficit financed by a permanent capital inflow. (It is necessary to suspend any scepticism about the possibility of that being permanent by remembering that we are assuming perfect capital mobility.) The price level p must, on the other hand, remain unchanged, since none of the other arguments in the demand for money function, equation 14.9, is changed.[14] Thus the new equilibrium E' must occur where $X'X'$ reaches the original price level p_0. PPP rotates to PPP' because a lower real exchange rate is needed to avoid excess demand by generating a current account deficit that matches the fiscal expansion. Investors can see what has happened and have confidence that it will continue, so the AA curve shifts to $A'A'$. The exchange rate falls immediately to e_1, without overshooting or indeed any subsequent gradual adjustment.

Note that in most respects these conclusions are very similar to those of the Mundell–Fleming model (with perfect capital mobility). In both models, a monetary expansion leaves the current balance unchanged, depreciates the currency and increases nominal income: the only difference is that the increase in income is real income in Mundell–Fleming and inflation in Dornbusch. A fiscal expansion has identical effects in the two models: income is unchanged, absorption rises, the currency appreciates and the current account goes into deficit. But the one difference is, of course, a crucial one: the Mundell–Fleming model pictures an expansionary monetary policy as a valuable instrument for increasing employment, whereas models with price flexibility suggest that it will instead tend to generate inflation.

In fact, Jeffrey Sachs (b. 1954) has shown that if we postulate that *real* wages are constant, in place of the Mundell–Fleming assumption of constant nominal wages, the traditional result is precisely reversed: monetary expansion *cannot* increase employment, but fiscal expansion *can*. The reasons are as follows. In the Mundell–Fleming model, monetary expansion increases the real exchange rate, and income therefore rises; but real wages fall as a result of the increased import prices. If real wages cannot fall because of real-wage resistance, the depreciation must result in inflation equal to the initial depreciation, thus restoring the initial real exchange rate and frustrating the income expansion. In contrast, a fiscal expansion leads to a real appreciation, which raises real wages at the initial employment level. Restoration of the initial real wage requires an output expansion to the point where the increase in the real wage permitted by the current account deficit is offset by the decline in the real wage resulting from diminishing returns.

The general conclusion suggested by these results is that fiscal expansion raises income at the expense of a bigger current account deficit but without much inflationary impulse, while monetary expansion can raise income without much payments cost but at a definite cost in terms of inflation. Hard choices still have to be faced by those conducting economic policy in an environment of floating rates.

So much for the case of perfect capital mobility. Let us now take a brief look at the implications of *imperfect* capital mobility: that is, of portfolio effects. We consider a simple model due to Kouri. Suppose that investors have a portfolio choice restricted to two assets (moneys) each of which has a constant (perhaps zero) rate of interest. Then the opportunity cost of holding the peso is its expected rate of depreciation.

Assuming that there is an equilibrium exchange rate which is known to the public and that any deviation from that equilibrium will arouse expectations of a return towards it (a regressive pattern that can, as before, be justified by appeal to rationality), one again has equation 14.8 and the relationship that a high e implies an expected future appreciation. That means that a high e will persuade investors to put a relatively large part of their portfolios into the domestic money and be satisfied with a small quantity of the foreign asset F.[15] Thus the asset market equilibrium curve AA of the right-hand quadrant of Figure 14.8, which shows the exchange rate as a function of the country's stock of foreign assets for a given money supply, is downward sloping. In the left-hand quadrant are shown absorption and output. Output is assumed fixed at full employment, while absorption declines as the exchange rate rises for absorption-approach reasons, as shown by the XX schedule.

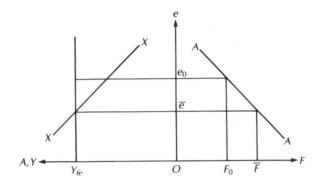

Figure 14.8 The Kouri model of portfolio adjustment

Suppose that initially the country has a stock of foreign assets F_0. To ration out this limited stock among investors, the price e of foreign exchange has to be high, at e_0. That high exchange rate implies high domestic prices and thus limited absorption, which generates a current account surplus, the excess of Y_{FE} over A. But with floating rates a current surplus implies a capital outflow, which involves an accumulation of F. Thus F gradually increases towards its equilibrium $\bar{F}$. As it does so, the greater availability of foreign exchange to investors induces a fall in e. Equilibrium is characterized by that stock of F which, given the money supply, persuades investors to hold the two assets at the exchange rate $\bar{e}$ where absorption is equal to output. In this model it is variations in the relative stocks of the assets rather than in their rates of return that serve to equilibrate demand and supply.

There is an important question we have commented on previously in this chapter but not as yet in the context of the asset market approach: the insulating properties of a flexible exchange rate. The basic conclusion is that *permanent* changes in either income or prices (but not interest rates) will be insulated, as in the Mundell–Fleming model, but that *temporary* changes will not be. The reason is that speculators who know that a change is temporary will realize that the exchange rate will return to normal after the temporary shock disappears, and will therefore be prepared to buy (or sell) the domestic currency when it has deviated sufficiently from its equilibrium value for the rebound to equilibrium to compensate them for the trouble and risk of making a portfolio shift. In practice, price-level changes are typically permanent, in the sense of not being reversed; indeed, inflation is highly serially correlated. This characteristic means that inflation differentials can be effectively neutralized through exchange-rate flexibility exactly as the simple models suggest. In contrast, real income has important deviations around its trend growth which are fairly clearly temporary, and the market will therefore not allow these deviations to push the rate too far away from equilibrium. This is a part of the explanation why the business cycle has remained synchronized since the adoption of floating rates, contrary to the predictions of the pre-1970s models.

The other part of the explanation has to do with the differing length of lags involved in the reaction to income changes on the one hand and to price changes on the other. The empirical evidence shows that a change in income is very quickly reflected in a change in imports, within a quarter or so, whereas we noted in section 12.3 that changes in competitiveness bring their effects only gradually over two or three years. This implies that it would not be possible for exchange-rate adjustments to offset the impact of income changes on the trade balance in the short run as is pictured in the current balance model. Such changes in the trade balance *have* to be financed in one way or another, with a crucial question being whether speculators are prepared to provide the finance in response to a moderate shift of the rate away from equilibrium, as implied in the preceding paragraph, or whether the degree of uncertainty as to where the equilibrium rate lies (and/or the low degree of substitutability between assets denominated in different currencies) means that rates will have to swing wildly in order to generate the necessary supply of finance. In either event, however, a floating system behaves much like a fixed-rate system in regard to the synchronization of the business cycle.

14.5 News, bubbles and chaos

The asset market approach, like its predecessors, predicts a rather orderly foreign exchange market. Exchange rates will be largely pinned down by the real forces that determine the solution to the Mundell–Fleming model, give or take a premium or discount reflecting the relative tightness of monetary policy and/or the net external wealth position. True, the Dornbusch analysis showed how the exchange rate could overshoot in response to a change in monetary policy, but monetary policy does not change every month, let alone every day or every hour. Yet floating exchange rates are forever bobbing around. Why?

The first attempt to explain the observed volatility of floating exchange rates ran in terms of the continuous arrival of 'news'. Suppose that the current market exchange rate reflects a balance between those expecting appreciation and those expecting depreciation on the basis of existing information, when something unexpected happens. (If it was not unexpected, it does not constitute news.) Market operators ask themselves what this implies about the outlook for exchange rates. If there is general agreement, the rate will jump to a new level with relatively little trading. If perceptions differ greatly, there will tend to be a lot more trading and it may take more time for rates to settle down again. But in either event the arrival of news will in general cause exchange rates to change. Volatility is explained by the continual arrival of news in the uncertain world in which we live.

Perhaps news can explain short-run volatility, but can it also explain what have come to be termed 'misalignments', meaning substantial and prolonged departures of exchange rates from equilibrium levels? There is no longer much doubt that misalignments occur: no one has seriously tried to claim that the dizzy heights to which the pound rose in 1980–1 or to which the dollar rose in 1983–5 were explicable in terms of a decrease in the equilibrium real exchange rate. Calculations by Paul Krugman demonstrated that the overvaluation of the dollar in 1985 was much larger than could be justified by the interest differentials posited as the crucial factor in pushing exchange rates away from medium-run equilibrium in Dornbusch's over-shooting analysis, and the US net external wealth position was already eroding so that Kouri's portfolio model could not help.

Since the models failed to explain what was happening, economists began to wonder whether they were observing a speculative bubble. A 'bubble' is a price increase that cannot be justified by the fundamentals, but that arises because past price increases create a belief that prices will rise even more in the future (i.e. expectations are extrapolative). Seeing a bandwagon develop, speculators rush to jump on before it is too late, in the process driving prices up even further. Since bubbles (like Ponzi games) cannot last for ever, economists had appealed to trans-versality conditions to argue that they could never start. The evidence that they sometimes do, from tulip mania in seventeenth-century Holland to the Wall Street crashes of 1929 and 1987, was ignored.

One thing that helped persuade economists that they should take the possibility of bubbles seriously was the development of a model of a 'rational bubble' by the French economist Olivier Blanchard (b. 1948). Consider a speculator who knows perfectly well the equilibrium price that is justified by the fundamentals, but who observes that the price is increasing even though it is already above equilibrium. Is it necessarily rational for him to sell? He knows that some day the price will go back to equilibrium. Suppose all the speculators assume that, when the price does drop, it will crash the whole way back to equilibrium instantaneously. In each period there is nonetheless a certain probability that the bubble will persist and the price will rise further. The price must rise faster the further it rises above equilibrium, in order to compensate the speculator for the increasing risks he knows he is running. The point is that the appeal to rational expectations is unable to rule out such bubble paths: at any time the expected profit of holding can be the same whether the price is on a bubble path or at equilibrium.

Another development that forced economists to take the possibility of bubbles seriously was evidence unearthed by Jeffrey Frankel (b. 1952) and Kenneth Froot (b. 1957). They examined survey evidence on the expectations held by foreign exchange traders during the years of the dollar's appreciation up to 1985, and found a consistent pattern. Traders had regularly predicted a *decline* in the dollar in the medium run, but a further *appreciation* in the short run. It is short-run expectations that drive actions in a market where everyone feels that they can liquidate their position in a matter of minutes should the need arise, and hence the dollar went on rising for several years after most market participants recognized that it was above its equilibrium level.

In 1990 the Belgian economist Paul De Grauwe (b. 1946) demonstrated that an inoffensive-looking model could produce a chaotic pattern of exchange rates. 'Chaos theory' is that branch of mathematics that analyzes systems in which a small differ- ence in initial conditions can make a large difference in subsequent trajectories, and in which the trajectories need not converge to equilibrium. De Grauwe's model of four rather standard equations, which included a J-curve and a mix of fundamentalist and extrapolative elements in expectations formation, generated just such behav- iour. This at last began to offer some understanding of the famous result of Meese and Rogoff (1983) which showed that for horizons up to two years a random- walk specification could outperform any of the standard models of exchange-rate determination.

14.6 Exchange-rate policy

The debate on exchange-rate flexibility was launched in the early 1950s, by two great economists of very different ideological persuasions, Milton Friedman and James Meade, arguing in favour of replacing the post-war system of (more or less) fixed exchange rates by floating rates. Friedman made two important positive arguments in favour of flexibility and one criticism of the case against. First, he argued that a floating exchange rate would give a country the freedom to choose its own monetary policy without having to be concerned about the balance of payments impact this would have: any inconsistency between its monetary policy and that of the rest of the world would be absorbed by a change in the exchange rate, rather than leading to reserve losses or gains that would feed back on the rate of monetary expansion. This was a point of crucial importance to Friedman, given his belief that a slow but steady expansion of the money supply was the key to achieving macroeconomic stability. Second, he argued that when it was necessary to achieve a change in the real exchange rate in order to adjust the balance of payments, it was much easier to do this by a single change in the nominal exchange rate rather than by revising thousands or millions of individual wages and prices in terms of national currency so as to have the same effect by changing the internal price level.

His criticism of the case against floating related to the question of destabilizing speculation, as it was then called. The Estonian economist Ragnar Nurkse (1907–59) had, during the Second World War, supervised a study of the inter-war experience with floating exchange rates, in which it had been concluded that speculative pres- sures had time after time resulted in floating rates being violently unstable (or volatile, in the terminology used above). Friedman countered this with the simple but powerful argument that speculators who really destabilized rates, in the sense of pushing them away from equilibrium (rather than making disequilibrium rates change suddenly), must lose money! Why? Because a speculator makes money by buying something when it is relatively cheap and selling when it is relatively dear, which raises prices at the trough and reduces them at the peak: that is, *stabilizes* rather than destabilizes. A speculator who does the opposite must lose money. Since this is not what the game of speculation is supposed to be about, the key to the observed volatility of exchange rates must lie elsewhere. Ever since, monetarists have been convinced that that key lies in unstable government policies (especially monetary policy).

In contrast to Friedman's *laissez-faire* desire to minimize the role of government, Meade's attitude was that of the technocratic manager seeking tools adequate to the job. Monetary policy was one such tool, but the analysis of section 12.5 (which we eventually decided in section 13.2 was not rendered redundant by Mundell's introduction of capital mobility) argued that it was not sufficient alone, or in combination with fiscal policy: it needed to be combined with an expenditure-switching policy. Exchange-rate policy provided the natural candidate (inasmuch as it alone does not involve creating microeconomic distortions). Meade also discussed the threat of destabilizing speculation. He did not share Friedman's confidence that this phenomenon could be ruled out on the grounds that it would be inimical to the interests of the speculators, but instead argued that it could be overcome by strong and internationally co-ordinated intervention policies. Although the matter is still not finally settled, the volatility of rates observed since 1973, which the new models of news, bubbles and chaos attempt to explain, would suggest that Meade's fears on this score were more realistic than Friedman's confidence that it could not happen. A possible explanation is that the speculators who lose money are not the core of professionals in the market, who would surely get out of the business if they could not beat the market and make money, but a part of that large fringe of traders, tourists and even central banks who take open positions in foreign exchange, sometimes because it is too much trouble not to, but to whom the activity is peripheral.

Opponents of flexible exchange rates developed a series of counterarguments in the years that followed, to supplement the fear that floating would mean volatility because of speculation. In the first place, they argued that this volatility would tend to make international trade and investment more risky and would therefore impede international integration. Second, they argued that removing the constraint on monetary policy provided by the need to defend a fixed exchange rate should be counted as a cost and not a benefit: countries need a discipline of that sort to prevent their political leaders engaging in irresponsible inflationary finance. Some supporters of flexibility replied that the democratic process and not the need to defend a fixed exchange rate should be allowed to decide how much inflation a country has. Others argued that under floating inflationary finance would quickly lead to a depreciation and thus to internal inflation, which hits the public directly in a way that reserve losses do not, so that discipline would actually be more effective under floating. Third, opponents of floating argued that a fixed rate provided a built-in stabilizer: a boom or recession would draw in more or fewer imports with a fixed rate and thus tend to dampen the change in income, whereas the income expansion would be bottled up at home by a floating exchange rate, leading to inflation or slump. This effect can be seen in Figure 14.2, reinterpreting the cause of the shift in XX as a domestic boom or recession. Supporters of flexibility retorted that this effect is crucially dependent on the assumption of no capital mobility, since a domestic boom would tend to raise interest rates and thus draw in capital rather than depreciate the currency where capital is mobile.

Two further arguments against floating were added in the 1970s, mainly by the global monetarists (who thus adopted a position on this issue opposed to that of old-fashioned monetarists). First, they argued that exchange-rate changes could produce expenditure-switching effects only if there were money illusion; in its absence, a devaluation would simply induce an offsetting inflation rather than a payments improvement. This issue has never been completely resolved, but the claim is certainly not universally accepted: what absence of money illusion *plus* the strong but usually unmentioned assumption of the uniqueness of equilibrium jointly imply is that a devaluation *alone* will not have a lasting effect in altering competitiveness. However, the sophisticated advocate of exchange-rate policy envisages its use as a part of a package, not as an isolated policy instrument (remember the absorption approach), and there is no reason for believing that it cannot be useful in that context just because money illusion is absent – as it surely is. Second, it was argued that exchange-rate flexibility would tend to accelerate the average rate of inflation because of ratchet effects: a depreciation would produce a proportionate inflation, whereas an appreciation would not reduce prices proportionately because of downward stickiness, so that variable exchange rates would ratchet up the price level. This sounds pretty plausible, but no decisive empirical evidence in favour of the hypothesis has yet been presented (and not for want of trying).

In parallel with the long-running debate on fixed versus floating exchange rates, there emerged in the 1960s a literature on intermediate options. One strand of this was initiated by Robert Mundell, with a paper that asked: what is the *optimal currency area*? By this, he meant the optimal area within which exchange rates should be fixed. Typically, each country has a single money, and different countries have different moneys, so that exchange rates are fixed within countries but may vary between them. But is there necessarily any logic in this? Mundell argued that one should ideally have one money for each area within which factors were mobile but between which they were not, since factor mobility would make exchange-rate changes redundant, while a change in the exchange rate could provide a helpful substitute for factor mobility where this was absent. Shortly afterward the Canadian-born Ronald McKinnon (b. 1935) argued that the critical factor was the openness of the economy rather than the degree of factor mobility, since a relatively closed economy could hope to use a devaluation to promote expenditure switching, while in a highly open economy the main result would be to raise the price level. Later participants in the debate argued that the key factor was the willingness to accept the same rate of inflation. Others pointed to the necessity for a common fiscal system, in order to provide an alternative mechanism for easing interregional adjustments in the form of fiscal transfers (a criterion that suggests the normal practice of having one money per country is rational). Today, the dominant tendency is to argue that schemes for currency unification should be judged on the basis of a cost–benefit appraisal involving all these factors, rather than appealing to some single criterion to the exclusion of all others.

A second strand to the debate on intermediate options arose from the observation that there are more alternatives available than free floating and permanent fixity. For example, there are also the two other systems that have in fact been widely employed in the post-war world: *managed floating*,[16] where there is no particular rate that the authorities are committed to defend, but where they nevertheless intervene at their discretion; and the *adjustable peg*, where the authorities accept a commitment to defend the rate at the particular level where it is currently pegged, but where they reserve the right to change that rate under certain circumstances. There is also a fifth possible exchange-rate regime, generally known as the *crawling peg*. This involves a country accepting a parity (or peg) for its currency, but changing this gradually over time in a series of small steps rather than in the sudden discrete changes that are characteristic of the adjustable peg. Such changes may be determined according to a formal rule – for example, revalue when reserves rise and devalue when they fall – or they may be determined by discretionary decisions – either announced in advance or made as the occasion arises in response to what are considered relevant criteria. The country that has employed the crawling peg for longest, Colombia, is guided largely by the objective of maintaining PPP with the United States so as to neutralize the effect of its high domestic rate of inflation.

The crawling peg is an intermediate regime that fits naturally into the scheme of those who see exchange-rate flexibility as a technocrat's tool. It gives a country the power to reconcile any internal rate of inflation with continued external balance: as noted in the previous section, the one thing that exchange-rate flexibility really can neutralize efficiently is differential inflation. This power has up to now been used to allow countries to inflate faster than the world average, but it could equally well be used as a tool to enable countries to repel imported inflation and enjoy a greater degree of price stability than the norm. Second, a crawling change in the exchange rate can be used to promote expenditure switching when this is needed. But one thing that the crawling peg cannot do is to liberate monetary policy. On the contrary, monetary policy has to be subordinated to the preservation of the interest arbitrage condition $i = i^* + E\hat{e}$: the incentive to export capital created by a known gradual devaluation has to be offset by accepting a more or less commensurate rise in the domestic interest rate if reserve losses are to be averted. Another thing it excludes is having the exchange rate do the immediate adjusting to an exogenous shock, in the manner portrayed by the jump from e_0 to e_1 in Figure 14.7(a). Evaluations of the crawling peg tend to depend on whether those two constraints on policy are judged to be potentially serious.

A third strand to the debate on intermediate options concerned another form of limited flexibility, known as the *wider band*. The band refers to the degree of variation around parity within which the exchange rate is allowed to fluctuate in response to market forces. In the Bretton Woods system as it prevailed up till 1971, countries agreed to hold their exchange rates within a 2 per cent band: that is, within margins 1 per cent either side of parity. The wider band or band proposal envisaged widening the band of 2 per cent to something in the range of 5 per cent to 10 per cent. The main idea was to provide somewhat more freedom for contracyclical monetary policy to vary between countries. For example, a country wanting to fight a recession by low interest rates could engineer a temporary expansion in the money supply to push the interest rate down. Its currency would depreciate towards the top of the band, but, so long as the market accepted that the parity would remain unchanged, there would be an expectation of a subsequent rebound of the rate towards parity which would compensate for the low interest rate and preserve the interest arbitrage condition $i^* = i - E\hat{e}$. A second aim was to make speculation on parity changes more costly and less profitable.

A new topic has become important since the move to floating exchange rates by the principal industrial countries in 1973. This concerns the exchange-rate policy to be pursued by the remaining countries, who include virtually all of the developing countries. It is conventionally argued that it would be unwise or even impractical for these countries to adopt floating rates, because of the limited scale of the market and the lack of depth of domestic capital markets. Prior to 1973, the only question that was left was when and how to change one's parity: for example, by adopting a crawling peg. But nowadays it is necessary to decide not merely *whether* to peg but also *to what* to peg. When all the major currencies were pegged to each other, pegging to the dollar meant pegging to everything else; now that the major currencies are floating, pegging to the dollar means having one's rate fluctuate in terms of everything else. These fluctuations may have some logic for the United States, but to a small country pegged to the dollar they have none whatsoever, and are pure shocks. Hence the question has arisen of how the country can choose a peg – in the sense of a currency or basket of currencies to which to peg – with the object of minimizing the damage done by the exchange-rate fluctuations between the major currencies. This has become known as the question of choosing an *optimal peg*. Broadly speaking, the answer is that countries should seek to stabilize their effective exchange rates by pegging to a basket of currencies. The effective exchange rate is defined as the trade-weighted geometric mean of the bilateral exchange rates with a country's trading partners and competitors. Stabilizing the effective exchange rate means that, although exchange-rate changes between the major countries will still influence the competitive positions and costs of individual industries and firms, at least these effects will tend to balance out over the economy as a whole and so not disturb *macroeconomic* equilibrium. A possible disadvantage of pegging to a basket, which has to be weighed against the macroeconomic benefit, is the microeconomic risk imposed on individual traders when they no longer have a major international currency in which they can write contracts and against which their own currency is reasonably stable.

14.7 Summary

The evidence since the adoption of widespread floating in 1973 is that floating rates are volatile and sometimes become seriously misaligned. Instead of the smooth and moderate adjustments that most economists had expected to prevail (largely because that was what the Mundell–Fleming model suggested would happen, and also because of the way the Canadian dollar had behaved when it was floating in the 1950s), rates have often jumped around wildly: by 2 or 3 per cent in a single day, with cycles of well over 20 per cent, and with occasional appreciations or depreciations of as much as 40 per cent to 60 per cent. (The extreme case is that of Britain, whose pound appreciated by over 55 per cent against the dollar from its trough in late 1976 to its peak in late 1980, despite some 10 to 20 per cent *more* inflation in Britain over the period.) Since in the short run national price levels are pretty sticky, these exchange-rate fluctuations have brought with them large variations in real exchange rates. Countries suffering exaggerated appreciations have had their tradable goods sectors threatened with serious damage (for example, Switzerland in late 1978, Britain in 1980–2, the United States in 1983–5), while exaggerated depreciations have imposed severe inflationary pressures (Britain in late 1976, the United States in late 1978, Germany in mid-1981).

How far does the theory that has been studied in this chapter go towards explaining these variations? The following list shows factors that are capable of altering the value of a floating exchange rate:[17]

1. The equilibrium nominal exchange rate may change because of differential inflation $\hat{p} - \hat{p}^*$ to preserve PPP (maintain the real exchange rate constant, from section 14.2. To preserve asset market equilibrium an anticipated inflation differential must be offset by an equal interest differential $(i - i^*)$ under perfect capital mobility; or by some combination of interest differential, real depreciation (remember the Kouri model) and financing through a reserve outflow under imperfect capital mobility.

2. The equilibrium real exchange rate may change for various reasons: differential productivity growth or exogenous changes in the terms of trade (section 14.2), changes in the underlying rate of capital inflow or permanent changes in real income. Any of these require a change in competitiveness which, for given price levels, implies an exchange-rate change.

3. The exchange rate may be returning to equilibrium along a correctly forecast path, having deviated because the interest rate temporarily diverged from its normal level (the Dornbusch model, or the band proposal).

4. A current imbalance may change the stock of foreign assets available and thus lead to an exchange-rate change to maintain portfolio balance (the Kouri model).

5. Expectations of any of the above may change, because of policy changes, because of news (unexpected developments that alter expectations of future policy or assessments of the value of a country's resources, or unexpected outcomes for relevant variables like the current account) or because of revisions to the assessment of previously available information. Factors of the first two sorts generate movements

of the asset market equilibrium curve in the Dornbusch model and may cause sudden jumps in the exchange rate. Revised expectations of inflation need cause no immediate movement of the exchange rate at all, provided that real interest rates remain constant. The common idea that high, even differentially high, inflation can be blamed for exchange-rate volatility is wrong. (On the other hand, there is *no* exchange-rate adjustment that can restore portfolio equilibrium under perfect capital mobility if the expected permanent inflation differential changes without an equal change in the nominal interest differential.)

6. Although the proposition is still controversial, many economists would now add that exchange rates are subject to speculative runs in which market rumours feed on themselves to produce an exchange rate out of touch with the underlying fundamentals. Many market participants seem to use 'chartist' techniques to guide their trading, which often amounts to allowing expectations to be formed extrapolatively rather than rationally, at least within a certain range. Such behaviour can result in exchange rates following the disorderly processes characterized by chaos theory – a far cry from the dominant theoretical model in which the current exchange rate is the anticipated future rate pinned down by long-run fundamentals discounted to the present by the differential between domestic and foreign interest rates.

14.8 Addendum: the large economy

The main implication of relaxing the small-country assumption relates to the Mundell–Fleming model. Two of the theorems developed in section 14.3 were that, with perfect capital mobility, monetary policy is ineffective under a fixed exchange rate and fiscal policy is ineffective with a flexible exchange rate. Both theorems fail in the case of the large country.

In the case of monetary policy, the analysis is obvious: a monetary expansion has a non-negligible effect in expanding the world money supply, and therefore the national money supply increases by a non-negligible proportion. (In the simple case of equal reserve ratios and money demand elasticities, the proportion of the monetary expansion that stays at home to reduce interest rates and increase income is equal to the country's money supply as a proportion of the world money supply.)

Similarly, a fiscal expansion by a large country will have some effect in stimulating income even with floating rates and perfect capital mobility. The reason is that the appreciation of our currency stimulates world income by a non-negligible amount, which then exerts pressure for our currency to depreciate once again, thus stimulating our income. Equilibrium requires a higher interest rate, and higher income distributed throughout the world. Crowding out is incomplete.

14.9 Bibliography

The classic analysis of the current balance model is chapters 17 and 18 of Mundell (1968), although there were many previous, less systematic, treatments. The Laursen-Metzler effect was developed in Metzler and Laursen (1950).

Cassell's major work on PPP was Cassell (1922). The analysis of differential productivity growth ('productivity bias') was developed in Balassa (1964). The international comparisons of real income made by the Pennsylvania team are presented for 130 countries over the period 1950–85 in Summers and Heston (1988), while the most complete description of the project is to be found in *World Product and Income* (1982) and a survey is provided by Kravis (1984). For the Scandinavian model of inflation, see Edgren, Faxén and Odhner (1969). Harry Johnson's formula for the impact of growth on the PPP inflation differential is in Johnson (1954), reprinted in Johnson (1958); the most famous empirical estimates along those lines are in Houthakker and Magee (1969). A survey of the literature on PPP is provided by Officer (1976). The reference to 'helicopter distribution' of additional money is from Friedman (1969, ch. 1).

Mundell's presentation of the Mundell–Fleming model can be found in chapter 18 of his *International Economics* (1968), while that of Fleming is in Fleming (1962), reprinted in Fleming (1972).

The asset market approach was launched in papers by R. Dornbusch, J. A. Frenkel, P. J. K. Kouri and M. Mussa at a conference in Saltsjobaden, Sweden, in 1975. They were printed in the *Scandinavian Journal of Economics*, 1976, vol. 2, and reprinted in Herin, Lindbeck and Myhrman (1977). The Dornbusch model presented in the chapter originates from Dornbusch (1976), also covered in chapter 11 of his *Open Economy Macroeconomics* (1980). The founding work on rational expectations is Muth (1961). The theorem that the effects of monetary and fiscal policy on real income are the opposite of those in Mundell–Fleming with a fixed real wage is proved by Sachs (1980).

The debate on exchange-rate flexibility was launched by Milton Friedman, in 'The case for flexible exchange rates' in Friedman (1953), and by James Meade (1955a). The 'orthodox view' of destabilizing speculation attacked by Friedman was developed in a League of Nations report written by Nurkse (1944). The debate on optimum currency areas was launched by Mundell (1961b), reprinted in his *International Economics* (1968); it was taken up in an article with the same title in the same journal by McKinnon (1962), and has been usefully reviewed by Tower and Willett (1976). An account of the debate on the crawling peg can be found in Williamson (1981). The band proposal was pioneered by Halm (1965); the most penetrating theoretical appraisal of the idea is in McKinnon (1971). The standard reference on the concept of the effective exchange rate is Rhomberg (1976). A survey of the literature on the optimal peg is provided in Williamson (1982).

'News' was emphasized by Frenkel (1981), Blanchard bubbles were presented in Blanchard (1979), the evidence that foreign exchange traders formed short-run expectations extrapolatively was presented in Frankel and Froot (1990), and chaos was unveiled by De Grauwe and Vansanten (1990). The interest parity condition developed in appendix B originated in Keynes (1923).

Appendix A: The algebra of Mundell–Fleming

The Mundell–Fleming model analyzed graphically in the text may be represented algebraically by three equations. The first, equation 14.13, is the *IS* curve, representing equilibrium in the market for goods; output depends positively on the real exchange rate, foreign income and fiscal policy, and negatively on the interest rate. The second, equation 14.14, is the *LM* curve, representing equilibrium in the market for money. The third, equation 14.15, is the *BP* curve, representing equilibrium in the balance of payments. Equation 14.15 is the case of perfect capital mobility, while 14.15b assumes imperfect capital mobility (or complete immobility with $\lambda = 0$).

Letters have the same meanings as we have been giving them, except that all have been written in lower-case form and are to be interpreted as logarithms of the variables in question: this is because the specification supposes that the model is log linear. (An exception concerns the interest rate: i has to be interpreted as unity plus the rate of interest in fractional form: for example, a rate of interest of 5 per cent is represented by $i = 1.05$ and not by log 5 or log 0.05.) Greek letters represent parameters, which are in fact elasticities in view of the log-linear specification. Ignoring constant terms – that is, considering deviations from an initial equilibrium – the model is then:

$$y = \alpha(e + p^* - p) + \beta y^* - \gamma i + \delta g \tag{14.13}$$
$$h - p = \xi y - \eta i \tag{14.14}$$
$$i = i^* \tag{14.15a}$$
$$\alpha(e + p^* - p) + \beta y^* - \theta y + \lambda(i - i^*) = 0 \tag{14.15b}$$

Note that, while it is entirely natural to put the same coefficient β in 14.13 and 14.15b, putting the same α in both involves assuming that the terms of trade are exogenous.

Consider first the benchmark case of a fixed exchange rate and zero capital mobility. This involves treating 14.13 and 14.14 as two simultaneous equations in the two endogenous variables y and i, and not imposing either version of equation 14.15. (Under the gold standard rules, the change in the money supply would be a positive function of the value of the balance of payments determined by 14.15b, with λ set equal to zero.) In matrix form, this gives:

$$\begin{bmatrix} 1 & \gamma \\ \xi - \eta \end{bmatrix} \begin{bmatrix} y \\ i \end{bmatrix} = \begin{bmatrix} \alpha(e + p^* - p) + \beta y^* + \delta g \\ h - p \end{bmatrix}$$

Inverting the matrix to solve for the endogenous variables, one gets:

$$\begin{bmatrix} y \\ i \end{bmatrix} = \frac{1}{\Delta} \begin{bmatrix} -\eta & -\gamma \\ -\xi & 1 \end{bmatrix} \begin{bmatrix} \alpha(e + p^* - p) + \beta y^* + \delta g \\ h - p \end{bmatrix} \tag{14.16}$$

where $\Delta = -\eta - \gamma \xi < 0$.

The effect of monetary expansion under fixed exchange rates is found by taking the total differential from equation 14.16:

$$dy/dh = -\gamma/\Delta > 0.$$

This is the magnitude that was defined as y_1 in Table 14.1.

The effect on income of a given expansion in the money supply is exactly the same under (finite) capital mobility. What differs, of course, is the size of the domestic credit expansion needed to achieve a given monetary expansion (since part of the increased credit leaks out abroad).

In the case of perfect capital mobility, we have 14.15a as well as 14.13 and 14.14. Substitution of 14.15a into 14.13 and 14.14 gives us two equations in the one endogenous variable y. The contradiction is resolved by recognizing that y is immediately determined by 14.13; h becomes an endogenous variable, which is determined by 14.14. Attempts to change h via monetary policy will fail; monetary policy is impotent.

Under floating exchange rates, e becomes an endogenous variable. The simplest case is that of perfect capital mobility, where substitution of 14.15a into 14.13 and 14.14 gives us two simultaneous equations in the two endogenous variables y and e:

$$\begin{bmatrix} 1-\alpha \\ \xi \quad 0 \end{bmatrix} \begin{bmatrix} y \\ e \end{bmatrix} = \begin{bmatrix} \alpha(p^* - p) + \beta y^* - \gamma i^* + \delta g \\ h - p + \eta i^* \end{bmatrix}$$

Inverting the matrix to solve for the endogenous variables, one gets:

$$\begin{bmatrix} y \\ e \end{bmatrix} = \frac{1}{\Delta} \begin{bmatrix} 0 & \alpha \\ -\xi & 1 \end{bmatrix} \begin{bmatrix} \alpha(p^* - p) + \beta y^* - \gamma i^* + \delta g \\ h - p + \eta i^* \end{bmatrix} \tag{14.17}$$

where $\Delta = \alpha \xi > 0$.

Extracting the total differential, one finds:

$$dy/dh = \alpha/\Delta = 1/\xi$$

which is positive and larger than dy/dh under fixed rates, given that $\eta > 0$.

The case of imperfect capital mobility incorporating 14.15b instead of 14.15a is somewhat more complex, since we now have three endogenous variables y, e and i and three equations:

$$\begin{bmatrix} 1 & -\alpha & \gamma \\ \xi & 0 & -\eta \\ \theta & -\alpha & -\gamma \end{bmatrix} \begin{bmatrix} y \\ e \\ i \end{bmatrix} = \begin{bmatrix} \alpha(p^* - p) + \beta y^* + \delta g \\ h - p \\ \alpha(p^* - p) + \beta y^* - \lambda i^* \end{bmatrix}$$

Matrix inversion yields:

$$\begin{bmatrix} y \\ e \\ i \end{bmatrix} = \frac{1}{\Delta} \begin{bmatrix} -\alpha\eta & -\alpha(\lambda + \gamma) & \alpha\eta \\ \lambda\xi - \theta\eta & -(\lambda + \gamma\theta) & \eta + \gamma\xi \\ -\alpha\xi & \alpha(1 - \theta) & \alpha\xi \end{bmatrix} \begin{bmatrix} \alpha(p^* - p) + \beta y^* + \delta g \\ h - p \\ \alpha(p^* - p) + \beta y^* - \lambda i^* \end{bmatrix} \tag{14.18}$$

where $\Delta = -\alpha\eta(1 - \theta) - \alpha\xi(\gamma + \lambda) < 0$, since $\theta < 1$.

Hence:

$$dy/dh = -\alpha(\lambda + \gamma)/\Delta$$

which is positive whether capital mobility (λ) is zero or positive, and in fact increases as λ increases. But even in the case $\lambda = 0$, the expression is larger than dy/dh under fixed rates, given that $\theta < 1$.

The student should similarly evaluate dy/dg from 14.16 to 14.18 in order to confirm the theorems summarized in the second row of Table 14.1. A more challenging exercise is to introduce commercial policy into the model as well.

The other set of theorems that can be extracted from the model concern the impact of changes in the foreign variables y^*, i^* and p^* under floating exchange rates. Under perfect capital mobility, one extracts from equation 14.17:

$$dy/dy^* = 0, \qquad de/dy^* = -\beta/\alpha < 0$$

With perfect capital mobility an increase in foreign income still causes an appreciation of the domestic currency sufficient to prevent any increase in domestic income: the business cycle would be desynchronized internationally. Second:

$$dy/di^* = \eta/\xi > 0, \quad de/di^* = \gamma/\alpha + \eta/\alpha\xi > 0$$

The increase in the foreign interest rate is transmitted to the domestic economy by incipient interest arbitrage, which causes the currency to depreciate and income to rise by as much as is needed to restore the demand for money (which fell because of the higher interest rate) to equal the unchanged supply. Finally:

$$dy/dp^* = 0, \qquad de/dp^* = -1$$

The currency appreciates to neutralize the foreign inflation and leave income unchanged. Thus with perfect capital mobility the only foreign shock that influences the domestic economy is one to the interest rate, and this has an effect *opposite* to that under fixed rates: a higher foreign interest rate stimulates domestic income.

Before leaving the case of perfect capital mobility, it is worth checking that a neutral domestic inflation – that is, an equal proportionate rise in the money stock h and domestic prices p – can be neutralized through a proportionate depreciation:

$$dy/dp|_{dp = dh} = 0, \qquad de/dp|_{dp = dh} = 1$$

In the case of imperfect capital mobility, one extracts the relevant total derivatives from equation 14.18:

$$dy/dy^* = 0, \qquad de/dy^* = -\beta/\alpha < 0$$
$$dy/di^* = -\alpha\lambda\eta/\Delta > 0, \quad de/di^* = -\lambda(\eta + \gamma\xi)/\Delta > 0$$
$$dy/dp^* = 0, \qquad de/dp^* = -1$$
$$dy/dp|_{dh = dp} = 0, \qquad de/dp|_{dh = dp} = 1$$

With the exception of the more complicated (but still qualitatively similar) formulae for the effect of a change in the foreign interest rate, these results are identical to those in the case of perfect mobility. A floating exchange rate still insulates the domestic economy from everything except interest-rate changes, where the direction of effect remains the opposite of that in the fixed exchange-rate case, and it still neutralizes the external effects of a neutral domestic inflation. The intuitive explanations given for the case of perfect mobility remain valid.

Appendix B: The forward exchange market

The analysis in the chapter was conducted as though all transactions take place in the spot market: that is, the market for immediate delivery or receipt of foreign exchange. In the case of the major currencies, these spot markets are supplemented by forward markets. These are markets in which contracts are signed now to sell one currency for another on a specified future date (typically in three or six months' time) at a price agreed now.

There are three types of activity that can be undertaken in the forward market. It is descriptively inaccurate but pedagogically useful to identify each of these with a distinct class of actors.

Hedging is undertaken by traders who sign a contract now in order to arrange for the future receipt or sale of foreign exchange that they know they will need or acquire, respectively, at the given date in the future. This avoids (or at least reduces – there may still be a lag before cover can be taken) exposure to exchange risk.

Arbitrage is undertaken by financiers, typically banks, in search of a riskless profit. They simultaneously sell one currency, say the peso, spot, and buy it back forward in three months' time, for example. They then invest the proceeds in dollars for those three months.

Speculation is undertaken by speculators who seek to make a profit by *accepting* exchange risk – by promising to buy or sell foreign exchange at a price decided now at some future date in the hope that on that date they will be able to sell or buy, respectively, in the spot market at a rate that will leave them with a profit. Obviously this is an activity that will actually yield profits only to those who on average have a certain degree of success in forecasting the future spot rate. Speculators are in practice a diverse group: multinationals, banks, central banks and traders who at times accept exchange risk deliberately.

Suppose that there is a single maturity in the forward market: for example, one year, for simplicity. Let the forward exchange rate – the peso price of a dollar for delivery at the end of that period – be f. Then f will be determined at the level that clears the forward market, where:

$$EDH + EDA + EDS = 0$$

where EDH is the excess demand by hedgers, etc.

It is possible to conceive of the forward market operating with only traders in the market. Every day, the value of import contracts hedged would have to equal the value of export contracts hedged. The traders undertaking these hedging operations would all be reducing their risk exposure, so there would be no reason to expect a risk premium – a systematic deviation of f from the e for the same date – to emerge. However, one would expect the rate f to be highly volatile: on a day when importers were signing a lot of contracts relative to exporters, it would be necessary for f to rise to the point where some importers were induced not to cover or not to sign their contracts after all or exporters were induced to cover more or to sell more.

The interest arbitrageurs would see money to be made in this volatility. Consider the case above where there is a forward discount on the peso: that is, where $f > e$. If interest rates were the same at home and abroad, it would pay financiers to sell pesos spot, invest the proceeds in dollars and sell the dollars forward at their high price f. In general, there is an incentive to undertake this operation so long as:

$$(1 + i^*)f/e > (1 + i).$$

This *covered interest arbitrage* is free of exchange risk. In the absence of effective exchange controls or different political risk at home and abroad, this means that we can rely on arbitrage to continue to the point where the inequality is replaced by an equality. At that point the forward discount $(f - e)/e$ is equal to:

$$\frac{f}{e} - 1 = \frac{1 + i}{1 + i^*} - 1 = \frac{i - i^*}{1 - i^*} \approx i - i^*$$

This is the condition of *interest parity* first derived by Keynes in 1923: the forward discount on our currency must equal the excess of our interest rate over the foreign interest rate. (In applying this formula, the forward discount and the interest rate differential must apply to the same time period – one cannot compare directly a three-month forward discount with an annual interest differential.)

The interest parity condition bears a close relation to equation 14.7, the condition for equality of yields $i = i^* + E\hat{e}$. The two together imply that the forward discount is equal to the expected rate of depreciation, which is the same thing as saying that the forward rate is equal to the expected future spot rate. This is to be expected: perfect capital mobility means precisely that investors will be prepared to pursue any additional expected yield, no matter how small, even at the cost of exchange exposure. Similarly, any deviation between the forward rate and the expected future spot rate implies an expected gain, which will be sought out by speculators regardless of risk under the postulate of perfect capital mobility. Risk-neutral speculators are the necessary and (with rapid adjustment) sufficient condition for perfect capital mobility.

Conversely, with imperfect capital mobility, f_{+1} can deviate from Ee_{+1}. If there is a preponderance of importers wishing to cover forward or if the domestic interest rate is higher than the foreign interest rate, the peso will be driven to a forward discount. As the discount widens, so speculators will enter the forward market to buy pesos cheap in the hope of being able to sell them on the spot market at a profit when their contracts mature. But the speculators have to be compensated for undertaking this risk: a risk premium $(f_{+1} - Ee_{+1} > 0)$ is necessary. Persuading speculators to take a greater open position, so as to finance a current account deficit or cover a capital inflow, requires that the risk premium rise.

What this implies is that the sort of analysis of macroeconomic policies undertaken in the chapter is not affected by the existence of a forward market (which is why the subject has been relegated to an appendix). Forward markets help reduce total risk (where there is two-way hedging) and permit a division of labour between traders, arbitrageurs and speculators. These are valuable microeconomic functions, but they are unimportant to an understanding of the macroeconomics of exchange rates.

Notes

1. It was in fact argued by Laursen and Metzler (1950) that a foreign boom would tend to cause a *fall* in our income under a floating rate – the exact opposite of the result of the foreign trade multiplier under a fixed rate. The reason is that the foreign boom causes our currency to appreciate, which improves our terms of trade, which raises our real income in terms of a price index of final goods, which raises both consumption and saving in terms of *that* price index – but *reduces* consumption in terms of a price index of home goods alone, which means that it increases unemployment. To show this, postulate that consumption is the only element of home demand, and:

    $C/p = \alpha + \beta(Y/p)$, or $C = \alpha p + \beta Y$

    where p is the price index of final goods:

    $$p = p_n{}^\gamma p_m{}^{(1-\gamma)}$$

    Current balance implies $X = M$ (in nominal terms), so:

    $$Y = C + X - M = C = \alpha p + \beta Y$$

    implies:

    $$(1 - \beta)Y = \alpha p_n{}^\gamma p_m{}^{(1-\gamma)}$$

    or:

    $$Y/p_n = [\alpha/(1-\beta)]p_m{}^{(1-\gamma)}p_n{}^{(\gamma-1)}$$

    so:

    $$\frac{\delta(Y/p_n)}{\delta p_m} = \frac{\alpha(1-\gamma)}{(1-\beta)} \cdot p_n{}^{(\gamma-1)} \cdot p_m{}^{-\gamma} > 0$$

    Thus a boom in the rest of the world, which cuts the domestic currency price of imports as a result of the induced appreciation, *reduces* income in terms of home goods. Although this Laursen–Metzler effect of an inverse cycle is famous, it is a second-order effect.

2. When the Laursen–Metzler effect exists (see note 1), *FF* actually shifts down *more* than *XX* and in consequence employment *falls* as a result of increased protection!

3. See the relevant references cited in the last paragraph of section 13.6.

4. Empirically, this is an exaggeration. However, the wage shortfall in the service sector does not increase systematically, and certainly not rapidly enough to dominate the differential productivity growth.

5. Proof. Define n, n^* as the price–wage ratios in the N-industries in the two countries, and m, m^* as the price-wage ratios in the M-industries. Then W's higher productivity and the stylized fact of greater technical progress in the M-industry imply $n/m < n^*/m^*$. Assuming the price index to have the Cobb–Douglas form $p = p_n{}^\alpha p_m{}^{1-\alpha}$, substitution of $p_n = nw$, $p_m = mw$, yields $p = (n/m)^\alpha p_m$. Similar substitution in the formula for p^* yields $p^* = (n^*/m^*)^\alpha p_m{}^*$. Given the perfect arbitrage hypothesis $p_m = ep_m{}^*$, it is clear that:

    $$p = (n/m)^\alpha p_m < ep^* = (n^*/m^*)^\alpha ep_m{}^* = (n^*/m^*)^\alpha p_m$$

    so long as $(n/m) < (n^*/m^*)$ as postulated.

6. Proof. From the logarithmic time derivative of equation 14.4, PPP will be preserved at a fixed exchange rate if:

    $$\hat{\pi} = \hat{p}^* - \hat{p}$$

Substituting from equation 14.5 and the equivalent result $\hat{p}^* = \hat{p}_m + \alpha\rho^*$:

$$\hat{\pi} = \hat{p}_m{}^* + \alpha\rho^* - (\hat{p}2I_m{}^* + \alpha\rho) = (\rho^* - \rho)$$

7. This expression can be further amplified to take account of growth, which makes it necessary to introduce price and income elasticities of demand for exports and imports, as developed in Johnson (1954).

8. In the long run, the payments deficit would lead to *LM* migrating leftward until it again intersected *IS* at *E*, assuming an absence of sterilization.

9. Proof. Higher income implies higher savings *S* and tax revenue *T*, while *G* is constant by assumption and $(X - M)$ is unchanged with a floating exchange rate and zero capital mobility. Thus from equation 11.2 we can see that *I* must be larger, which requires that *i* be lower.

10. Once again, with the Laursen–Metzler effect the new equilibrium would actually lie to the left of *E*.

11. Quite a long time after – the idea took about ten years to be noticed!

12. This is equivalent to the regressive expectations formula previously given, $Ex_{+1} = \alpha x + (1 - \alpha)\bar{x}$ when we put $e = x$, so $E\hat{e} = Ex_{+1} - x$, and $\theta = 1 - \alpha$ since then:

$$E\hat{e} = \alpha x + (1 - \alpha)\bar{x} - x = (1 - \alpha)(\bar{x} - x) = \theta(\bar{e} - e).$$

13. This is another of those regrettable cases, like the demand and supply diagram, where economists have been careless enough to adopt a diagrammatic representation that puts what is usually the independent variable on the vertical axis.

14. Actually, this result depends on import prices not entering the price deflator.

15. Note that *F* has now reverted to representing foreign assets, rather than liabilities.

16. Those who dislike exchange-rate management use the pejorative term 'dirty floating' instead.

17. This is not the only possible way of organizing such a list. No doubt some would prefer a classification by the type of shock involved (changes in money supplies, changes in prices, etc.) rather than our classification by the channels through which shocks operate.

V

Development

This part of the book considers the relevance of international factors to the process of economic development. Chapter 15 concentrates on trade aspects, while Chapter 16 is devoted mainly to resource questions.

15

Trade and development

Economic development may be defined as the process by which a traditional society employing primitive techniques and therefore capable of sustaining only a modest level of per capita income is transformed into a modern, high-technology, high-income economy. The process involves the replacement of labour-intensive subsistence production by techniques that use capital, skilled labour and scientific knowledge to produce the wide variety of different products consumed in an affluent society. In the subsistence economy, production is essentially for own-use and exchange is marginal; in the modern economy, there is an advanced division of labour in which everyone specializes in producing goods that would satisfy only a minute part of total needs, so that production is essentially for the market and own-use is marginal.

It is clear that the indispensable prerequisite for this transformation of the nature of economic activity is the accumulation of those factors of production that are necessary to exploit scientific knowledge and utilize sophisticated production techniques. In a very broad sense, one may call those additional factors capital; but that concept must be interpreted to include not just physical capital goods but also human capital and intangible capital (relevant scientific knowledge).

A given rate of factor accumulation may, however, have very different implications for the rate of economic growth, depending on the goods that the extra factors are used to produce. The choice of which goods will be produced or of an environment in which that choice will be made by the microeconomic decision-makers has come to be known as the choice of a development strategy. It is a choice that has to pay attention to various factors. In particular, it has to consider where the *markets* for the increment to output will come from, and it has to ensure access to supplies of such *intermediate goods* as may be necessary to operate the new production processes. It is because international trade can be relevant to both the development of markets for output and the acquisition of intermediate inputs that the choice of a development strategy is a part of international economics.

15.1 Alternative development strategies

Development typically starts (or started, since the initial steps have now been taken virtually everywhere) when a small export sector develops alongside the subsistence economy. This produces a narrow range of goods based closely on the country's resource endowment – typically plantation crops, fibres or minerals, although occasionally peasant crops (like cocoa) are important. A monetized service sector develops to serve the export sector, parallel with the traditional services produced within the subsistence sector. Export proceeds are used to buy consumer goods, capital goods and intermediate goods for the modern sector. To the extent that the modern sector buys consumer goods from the traditional sector, the latter also acquires money that can be used to purchase imported consumer goods.

If a country that has reached this stage begins to generate increasing supplies of the factors of production needed to expand its modern sector, the question then is where those supplies should be deployed to ensure that the resulting output finds a market and necessary supplies of intermediate goods are forthcoming. There are three alternative strategies in the literature.

Balanced growth. When economists first began thinking of how policy could deliberately stimulate the development of underdeveloped countries, in the 1940s, a popular answer was that it was necessary to organize a simultaneous expansion of output over a wide range of industries. The Austrian-born economist Paul Rosenstein-Rodan (1902–86) and Ragnar Nurkse became the leading exponents of what was termed 'balanced growth'. They argued that an isolated expansion of output by one or two industries was bound to fail because there would be no increase in purchasing power elsewhere in the economy to buy the additional output; as a result only by a drastic cut in prices could an unbalanced increase in output by a particular sector be sold, which would make the expansion unremunerative. Their solution to this dilemma was balanced expansion by a large number of sectors, each thus providing additional purchasing power to help raise demand for the output of – and/or provide needed intermediate inputs to – all the other sectors. Thus a bold simultaneous advance might succeed where a series of piecemeal unbalanced initiatives would fail.

Although the basic insight on the nature of the problem is correct, time has not dealt kindly with the idea of balanced growth. There are two reasons. First, it is now clear that a simultaneous advance across a broad field is not practical, especially in small countries, because of economies of scale (see Chapter 5). In many industries, profitable operation requires the attainment of some minimum scale of operation. But the sum of the factor requirements needed for a simultaneous expansion of the minimum efficient size in a wide range of industries will exceed the sum of the additional factors becoming available over the normal investment period of a couple of years – indeed, in small countries this excess may be very large. This would mean that a balanced expansion would have to be programmed over a longer period than the normal investment period. But no firm will be willing to start investing now when it knows that returns would start accruing only long after the investment was complete. Therefore, balanced growth would never get off the ground.

Second, balanced growth is not necessary because the international economy provides an alternative source of markets and of supplies of intermediate goods. Additional output can be sold abroad or can take over a domestic market currently supplied by imports, and the foreign exchange thus earned or saved can be used to buy intermediate goods. The alternative strategies all give a central role to the international economy in sidestepping the need for balanced growth.

Export promotion. An alternative is to direct the additional factor supplies to export sectors. These may involve industries already engaged in export production, which by virtue of that fact presumably are those sectors where the country has a comparative advantage. Foreign rather than domestic markets are thus relied on to provide the additional demand, which – especially for a small country without influence on its terms of trade – they can certainly do. The proceeds of the exports can be used to purchase needed inputs abroad. It is possible to extend the strategy to the development of new (non-traditional) export sectors. Again foreign rather than domestic markets provide the addition to demand and the export proceeds finance the purchase of necessary inputs from abroad.

Import substitution. The last possibility is to establish new industries to replace imports. The market is thus domestic rather than foreign but, unlike the first case, it is possible for import substitution to take place sector by sector. The elimination of some imports releases foreign exchange for the purchase of needed inputs on the world market, or some intermediate goods may be among those for which local production is initiated.

15.2 Historical experience

Chapter 1 described the process of economic growth that first developed in Britain in the late eighteenth century and subsequently spread to embrace more and more countries during the nineteenth and twentieth centuries. To understand the post-war debate on the best development strategy, it is helpful to have some idea of the role of export expansion and import substitution as engines of growth in earlier periods.

The first experience of sustained economic growth, that of Britain, was fuelled by an expansion of industrial exports. The technical advances that were realized in Britain made it possible for British textiles and subsequently engineering products to penetrate and indeed dominate world markets. To some extent the reductions in prices and innovations in quality served to expand total world demand. The rest came from displacing traditional supply sources, as has usually been the dominant factor in export-led growth. The effect on traditional suppliers was painful, the more so because the increased British production involved an expansion that was large in relation to the size of the world market.

The pattern was fairly similar in the next two countries to start to industrialize, Belgium and France. There was somewhat more scope for import substitution on the basis of the internal markets that had been developed by British exporters, and the impact on third markets may have been somewhat less, but the basic picture is again of manufactures produced for export constituting the leading sector.

From then on there was a major change in the pattern of development. The nucleus of a group of industrializing countries created a growing demand for raw materials and later food, which presented opportunities to other countries to come in as suppliers. The typical development strategy for the remainder of the century of relative peace (1815–1914) involved a central role for a traditional export sector – not always traditional in the sense of exporting products that had long been sold abroad, but traditional in the sense of comprising primary products closely related to the country's natural resource endowment. Thus the United States exported cotton and later wheat, meat and a wide range of other primary products; Japan exported silk; Canada, Australia and Argentina exported wheat and beef; New Zealand exported butter and lamb; South Africa exported gold and diamonds; Sweden exported timber; Russia exported wheat; Brazil exported rubber and coffee; West Africa exported cocoa; India exported tea; and so on.

The above list contains some countries that had entered the ranks of the developed by 1914 (the United States, Canada, Australia, New Zealand), others that were still developing in 1914 but had certainly graduated by the 1960s (Japan and Sweden), marginal cases (Argentina, South Africa and Russia), as well as countries that are still among the developing (Brazil, West Africa and India). Clearly the mere establishment of a significant export sector is no guarantee that a take-off into sustained growth will be achieved. A look at what governs factor accumulation explains why some countries made the transition while others did not. For countries in close cultural contact (through geography or migration) with societies where growth had already taken root, the acccumulation of human capital was relatively easy. An expanding export sector providing raw materials to the industrial centre of the world economy generated demands to which the rest of the economy was capable of responding by building up import-substituting sources of supply. Export receipts, supplemented by foreign borrowing (which was feasible because the country's export performance gave assurance of ability to service its foreign debt), provided both the savings and the foreign exchange necessary to finance capital formation. Technical advances were applied in the production of food for local consumption, as well as in the modern export and import-competing sectors, so that the supply price of labour to the export sector rose. Thus the export sector avoided competing its price down to levels equivalent to a bare subsistence wage.

Things were very different in those countries where the population in general had no contact with the ways of the modern world. Without the ability to implement technical change or the entrepreneurial attitude to conceive of the possibilities, the expansion of the export sector did not set in motion other forces for modernization. Indeed, in many cases the export sector was itself the result of outside initiatives – of plantations or mines financed and managed by foreigners (typically from the colonial power) and drawing on the local economy only for unskilled labour and (the virtually free use of) natural resources. In these circumstances the modern export sector formed an isolated enclave, which generated little income locally – not much more than the subsistence-level wages of unskilled labour. The bulk of the income accrued to the foreign owners, who either repatriated the proceeds directly or spent them on buying imports. The isolation of the exporting enclave sector from the rest of the economy was at times extreme, as when the gentlemen of Manaus (the centre of the late-nineteenth-century rubber boom in the Amazon region of Brazil) sent their shirts to Lisbon to be laundered.

While export-led growth was the pattern typical of the liberal nineteenth century, it was not the only pattern. It was at times mixed with, and in some cases dominated by, that of import substitution. The classic case was that of Germany. Following the formation of a customs union, the Zollverein, between the then-independent German states in 1834, the enlargement of the internal market gave a stimulus to the development of domestic industry. Germany continued to follow protectionist policies following the unification engineered by Bismarck in the 1860s, and industry expanded at a rapid rate, especially in sectors like steel and chemicals. By the 1890s these industries had emerged as important export sectors. The outcome (though not necessarily the result) of this policy episode was what the proponents of infant-industry protection expected: temporary protection establishing industries producing first for the home market and subsequently for foreign markets.

Protection of the import-competing sector was also a feature of the industrialization of other countries – notably the United States and Japan, also in the less successful development efforts of Austria-Hungary and Italy, and after the First World War, in the countries of recent settlement. In fact, the only countries that have industrialized and not protected their incipient manufacturing industries producing for domestic markets are Britain and Hong Kong. The strategy of import substitution fostered by protection acquired a new importance in the inter-war period. Because of the relapse into protectionism by the developed countries, especially after the onset of the Great Depression in 1929, the option of export expansion was almost closed, except for countries with oil to export. (Not completely closed, as the Japanese example showed – but Japanese attempts to expand non-traditional exports encountered strong resistance from the developed countries, and insecurity in its dependence upon world markets played a major role in propelling Japan into the imperialist expansion that culminated in the national disaster of the Second World War.) Moreover, the forced import substitution in the periphery during the First World War, when the traditional suppliers were too busy fighting each other to attend to their traditional export markets, had demonstrated that a significant measure of industrialization was a feasible option for countries that had traditionally been suppliers of primary products.

For the world as a whole the 1930s was a disastrous decade, with a collapse of income in the early years followed by hesitant recovery and a shrinkage and distortion of trade as the income changes were first reinforced and later (when income started to recover) offset by protectionist pressures. However, some individual countries managed to do better than others and to avoid the worst of the recession. These were the countries that adopted the most protectionist and nationalist policies (and adopted them first): newly protectionist Britain and Nazi Germany, the Soviet Union and the larger Latin American republics that early rejected monetary orthodoxy and opted for devaluation, monetary expansion and protection – Argentina, Brazil, Chile, Colombia and Mexico. The countries that remained bound to the orthodoxy of fixed gold parities, the gold standard rules of the game, balanced budgets, free trade and letting insolvent banks collapse suffered the greatest fall in real income. Until the administration of President Franklin Roosevelt took office in 1933, the leading example of orthodoxy was the United States; subsequently, the 'gold bloc', led by France and encompassing Switzerland and Benelux, maintained an orthodox stance, at great cost, for another three years.

This then, was the historical background for the great debate on development strategy which was joined in the late 1940s, following the end of the Second World War and the conscious adoption by the member nations of the ideals of human betterment embodied in the United Nations Charter. There had been a golden age when trade had acted as an engine of growth, and it had been possible for a country to prosper as a supplier of primary products to the booming markets of the industrial centres of the world economy. That age had, however, been supplanted by one in which trade had grown much more slowly than income and a number of countries had demonstrated the feasibility of a strategy of import substitution. It was inevitable and perfectly proper that these experiences would influence the debate on development strategy. It was not inevitable, but it was perhaps natural, that the more recent experiences should have had the dominant impact.

15.3 Import substitution versus export promotion

Once the initial argument in favour of balanced growth had lost its appeal, the debate over development strategy settled into one between the relatively autarchic option of import substitution fostered by protectionism and the outward-looking option of export expansion. For the first few years the debate was dominated by those favouring import substitution. The most influential school arguing that case was based at the Economic Commission for Latin America (ECLA), in Santiago, Chile, whose dominant force was the Argentinian economist Raul Prebisch (1901–85). Prebisch had played a leading role in guiding the rather successful heterodox policies adopted by the Argentine Central Bank in the 1930s, so that he already had a close acquaintance with a case of import substitution.

The principal arguments in favour of import substitution – in addition to the emotive appeal of escaping from a role often perceived as that of hewers of wood and drawers of water – ran as follows: since balanced expansion of the domestic economy was impractical, the sale of additional output required winning new markets, either domestic or foreign. Furthermore, the expansion of output required the importation of capital goods and of intermediate inputs, which meant that additional foreign exchange must be made available. The question was whether it would be more advantageous to expand the slice of the domestic market supplied from domestic sources or to win a larger share of the world market. The latter meant either starting to export additional products or expanding exports of the products that the country had traditionally supplied. Exporting additional products – developing non-traditional exports – means principally industrial products. It was argued that such an option was not viable, for two reasons: the lack of a comparative advantage in the production of such goods and the problem of incipient protection by the developed countries that were the potential importers. The inter-war experience of Japan suggested that the liberal trading principles proclaimed by the West as a part of the brave new post-war world would be thrown to the winds if in fact developing countries did begin to establish a comparative advantage in the production of manufactures which might make substantial inroads into Western markets. Just how great was this pessimism of the West's unwillingness to absorb significant quantities of imports of manufactures from developing countries can be judged from a United Nations report of 1960 estimating the growth of LDC manufactured exports over the following decade at 60 per cent.

A strategy of export expansion was therefore assumed to involve putting additional resources into production of the primary products that a country had traditionally exported because of its comparative advantage based essentially on its endowment of natural resources. Despite the historical evidence that such a strategy had yielded dividends in the golden age of booming world trade prior to 1914, there were various reasons for arguing that this strategy was unlikely to offer the same advantages in post-war conditions. First, world trade had not boomed since 1914. Second, the export sectors that developing countries had previously built up had typically led to an enclave pattern of development rather than setting in motion forces leading to generalized growth. The income from additional traditional exports accrued largely to a limited class of rural (or, worse, foreign) landlords or mineowners, who lacked the interest or aptitude to invest outside their traditional activities and preferred to buy imported consumer goods rather than provide growing markets for domestic manufactures.

The third reason given has subsequently generated a substantial debate. It was argued that additional exports of primary products would turn the terms of trade against the exporting country (see the analysis of the large economy and the terms of trade in section 7.6). At best, this would mean that a part of the additional real income would accrue to the developed importing countries rather than to the developing exporters. At worst, where demand is price inelastic, it might lead to the phenomenon now called *immiserizing growth* (see section 16.9), since the terms of trade would deteriorate so much that the country actually would be worse off as a result of producing and selling more. It was asserted that these fears were not hypothetical possibilities, but that there had in fact been a historical tendency for the terms of trade of the primary-product-exporting countries to deteriorate as a result of supply running ahead of demand.

There was a great deal of subsequent criticism of the thesis of a secular deterioration in the terms of trade of primary producers. Critics were able to show that, by changing the period over which comparisons were made or the basket of commodities, the statistical evidence of such a deterioration vanished. (For example, consider a basket of primary commodities that includes oil and a time period that ends in the early 1980s.) But it was also argued that such historical comparisons were missing the central point. Sir Arthur Lewis asserted that the real source of the sense of injustice felt by developing countries lies in what are technically known as the double-factoral terms of trade:[1] the enormous disparity between the person hours that have to be expended in a developing country to buy the fruit of an hour's labour in a developed country, as compared to the fraction of a person hour that has to be expended in a developed country to buy the fruit of an hour's labour in a developing country.

There was also criticism of the idea that countries should avoid activities just because they may involve a deterioration in the (commodity) terms of trade. It was argued that any individual country could expand its exports without having a major effect on its terms of trade, given that there are few countries with much monopoly power in the supply of their exports. However, this does not really dispose of the terms-of-trade objection to the strategy of expanding sales of traditional exports. It means that an *individual* country may indeed be able to expand its export earnings by producing more, but this will be at the expense of a *greater* loss in earnings for other developing countries where total market demand is price inelastic. Especially where developing countries collectively supply the whole world demand for a good, as is true of all specifically tropical products, these countries may *collectively* suffer when one of them increases supply to the world.

The path of import substitution seemed attractive in comparison to these perceived problems and disadvantages of export expansion. It was conceded that import substitution might be a more expensive way of relieving a foreign exchange shortage in the short run, but the infant-industry argument for protection had long provided a rationale for accepting a degree of additional short-run cost in return for the future benefits of establishing a dynamic industrial sector. Furthermore, any terms-of-trade effects would be beneficial rather than harmful, while the sector that would benefit from protection would be (it was hoped) the dynamic industrial sector that could and would reinvest the bulk of its profits in further expansion. This mixture of infant-industry, income-distribution and terms-of-trade arguments for protection proved to have wide appeal, and in the 1950s there was a very general adoption of protectionist, import-substituting policies as concern to promote development spread to the farthest corners of what used to be known as the periphery.

The early results of the policy of import substitution appeared promising. At least in most of Asia and Latin America, where the educational system was already producing substantial numbers of trained personnel, industry responded to the chance of taking over the home market. Subsequent difficulties with import substitution policies have, however, led to a closer examination of those experiences. It is now argued that the first stage of import substitution is characteristically easy because it involves the production of non-durable consumer goods whose production requirements are well suited to the conditions existing in countries without previous industrial experience. These goods are intensive in unskilled labour. The efficient scale of output is small. Technology is unsophisticated. There is no need for a network of suppliers of parts, components and accessories. In short, countries with low wage levels should be able to produce economically their own non-durable consumer goods like clothing, shoes and simple household goods, together with many of the necessary intermediates like textiles, leather and wood.

In the early 1960s policies began to diverge. Some countries, like India and most of Latin America, pushed on to a second stage of import substitution based on their domestic markets, involving the establishment of industries to produce durable

Table 15.1 Trade orientation and economic performance

	Strongly outward-oriented countries		Strongly inward-oriented countries	
	1963–73[1]	1973–85[1]	1963–73[2]	1973–85[3]
Annual average growth of real GDP (%)	9.5	7.7	4.1	2.5
Annual average growth of real GNP/head (%)	6.9	5.9	2.7	1.0
Annual average growth of manufacturing value added (%)	15.6	10.0	5.3	3.1
Annual average growth of merchandise exports (%)	10.8	11.2	8.8	2.5
Annual average growth of manufactured exports (%)	14.8	14.2	5.7	3.7

[1] Korea, Singapore and Hong Kong.
[2] Dominican Republic, Ghana, India, Sri Lanka, Tanzania, Pakistan, Sudan, Uruguay, Ethiopia, Peru, Chile, Turkey, Bangladesh, Burundi, Zambia and Argentina.
[3] As in 1963–73 period except excludes Sri Lanka, Pakistan, Uruguay, Chile and Turkey, and includes Nigeria, Madagascar and Bolivia.
Source: Adapted from Greenaway and Nam (1988), tables 2 and 3.

consumer goods and more capital-intensive intermediates, like steel and petro-chemicals. In some cases, especially in Latin America, an attempt was made to assist this second-stage import substitution by the formation of regional trading blocs intended to provide a wider market for the newly established industries (see section 8.5 for the theory and Chapter 17 for a description of the blocs).

Other countries broke with the policy of import substitution more or less as soon as the easy first stage had been accomplished, and adopted instead an outward-looking strategy that favoured the growth of non-traditional exports. The leading examples, subsequently dubbed the 'Gang of Four', were Hong Kong (which indeed never had an initial protective phase), Korea, Singapore and Taiwan. Their example was partially followed in the later 1960s by some of the Latin American countries, notably Brazil and Colombia, which at that stage were already well into the second stage of import substitution in which durable consumer goods industries were established, but with high import requirements for intermediate inputs and capital goods.

The growth rates since 1963 of certain countries that have been identified as pursuing particularly outward-looking or particularly inward-looking policies are compared in Table 15.1. They do suggest that outward orientation has been more conducive to growth in general, to growth of manufacturing activities and to export expansion than inward orientation. Some caution must be attached, of course, to this type of comparison. First, there are a small number of observations for the strongly outward-oriented group. Second, the growth differences of the moderately outward- and inward-oriented countries (not shown in the table) are less clear. Third, per capita incomes are lower in the strongly inward-oriented countries than in the outward-oriented countries, and growth potential may decline as per capita income falls. It is worth pointing out, however, that Korea was one of the world's poorest countries in the mid-1960s! Thus, although a causal link between growth and outward orientation (export promotion) strategies cannot be proved with this type of empirical evidence, it is at the very least suggestive.

The hypothesis of a causal relationship between outward orientation and growth remains subject to criticism by the advocates of import substitution, but is widely accepted by agencies such as the World Bank, which has sponsored liberalizing trade policy reform in developing countries in the last decade. It is also pointed out by those defending outward orientation that domestic income distribution in the successful exporting countries has remained comparatively egalitarian. Furthermore, those pursuing the more outward-oriented policy seem to have exhibited more resilience in responding to additional burdens imposed by oil price increases.

In order to understand this success for the strategy of promoting non-traditional exports, it is necessary to understand the disadvantages of second-stage import substitution. While the non-durable consumer goods industries that are normally developed in the first stage of import substitution are technically suited to a country with little industrial expertise, this becomes less and less true the further import substitution is pushed. The additional industries are more capital intensive and skill intensive. Economies of scale are important: the minimum efficient size of plant is large relative to the scale of the market. Supplies of parts and components become an increasingly important consideration. Thus the country finds itself trying to establish industries in which it is less and less likely to have a comparative advantage.

A useful concept that has been developed to study this question is that of the *domestic resource cost* (DRC) of saving a unit of foreign exchange. The DRC of saving a dollar by import substitution is the total value (the social opportunity cost) of the domestic factors of production – labour, capital and natural resources – used in increasing the domestic output of a good that was previously imported,[2] expressed relative to the foreign exchange saved (valued at the shadow exchange rate).[3] A DRC ratio of less than unity indicates net cost savings to the economy from the activity in question. A ratio in excess of unity shows that foreign exchange savings on displaced imports (less any increase in foreign exchange payments needed to sustain domestic production – to buy imported intermediates or capital goods or to hire foreign technicians or to pay the profits of multinationals) are smaller than the resource costs of domestic production. The problem with second-stage import substitution is that it tends to involve escalating DRC ratios.

The concept of DRC can also be applied to export promotion. The DRC of earning a dollar through exports is the value of the domestic factors of production utilized divided by the net earnings of foreign exchange, after deducting costs of imported intermediates or other foreign exchange costs of generating exports. Clearly allocative efficiency requires that the domestic resource costs of importables and exportables production, of saving and earning foreign exchange, are equalized. What the supporters of an outward-oriented strategy maintain is that, once the easy first stage of import substitution has been accomplished and an initial industrial base has been established in non-durable consumer goods, the DRC ratio from exporting some of those (or similar) products is likely to be lower than that involved in further import substitution. Even if increasing and diversifying exports involves increases in DRC ratios, these are unlikely to be as large as from further import substitution. In the case of exports the rate of resource cost increase is set by the absorptive capacity of the world market or by the domestic supply side, rather than by the limited domestic market as with import substitutes.

There are several other reasons for maintaining that the DRC ratio will, after the first stage of import substitution, be lower for non-traditional exports than for further import substitution. One is that those first industries established use the factors that are abundantly available in countries lacking a past industrial history, notably unskilled labour, whereas further import substitution requires increasingly large proportions of scarce capital and skilled labour. For this reason an export-oriented strategy often creates a strong demand for the abundant factor of unskilled labour, so that the Stolper–Samuelson theorem helps explain why countries that have developed in this way have had a comparatively egalitarian income distribution. (In other cases, however, export orientation may involve emphasis on land-intensive products like soya beans, which will lead to income concentration unless the land is widely distributed among peasants.) A second reason is that an export orientation provides the chance to exploit economies of scale. There are some industries where the home market is large enough to sustain a domestic industry able to realize scale economies, but beyond some point (which seems to arise quite soon in small countries) this ceases to be true. A domestic industry limited to the home market will therefore involve the operation of plant below the minimum economic size. In contrast, exporting enables a country to concentrate on a limited number of sectors, each of which can be large enough to exhaust scale economies. Third, even where the domestic market is large enough to sustain a plant of minimum efficient size, this is not necessarily enough. Guaranteeing the domestic market to a single supplier invites all the ills of monopoly, notably high prices and lack of incentive to ensure efficiency. The need to compete on the world market provides a potent discipline that is all too often absent in countries adopting the import substitution strategy. Thus, whether we think in Heckscher–Ohlin terms of relative factor supplies or in Krugman–Lancaster terms of differentiated products offering scale economies, the DRC ratio of non-traditional exports is less likely to rise quickly than that of import substitutes.

Advocates of import substitution have traditionally feared that making oneself too comfortable on the bottom of the development ladder may impede subsequent efforts to climb higher. Not so, reply the proponents of an outward orientation: as a country accumulates more capital and industrial skills, it will naturally develop new industries which are intensive in the now-more-abundant factors. As comparative advantage changes, so will its mixture of industries: this is the optimistic message of dynamic comparative advantage. Attempts to drag a part of the economy prematurely up the ladder are likely to depress total income, and therefore savings, and therefore factor accumulation. This argument is not conclusively settled: it can be counter-argued that establishing industries with a strong demand for technical labour will increase the salaries of such persons and thereby the incentive to acquire such skills. For this reason some economists who have been impressed by the general argument for an outward-oriented strategy might still favour the maintenance of incentives towards a broadening of the industrial base.

What policy measures are called for to implement an outward-looking development strategy? Basically, the avoidance of import restrictions (tariff and non-tariff) on a scale that creates a significantly greater incentive for domestic producers to produce for the local than for the export market, and the maintenance of a realistic exchange rate.[4] The market will then provide an incentive for resources to be allocated between and within firms, industries and sectors to equalize DRC ratios between production for alternative markets. With the heavy protection called for by the import substitution strategy, payments equilibrium requires that the currency appreciate to the point where the growth of both traditional and non-traditional exports is impeded. It is noteworthy that countries that have adopted a strategy of promoting non-traditional exports have also had stronger growth of traditional exports than have the import substituters.

Two other arguments advanced in favour of an outward-oriented strategy are worthy of note. The first is that an import substitution strategy is more prone to create opportunities for bribes and corruption. Especially where the domestic market is too small to permit more than one firm and where the technology dictates that this be a multinational, the decision as to which firm will be established is essentially administrative and the temptations are evident. Furthermore, where protection is administered by quantitative restrictions rather than by tariffs, there are all the temptations that can arise from the need to distribute import licences, as noted in Chapter 8.

The second argument is that an export-oriented economy inherently has more flexibility to respond to shocks than a relatively closed economy, where the only goods imported are intermediate goods essential to the maintenance of domestic output and capital goods essential to the maintenance of economic growth. The existence of a margin of imports of consumer goods means that a combination of expenditure-reducing and expenditure-switching policies can adjust the balance of payments without the need to deflate output or curtail growth. This possibility still exists in a country without consumer goods imports, but only over the longer time period needed to change the pattern of output through additional investment in the traded goods industries. This presumably explains why the East Asian new industrial countries (NICs) seem to have experienced less trouble adjusting to the oil price increase than did less open economies, even ones on which the direct impact was smaller. However, the extra flexibility in adjustment must be bought at the cost of additional vulnerability to certain types of shock. There is evidence to suggest that the oil price increases in fact had a bigger impact on the outward-oriented, but their greater flexibility outweighed this disadvantage and enabled them to maintain growth better.

In fact, vulnerability to the state of the world economy remains the enduring worry about the viability of a strategy of export-led growth. The success of outward-oriented strategies in the 1960s and 1970s was possible only because the developed countries absorbed large quantities of manufactured imports from the NICs. In retrospect, we know that the sluggish trade growth of the period 1914–45 had given way to a new boom in trade from the early post-war period on, in which trade expanded more rapidly than output. Instead of the 60 per cent increase in LDC manufactured exports forecast in 1960 for the following decade, the actual increase was 500 per cent. It should not be thought that the expected defensive reactions to limit LDC manufactured exports were absent: as was noted in more detail in Chapter 9, the industrialized countries resorted to a series of subterfuges to restrict their imports in those cases (like textiles) where the NICs threatened to decimate their industries. But overall the old industrial countries proved more willing to accept NIC exports, and the NICs proved more capable of adapting themselves to produce goods that their customers found attractive, than the economists who had thought about these things in the 1950s had believed possible. Planning for an export-oriented strategy in the future does require an element of faith that the future will prove more like the post-war period has so far been than like the 1930s.

At least in the world conditions of the past thirty years, the 1950s pessimism about the feasibility of a strategy of non-traditional export expansion proved unfounded. The combination of successful practice with the convincing theoretical reasons analyzed earlier for expecting superior performance from an outward-oriented policy has proved persuasive. The result has been to make non-traditional export expansion into something of a new orthodoxy, especially in the World Bank, where its leading advocate was for long the Hungarian-born Bela Balassa (b. 1928) and subsequently, during her time as chief economist (1982–7), Anne Krueger. Quite a number of countries have adjusted their policies in that direction in the past two decades, especially in South-East Asia and South America. There have been stirrings also in South Asia, with a notable liberalization by Sri Lanka in 1976. Even in Africa, where the old objective of reducing the degree of integration with the world economy had a very strong influence on policy formulation, there have been a number of substantial trade liberalizations in recent years (e.g. Ghana, Tanzania). Much of this trade policy reform has been inspired by the World Bank, as a condition for structural adjustment loans. It is to a consideration of the trade component of such policy-conditioned lending that we now turn.

15.4 Conditional lending and trade policy

The second oil shock (see section 20.4) created severe payments problems for many developing countries. One response to this crisis was the initiation of a programme of structural adjustment lending by the World Bank. Although World Bank lending to developing countries traditionally involved some conditions (albeit often informal and imprecisely specified) about policy reform before this development, structural adjustment loans (SALs) constitute a systematic and overt attempt to sponsor policy reforms in developing countries aimed at 'getting prices right', opening up the economy and mobilizing domestic resources. Traditionally, World Bank lending concentrated on specific project loans, plus some sector loans and to a lesser extent loans for technical assistance. The SAL programme was initiated only in 1980, and by 1988 policy-conditioned lending accounted for $4.5 billion, some 25 per cent of total World Bank lending. Its size reflects the importance attached by the World Bank to the need for policy reform.

The SAL programme involves a commitment to agreed policy reforms in exchange for the right to borrow funds not tied to specific projects. In contrast to IMF stabilization loans, which are also conditional and tend to focus on short-run demand management and stabilization measures, SALs are conceived of as medium-term loans conditional upon predominantly supply-side reforms which are likely to require longer to be effective. Although IMF stabilization programmes are a necessary prerequisite for a SAL agreement, the two elements of stabilization and liberalization/ adjustment were viewed originally by the respective international agencies as separate and separable programmes. In the event there has been more overlap between the programmes than envisaged at the outset, and as a result there has at times been tension between the organizations about the nature of desired reforms and the timing and sequencing of reforms.

Trade policy reforms (narrowly defined) and reforms to closely related policies, such as exchange-rate and industrial policy, have been a major element of the SAL programme thus far. There is an extensive academic literature comparing the performance of economies pursuing different trade strategies, but until recent years less attention has been paid to the transition from one to the other. Indeed, there was relatively little empirical and case-study evidence available, prior to the start of SAL programmes, to guide the negotiations between the World Bank and the governments of developing countries about the form and pace of reform.[5] As a result the detailed form and sequencing of reforms have varied substantially between countries. This diversity of experience now provides a rich source of information for studying the process of trade liberalization. Research is now asking questions about the optimal form, timing and sequencing of trade and related policy reforms and about the conditions that affect the sustainability and success of the reforms. Although there are not, as yet, unambiguous and unique answers to many of these questions, some general principles are beginning to emerge.

Reform of direct instruments of trade policy under SALs has involved, to varying degrees, one or more of the following:

- the lowering or dismantling of quantitative restrictions against imports;
- the reform of tariffs;
- direct promotion of exports.

It is widely accepted that moving from non-tariff to tariff forms of protection is desirable because tariffs are more transparent, allow competition at the margin on the home market and tend to be less protective as demand expands. (See Chapter 8 for a fuller elaboration of these points.) Thus a liberalization policy often starts with the elimination of quantitative restrictions (QRs) even if this means higher tariffs than before. But the *immediate* conversion from QRs to tariffs is only one option. Since it is difficult in practice to measure, even approximately, the tariff equivalent of a quantitative import restriction, there is a danger either that the new tariff will prohibit imports or that it will lead to the rapid increase of imports that policy-makers fear. Rapid import increases may threaten the sustainability of reform. In such circumstances there may be a rationale for removing QRs in a manner that avoids large, short-run changes in the volume and composition of imports.

More gradual QR liberalization is possible through the gradual raising of quota ceilings (with elimination when they become non-binding) or by eliminating QRs sequentially on a product-by-product basis. But gradualism may mean that the wrong signals are given. The private sector may have difficulty in translating a schedule of quota ceilings into price and protection levels. Indeed, the short-term signals may be perverse. If the product-by-product elimination of quotas liberalizes the least politically sensitive items, such as raw material and component imports, first, then this will raise (rather than lower) the effective rate of protection of final goods. Moreover, a 'tariffication' of QRs would increase government revenue, as quota revenues are transferred from holders of import licences to the government, and this benefit is forgone with a gradual easing of QRs. Thus a mixed strategy of gradual QR liberalization and some (temporary) compensatory tariff-rate increases may offer a viable solution.[6] An alternative possibility is to auction off the quotas for the first year or two, set the new tariffs at the revenue level realized in the auction and subsequently reduce the tariffs gradually.

Tariff reform has been concerned with both the rationalization and reduction of tariffs. Given that QR liberalization is likely to precede tariff reduction, the first stage of tariff reform is likely to be mainly concerned with rationalization. At this stage, rationalization may seek to reduce the number of border taxes on imports and the number and dispersion of tariff rates that apply against particular categories of imports; reducing the number of taxes increases the certainty and transparency of the protective structure, while reducing the dispersion of tariff rates increases the neutrality of the system and curtails the opportunities for corruption. But ultimately, rationalization and liberalization are interelated considerations. Greater uniformity or neutrality can be achieved, for example, by raising tariffs (or eliminating duty exemptions) on intermediate and raw material imports while leaving tariffs on final goods unaltered on average. The net effect would be to lower levels of effective protection for domestic producers of final goods. On the other hand, lowering tariffs on intermediate goods would raise effective protection if tariffs on final goods remained unaltered.

Clearly it is necessary to be careful when designing the sequence of tariff reforms if they are to increase neutrality and reduce protection. As a rule, simple schemes widely applied work better than fine tuning tariff-line by tariff-line. Some tariff reforms have attempted to target the effective, rather than nominal, rates of protection (the Philippines reforms of 1981–5 and the Ivory Coast reforms of 1981–6 are examples). Such complicated reforms have tended to be unsuccessful because of measurement problems and the excessive demands they have imposed on administrative systems. As was indicated in the discussion of optimal taxation in Chapter 10, there are strong practical arguments in favour of relatively uniform tariffs across and within different categories of imports. This may justify raising tariffs and/or removing duty exemptions on intermediate goods in the early stages of reform. This should be beneficial for government revenue and the balance of payments. The extent of the adjustment costs for final producers whose levels of effective protection are reduced by higher input tariffs will be influenced by the extent of QR liberalization as well as the speed and extent of input-tariff increases. Some argue that, to help business plan a rational adjustment strategy, future tariff changes should be clearly announced and rigidly adhered to. Others argue that the rate of trade liberalization should vary with macroeconomic conditions, slowing down further liberalization when the economy is in recession or subject to severe payments strains.

Medium-term tariff reduction following the liberalization of QRs and initial tariff rationalization should again exploit simple tariff-cutting rules. One such procedure is the 'concertina approach': an initial tariff ceiling is set, all tariffs above that ceiling are lowered according to an agreed timetable and this procedure is then repeated for a new, lower ceiling. This helps to minimize adjustment costs and achieve greater uniformity of effective protection across and within industries. The speed of such tariff reform is a subject of debate. A lengthy time period may ease adjustment costs and thereby help to sustain reform, but it may create a danger that the adjustment will not be viewed as credible by a private sector that may anticipate being able to block further reform through its lobbying activity.

The logic of trade liberalization is that import protection should be as low as possible. But, even in the medium to long term, average tariffs may well be positive and non-negligible. In the case of Chile, a country that underwent a major economic liberalization during the 1970s, the tariff ended up at a uniform rate of 10 per cent. Revenue, protective and balance of payments factors may account for a reluctance to liberalize imports completely. In any event, little harm is done by uniform tariffs as low as 10 per cent.

Where import tariffs remain significant, however, some anti-export bias is likely to result. The bias against exports may be of two analytically distinct forms. Positive protection for import-substituting activities will discriminate between different types of tradable goods, discriminating in favour of importables production and against exportables production if exportables are not subsidized by a similar amount. Import protection will also tend to induce overvaluation of the real exchange rate; this may reduce the competitiveness of exports in foreign markets and provide an incentive for resources to be pulled out of the production of tradable goods into that of non-tradable goods. Where significant import protection remains, export promotion therefore requires that excessive currency overvaluation is avoided. It may also provide an incentive for considering direct export promotion measures that compensate exporters for the implicit subsidy to import-substituting activities from tariff protection. (Export subsidization measures were considered in greater detail in Chapter 9.) There are problems, however, associated with direct export promotion. It may pose administrative problems where selective support is given for production destined for foreign, but not domestic, markets. It often requires significant budgetary resources. Domestic rent-seeking activity and trade conflicts with importing countries may also be encouraged. Indirect export promotion via import liberalization is likely to be more effective than compensatory export promotion measures in the longer term.

The design of trade policy reform remains a controversial area. Even among those who accept the rationality of liberalizing trade, there are those who are critical of an infringement of national sovereignty in having international agencies 'bribe' countries into making such reform. However, pragmatic technocrats often welcome SAL conditionality as a weapon that can help overcome mercantilist prejudices of politicians and rent seeking by vested interests. On the more technical issues, there is wide agreement on the need to start the process of trade policy reform by achieving a competitive exchange rate to promote exports and abolishing QRs, but substantial disagreements persist about the speed of liberalization and the wisdom of sticking to a rigid timetable.

15.5 Summary

A developing country that is succeeding in accumulating capital and skilled labour has to determine in which sectors these factors should be deployed to promote development. The relevant considerations are that new markets must be found and necessary intermediate goods must be acquired. One possible solution to this problem, balanced growth, is ruled out by the importance of scale economies. The alternatives involve international trade, either by increasing exports or by substituting for imports. Prior to 1914 peripheral countries were able to base their development on the expansion of primary-product exports, for which their natural resource endowment gave them a comparative advantage, to the growing industrial markets of the centre. In the age of crises from 1914 to 1945 this strategy was undermined by the sluggish growth in trade that resulted from the combination of slow growth and protectionism in the centre, and some countries ameliorated the effects of recession by adapting their policies to the circumstances of the times, giving protection to import substitutes. The development orthodoxy of the 1950s, assuming this world environment would continue, prescribed import substitution as the best development strategy, and this advice was widely heeded. However, world markets were far more buoyant than had been expected and gave ample opportunities for growth through the expansion of non-traditional – principally industrial – exports. Where feasible, this strategy offers many advantages in comparison to import substitution: it exploits rather than fights comparative advantage and economies of scale; it leads to more demand for unskilled labour and thus to a less concentrated income distribution; it permits the maintenance of competition and is less conducive to the creation of opportunities for corruption; and it gives more flexibility in adjustment. This strategy has therefore become a new orthodoxy and has been quite widely adopted in recent years.

The judgement that the new orthodoxy is essentially correct merits some further elaboration. First, the extent of the success of the strategy of export promotion depends on the state of the world economy, although it has to be said that second-stage import substitution would look a pretty unpromising alternative even if the industrial world went into recession or turned strongly protectionist. A second issue relates to whether exporting labour-intensive manufactures will remain an attractive option if too many other developing countries adopt the same strategy. The fear is that developing countries would compete the benefits of trade away. But it has also been argued that this need not happen, since, as new countries start to industrialize and export the simplest labour-intensive commodities, the present NICs will have acquired the skills to move upmarket and supply the more sophisticated goods that are now still the preserve of old industrial countries. (Signs of this trend can already be detected in the increasing weight of engineering products, including capital goods, among the exports of countries like Brazil, India and Korea.) A third issue is the sequencing of reform. It is widely agreed that a reform-minded country should start by liberalizing QRs, but a lively debate is still in progress over other questions, such as the speed of liberalization and the rigidity of the timetable for dismantling trade restrictions.

15.6 Bibliography

The literature on balanced growth was initiated by Rosenstein-Rodan (1943). For an authoritative statement of the arguments for import substitution, see Economic Commission for Latin America (1950). An early paper favouring export promotion was Macarro (1964). The main counter-revolution in favour of export promotion was led by Balassa (1970) and Little, Scitovsky and Scott (1970). Useful papers on the debate include Diaz Alejandro (1975), Balassa (1980), Krueger (1984), Kirkpatrick (1987), and Lal and Rajapatirana (1987). There are also a number of papers in both Greenaway (1988) and Milner (1990) which deal with the current theoretical and empirical issues in this area.

For the debate on the secular tendency of the terms of trade of primary products, see Findlay (1981) and Sapsford (1988). A detailed outline of the domestic resource-cost methodology is provided by Bruno (1972) and Krueger (1972). An up-to-date review of theory and evidence on DRC estimates is provided in Greenaway and Milner (1991).

Work on policy-conditioned lending inspired or sponsored by the World Bank itself is reported in Choksi and Papageorgiou (1986) and World Bank (1988). An alternative perspective is provided by Mosley, Harrigan and Toye (1990).

Notes

1.   The terms-of-trade concept used up to now is the commodity or net barter terms of trade, p_X/p_M, which measures the quantum of imports that can be bought with a given volume of exports. The 'single-factoral terms of trade', w/p_M, measures the quantity of imports that can be bought with a given quantity of domestic labour. The 'double-factoral terms of

trade', w/ew^*, measures the quantity of foreign labour that can be 'bought' with a given quantity of domestic labour.

2. Note that if there is a good reason to suppose that the market price of some domestic factor(s) misrepresents its social value – for example, because the marginal product of labour in its alternative (subsistence-sector) use is much less than the wage it will receive in the modern sector – then for the purpose of this calculation it is rational to represent its social value by a shadow price that reflects the social opportunity cost.

3. A shadow price refers to the marginal value of a scarce resource. The shadow exchange rate therefore represents the social value of an additional unit of foreign exchange. In highly distorted economies where macroeconomic management is weak, the actual exchange rate typically underestimates the social value of foreign exchange. In principle the shadow rate could be estimated from a model of the economy where social welfare is maximized subject to all current and future production constraints. In practice, *ad hoc* adjustments are often made to the actual exchange rate in the light of guesstimates of exchange-rate misalignment.

4. Some countries, like Brazil and Colombia, that had already undergone second-stage import substitution when they adopted an outward orientation, chose to maintain high tariffs and an overvalued currency and to compensate for the disincentive to non-traditional exports by subsidizing the latter. This enabled the established import-substituting industries to survive, but penalized the development of traditional (non-subsidized) exports. The implications of this 'mixed' approach are considered in section 15.4.

5. The principal exception was by Krueger (1978), a multi-country study of foreign trade regimes which examines the relationship between liberalization and stabilization.

6. One possibility in this case would be the use of tariff quotas: imports to a given quantity enter at the existing tariff rate and imports in excess of the quota enter at a higher rate.

16

Factor accumulation in the open economy

The fundamental prerequisite of economic growth is accumulation of larger stocks of the factors of production (including knowledge). If growth is to lead to higher living standards, then the factors accumulated must be factors other than unskilled labour. The topic of this chapter is how this process of factor accumulation is influenced by the openness of the economy.

The traditional two-factor model used to analyze questions of economic growth assumes that factors of production can be aggregated into homogeneous capital and homogeneous labour. Labour growth is assumed either to be exogenous or else to decline as per capita incomes rise, representing the effect of higher income levels in raising aspirations, reducing desired family size and increasing knowledge of birth-control techniques. In either event, the key to economic progress, interpreted as raising per capita income, is to be found in capital accumulation.

16.1 Capital accumulation in the closed economy

There are at least three different visions of what drives the process of capital accumulation in a closed capitalist economy. These may be identified with neo-classical, Marxist and Keynesian schools of thought.

The neo-classical view treats investment as determined by savings, and savings as the result of the intertemporal consumption decisions of households. This is, for example, the situation in the neo-classical growth model, where there is continual full employment and capital accumulation is that part of full-employment output that households choose not to consume. A critical question is: what is supposed to maintain continual full employment? The only logically satisfactory answer is that this must be the result of price flexibility (including interest-rate variations). The problem with the more realistic answer, that the government may adopt an active fiscal–monetary policy to maintain full employment, is that in that event the savings ratio will depend upon the necessity for, and the form of, the government's demand management policy, rather than simply reflecting household consumption prefer-ences.

Assuming that the story of price flexibility is sufficiently convincing to make the neo-classical model worth further consideration, there are two ways in which it can

302

be extended. One is to modify the simple assumption that households always consume a constant fraction of their income and assume instead that they make an attempt at intertemporal optimization. This has the effect of introducing wealth and interest rates as determinants of the level of savings. A consequence of this modification is to rule out certain implausible possibilities that arise with the fixed savings ratio, such as society saving too much for its own long-run good.[1] A second extension involves disaggregating goods into a consumer good and a capital good, and positing a concave production possibility curve between them. This means that any attempt to increase the rate of growth would tend to run into diminishing returns, since a cut in the output of consumption goods would not permit a proportionate increase in the output of capital goods.

The analysis of the German economist, sociologist and philosopher Karl Marx (1818–83), the founder of socialism, centred on the process of capital accumulation. It is therefore not surprising that he presented a distinctive view on the subject. This view coincides with the neo-classical one in assuming that it is savings that determine investment, but differs in identifying the main determinant of the savings ratio as the distribution of income between wages and profits rather than the consumption preferences of households. In its extreme form, the Marxist savings hypothesis says that workers spend all their income while capitalists save (and invest!) all theirs, but the qualitative flavour of the analysis is retained so long as capitalists save a higher proportion of their income than do workers.

The Marxist savings hypothesis has proved popular with a number of non-Marxist economists, such as the Hungarian-born British peer Lord (Nicholas) Kaldor (1908–86) and some of his Cambridge colleagues. It also plays a central role in Sir Arthur Lewis's famous analysis 'Economic development with unlimited supplies of labour' (1954). In that model, a small modern manufacturing sector is assumed to be implanted by local capitalists in a predominantly subsistence economy where the marginal product of labour is close to zero but everyone receives a subsistence income equal to the average product of labour because of the extended family system. The modern sector can therefore draw on an unlimited supply of labour at a real wage that exceeds the average product of labour in the subsistence sector by enough to tempt unskilled labourers to leave their homes and traditional way of life. The excess of the output of the modern sector over the subsistence-plus wages paid to labour constitutes a surplus for the capitalists which they plough back into expanding the size of the modern sector. Barring crises, the process of expansion of the modern sector will persist for decades, but one day the whole of the surplus labour will have been absorbed by the modern sector and real wages will start to rise, thus exerting pressure for modernization in the traditional sector as well.

A third view of capital accumulation, pioneered by the Austrian economist Joseph Schumpeter (1882–1950) but now mainly associated with Keynesian thought, sees savings as determined by investment rather than vice versa. In Keynes's graphic phrase, investment is determined by the 'animal spirits' of the entrepreneurs rather than by a passive decision of capitalists to invest all. (To be sure, Marxists also recognize the possibility that the profitability of investment may decline to the point where capitalists lose interest in investing, but then excitement at the prospective crisis leading to the demise of capitalism tends to displace further analysis.) Given investment, income adjusts to generate that level of savings, so long as income does not run into the full-employment constraint. If investment exceeds full-employment savings, a variety of adjustment mechanisms may come into play: interest rates may rise, thus curtailing investment and perhaps also stimulating savings in a neo-classical way; prices may rise more than wages, redistributing income from wages to profits and so increasing savings according to the Marxists savings hypothesis; the government may deflate, either cutting investment or increasing savings; or inflation may develop, adding to savings through the inflation tax.

Of these three visions of what drives the process of capital accumulation, the most popular among economists has traditionally been the neo-classical view and the least popular has been the Keynesian. Unfortunately, this order of popularity reflects the ease with which the respective hypotheses can be embodied in elegant and self-contained models rather than their usefulness in illuminating the real world. Circumstances do exist in which the neo-classical or Marxist models can be useful, as noted above in the discussion of the various adjustment mechanisms when investment exceeds full-employment savings. But one always needs to consider whether investment is constrained by the lack of incentive to invest or by a shortage of savings, rather than reasoning automatically in terms of a model which takes it for granted that only a savings constraint can exist.

16.2 Borrowing or lending to enhance income

In a closed economy, investment is constrained by the ability of the domestic economy to generate savings. In an open economy, this constraint can be relaxed by foreign borrowing. Alternatively, an economy where investment falls short of full-employment savings may develop a current account surplus and lend its excess savings abroad, rather than allow the potential savings to run to waste through recession.

Borrowing gives a country the ability to finance a trade deficit, which permits absorption to rise above output. When the country ceases borrowing and has to service its debt, either by paying interest or by repaying the principal (or amortizing its debt, as repayment by stages is called), the contrary occurs: it has to restrict absorption to a level lower than income in order to generate a trade surplus. Borrowing therefore involves an early period when absorption exceeds income, followed by a later period when income exceeds absorption. Conversely, lending involves an initial period when income exceeds absorption, followed by a later period when the lender can enjoy the fruits of earlier abstinence by absorbing more than his or her income.

The first motivation for borrowing (or lending) that we shall study is that of enhancing the stream of income over time. Consider the standard type of Keynesian investment function shown in Figure 16.1, in which the marginal efficiency of investment (*MEI*) is a declining function of the rate of interest. Suppose also that savings are interest inelastic as in standard Keynesian models, so that the savings

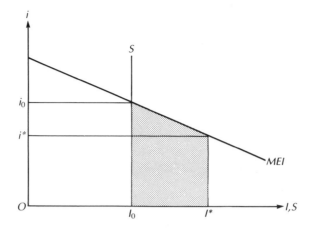

Figure 16.1 Investment-savings equilibrium

schedule is vertical as shown. Then the interest rate consistent with macroeconomic equilibrium in a closed economy would be i_0. If the government tried to use monetary policy to push the interest rate down below i_0 and so stimulate investment to raise growth, it could succeed only to the extent that the monetary expansion created inflation and so generated forced savings. The wisdom of such a policy of inflationary finance is very questionable, and we shall instead assume that the country avoids these temptations and selects its monetary policy to generate the equilibrium interest rate i_0 and hence the level of investment I_0.

Now suppose that our country discovers that it has the option of borrowing unlimited sums on the world capital market at the going world interest rate i^*. (This assumes that creditors would not start to worry about the debtor's creditworthiness as its indebtedness mounted, as well as that the country is small in the world capital market.) Clearly it will be advantageous for it to borrow $(I_1 - I_0)$ and expand investment up to the point I_1 where the marginal efficiency of investment is equal to the world interest rate. This increases future income by a sum equal to the shaded area. Of that, the rectangular part has to be paid as interest to the foreign lenders, while the triangle remains as a net benefit to the country. As and when debt-service payments come to exceed capital inflows, our country will need to generate a trade surplus, and absorption will in consequence fall short of income. But as long as our country never overborrows, in the sense of contracting loans with a higher interest cost than the return on the additional investment they are used to undertake, then the country will necessarily be better off for having borrowed and invested the proceeds.

The impact of such productive loans on the time path of income and absorption is shown in Figure 16.2. The lower curve shows the path that income (equals absorption) would take under capital account autarchy. However, when the marginal efficiency of the investment financed by domestic savings exceeds the world rate of interest, it pays to borrow, which enables A to exceed Y by the amount of the capital

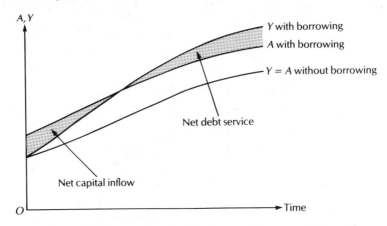

Figure 16.2 Impact of productive loans on income and absorption

inflow. Because of the additional investment, Y grows faster than it otherwise would,[2] as shown by the curve Y *with borrowing*. Absorption starts off above Y and remains above so long as capital inflows exceed debt service (that is, so long as the net resource transfer[3] is positive), but eventually net resource transfer turns negative and in consequence A falls below Y *with borrowing* (though remaining above the $Y = A$ curve), as shown by A *with borrowing*.

In the case just discussed, the forces of thrift and productivity led the country to borrow. But it is evident that, had the savings curve of Figure 16.1 lain to the right of the point I_1 (where the *MEI* falls to i^*) instead of to the left, the whole argument would have had to go into reverse. Our country would then have found it advantageous to lend the excess of its saving over and above the domestic investment that was expected to generate a return as high as the world interest rate. So long as this net lending was in progress, absorption would have fallen below income. But as and when interest earnings and amortization came to exceed new lending, the net resource transfer would become positive and absorption would rise above income. Later A would also rise above the $Y = A$ curve of capital autarchy, assuming that the country did not overlend. Lenders, as well as borrowers, can hope to gain through this process of international investment, which increases world output by relocating investment from areas where returns would be low to those where they are high. That is why one is not surprised to find that capital has generally flowed from the capital-rich industrial countries or the oil-producing surplus states with small populations to the capital-poor developing countries and the resource-rich primary producers, neither of which generate enough domestic savings to exhaust the investment opportunities that are profitable at the world interest rate. Its failure to continue flowing in that direction in the 1980s following the debt crisis led to many complaints about 'negative transfers'. How surprised should one be at this development? Let us consider the model of a debt cycle.

16.3 The debt cycle

Imagine a country that first comes into contact with the modern world. Since it has a low capital stock (per capita), the marginal productivity of capital will presumably be high. On the other hand, savings will be limited by the low level of output and therefore income. This is the classic situation in which it will pay a country to borrow abroad in order to accelerate the process of capital accumulation. The country enters the first stage of the debt cycle, that of a net borrower with an inward real-resource transfer.[4]

Over time the country builds up both its capital stock and its international debt. The higher level of capital increases output, a part of which is diverted into servicing the external debt. In due course debt service comes to exceed the capital inflow, and the resource transfer becomes negative: this is the second stage of the debt cycle.

The third stage arises if and when the country generates domestic savings larger than its domestic investment requirements, and exports the excess savings abroad. This increases the negative resource transfer, but the benefit is that external debt gradually decreases.

The fourth stage of the debt cycle comes about if the country remains a capital exporter long enough to repay its (net) external debt and become a creditor. Initially the resource transfer remains negative, since its capital outflow exceeds its interest receipts, which become positive once the country becomes a net creditor.

As the build-up of external assets continues, a time may come when debt service exceeds the capital outflow and the country moves to stage 5. This is the position of a 'mature creditor', which enjoys a positive resource transfer as it ploughs back a part of its foreign investment income into new investment and uses the remainder to increase its consumption.

The sixth and 'final' stage of the debt cycle arises if and when a mature creditor starts to live off its (foreign) capital, consuming not merely its interest income but importing capital as well.

Must countries necessarily go through the full six stages of a debt cycle, or can a steady state develop before the cycle is played through? For example, could a country remain in stage 1, a capital importer enjoying a positive resource transfer, in the long run? Only if the rate of interest is less than 'the' rate of growth: in that event the ratio of debt to whatever is growing will fall continuously, so that the country's debt burden declines over time even while it has a positive income transfer. The Brazilian economist Mario Henrique Simonsen (b. 1935) has termed this a situation of 'pleasant debt arithmetic', which middle-income countries experienced while they borrowed from the banks in the 1970s.

What is the relevant magnitude whose growth should be compared to the interest rate? The usual candidates are exports and GNP: the former provides a measure of current debt-servicing capacity, while the latter is relevant inasmuch as in the long run resources are fungible and the factors producing non-traded goods could be redirected to the external market. The long run could not, however, last literally for ever. We know that growth rates cannot exceed the interest rate for ever, because if they did present values would be infinite. A country with a growth rate exceeding the world interest rate would therefore become large relative to the world economy, at which point it would bid the world interest rate up to exceed its growth rate. Its interest payments would then come to exceed its new borrowing, so it would move to stage 2. Thus although countries may under certain circumstances remain in stage 1 a long time, provided they remain 'small', this is not a position where steady state is possible.

Countries with relatively high savings rates, resulting in the neo-classical view from a rate of time preference less than the world rate of interest, will in any event move into stage 2 even while their own growth rate may exceed the world interest rate. These thrifty countries are the ones that will move on into stages 3, 4 and 5. But less thrifty countries will also move into stage 2 when creditors call a halt to further increases in the debt–export (or debt–GNP) ratio: at that point the rate of growth of debt must fall to the rate of growth of exports (or GNP), which, as argued above, must ultimately be less than the interest rate, implying that debt service will exceed the capital inflow. There is no reason why such a situation should not persist indefinitely: indeed, stage 2 seems the natural steady state for an 'impatient' country. In fact, a particularly myopic country might reach stage 2 by using its stage 1 borrowing to finance a consumption binge rather than added investment.

Stage 3 certainly cannot be a steady state, for eventually an indebted capital-exporting country will repay all its debt and move into stage 4. Could a country remain in stage 4, building up its foreign assets, for ever? Once again, this would be possible if and only if the growth rate (of foreign lending, in this case) exceeds the interest rate, for otherwise debt service must eventually come to exceed the capital outflow. That is certainly not an outcome that would be predicted by economic theory: accumulating wealth is expected to lead to increasing consumption. Intertemporal optimization implies that the fruits of wealth accumulation will eventually be in part consumed.

Thus the expectation is that a thrifty country will eventually move on into stage 5. This is perfectly consistent with steady state: foreign assets could grow along with the rest of the economy, with the excess interest income being consumed. Indeed, one might expect such a steady state to be the norm: only a country that becomes less thrifty will move on into stage 6, of living off its capital. Clearly this is possible only for a finite time, and eventually such a country must move back into one of the earlier stages.

Thus the two stages where one expects to find countries for a lengthy period are stages 2 and 5, with spendthrift countries in the former stage and thrifty countries in the latter stage. Paradoxically the spendthrift countries will have a negative resource transfer and the thrifty countries a positive transfer.

The two best examples of countries going through a full debt cycle are Britain and the United States. A positive resource transfer helped Britain to finance the start of the industrial revolution in the late eighteenth century, although in this case expropriation of the hapless Bengalis following their conquest in the Seven Years War may have played a bigger role than borrowing. An advantage of expropriating foreigners rather than borrowing from them is that stage 2 can be omitted, so Britain emerged as a creditor early. It built up a vast creditor position by the eve of the First World War, when it was a mature creditor receiving over 10 per cent of its GNP from investment income and reinvesting about half of that to increase its foreign assets. This vast treasure was used to finance the two world wars, after the second of which Britain's net external assets had practically vanished.

The United States borrowed abroad to help finance its railroads, Civil War and early industrialization. By the end of the nineteenth century it had started to export capital, though it was still a net debtor (stage 3). It became a net creditor during the First World War and a mature creditor after the Second World War. In the 1980s President Reagan's 'politics of joy' – cut taxes in the implausible hope that this will increase revenue, savings and the trade balance, rather than lead to twin deficits – took the United States through stage 6 in a few years and back to its current position in stage 1.

16.4 Borrowing or lending to modify the time path of absorption

The second general motivation for international capital flows is that of modifying the time path of absorption. To permit a sharp distinction between this case and the previous one, we must suppose that the time path of domestic investment is given, which implies that the path of income (GDP) is independent of capital flows. Given that assumption, Figure 16.3 shows the three cases that may arise.

Figure 16.3(a) shows the use of the international capital market to postpone consumption. (Given that investment is being held constant, postponing absorption is the same thing as postponing consumption.) This describes the situation of one of the low-absorbing oil exporters in the era of high oil prices. They enjoyed a high level of gross[5] domestic income, which should have been expected to fall off in the medium term. Instead of splurging all this income on consumption, and then facing the next

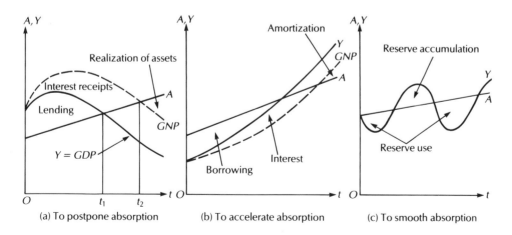

Figure 16.3 International capital flows to modify the time path of absorption

generation with the need to accept a fall in its standard of living, it is natural and rational for such a country to run a current account surplus in the short run and invest the proceeds abroad. This will permit the maintenance of constant or rising consumption even after domestically generated income starts to decline. There will come a time (t_1 in the diagram) when absorption will overtake GDP and the country will start to live off its investment income. For a time the country will in fact continue to make additional loans of a value less than the interest income (shown as the excess of the dotted curve over the Y-curve), but eventually (beyond t_2) it may start to realize its assets. Note that the equation describing the sources and uses of income is:

$$Y + iF = A + \dot{F} \tag{16.1}$$

where F is the country's stock of foreign assets. From equation 16.1 it follows that $\dot{F} = iF$ at time t_1 and $A = Y + iF$ at time t_2.

The converse case is shown in Figure 16.3(b), a country that borrows in order to raise present consumption at the expense of future consumption. Such consumption loans are sometimes attacked as irresponsible because they mortgage future generations. That can and does occur. But where there is a country with strong growth prospects, as pictured in Figure 16.3(b), it is not at all evident that the present generation is to be condemned for taking some of the benefit of that future growth for itself instead of leaving all the benefits for the next generation (which is in any event going to live better than itself) while bearing all the costs that make that future growth possible. Such consumption loans will take place to the extent that savings are interest elastic, as Figure 16.4 shows. Taking advantage of the world capital market raises investment from I_0 to I_1, and also cuts savings from I_0 to I_2, so that the proportion $(I_1-I_0)/(I_1-I_2)$ of the capital inflow is a production loan and the proportion $(I_0-I_2)/(I_1-I_2)$ is a consumption loan.

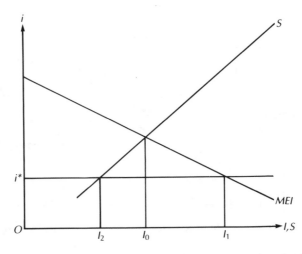

Figure 16.4 Savings-investment equilibrium with interest-elastic savings

Figure 16.3(c) shows a third possibility, using the international capital market to smooth out absorption in the face of variations in income. Traditionally, this has been regarded as a principal reason for holding reserves, so the diagram is labelled on the assumption that reserves are used for this purpose, but there is no reason why a country need use reserves rather than borrow, or accumulate reserves rather than lend in other ways. (Interest payments are omitted from the diagram for reasons of simplicity.) The most important variations in income are those stemming from changes in the terms of trade and crop failures. The oil price increases of 1973 and 1979 caused important adverse movements in the terms of trade of oil-importing countries, which they largely accepted as increased current account deficits in the short run, and financed by borrowing or reserve decreases. Exporters of primary products often face equally dramatic changes in their terms of trade as a result of a rise or fall in the price of a principal export product. Or else countries may experience a crop failure that deprives them of a principal export product or creates the need to import to substitute for lost domestic production. These events may easily be linked: the loss of a large part of the Brazilian coffee crop from frost in 1976 caused a rise in the price of coffee which benefited the terms of trade of other coffee exporters like Colombia. There will sometimes be a problem in being confident that swings in the terms of trade are temporary. But to the extent that a government believes that it is able to diagnose temporary swings, there is a strong case for financing them rather than forcing absorption to follow the fluctuations in income. Indeed, there is evidence from countries as far apart as Costa Rica and Kenya that coffee producers tried to engage in such consumption smoothing by building up foreign assets when prices were high, until governments tried to monopolize the holding of foreign exchange.

On a substantially longer time scale countries may also be able to benefit by borrowing or lending motivated by different demographic positions. The basic idea stems from the life-cycle hypothesis of the Italian-born Nobel laureate Franco Modigliani (b. 1918), which postulates that the major motive for saving is to even out consumption in the post-retirement years when income falls off. In fact the high-savings years tend to be the ten or twenty years prior to retirement, when houses have already been bought and furnished and children have left home.

Thus societies with a high concentration of the population in the pre-retirement years tend to have a high propensity to save; if their labour force is also relatively stable, they will have correspondingly modest investment needs and hence are likely to be capital exporters (as Japan has been in the 1980s). Countries with a growing labour force and the bulk of the population still childbearing, as the baby boom generation is in the United States today, may well be capital importers: the US emergence as a net debtor in the 1980s may be in part a rational response to its relative demographic situation. Countries with a large proportion of elderly in the population are likely to save less and may even liquidate foreign assets to meet a period of peak consumption demand. These demographic factors can cause quite rational departures from the pattern of progressive movement from debtor to mature creditor suggested by the model of the debt cycle.

16.5 Investment and the exchange rate

In the preceding analysis of international investment, a capital inflow simply adds to the total of goods available for consumption or investment. Those goods are treated as a single homogeneous good. If the additional goods are invested, we have the case of borrowing to enhance income (see section 16.2); if they are consumed, we have the case of borrowing to modify the time path of consumption (see section 16.4).

The analysis of section 16.1 suggests further ways in which the openness of the economy may influence the process of capital accumulation. The first is through the Keynesian channel of influencing the *incentive to invest*. Especially regarding the incentive to invest in the production of tradable goods, an important determinant is the expected future level of the real exchange rate. When businesses see their currency becoming overvalued and believe that state of affairs is likely to be allowed to continue – or even if they feel great uncertainty whether it will be allowed to continue – their natural defensive reaction is to cut back on investment. Assurance of a competitive exchange rate is therefore an important element in stimulating investment.

It is also true that an *undervalued* currency can hold back investment. The reason is that an undervalued currency tends to generate a current account surplus, which reduces the savings available for domestic investment. When the level of savings is the effective constraint on investment, an increase in competitiveness – that is, a rise in the real exchange rate – will tend to reduce the level of investment. In fact, a condition for maximizing the rate of investment and therefore the rate of growth is that the real exchange rate equates the *ex ante* level of investment to full-employment savings plus the capital inflow. A higher real exchange rate will reduce the current deficit below the capital inflow and thus cut investment below its potential. A lower real exchange rate will cut the incentive to invest, and the excess potential savings will be wasted in unemployment rather than translated into more capital. Maximizing growth involves having an appropriate real exchange rate.

16.6 The two-gap model

Another way in which openness of the economy may influence capital accumulation is through the requirement that some part of the capital goods be imported. When capital goods and consumer goods are distinct, as in the two-good extension of the neoclassical model, the home country may be able to produce one of them only at great cost or conceivably not at all. In reality it is capital goods that are typically imported, especially by developing countries. The technology of producing capital goods is generally more complex, their production is skill intensive and demand is smaller relative to the minimum-cost level of production, thus denying scale economies to countries that seek self-sufficiency. The result is that even the industrially more advanced of the developing countries, or for that matter developed countries, continue to import a relatively high proportion of their capital goods. The less developed of the developing countries rely on imports for the vast bulk of the capital goods they install.

In developing countries, growth is generally constrained by the lack of resources to make investments rather than by the lack of an incentive to invest. Hence the two important ways in which openness influences capital accumulation are generally through the possibility of supplementing domestic savings by foreign borrowing and via the necessity of importing a part of the capital goods invested. The interrelationship between these two influences has been formalized in the two-gap model first developed by Hollis Chenery (b. 1918) and the Israeli economist Michael Bruno (b. 1932). The model has been quite influential in guiding the policies of the World Bank, especially with regard to the international distribution of aid flows. It derives its name from the dual role played by an inflow of foreign exchange, in reducing both the savings gap and the foreign exchange gap.

The model treats the extreme case where production requires the combination of two distinct types of capital goods in fixed proportions. One of these capital goods, K_f, is not made at home and therefore has to be imported. The other, K_d, can be made at home, although it can also be imported. Let the fixed input coefficients per unit of output be a α of K_f and β of K_d. Assume also that production requires the utilization of a fixed quantity of an imported intermediate good (oil, for example), and let the import content per unit of output be m. Finally, assume that exports are limited to some fraction γ of total output Y because only that fraction of productive capacity has been designed to produce exportables.

According to these assumptions, one limit to total output Y is set by the availability of the two forms of capital goods (it being implicitly assumed that labour is available in unlimited supply from the subsistence sector):

$$Y \leqslant \min. [K_f/\alpha, K_d/\beta]$$

If the economy is initially at full employment and the two types of capital are in appropriate balance, with neither in excess supply, then:

$$Y = K_f/\alpha = K_d/\beta$$

Any *increase* in Y (ΔY) will require an increase of both $\Delta K_f = \alpha \Delta Y$ and $\Delta K_d = \beta \Delta Y$. Hence the savings necessary to finance growth of ΔY would be:

$$S = (\alpha + \beta) \Delta Y \qquad (16.2)$$

According to the neo-classical savings hypothesis, domestic savings S_d are a fixed proportion of income. Income is the net value of output, after deducting the import content, so:

$$S_d = s(1 - m)Y \qquad (16.3)$$

Note that equations 16.2 and 16.3 reduce to a simple Harrod–Domar growth formula for the case of a closed economy ($\alpha = m = 0$, $S = S_d$):

$$\Delta Y = S/\beta = (s/\beta)Y$$
or $\quad g = \Delta Y/Y = s/\beta$

that is, the growth rate is equal to the savings ratio divided by the capital–output ratio. The Harrod–Domar model can in turn be regarded as a short-term approximation of the neo-classical growth model, valid over such a period of time as the capital–output ratio can be considered a constant rather than increasing with capital accumulation due to diminishing returns. Since there is little reason to expect diminishing returns to set in during the period of industrialization while the modern sector is drawing labour from the subsistence sector at a constant real wage, the technological assumptions can be regarded as acceptable for the purpose in hand.

The capital–output ratio, or strictly speaking the incremental capital–output ratio (ICOR) $\Delta K/\Delta Y$, varies considerably both between sectors and between countries. It tends to be high in utilities and urbanization and low in agriculture, with a wide range in manufacturing. Since second-stage import substitution normally involves the establishment of capital-intensive industries while an outward-oriented strategy involves the growth of labour-intensive exports, one would expect ICORs to be higher in countries pursuing a strategy of import substitution. The differences are in fact large. While a value of 3 used to be taken as a typical figure for an ICOR, Balassa quotes figures for ICORs for the period 1960 to 1973 that vary from 1.8 in Singapore, 2.1 in Korea and 2.4 in Taiwan, to 5.5 in Chile, 5.7 in India and 9.1 in Uruguay.

In the open economy, domestic savings S_d may be supplemented by an inflow of capital or aid. Denote that inflow S_f. It has been customary to assume that the ratio of capital/aid inflow to income can be treated as a constant, which we may denote by ζ. The savings constraint on the growth rate then takes the form:

$$\Delta Y \leqslant S/(\alpha + \beta) = (S_d + S_f)/(\alpha + \beta) = [s(1-m)+\zeta]Y/(\alpha + \beta)$$

or $$g = \Delta Y/Y \leqslant [s(1-m)+ \zeta]/(\alpha + \beta) \tag{16.4}$$

Equation 16.4 makes excellent intuitive sense: an increase in the propensity to save or in the capital inflow raises the feasible growth rate, while an increase in the technically necessary quantity of either form of capital reduces feasible growth.

Figure 16.5 illustrates the way in which the growth rate depends on the inflow of capital or aid (as a proportion of income), ζ. Equation 16.4 provides the first constraint on the growth rate, that coming from savings. The savings constraint has a positive intercept on the vertical axis at a value of $s(1-m)/(\alpha + \beta)$: even without a capital inflow domestic savings will be sufficient to finance a certain positive rate of growth, assuming only that $m < 1$ (which had better be true, or the country would be better off producing nothing at all!).[6] It has a positive slope equal to $1/(\alpha + \beta)$: each additional unit of inflow provides enough to finance the purchase of two capital goods in quantities that will permit output to rise by that much. Growth is confined to the rate on or below the savings constraint.

So far as Figure 16.5 is concerned, it would make no difference if savings were generated by a Marxist rather than by a neo-classical savings function. There would still be a determinate level of domestic savings generated at full employment, and that level could still be expected to rise more or less proportionately with the level of income. Foreign savings could still supplement domestic savings and thus generate an upward-sloping savings constraint.

The second constraint on growth arises from the limited availability of foreign exchange. Ignoring changes in reserves, on the grounds that a rundown in reserves

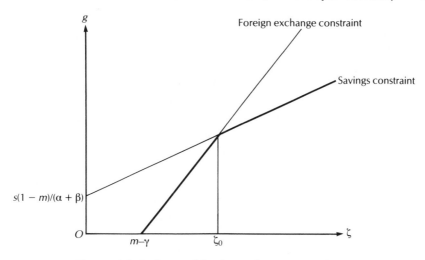

Figure 16.5 Savings and foreign exchange constraints

cannot normally be maintained long enough to boost the growth rate significantly, the balance of payments equation says that exports plus the inflow of capital-aid will equal imports of intermediate goods and final goods:

$$X + S_f = mY + \Delta K_f$$
or $\qquad \gamma Y + \zeta Y \geq mY + \alpha \Delta Y$

Since there is no limitation on reserve *accumulation*, this may be rearranged to express the foreign exchange constraint on growth:

$$g = \Delta Y/Y \leq (\gamma - m + \zeta)/\alpha \qquad\qquad (16.5)$$

The foreign exchange constraint of equation 16.5 can also be shown in Figure 16.5. It may intercept either axis, depending on whether $\gamma \gtrless m$. When $\gamma > m$, the country's exports exceed its imports of intermediate goods, so it has some foreign exchange left over to buy imported capital goods even without an inflow of capital/aid. When $\gamma < m$, exports are insufficient even to keep the economy operating at full capacity, and an inflow of capital or aid is essential to permit any growth at all. In either event the foreign exchange constraint has a slope $1/\alpha$, which is necessarily greater than that of the savings constraint $(1/(\alpha + \beta))$. Growth cannot exceed the level permitted by the foreign exchange constraint.

Considering the two constraints together, growth is limited to the area below both curves, bordered in Figure 16.5 by the heavy line. The main conclusion is that up to a certain critical level (ζ_0 in the figure) an inflow of capital or aid is likely to be of strategic importance to the development process in easing a foreign exchange bottleneck. In this range the rate of return will be very high. Despite this, a country may fail to attract a capital inflow on commercial terms if it is considered to be a bad credit risk. The policy conclusion is that aid should be allocated in such a way as to fill such gaps. Once the inflow passes the critical level ζ_0, it will still permit an increase in the growth rate, but it will be less effective inasmuch as it now has to finance the purchase of *all* the additional capital goods rather than just those that cannot be produced at home.

There has been much debate about whether a foreign exchange constraint independent of the savings constraint really exists. A neo-classical view suggests that there are likely to be possibilities of substitution in production, to boost the export proportion γ and/or to cut the import coefficient m, or even to increase β at the expense of α. Such possibilities imply that the foreign exchange constraint can be relaxed and that the only real constraint on growth is that furnished by the savings constraint.

No doubt in the long run the type of flexibility suggested by the neo-classical analysis exists. The proportion of output exported can be increased, and import substitution can reduce both m and α. But long-run considerations are not the only ones that are relevant. Nasty things can happen in the short run during which inflexibilities persist: people may starve, the people may revolt, or generals starved of new arms in the cause of reducing m may stage a coup. Relaxing the foreign exchange constraint can therefore be an important objective of policy, and it makes no sense to design policy on the assumption that no such constraint ever exists. After the debt crisis broke in 1982, even semi-industrialized countries found the foreign exchange constraint had again become painfully operative.

Indeed, it has even been argued in recent years by the Brazilian economist Edmar Bacha (b. 1942) that there is a third constraint, which the debt crisis may have made the binding one. This third constraint is public investment in infrastructure and the like, which is asserted to be an essential complement to private investment. If public-sector finances are extremely strained, *inter alia* by the need to raise the local funds to service foreign debt, a country may have to cut back its infrastructure investment to a point that curtails growth more than either the savings or foreign exchange constraint does. Once again, such a constraint can hardly be taken to be a natural constant in the long run (it can be relaxed by fiscal policy or by privatization), but that does not mean that it may not be troubling in the short run.

16.7 Technology

Studies of the determinants of economic growth, such as those undertaken by Edward Denison (b. 1915), have typically concluded that the largest single contributing factor is technological progress, as opposed to capital accumulation, improved education or any other specific factor. The studies in question have, admittedly, concentrated on explaining growth (in supply) in the leading countries, especially the United States. It is in principle more difficult to separate the effect of technical progress from that of capital accumulation or education in countries that are in the phase of catching up. The essence of the growth process in that phase is that unskilled labour is drawn out of the low-productivity subsistence sector and employed, along with a mixture of suitably skilled labour, in a modern sector that is being expanded by investment in new capital goods that embody modern technology. When ample supplies of unskilled labour are available from the subsistence sector, and ample supplies of skilled labour are being produced by the educational system, this process can sustain 'miracle' rates of growth of upwards of 6 per cent per annum. But the technological improvement is an integral part of the process of investment. While it is an indispensable condition for the growth, however, it is impossible to say that x per cent of that growth is due to the investment and y per cent to the technological advance.

Technology is analogous to capital in that resources currently devoted to investment in making technological improvements are expected to permit larger output to be realized in the future. However, there is a very important difference between capital and technology, deriving from the public-good characteristics of the latter. When a capital good is constructed, it is clear to whom it belongs and hence who is entitled to receive the income that it generates, and because of this there is an incentive to make investments whenever the projected returns outweigh the costs. When a new invention is made, on the other hand, it is rather difficult to prevent others copying it. Moreover, *given* that the invention has been made, it is undesirable to stop others imitating, inasmuch as their making use of the invention does not diminish the possibility of the inventor using it – the invention is in that sense a public good. The problem is that no one would have an incentive to invest in making inventions which could immediately be copied by everyone, since the imitator would compete the price of the original down to a point that would deprive the inventor of any profits to compensate him or her for the costs of making the invention.

There is no universal or perfect solution to this dilemma, but societies use a variety of ways to reach tolerable compromises. One possibility is to resort to the classical solution to the public-good problem, which is to have the state provide the service in question. Hence one finds research centres and universities supported by the state, especially for pure research and for research in sectors like agriculture where productive units are so small that there are few realistic alternatives if any research at all is to be done. The problem with this approach is that research tends to be too far removed from the point of application – the researchers may be out of touch with the day-to-day problems that determine which approaches are feasible and suggest where effort would be best expended. Hence an alternative possibility, that of creating a *patent system*, may also be employed. A patent is a legal grant of the monopoly right to use a certain invention for a limited period of time (typically fifteen to twenty years). By granting a patent to an inventor, the state gives him or her the opportunity to recover the funds invested and to make a profit out of the monopoly profits available during the lifetime of the patent, in return for which the invention is made freely available to everyone when the patent expires. Large oligopolistic firms employing specialized technologies or selling capital goods might find it worthwhile to engage in research and development even without the protection afforded by a patent system, on the reckoning that they can keep the know-how secret sufficiently long to more than recover their costs, by continually renewing their product range and making it more attractive.

It is the public-good characteristics of technology that are responsible for the fact that present-day developing countries have the chance of making the transition from subsistence economy to affluence so much more rapidly than did the first industrial countries. (Britain took perhaps 150 years to accomplish what Singapore did in the last quarter of a century.) Present-day capital goods which can be bought off the shelf embody a range of technical advances that reflect the investments in technology of some 200 years. In itself, this is an enormous advantage, but it does not mean that developing countries face no problems of access to suitable technology. There are in fact two important problems.

The first concerns the general question of what balance to strike between providing an incentive to innovate and allowing progress through imitation. Some have argued that, in view of the vast opportunities for imitation open to present-day developing countries, it makes no sense for them to invest resources in innovating or to limit the access of their firms to available technologies for the sake of stimulating local innovation. Two important points are raised in reply. First, it is argued that efficient employment of modern technology requires not just the use of potential information but also the deployment of a range of know-how that is only half in the public domain, and that a patent system is important in giving multinationals the security to enter the country and bring their latest know-how with them. Second, it is argued that there is a need to encourage inventions adapted to the specific conditions of developing countries – which means in part to their generally tropical climate, but above all to their factor endowment. The idea is that the form of innovation responds to economic stimuli, so that in capital-rich countries with high labour costs the incentive is to develop labour-saving inventions, whereas capital-saving inventions would be far more useful to the typical developing country with its abundant supply of unskilled labour. According to this argument, innovation to develop appropriate technology, rather than just taking techniques over from the developed countries, is much to be desired.

The second problem that arises in securing the adoption of appropriate technology in developing countries is that, even if suitably labour-intensive production techniques exist, it may not pay firms to adopt them. The rates of pay to urban labour may substantially exceed the opportunity cost of labour in the subsistence sector. The reasons why this distortion frequently occurs include the power of trade unions, the greater political influence of the urban proletariat as opposed to the rural poor (especially under left-wing governments), and the tendency for labour to receive its average product rather than its (supposedly smaller) marginal product in the subsistence sector.

There are lots of opinions but no very firmly established generalizations as to the relative and absolute importance of these considerations. Fragmentary evidence from Latin America suggests that local private-enterprise firms tend to be more innovative in adapting Northern technology to a more labour-intensive form than are multinationals, while the latter in turn exhibit more flexibility in this regard than do state enterprises. This suggests that, even though market forces may be blunted by excessive urban real wages, some market incentive to innovate nevertheless exists. It also suggests that it is naive to assume that state enterprise can necessarily be relied upon to undertake actions more in accord with social needs than those induced by private incentives.

16.8 Human capital

The other essential element in the development process is the education of the labour force in the wide range of skills that are essential to the operation of a modern economy. One may summarize the skills needed as those of engineers, to operate the necessary technical processes, and of entrepreneurs, to perceive and exploit the opportunities of applying those processes. But in reality there are many other professions that have a role to play, including that of the economist – even if his or her role must often be the negative one of trying to restrain ideologues from foolish acts like imposing marginal tax rates of 100 per cent odd, or expecting supply-side miracles from cutting tax rates a mere fraction of that.

Acquisition of skills again involves a process of investment. Teachers and students devote their time to imparting and acquiring skills that will subsequently permit increased production, whereas they could be producing output for current consumption. Some thirty years ago economists started to exploit the analogy between the formation of physical capital and of human capital. Many studies were undertaken on the rate of return on investment in education, leading to the general conclusion that this is indeed a sensible form of investment yielding a competitive rate of return. Of course, none of this is to deny that education may be worthwhile for general cultural reasons quite unrelated to anything that can be measured in the GNP statistics. It demonstrates rather the reverse: that even philistines who attach no value to culture should be prepared to support a strong educational system on crude economic grounds.

The special economic characteristic of investment in human capital is that a large part of its return accrues in the form of increased earnings for the particular individual in whom the investment was made. There is no market mechanism that would permit an investor with surplus cash to decide that the best way to invest it would be in the education of the most talented (although the investor might decide to spend it on educating his or her own family). Where markets fail, the state tends to step in; and so one finds most educational spending being undertaken or at least subsidized by the state. But this solution still leaves a large part of the returns accruing to the individuals who receive the education rather than to the society that makes the investment. The result is highly inegalitarian: middle-class children are subsidized by the population at large to enhance their own earning ability. It is something of a mystery why this inequitable arrangement is tolerated so readily, with virtually no attempt to mitigate the inegalitarian impact by financing education through loans. Even so, it may well be that state expenditure on education is less inegalitarian than many other ways of encouraging growth, like subsidizing private investment.

One danger of investing heavily in higher education is that many of the beneficiaries will join the 'brain drain', and thus that even less social benefit will be reaped by the societies that made the investments. This has become a major problem for many developing countries in the world of high mobility for those with marketable skills in which we live today. A visionary proposal to deal with this problem was once advanced by Jagdish Bhagwati: the establishment of co-operative international arrangements for the payment of special taxes by immigrants, with the taxes being levied by the countries of settlement and paid over to the countries of origin. It evoked not a flicker of interest in the North–South negotiations then in train.

Another international dimension of investment in human capital is worth note. The import component of investment in human capital tends to be smaller than that of investment in physical capital. Nevertheless, the import component is not negligible at early stages of development – foreign teachers are hired, and students go to foreign universities. Import substitution takes place in the educational sector as in any other, starting at the primary level and ending up with Ph.D. programmes. Foreign borrowing can be used to invest in human capital as much as for any other purpose, either to pay for the import content or to import consumer goods that permit more domestic resources to be released for an expanded educational and training programme. There is an opinion, apparently based largely on the experience of Korea, that the best way of telescoping the development process is to invest very heavily in education at the initial stages. There is also a view, based primarily on German success, that a first-rate system of vocational training is an excellent form of investment.

16.9 Immiserizing growth

The key to growth is factor accumulation. But around the mid-1950s economists started finding cases in which factor accumulation and the resulting growth in output actually made an open economy worse off, or 'immiserized' it.

The first example in which this can occur was produced by Jagdish Bhagwati, and arises from the possibility that increased output would turn the terms of trade against the growing country. At constant prices, the outward movement of the production possibility curve generated by factor accumulation increases the excess supply of exportables and the excess demand for importables. This will tend to worsen the terms of trade if the country is large enough to be able to influence its terms of trade at all. It is possible for this deterioration in the terms of trade to be so large as to outweigh the physical increase in output and leave the country worse off than before. On the other hand, it can be shown that this is not possible if the country is imposing an optimum tariff (see section 10.6.) Although the large-economy assumption needed to permit immiserizing growth may rule out the possibility when considering the isolated growth of a single developing country, it cannot be ruled out when the simultaneous expansion of all the developing countries is considered.

A second case of possible immiserizing growth, demonstrated by Harry Johnson in the mid-1960s, stems from technical progress in the import-competing industry or accumulation of the factor of production used intensively in that industry. The argument is simplest in the case of technical progress as shown in Figure 16.6. The

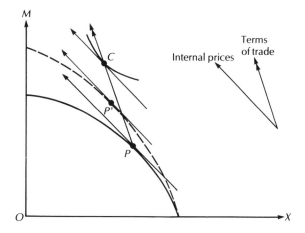

Figure 16.6 Immiserizing growth with technical progress

diagram with the solid production possibility curve is basically the same as Figure 8.1(b), except that it omits details of the free-trade equilibrium. Production with the tariff is at P, while consumption is at C. Suppose now that there is technical progress in the M industry, so that the ppc moves up to the dotted position. Then it is clear that for a small economy, which therefore faces unchanged prices, the new production point P' must lie above and to the left of P. The critical question is: on which side of the line CP does it lie? In particular, one cannot exclude the possibility that it will lie to the left-hand side, as shown, in which case it is clear that the new consumption point must lie on a lower indifference curve than C.[7]

The intuitive explanation of this case of immiserizing growth is quite simple. Technical progress increases potential output per head, but it also shifts resources towards the industry in which progress occurs. Where this is a protected import-competing industry, the social value of the output is less than it was in the export industry from which the resources were withdrawn. It is possible for the cost of this increased distortion to outweigh the benefit of the increase in potential output. This would not be possible if the country were employing an optimal tariff, which in this case is zero.

A third case, which has been analyzed by the Canadian Richard Brecher (b. 1951) and the Cuban-born Carlos Diaz Alejandro (1937–85), arises when foreign capital is attracted by a national tariff. They show that immiserization is in this case not just possible, but (admittedly on the assumption that the profits of the foreign investor are not taxed) *inevitable* over a certain range. The reason is shown in Figure 16.7. P is again the original production point, and C the point of consumption. Suppose that in response to the tariff there is an inflow of capital that shifts the ppc out, and that the new point of tangency is a point P' as analyzed above. We already know that growth would be immiserizing in the case considered in the previous section where P' lies to the left of PC, so consider the case where it lies to the right as shown. That implies that if the increased capital stock belonged to domestic residents, consumption could rise to the point C' (assuming a linear income–consumption path). But in fact the foreign investors must be paid. In the absence of taxation they receive the marginal product of capital, valued at domestic prices, multiplied by the size of the capital inflow. Measured in terms of the exportable good, the increment in output due to the capital inflow is ZP' (since Z has the same value as P measured in domestic prices). But the level of consumption attainable from Z is only C'', which is less than C. Thus growth has once again immiserized and must do so unless profits taxation is high enough to leave the foreign capitalists with a sufficiently small part of their profits as to place the domestic consumpion to the right of PC.

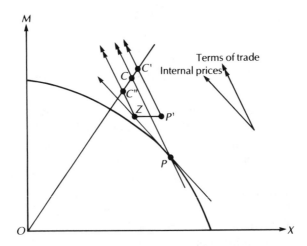

Figure 16.7 Immiserizing growth with foreign capital

Once again, immiserizing growth was possible only because of a distortion. This is in fact the common theme to emerge from these examples: that the circumstances under which growth would immiserize are not far-fetched, but they all depend upon policy creating some distortion (classifying a deviation from the nationally optimal tariff as a distortion). Countries that follow sensible policies have nothing to fear.

16.10 Summary

Economic development depends upon capital accumulation, using the phrase broadly to cover the intangible capital of technical knowledge and the human capital of skilled labour, as well as physical capital. The international dimension is important to the process of capital accumulation in influencing (1) the incentive to invest; (2) the availability of savings; and (3) the availability of imported capital goods. The classical motive for foreign borrowing is that of securing a transfer of real resources from countries where savings are abundant relative to investment opportunities to those in an opposite situation. This suggests that developing countries will typically import capital and become debtors, while the more thrifty countries will eventually repay their debt and emerge as external creditors, in a 'debt cycle'. Both debtors and creditors can increase their welfare through international, intertemporal resource reallocation, either by enhancing their level of income or by modifying the time path of absorption relative to that of income, or both.

At least, there is the potential for mutual improvement of welfare. It has not always been realized, as will become evident when we study the debt crisis in section 18.4. Countries sometimes overborrow, in the sense that they have to repay when resources are scarcer than they were at the time of borrowing. Perhaps the most flagrant case of misuse of the international capital market in history was the foreign borrowing undertaken in the 1970s by Romania's erstwhile dictator Ceauşescu to finance unproductive white elephants when foreign exchange was relatively abundant, and then repaid in the 1980s by bleeding his subjects dry when the international environment turned inhospitable.

The interaction between the availability of savings and the availability of imported capital goods is analyzed by the two-gap model, which shows that access to additional foreign exchange is of particular value when it breaks a foreign exchange constraint. But mere factor accumulation does not guarantee that a country will benefit; in the presence of sufficiently misguided policy, growth can immiserize. The ICOR statistics quoted in section 16.6 suggest that, even short of the case of immiserizing growth, a rational microeconomic policy is essential to making good use of the macroeconomic sacrifices that a policy of development requires.

16.11 Addendum: the large economy

The analysis of sections 16.2 and 16.4 is based on the assumption that the country is unable to influence the world interest rate i^* at which it borrows and lends. This is, of course, a small-economy assumption. A large economy will tend to push i^* up the more it borrows and push it down the more it lends.

Ability to influence the world rate of interest introduces considerations into welfare analysis analogous to those in the optimum tariff literature (section 10.6). A large country concerned with maximizing its national welfare (and able to count on an absence of foreign retaliation) will seek to restrict its export of capital, if it is a creditor, or its import of capital, if it is a debtor, so as to move the capital terms of trade in its favour. (Even small debtor countries may have an incentive to act in this way to the extent that they face a national borrowing cost that increases with the level of their indebtedness, because of fears as to their continued creditworthiness.)

The standard analysis would suggest that the United States, as a large creditor country, could be expected to restrict its capital exports. While the United States did in fact try to restrict the outflow of capital in the 1960s, the motivation for this was concern over the balance of payments: the United States was keen to liberalize those restrictions, while many of the capital-importing countries (at least the developed ones) were urging they be maintained or strengthened. These facts appear paradoxical from the standpoint of the theory that countries try to manipulate their capital terms of trade in pursuit of national advantage. They can, however, be neatly explained by the Marxist hypothesis that governments are the creatures of their capitalist ruling classes rather than dedicated to pursuit of the general social good as usually interpreted by economists, since United States capitalists stood to gain and foreign capitalists to lose by free export of capital from the United States.

The small-country assumption was also abandoned at places in section 16.3, where it was argued that small countries could not grow indefinitely at a rate above the rate of interest because if they did they would become 'large' and increase the interest rate.

16.12 Bibliography

Arthur Lewis (1954) presented his model of economic development with unlimited supplies of labour. Figures 16.2 and 16.3 are adapted from Lessard (1981). The concept of the debt cycle seems to have been introduced into the English-language literature by Crowther (1957, pp. 352–60), but it goes back at least to the 1920s in the German literature (e.g. Eulenberg 1929). It has been given mathematical formulations by Fischer and Frenkel (1972) and by Horst Siebert (1989). The analysis of the implications of demographic differences for payments imbalances is in an early stage of development, with the most authoritative treatment as this goes to press being Masson and Tryon (1990). MacDougall (1960) provided a pioneering analysis of the welfare effects of foreign investment, while Bhagwati (1979) has a more recent review of the literature in this area. Balassa and Williamson (1990) apply the analysis of section 16.5 to analyze exchange-rate policy in the East Asian NICs.

The two-gap model was developed in Chenery and Bruno (1962) and given its sharpest formulation in McKinnon (1964). The three-gap extension is in Bacha (1989). 'Growth accounting', the attempt to decompose the (supply-side) determinants of economic growth, was pioneered by Denison (1967). An advanced survey of the work on human capital formation is provided by Blaug (1976). The theory of immiserizing growth was developed by Bhagwati (1956), Johnson (1967) and Brecher and Diaz Alejandro (1977): the latter two are reprinted in Bhagwati (1987). Bhagwati's proposal to tax the brain drain was originally presented in Bhagwati (1972).

Notes

1. This is strictly true only if individuals are infinitely long lived. Another consequence is that the possibility of the growth rate being raised by resort to inflationary finance, which is suggested by the literature on money in growth models, is reduced.
2. The relevant concept of income here is GDP (gross domestic product) rather than GNP. For the difference, see section 11.4.
3. The net resource transfer (or the net transfer of real resources) is defined as the capital inflow minus interest payments. It is equal to the balance of goods and non-factor services (see section 11.2). A positive resource transfer involves a deficit on goods and non-factor services (an inflow of real resources) financed by a capital inflow greater than interest payments.

4. The debt cycle can be modelled formally, but a simple formalization in which output depends on the stock of capital, and investment increases the capital stock peso for peso, yields the conclusion that the capital stock will be increased to its steady-state level in a single jump once foreign borrowing becomes possible. Thus the text is restricted to a verbal description of the more realistic case in which diminishing returns to the rate of investment yield a gradual accumulation of capital.

5. Conceptually correct (though not currently conventional) accounting would treat the depletion of oil reserves in the ground on a par with the depletion of produced capital goods. This would mean that the overwhelming part of oil revenue would not qualify as a part of net domestic product, although it does of course contribute to GDP. The point is important in assessing the income level of the oil producers relative to that of the industrial countries, which is grossly exaggerated by current accounting practices.

6. The condition $m < 1$ is the simplest form of what are known as the Hawkins–Simon conditions, which are necessary for an economic system to be 'productive' in the sense that it is capable of producing more than it consumes in intermediate inputs.

7. An increase in the stock of the factor used intensively in producing M would shift the ppc outward throughout its length, rather than leaving the intercept on the x-axis unchanged as in the case of technical progress. However, the Rybczynski theorem tells us that P' will lie above and left of P, so that the possibility of immiserizing growth again arises.

VI

World economy

The previous parts of the book have focused on the interaction between an individual country and a rest of the world that was considered to be parametric. At this stage, the point of view changes. This last part of the book aims to examine the characteristics and logic of the world economic system. Chapter 17 deals with international trading arrangements, Chapter 18 with the world capital market and Chapter 19 with monetary arrangements. The final chapter discusses the series of global economic problems that have dominated debate among the industrial countries since 1960.

17

The international trading system

The historical account opening this book recalled how the era of free trade before the First World War gave way to unprecedented economic nationalism in the 1930s, during the Great Depression. This economic nationalism took various forms: protectionism, exchange control, bilateral trade deals, competitive devaluation. Some of the countries that took the lead in abandoning the old ideals of free, multilateral trade and exchange suffered less than most, but their gain was in part at the expense of others. Not only did this vicious competition bring economic loss to the world, but it fanned the flames of a new war. The militarists who took control of Japan could appeal not just to xenophobia but also to quite rational concerns for economic security in the face of foreign protectionism, which threatened the ability to earn the foreign exchange essential to the purchase of imports of materials. Territorial expansion was in part a response to that threat, which in due course provoked the announcement of an oil blockade by the United States. The attack on Pearl Harbor was a pre-emptive strike to break that incipient blockade – the climax to a chain of mutual provocations that originated in part in protectionism, not a bolt from the blue as often painted in Western accounts.

Fortunately Western economic statesmen were not deceived by their own propaganda but started to think about how a liberal international economic order could be restored even while the Second World War was at its peak. Their designs came to fruition in certain respects: specifically, they created the World Bank and a monetary order supervised by the IMF that more or less functioned till 1971. But their ambitious plan for a comprehensive International Trade Organization (ITO) was not accepted; differences between the United States and Britain over the extent to which an international organization should circumscribe the authority of national governments prevented ratification by the United States Congress. As a result a temporary agreement on tariffs and trade, prepared while countries were discussing the ITO, became the main vehicle for managing post-war trade relations. The General Agreement on Tariffs and Trade (GATT), initialled by twenty-three nations in 1947, has proved remarkably robust and durable. It has grown into an organization with a permanent secretariat in Geneva and with a substantially increased number of members ('contracting parties'). It remains the dominant vehicle for negotiating multilateral reduction of trade barriers and for constraining further trade restriction.

The characteristics of international trading relationships have nonetheless changed dramatically over the post-war period, and the aim of this chapter is to examine how these changes have fashioned the functioning of commercial policy both inside and outside GATT.

17.1 General Agreement on Tariffs and Trade

The original objectives of GATT were thoroughly fashioned by a desire to avoid repetition of the inter-war experiences. Thus GATT sought to provide a framework for the orderly conduct of trading relations (codes of conduct in Parts I and II of the Agreement restrict unilateral action by countries) and for the progressive elimination of trade barriers.[1] A number of basic principles underpin these obligations; these include *non-discrimination*, *reciprocity* and *transparency*.

The 'most favoured nation' (MFN) rule embodied in Article 1 is probably the most important principle of the GATT. Its aim is to ensure that any trade concessions or barriers are applied in a non-discriminatory fashion. Thus if country A agrees to reduce its tariff on a certain product on imports from B, this concession must be extended to all other contracting parties. *Non-discrimination* provides a strong incentive for countries to participate in bargaining for tariff liberalization, especially since tariff reductions are 'bound' by GATT against future arbitrary increases. Any concession gained from country B by country A can be viewed as permanent, and country A cannot be excluded from the benefits of any other agreement by country B with another contracting party.

The *reciprocity* obligation requires a country accepting a tariff concession to offer comparable concessions in return. In the absence of the obligation to offer reciprocal tariff concessions, mercantilist-minded governments would be pleased to benefit from lower trade barriers in their export markets without reducing their own barriers against imports (to 'free-ride'). Given the simultaneous existence of such sentiments in many country's, trade liberalization might never get under way. The reciprocity obligation helps to create domestic producer lobbies with an interest in lowering their own countries' trade barriers. Export industries will anticipate benefits, i.e. more exports, following the offer of concessions that are reciprocated by the countries to which they export. Thus this principle serves to counteract the domestic political influence of producer lobbies with an interest in resisting tariff liberalization.

To some extent MFN and reciprocity are conflicting principles: strict or unconditional adherence to non-discrimination would permit 'free-riders' and thereby undermine the incentives to multilateral liberalization provided by reciprocity. But, in what is after all ultimately a negotiating framework, compromises allow the obligations not to be rigidly enforced. Differences in countries' 'ability to offer' concessions are implicit in the negotiation processes, and are explicitly recognized in specific exceptions embodied in other articles of the General Agreement. We return to the issue of exceptions or special cases below. At this stage it is important to emphasize that the core principles of GATT, namely of non-discrimination and reciprocity, are underpinned by the logic that governments perceive benefits primarily from increased exports rather than unilateral free trade. From the analysis of trade policies in Chapters 8–10 we know that, on economic grounds, (unconstrained) governments of countries so small as to have no ability to bargain down the trade barrier of their partners have an unambiguous interest in liberalizing unilaterally. But political economy considerations suggest that we need an international agreement, like GATT, that does not rely on governments recognizing that logic to motivate mutual restraint regarding trade restrictions.

The last of the principles listed earlier is the transparency principle. Article 11 outlaws the use of direct controls on trade flows, in particular the use of quotas and similar quantitative restrictions. One of the reasons for this is the desire for greater transparency: that is, for the use of instruments whose economic effects are more visible and more certain. GATT incorporates the liberal sentiment that price signals allow markets to operate effectively and therefore efficiently. Given that the initial signatories of GATT at the start of the post-war period were largely the non-Communist industrial market economies of North America and Western Europe, such a sentiment is not surprising. These countries had, in any case, experienced the illiberal policy environment of the inter-war period, and the GATT principles were strongly fashioned by the desire to avoid repetition of that experience.

There are exceptions, however, to the transparency and other principles. Thus GATT, while stating a general preference for tariff protection, allows direct controls under certain circumstances such as temporary balance of payments difficulties and temporary market disruption caused by import growth in specific industries. Similarly, discriminatory action, such as countervailing duties against dumped imports from specified countries, is permitted under certain circumstances. An even more significant exemption from the non-discrimination principle is embodied in Article 24. This lays down the rules for the establishment of free trade areas and customs unions, within which tariffs or other restrictions may discriminate between trading partners and non-partners.

Exceptions to the non-discrimination principle have also been added over time. Thus waivers of the principles have been given in order to 'legalize' the tariff preferences given by developed to developing countries. (We return to the issue of the Generalized System of Preferences in section 17.7.) Subsequent to the original agreements, developing countries have also been effectively exempted from their reciprocity obligations.

The significance of these exceptions to the general rules tends to change with the passage of time and changes in economic circumstances. Thus the United States has become more concerned over time with the amount of trade diverted to within the EC. The exception to allow regional integration was aimed originally at encouraging reconstruction in Western Europe. But ultimately it must be recognized that GATT provides a framework for the conduct of commercial policy negotiations; it was not designed to be an international agency to 'police the rules of the system'. *De facto* the rules tend to reflect the inter-country realities of economic power. Thus, as some of the NICs have expanded their industrial base and become more important in world trade, so they have come under pressure from the industrial countries to 'graduate' to the principle of reciprocity.

GATT's bargaining framework proved successful in dismantling the old protectionism, but has faced greater difficulties in trying to cope with the new. Let us consider the more successful episode in the operation of GATT first.

17.2 Dismantling the old protectionism

GATT does have a continuing or 'day-to-day' role in seeking to maintain an orderly framework for trade. It provides information and conciliation services and has a research department. But the GATT secretariat is modest by international agency standards, and it is the outcome of the 'round' of trade negotiations conducted under the aegis of GATT that is the tangible and publicized GATT activity.

Since quotas were outlawed *in principle* from inception, attention has always been focused on reducing the tariff rates inherited from the pre-war period. The negotiators who gathered in Geneva in 1947 to sign the General Agreement also agreed to make tariff concessions on items covering about one-half of world trade at that time. Item-by-item bargaining continued in a number of subsequent rounds through the 1950s and early 1960s. But the pace of trade liberalization associated with the early rounds could not be maintained. This was due in part to the cumbersome nature of item-by-item bargaining on a multilateral basis. More important, however, was the fact that the process encountered political resistance. In the early rounds, item-by-item bargaining proved acceptable because it permitted negotiators to select items for concessions where tariff redundancy allowed 'liberalization' with limited need for adjustment, but eventually countries with relatively low tariffs were concerned that a continuation of the item-by-item process would eventually leave them in an exposed position relative to countries with high tariffs.

As a response to dissatisfaction with item-by-item negotiation it was suggested as early as 1951 that tariffs be lowered on an across-the-board basis, and that the reductions should be planned and staged. This proposal was not endorsed by the United States or Britain, and the continental European nations channelled their energies into economic integration instead. The outcome was the creation of the EEC in 1956 and the European Free Trade Area (EFTA) in 1959. This preoccupation with regional liberalization undoubtedly undermined interest in multilateral liberalization via GATT in the 1950s.

The Kennedy Round of negotiations (1964–7) stands out as something of a landmark in the rounds system. The round was far more ambitious than previous rounds, and introduced across-the-board cuts. There was some dispute over the form which any across-the-board reduction should take. The United States tended to favour a linear cut which would apply to all commodities. The EEC, on the other hand, favoured some attempt at harmonization: that is, higher rates of reduction on high-tariff items. (The dispersion of Western European tariffs was much narrower than that of United States tariffs.) Ultimately agreement was reached in 1967 on tariff cuts which affected about 75 per cent of total industrial trade. The average tariff reduction amounted to a cut of something over 36 per cent. In addition, some degree of harmonization took place.

In terms of tariff liberalization, these results were quite the most spectacular of any of the GATT rounds to date. We should note, however, a number of qualifications:

1. The liberalization was concentrated on industrial goods. Industrial countries continued to protect their agricultural sectors, largely for non-economic reasons, and even after the Kennedy Round agriculture remained a highly protected sector in most industrial countries.
2. There were exceptions among manufactured goods. Most significant were the relatively low cuts which applied to textiles, a 'sensitive' sector on which special-case status had been conferred as early as 1961 by the Long Term Arrangement on Cotton Textiles. Textiles continued to be excluded from the multilateral liberalization process.
3. In the pre-Kennedy rounds, there had been a tendency on the part of the industrial countries to reduce tariffs on primary commodities and raw materials to a greater extent than on finished goods. The consequence of such a pattern of liberalization is to raise effective rates of protection on finished goods. Little was done by the Kennedy Round to reverse this process.

The Kennedy Round was in many ways a major step towards freer trade among the industrial countries. With the average tariff on actually traded industrial goods standing at 7.2 per cent at the start of the 1970s, the round had succeeded in dismantling much of the old protectionism. As Table 17.1 forcibly demonstrates, it is intra-industrial country or 'North–North' trade in manufactured goods that has been fostered by this tariff liberalization process. However, the special cases identified above imposed problems on later rounds, while changing economic conditions have created new problems.

The process of dismantling the old protectionism mainly involved a relatively small number of industrialized countries and was focused on the liberalization of trade in industrial goods. This focus in commercial policy negotiations reflected the prevailing pattern of international economic power. But the location of economic power was already changing during the 1950s and 1960s, as reconstruction in Western Europe was completed and Japan emerged as a major trading nation. Since the 1960s the patterns of international trade and economic power have been subject to further substantial changes. In order to understand the current issues in global commercial policy, it is necessary to examine the nature and significance of three major developments:

1. The entry of new competitors into international markets for industrial products.
2. The influence of industrial trading blocs on the direction of trade.
3. The oil price changes.

17.3 New industrial competitors

We referred above to the emergence of Japan during the 1960s as a major trading nation. With GNP growth rates more than twice those of the United States and

Table 17.1 Direction and composition of world exports, 1987

	Exports to ($ billion)			Share of merchandise trade (%)	
	'North'	'South'	'East'	Primary	Manufactured
Exports from:					
Industrial countries[1] ('North')	1,288	351	39	19	81
Developing countries[2] ('South')	348	159	37	45	55
Socialist countries[3] ('East')	39	34	n.a.	n.a.	n.a.

[1] OECD members.
[2] Low- and middle-income developing countries.
[3] USSR, Albania, Bulgaria, Cuba, Czechoslavakia, East Germany, Mongolia, North Korea, Hungary, Poland and Romania.
Sources: *Direction of Trade Statistics* (IMF 1988); *World Development Report* (1988).

Europe, Japan's share of the output of the industrial countries increased from about 4½ per cent in 1960 to nearly 10 per cent in 1970. But Japan's export share grew even more rapidly (Table 17.2). In 1960 Japan's exports were one-fifth of those of the United States, but by 1970 they were nearly a half. This increased competition, in particular in traditional industries in the United States and Europe, induced protectionist pressures just when the Kennedy Round tariff reductions were being implemented. The United States Congress began to consider bills that would have put import quotas on a range of products, from textiles to steel. The United States administration was able to avert formal and overt trade restrictions by negotiating 'voluntary' restrictions on exports to the United States in 1968: for example, Japan and several European countries were persuaded to impose voluntary export restraints on basic carbon steel. This use of new and hidden forms of protection was to proliferate in the 1970s. The rounds of GATT negotiations since this time have had to cope with this new protectionism, discussed in section 17.4.

The challenge to the traditional industrial countries of new industrial competitors has continued to intensify since the 1970s. The NICs achieved rapid industrial growth in the 1970s, and expanded their exports – albeit of a relatively narrow range of products, such as labour-intensive textiles and clothing and low-tech, capital-intensive products like steel – quite dramatically. As Table 17.2 shows, they increased the value of their exports about tenfold in nominal terms between 1970 and 1980, which even exceeded the growth rate of Japanese exports. Although the NICs' share of world trade was still relatively small in 1980, the nature of the import competition in

Table 17.2 Global exports, 1950–90 ($ billion)

	1950	1960	1970	1980	1989
World	60.8	128.3	313.9	1,988.0	2,912.2
Developed market economies	37.0	85.8	224.9	1,270.3	2,125.4
Of which:					
United States	10.1	20.4	42.6	216.7	363.8
EEC	16.3	42.1	112.4	665.3	1,133.7
Japan	0.8	4.1	19.3	129.2	274.6
Developing market economies	19.2	27.1	55.7	540.4	786.8
Of which:					
OPEC	4.0	7.8	18.0	296.4	154.8
(Saudi Arabia)	0.3	0.8	2.4	109.1	31.9
Some NICs[1]	3.5	3.9	8.9	87.5	239.5
Centrally planned economies	4.6	15.4	33.3	177.3	73.5

[1]This grouping of newly industrializing countries comprises Hong Kong, Korea, Singapore, Brazil and Mexico.
Source: compiled from *Direction of Trade* (IMF, various).

the traditional industrial markets, especially the United States, posed particular difficulties for the maintenance of liberal policies. Competition was concentrated in labour-intensive industries where adjustment problems tended to be particularly severe. This was against a background of poor growth performance during the 1970s and early 1980s in industrial countries. The concentration of competition also encouraged the protectionist lobbies in the adversely affected industries to claim that targeted or predatory marketing strategies were being employed. Given also the less open economies of the new industrial exporters, and other cultural, institutional and policy differences between the new and traditional industrial countries, protectionist pressures in the United States and EEC mounted. The expansion of the industrial camp increased the range of trade issues, the complexity of negotiating and the resistance to non-discriminatory liberalization.

17.4 Industrial trading blocs

Exception from the non-discrimination principle of GATT for regional trading blocs was seen by the United States as a way of encouraging post-war reconstruction in Europe. Increasingly, however, the United States has become sensitive to the potential diversion of trade away from it caused by the European Community.

GATT rules permit discrimination in favour of other countries that are fellow members of a customs union or free trade area, including a bloc in process of formation where internal tariffs have still not been completely abolished. In principle it is only full unions, involving the ultimate complete abolition of internal tariffs, that are permitted. Some arrangements that created preferential arrangements by internal tariff reductions and then ceased to advance further have been tolerated, or have been permitted under the special and differential arrangements that apply under GATT for developing countries. GATT also acquiesced in the classification of preferential trading arrangements between the European Community and its associated states as 'free trade areas'.

A brief idea of the constitution and achievements of the industrial trading blocs that have functioned since the early 1960s follows. (We discuss regional integration among developing countries in section 17.8.)

European Economic Community (EEC or EC)

The EEC, or the EC (European Community) as it now prefers to be known, is based on the 1957 Treaty of Rome. The members started to cut tariffs in 1958. The initial members were Belgium, France, Germany, Italy, Luxemburg and the Netherlands, with headquarters in Brussels. The Rome treaty provided for the establishment over a ten-year transitional period of a customs union in industrial products: that is, internal free trade and a common external tariff (set at the average of the previous tariffs of the members). It was also planned to create a common, though controlled, market in agricultural products, and this was duly done. Details vary from one product to another, but the typical pattern is that the Community sets each year a minimum support price at which it acts as residual buyer, while preventing producers in the rest of the world benefiting from this price by imposing a variable levy on imports to the Community equal to the excess of the support price over the foreign supply price. When support prices are set high enough to induce an excess of EC supply over demand, the excess is put into stock (forming a 'butter mountain' or a 'wine lake') and eventually dumped on the world market for whatever price can be obtained, to the not-surprising indignation of competitive suppliers. In addition to the basic plan for a common market in industrial and agricultural products, the Treaty of Rome provided for free internal movement of labour, a co-ordinated anti-monopoly policy and ambitions towards monetary union (see section 19.7).

There is no doubt that the common market in industrial products was a great success. It was estimated that EC intra-trade in manufactures grew some 50 per cent more than would otherwise have occurred in the decade following the Rome treaty. (Table 17.2 shows that by 1988 the combined exports of the EC were more than 200 per cent higher than those of the United States; in 1950 they were only 50 per cent higher.) Although the orthodox triangles (of consumer's and producer's surplus) analysis of the welfare implications of trade liberalization is dismissive of the benefits of even such a large expansion of trade, some reasons were given in section 8.5 for believing that the orthodox analysis is seriously incomplete, and there was certainly a widely shared perception in Europe that the EC was a major factor in promoting the prosperity of the 1960s. The common agricultural policy was less of a success, the main problem being that the farm lobby managed to set and maintain support prices too high, with a consequent chronic tendency to induce wasteful excess supply. Common policies were put in place on other issues as well, with results that varied from the marginally useful to the mildly comic.

The early success of the EC led Britain to regret its initial decision to stand aside, and twice during the 1960s it applied for admission, only to be rejected by de Gaulle's France. A third application submitted after de Gaulle's retirement and death was successful, and in 1972 the EC was enlarged by the entrance of Britain, Denmark and Ireland. Although the expansion of intra-trade among the original members showed signs of slowing down in the 1970s, trade involving the new members grew sharply. This benefit was, however, somewhat overshadowed by the general stagflation and disputes about payments into the EC budget (mainly used to finance agricultural subsidies), so that the EC no longer exuded that dynamism that it had done in its first decade. Despite that, it has attracted new applicants for membership: Greece, Portugal and Spain. This *widening* process is likely to continue with the opening up of Eastern Europe and the reunification of Germany.

The process of economic integration in Europe will be *deepened* after 1992 with the 'completion of the internal market'. Although tariff and quantitative import restrictions have been eliminated on intra-EC trade, there are technical and administrative barriers – customs controls, differences in technical regulations, etc. – which continue to restrict intra-union trade. It is unlikely that the removal of technical, fiscal and administrative differences between member countries will be achieved immediately after 1992. But the process of creating a European internal market after 1992 can be expected to increase allocative efficiency and competition within the EC. This can also be expected to increase intra-union trade, and the induced efficiency and scale advantages for EC producers will increase their competitiveness also in extra-EC markets.

The widening and deepening of the EC makes access to this market very important for non-members. The Community has concluded association agreements with a large number of countries. These provide for preferential access to the EC market of specified quantities of various goods. Most countries bordering on the Mediterranean, from Algeria and Morocco to Israel and Turkey, have concluded such agreements. These used to provide that the associates would grant preferences in their markets for imports of certain goods from the EC, but under pressure from competing suppliers these reverse preferences have tended to be dropped. Only with EFTA members, with whom the EC now has virtual free trade in industrial products, do reverse preferences still exist.

European Free Trade Association (EFTA)

When Britain found to its surprise in 1958 that the six original members of the EC were in earnest about creating a common market from which it would be excluded, it responded by trying to organize most of the excluded European countries into a free trade area. This was the origin of EFTA, whose members, besides Britain, were Austria, Denmark, Finland, Iceland, Norway, Portugal, Sweden and Switzerland.

Despite its anomalous shape, EFTA proved quite successful in promoting intra-trade in manufactures, although there is evidence that a much higher proportion of this (perhaps 50 per cent as against 25 per cent in the case of the EC) represented trade diversion – overwhelmingly at the expense of the EC. The intuitive reason for expecting a higher percentage of trade diversion in the EFTA case is that the EFTA economies were more heterogeneous in resource endowments and income levels than the EC economies, so that there were relatively more opportunities for changing the source of what had to be imported anyway than there were for importing what was primarily produced at home. EFTA has continued to exist even after the withdrawal of Britain and Denmark, and now enjoys virtual free trade in industrial goods with the EC. The completion of the EC internal market after 1992 will, however, put pressures on firms in EFTA countries to reorganize production and marketing strategies, to remain on the same 'level playing field' as EC producers.

Council for Mutual Econonic Co-operation (CMEA or COMECON)

The members of the CMEA, which was founded in 1949, were those Communist states that, until the reforms in Eastern Europe, looked to the Soviet Union for political leadership: Bulgaria, Cuba, Czechoslovakia, East Germany, Hungary, Mongolia, Poland, Romania and Vietnam, as well as the USSR itself. The aim was not to free trade, which was neither possible nor desired given that trade was a state monopoly in each of the member countries, but rather to plan production on a joint basis and to seek to ensure that the resulting trade flows balanced. For some reason that is incomprehensible to a Western economist, CMEA sought to establish *bilateral* trade balance between each of the member states rather than simply requiring that each was in overall balance and then transferring claims between them in some convertible currency. A requirement of bilateral balance is virtually guaranteed to lead to inefficiency, since only by coincidence would the trade pattern that emerges from each country maximizing its overall utility subject to a single constraint of balanced trade (or a given level of imbalance) also satisfy the additional constraints imposed by the requirements of bilateral balance. Perhaps this explains why the CMEA has not been a great success, as manifest by the preference members display for selling to the West (where they earn convertible currency) rather than selling to their partners. The economic reforms taking place in Eastern Europe and the Soviet Union, and the reunification of Germany, make the dismemberment of the CMEA – at least as it has functioned in the past – a virtual certainty.

US–Canada Free Trade Area

In 1988 the United States and Canada signed a free trade agreement.[2] As from the beginning of 1989 the two countries began to phase in (over a ten-year period) the elimination of *all* tariffs and *many* non-tariff barriers against trade in goods and services between the two countries. Arguably the agreement may not be viewed as very important, especially in terms of its immediate effects. Even before the agreement, nearly three-quarters of US trade with Canada was duty free and the average duty on the remainder was quite low. The United States is overwhelmingly Canada's major trading partner. Canada is the second most important single trade partner for the United States, after Japan, but it accounts for only about one-fifth of United States trade. Thus the agreement may be viewed as more important for Canada than the United States. But the free trade area may be a tentative first step towards a North American common market: the United States has already initiated negotiations with Mexico for a free trade agreement. The existing agreement with Canada does not establish a common external commercial policy; labour mobility will remain highly restricted, and there is no intention as yet to harmonize or co-ordinate macroeconomic policies.

17.5 Trade in oil

From the time that the oil trade started, around the turn of the century, until the early 1970s, the trade in oil was conducted overwhelmingly on an intracompany basis. With the exception of the United States, the countries where major oil discoveries were made lacked the technology necessary to exploit them. They therefore granted exploration and production rights to one of the major oil companies.

The main impact of the oil industry on the economies of the exporting countries stemmed from the royalties received by their governments. Although these were rather modest, they were still sufficient to make the low-population oil exporters the aristocrats of the developing world. Their governments became unhappy, however, when competition led to a fall in the price of crude oil and therefore in their royalty receipts, as happened in the late 1950s. The main oil exporters decided to form a producers' association to prevent further erosion of their receipts, and in 1961 the Organization of Petroleum Exporting Countries (OPEC) came into being. Currently, and for some years past, OPEC has had thirteen members: Algeria, Ecuador, Gabon, Indonesia, Iraq, Iran, Kuwait, Libya, Nigeria, Qatar, Saudi Arabia, the United Arab Emirates and Venezuela.

For the first decade of its existence, no one except specialists had heard of OPEC. It succeeded in the initial aim of preventing further erosion in royalites. Although the oil price continued to edge down even in nominal terms through most of the 1960s, the oil companies agreed to pay royalties on the basis of a fictional posted price rather than on the price they were using in intracompany transactions. The low and declining real price of oil energy led to a rapid growth in demand. The world became increasingly dependent on oil and, in particular, on Arab oil. By the early 1970s the producing countries were already nationalizing the activities of the oil companies in their territory, but this was regarded as a problem for the oil companies rather than for the oil-importing countries.

This fool's paradise came to an abrupt end following the Egyptian–Israeli war of 1973. To put pressure on the West to lean on Israel following the fighting, the Arab oil exporters decreed a cutback in oil exports. OPEC took advantage of the prospective supply shortage to quadruple the price of oil within three months. The real price of oil then remained fairly steady until 1979 and then took another upward bound.

The process of nationalization was quickly completed following the act of OPEC self-assertion in 1973. Since then, oil has been produced by companies owned by the producing countries; these companies contract foreign technicians and technical services as necessary. It is sold by the producers, in part under contract to the oil companies of the importing countries, but now principally on a competitive flexprice market.

There are three stories about the correct way to characterize the post-1974 oil market. A first is to picture it as a cartelized market. According to this view, which has been the dominant one in the oil-importing countries, the competitive price is more or less that which prevailed (in real terms) up to 1973. The fact that the real price has been much higher since then, especially until 1986, is attributable to the success of OPEC in organizing the producers into a cartel that holds the price above the competitive level and persuades producers to supply less than they would choose to on the basis of calculations of nationally optimal supply levels, so as to sustain the cartelized price.

A second version treats the oil price as being set on the basis of calculations of intertemporal optimization by the holders of an exhaustible resource. A basic theorem about the pricing of an exhaustible resource says that its price should rise over time at a rate equal to the rate of interest, so as to make holding the resource in the ground as attractive an investment as any other. The *height* of the price path should be such as to ration out the supply of the resource over time, avoiding both unduly rapid depletion, which would leave the world short of an essential resource before a satisfactory substitute was developed, and unduly slow use, which would delay development in the short run to an extent that outweighs greater availability of the resource in the more distant future. Naturally, the oil exporters tend to take this view of the oil market, arguing that the pre-1973 price was unduly low and therefore induced wastefully rapid depletion.

The third story about the oil market argues that the increase in the oil price could be maintained because the supply curve of oil is backward bending. Prior to 1973, the producing countries had to pump all the oil they could in order to earn enough cash to finance the imports they wished to buy. After the price rise, however, they were able to satisfy all their import needs and still have cash left over. Rather than invest it all in the paper assets issued by the importing countries, it made sense to invest some in larger stocks of oil in the ground – that is, to reduce the supply they placed on the world market. Adherents of this story point to the fact that in the 1979–80 oil price increase it was the price on the free market that *led* the rise, with OPEC raising its price periodically towards the free-market level. This hardly seemed consistent with the story of a cartelized market, since a cartel typically dictates a price rise and then spends its time policing those of its members who cheat by offering discounts.

Nevertheless, in 1986 the oil price collapsed, and when it did so the reason was that OPEC found itself unable to persuade the non-Saudi members to share the burden of restraining output. This makes it difficult to deny that OPEC did function as a

Table 17.3 Tokyo round: average tariff changes (%)

	United States	EEC	Japan
Raw materials			
Pre-Tokyo	0.9	0.7	1.5
Post-Tokyo	0.2	0.2	0.5
Semi-manufactures			
Pre-Tokyo	4.5	5.8	6.6
Post-Tokyo	3.0	4.2	4.6
Finished manufactures			
Pre-Tokyo	8.0	9.7	12.5
Post-Tokyo	5.7	6.9	6.0

Source: Adapted from Kenen (1989), table 11.2.

cartel, but the other two theories help explain why it was such a successful cartel for so long.

The oil price shocks of the 1970s added to stagflationary pressures of the period. They reinforced the challenge from the NICs in creating a climate conducive to protectionist pressures.

17.6 GATT II: Coping with the new protectionism

Against the background of international monetary crisis (see section 19.4) and of rising protectionist pressures in the United States, the Nixon administration called in 1971 for a new round of GATT negotiations to be aimed at what the United States saw as 'unfair' trade practices. Despite the inauspicious conditions (stagflation and the growth of the new protectionism), a GATT meeting in Tokyo in 1973 agreed to an ambitious agenda, including further tariff liberalization, special efforts to liberalize trade in agricultural products, reduction of non-tariff barriers and preparation of codes of conduct to prevent unfair trade practices.

The Tokyo Round lasted until 1979 and covered a large part of its agenda. The question of tariff liberalization proved to be relatively uncontroversial, largely because pre-Tokyo Round average tariffs on (industrial) goods were already quite low. The tariff cuts agreed were in similar form and size to those of the Kennedy Round. They are summarized in Table 17.3. The tariff reductions agreed (about 34 per cent on industrial products for all industrial countries)[3] were implemented from the beginning of 1980, and phased in over an eight-year period.

Given tariff liberalization comparable with the Kennedy Round, the Tokyo Round might have been viewed as another clear success. But a number of qualifications are in order. First, the concessions applied mainly to industrial products. Agriculture continued to be highly protected in industrial countries. Second, the concessions did not apply to all industrial products. 'Sensitive' items such as textiles, leather and footwear were subject to lower or no tariff reductions. Third, the significance of the tariff reductions was substantially reduced by the increased use during the 1970s of the trade instruments of the 'new protectionism' (the hidden, non-tariff measures, which were discussed in detail in Chapter 9). In terms of dealing with the significant issues of non-tariff protection and fair trade, the Tokyo Round was much less successful.

The Tokyo Round made some progress on the more identifiable and quantifiable non-tariff barriers, such as the standardization of customs procedures and the strengthening of anti-dumping codes. But little was ultimately achieved in terms of dismantling or restricting the growth of quantitative and discriminatory import barriers (such as VERs). Some commentators interpreted the Tokyo Declaration as the twilight of the liberal order. It may be better viewed, with hindsight, as a successful holding operation: faced with unfavourable conditions it managed to maintain a relatively open and orderly trading system. The unfinished business had to wait until circumstances were more favourable.

Unfinished business

In 1986 a Ministerial Conference at Punta del Este in Uruguay launched an eighth round of multilateral trade negotiations (MTN). The Uruguay Round was scheduled for completion at the end of 1990. Tariff reduction was again sought. But much more was on the agenda: unfinished business from previous rounds (e.g. non-tariff barriers and safeguards), issues avoided by previous rounds (the 'special cases' of agricultural protection and the Multi-fibre Arrangement) and new issues (e.g. trade barriers against services). In some respects the conditions are more favourable for agreement than in the case of the Tokyo Round. Since the early 1980s growth rates and employment have recovered in the major industrial countries. Budgetary costs of agricultural support have become an increasing strain on public finances in the USA and EC. Coalitions of developing and other agricultural exporting countries (e.g. Australia and New Zealand) have lobbied more actively and effectively than previously for the reform of agricultural trade.

There are, however, also reasons for suspecting that the prospects for substantial reforms are limited. First, a number of the issues on the agenda are very complicated: for example, about how to liberalize or replace the quantitative import restrictions on textiles, or how to introduce trade in services into GATT's legal framework. Second, the agenda is very ambitious and there are complex 'linkages' between issues: the EC is likely to concede one issue only if the United States concedes on another, which in turn depends on Japan's willingness to accept reforms elsewhere. Third, there are more countries actively involved in the negotiations this time: the developing countries have played a more active role in the negotiations than in previous rounds, where they felt the agenda had been set largely by the major industrial countries. Finally, a number of the major 'players' in the negotiations have other issues that may deter them from accepting substantial further change. The EC is concerned with integrating its lower-income new entrants, completing the internal market, the reunification of Germany and developments in Eastern Europe. The

United States has severe budget and trade imbalance problems, not to mention new military involvement in the Middle East. Progress had apparently been limited even before these distractions, so the outcome of the Uruguay Round may fall short of its ambitious aims.

Perhaps, as before, the negotiations will be saved by the 'eleventh hour' rule – countries holding out until the last minute before making concessions. Certainly it is to be hoped that the rule applies, since the price of failure to complete the round successfully could be high. But by February 1991 there was still no agreement, and little sign that the EC was willing to concede the US demands for radical liberalization of agricultural trade.

Probably the most important achievement of GATT has been the promotion of multilateralism. This is ultimately what is at stake in the Uruguay Round and in the 1990s. The proliferation of discriminatory, often bilateral, restrictions in the 1970s and 1980s challenged this principle and the credibility of GATT. A failure of the Uruguay Round would encourage growth of the new protectionism. This would be particularly serious because of other developments which have created more propitious circumstances for bilateralism. These developments are the 'deepening and widening' of the EC (see section 17.4) and the 1988 United States Omnibus Trade Bill.

The 1992 programme of the EC is aimed at revitalizing the process of economic integration in Western Europe. If fully implemented, it will create the world's largest fully integrated market. In itself the programme is not inconsistent with GATT or with multilateralism. But complete liberalization of trade among the existing members, and perhaps more when membership increases, is likely to have important implications for the conduct of the EC's commercial policies with non-members. The possibility of a 'fortress Europe' has created some concern outside the EC. One concern is that producer lobbies faced with increased internal competition might seek to restrict imports from outside the EC. As the opportunity for individual member countries to use bilateral measures, such as VERs on Japanese cars, disappears after 1992, then EC 'administered' protection against 'foreign' competition (through, for instance, technical standards or anti-dumping legislation) may become the refuge of EC producer lobbies. A further possibility is the 'entry-price' scenario. A 'deepened and widened' EC will be a large and lucrative market for firms from non-member countries, for which they may be willing to 'pay' an entry fee of some form. Where inward investment is involved, payment could be in the form of additional local content requirement. Or there might be demands for preferential access for EC producers in foreign markets.

Of course such things could happen whatever the outcome of the Uruguay Round. Their probability, however, will be higher if the Uruguay Round fails to deal a blow at bilateralism.

A major theme running through recent discussions of trade policy in the United States has been the 'level playing field'. The term has been used widely by politicians, administrators and producer lobbies. It reflects a belief that the United States producers are playing by the rules of the game, but that many of their trading partners are not. Most of these allegations are directed at Japan and the NICs, although the EC has not escaped criticism. Irrespective of the merits or otherwise of these arguments, and notwithstanding the fact that the United States already had legislation in place to deal with unfair trading, the 1988 Omnibus Trade Bill introduced several new provisions designed to 'level the playing field'. The most important provision is the so-called *Super 301*. This allows the United States to name trading partners engaged in 'unfair trading'. Once named, these countries are called on to enter bilateral negotiations intended to alter their behaviour. If no agreement is reached within eighteen months, retaliatory action can be taken. The mechanism came into force in May 1989. Three countries were named: Japan (for practices in forest products, government procurement practices, restrictions on satellites and super-computers); Brazil (for a restrictive import licensing system, standards and technical barriers); and India (for performance requirements and barriers to trade in services). In addition, eight countries were placed 'on remand'.

With this legislation the United States took an important step down the road to bilateralism. Rather than trying to resolve trade disputes through GATT procedures, it chose to act independently. As with 'fortress Europe' scenarios, this poses a threat to multilateralism irrespective of the outcome of the Uruguay round. Again, however, the probability of the Super 301 provisions being more widely used is higher if the Uruguay Round fails. Of course Super 301 and 'fortress Europe' are not independent of each other. If the United States' demands for 'greater reciprocity' are pursued more widely through Super 301, the EC may respond in kind. Similarly, a willingness of the EC to restrict access to its enlarged market may provoke a more energetic use of Super 301 actions.

Escalation of such use of bilateral restrictions is not in the long-term interests of the United States and European Community, or of the rest of the global trading system. There is a danger too of proliferation as other regional trading alliances might be drawn away from multilateralism. Indeed this tendency towards regionalism and fragmentation may be strongest among the developing countries, which tend to view the rules of the international trading system as having been designed to benefit the northern industrialized countries. This provides a strong incentive to search for 'southern' solutions.

17.7 Developing countries and the trade system

The preceding analysis of GATT and the conduct of commercial diplomacy in the last forty years or so has focused overwhelmingly on the 'North'. Both the 'rules' of the system and the nature of the trade problems of the developing countries (the 'South') are quite different from those of developed, industrialized countries.

Primary products

Table 17.1 records the greater dependence of the developing countries on exports of primary products. Unlike trade in industrial products, which are generally sold in fixprice markets, most primary products are traded in flexprice markets. The bulk of world trade in primary products, excluding diamonds, fruit and iron ore, is conducted on the basis of prices determined in organized commodity markets, in which the price fluctuates from day to day and hour to hour to clear the market. These commodity markets are mainly located in London, New York and Chicago. By no means all the trade in these products is carried out on the basis of contracts concluded on those markets, but the prices agreed in contracts signed off-market are strongly influenced by ruling market prices.

The outstanding stylized fact about the markets of most primary commodities is that both demand and supply tend to be distinctly inelastic with respect to price in the short run. By and large demand is inelastic either because primary products provide the basic staples of life or because their cost is only a small fraction of users' total cost of production. And supply is usually inelastic in the short run because of technological factors: once the mines are sunk, the trees are planted or the crops are sown, there is not much scope for varying output in response to a change in price.

Figure 17.1 shows a competitive market for a typical primary product, with inelastic demand and supply curves. Initial price is p_0 with the corresponding equilibrium quantity q_0. Now suppose that the supply curve shifts right, to S', perhaps because of unusually favourable weather conditions. There is no contradiction between the hypothesis of inelastic supply and the hypothesis that supply may be subject to big shocks: one refers to movements along, the other to shifts of, the supply curve. The new equilibrium is characterized by a lower price p_1 and a higher quantity q_1; because the demand curve is inelastic, the total revenue (pq) *falls* as a result of the increase in supply.

Shifts in demand produce even more violent variations in the incomes of primary

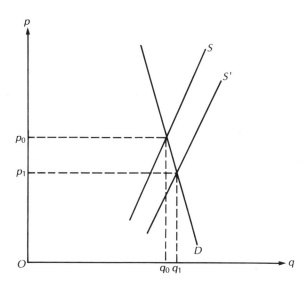

Figure 17.1 Market for a typical primary product

producers, since price rises a lot because of the inelasticity of supply, while, to the extent that quantity does vary at all, it reinforces rather than counters the effect of the increase in price. (Imagine a rightward shift of the demand curve in Figure 17.1). Once again, such shifts in demand are in no way inconsistent with inelasticity of the demand curve, and in fact the demand for many primary products does fluctuate. Specifically, a cyclical boom in the developed countries strengthens demand for basic materials, especially metals, and thus leads to big increases in the value of primary product exports. Conversely, world recession leads to a sharp fall in the value of exports of primary products, and therefore in the export receipts of the typical developing country. Thus shocks to either demand or supply can create fluctuations in the receipts of countries exporting primary products.

There is, of course, an important influence in many primary product markets that has not yet been mentioned: speculation. With any storable commodity one should expect to find people attempting to profit by buying when the product is relatively cheap and selling when it is dear. To the extent that they succeed, they will perform the social service of financing a carryover of stocks from periods of plenty to those of scarcity, in the process diminishing the fluctuations in price that provide the incentive to speculate. Speculation does indeed occur in the markets for the storable primary commodities. Nevertheless, judging by the price swings that continue to occur, it is not very successful.

Not unnaturally, those whose foreign exchange receipts depend heavily on sales of a few primary commodities with volatile prices have tended to regard the present organization of the primary product markets as unsatisfactory. There have in fact been a number of attempts to manage markets with a view to reducing the volatility of prices and income. These have taken two general forms: limitations on supply and the establishment of buffer stocks.

Supply limitations are difficult to administer. The same reasons that make supply curves inelastic serve to give an incentive to individual suppliers (whether peasants, companies or countries) to avoid their share in the necessary total cutback in supply. Since a limitation on supply in weak periods does nothing to raise supply in periods of strong demand, the average rate of return rises and attracts new entrants, further compounding the difficulty of limiting supply. The leading historical example of supply limitation was that unilaterally practised by Brazil in the 1930s, when it had a near-monopoly of the supply of coffee. Burning coffee made sense from a national if not from a cosmopolitan Pareto standpoint – at least in the short run. But new entrants flooded in (now over seventy countries export coffee), and in the long run Brazil lost its near-monopoly.

The alternative is to establish a buffer stock, which is an attempt to do through official channels what the private speculators have failed to do satisfactorily: to buy when the price is low and sell when it is high to reduce the swings in prices. Figure 17.2 illustrates the principle. Given that you know (at least approximately) the average position of the demand and supply curves over the long run and can there-fore estimate the average equilibrium price p_e, you set a ceiling price above that level and a floor price below. If the supply curve shifts right and the demand curve shifts left to the point where the price falls to the floor, the buffer stock comes in as residual buyer to prevent any further price decline. Conversely, a combination of a positive demand shock and/or negative supply shock, such as to threaten to raise the price above the ceiling, leads the buffer stock to act as residual seller. Price is therefore constrained to the range between the floor and ceiling, with a reduction in the fluctuations in export receipts.

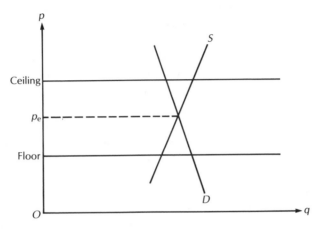

Figure 17.2 Buffer stock

Buffer stocks have functioned off and on for several commodities since the 1920s, most especially for tin and cocoa. Sometimes they have operated as intended, for a while. But sooner or later they have usually either run out of their commodity, at which point the price has shot above the ceiling, or run out of money, at which point the price has dropped through the floor. One could always avoid the latter problem by giving the buffer stock manager more money, but there is a point at which those putting up the money (especially when these are the consumer nations) wonder whether they are making a sensible investment. A buffer stock which delayed the initiation of adjustment in response to a fall in the equilibrium price by holding prices artificially high for a while could in the end magnify the adjustment problem for the producers as well. The fact is that a successful buffer stock needs much the same forecasting abilities as a successful speculator in the private sector, and the basic problem is simply that the world is not that forecastable. Many economists never-theless intuitively feel that it must be possible to do better than in the past, but even a sympathizer has to admit that at the present time this conviction is sustained more by hope than by evidence.

Potential instability of primary product prices and the threat of secular decline in the terms of trade have been among the factors that have encouraged policy-makers in developing countries to promote manufactured exports. The promotion of infant export industries was seen by many as requiring discriminatory action in favour of developing countries.

'Differential and more favourable' treatment

The origins of differential treatment for developing countries within GATT can be traced back to the 1940s when the institutional framework for the post-war international economic order was being designed. The developing countries tabled numerous amendments to the draft charter of the International Trade Organization, calling in effect for their exemption from the requirements for reciprocity, non-discrimination and liberalization of quantitative restrictions. There was, in particular, growing interest in inward-oriented development strategies in newly independent nations.

The original GATT articles met relatively few of the developing countries' demands. Article XVIII, on 'Government Assistance to Economic Development', allowed contracting parties in early stages of development to use quantitative and other restrictions to protect infant industries (and, after 1955, for balance of payments control). Although the implementation of this dispensation was in principle subject to GATT approval, the relatively few developing countries that were early members of GATT were allowed *de facto* to pursue relatively autonomous trade policies (free from threat of retaliation by the industrial countries). The industrialized countries were in practice indifferent to the policies of the developing countries because they saw very limited export prospects at that time. It took the industrial countries rather longer to concede formally most of what the developing countries were demanding.

By the mid-1950s it was evident that export growth, especially of manufactured goods, and economic growth in general were being achieved by the developed countries, but not at comparable rates by the developing countries. Indeed, the developing countries were losing market share in many primary exports. No doubt the trade policies of the developed countries, notably the concentration of liberalization on products other than those in which developing countries had a comparative advantage, were a contributory factor to this apparent failure of the international order to satisfy the needs of the developing countries. But many policy-makers in developing countries, as well as academics, became convinced 'export pessimists': fears of 'unequal exchange' and secular decline in the terms of trade abounded, and inherent structural deficiencies and rigidities were believed to preclude the growth of their manufactured exports. Such arguments provided a rationale for continuation of protectionist policies. The ascendency of structuralist thinking within the development literature provided an intellectual basis for import-substituting industrialization strategies.

Import substitution policies themselves contributed to poor export performance. By the 1960s the developing countries tended to view themselves as a homogeneous grouping (the 'South') all subject to an external constraint. The alleviation of this external constraint suggested that they negotiate collectively with the 'North' (the 'rich man's club'). Demands in GATT for the reduction of the North's obstacles to their exports were unsuccessful. The addition of a Part IV to GATT on 'Trade and Development' in 1964, which relieved developing countries of reciprocity obligations to concessions made by other GATT members, was seen by the South as a disappointing outcome of the Kennedy Round. The developing countries then proceeded to press their claim for differential treatment outside the GATT framework.

Generalized System of Preferences (GSP)

Until the early 1960s, the struggle for political independence had pushed economic questions into the background except in Latin America. But after the decolonization of Africa (around 1960) economic development became the top priority. Discontent with existing trade arrangements led to pressures to create a new organization, and the first meeting of the United Nations Conference on Trade and Development (UNCTAD) was accordingly convened in 1964.

The only issue on which UNCTAD has been successful in getting a major change in international rules concerns the tariffs applied by developed countries to imports from developing countries. The EC started in the 1960s to give preferential access to its market for certain imports from signatories of the Lomé Convention and other associates, and this led to the exclusion of competitive products from Latin America and other areas not eligible for associate status. UNCTAD argued that the principle of allowing preferential access for the exports of developing countries was right, but that the practice of restricting such concessions to a limited number of developing countries and thus diverting trade was wrong. Such tariff preferences should be generalized to apply to all developing countries.

After much negotiation, a limited scheme for generalized preferences, the GSP, entered into force in 1971. This scheme provides for each of the developed countries – with the EC acting as a single country in this respect, as in other questions of commercial policy – to draw up its own individual list of the products in which it will make tariff concessions on imports from 'all' of the developing countries. The word 'all' is in quotes because when a country has too much success in building up a large volume of exports, it may find its name withdrawn from the list of beneficiaries for the product in question. Given that the quantity of imports that is going to be accepted on preferential terms is limited, there is in fact a certain logic in excluding countries that have successfully established themselves as exporters of a particular product. This is consistent with the scheme's objective of acting as a stimulus to infant exporters, and so helps in the critical first stage of launching non-traditional exports in the markets of the industrial countries.

A main criticism of the GSP by the developing countries is its limited scale of operation. Less than 20 per cent of LDC exports to industrial countries (even excluding petroleum) enter on preferential terms under the GSP. GSP-eligible trade has also been dominated by a relatively small number of the successful NICs, though this should decline as countries are 'graduated'.

The arguments for differential and preferential treatment have been challenged in recent years. In particular, it is now widely held that it was a mistake for developing countries to seek exemption from the reciprocity requirement. This made it far too easy for governments to surrender to pressure-group demands for import restrictions, and removed one source of external pressure to avoid pushing import substitution too far. The performance of developing countries that have unilaterally liberalized in the last two decades confirms that import protection has been a significant barrier to exports: by raising domestic prices above world prices and overvaluing the currency, import substitution strategies reduce the incentive to produce for export.

The critique of the GSP is less fundamental: it is simply not very important. In itself the GSP is unlikely to do any harm and is probably of some help,[4] but the export success of the Asian NICs in fields not covered by the GSP has shown that it is not necessary, and the failure of other countries to develop successful export industries despite the GSP shows that it is not sufficient.

The developing countries have taken a more active role in the Uruguay Round of GATT negotiations than they did in earlier rounds. Coalitions of developing countries were active in launching the round and in drawing up the agenda for the negotiations. Indeed, the width of the agenda reflected the greater involvement of developing countries, including negotiating groups on non-tariff measures, natural resource-based products, textiles and clothing, tropical products and agriculture. Much of the coalition activity was by countries united by common interest rather than a North–South ideological split. It is to be hoped that this activism is rewarded by worthwhile benefits, and that in future developing countries participate as full members of the global trading system.

17.8 'South–South' trade

Although the case for greater outward orientation is now widely accepted in developing countries, interest remains in discriminatory export promotion: interventions that promote South–South exports, but reduce dependence on North–South trade.

The calls for a discriminatory policy favouring South–South trade are based on a variety of more or less convincing arguments. Some analysts explain the South's dependence on capital and high-technology goods from the North as part of a vicious cycle that cannot be broken without some governmental intervention. For instance, northern manufacturers can mass-produce sophisticated goods at lower costs because a huge global market for them exists simply because southern producers are not producing the goods themselves. Southern manufacturers cannot enter the market because of the high costs (and thus high prices) at initial low levels of production.

In his lecture on being awarded the Nobel prize, Arthur Lewis (1980) resurrected the hypothesis of trade as an engine of growth and pointed to a stable long-run relationship between growth in the industrial market countries and growth in the developing countries. Because growth in the former has slowed and shows few signs of regaining the trend levels of 1948–73, it follows according to this argument that growth in the latter will suffer unless South–South trade expands to fill the gap. Lewis argues that policy intervention is necessary for South–South trade to expand.

The growth of the new protectionism in the North has provided another reason

Table 17.4 Trade integration arrangements among developing countries, 1989

Region and organization	Participating countries
Africa	
Communauté Economique de l'Afrique de l'Ouest (CEAO)	Benin, Burkina Faso, Côte d'Ivoire, Mali, Mauritania, Niger, Senegal
Mano River Union (MRU)	Guinea, Liberia, Sierra Leone
Economic Community of West African States (ECOWAS)	CEAO members, MRU members, Cameroon, Gabon, Gambia, Ghana, Guinea-Bissau, Nigeria, Togo
Union Douanière et Economique de l'Afrique Centrale (UDEAC)	Cameroon, Central African Republic, Congo, Gabon, Chad, Equatorial Guinea
Communauté Economique Pays des Grand Lacs (CEPGL)	Burundi, Rwanda, Zaire
Communauté Economique des Etats de l'Afrique Centrale (CEEAC)	UDEAC members, CEPGL members, Chad, Equatorial Guinea, São Tome and Principe
Southern African Customs Unit (SACU)	Botswana, Lesotho, Swaziland
Preferential Trading Arrangement for Eastern and Southern African States	Burundi, Comoros, Djibouti, Ethiopia, Kenya, Lesotho, Malawi, Mauritius, Mozambique, Rwanda, Somalia, Swaziland, Tanzania, Uganda, Zambia, Zimbabwe
Southern African Development Co-ordination Conference (SADCC)	Angola, Botswana, Lesotho, Malawi, Mozambique, Swaziland, Tanzania, Zaire, Zimbabwe
Asia	
Association of South East Asian Nations (ASEAN)	Brunei, Indonesia, Malaysia, Philippines, Singapore, Thailand
Latin America and the Caribbean	
Caribbean Community (CARICOM)	Antigua and Barbuda, Barbados, Belize, Dominica, Grenada, Guyana, Jamaica, Montserrat, St Kitts and Nevis (including Anguilla), St Lucia, St Vincent and the Grenadines, Trinidad and Tobago
Eastern Caribbean Common Market (ECCM)	Special regime within CARICOM for its less developed members
Latin American Integration Association (LAIA), successor to Latin American Free Trade Association (LAFTA)	Mexico plus all South American countries except French Guiana, Guyana and Surinam
Central American Common Market (CACM)	Costa Rica, El Salvador, Guatemala, Nicaragua, (Honduras)[1]
Andean Group	Bolivia, Colombia, Ecuador, Peru, Venezuela, (Chile)[1]

Source: Greenaway and Milner (1990).
[1] Former members shown in brackets.

for looking to South–South trade. Why expand exports to northern markets if the response in those markets is likely to be the erection of protective barriers?

The obvious way of promoting South–South trade is through the establishment of common markets or free trade areas in the South. There is in fact a relatively long history of such attempts. During the 1960s many regional integration arrangements were initiated between developing countries; there are currently considerably more southern integration arrangements than industrial trading blocs. Table 17.4 lists the current arrangements among developing countries.

Following revisions to GATT in 1979, developing countries were exempted from the requirements that only full customs unions or free trade areas were GATT-legal. As a result these southern integration arrangements are invariably only loosely organized preferential trading areas (PTAs). This may be one of the reasons why the arrangements have not been very successful in terms of stimulating intra-group trade. Table 17.5 provides information on the growth and share of intra-group trade over the period 1960–83 for some southern arrangements and contrasts this with the EEC's record.

The reasons for the poor record of South–South arrangements in stimulating trade expansion are not hard to find. One significant problem has been that the members of some of the unions not only have small markets and low incomes but have comparable production structures. A union among similar economies presumes that trade expansion will come from intra-industry specialization and product differentiation. Such expansion has been found among the members of the EC, where market size and incomes can support such specialization, but it is far less possible among comparable but poorer markets. A second problem arises from the content of the various agreements. Details vary, but tariff concessions negotiated under PTA arrangements have usually been negotiated item by item rather than across the board. Negotiating in this fashion is cumbersome and costly and encourages members to be selective in the offers they make, so that exclusions are numerous, whereas preferences are often idiosyncratic. Moreover, PTAs typically cover tariffs only and exclude the full range of non-tariff barriers, such as legal and administrative requirements and health and safety standards. The effects of a particular tariff cut can be subverted by a specific non-tariff intervention, which can also be deployed competitively in bids to attract foreign direct investment.

Another crippling feature of these arrangements has been their lack of redistributive mechanisms (see section 8.5). Invariably some members of an agreement gain more than others, especially when they are at different stages of development. Without a formal mechanism for redistribution political tension among the members has tended to undermine commitment and can eventually destroy the union, as it did in the case of the East African Community.

The history of South–South integration arrangements thus far is not encouraging. Nonetheless, new proposals continue to be floated. In 1986 the Group of 77 (developing countries) concluded an agreement that provides a legal framework for a South–South version of a system of general trade preferences. A southern free trade area has also been suggested. Argentina, Brazil and some of their neighbours have renewed efforts to reduce barriers among themselves, encouraged by President Bush's call to consider a Western Hemisphere free trade area. There need not necessarily be a conflict between such regional trade liberalization and the continued reduction of barriers against the rest of the world, any more than there was in Europe. The real question is in both cases whether developing countries have now absorbed the logic of trade creation.

Table 17.5 Intra-trade of economic groupings of developing countries, 1960 and 1970–83 (selected years)

Economic grouping[1]	Intra-trade (US$m)					Intra-trade of group as % of total exports of each group				
	1960	1970	1976	1980	1983	1960	1970	1976	1980	1983
ASEAN	839	860	3,619	11,918	17,080	21.7	14.7	13.9	17.8	23.1
UDEAC	3	33	75	200	80	1.6	3.4	3.9	4.1	2.0
CACM	33	299	653	1,141	840	7.5	26.8	21.6	22.0	21.8
CARICOM	27	73	212	354	360	4.5	7.3	6.7	6.4	9.3
LAIA	564	1,290	4,434	1,027	1,200	7.5	10.2	12.8	13.5	10.2
Of which:										
Andean Group	25	109	594	955	1,037	0.7	2.3	4.2	3.5	4.3
CEAO	6	73	177	296	406	2.0	9.1	6.7	6.9	11.6
ECOWAS	17	61	478	1,056	860	1.2	2.1	3.1	3.9	4.1
CEPGL	–	2	3	5	5	0.0	0.2	0.1	0.2	0.2
MRU	–	–	2	2	7	0.0	0.1	0.2	0.1	0.1
For reference:										
EEC	10,300	43,400	n.a.	747,000	298,900	34.6	48.9	n.a.	52.8	52.4

[1] See Table 17.4 for membership.
Source: Robson (1987).

17.9 Summary

Trade in industrial products between industrial countries ('North–North' trade) has expanded rapidly in the post-war period under the twin influence of multilateral liberalization in the GATT framework and liberalization in regional trading blocs. By the end of the 1960s trade was probably freer than that at any time in history. Since then some further tariff liberalization has been achieved through multilateral trade negotiations. There has, however, been a serious threat to the maintenance of a liberal order through the emergence of the 'new protectionism', a series of restrictions on the exports of Japan and the NICs. In fact the NICs have continued, despite the restrictions, to increase their exports, due to increasing competitiveness and circumvention of the restrictions through export diversification.

The efforts to maintain GATT's multilateral approach to commercial policy are constrained both by legacies of the past and by new pressures for bilateralism and fragmentation. Legacies of the past include the hitherto 'special cases' of agriculture and textiles. New pressures for bilateralism include the US Omnibus Trade Act of 1988 and might result from the widening and deepening of the EC after 1992.

The South has recently taken a more active role in global trade negotiations, as befits the move towards outward orientation. Its efforts at regional integration have so far been disappointing, but outward orientation is potentially consistent with both full participation in the multilateral system and a renewed commitment to regional integration.

17.10 Bibliography

A detailed though now somewhat dated discussion of the functioning of GATT is contained in Dam (1970). A comprehensive account of the formation of GATT and its activities in the pre-Kennedy Round period can be found in Curzon (1965). There are several good reviews of the details and backgrounds to the Kennedy and Tokyo rounds: Meier (1973), Baldwin (1979) and Greenaway (1983). For a thorough review of issues and background to the Uruguay round, see Finger and Olechowski (1986). The developing countries' interests in the Uruguay Round are comprehensively investigated in a symposium issue of *World Bank Economic Review* (1987, no. 4). This and the previous reference include papers on 'differential and more favourable' treatment for developing countries. Tariff preferences are examined in Murray (1977) and Langhammer and Sapir (1987). The GATT Annual Report is worth consulting to keep up to date with developments.

A useful series of papers on the EEC, including a review of attempts to measure its impact on trade, can be found in Balassa (1975). For a consideration of recent developments in regional trading arrangements, see Greenaway, Hyclak and Thornton (1989).

The most thorough investigation of trade integration among developing countries is by Cline and Delgado (1978) on the Central American Common Market. This and other empirical work is evaluated in Greenaway and Milner (1990).

There is a large literature on the instability of the export earnings of primary producers. For a review of the evidence, see Macbean and Nguyen (1988). An important pioneering study on commodity price stabilization is Newbery and Stiglitz (1981).

Notes

1. Part I (Articles 1 and 2) sets out basic obligations on all contracting parties, and Part II (Articles 3 to 23) provides in effect a code for fair trade. There are also two other parts: Part III (Articles 24 to 35) deals with procedures for application and conditions for amendment of articles, and Part IV (Articles 36 to 38), which was added later, deals principally with the trade of developing countries.
2. The USA already had a free trade agreement with Israel.
3. The so-called 'Swiss formula' employed allowed a degree of harmonization as well as reduction. The average tariff cut varied between countries, higher average-tariff countries conceding higher average costs.
4. Where tariff preferences increase exports in activities for which countries have genuine comparative advantage, they are unambiguously beneficial. In principle, large preferences could encourage exports of goods for which a country does not have a comparative advantage. In this case tariff preferences would divert a country's production into activities where it was unable to expand its output and exports progressively, and could thus worsen its position.

18

World capital markets

There are two polar idealizations of how a world capital market might function. One involves a centralized international market in which participants from the various national markets place their excess funds or relieve their cash shortages by borrowing. The other involves the series of individual national markets being linked together through the residents of one country participating in the markets of other countries, by lending or borrowing. From the point of view of the real effects of capital flows (see Chapter 16) or their payments implications (see Chapter 13), it makes little difference which of these institutional forms the international capital market takes. But from the point of view of understanding the functioning of the market, the distinction is worth noting.

In reality the world capital market contains important elements of both forms. The Euromarkets, alternatively referred to as the offshore markets, are not completely centralized, but they nevertheless approximate the first form, inasmuch as they consist of an international meeting place for the participants from different national markets. Parallel to these, there exist a number of ways in which the residents of one country can deal in the financial markets of other countries – through overseas bank branches, bond flotations in foreign markets, the purchase of equities or bonds in foreign markets, the issue of export credits, shifting bank deposits (especially through the accounts of multinationals), the purchase and sale of shares that are quoted on more than one stock market, and so on.

Another distinction is whether capital moves through the public or the private sector. The critical criterion in distinguishing between the two relates to the identity of the *lender* rather than the borrower: a large part of what are normally classified as private international capital movements involve loans made to public-sector borrowers. What are considered public-sector international capital movements involve aid given, or loaned, by governments, export credits guaranteed by public entities, and loans made by the multilateral development banks.

18.1 Eurocurrency markets

About 60 per cent of all Eurocurrency deposits are denominated in dollars. Next in importance come the Deutschmark (DM) and the Japanese yen, followed by the

European currency unit (ECU, see section 19.7), the Swiss franc, the pound sterling, the French franc, the Dutch guilder, the Belgian franc, the Italian lira, the IMF's SDR (see section 19.5), and perhaps small quantities of some other currencies as well. It will be convenient to speak of Eurodollars in the analysis that follows, but an equivalent analysis can be performed for any of the other currencies with an active Euromarket.

A Eurodollar deposit is simply a bank deposit denominated in dollars on the books of a bank outside the political jurisdiction of the country that issues dollars, namely the United States. They are called Eurodollars because the first banks to accept such deposits were located in Europe and that is still where the bulk of the market is. London remains the leading centre with about a third of all deposits. Other important European centres are Amsterdam, Brussels, Frankfurt, Luxemburg, Milan, Paris and Zurich. The market has, however, extended to the Middle East, Asia and the Caribbean. The main centre in the Middle East used to be Beirut, but the Lebanese civil war and competition from the Persian Gulf led to Bahrain becoming pre-eminent. The Asiadollar market is centred in Singapore, with Hong Kong also important. The main Caribbean centres are the Bahamas, Barbados, Bermuda, Panama, the Cayman Islands and the Virgin Islands.

Eurodollar deposits are time deposits, not demand deposits. Their term may be very short – a few days, or even overnight – but it is not possible to withdraw on demand or to use them as a medium of circulation to write cheques. Accordingly, it is appropriate to exclude Eurodollars from narrow measures of the money supply (M1-type). Typically, terms are for a month or less, three months, or six months, which suggests that in principle Eurodollar deposits owned by a country's residents should be included in wide (M3-type) measures of the money supply.

Banks that accept Eurodollar deposits typically use those funds in order to extend loans, which are also denominated in dollars, and hence are referred to as Eurodollar loans. Borrowers normally wish for loans with maturities longer than the few months for which lenders are prepared to deposit their funds. The banks responded to this inconsistency between the preferred maturities on the two sides of their balance sheets by inventing the *rollover loan* with a *floating interest rate*. A borrower receives what is in form a six-month credit, but with a guarantee that it will be renewed – rolled over – at the end of that period, and at the end of every subsequent six months for the *de facto* life of the loan, which is anything up to eight years and may on occasion range up to ten or twelve years. Each six months the interest rate is adjusted, according to a formula, in order to keep it in line with the market interest rates that the bank is having to pay on its deposits. In this way the risks of maturity transformation – as the normally risky process of borrowing short to lend long is known – are kept down to what the market practitioners claim is a safe level.

The normal formula for a floating interest rate is:

$$\text{Interest charge} = \text{LIBOR} + \text{spread}$$

LIBOR stands for the London interbank offer rate. This signifies the rate that the Eurodollar banks charge on the loans that they extend to one another – a large proportion of the deposits placed in the market are shuffled around between the banks, before coming into the hands of a bank that needs the funds to extend a loan to a final borrower. LIBOR is determined competitively day by day, as the banks borrow or lend in order to balance their books without carrying excess liquidity. Banks normally aim to pay something less than LIBOR on the deposits they take from non-banks. The LIBOR element of the interest charged on a rollover loan for a six-month period is typically the average value of LIBOR over the month preceding renewal: this means that in a period of rising interest rates a bank may have to pay more than it receives for a while, but the danger of losing out seriously is minimal as long as the borrower services its debt.

The spread is a charge specific to each loan. It is set at the time the loan is granted. It covers the administrative costs of the bank, as well as its gross profits, including compensation for the risk inherent in lending. Banks' perception of risk is, in fact, a principal determinant of the spread charged. Risk can be broken down into two elements: (1) country risk – the risk that borrowers from a particular country will have to interrupt debt-service payments because of a government decision, usually motivated by balance of payments problems; and (2) borrower risk – the risk of bankruptcy of the borrower. Since the Euromarket usually lends only to blue-chip borrowers, country risk is in practice the dominant element in determining whether the spread is a fraction of 1 per cent or over 2 per cent.

Depositors in the Euromarkets consist of commercial banks that have more cash than they can advantageously deploy in their domestic markets, some central banks, other government units, multinational corporations, and large national companies or even wealthy individuals from countries with liberal exchange control regulations. Geographically, depositors are very widely spread, with about 50 per cent of deposits coming from Western Europe and with OPEC also much overrepresented in proportion to its weight in the world economy. However, there are also depositors from the other areas, including the developing countries and Communist countries. The latter are reputed to have played a crucial role in the creation of the Eurodollar market in the late 1950s, when the Soviet Union and other East European countries were anxious to hold dollar deposits but also anxious to avoid holding them in the United States where they would have been vulnerable to freezing by the United States government. Inventive London bankers resolved the problem by accepting dollar deposits in London banks, and the Eurodollar market has never looked back.

Borrowers in the Euromarkets consist of commercial banks that want to increase their domestic lending (see the Frenkel model in section 13.3); governments; more often, state enterprises; multinationals; and large private companies of individual countries. Geographically, borrowers are also widely spread, with Western Europe again accounting for about half the market. The middle-income developing countries and the Communist countries are heavy net borrowers, while Japan, OPEC, Switzerland and Taiwan are the heavy net lenders. OPEC used the Euromarkets to recycle a substantial part of the oil surplus, while Swiss banks use it to recycle a substantial part of the funk money placed in anonymous bank accounts from who-knows-where.

Eurobanks normally hold small working balances with New York banks. These are used for making payments to the bank's customers when someone who has received a loan wishes to draw it down or when someone whose deposit has matured wishes to call it. These working balances are normally a very small proportion of total deposits, perhaps 1 or 2 per cent. This observation gave rise to a debate about whether or not there was a Eurodollar multiplier at work whose operation could explain the rapid growth of the Eurodollar market through the 1960s and 1970s.

One school of thought argued, by analogy with domestic monetary theory, that, if working balances were only 2 per cent of Eurodeposits, there must be a money multiplier of 50.[1] However, it was soon pointed out that the traditional formula applies to a *closed* banking system, in which it can be assumed that every recipient of a loan and everyone who receives payments from him or her will redeposit the proceeds of the loan in a bank that is a part of the system. This certainly does not describe the Eurodollar system. A few recipients of loans may redeposit their receipts in Eurobanks or pay multinational corporations which deposit there, but in general a recipient of a Eurodollar loan uses the funds to switch into his or her domestic currency, since this is what he or she normally needs in order to make payments. Those funds will then get fed back into the Euromarket only to the extent that the central bank of the country of the borrower chooses to deploy its extra reserves in the Euromarket rather than elsewhere. In other words, there is a very high leakage of funds from the Euromarket – and such leakages form a *second* element that enters the money multiplier formula. In fact, with a redeposit ratio α, the money multiplier formula becomes[2] $1/[1 - \alpha(1 - \phi)]$, which is $1/\phi$ for the closed monetary system where $\alpha = 1$, but falls to unity for a completely open monetary system where $\alpha = 0$. It is now generally accepted that leakages from the Euromarkets are sufficiently high to ensure that the multiplier is not much above unity, and also that it is variable as a result of instability in the size of the leakage. (Nowadays the Euromarket is so closely integrated with the national markets of the countries that have abolished exchange controls that the Bank for International Settlements no longer publishes data on the size of the Euromarket. But at the end of 1986 total bank deposits in a currency other than domestic currency were about 23 per cent of the value of the money supply[3] of the industrial countries.)

A multiplier equal to 1 implies that any expansion in the size of the market occurs only because someone decides to switch more funds to hold there, rather than because of the internal dynamics of the market itself. It is a fact, illustrated in Table 18.1, that the Eurocurrency market grew very rapidly after its inception in the late 1950s. If this rapid growth cannot be explained by a multiplier process, the question arises as to how it can be explained. Why should there have been a continuing shift of portfolio preferences towards holding an ever-larger proportion of liquid assets in the Euromarkets, over a quarter of a century?

Various answers have been given to this question. In the early years, potential users were discovering the market for the first time, and so it was natural that there should be a portfolio shift as the attractions of the market became more widely known. These attractions include such factors as the convenience of being able to hold short-term dollar deposits in a bank in the same continent, and especially the

Table 18.1 Estimated net size of the Eurocurrency
market (end of year, $ billion)

1964	9
1967	18
1970	57
1973	132
1976	147
1979	475

Source: Bank for International Settlements, *Annual Report*, various years.

same time zone, as one's business; the freedom of the market from bank regulations, which enables the banks to offer relatively more attractive interest rates since they do not need to tie up a part of their portfolio in holding non-interest-earning reserves; the absence of tax withholding on interest income; and the freedom from fears of freezing and of capital controls by the United States authorities. From 1963 to 1974 another factor promoting the expansion of the Eurocurrency market was the attempt of the United States to cure its balance of payments deficit through a programme restricting capital outflows: United States banks were (with certain exceptions) forbidden to lend abroad from their domestic branches. This tended to raise interest rates abroad, including in the Euromarkets, relative to those in the United States. But foreign corporations (in particular) were not prohibited from switching their dollar deposits from United States banks to Eurobanks, which they naturally did to take advantage of the higher interest rates available there. ('Money is fungible', as critics of the United States capital controls used to say.)

After 1974 a new factor came into play. Some of the wealth-owners who had already decided to hold a substantial part of their portfolio in Eurodeposits were the central banks of OPEC countries. With the sudden emergence of a large OPEC current account surplus in 1974, the financial wealth of these countries grew far more rapidly than before; the redistribution of wealth, with given portfolio preferences on the part of each holder, led to an expansion of the Euromarket. Indeed, the same factor has probably been operating, if in a less graphic way, ever since the 1950s: that part of the world economy that is likely to think of placing a part of its liquid assets in the Euromarkets – notably the multinationals but also the more entrepreneurial central banks (typically of OPEC and NIC countries) – has been expanding relative to the rest.

In fact, the Euromarkets played a key role in recycling the oil surplus after 1974. An example of how this recycling occurs can help one understand the operation of the Euromarkets. Consider the case of a Brazilian oil deficit with Venezuela. A particularly simple case would occur if Brazil settled its debt by drawing down its holdings of United States Treasury bills to get the dollars to write a cheque on a New York bank; if Brazil paid this cheque to Venezuela, which then deposited it in the Euromarket; if the Eurobank made a loan to a Brazilian state enterprise, which then converted its borrowing into cruzeiros with the Brazilian central bank; which then completed the circle by using its dollar receipts to buy United States Treasury bills. Obviously one does not expect that the circle was usually closed in this way, but the example serves to illustrate the important principles. In particular, the Euromarket created reserves (for Venezuela) and acted as a financial intermediary for passing Venezuela's savings on to Brazil, which could thus finance its current account deficit without losing reserves and avoid the cutback in investment or consumption that would otherwise have been necessary.

There has been much debate about whether the Euromarkets pose a threat to financial stability. One fear is that the Euromarkets manufacture additional liquidity, outside of any national control, which may have inflationary consequences. We have already examined, and rejected, one theory that often underlies this view – namely, that there is a high Eurodollar multiplier. But even those who accept that the Eurodollar multiplier is little different from unity need to recognize that a switch of dollar deposits to the Euromarket will have a net expansionary impact on global liquidity, due to such factors as the absence of reserve requirements against Euro-dollar deposits. The policy question is whether that effect is sufficiently important to justify an attempt to regulate the Euromarkets – for example, by imposing reserve requirements against Eurodeposits – or whether it can be ignored in the same way that the liquidity-creating potential of non-bank financial intermediaries is customarily ignored in the formation of national monetary policy.

The main fear is that the Euromarkets are vulnerable to a financial panic. Since the banks lend extensively among themselves, especially in the London interbank market, the worry is that default by an important borrower could trigger a chain of bank failures. In a national market, a central bank would step in to lend to a bank suffering liquidity difficulties or would even bail out a bank faced with insolvency, if this were judged advisable, and so prevent a default leading to a general collapse. But there *is* no central bank that takes a clear responsibility for administering the Euromarkets – in part because the central banks of the countries where the market is physically located fear that attempts by them to control the market would simply drive it away to other centres. However, countries have now tightened prudential supervision of the loans extended by their own banks, including their foreign branches, in an attempt to ensure that default by a single borrower could never threaten bank solvency. Moreover, the principal central banks have agreed in the course of their discussions at the Bank for International Settlements in Basel on the basis of a formula to determine which of them would be responsible for giving aid to the Euromarket as lender of last resort should that some day prove necessary. Most bankers seem convinced that these measures are sufficient to minimize the threat of collapse.

18.2 Other private markets

While the Euromarkets are the best-known part of the international capital mar-ket, they are not in fact the quantitatively dominant part: less than one-half of international bank lending is undertaken by the Eurobanks. Instead, for example, Citibank (New York) may make a loan – almost always expressed in dollars – directly to a foreign borrower, which may well be one of its own subsidiaries. In the latter case, the local branch of Citibank acquires additional funds with which it can expand its loan portfolio in the borrowing country, as analyzed in section 13.3. It is the initial foreign borrower – which in the example just mentioned is the local foreign branch of Citibank – that takes the exchange risk, for which it will normally expect to be compensated (as was hypothesized in the Frenkel model of section 13.3).

Under certain ideal circumstances it makes no difference at all whether a deposit is placed in a Eurobank or a United States bank. If the regulations applying to Euro- and United States banks were the same, if they both held their reserves at the Federal Reserve, and if the managers of the two sets of banks had identical behaviour patterns, it would make absolutely no difference whether Venezuela placed its newly acquired funds in a Eurodollar bank in London rather than in New York. In the latter event, the New York bank could just as easily extend a loan to Brazil as the Eurobank did in the example at the end of the last section.

Conversely, the process of intermediation will be affected if the various *ceteris paribus* assumptions made above are violated.

Different regulations. The most important way in which regulations differ between the United States market and the Euromarket is in respect of reserve requirements. There are no reserve requirements on Eurodeposits, whereas the Federal Reserve imposes a 3 per cent reserve requirement against time deposits held in United States banks. This means that a Venezuelan decision to hold deposits in New York rather than London would increase the demand for base money, reduce the sum available for lending and raise the interest rate that a bank lending to Brazil would charge.

Different reserve holdings. The major United States banks hold their working balances (as well as required reserves) at the Federal Reserve, whereas Eurobanks hold their working balances at United States commercial banks. This provides a second reason why a Venezuelan decision to place its deposits in New York rather than London would increase the demand for base money and exert a relatively contractionary effect on the global money supply.

Different behavioural patterns. It is a fact that the proportion of loans made to non-United States borrowers by Eurobanks is far higher than that of loans made by United States banks. However, this in itself is not necessarily very important. It is surely true that California banks lend more of their portfolio to California farmers than do New York banks, but no one would conclude from that that a switch of deposits from California banks to New York banks would squeeze the borrowing ability of California farmers. The reason is that the United States capital market is so integrated that funds would be promptly arbitraged back from New York to California to permit the distribution of final loans to remain determined by considerations of economic efficiency. Similarly, a switch of Venezuelan deposits from London to New York would not deprive Brazil of access to bank credit, even if New York bankers were entirely incapable of visualizing making loans to Brazil, so long as there were no capital controls separating the United States market from the

Eurodollar market. An incipient rise in the Eurodollar interest rate relative to the New York interest rate would encourage the funds to be arbitraged back to London for lending to Brazil. One may conclude that, given the current absence of capital controls by the United States, differences in lending patterns by particular groups of banks will not influence significantly the result of the intermediation process.

A second form in which national capital markets are interlinked involves the bond market. An international capital market dominated by bank lending is, in fact, a historically recent phenomenon. In the previous great age of international lending, prior to the First World War, the dominant instrument was the bond. A company, typically a utility, or a government, would issue a fixed-interest bond denominated in the currency of the lender, and sell it in the lender's market. Local individuals (or companies, though institutions like pension funds were unimportant in those days) would buy the bonds, and the borrower would switch the cash into his or her national currency to finance investment or use it directly to pay foreign bills.

International capital flows through bond issues revived earlier than the expansion of international bank credits, though on a much smaller scale. A factor that contributed to limiting the size of the bond market in the 1970s was uncertainty over future inflation. Any certain future rate of inflation can be allowed for by a corresponding increase in the nominal interest rate. But *uncertainty* of the future inflation rate creates a problem for a traditional bond market: an interest rate that would provide a minimal real return to the lender with 15 per cent inflation would prove a crippling financial burden to the borrower if inflation turned out to be 5 per cent.

The bankers largely circumvented this difficulty by inventing the rollover loan with a floating interest rate. An equivalent technique in the bond market, the *floating rate note* whose interest yield is adjusted in line with market rates, was developed in the early 1980s. It proved to be the key to revival of the bond market, which now once again rivals the scale of international lending via bank credits. However, the bond market is largely restricted to maturities no longer than those of bank credits, in contrast to the twenty or thirty years that were commonplace prior to 1914. (Another possible solution to the problem of uncertain future inflation, the use of index-linked bonds, has been ignored in the international capital market to date.)

A form of capital flow that has developed rapidly in the 1980s involves foreign purchases of equities (stocks). This can occur in two ways: through a company listing its shares (or issuing new shares) on a foreign stock market, or through foreign investors purchasing shares listed or issued on the company's local stock market. More and more multinationals are now seeking to have their shares listed on several of the leading stock markets, in the belief that easy access of their shares to more investors will bid their price up and thus reduce the company's cost of capital. Equally, more and more institutional investors (especially pension funds and insurance companies) are becoming accustomed to placing a part of their portfolios in equities listed on foreign stock markets, often by buying into mutual funds that specialize in such investments. The big attraction of such investments is that the risks faced by firms in different countries tend to be less closely correlated than those faced by firms within a single country, thus permitting international portfolio diversification to improve the risk/return trade-off (section 13.3). International equity investment mainly involves flows among the industrial countries, although a substantial flow to the more capitalist developing countries (principally in East Asia) has got under way since 1985.

Export credits involve bank loans either to exporters who then grant extended credit to their foreign customers or direct to the foreign importers. Their distinctive characteristic is that the availability of the loan is conditional on purchase of goods in the country granting the credit and normally limited to the value of the exports involved. Exports of capital goods are typically financed by medium-term export credits of up to eight or ten years: indeed, it would be difficult to sell capital goods internationally without credit attached. Export credits were an important form of LDC capital import in the earlier post-war period, but they were dwarfed by regular bank credits during the lending boom of the 1970s. At times countries have competed for exports by offering low-interest export credits, but the OECD now sponsors an agreement among its members providing for minimum rates of interest on such loans.

The final form of capital mobility that merits mention is that of shifting bank deposits. Anyone – or, more relevantly, any company – with bank accounts in more than one currency can shift money from one account to another. Obviously this is used mainly for short-term speculative capital movements. Indeed, in the presence of exchange controls, most forms of capital mobility can be impeded, but it is difficult to prevent leads and lags – accelerated payment of bills denominated in a currency that is expected to rise in value and delays in the payment of bills denominated in a currency that is expected to fall in value. The companies in the best position to evade exchange controls through leading and lagging are the multinationals, which indeed can switch funds directly between their bank accounts in different currencies and within wide limits justify this by choosing which of the various trade credits between their branches are being settled.

There are, of course, other channels through which capital movements can and do occur: 'money is fungible'.

18.3 Aid and the multilateral development banks

Aid consists of the donation of financial or real resources by one country to another without the expectation of an equivalent payment in return. In fact, pure – or grant – aid involves a donation, for which nothing is expected. For other aid, the grant element is calculated as the excess of the sum donated over the present value of the repayment obligations, where that present value is calculated using a conventional discount rate, customarily 10 per cent.

Aid provided by the United States through the Marshall Plan to Western Europe, amounting to as much as 2.5 per cent of the donor's GNP, played a vital role in securing European recovery from the Second World War after 1948. As the European Recovery Program achieved its objectives, in the 1950s, there was an international move to redirect the flow of aid to support the cause of development

Table 18.2 The aid record

Year	OECD (DAC members)		OPEC
	(Net resource flow)/GNP	ODA/GNP	ODA/GNP
1960	0.88	0.51	n.a.
1965	0.77	0.49	n.a.
1970	0.78	0.34	n.a.
1975	1.17	0.36	2.59
1980	1.04	0.37	1.36
1985	0.55	0.35	0.05

Source: World Bank, *World Development Report 1981* app. table 16; used by permission. Organization for Economic Co-operation and Development, *Development Assistance*, 1971, *Development Assistance Efforts*, 1980, and *Development Co-operation*, 1987.

and to enlist the newly recovered rich nations of Europe – and subsequently Japan and Australia as well – as donors. The United Nations adopted targets for donor countries' aid: the most famous was that each donor was supposed to aim at a total net resource flow to the developing countries of at least 1 per cent of GNP. Since virtually anything could be included in this total – export credits, direct investments or loans on commercial terms – that target has in general been achieved (see Table 18.2), but at the same time it does not really mean very much, since the bulk of what it includes is not really aid at all. The more serious target is that 0.7 per cent of GNP should be donated as official development assistance (ODA). The OECD Development Assistance Committee (DAC), which has tried to goad its members into living up to their responsibilities, further prescribed that ODA should have a grant element of at least 80 per cent. That last target has been achieved for some years, but the total level of ODA has fallen far short of the 0.7 per cent target, as Table 18.2 shows. In fact, the only OECD donor countries that have achieved the 0.7 per cent target are Denmark, the Netherlands, Norway and Sweden.

Aid is distributed both bilaterally and multilaterally. Bilateral aid, as the name implies, is a payment made directly by one government to another country – typically to the government of that country. It is frequently used as an instrument of foreign policy, so that the recipients tend to be those whom the donor wishes to promote, often out of ideological or religious sympathy.

Multilateral aid is channelled through the multilateral development banks (MDBs), of which the leading example is the World Bank. The International Bank for Reconstruction and Development, to use its official name, was created as a sister institution to the IMF following the Bretton Woods conference of 1944, with the object of providing a flow of long-term finance to substitute for the then-vanished private capital market. Its resources proved inadequate to the task of playing a major role in post-war reconstruction, in which capacity it was overwhelmed by the Marshall Plan, but it emerged subsequently as a significant source of development finance. The Bank raises money by issuing bonds on commercial terms, and lends these funds to developing countries, so that the only element of aid provided is the Bank's ability to borrow on somewhat better terms than individual developing countries could – a possibility helped by the guarantee that the developed countries provide on the Bank's borrowings. However, in 1960 the Bank established an affiliate, the International Development Association (IDA), to provide highly concessional assistance (fifty-year loans with a zero interest rate and a substantial grace period) to the poorest countries. This is financed with funds specifically provided by the donor countries: negotiating IDA replenishments to keep IDA in business is a perennial diplomatic problem.

Since the funds provided by the World Bank and, even more, by IDA are on concessional terms, there is, not surprisingly, a potential excess demand for such loans. As always, some rationing mechanism is needed to choke off the excess demand. In the case of the World Bank, this traditionally took the form of limiting lending to the foreign exchange component of approved projects. There is really no compelling economic rationale for only providing foreign exchange to finance particular projects, or for refusing to finance the local currency cost. After all, foreign borrowing is basically needed to provide additional real resources to sustain a higher level of investment overall, and it is possible that the most efficient way of accomplishing that is to import more intermediate goods to produce more consumer goods to enable labour to be redeployed to an investment project with a zero component of imported capital goods. But insisting that only project loans are eligible has the administrative advantage of restricting demand to a part of the cost of those projects for which a serious economic case not only can be made but actually has been made, which requires much bureaucratic effort and thus provides a rationing mechanism. There is a second advantage to insisting on project lending: it requires the technocrats of the borrowing countries to keep up to date with the latest thought on project appraisal, as well as giving the World Bank's staff opportunities to undertake detailed studies of the borrowers' economies, and in these ways contributes to the Bank's educational role in the world.

Nevertheless, these bureaucratic advantages were increasingly outweighed by economic realities in the 1980s. Many countries that were constrained by a foreign exchange shortage – for example, as a result of the debt crisis – found that it was economically rational to cut back on new projects and use more of the available foreign exchange for maintenance or just to keep the economy operating. The World Bank responded to this change of circumstances by developing programmes for 'sector loans' and 'structural adjustment loans', which now account for around 25 per cent of its lending (see section 15.4).

There are other MDBs besides the World Bank: the regional development banks (the African Development Bank, the Asian Development Bank, the InterAmerican Development Bank and, since 1990, the European Bank for Reconstruction and Development); the International Fund for Agricultural Development sponsored by the Food and Agriculture Organization of the United Nations; the Islamic Fund for Economic Development; and the Arab Fund. Most of these follow policies broadly modelled on those of the World Bank, and seek to make project loans rather than to give general balance of payments finance.

18.4 The debt crisis

Against the expectations of the early post-war years, the international capital market revived in the 1950s, developed in the 1960s and came to embrace most countries other than the least developed in the 1970s. By the late 1970s it was generally regarded as a thoroughly benign institution. In particular, it was fulfilling the classic purpose of a capital market, of transferring funds from areas where savings were relatively abundant to those where they were relatively scarce and the return on investment was therefore relatively high. Its recycling of the oil surplus to the middle-income developing countries was perceived to have minimized the deflation that might otherwise have resulted. And its integration of the capital markets of the industrial countries was perceived to have reduced risk to savers (through diversification) and reduced borrowing costs to many investors.

The sanguine assessment of the benefits of capital mobility among the industrial countries is still prevalent, despite the existence of a few sceptics who blame it for exchange-rate misalignments or claim that its major motivation is tax avoidance. More and more industrial countries have therefore dismantled exchange controls. Britain abolished them in 1979, Japan followed suit in the early 1980s, while France and Italy – the last two major industrial countries to retain such controls – abandoned them in 1990. Many financial assets are now traded around the clock, in Tokyo, London or New York, depending on the time of day. In the jargon, the financial market has been globalized.

In contrast, the international capital market currently appears a much less beneficial institution from the standpoint of many developing countries, especially most of those that borrowed extensively in the late 1970s and early 1980s. The reason is, of course, the 'debt crisis': their loss of creditworthiness and resultant inability to continue borrowing voluntarily, which imposed a need for precipitate and costly balance of payments adjustment.

Until the recession of 1980–2, bankers had few qualms about the ability of the borrowing countries to service the debt they were running up. The value of exports was increasing about as fast as the level of debt, suggesting that the ability to service debt was not being eroded despite the debt build-up. Consequently, bankers remained ready – indeed anxious – to lend more. As long as that was true, the debtor countries encountered no difficulty in servicing their debt, for they could borrow more to pay their debt service (interest plus amortization) as well as to secure an inward transfer of real resources to expand investment. It was hoped that this would in turn generate additional exports that would thus help service the new debt and permit the benign process to continue until development had proceeded far enough to allow generation of a trade surplus that could service the debt without further borrowing.

This strategy was a good deal more sophisticated than most of the banks' critics-with-hindsight have ever recognized. Nevertheless the strategy was inherently a risky one, for the borrowing had a maturity (typically six to eight years) that was short relative to the investment being undertaken (which was essentially investment in the process of development). The risks that interest rates would rise, that the investment would prove unproductive and that the ability to service debt would decline were all borne by the borrowers. Moreover, the borrowing was pushed to excess: money was so easily available that the easiest reaction to any problem was to borrow more, even if the proceeds were not destined to increase productive investment.

Trouble did indeed come when the world economic environment deteriorated sharply in 1980–2. The decision by the major industrial countries to reduce inflation, rather than to allow it to be carried up to a new plateau by the second oil shock, led to recession. This depressed the borrowers' export earnings, especially by reducing the prices of their primary commodity exports, which cut into both the actual ability to service debt and the perception of that ability (which was typically measured by the debt/export ratio). But superimposed on this were two further effects that resulted from the particular form of inflation fighting that was chosen, and both of which bore particularly heavily on indebted countries. One was the rise in interest rates, as the industrial countries relied overwhelmingly on monetary policy to combat inflation. The other was the appreciation of the dollar, as the United States adopted a more expansionary fiscal policy, while the other industrial countries mostly did the reverse, as a result of which US interest rates rose relative to those in other countries and pulled the dollar up in the exchange markets. Since most debt was denominated in dollars while export income was earned in a mixed bag of currencies, this increased the burden of debt service still further.

All these factors eroded the ability of the debtor developing countries to service their debt. For a year or two they were able to counter the adverse trend by borrowing more, usually involving shorter maturities and higher spreads. But these expedients only postponed the day of reckoning. By August 1982 Mexico had exhausted its reserves and could borrow no more. It was forced to declare a moratorium on debt service. Bankers immediately decided that it was only a matter of time till other heavy debtors would reach a similar impasse, so they refused to extend new loans to other Latin American countries. This made it next to impossible for them to maintain normal debt service. The debt crisis had broken.

In terms of bank loans outstanding, Latin America was the principal area of the world to be engulfed by the crisis, but it was not the only one. Eastern Europe had already encountered similar difficulties, prompted by the Polish government's repression of the Solidarity trade union movement during the previous winter. Sub-Saharan Africa slid more slowly into an even deeper crisis, though one related more to the inadequacy of new financing than to the inability to service existing debt, which was overwhelmingly public debt with relatively low interest rates rather than debt to the private banks. Immediately after the Mexican moratorium there were fears that much of Asia, including Korea, might succumb as well. In the event Korea proved to be on the threshold of a remarkable recovery as a result of the adjustment measures implemented over the previous two years; only the Philippines lost voluntary access to capital markets for any length of time.

A response to the debt crisis was quickly developed by the International Monetary Fund, the traditional lender of last resort to countries in balance of payments difficulties. It consisted of three elements. First, each debtor country in difficulties would be expected to agree an adjustment programme with the Fund. Such programmes normally aim for gradual adjustment, and therefore imply a continued financing need in the interim. The second element of the strategy therefore involved the Fund lending a part of the needed finance, the amount being determined in a traditional way according to the country's quota in the Fund. But the third element of the debt strategy was novel, for it involved the Fund taking a lead to pressure the commercial banks into additional involuntary lending, as well as rescheduling of maturing debt, in order to close the financing gap.

The hope was that, in association with a vigorous recovery in the world economy, the agreed adjustment measures would induce a rapid switch towards export-led growth that would diminish the need for future borrowing. This would enable the debtor countries to re-establish their creditworthiness and dispense with the need for further rescheduling and involuntary borrowing, while avoiding the threats to the solvency of the lending banks and the future credit standing of the debtors that would arise if the debtors ceased to service their debts.

These hopes were not fulfilled. Most debtors continued to try to service their debts, although there were an increasing number of moratoria as time progressed. The financial viability of the commercial banks remained intact. The current account deficits of the debtor countries shrank dramatically: indeed, they began to export real resources on a substantial scale.[4] Unfortunately, however, this balance of payments improvement was secured by a reduced value of imports rather than by an increased value of exports: while the *volume* of exports increased substantially, this was offset until 1987 by the weakening of export prices, particularly of primary products. The continuing need to repress imports prevented the resumption of robust growth. Payments recovery has been inadequate to re-establish creditworthiness (as of 1990) with the exceptions of Korea and Turkey.

Recognition that the initial debt strategy was not working as hoped led to the initiation of several 'mid-course corrections'. The first of these was the 'Baker Plan' outlined by US Secretary of the Treasury James Baker at the IMF/World Bank Annual Meetings at Seoul in late 1985. This called for a reorientation of conditionality towards the resumption of economic growth, to be supported by increased capital flows of about $10 billion per year, of which it was envisaged that two-thirds would be provided by the commercial banks and one-third by the MDBs. The change in rhetoric was highly welcome to the debtor countries, but the details of implementation were rather vague: growth was to be promoted by supply-side reforms like privatization, and the World Bank was supposed to take over from the IMF as lead international agency. Vaguer still, the Baker Plan contained no mechanism by which the commercial banks were to be persuaded to play their part in lending more. In practice this meant a perpetuation of the previous situation in which each bank was expected to put up a proportion of the total agreed amount of 'new money' (involuntary lending) equal to its share in outstanding exposure to the debtor country as of the initiation of the debt crisis in 1982, and the big banks had to lean hard on the smaller banks to persuade them to participate.

By early 1987 the difficulties in persuading banks to participate in the Mexican new money package led the authorities to conclude that this process had reached its limit. In order to make new lending less unpalatable to the banks (all of which would have *individually* liked to reduce their exposure, though *collectively* this would have been suicidal since it would certainly have provoked a moratorium), it was agreed that in future the banks should have a choice between various ways in which they could satisfy their obligation to provide new money. In the Argentine package of mid-1987, where this second mid-course correction was first implemented, each bank could choose whether to extend a traditional bank credit, to buy a special issue of bonds or alternatively an 'exit bond' (a low-yielding bond that freed the purchaser of any obligation to participate in further new money packages), to capitalize an equivalent value of the interest due them, to swap debt into equity, or to place an equivalent sum in an account with the Central Bank of Argentina that they could subsequently on-lend to domestic Argentine borrowers.

This 'menu approach' still did nothing to address the great complaint of the critics of the debt strategy, which was that, although the debt crisis was the joint product of mistakes by both borrowers and lenders, the borrowers were being required to pay the entire cost of correcting the mistakes. Additional lending might be unwelcome to the banks, but it was on commercial terms that did not reduce the present value of future debt service payments: it did not, in other words, involve debt relief. Many creditor banks recognized that their loans were unlikely to be worth 100 cents on the dollar and hence a secondary market emerged where loans were sold at heavily discounted prices, but the purchasers of those loans were other investors and the debtor countries did not benefit.

Gradually, however, ways emerged by which the debtor countries were enabled to 'capture' at least a part of the discount. The first of these involved debt/equity swaps. A foreign investor desiring to make a direct (equity) investment in a debtor country was allowed to buy debt at its discounted secondary market price and then swap the debt for the currency of the debtor country, with which it could finance its investment. If the central bank of the debtor country redeemed its debt at par, the foreign investor got the secondary market discount as an investment subsidy. But to the extent that the central bank redeemed its debt at less than par, the debtor captured part of the discount. A major problem with debt/equity swaps is that they involve an increase in the money supply of the debtor, except where the funds are used to buy newly privatized assets from the government. It is no accident that the one country that secured a major reduction in its foreign debt through debt/equity swaps is Chile, a country whose government actively welcomed privatization on a massive scale.

An alternative way in which debtors were enabled to capture the discount was to buy back their own debt on the secondary market. The problem with this option was that it required the debtor to have some cash, and almost by definition troubled debtors are short of ready cash. Bolivia, the first country to mount a buyback (in March 1988), used cash provided by friendly donors impressed by its brave reforms, in order to buy back almost half its commercial bank debt at a price of 11 cents on the dollar.

Instead of using cash to buy back debt on the secondary market, it is possible to use it to collateralize principal and/or interest payments on newly issued bonds offered to creditors who are willing to swap their existing loans at a discount. Mexico initiated such debt/debt swaps in early 1988. Once again, however, their scale was limited by the cash that debtors could afford to devote to debt reduction.

Critics of the debt strategy such as Peter Kenen (b. 1932) sought to overcome the constraint on debt reduction imposed by the shortage of cash by urging creation of a new international institution that would buy up the debt of the banks at a discount and pass the saving in interest costs on to the debtors. Various suggestions were made as to the mechanisms that could be used to persuade the banks to sell their loans, such as the imposition of high reserve requirements against loans that were not sold. But in the event, when US Secretary of the Treasury Nicholas Brady came to formulate a new debt initiative in March 1989, he chose instead to propose that the IMF and World Bank make loans that could be used to finance voluntary debt reduction operations.

The strategy that he proposed, which quickly became known as the 'Brady Plan', has three key features. The first is that it limits help to countries that have undertaken extensive policy reforms, in the belief that generalized debt reduction could all too easily amount to throwing good money after bad and might even be a disservice to debtors since it could enable a country to perpetuate policies that badly need reforming. The second is that it retains an element of voluntarism, inasmuch as banks have an element of choice as to the form in which they make concessions, and except in extreme cases one of the choices is to provide 'new money' (which really means partial interest recycling) rather than to grant debt reduction. In any voluntary or quasi-voluntary scheme the debtor has to 'buy' debt reduction (e.g. through a buyback). The third key feature of the Brady Plan is that the money to buy debt reduction is provided by the Bretton Woods institutions, supplemented by Japan.

The first few settlements under the Brady Plan showed considerable variation in their details. They involved different combinations of buybacks, bonds with a lower face value or interest coupon but carrying 'enhancements' (such as collateralization), and 'new money'.

The impact of a debt reconstruction should be assessed in at least two dimensions: by its effect on the present value of the debt outstanding, and by its effect on cash flow. The first agreement, with Mexico, provided debt relief (a reduction in present value) of about 30 per cent, but it reduced cash flow (the negative resource transfer) by not much over half of that, essentially because part of the savings were offset by the cost of servicing the debt contracted to provide the enhancements that made the deal possible. The second deal involved the Philippines, and produced much less debt relief but a greater easing of the cash outflow. The third deal, with Costa Rica, gave about 65 per cent debt relief but *no* cash flow relief compared to the previous situation in which Costa Rica had been allowing arrears to accumulate; the agreement essentially legitimized the relief that was already being taken unilaterally.

Will the Brady Plan suffice to end the debt crisis? With luck, it will be just enough to enable debtors that have implemented serious policy reforms to re-establish confidence that the balance of payments position will allow them to resume growth even without the return of flight capital – at which point flight capital will indeed start to return and the debt problem will be over.

Even if that is true, there remain many other debtor countries in the world whose prospects are scarcely affected by the Brady Plan because most of their debt is owed to public-sector agencies rather than to the commercial banks. The least developed among these countries have already received some debt relief on their bilateral debt following the Toronto summit meeting in 1988, but more will doubtless have to be done yet, both for them and for middle-income debtors like Poland and Zimbabwe (who have so far received no debt relief at all).

18.5 Summary

The international capital market has come a long way since its re-establishment in the form of the offshore banking known as the Euromarkets in the 1950s. At its core are the major industrial countries that no longer have exchange controls, plus Hong Kong and Singapore, as well as the Euromarkets. Capital mobility within the area is quite high, though nowhere near perfect. (The main reason it remains imperfect seems to be the existence of separate currencies and the consequential presence of exchange risk.) Residents of these countries are able to reap the benefits of capital mobility both as investors, in supplementing domestic with foreign savings when interest rates are low abroad, and as savers, through diversifying their portfolios and lending abroad when returns are higher there. The price paid for these advantages is a severe limitation on the ability to pursue a macroeconomic policy at variance with that in the rest of the world, or, at least, in the rest of the core area. Under fixed rates, a monetary policy inconsistent with that of the rest of the core area is quickly overwhelmed by reserve movements; under floating rates, by exchange-rate swings so sharp as to undermine price stability (when a country tries to expand more than the group) or to threaten deindustrialization (when it tries to expand less).

Beyond this core group, a large number of countries participate in the market in a more limited way, principally as borrowers. Some, notably in Latin America, have been involuntarily marginalized by the debt crisis during the 1980s. They have lost the ability to tap foreign savings, and are struggling to service their outstanding debt. As a result they are suffering a negative transfer of real resource. The Brady Plan seeks to mitigate this state of affairs by lending funds to debtor countries that have implemented substantial policy reform, so as to enable them to 'buy' a measure of debt relief from the banks.

A third group consists of those countries that are at best marginal participants in the international capital market. These are most of the low-income countries except

China and India, plus most of the Communist countries. They are not significant borrowers because they are not considered creditworthy. And they do not lend (apart from the deposit of official reserves) because their governments fear that their citizens would take the same view of their creditworthiness as foreign bankers do, and therefore the governments impose stringent exchange controls in an attempt to prevent capital flight. These countries are almost entirely dependent on foreign aid and the loans of the MDBs to supplement their domestic savings.

18.6 Bibliography

For statistical material, see the Annual Report of the Bank for International Settlements, the *World Debt Tables* published by the World Bank and the Annual Report of the OECD's Development Assistance Committee. On the Euromarkets, see McKinnon (1977), McKenzie (1976) and Cohen (1981). On the World Bank, see Ayres (1983) and Feinberg *et al.* (1986).

The debt crisis has spawned a vast literature. Noteworthy early contributions were Diaz Alejandro (1984), Cline (1984) and Cuddington and Smith (1985), especially the paper of Mario Simonsen. Kuczynski (1988) provides a survey to 1987, and Sachs (1989) edited a major study. Kaletsky (1985) argues that the debtors were being too timid in not defaulting. Kenen (1990) expounds his longstanding proposal for a new institution. For a sympathetic early appraisal of the Brady Plan, see Williamson (1989).

Notes

1. Remember the money multiplier formula introduced in section 11.5, $k = 1/\phi$, where ϕ is the reserve ratio of the commercial banking system.
2. Proof. Consider an initial deposit B_0, which initially expands the monetary base by that amount. The bank receiving the deposit then increases its loan by $(1 - \phi)B_0$, which leads to a secondary expansion of deposits of $\alpha(1 - \phi)B_0$. Banks then loan $\alpha(1 - \phi)^2 B_0$, which leads to a tertiary rise in deposits of $\alpha^2(1 - \phi)^2 B_0$, etc. Summing the geometric series, the final increase in deposits is $[1/(1 - \alpha(1 - \phi))]B_0$.
3. On a wide concept of the money supply, covering the IMF's measures of money and quasi-money, plus Eurodeposits.
4. The transfer of real resources to countries that experienced debt-servicing difficulties went from an average inflow of $25 billion in 1980–2 to an outflow of $29 billion in 1985–7. (The real-resource transfer is essentially the current account deficit less net investment income payments: see section 16.2.)

19

International monetary arrangements

A traditional classification distinguishes three functions of money: providing a unit of account, medium of exchange and store of value. All three roles contribute towards eliminating the inconvenience of barter and permitting the division of labour that Adam Smith first recognized as the basis of a modern economy. Indeed, the phrase 'monetized sector' is virtually a synonym for 'modern economy'. Without a monetary unit to provide a common basis in which to express values, a monetary medium against which exchanges can be made and a monetary asset that can be held to permit desynchronization of sales and purchases, the division of labour simply could not be carried very far.

International monetary arrangements have a similar purpose at the international level. They enable transactions between the residents of different countries to be carried out without the need to ensure that the accounts between countries are always, continuously and bilaterally balanced. One can distinguish three requirements that must be satisfied in one way or another for that to be possible. First, there must be an *exchange-rate regime* which determines the rate of exchange at which one money is exchanged for another, so as to permit monetary (rather than barter) international transactions. Second, there must be a *reserve regime* defining the assets that will be transferred in settlement of residual surpluses or deficits when transactions are unbalanced. Third, while it is inherent in the nature of money that agents can escape from the need to maintain continuous and bi-lateral balance, it would ruin the incentives to microeconomic efficiency if they could escape from the need to maintain long-run and overall (multilateral) balance. That implies that an international monetary regime also involves *adjustment obligations*, covering both its requirements as to when imbalances should be adjusted rather than financed and who is to take what actions when adjustment is called for.

Naturally an evaluation, as well as a description, of those arrangements is of interest. A first test of a monetary system concerns its efficiency in facilitating microeconomic transactions. Does it permit financing of all Pareto-improving sets of transactions? Does its operation cost more than is necessary? Does it intermediate efficiently between borrowers and lenders? Does it avoid exposing transactors to unnecessary risks?

The second test of a monetary system involves its compatibility with macroeconomic stability. Microeconomic efficiency advantages of abandoning barter in favour of a monetary economy are bought at a cost, which is the possibility of macroeconomic instability. For example, Say's Law holds in a barter economy, so that there cannot be Keynesian unemployment. Equally, there is no such thing as inflation in a barter economy. But both unemployment and inflation are possible in a monetary economy as a result of individual and government decisions not summing to a total consistent with the macroeconomic constraints. The extent to which a monetary system accommodates such inconsistency and thus permits macroeconomic malfunctioning is self-evidently important.

It is the same with international money: the cost of the convenience of transactions that are unbalanced (in the short run) is the danger that the set of national policies will no longer add up to consistency with a global constraint. Individual countries can escape from the need for income to equal absorption by running current account imbalances, but the world cannot. Individual countries can all try to gain reserves, but if the supply of reserves is not elastic, they cannot all succeed. Individual countries may be able to cut unemployment and inflation simultaneously by tightening monetary policy and loosening fiscal policy and so engineering an appreciation of their currency, but this is not an option for the world as a whole.

This issue has arisen in various guises and received various names in the literature on international monetary economics. It has been called the $n-1$ problem, on the ground that in a system with n countries or exchange rates or balances of payments, there are only $n-1$ degrees of freedom. Once $n-1$ countries have adopted policies to determine their payments position, for example, the payments outcome of the nth country is determined as a residual, and any attempt by that nth country to seek a different outcome would threaten to generate conflict. It has also been called the *redundancy* problem, on the ground that the nth country's policy instrument is redundant – a terminology that neglects the possibility that the nth country will not be content to accept the residual outcome and that international conflict will ensue as a consequence. Perhaps the best term is that of Benjamin Cohen (b. 1937), who calls it the *consistency* problem.

19.1 The pre-1914 gold standard

Since every country on the gold standard defined its currency in terms of gold, the ratios between each pair of currencies – exchange rates – were essentially fixed. The only scope for variations arose from the costs of shipping gold between central banks, which allowed rates to fluctuate within what were known as the 'gold points'.

A country on the gold standard allowed its residents to ship gold abroad to finance a payments deficit, and the central bank stood ready to buy or sell gold with its currency. Thus gold served as the principal reserve asset. In the later years of the system, some countries began holding reserves in the form of currency (mainly sterling).

The gold-standard rules of the game specified adjustment obligations and provided an adjustment mechanism. Loss of gold signified an obligation to accept monetary contraction, and a gain of gold implied an obligation to expand. These policies did promote adjustment, as analyzed in sections 12.1, 12.6 and 13.4 – if not always through the price-specie-flow mechanism as conceived by David Hume, then through some combination of interest-rate effects on capital flows, of Ohlin's income effects and of Triffin's terms-of-trade effects on the periphery (see section 12.1).

In retrospect, the operation of the gold standard was idealized as a golden age in international monetary relations. The system certainly promoted microeconomic efficiency: trade could be financed without unnecessary restrictions or expense and there was a thriving international capital market intermediating funds mainly from British and French savers to investors in the lands of recent settlement and elsewhere. It has also been credited with solving the consistency problem. Gold provided a world monetary base whose redistribution among countries would cause some to expand and others to contract without imposing any net pressure for world inflation or deflation. Critics have pointed to the fact that financial panics occurred at irregular intervals even in the principal countries and that these panics usually brought sharp (though short-lived) recessions in their train. They have argued that current account adjustment tended to operate by the wasteful method of high unemployment. Triffin argued that the system worked comparatively well for the centre countries only because they were able to export a large part of the burden of adjustment, through inducing changes in their terms of trade, to the primary producers of the periphery. Golden ages are, perhaps, relative.

19.2 The gold exchange standard of the 1920s

Convertibility of their currencies into gold was suspended by all the belligerents except the United States during or shortly after the First World War. Paper currencies were exchanged for one another on the basis of floating rates. All countries inflated, though some much more than others. Once the war was over, the dominant aim became that of re-establishing pre-war normality, though Germany and several East European countries went through the traumatic experience of hyperinflation before dedicating themselves to the task of normalization.

In the monetary context, the normal was interpreted as the gold standard. There was, however, an obstacle to revival of the pre-war gold standard: the shortage of gold that resulted from the wartime inflation, given the determination of the United States and the United Kingdom to maintain and to restore, respectively, their pre-war gold pars.[1] A world economic conference held in Genoa in 1922 decided to solve this problem by two steps: encouraging nations to withdraw gold from circulation, and recommending that countries other than the main financial centres hold their reserves in the form of gold-convertible currencies rather than gold itself. A system with the latter feature is known as a 'gold exchange standard'. It came into being formally in 1925, when Britain re-established the gold convertibility of the pound at its pre-war par and most other independent countries soon followed, many holding a part of their reserves in currencies like sterling and the United States dollar.

The exchange-rate regime of the gold exchange stardard was in principle the same as that of the gold standard, a system of fixed rates. However, there was a difference in that the world had just undergone the experience of seeing fixed rates abandoned under pressure. The insistence on returning to the old pre-war pars may have been intended to promote confidence in the fixity of those rates, but – as often happens with the attempt to establish confidence by clutching at symbols instead of creating objective conditions that merit confidence – if so, it was counterproductive: the overvaluation of the pound sterling (in particular) bred nervousness as to how long Britain would be prepared to continue paying the price involved in keeping its exchange rate fixed. Confidence was further undermined when the French franc was stabilized at an undervalued level.

The reserve regime was now officially a gold exchange standard rather than a pure gold standard, so that leading currencies, as well as gold, were held in reserves. In practice, the change from pre-war days was not all that sharp, since some countries were already building up foreign exchange reserves before the war, while others proved reluctant to accept the recommendation of the Genoa conference that they run down their gold holdings.

Adjustment obligations were in principle unchanged. In practice, however, governments were in full retreat from the *laissez-faire* philosophy that had allowed them to play by the rules of the game, and were embracing instead (with varying degrees of competence and enthusiasm) the commitment to internal balance. In particular, the Federal Reserve sterilized the flow of gold into the United States so as to avoid worsening inflation.

At the microeconomic level, the system worked well enough. However, the coherence that enabled the gold standard to function reasonably satisfactorily at the macroeconomic level had been destroyed. There were two problems. One was that there was no longer any assurance of adjustment with fixed exchange rates, both because of the tendency to abandon the rules of the game and also because of the growing downward inflexibility of wages. The second was the fact that any decision by central banks holding reserves in foreign exchange to exercise their right to convert them into gold would result in a net destruction of gross reserves (since the converting central bank simply changed its reserve composition, while the reserve centre suffered a reserve loss), thus exerting asymmetrical contractionary pressure on the system. Add to that the recent reminder that exchange rates were not immutable and the financial incentive that any central bank holding foreign exchange has to shift out before a devaluation of its reserve currency occurs, and a crisis was inevitable sooner or later. It came as part of the Great Depression (and is indeed one of the factors that made the depression great). The Wall Street crash of 1929 led to a virtual cessation of United States capital exports, which had previously been a major source of the money used by Germany to pay reparations. Reinforced by the cut in United States imports caused by the depression and the ultraprotectionist Smoot–Hawley Tariff Act of 1930, Germany stopped making reparations payments, which undermined the fragile structure of intra-European credit. The French had already cashed in their sterling deposits for gold, and others were restrained from following their example only by solemn British assurances of the immutability of sterling's link to gold. Then in 1931 came the crash of the Austrian bank Creditanstalt, and a wave of bank runs spread over Europe. In due course this caused a run on sterling, and on 21 September 1931 Britain 'went off gold'.

19.3 The monetary chaos of the 1930s

That decision ushered in the monetary anarchy of the 1930s. Countries coalesced into currency blocs: a sterling bloc based on Britain and the Commonwealth (except for Canada) plus a number of other countries with close historic and financial links to London; a dollar bloc based on the United States; and a gold bloc of south and west Europe headed by France. The ideologically autarchic – Germany, Japan and the Soviet Union – stood alone.

Some currencies floated, with intervention by the central banks of the countries involved. Others remained pegged to gold, though their gold pars no longer carried much assurance of fixity; the dollar was devalued in the period 1933–4, while the gold bloc held out till 1936. Others pegged to intervention currencies. Many countries welcomed depreciation as a method of stimulating aggregate demand. Only with the Tripartite Agreement of 1936 between Britain, France and the United States was a minimal measure of agreement to restrain competitive devaluation achieved even amongst the leading currencies.

Foreign exchange reserves were largely liquidated in the crisis of 1931, so that, although the members of currency blocs continued to hold working balances in dollars and sterling, gold became once again the dominant reserve asset. The value of gold reserves was much increased by the devaluation of the dollar in 1933–4.

Countries acknowledged no obligations with respect to when or how they should adjust, although they remained subject to a reserve constraint, which implied that they had to initiate adjustment when they ran short of reserves. A powerful new instrument, exchange control, was invented with the deliberate purpose of enabling countries to avoid the traditional adjustment mechanism, by rationing scarce foreign exchange rather than reducing the demand for it through deflation or devaluation. Commercial policy, as well as devaluation, was used as an expenditure-switching weapon in attempting to increase output relative to absorption at a time when there was an acute global deficiency of demand.

The international monetary arrangements of the 1930s were an unmitigated disaster in terms of both microeconomic efficiency and macroeconomic consistency. Trade fell drastically in the Great Depression and failed to regain earlier trends even when output recovered in the mid-1930s. Not only was trade reduced in volume, but it was diverted from its previous and efficient pattern by a web of preferential tariffs and bilateral payments agreements. The international capital market ceased to function. The countries that came closest to prospering were those that were most ruthless in pursuing their national advantage without concern for the repercussions on others. The arrangements contained no inducements to countries to eschew such beggar-my-neighbour arrangements in favour of policies that would help to relieve the shortfall of global aggregate demand. The lack of international monetary organization must therefore be assigned a share of the blame for the disasters of the 1930s.

19.4 The Bretton Woods system

Negotiations between Britain and the United States on post-war economic planning started almost as soon as the United States entered the Second World War at the end of 1941. Although the phrase was not used, there was a clear intention of creating a new international economic order. Despite occasional British hesitations, from no less a figure than the chief British thinker and negotiator, Lord Keynes, among others, the conscious aim was that of creating a liberal, multilateral order that would be the polar opposite of the restrictions and bilateralism of the chaotic 1930s. As conceived, this new liberal order would be supervised by a triad of new international economic institutions: the International Trade Organization (ITO), whose premature death was noted at the beginning of Chapter 17; the World Bank, whose functioning was examined in section 18.3; and the International Monetary Fund (IMF).

Having first achieved a substantial measure of bilateral agreement on the basic issues, Britain and the United States invited the other wartime allies to a conference to draft the Articles of Agreement of the World Bank and the IMF. This conference met in July 1944 in the mountain resort of Bretton Woods in New Hampshire – a township that thereby lent its name to the international financial order planned for the post-war world. This order, and the principal controversies surrounding its design, can again be described under the headings of the exchange-rate regime, the reserve regime and adjustment obligations.

Exchange rates were normally to be fixed, except for a margin of ±1 per cent to emulate the old gold points and provide an incentive for commercial-bank clearing of most exchange transactions. The par values of all exchange rates were to be expressed in terms of gold. A par value could, however, be adjusted if the country so requested and the IMF agreed that a change was necessary to correct a 'fundamental disequilibrium'. This concept was never formally defined, but it was intended to refer to a situation in which a country was unable to maintain external balance over the trade cycle as a whole without a significant departure from internal balance or from its obligations with respect to the maintenance of liberal trade and payments. By allowing devaluation (or revaluation, though that was not an option in anyone's mind in 1944) but only subject to international approval, the negotiators hoped they had found a middle way between countries being forced to sacrifice their internal economies to the defence of a fixed exchange rate, as had happened to Britain in the 1920s, and the dangers of a repeat round of competitive devaluations, as had occurred in the 1930s.

In the early Anglo-American discussions on post-war financial planning, Britain had proposed the Keynes Plan for creating a radically new reserve regime. In place of the IMF there would have been an International Clearing Union (ICU), which would have acted as a central bank for central banks. Each central bank would have had an account at the ICU in terms of a new international money called 'bancor'. Countries could have acquired bancor balances by depositing gold or by receiving bancor from deficit countries – which they would indeed have been obliged to accept in settlement of deficits. Each member country would have had a right to a certain overdraft, related to the size of its trade, which would thus have provided leeway for deficit countries to finance their deficits. The proposed overdrafts were on the generous side (the European overdrafts would have come to much the same total as Marshall aid finally did), so the United States rejected the idea as a British plot to soak the surplus countries, which they automatically equated to themselves. The British therefore had to be content with the main outlines of the White Plan, named after the chief United States negotiator Harry Dexter White (1892–1948), later hounded as a supposed Communist. This plan merely proposed creating a pool of gold and currencies in the hands of the IMF, which could be lent to countries suffering a temporary deficit to supplement their holdings of the existing reserve assets. Those existing reserves were still overwhelmingly gold, with sterling and dollars – in that order – as reserve currencies.

The Keynes Plan included a provision whereby countries would have had to pay interest not only on their borrowing from the ICU, but also on excessive *credit* balances. The purpose was to spell out the obligations of both deficit *and* surplus countries as to when they should adjust and to provide an incentive for them to respect those obligations. This idea was another early casualty of the bilateral Anglo-American negotiations. Nevertheless, the Bretton Woods agreement (the IMF Articles) did contain an endorsement of the idea that surplus countries had a responsibility to play a role in promoting adjustment. A scarce currency clause enabled the Fund to declare a currency scarce if its holdings of that currency were becoming exhausted as a result of many countries borrowing it (to settle deficits with a chronic surplus country), whereupon Fund members would have been authorized to discriminate against imports from that country. (The clause was never invoked and has now been abolished.) Deficit countries were still subject to the discipline imposed by limited reserves, ameliorated by loans from the IMF if the Fund saw fit. Although no one worried much about the United States becoming a deficit country, it is worth noting that there was no suggestion that the special position accorded the United States dollar in the Bretton Woods agreement would limit the United States' responsibility for initiating adjustment. This special position consisted of the United States defending the dollar by buying and selling gold, while other countries de-fended their currencies by buying and selling dollars. However, if surplus countries had used all the dollars acquired in intervention to buy gold from the United States, the United States would have been exposed to the same pressure to adjust when in deficit as any other country.

Bretton Woods did not spell out very explicitly how countries were supposed to adjust when adjustment was called for. The general principles implicit in the system were that a high priority should at all times be accorded to the preservation of internal balance; that temporary imbalances should be financed rather than adjusted; that modest but persistent imbalances should be met by trimming fiscal–monetary policy as long as this did not involve a major departure from internal balance; and that large and persistent imbalances not due to deviations from internal balance could be met by exchange-rate changes. It was accepted that destabilizing capital movements could be suppressed by exchange controls.

The Fund was formally created in 1946, but it accomplished little in its first decade primarily because the limited resources with which it had finally been endowed were insufficient to make any impact on the main issue of the day – post-war reconstruction and its counterpart, the chronic European payments deficit. The problem of an acute shortage of dollars (the dollar problem) was finally resolved by Marshall aid. (This, by a nice historical irony, might never have been necessary had the United States accepted the Keynes Plan, in which case the United States could have lent what eventually it gave away.) To keep some control over who was receiving what, it was agreed that countries receiving Marshall aid would not also draw from the IMF. That left the Fund with the responsibility of approving devaluations, of which by far the most important was the round of 1949 devaluations of most of the non-dollar currencies that laid the basis for the end of the dollar shortage, and the role of making loans to its Latin American members. These provided the testing ground for the principles of Fund conditionality and the stimulus for the emergence of the Fund's version of the monetary approach to the balance of payments (see section 12.6).

The Fund began to emerge from the twilight in 1956, when Britain and France needed bailing out from the financial consequences of their Suez escapade. But by two years later a fundamental change in the world economy had become manifest: the dollar shortage had vanished and been replaced by a dollar glut. (In those two years the phrase 'dollar problem' came to mean an excess supply of, instead of an excess demand for, dollars.) The Europeans at last declared their currencies convertible at the end of 1958, thus accepting the obligations that brought the Bretton Woods system into operation. The United States sought to adjust its balance of payments, but without devaluing or doing anything else that might hurt too much. Until the hoped-for adjustment took effect, it sought to persuade other countries to hold their dollars instead of converting them into gold.

In terms of microeconomic efficiency, the Bretton Woods system of the following decade was an unbridled success. Transaction costs fell, many restrictions disappeared, risks were low, trade flourished and the reborn international capital market expanded dramatically.

In terms of macroeconomic consistency, the record was more mixed. From a short-run standpoint, the early 1960s were highly satisfactory. Keynesian demand management was in its heyday, with the efforts of countries to 'fine tune' demand to match capacity being internationally co-ordinated, to take account of spillover multiplier effects, by the OECD (see section 20.2). Inflation, though modest, provoked attempts to design incomes policies to reduce it still further without sacrificing employment targets. It was an era of relatively non-inflationary full employment with rapid real growth and modest payments imbalances.

The great question was whether this prosperity was sustainable in the longer run. At the domestic level, the issue was whether maintenance of high levels of employment through active demand management would not stimulate accelerating inflation (a doubt clearly formulated by economists in 1967 with the work of Friedman and Phelps). At the international level, analogous doubts about the sustainability of the system had been formulated much earlier, even as the Bretton Woods system was moving into its golden age at the end of the 1950s.

The main prophet was Robert Triffin. He argued that the growth in dollar reserves being generated by the United States payments deficit and not being converted into gold was necessary if world economic expansion were to be maintained; countries needed growing reserves as trade expanded if a given degree of trade liberalization was to be maintained, and there was no other significant source of reserve growth. (Commercial demand for gold was fast catching up with supply at the official, supposedly eternal, price of $35 per ounce that had been set by President Franklin D. Roosevelt in 1934.) However, if the short-run dollar liabilities of the United States continued to expand while its gold assets remained constant or even shrank, it was only a matter of time before the credibility of the commitment to sustain the $35 gold price was called into question. At that point central banks would rush to convert dollars into gold, just as had happened to Britain in 1931. Thus the system faced a dilemma, quickly dubbed the *Triffin Dilemma*: either the United States would succeed in curing its payments deficit, in which case world growth would be strangled by the emergence of a progressively more acute liquidity shortage; or its deficit would continue, in which case a crisis of confidence would sooner or later be inevitable. The system as constituted was inherently incapable of solving simultaneously what later analysts called the *liquidity problem* – how to ensure that reserves grow at an appropriate rate – and the *confidence problem* – avoiding crises of confidence.

Another problem with the Bretton Woods system was termed the *adjustment problem*. This referred to restoring and maintaining payments equilibrium (where equilibrium should be interpreted as external balance in the sense of section 13.2). Until about 1960 the Bretton Woods system had had a functioning adjustment mechanism, in the form of progressive trade liberalization by Europe and Japan: a tendency towards excessive surplus was exploited to take another step towards fulfilling paper obligations of freer trade and payments. But by 1960 those obligations were being fulfilled, and thus there remained no further scope for differential trade liberalization to be exploited as an adjustment weapon. Nothing else took its place. Fiscal–monetary policy was ruled out, except to the most marginal extent, by the near-universal commitment to full employment. Exchange-rate policy was being ruled out by a reinterpretation of the rules of Bretton Woods, which were read as implying that devaluation was an ultimate weapon whose use was a national disgrace – a reinterpretation generated by the need to prop up confidence by denying that you were about to devalue, which naturally created an interest in not breaking one's word. So the only 'adjustment mechanism' left was a Mundellian manipulation of the fiscal–monetary mix, which is really a means of financing rather than of adjustment, and as such is at best a temporary solution (see section 13.2).

In the short run the situation was viable. Payments imbalances were not particularly large, so that the lack of an adequate adjustment mechanism was not too pressing an issue. And most central banks (with the exception of the Banque de France during de Gaulle's presidency) were willing to go along with the United States in financing its deficit by mainly holding rather than converting dollars, at least for a time. Once the official world had been convinced that there was a problem of long-run viability of the system, negotiations on international monetary reform got under way (see section 19.5). The dominant view was that measures like restraint in converting dollars into gold were buying time until a reform could be negotiated. The main problem was, of course, the lack of a consensus as to the desirable direction of reform, which in the event prevented adequate changes being negotiated before the crisis finally broke.

The beginning of the end came in 1967, with the devaluation of the pound sterling, following repeated denials that this would occur and a period of five and a half years in which no major currency had changed its par value. This had the predictable effect of eroding confidence in the United States' commitment to defend the gold price, resulting in a run from the dollar into gold in early 1968. A hastily convened conference in Washington decided to create a two-tier gold market, with the price on the private market left free while the official price for transactions between central banks remained $35 per ounce. Since Bretton Woods had never involved an official commitment to trade with the private sector in gold, this did not change the formal rules of the system. But in fact it brought Gresham's law into play and virtually drove gold out of active circulation as a reserve asset, as well as making it clear to central banks that extensive recourse to their right to demand gold from the United States Treasury would almost surely provoke a withdrawal of that right. Since other countries *de facto* accepted that situation, the world came very close to being on a dollar standard.

The following years were marked by a series of speculative crises, of ever greater force, involving in particular runs from the French franc (1968–9) and sterling (1968) into the DM (1968–9), from the Belgian franc following devaluation of the French franc (August 1969) and into the Belgian franc following revaluation of the DM (October 1969), and into the Canadian dollar (May 1970). Politicians prated about how they would never devalue or revalue a few weeks before doing it, thus devaluing political assurances about financial policy. Eventually the long-feared run out of the dollar got under way, at least on the part of the private sector, following a notable easing of United States monetary policy in 1971. By August there were signs of uneasiness on the part of official holders as well. This combined with a growing conviction in Washington that the *de facto* dollar standard had not been serving United States national interests, in particular by allowing the dollar to become seriously overvalued. On 15 August President Richard Nixon's administration closed the gold window, as part of an effort to get other countries to revalue against the dollar. Most economists mark the death of Bretton Woods from that date.

The United States' suspension of gold convertibility left the other major countries with little alternative but to float, which they did with great reluctance. Accordingly everyone agreed that negotiations to construct a new international monetary system to succeed the defunct Bretton Woods system were an urgent necessity. The first step in this reconstruction was agreed to be the re-establishment of a new structure of pegged exchange rates. This was accomplished at a conference held in the Smithsonian Institution in Washington in December 1971, involving a small (8 per cent) devaluation of the dollar in terms of gold and some revaluation of the stronger currencies. This agreement started to unravel a mere seven months later, when a run on the pound led to a British decision to let sterling float again. The next February came more speculative runs, leading to a new wave of currency realignments, which this time lasted only a couple of weeks before being overwhelmed by further speculative pressures. The adjustable peg had, quite patently, become unworkable, and the major countries finally accepted that fact by moving to a system of generalized floating. At that point, all that remained of Bretton Woods was the IMF.

19.5 The reform debate

Triffin's diagnosis of the dilemma facing the gold exchange standard led him to a prescription for its reform. He argued that a mechanism was necessary for creating additional international reserves which would both bring the total growth of reserves under purposive international control and avoid progressively undermining confidence. Triffin proposed a solution somewhat reminiscent of the Keynes Plan, involving an expansion of the IMF into a deposit bank for central banks. Each member would have undertaken to hold a certain proportion of its reserves as deposits at the IMF, while the Fund could have expanded reserves by granting loans (medium or long-term) or by buying securities.

Promulgation of the Triffin Plan initiated a wide-ranging and long-running debate on reform of the international monetary system. It started off with academic economists inventing rival plans, and the official world brushing aside all these suggestions with assurances that revolution was unnecessary because a satisfactory process of evolution was already under way. The academics retorted that such 'ad hockery' was not enough, and in the surprisingly short time of about three years the official world came around to their view and initiated discussions on the desirable nature of reform. Academic participation was not invited, to the annoyance of the leading academics, who thereupon set up their parallel Bellagio group with the aim of clarifying the issues. It was the first report of this group that classified the problems of the Bretton Woods system into the triad of adjustment, liquidity and confidence already used in the last section. Subsequently the academics and officials made their peace, and the Bellagio group was broadened into a meeting place between the two sides, in which the academics could keep up to date with the evolving issues and the officials could draw on the fruits of academic analysis. The interaction of theory and practice that characterized the reform debate owed much to these meetings.

At least five reasonably distinct schools emerged during the debate. The first was that inspired by Triffin. The essential underlying idea was that the world reserve stock provides a world monetary base that has to grow at an appropriate rate if harmful inconsistencies in national policies are to be avoided. If the stock of reserves grows too fast, countries in general are enabled or encouraged to pursue overexpansionary demand policies, and inflation results. If reserves grow too slowly (or, even worse, if they fall because of a switching of reserve currencies into gold in the course of a confidence crisis), the result is likely to be deflation, competitive devaluation and/or rising protectionism. The programme of action suggested by this vision was that of creating a new reserve asset and limiting the supply of alternative forms of reserves to bring the total supply under purposive control. This was the dominant view inspiring official negotiations through the 1960s and right up to the failure of the reform exercise in 1974.

A second school looked to markets to solve most problems, including those of adjusting balances of payments and producing consistency between the policies adopted by different countries. For these purposes, they wanted to allow exchange rates to float. This school was much more influential among academics than among officials, although there was some sympathy in this direction in the Nixon administration.

A third school wanted to reinstate gold, starting off by increasing its price. The hard members of this school, headed by de Gaulle's confidant the French economist Jacques Rueff (1896–1978), wanted to go back to the classical gold standard, including reliance on the monetary mechanism of adjustment to solve the adjustment problem and reliance on the symmetry of that mechanism to ensure policy consistency. France espoused these views during de Gaulle's presidency, while global monetarists began to endorse them in the 1970s. There was also a soft version of the school, which thought that Bretton Woods could be revitalized by increasing the gold price, since no one would want to shift from dollars into gold once the prospect of a gold price increase in the near future were banished. They also argued that this would resolve the consistency problem, which they perceived as arising from competition to generate current account surpluses. They expected a higher gold price to generate a net inflow of gold into reserves, which would have enabled the world as a whole to generate a net current account surplus.[2]

A fourth school favoured a dollar standard, a system under which the dollar is the basic reserve asset, convertible into nothing else. Other countries peg to the dollar, and if they do not like their payments outcome, they adopt adjustment policies, while the United States treats its balance of payments with benign neglect. This provides a resolution of the consistency problem, since one country allows its balance of payments to be determined as a residual, which it is in a financial position to do in view of the willingness of other countries to hold its currency. This school was dominated by United States academics and found a fair measure of sympathy in the Nixon administration prior to August 1971.

The fifth school believed that one needed both control of the reserve supply *and* limited exchange-rate flexibility, especially a crawling peg. The former was envisaged as necessary to resolve the liquidity problem, while the latter would provide a solution to the adjustment problem without undermining confidence. Consistency in aims would have been provided by control of the reserve stock as in Triffin's model, while that consistency could have been translated into action through the existence of a usable adjustment mechanism.

Negotiations on international monetary reform started in earnest among the ten major financial powers constituting the Group of Ten[3] in 1965, after the United States endorsed (at least pro tem) the Triffinesque orthodoxy of the first school. Despite French opposition based on de Gaulle's support for the alternative of a revived gold standard, the negotiations to create a new reserve asset were brought to a successful conclusion at the IMF's Annual Meetings in Rio de Janeiro in 1967. The new reserve asset was called a Special Drawing Right (SDR), the odd term being a linguistic attempt to mollify the French for having lost out on the substance of the argument. The SDR was defined as having a value of 1/35 of an ounce of gold, the same as the value of the dollar at that time. It carried an interest rate of 1.5 per cent per annum. It was to be used in much the same way as gold, to be sold by a country in deficit to a strong-currency country in exchange for currencies that would be usable in intervention in the exchange markets. The IMF would designate which strong-currency country would receive SDRs, while the use of SDRs was restricted to countries in deficit to avoid adding to the confidence problem.

SDRs were created by allocating them to members in proportion to their quotas in the Fund: that is, on a given day the Fund simply credited the accounts of participants with a certain number of SDRs, which they were thenceforth able to use to finance deficits. They did, however, accept the obligation to pay interest on their past allocations, so that the system was self-financing. How new allocations of SDRs should be distributed between participants was, naturally, a controversial question. Initially the industrial countries had thought of limiting the issue of a new reserve asset to themselves, on the ground that countries receiving an allocation were taking responsibility for guaranteeing the asset, which would make sense only if restricted to highly responsible countries. The developing countries countered by a proposal that became known as 'the link',[4] under which they would have received a disproportionate portion of allocations, partly on the ground that that would enable the industrial countries to run a collective current account surplus just like gold inflows would, and partly on the ground that, if there was 'seigniorage'[5] around, it should go to the most needy. The compromise of basing allocations on IMF quotas was supposed to be distributionally neutral, which it would be if quotas were a good index of average reserve holdings.

The first SDRs were allocated on 1 January 1970, after everyone had argued themselves into more or less believing that there was a liquidity shortage developing and therefore a need to relieve it by creating SDRs. But even as that was being done, United States monetary policy was easing. There was a vast outpouring of dollars in the following years, which, in the attempt to prop up the fixed exchange rates of Bretton Woods, were absorbed by the central banks of other countries. (Reserves rose by 61 per cent in the period 1970–1 alone, as opposed to 22 per cent in the whole of the 1960s.) Hence when the Bretton Woods system collapsed, the perception of the Triffin school, which included the European–Japanese bloc in the IMF, was that the essential step was to restore a workable convertibility-type discipline to the United States so as to limit further reserve creation to the level judged internationally desirable. That provided their basic objective in the reform negotiations that ensued.

Other countries had different views of what the reform negotiations should be achieving. The United States had by this time lost sympathy with the Triffin school, having been partly seduced by the prestige and convenience of having the world on a dollar standard and partly convinced by the advocates of exchange-rate flexibility. On the other hand, the United States negotiators realized the importance that other countries were attaching to a restoration of convertibility in some form or other. Given the tensions between these mutually contradictory positions, the United States showed considerable ingenuity in fashioning a set of reform proposals. Their centrepiece was a system of reserve indicators, under which each country would have had a normal level of reserves and been expected to take adjustment action as necessary to keep its reserves within specified margins about its norm. This looked ironically like Keynes' proposals for penalizing countries whose bancor holdings deviated too far from zero in either direction, which the United States had summarily rejected almost thirty years before. These reserve indicators were to be accompanied by a restoration of dollar convertibility, essentially into SDRs rather than into gold, for countries that stayed suitably close to their reserve norms. Thus there was a limited restoration of convertibility to placate other countries; a limit on that convertibility to safeguard against the United States being subject to excessive pressures of a sort that the dollar standard had eliminated; and reserve indicators that would more or less oblige countries to alter exchange rates when adjustment was necessary.

The third major group of countries in the negotiations consisted of the developing countries. The fact that they were included at all was noteworthy, given that the industrial countries had previously dominated the crucial negotiations on monetary issues. In 1972 it was agreed that the attempt to design a successor system to Bretton Woods would be done by a committee whose composition would parallel that of the IMF Executive Board, which gave nine of the twenty places to the developing countries. Their general position was sympathetic to a structured system, with pegged exchange rates and the SDR as the principal reserve asset. They also used the occasion to pursue their own distinctive interest in a system that would promote a transfer of real resources to themselves: the principal mechanism that they sought to give effect to that objective was the link.

The Committee of Twenty (C–20), as the committee charged with designing a reform was termed, held periodic meetings during the years 1972–4, where it discussed the various reform proposals at great length. There was, however, no meeting of minds on the basic shape that a reformed system should take, and there was no hegemonic power with the ability to force its will on the others in the absence of their voluntary assent. Accordingly, the Outline of Reform that expressed the results of the committee's deliberations was largely limited to recording the general principles on which all had agreed – an 'effective and symmetrical adjustment process', 'co-operation in dealing with disequilibrating capital flows', 'better international management of global liquidity, with the SDR becoming the principal reserve asset', etc. – and a host of alternative mechanisms for effecting those principles on which they had not agreed. Even in the rare case where there was supposed to be agreement, this tended to be unrealistic, as in the case of the resolve to restore 'stable but adjustable exchange rates' – the very system that broke down during the committee's deliberations and that even its original supporters were recognizing to be unrealistic by 1974.

In that year, the oil price increase provided a convenient alibi for declaring the reform to be postponed, and the committee turned its attention to more immediate issues before abolishing itself. It approved three specific decisions.

First, the value of the SDR was redefined to make it equal to the value of a basket of the sixteen major currencies.[6] Some such step was essential to enable the SDR to function effectively in a world of generalized floating, since the value of gold, the previous measure, no longer had an unambiguous meaning. Defining the SDR as equal to a basket of currencies enabled it to serve as a unit of account equal to an average of the major currencies. Allied to this change was a decision to raise the interest rate on the SDR about half-way towards a market rate. A second decision involved the promulgation of a set of guidelines for floating exchange rates – a code of good conduct for the authorities of countries with floating rates, encouraging them to intervene to smooth out erratic fluctuations while proscribing aggressive intervention to promote competitive depreciation or appreciation. The third decision involved the creation of a high-level committee, modelled on the C–20 itself, to meet about twice a year to supervise the IMF. It was envisaged that this might some day be a formal council with executive powers, but sixteen years later it remains an informal Interim Committee with advisory powers only.

Matters could not be left where they were at the end of the C–20, however, since all the major members of the Fund were in transgression of the IMF's Articles, which prohibited floating rates. Furthermore, the major holders of gold were dissatisfied with the extent to which gold had been immobilized. The private gold price had risen far above the official price, but central banks were forbidden to sell above the official price – making their gold totally unusable except through elaborate deals in which it served as collateral for borrowing. There then followed eighteen months of haggling to find a form of words that would recognize the facts of life and legalize what everyone was doing or determined to do. Agreement was finally achieved at a meeting of the Interim Committee in Jamaica in 1976.

19.6 The non-system

The non-system that had come into being in March 1973 was legalized by the Interim Committee decisions at Jamaica in January 1976. It is called a non-system because it makes no attempt to subject countries to obligations or to impose any order, as the gold standard and Bretton Woods had done. A description of these arrangements under the same three headings previously used to characterize earlier regimes will make this clear.

The revised IMF Articles allow countries to float or to peg. If they float, they are supposed to be subject to IMF surveillance, but since the Fund has failed to specify any norms, this has not amounted to much in practice. (Even the guidelines adopted in 1974 were dropped in 1976.) If they peg, they can peg to anything they like – except gold! This includes the possibility of pegging not just to a single currency but also to a basket or to the SDR, or for a number of currencies to peg to each other. There are no limits on the margins within which pegged exchange rates are allowed to fluctuate, and no rules as to whether pegs should be changed in large steps, as under Bretton Woods, or small steps, as under the crawling peg.

Countries in fact employ a wide variety of exchange arrangements. In general the currencies of the major industrial countries have been allowed to float, though the central banks have intervened to attempt to smooth out fluctuations – with the United States usually having been less disposed to intervene than the others. There is a group of EC countries, however, that peg their currencies to each other (while they float against other currencies) in what is now known as the European Monetary System (EMS, see section 19.7). About thirty currencies are still pegged to the dollar – mostly in the Caribbean or the former Communist bloc, plus a few countries scattered over Africa, Latin America, the Middle East, Asia and Oceania. Fourteen francophone African countries remain pegged to the French franc, and a handful of other currencies are pegged to other single currencies, normally of the former colonial power or a near neighbour. Some thirty currencies are pegged to a basket and about five to the SDR. Some of the pegged currencies still change their pegs according to the old Bretton Woods practice of making substantial changes at infrequent intervals, but about fifteen operate a crawling peg. Several developing countries now float. A number of those that claim to peg to a basket announce neither the composition of their basket nor when they are changing the peg, so that it is difficult to know what they actually do. Others change their rate by administrative fiat without pretending to explain any principles.

The reserve regime is equally anarchic. There are no rules on what countries may hold as reserves or where they may hold them, nor on permitted levels of reserves, such as were sought in the C–20 negotiations. The dominant reserve asset, constituting about 75 per cent of total liquid reserves, is foreign exchange. About 65 per cent of these exchange reserves are still held in United States dollars; since 1978 there has been a strong tendency for the holdings of other reserve currencies to increase. The other currencies with a significant reserve role are the DM, the Japanese yen, the pound sterling, the Swiss franc, the French franc and the Dutch guilder. An increasing part of foreign exchange reserves, especially of developing countries, is held in the Euromarkets. The other components of liquid reserves consist of the reserves created by the operations of international organizations, the IMF and the European Monetary Co-operation Fund (the agent of the European Monetary System). The IMF can create SDRs, as already described, although none have been created since 1981. Members also gain reserve positions in the Fund, which count as an element of reserves, when other countries borrow their currencies from the IMF. EMS members deposit 20 per cent of their dollars and gold with the European Monetary Co-operation Fund and receive European currency units (ECUs) in return. The composition of the reserve stock is shown in Table 19.1.

In addition to the foregoing elements of reserves, central banks still carry gold on

Table 19.1 Official reserves (in billions of SDRs at year's end)

	1970	1975	1980	1985	1988
Foreign exchange:					
US dollars	35.2	116.8	173.0	182.4	240.2
Other[1]	10.2	20.5	68.3	127.7	202.6
Reserve positions in					
the Fund[2]	7.7	12.6	16.8	38.7	28.3
SDRs	3.1	8.8	11.8	18.2	20.2
ECUs	–	–	52.2	37.7	50.4
Total liquid reserves	56.2	158.7	322.1	405.2	541.6
Gold:					
At SDR 35 per ounce	37.0	35.6	32.8	33.2	33.1
At London market price	39.5	121.9	433.5	282.6	288.2

[1] Including unidentified currencies.
[2] The fall after 1985 was due to overall net repayments to the Fund.
Source: International Monetary Fund, Annual Reports.

their balance sheets as though it were a reserve asset. In fact it long ago ceased to merit that classification according to the standard definition of a reserve asset, which is an asset unconditionally available at short notice to support a country's currency in the foreign exchange market. But since central banks have still not brought themselves to reclassify gold as the speculative commodity that it has become, but like to show it in their balance sheets as a reserve asset, a concession is made to their feelings by including it as a non-liquid asset in Table 19.1.

The penultimate row of the table shows the value of gold holdings at the old official price of SDR 35 per ounce, which was abolished at Jamaica. The final row shows the value at the price prevailing in the London gold market, which is a price that is now somewhat relevant because it was also agreed at Jamaica to abolish the prohibition against selling at the market price. It is only 'somewhat' relevant, however, because if any major central bank tried selling a significant part of its gold on the market it would bid the price down, and central banks do not like depressing the book value of their assets. This is one of the factors that makes gold an illiquid asset. But, even if an illiquid speculative asset, and despite two major price declines, gold was a great speculative success over the 1970s as a whole, as the contrast between the last two lines of Table 19.1 shows. In 1982, however, its price fell back to around $400 per ounce, and it has since oscillated in a wide range around that level. The developing countries, who hold little gold, were aggrieved at the contrast between the way the developed countries allowed their own gold holdings to be revalued and the way they rejected pleas for the link.

The non-system is also permissive in its specification of adjustment obligations and adjustment mechanisms. Even the old discipline of limited reserves has been much eroded by the international capital market, which allows most of the industrial countries (though no longer many of the developing countries) considerable latitude to finance current account deficits by going into debt. There are no agreed rules, or even conventions, as to the mix of exchange-rate policy, monetary (credit) policy and fiscal policy that countries should adopt. For a time policy in the major countries was dominated by the attempt to secure a preannounced rate of growth of the money supply as recommended by Friedmanian monetarism.

At the microeconomic level, the non-system has been inferior to its predecessor. Transaction costs have risen: buy–sell spreads in the foreign exchange markets are now typically about four times what they were, though they remain small as a percentage of the value of transactions. Exchange rates have proved extremely volatile, on any measure. Exchange risk has increased in consequence, and misalignments – deviations of real exchange rates from underlying equilibrium – have widened rather than being reduced, as most advocates of greater exchange-rate flexibility had expected. Nevertheless, markets have continued to function: there has been no seizing-up of trade or capital flows. Some economists believe that the greater uncertainty being generated by volatile exchange rates must be having bad effects, like discouraging trade, ratcheting up the rate of inflation and bankrupting businesses in countries with overvalued currencies. To date, however, there is only limited evidence to support these conjectures.

In the early years of the non-system it was often argued that flexible interest rates and exchange rates must be capable of establishing a satisfactory global macro equilibrium. If, for example, there were inconsistent national ambitions towards current account surpluses, then interest rates would be bid down until some countries were tempted into borrowing more and others wanted to lend less. Freedom from the need to treat the exchange rate as a constraint could only help countries to achieve their national inflation targets. Such arguments have fallen under suspicion as experience with floating has accumulated, and the world has again started to search for alternatives.

19.7 The European Monetary System

The first attempt to return to more formal exchange-rate arrangements took place in Europe. Indeed, a core of European countries never allowed their currencies to float against one another. In the early 1970s the members of the European Community endorsed a plan to move to complete European Monetary Union (EMU) by 1980. The first stage of this plan was implemented in 1972, before the major currencies started floating. It involved a narrowing of the intra-European margins: the EC countries agreed to limit the deviations of their cross-rates to less than was allowed by their intervention points against the dollar. The dollar intervention points provided a 'tunnel', and the European currencies snaked around together within those limits, so that this arrangement was dubbed the 'snake in the tunnel'.[7]

The pound sterling was taken out of the snake in response to a speculative crisis after only a few weeks, in June 1972. Then, in March 1973, the move to generalized floating meant that the snake broke out of its tunnel, but it held together and even collected Norway and Sweden for a while. However, both France and Italy dropped out eventually, so that by 1978 the snake was reduced to the DM and Germany's small Benelux and Danish neighbours.

The weakness of the dollar in 1977–8 prompted the German Chancellor Helmut Schmidt and the French President Valéry Giscard d'Estaing to develop a new initiative aimed at creating a 'zone of monetary stability' in Europe. This was the origin of the European Monetary System (EMS), which was established in early 1979. Its core is a revitalized 'snake', in which all the participating currencies are held within margins of ±2¼ per cent around a set of bilateral parities. But it is broader than the snake in a series of key respects: in the countries that participate; in the creation of an embryonic monetary unit, the 'European currency unit' (ECU); in the attempt to co-ordinate policy; and in the ambition to move on to closer monetary union in the future.

So far as participation is concerned, all members of the European Community are formally members of the EMS. This means that Britain, France, Ireland and Italy joined on its establishment in 1979, while Greece, Portugal and Spain joined on their accession to the Community. But what really counts is membership of the exchange rate mechanism (ERM) – that is, acceptance of the commitment to maintain exchange rates within margins – rather than of the EMS *per se*. Britain refused to accept this obligation in 1979 and maintained its refusal until late 1990, when it accepted the obligation in qualified form with wide margins of ±6 per cent. Italy had entered on a similar basis in 1979, though it moved to the conventional ±2¼ per cent margins in 1990. Spain joined, with wide 6 per cent margins, in 1989. As of February 1991, the participants in the ERM are thus Belgium–Luxemburg, Denmark, France, Germany, Ireland, Italy, the Netherlands and (with wide margins) Spain and Britain.

The ECU is the accounting unit of the European Community. It is defined, like the SDR, as a basket of currencies. All the Community currencies, whether or not they participate in the ERM, are in the ECU basket, with weights varying from 30.1 per cent for the Deutschmark down to 0.8 per cent for the Greek drachma and the Portuguese escudo. Although the official ECU has served as little more than a unit of account, the market has created 'private ECUs' by bundling up the constituent currencies. This private ECU has become fairly widely used as an international currency: by early 1990 it had the fifth largest value of Eurobonds outstanding (after the dollar, DM, yen and sterling), as well as offering a fairly full array of financial products like bank loans and deposits, Treasury bills, options, swaps and futures. Some trade is now being denominated in ECUs, though this has been slow to develop. The European Commission has provided 'infant currency protection' by encouraging such institutions as the European Investment Bank to denominate their bonds in ECUs. The main attraction of the ECU is that, because of its definition as a basket of European currencies, it provides built-in hedging for enterprises with diversified European operations.

The most important difference between the EMS and its predecessor, the snake, is that the EMS aims to co-ordinate the macroeconomic policies of its members. The original plan was to utilize a 'divergence indicator', which showed how far a currency was out of line with the average of the other currencies in the EMS in order to decide which countries needed to adjust their policies (or their parities). And in its early years the EMS did function somewhat in this way: parity changes were relatively small and frequent, going a large part of the way towards offsetting differential inflation, so that the EMS functioned more like a system of fixed *real* exchange rates than one of fixed *nominal* rates.

As time progressed, however, more and more of the member countries came to view the EMS as a mechanism for making economic policies *better* rather than simply *more convergent*. In particular, they came to believe that it was possible to use the promise of a fixed exchange rate against the currency with the best inflation performance (the DM) as a way of increasing the credibility of their own anti-inflationary promises, thus reducing the output cost of disinflating. The result is that the EMS is now effectively a DM zone with what are intended to be fixed nominal exchange rates, in which the Bundesbank chooses its monetary policy to stabilize the German economy and the other member countries vary their monetary policies to maintain their exchange rates. There was in fact only one realignment from 1987 until this went to press in 1991, and that was a devaluation of the lira's central rate – but not of its lower margin – at the time that the lira's margins were reduced to 2¼ per cent in January 1990.

Some economists question whether this stability of nominal exchange rates can persist. The process of achieving inflation convergence gave rise to a undervaluation of the DM and overvaluation of most other EMS currencies that by early 1990 had produced a massive German surplus offset by deficits in other European countries. Add to this the need for a real appreciation of the DM to help Germany use some of its external surplus to finance the reconstruction of East Germany, and the likelihood of at least one further realignment seems quite high.

The final difference between the EMS and the snake is that the EMS is envisaged as merely the first step on the road to monetary integration. Once again, the EMS has not worked out as planned, since the participants were originally expected to pool their reserves in a European Reserve Fund by 1981. That never occurred, but instead the European Community eventually decided (despite vigorous opposition from Mrs Thatcher) to pursue the objective of monetary union. In 1988 the heads of government set up a committee to recommend how this could be achieved. Its report, the so-called Delors Report (after its chairman, the President of the European Commission), was published in 1989. It recommended a three-stage process for moving to complete monetary union (a single money) by an unspecified date.

The first stage would involve all members joining the ERM and all capital controls being abolished (except by the poorer countries like Greece and Portugal). The second stage would be marked by the creation of a European System of Central Banks (i.e. a central bank with a federal structure like the Federal Reserve System in the United States). Exchange-rate parities would be irrevocably frozen in the third stage, and thereafter the various national moneys would be replaced by a single European money issued and managed by the European System of Central Banks. This ambitious blueprint is still controversial.

19.8 New efforts at global reform

In the course of 1985 it transpired that the previous principal supporter of the non-system, the United States, had become disillusioned with its operation. Floating exchange rates had allowed the dollar to become vastly overvalued. Without policy co-ordination the United States had undertaken a large fiscal expansion while Japan and Europe were in the process of fiscal consolidation. Together these developments had produced a vast US current account deficit matched largely by the surpluses of Japan and Germany. American tradable goods industries were screaming for protection and the United States was being transformed from its old position as the world's largest net creditor to its current status as the world's largest net debtor. The new team that took control of the US Treasury in President Reagan's second term, headed by Treasury Secretary James Baker, judged these developments intolerable.

The essence of the non-system had been willingness to treat the exchange rate as the residual in the process of policy determination. Abandonment of this attitude dates from the Plaza Agreement of the Group of Five[8] in September 1985. The communiqué announced agreement that prevailing exchange rates did not reflect the fundamentals and that an orderly appreciation of the non-dollar currencies was therefore to be desired, which is of course the diplomatic way of saying that the dollar was overvalued and should therefore depreciate. This it duly did in the following months, with some help from the central banks, mainly in the form of intervention to sell dollars.

Once the authorities had concluded that the non-system was inadequate, it was natural that they should seek an alternative. One idea on the table, advocated by Ronald McKinnon, suggested a 'gold standard without gold'. In the strongest version of this proposal, the three major economic powers (Germany, Japan and the United States) would agree on a set of fixed exchange rates among themselves and a rate of monetary expansion for the group of countries together. Each country would commit itself to a fixed rate of domestic credit expansion (DCE) and then undertake un-limited unsterilized intervention in order to stabilize exchange rates: the *distribution* of monetary expansion could thus respond to the intervention that proved necessary, but the *total* 'world' monetary expansion would not, since intervention would net out. Each country's DCE would be set equal to its trend growth of nominal income when the price of tradable goods is stable multiplied by its estimated income elasticity of demand for money, so as to achieve stable prices for tradable goods.

The standard criticism of the McKinnon proposal is that it takes a fairly ex-treme monetarist position in denying the relevance of fiscal policy and the need for any attempt to direct macroeconomic policy at 'internal balance' other than to achieve secular price stability of traded goods. An alternative approach took a more traditional stance on those issues, but still suggested the establishment of 'target zones' for currencies. It represented a development of the limited flexibility proposals of the late 1960s (see section 14.6). It envisaged the major countries agreeing target zones for their real effective exchange rates, and undertaking to modify their policies, especially monetary policy, in order to discourage exchange rates moving outside those zones. The centres of the zones would be chosen as the exchange rates estimated to reconcile internal and external balance in the medium term. The proposal to have rather wide zones was justified both by the impossibility of estimating sensible target exchange rates at all accurately and by the desirability of allowing exchange rates to fluctuate to accommodate differences in conjunctural (anti-cyclical) policy and speculative pressures. Nominal exchange-rate targets would be adjusted automatically to offset differential inflation to maintain the real zones constant, while the real zones could be adjusted if needed to support adjustment in response to real shocks.

The main criticism of the target zone proposal was that stabilizing exchange rates without co-ordinating other policies could make things worse rather than better. Suppose, for example, that the United States had been committed to a target zone for the dollar in the early 1980s. Then, to limit the dollar's appreciation after the 1981 tax cuts, the Fed would have been obliged to relax monetary policy, which would have thwarted the disinflation that the tight monetary policy was designed to achieve. Supporters of target zones retorted that these pressures might instead have encouraged the US government to curb the fiscal deficits that have plagued the United States, and indeed the world economy, ever since, but this possibility was dismissed as politically naive by the critics.

What both sides could agree on was that it would be better if any exchange-rate agreement was part of a more comprehensive plan for policy co-ordination. This was in fact the path pursued by the major countries, for at the Tokyo summit of May 1986 the Group of Seven[9] agreed to construct a set of 'indicators' to help co-ordinate their economic policies. The Group of Seven now lay out their projections (targets?) for a set of key variables with a view to allowing the IMF (which provides the technical back-up) to check the mutual consistency of their policy intentions. The variables monitored in this way are the growth of real GNP, inflation, the balance of payments on current account, fiscal and monetary policies and exchange rates.

Although the governments gave the impression in 1986 that they had rejected target zones, their next major agreement was very much in the spirit of that proposal. Specifically, the Louvre Accord of February 1987 declared that the dollar had fallen enough. Thereafter an attempt was made, largely by unsterilized intervention, to stabilize exchange rates within rather narrow zones. The trouble has been that the critics of the target zone proposal are right in arguing that exchange-rate commitments need backing up by appropriate fiscal policies, while only Japan (with a well-timed fiscal expansion in spring 1987) has shown any willingness to adjust its fiscal policy when the need arose. The United States did little to curb its massive deficit; Britain refused a needed fiscal contraction in 1988 on the ground that it already had a fiscal surplus; Germany refused to expand in the mid-1980s, when this was called for, and promised instead a delayed tax cut that took effect in 1990 – just as the economy was booming.

In an attempt to provide some fiscal guidelines that might help avoid such nonsense, the target zone proposal was embedded into a comprehensive 'blueprint' for policy co-ordination in 1987. This blueprint is based on a standard Meadean framework of using the two instruments of monetary and fiscal policy to pursue simultaneously two intermediate targets, one for the growth of nominal domestic demand and the other for the level of the real effective exchange rate. The intermediate targets are themselves chosen with the aim of leading the economy gradually, over a period of five years or so, to a position of simultaneous internal and external balance. In particular, the centre of the target zone for the exchange rate is supposed to be chosen to produce a current account balance corresponding to a sustainable and welfare-maximizing capital flow when the economy is at non-inflationary full employment. Moderate deviations of the exchange rate from that level would be tolerated, so as to allow monetary policy to be used on a routine basis for managing domestic demand, but the threat of a major misalignment (defined as a deviation of 10 per cent or more from the centre of the target zone) would prompt a corrective change of interest rates. Any undesired effects of such monetary changes on domestic demand would be countered by a temporary adjustment in the fiscal stance.

The G–7 policy co-ordination of the late 1980s was not, however, based on any such set of articulated principles. Fiscal policy was largely frozen, and hence only one serious policy instrument, namely monetary policy, was available. This has been devoted mainly to managing domestic demand. When exchange rates threatened to become seriously misaligned, the G–7 balked and intervened. This proved more effective than many economists might have expected (which has prompted a re-examination of the conventional wisdom that sterilized intervention is ineffective): a bear squeeze mounted by the central banks stopped the plunge of the dollar in the first days of 1988, after the stock market crash had unleashed forces that seemed likely to lead the dollar to a 'hard landing'. Similarly, when the dollar had again become overvalued in the summer of 1989, a G–7 communiqué in September followed by determined intervention and backed up by modest changes in interest rates succeeded in reversing its rise, at least against the European currencies.

Nevertheless, the G–7 policy co-ordination process still leaves a lot to be desired. Admittedly not everyone is worried by its limitations to a fire-fighting role. Some argue that in the brave new world of global financial markets the traditional concern about payments deficits has become redundant. (Sceptics note that similar claims have been made before: for example, in relation to Latin America in the 1970s.) Others argue that policy co-ordination is an unimportant enterprise because governments can get close to an optimum outcome anyway simply by pursuing their own national self-interest irrespective of what other countries are doing. (This claim is based on a highly contentious approach to identifying a country's national interests, which relies on the assumption that in the years prior to G–7 policy co-ordination countries actually achieved the best outcomes available to them.) Still others remain stoically indifferent to the behaviour of exchange rates, on the ground that the only way of having a dependable influence on the exchange rate is via monetary policy, and a monetary expansion cannot be expected to reduce a balance of payments deficit even though it will depreciate the exchange rate, since it will also increase imports through a positive income effect. (This is true but not really relevant, inasmuch as the aim is to improve the balance of payments at a given output level – which indeed requires a fiscal contraction as well.) The debate continues.

19.9 Summary

The world has experienced a variety of international monetary regimes over the past century. The two most successful regimes were the two that were most structured, the gold standard and Bretton Woods, but it would be quite unrealistic to seek to restore either of them. The two least successful were, conversely, the two that were least structured, the free-for-all of the 1930s and the non-system of 1973–85. The EMS is already pointing the way towards a restored monetary order at the European level, and the G–7 has established arrangements for policy co-ordination that could provide the basis for a restored world system.

19.10 Bibliography

A lucid and fairly detailed account of international monetary history up to 1974 is to be found in part 2 of Yeager (1976), and up to about 1980 in Solomon (1982).

On the gold standard, see Bloomfield (1963), Ford (1962), Lindert (1969), Triffin (1964) and, for a monetarist interpretation, McCloskey and Zecher (1976). On the inter-war period, see Nurkse (1944) and Eichengreen (1990).

A readable account of the negotiations that led up to Bretton Woods is contained in chapter 13 of Harrod (1951). More detail is provided in Gardner (1969) and the official history of the IMF (Horsefield 1969). Keynes's papers are in volumes XXV and XXVI of his collected works (Johnson and Moggridge various years).

Triffin's diagnosis of the weakness of the Bretton Woods system and his proposals for reform are in Triffin (1960). The adjustment–liquidity–confidence classification was introduced in Machlup and Malkiel (1964). A brief history of the Bretton Woods system is provided in chapter 1 of Williamson (1977), the rest of which is centred on the C–20 negotiations.

For a useful summary of the EMS experience, see Gros and Thygesen (1989) or Giavazzi and Giovannini (1989a), and for more extensive analysis consult Giavazzi, Micossi and Miller (1988) or Giavazzi and Giovannini (1989b). The Delors Report is in the Committee on the Study of Econonic and Monetary Union (1989).

McKinnon (1988) provides a representative statement of his proposal. The target zone proposal was first elaborated in Bergsten and Williamson (1983), and developed further in Williamson (1985). The blueprint was presented by Williamson and Miller (1987). For a critical view of exchange-rate targeting, see Frenkel (1987). Oudiz and Sachs (1984) and Feldstein (1988) present sceptical and hostile views respectively on policy co-ordination. Marris (1987) and Makin (1990) give views for and against worrying about the US payments deficits.

Notes

1. A par, or par value, is the official central rate declared for a currency in terms of the system's unit of account, or numeraire. A parity is the ratio of two par values, the official central rate of one currency in terms of another.
2. This arises from an accounting asymmetry. The gold producer counts gold exports as a normal commodity, while the country importing gold puts it in the monetary account. This enables the sum total of world current accounts to be positive.
3. The initial members of the Group of Ten were Belgium, Canada, France, Germany, Italy, Japan, the Netherlands, Sweden, the United Kingdom and the United States. Switzerland had observer status; it has since been admitted as a full member, but the name of the Group has not been changed.
4. The 'link' was initially a part of the phrase 'a link between reserve creation and development assistance', signifying that newly created reserves would have accrued in a way that financed development programmes, but the phrase was subsequently abbreviated.
5. 'Seigniorage' originally (in the Middle Ages) referred to the profit the crown reaped on minting metal into coins, but it has now been broadened to refer to the profit that accrues to the first spender from the ability to issue money in any way.
6. The basket consisted of 33 per cent US dollar, 12.5 per cent Deutschmark, 9 per cent pound sterling, 7.5 per cent each French franc and Japanese yen, 6 per cent Canadian dollar and Italian lira, 4.5 per cent Netherlands guilder, 3.5 per cent Belgian franc, 2.5 per cent Swedish krona, 1.5 per cent each Australian dollar, Danish krone, Norwegian krone and Spanish peseta, and 1 per cent each Austrian schilling and South African rand. The composition of the sixteen-currency basket was subsequently updated so that it continued to contain the currencies of the sixteen countries with largest exports. It was then simplified to the five major currencies on 1 January 1981, with shares of 42 per cent for the US dollar, 19 per cent for the Deutschmark and 13 per cent each for the French franc, Japanese yen and pound sterling. The share of the yen was subsequently increased to 15 per cent, at the expense of 1 per cent each for the franc and the pound.
7. The Benelux currencies kept closer still, a relationship known as the 'worm in the snake in the tunnel'.
8. The Group of Five consists of the five major countries whose currencies now constitute the SDR basket: France, Germany, Japan, the United Kingdom and the United States.
9. The Group of Seven was constituted by expanding the Group of Five, adding the two other countries that participate in summit meetings, Canada and Italy.

20

Global economic problems

This final chapter is devoted to a review of the principal economic problems that have dominated global concerns since post-war reconstruction was completed about 1960. It focuses on the issues that have headed the agenda of the major powers, rather than that of the developing countries. There has been a continuing effort to promote development, even though it has not matched up to the hopes of the developing countries, but the attempt made in the 1970s to push development to the top of the agenda – by the creation of a 'new international economic order' – did not succeed. However, the issues of most concern to the industrial countries have increasingly been ones on which the developing countries are major actors.

The chapter starts by outlining the various aggregates into which countries are customarily grouped for purposes of presenting data and analyzing global developments. It then proceeds to discuss the major issue of the 1960s, which was the international interaction of demand management policies and the business cycle. In the early 1970s this was overshadowed – though not displaced – by concern over the worldwide explosion of inflation. The first oil shock superimposed a new dominant problem, the oil deficit, on continuing worries about the level of activity and inflation. In the 1980s the major problem became international debt: not just the Third World debt crisis already discussed in section 18.4, but also the dangers posed by the build-up of US debt. The chapter concludes by examining what promises to be the most difficult international economic issue of the 1990s: namely, how to develop policies and institutions to cope with the environmental dangers confronting the world.

20.1 Aggregates

The four main country groupings to be found in most data presentations or analyses have for years been the industrial countries, the centrally planned economies, the oil exporters and the developing countries. The names given to these groups and the boundaries between them have differed somewhat, depending on both the analytical purposes and the political sympathies of the user. The groupings may also be disaggregated.

The following brief discussion of the names and country composition of each of those four groupings, of their common characteristics and of ways in which they are frequently disaggregated, should be read in conjunction with Table 20.1, which provides leading statistical data on all the larger countries (defined as those with a GNP estimated at over $10 billion in 1988, or $6 billion in sub-Saharan Africa). Countries are allocated among the four groups, with a further disaggregation between middle-income and low-income developing countries, and listed alphabetically within each group. Marginal cases have been distributed between the groups on the basis that seems most natural.

The first column in the table shows population as of mid-1988. The second column shows 1988 GNP, calculated in the conventional way by converting local-currency GNP into dollars at the market exchange rate: this gives an idea of the relative size of different economies. The third column gives an idea of per capita income in different countries, for which purpose the estimates of the International Comparisons Project using purchasing power comparisons are more suitable than conventional estimates of GNP per capita. The latest year for which such figures are available is 1985. But these figures still seem to have some quirks. Italy is ranked surprisingly (implausibly?) low, while the former centrally planned economies – especially the Soviet Union and China, for which the data were least adequate – are surely ranked too high.

Column 4 shows average growth in real per capita GNP during the 1980s, up to 1988. Column 5 shows openness as measured by the ratio of imports to GNP (or to GDP, where no figure for GNP is available) in the most recent year for which data are available. This is usually 1988, though a few entries go back to as far as 1983; but this is not a ratio that varies sharply in the short run. The final column gives the average rate of inflation in the 1980s, up to 1987.

Industrial countries

The industrial countries, industrialized countries or developed countries, as we have referred to them, are also called the industrial market economies (by the United Nations and World Bank) or the advanced capitalist countries (by those with Marxist sympathies). The fourteen core members of the group are Belgium, Canada, Denmark, France, Germany, Italy, Japan, Luxemburg, the Netherlands, Norway, Sweden, Switzerland, the United Kingdom and the United States. Some or all other members of the OECD may be included in the group, most regularly the high-income ones: Australia, Austria, Finland, Iceland, Ireland, New Zealand and Spain. The other OECD members in southern Europe, namely Greece, Portugal and Turkey, as well as Yugoslavia, are more often grouped with the middle-income developing countries. Israel is also occasionally placed among the industrial countries. The same used to be true of South Africa, presumably because the white minority – which has long enjoyed industrial-country living standards – was implicitly being treated as the real nation separate from the black majority.

The common economic characteristics of the industrial countries are that they have relatively high per capita incomes, that they have completed the transformation from a subsistence economy to a modern economy and that they have market-oriented (capitalist or mixed) economic systems. In addition, all now have liberal-democratic systems of representative government.

The most frequent disaggregation involves picking out some of the large economies, notably the United States, Japan and Germany, and quite often all seven of the large economies (which involves adding Canada, France, Italy and the United Kingdom, to give the membership of the G–7). The remaining small industrial countries may be treated as a group. Alternatively, the industrial countries may be disaggregated geographically into North America, Europe and Japan plus Australia and New Zealand. The EC may also be treated as a subaggregate.

Centrally planned economies

The centrally planned economies, as they were long referred to by the United Nations, were also called the non-market economies, the Communist countries (usually by capitalists), or the Socialist countries (usually by Communists). The core group consisted of Bulgaria, Czechoslovakia, East Germany, Hungary, Poland and the Soviet Union. Romania, the poorest European member of the CMEA, was also usually included, though the World Bank listed it and all other countries with Communist governments among the developing countries. The non-European members of the CMEA – that is, Cuba, Mongolia, North Korea and Vietnam – are also usually included. The other obvious candidates are Albania (probably the world's most closed economy), China (the most populous country), Kampuchea (formerly Cambodia), Laos and conceivably Yugoslavia. Other Third World countries with Marxist-oriented governments (like Angola, Ethiopia, Mozambique and South Yemen) were left in the category of developing countries, presumably because their regimes did not look sufficiently securely entrenched to merit the trouble of reclassification.

The obvious common characteristics of the countries in the group were that they all had governments that called themselves Socialist–Communist–Marxist and looked fairly permanent (more permanent than they have proved to be); they had all undertaken a major socialization of the economy; and they all relied on central planning rather than the price mechanism for important economic decisions. Per capita incomes range down from the maximum in East Germany, which is about equivalent to that in one of the poorer industrial countries, to levels typical of low-income LDCs.

It transpired in 1989 that the ideological orientation of many of these countries was much less permanent than had previously been supposed. Most of them are now committed to the objective of transforming their command economies into market economies, and how well they succeed is one of the great issues of the 1990s. One consequence of that outcome will doubtless be the way in which they are classified and described in future official international publications, but this is still an open question in 1990. It has already taken place, however, in the case of East Germany (the former German Democratic Republic) as a result of its absorption into the Federal Republic of Germany.

Oil exporters

After the 1973 oil price increase it became customary to treat some group of oil-exporting countries as a separate aggregate. The simplest basis for drawing this distinction is to select the thirteen members of OPEC (Algeria, Ecuador, Gabon, Indonesia, Iran, Iraq, Kuwait, Libya, Nigeria, Qatar, Saudi Arabia, United Arab Emirates, Venezuela). The objection to this procedure is that membership of OPEC is not a particularly good indicator of the importance of oil to a country's economy. Some OPEC members like Indonesia and Nigeria have quite large, diversified economies to which oil is, while more than marginal, fairly minor. Others, like Ecuador and Gabon, provide only a tiny fraction of the world oil supply. On either criterion some non-OPEC members are now stronger candidates for inclusion than some OPEC members.

These considerations have led to rival alternative classification schemes. First, those countries with economies dominated by oil, and few alternative productive resources, and which therefore had payments surpluses on current account throughout the period 1974–85, are called the low-absorbing or capital surplus oil exporters. These are the core oil exporters, which are always placed in this category: Kuwait, Libya, Qatar, Saudi Arabia (the dominant member of the group) and the United Arab Emirates. Iraq was a marginal case, although it went into deficit during the 1979–88 war against Iran. Second, the IMF calls the oil-exporting countries those whose oil exports comprise more than two-thirds of their total exports and more than 1 per cent of total world exports: as compared to the membership of OPEC, this has the effect of excluding Ecuador and Gabon and including Oman. Third, the World Bank distinguishes the countries for which exports of petroleum and gas account for at least 30 per cent of merchandise exports: this criterion includes all the above plus Angola, Brunei, Bahrain, Cameroon, Congo, Egypt, Mexico, Norway, Syria, Trinidad and Tobago, and the USSR. But then one could of course ask: why only hydrocarbons, why not all forms of energy? Or why only energy, why not other forms of mineral wealth? As usual, there is no perfect basis for aggregation.

Developing countries

All countries not included in one of the preceding aggregates are put in the category that has in recent years usually been referred to as the developing countries. They started off being called the poor countries, a term progressively modified to underdeveloped, less developed (from which the LDC acronym still sticks), and then developing, in an attempt to find a term that would not offend national pride. But given that the major criterion for inclusion is in fact per capita income rather than its rate of increase, the nomenclature leaves much to be desired. However, even per capita income is no longer a reliable criterion: both Hong Kong and Singapore have now overtaken a number of developed countries in income per head, but resist reclassification. Developing countries are often split into two groups, on the basis of per capita income: middle-income and low-income countries. This is done in Table 20.1.

Table 20.1 Summary statistics of the larger economies

	1988 population (millions)	1988 GNP (exchange-rate basis: US $ billion)	1985 GDP per capita (purchasing power basis: international dollars)	Average growth in per capita GNP 1980–8 (% per annum)	Imports/ GNP, latest year (%)	Average rate of inflation 1980–7 (% per annum)
Industrial countries						
Australia	16.5	204	11,730	1.7	18	7.8
Austria	7.6	118	11,830	1.7	35	4.3
Belgium	9.9	144	12,880	1.4	66	5.1
Canada	26.1	437	16,160	2.3	27	5.0
Denmark	5.1	95	14,420	2.3	31	6.8
Finland	4.9	92	12,210	2.7	25	7.2
France	55.9	899	13,140	1.2	21	7.7
W. Germany	61.0	1,131	14,190	2.0	27	2.9
Ireland	3.6	27	6,900	0.0	62	10.2
Italy	57.5	765	9,840	1.7	18	11.5
Japan	122.4	2,577	12,520	3.4	10	1.4
Netherlands	14.8	214	12,050	1.1	51	2.3
New Zealand	3.3	32	10,600	0.6	28	11.5
Norway	4.2	84	16,730	3.8	37	6.1
Spain	39.0	302	8,530	2.0	21	10.7
Sweden	8.4	160	13,120	1.9	32	7.9
Switzerland	6.5	178	14,100	1.6	34	3.9
UK	57.0	730	11,500	2.8	27	5.7
USA	245.9	4,864	16,600	2.1	11	4.3
Centrally planned economies						
Bulgaria	9.0	n.a.[1]	6,770	3.5[2]	n.a.	n.a.
China	1,083.9	356	3,240	n.a.	n.a.	4.2
Cuba	10.4	n.a.	n.a.	n.a.	n.a.	n.a.
Czechoslovakia	15.6	n.a.	9,840	1.5[2]	n.a.	n.a.
E. Germany	16.7	n.a.	10,460	4.6[2]	n.a.	n.a.
N. Korea	21.9	n.a.	n.a.	n.a.	n.a.	n.a.
Hungary	10.6	26	7,640	1.4[2]	35	5.7
Poland	37.9	70	6,510	1.7	20	29.2
Romania	23.1	n.a.	5,660	4.0[2]	n.a.	n.a.
USSR	285.7	n.a.	8300	2.7[2]	n.a.	n.a.
Vietnam	66.7	n.a.	n.a.	n.a.	n.a.	n.a.
OPEC						
Algeria	23.8	58	2,840	0.0	59	5.6
Ecuador	10.2	11	3,160	−1.1	31	29.5
Indonesia	174.8	76	1,660	1.7	23	8.5
Iran	48.6	n.a.	5,200	n.a.	9	n.a.
Iraq	17.7	n.a.	3,730	n.a.	n.a.	n.a.
Kuwait	1.9	26	19,700	−2.5	34	−4.6
Libya	4.2	23	n.a.	−9.9	n.a.	0.1
Nigeria	110.1	32	770	−4.3	15	10.1
Saudi Arabia	14.0	87	7,910	−5.9	48	−2.8
U Arab Emirates	1.5	24	16,440	−9.0	44	−0.3
Venezuela	18.8	59	4,700	−2.4	28	11.4

Table 20.1 Summary statistics of the larger economies (continued)

	1988 population (millions)	1988 GNP (exchange-rate basis: US $ billion)	1985 GDP per capita (purchasing power basis: international dollars)	Average growth in per capita GNP 1980–8 (% per annum)	Imports/ GNP, latest year (%)	Average rate of inflation 1980–7 (% per annum)
Developing countries: middle income						
Argentina	32.0	83	4,620	−1.6	11	298.7
Brazil	144.4	329	4,350	1.2	6	166.3
Cameroon	11.2	11	1,450	3.0	19	8.1
Chile	12.8	19	4,620	−0.1	27	20.6
Colombia	30.0	37	3,440	1.2	13	23.7
Egypt	51.4	33	1,570	2.8	24	9.2
Greece	10.0	48	5,910	0.1	31	19.7
Hong Kong	5.7	52	12,050	5.7	n.a.[2]	6.7
Israel	4.4	38	8,310	1.5	52	159.0
Korea	42.6	150	4,050	7.7	33	5.0
Malaysia	16.9	32	4,520	1.3	61	1.1
Mexico	83.6	152	5,280	−1.4	13	68.9
Morocco	23.9	18	1,620	0.8	25	7.3
Pakistan	105.7	37	1,530	3.0	17	7.3
Peru	20.7	29[3]	2,800	−1.2	21	101.5
Philippines	59.7	38	1,800	−2.4	24	16.7
Portugal	10.2	37	4,940	1.9	37	20.8
Singapore	2.6	24	13,030	5.8	140	1.3
South Africa	33.9	78	5,150	−1.0	25	13.8
Syria	11.7	20	3,840	−3.1	42	11.0
Taiwan	19.9	125	4,740	7.0	43	2.9
Thailand	54.5	55	2,520	3.8	37	2.8
Turkey	53.8	69	3,360	3.0	22	37.4
Yugoslavia	23.6	63	6,710	−0.1	23	57.2
Zimbabwe	9.3	6	1,260	−1.0	26	12.4
Developing countries: low income						
Bangladesh	104.5	18	860	0.8	n.a.	11.1
Ethiopia	46.1	6	410	−1.4	24	2.6
India	814.0	271	990	3.3	8	7.7
Kenya	23.0	8	790	−0.2	28	10.3
Myanmar (Burma)	40.2	n.a.	740	n.a.	5	n.a.
Sudan	23.8	11	720	−4.2	n.a.	31.7

[1]   n.a. = not available.

[2] Growth in net material product per capita, 1980–5.

[3] 1987.

Sources: Cols 1, 2 and 4, *World Bank Atlas*, 1987) col. 3, Summers and Heston (1988); Col. 5, *International Financial Statistics*; co. 6, *World Development Report*, 1989.

One thing the developing countries tend to have in common is their dissatisfaction with the international status quo. This is manifest in their frequent joint action in fora like the United Nations, UNCTAD and the Group of Seventy-Seven – a pressure group originally formed by the seventy-seven LDC participants in the first UNCTAD conference, which retains its original name although it now has over 100 members.

The middle-income countries are defined in Table 20.1 as those with 1985 per capita incomes measured by PPP in excess of $1,000, The majority of these countries had significant access as borrowers to the international capital market in the 1970s, though not many of them allow their residents to lend extensively, and most lost their access as borrowers in the 1980s. An important subcategory is the semi-industrial countries, or NICs, or exporters of manufactures: the World Bank lists Brazil, China, Hong Kong, Hungary, India, Israel, Korea, Poland, Portugal, Romania, Singapore and Yugoslavia in this category. A new subcategory that developed in the 1980s is that of the highly indebted countries: Argentina, Bolivia, Brazil, Chile, Colombia, Costa Rica, Côte d'Ivoire, Ecuador, Jamaica, Mexico, Morocco, Nigeria, Peru, the Philippines, Uruguay, Venezuela and Yugoslavia. Finally, the developing countries are often disaggregated on a geographical basis: the World Bank distinguishes sub-Saharan Africa (which still excludes South Africa); developing countries of Europe, the Middle East and North Africa; East Asia; South Asia; and Latin America and the Caribbean.

The low-income countries as defined in Table 20.1 are those with a per capita income (using PPPs) of under $1,000 in 1985. Most of them have very little creditworthiness with the private market. All except India are overwhelmingly exporters of primary products. An important subcategory, characterized by both very low per capita income and the absence of any significant modern sector, are the least developed. The United Nations list comprises Afghanistan, Bangladesh, Benin, Bhutan, Botswana, Burundi, Burkina Faso, Burma, Cape Verde, Central African Republic, Chad, Comoros, Djibouti, Equatorial Guinea, Ethiopia, Gambia, Guinea, Guinea Bissau, Haiti, Kiribati, Laos, Lesotho, Malawi, Maldives, Mali, Mauritania, Mozambique, Nepal, Niger, Rwanda, Samoa, São Tome and Principe, Sierra Leone, Somalia, Sudan, Tanzania, Togo, Tuvalu, Uganda, Vanuatu and Yemen. The United Nations has urged the international community to make special efforts to help these countries and has to that end established a separate aid target for them, involving donors giving at least 0.15 per cent of their GNP to the group.

20.2 Demand management in the 1960s

The 1930s provided graphic evidence of the international interdependence of economic activity. The lesson was not forgotten in the early post-war years, when people used to talk of how 'Europe would catch pneumonia if the United States sneezed', meaning that any United States recession would spread to, and have magnified effects in, Europe. Then came 1958 and the most severe post-war recession prior to the oil price increase, from which Europe recovered rapidly while President

Eisenhower's caution sent the United States into a new recession almost as soon as recovery had started. That served to lay to rest the worries about European dependence on the United States.

It did not, however, lead decision-makers to the false conclusion that demand management policy should be treated as a purely national problem. It so happened that the Organization for European Economic Co-operation (OEEC) had just worked itself out of a job, with the successful completion of post-war reconstruction in Europe and the winding up of the European Payments Union. However, one can never abolish a bureaucracy, especially an international bureaucracy, so it was necessary to find it a new job. The solution adopted was to enlarge it (to include the United States and Canada, then Japan, and subsequently Australia and New Zealand), change its name (to OECD) and charge it with the task of co-ordinating economic policy. Although OECD has concerned itself with myriad aspects of economic policy over the last twenty years, from fisheries to technology to pollution to energy to trying to get its members to shame one another into stepping up aid, a central part of its work has always been the co-ordination of conjunctural policy.

In the 1960s this was conceived as a topic that was relevant only to the industrial countries. The others were regarded as having neither any significant degree of policy autonomy capable of influencing the course of the world economy nor any worthwhile expertise to offer to those who had. Consequently, it was deemed natural and appropriate to discuss conjunctural co-ordination within the limited confines of what outsiders dubbed the rich men's club. This became the province of the OECD's Economic Policy Committee and its Working Party No. 3, whose terms of reference committed it to supervision of the process of balance of payments adjustment. Senior civil servants converged on Paris every six or eight weeks to scrutinize one another's policies with regard to demand management and payments adjustment. It was not possible to divorce discussion of the two topics because, as noted in section 19.4, the Bretton Woods system after about 1960 had no adjustment mechanism other than the trimming of demand management policy to the needs of external balance (apart from the last-resort technique of exchange-rate changes).

The spirit of the 1960s, especially the early 1960s, was overwhelmingly Keynesian. It was taken for granted virtually throughout the Atlantic Community (a geopolitical concept that came to include Japan) that it was possible and desirable to manipulate monetary and especially fiscal policy with a view to pursuing those targets that we have been calling internal balance and external balance. Policy was not confused by the parallel existence of financial targets like preordained growth rates of the money supply or balanced budgets (usually three years in the future), as it was in the 1970s. If unemployment rose above target, the government raised its spending, cut taxes and, since monetary policy was generally dedicated to maintaining the interest rate constant, financed part of the resulting increase in the budget deficit by monetary expansion. If the economy showed signs of becoming overheated, those policies were put into reverse. A payments deficit induced similar reactions, though with a greater component of monetary restriction thrown in (a reflection of Mundell's argument about manipulating the fiscal–monetary mix). A payments surplus tended to induce some easing of policy, though rarely enough to deflect sermons being delivered in Paris about the responsibilities of surplus countries.

In retrospect, one looks back on the 1960s as a *belle époque* when governments wielded their policy instruments in a rational way and achieved an impressive measure of success. At the time, however, the problems looked real enough. And, indeed, one can now see that the failure to meet some of those problems at the time – especially those of inflation and the United States payments deficit – undermined the continued viability of the *belle époque*.

Richard Cooper, the major analyst of the 'economics of interdependence' of the period, diagnosed three general problems. The first was an insufficiency of instruments. The second was a possible inconsistency in targets. The third was dynamic inefficiency when policy instruments with strong international spillovers were adjusted by national policy-makers in an uncoordinated way. All three were problems which, although they had always existed to some degree, were magnified in importance by the dramatic increase in interdependence within the Atlantic Community after 1958.

The two instrument insufficiencies that most worried observers related to the balance of payments on the one hand and inflation on the other. Demand management policy was pre-empted for an internal balance target, interpreted as a particular level of employment. Given the unwillingness to use exchange-rate changes or commercial policy, and the inadequacy of merely financing rather than adjusting current imbalances, there was one instrument too few to achieve the external balance target. The desire to remedy this deficiency provided one of the bases for advocacy of greater exchange-rate flexibility. Similarly, the employment target was thought of as implying a particular outcome for the inflation rate (by the Phillips curve). Opinion divided as to what to do when that outcome was unacceptable. The Germans[1] argued that priority should be given to combating inflation, if necessary by adjusting the employment target to a rate consistent with price stability. This argument eventually triumphed among the Anglo-Saxons as well, after Phelps and Friedman had called the implied employment target 'the natural rate of unemployment' and experience had demonstrated that there was something in the idea that attempts to hold unemployment lower would lead to accelerating inflation. But there was another reaction as well, which at the time was more influential within the OECD. That was to search for another policy instrument, capable of reconciling full employment and price stability. That was the birth of the search for incomes policies. It is a search that was not conspicuously successful and was largely abandoned in the 1980s, though not necessarily for good.

The second general problem was that of target inconsistency. The inconsistencies that caused concern were those regarding the balance of payments – the $n-1$ or consistency problem again. We already discussed in section 19.5 how one of the arguments in favour of the creation of a new reserve asset was the desire to be able to increase the stock of reserves to reconcile reserve accumulation objectives that might otherwise be inconsistent. The solution to the $n-1$ problem was, therefore, that of providing an nth degree of freedom to the system. But there was another type of

Table 20.2 OECD estimates of international demand spillovers

Country expanding demand (1)	Domestic multiplier (2)	OECD multiplier / Domestic multiplier (3)	Effect on OECD (4)
USA	1.47	1.23	0.74
Japan	1.26	1.46	0.21
Germany	1.25	1.90	0.23
France	1.21	1.68	0.18
UK	1.17	1.98	0.13
Italy	1.24	1.96	0.09
Canada	1.27	1.83	0.10
Netherlands	0.73	2.69	0.04
Total OECD	n.a.	n.a.	2.04

Source: *The OECD International Linkage Model*, Organization for Economic Co-operation and Development Occasional Studies, January 1979, table 8.

inconsistency in payments objectives to which the solution was not so easy: objectives for the current account of the balance of payments. Cooper (1968, pp. 156–7) records that in 1962 all the major industrial countries were simultaneously wishing to increase their current account surpluses or decrease their deficits. True, they could have accomplished that if the rest of the world had correspondingly increased its current account deficit, and this was indeed one of the arguments deployed in favour of the link (see section 19.5). But that solution did not prove to have much appeal to the OECD countries, which instead settled down to years of debate as to how they should divide up between themselves the total current account deficit that the rest of the world could finance. Critics regarded this debate as rather sterile, inasmuch as the countries did not actually wield any policy weapons capable of accomplishing much effect of any sort, including harm to the system, if they set about pursuing inconsistent targets.

The third problem was that of dynamic inefficiency when policy instruments with strong international spillovers were adjusted by national policy makers in an uncoordinated way. The fact that international spillovers are significant is illustrated by the estimates shown in Table 20.2. These come from simulation exercises undertaken on the OECD model called INTERLINK, which is a model that consists of thirty-one submodels (of twenty-three OECD countries and eight non-OECD regions) linked together through a world trade model. All estimates refer to the first-year impact of an exogenous fiscal expansion equivalent to 1 per cent of GNP by the country listed in the first column. The second column then shows the domestic multiplier: for example, a fiscal expansion equal to 1 per cent of GNP in the United States would increase US GNP by 1.47 per cent. Note that this *includes* the foreign repercussion of section 12.9. There is clearly a tendency for the domestic multiplier to decline as the economy becomes smaller and more open, reaching a value of less than unity (0.73) for the Netherlands. The third and critical column shows the ratio critical column shows the ratio between the multiplier for the whole of the OECD area and the domestic multiplier. Even for the relatively closed United States and Japanese economies, it is estimated that the multipliers for the whole OECD are almost a quarter and a half larger, respectively, than the domestic multipliers. The ratios are higher for other countries: almost double for the other large countries, and almost three times as large for the Netherlands. If one had an estimate of the world multiplier rather than the OECD multiplier, the spillover would be relatively more important still.[2]

The final column shows the estimated percentage effect on OECD GNP of a 1 per cent fiscal expansion in each country. Obviously this effect is larger in the bigger countries: thus a 1 per cent United States fiscal expansion is estimated to raise OECD GNP by 0.74 per cent, while a 1 per cent fiscal expansion by the Netherlands would raise it by only 0.04 per cent (despite the fact that, dollar for dollar, Dutch expansion is actually more effective than United States expansion). The last line of that column shows that the total OECD multiplier is just over 2: that is, a 1 per cent fiscal expansion in all the OECD countries simultaneously would increase OECD GNP by an estimated 2.04 per cent.

Why should this interdependence constitute a problem for policy? Given that the national policy-makers control sufficient instruments and that the targets they are pursuing are mutually consistent, there is no reason to suppose that the system would not in due course approach equilibrium just because the policy instruments are wielded without conscious co-ordination. The situation is analogous to that which arises in the case of Mundell's assignment problem illustrated in Figure 13.2: there the policy instruments were wielded by independent agencies within a single country, whereas here instruments are controlled by policy-makers in different countries. But no one has ever suggested that there is any danger of an assignment of domestic full employment and national payments equilibrium to the authorities of each country turning out to be unstable.[3] Hence those who are convinced by Mundell's analysis should presumably reject Cooper's concerns. But it will be recalled that in section 13.2 we argued that it made little sense to have the economy pursue a zig-zag path from its initial position at E_1 to its desired equilibrium at E (in Figure 13.2(b)), as is implied by uncoordinated manipulation of fiscal and monetary policy by the Ministry of Finance and central bank, when co-ordination between the two would let them guide the economy straight to E. Co-ordination of policy instruments is, in other words, intended to reduce the time the economy spends away from the desired equilibrium.

Cooper argued that exactly the same thing was true in the international context. A lack of policy co-ordination could be expected to delay the achievement of policy objectives (as well as increasing the need for international reserves to finance the payments imbalances that would arise on the path to equilibrium). Moreover, he showed that the costs of a lack of co-ordination, in terms of delays in achieving objectives and increased reserve needs, increase with the degree of interdependence. For example, suppose that Europe were at internal balance when the United States ran into excessive demand pressures and therefore decided to deflate. Then the higher the United States import propensity, the greater would be the impact of United States deflation on European income, and therefore the greater would be the need for Europe to embark on prompt reflationary measures if undesired unemployment were to be averted.

The OECD consultations on co-ordination of economic policy therefore involved swapping experiences of attempts to widen the range of instruments available, attempting to secure consistency in national policy objectives (mainly with respect to the balance of payments), and ensuring that demand management policies for the OECD area as a whole added up to a stance consistent with a satisfactory level of activity for the area as a whole. The task that involved the most continuous monitoring was the third of these. In principle, it covered the pursuit of external as well as internal balance, but in view of the insufficiency of policy variables, it was the latter that was important. In the 1960s governments had no qualms about using fiscal–monetary policy in pursuit of an employment target. And in general the OECD area did stay close to full employment, though some have questioned to what extent policy co-ordination contributed to that success.

One potential danger of co-ordinating demand policies is that exhortations to expand or contract, issued because of the state of the world conjuncture, will induce parallel policies in most countries. Given that all demand policies act with a substantial lag, it is entirely possible that the business cycle might be amplified rather than reduced. It was indeed argued that this happened in the early 1970s, when the urgings to expand out of the 1971 recession led to the synchronized world boom of 1973, and the restrictive actions induced by that boom magnified the simultaneous recession of 1975. The conclusion drawn from these experiences by the OECD was the need to foster cyclical desynchronization. That gloss has been one factor modifying the policy recommendations of the OECD since then. But a far more important factor has been the problem of inflation.

20.3 The outbreak of world inflation

Although the world never returned to price stability after the Second World War, it got close to it in the 1950s. The IMF's world average of the rate of increase of consumer prices was a mere 0.3 per cent in 1950 and 1 per cent in 1955. Even the United Kingdom recorded an inflation rate as low as 0.6 per cent in 1959, while actual price falls were recorded for about 13 per cent of industrial-country years in the 1950s (excluding the Korean War years). Inflation expectations were near zero; indeed, few economists were aware of the concept.

The uneven, gradual, but persistent acceleration of inflation from the mid-1950s through to 1974 is shown by the figures presented in Table 20.3. When concern about the persistence of inflation started to mount in the late 1950s and early 1960s, it was viewed as a series of national problems. The dominant theory of inflation at the time was the simple Phillips curve. Inflation occurred because governments were pursuing ambitious employment targets, and it was faster in countries like Britain and France that gave a greater weight to low unemployment than it was in other countries like

Table 20.3 World inflation, 1950–88 (% per annum increase in consumer prices)

	World	Industrial countries	USA	Japan	Germany	France	UK
1950	0.3	−0.1	−1.4	−7.1	−6.2	8.0	2.3
1951–2	6.8	6.7	5.1	10.8	5.0	14.8	8.1
1953–5	1.1	0.7	0.3	4.0	0.0	−0.2	3.4
1956–9	3.7	2.6	2.2	1.0	2.0	6.2	2.7
1960–4	3.5	2.2	1.2	5.4	2.3	4.0	2.6
1965–9	4.8	3.6	3.4	5.3	2.5	3.8	4.3
1970–2	5.9	5.2	4.5	6.1	4.7	5.8	7.6
1973	9.4	7.6	6.2	11.6	7.0	7.3	9.2
1974	15.3	13.2	11.0	23.2	7.0	13.7	15.9
1975	13.5	11.2	9.1	11.8	5.9	11.8	24.3
1976	10.7	8.3	5.8	9.4	4.3	9.6	16.6
1977	11.1	8.6	6.5	8.2	3.7	9.4	15.8
1978	9.4	7.3	7.6	4.2	2.7	9.1	8.3
1979	12.4	9.2	11.3	3.7	4.1	10.8	13.4
1980	15.7	11.9	13.5	7.7	5.4	13.3	18.0
1981	14.4	10.1	10.3	4.9	6.3	13.4	11.9
1982	12.7	7.5	6.2	2.7	5.3	11.8	8.6
1983	12.8	5.1	3.2	1.9	3.3	9.6	4.6
1984	10.6	4.6	4.3	2.3	2.4	7.4	5.0
1985	10.2	4.0	3.6	2.0	2.2	5.8	6.1
1986	7.2	2.3	1.9	0.6	−0.2	2.5	3.4
1987	9.3	2.9	3.7	0.1	0.3	3.3	4.2
1988	13.3	3.3	4.0	0.7	1.2	2.7	4.9

Source: *International Financial Statistics, 1989 Yearbook.*

Germany or the United States that gave a higher priority to combating inflation. The monetarist view at that time was not very different: monetarists preferred to argue straight from monetary policy to inflation rather than recognize the intervening effect on employment, but given that they thought of monetary policy as money-supply policy and regarded that as under national control, they still thought of inflation as a series of national phenomena. When national policies proved incompatible to the point of jeopardizing external balance, both schools accepted that the country that was out of line should change its exchange rate to restore PPP.

This view of inflation was challenged by two fundamental analytical developments in the late 1960s. Monetarists played an important role in both, while many Keynesians resisted both. The fact that events soon demonstrated that both contained substantial elements of truth perhaps did more than anything else to undermine the credibility of Keynesianism and entrench monetarism, despite the fact that the logical link to the rest of the monetarist creed is not particularly strong.

The first new development was of course the Phelps–Friedman accelerationist theory, or the vertical long-run Phillips curve, already sketched in section 12.5. This amounted to reinterpreting the Phillips curve as representing the net balance of desired *relative* price changes. To deduce the corresponding actual rate of price change, it is necessary to add the expected rate of inflation. Then, if you add the adaptive expectations hypothesis (see section 14.4), according to which expected inflation will adjust towards the rate actually experienced, one can conclude that any attempt to hold unemployment below the natural rate will generate accelerating inflation – such as the world experienced from the mid-1950s to the mid-1970s.

Taken by itself, the natural rate hypothesis would suggest that each individual country would experience an acceleration of inflation that depended on how close it was operating to full employment. But in fact the inflationary acceleration was more uniform across countries than that could have explained. This is where the second analytical innovation entered: the view that under a fixed exchange-rate system (such as the world largely retained till 1971, or even 1973) inflation was a single global phenomenon, rather than a series of national phenomena.

Monetarists advanced two main analytical grounds for this assertion. The first is that price levels are kept in line internationally by arbitrage. We already encountered this global monetarist claim in section 13.4 and concluded that the empirical evidence strongly refutes the extreme version of the hypothesis. But this is not to dismiss it altogether. Empirical price equations typically do find a role for foreign competitors' prices, as well as for domestic costs (with the former, quite plausibly, being more important in explaining export prices than domestic prices, and more important in small countries than in large ones). This implies that inflation will spill over from one country to its trading partners and hence that inflation rates will tend to move in parallel internationally.

The second principal channel that monetarists argued must maintain parallel inflation rates within a fixed exchange-rate area is the spillover of money through the balance of payments. An expansion in domestic credit in one country will tend to flow out through an increased payments deficit, on current or capital account or both, which will swell the reserves and – in the absence of complete sterilization – the money supplies of its trading partners. Thus monetary expansion gets spread around the world and generates inflation more or less equally everywhere so long as exchange rates remain fixed. The central question in understanding world inflation then becomes understanding how the world money supply is determined. Section 19.1 demonstrated how under a gold standard the world money supply is determined in large measure by the stock of gold reserves and that the reserve gain and consequent expansionary impulse in the surplus countries is offset by the increasing pressure to reverse their expansionary policies in the credit-creating deficit countries. However, the world was not on a symmetrical gold standard in the late 1960s but on a somewhat asymmetrical gold exchange standard that came close to being a totally asymmetrical dollar standard after creation of the two-tier gold market in 1968. This has strong implications for the world money supply process, as the Swiss economist Alexander Swoboda (b. 1939) has analyzed most extensively. Since dollars that flow out through a United States payments deficit were added to other countries' reserves rather than depleting the stock of United States reserve assets, the United States could afford to – and did – sterilize its deficit completely. Meanwhile those dollars provided high-powered money that generated monetary expansion in other countries. Thus under a dollar standard United States monetary policy provides the motive force driving world monetary expansion.

This analysis suggests that the key event in igniting world inflation was the superimposition of the Vietnam War on President Lyndon Johnson's ambitious Great Society social programme in the United States. Given the absence of an external payments constraint, it was all too easy to finance a good part of the resulting fiscal deficit by monetary expansion. In due course the United States payments deficit exploded, and other countries imported inflation. The abandonment of pegged exchange rates in early 1973 was, in this view, a consequence of the unwillingness of countries like Germany and Switzerland to continue importing inflation. Floating against the dollar gave them the option of appreciating instead of buying dollars, and thus permitted them to secure a lower rate of inflation – which is precisely what they proceeded to do.

Economists in the eclectic mainstream accept the basic notion that inflation rates within a fixed exchange-rate area cannot diverge very far, but they tend to argue that the monetarist version goes too far in some respects and not far enough in others. It goes too far when it argues that price levels are rigidly pegged together through arbitrage, that countries cannot inflate themselves into uncompetitiveness, that devaluation cannot improve competitiveness and that inflation can be brought down to the international norm without the threat of a drastic departure from internal balance simply by pegging the exchange rate. But it does not go far enough when it concentrates attention on arbitrage and money spillovers as the *only* channels tending to keep inflation rates in line internationally. One other channel that is certainly important in practice is the direct cost-push effect of increased prices of imported raw materials and intermediate goods. Another is the demand-pull effects that are generated by increased exports and import substitution when a country becomes more competitive as a result of foreign inflation not neutralized by an exchange-rate change. It is even possible – and was seriously suggested in the late 1960s, when the French Events of May 1968 were followed by increased labour militancy in other European countries – that a successful union wage push in one country can induce emulation in others.

An adequate theory of inflation needs to recognize the existence of a series of proximate sources of inflationary pressure. These include the pressure of domestic demand; domestic cost pressures (stemming, for example, from the attempts of labour to achieve collectively more real income than is available); imported inflation, stemming from foreign price rises; quasi-imported inflation, arising from exchange depreciation – which has similar effects, though not causes, to foreign price rises; and inflationary inertia, arising from inflationary expectations or indexation. If one wishes to think in Phillips-curve terms, one would say that the first factor determines the position on the Phillips curve, while all the others influence its position. Thus an upward shift of the short-run Phillips curve is produced by increased inconsistency of real-income claims, higher foreign inflation, depreciation, increased inflationary expectations or, where indexation is present, higher past inflation. There is no inconsistency between this eclectic view of the proximate sources of inflationary pressure and recognition that in the long run inflation in a closed economy will stay close to the growth rate of the money supply. Nor is this eclectic view in any way inconsistent with recognition that in the long run inflation in an open economy with a fixed exchange rate will stay close to inflation in the rest of the world. The eclectic view does, however, suggest that recognition of such long-run truths does not by itself furnish an adequate basis for policy formation, since the transitional consequences of anti-inflationary policy are critically important and can be profoundly influenced by the anti-inflation strategy that is adopted.

While certainly not dismissing the significance of the inflationary financing of the Vietnam War, an eclectic interpretation of the origins of the inflationary explosion of the early 1970s would suggest that there were other important reinforcing factors at work. First, there appears to have been a tendency in at least some countries for real-income aspirations to run increasingly far ahead of what the economy could generate. The outstanding examples were the French Events of May 1968 and the British wage explosion of autumn 1969. Second, there were adverse supply shocks, particularly in the form of the failure of the Soviet grain harvest in 1972 and the disappearance of the anchovy from the Peruvian coast due to past overfishing in 1973. Third, the cyclical expansion of 1973 was probably the most synchronized the world has ever seen. In the short run, GWP grew by almost 7 per cent in the year, a record. But the cost was to bid up the prices of raw materials in a commodity boom unprecedented since the Korean War and thus add yet another reinforcement to the inflationary momentum. What was a cost-push effect from the viewpoint of each individual country was a clear case of demand-pull at the global level.

The explanation for the breakdown of the exchange-rate system of Bretton Woods offered by the mainstream view is not very different to the monetarist interpretation already noted. Even with fixed exchange rates, countries could experience faster or slower inflation than their partners for a while. But if they did not ratify such a discrepancy by an exchange-rate change, the pressures to drag them back into line multiplied. Countries with above normal domestic inflationary pressures found themselves with overvalued currencies, and therefore confronted with a three-way choice between devaluation, chronic current account deficit and unemployment. Countries that succeeded in curbing domestic inflation found themselves in the converse situation, forced to choose between revaluation, increasing external surplus and importing inflation. As long as world inflation remained generally low, most countries found the common rate of inflation dictated by fixed exchange rates tolerable – although even before 1973 there were occasional changes in exchange rates caused mainly by some combination of differing cost-push pressures and differing determination to resist inflation. But as inflation accelerated, both countries like Britain that had allowed their internal inflationary momentum to get out of hand, and those like Germany, that resented having to import the common rate of inflation, found the situation intolerable. Agreed international monetary reforms relevant to the situation (like general crawling to allow inflation differentials to be accommodated or a restoration of dollar convertibility to discipline United States monetary policy) not being forthcoming, exchange rates were allowed to float from March 1973.

Floating allows inflation rates to diverge, which they duly did after 1973 (see Table 20.3). It also has profound repercussions on the nature of international spillover effects. Under fixed rates, an expansion of demand in one country increases demand in its trading partners and therefore has an inflationary impact involving a shift along the Phillips curve. In contrast, under floating a demand expansion – at least if engineered by monetary policy – causes the domestic currency to depreciate and hence foreign currencies to appreciate, which will help to counter their inflation, by shifting the Phillips curve. (It was also traditionally argued that a monetary expansion in one country would lead to a demand contraction in its partners, but this inverse transmission of the business cycle presupposed an absence of capital mobility and does not in fact occur.)

Floating also changes the terms of policy trade-offs. In particular, monetary expansion comes to imply depreciation rather than a loss of reserves. As noted in section 19.5, there has been an inconclusive debate as to whether this is likely to erode or to accentuate the discipline to avoid inflationary policies. In the case of the United States, however, where payments deficits had ceased to involve reserve losses under the dollar standard, there is a presumption that the move to floating strengthened the incentive to avoid inflationary monetary policies. In fact the industrial countries showed themselves willing to pay a high price, in terms of acceptance of higher levels of unemployment, in the attempt to bring inflation down. Despite that, it stayed stubbornly high through the 1970s. Two reasons can be suggested for this. One is that many countries largely limited anti-inflationary policy to adoption of a restrictive monetary policy, under the influence of the prevailing monetarist belief that the only factors relevant to the determination of inflation are the exchange rate, excess demand and expectations. (The more successful countries, like Austria, Germany and Japan, made a broader-based attack, not neglecting incomes policy.) The second reason is that the problem of inflation was much aggravated by the oil price increases – a new page of history, with the additional problems that emerged in 1974.

20.4 The oil deficit

In the last quarter of 1973 the price of the most important commodity in world trade quadrupled, thus transferring some 2 per cent of GWP from the importers to the exporters of oil. The immediate consequences included a further boost to the already rapid world inflation and the creation of historically unprecedented imbalances on current account. More fundamental still, the great boom finally petered out, to be replaced by an epoch of stagflation that was far more difficult for everyone except the oil exporters.

Unlike demand management in the 1960s or the inflationary explosion of the early 1970s, no one could interpret the oil shock as a matter of exclusive concern to the developed countries. In the first place, the change was a consequence of the success

Table 20.4 Global balance of payments summary, 1972–80 ($ billion)

	Current balance			Capital balance			Monetary balance		
	Industrial countries	OPEC	LDCs	Industrial countries	OPEC	LDCs	Industrial countries	OPEC	LDCs
1972	9.?	2.0	−13.6	−12.2	1.4	18.2	n.a.	n.a.	n.a.
1973	11.3	6.2	−8.7	−13.2	−1.9	19.0	10.1	4.3	10.5
1974	−9.6	66.7	−42.9	−5.3	−23.7	39.5	21.8	43.1	−0.3
1975	19.4	35.0	−51.3	−19.6	−15.0	43.1	8.3	20.1	2.0
1976	−0.5	40.0	−32.9	−4.6	−31.3	41.4	25.6	8.8	17.1
1977	−4.6	31.1	−28.6	3.6	−20.8	41.3	78.1	10.3	11.5
1978	30.8	3.3	−37.5	−18.1	−13.3	53.8	77.1	−10.0	15.3
1979	−7.8	68.4	−57.6	32.4	−54.4	67.5	−2.4	14.0	10.3
1980	−44.1	112.2	−82.1	51.3	−92.5	80.3	56.2	19.7	4.2

Note: There is an element of ambiguity in distinguishing capital outflows from reserve accumulation in some OPEC members. There is an important accounting asymmetry in Euromarket operations, since a reserve placement at a Eurobank permits a capital account inflow to the country that borrows from the Eurobank. This is the principal explanation of the regular world surpluses on both capital and monetary balances.
Sources: International Monetary Fund. *Annual Reports*, 1974, 1976, 1980, 1981.

of OPEC in increasing the price of oil. A group of non-industrial countries used their economic muscle to effect a major redistribution of income in their favour. Second, the victims of the oil price increase were not just the developed countries but included the oil-importing developing countries. Indeed, it is now clear that the area that suffered most was sub-Saharan Africa. Third, the middle-income developing countries exploited their newly established creditworthiness to adopt a strategy of debt-led growth. This had a significant effect in limiting the North's recession and quickly transferred the whole of the oil deficit – the counterpart to the OPEC surplus – away from the developed countries (see Table 20.4). In short, global macro-economics had become truly global: one could no longer hope to understand the evolution of the system by studying a limited part of it.

There are six ways in which the oil price increase had a significant impact on the evolution of the world economy, apart from the obvious effect of increasing potential income in the OPEC gainers and reducing it for the oil importers.

1. Higher oil prices gave a direct impulse to costs of production and thus to the rate of inflation. They also reduced the total available real income in the oil-importing countries, thus intensifying the inconsistency in real-income claims that was already generating inflation in many countries, and so made it more difficult and costly to reduce inflation through conventional policies of demand restraint.

2. Since the oil exporters lacked the inclination, not to mention the physical capacity,[4] to spend a large part of their extra income in the short run, the world propensity to save rose. This had a contractionary effect on world demand. In association with the restrictive fiscal–monetary policies that had been adopted in most of the leading industrial countries to combat inflation, it pushed the world into

the 1975 recession, the most severe since the Great Depression (at least prior to 1982).

3. The increase in the value of oil exports, without a corresponding short-run rise in the value of OPEC imports, resulted in unprecedented imbalances on the current account of the balance of payments (see Table 20.4). The OPEC surplus necessarily had as its counterpart a corresponding[5] current account deficit distributed between the other two groups – the so-called oil deficit. In 1974 (as again after the second oil price increase in 1979–80) this was indeed split between the two groups, but the contrast between the contractionary policies of the industrial countries and the attempt of the LDCs to resist a major slowdown in growth soon led to the whole of the oil deficit being carried by the LDCs. This was, of course, possible only because of their success in tapping the world capital market, which succeeded in recycling petrodollars from OPEC to the deficit countries, as analyzed in section 18.1.

4. Over time, the OPEC countries started to use their increased earnings to buy more imports and hire more foreign workers. This was the major reason for the near-disappearance of the oil surplus in 1978, when only the low absorbers remained in significant current account surplus. It provided an especially important cushion for countries close to the main OPEC markets, especially the non-oil Arab countries, but also India and Pakistan. The oil importers faced a potential transfer problem in switching resources to meet the increased OPEC demand, but in fact the transfer process encountered no dificulties.

5. The rise in the relative price of oil created incentives to modify production techniques and consumption patterns to economize on the use of petroleum and energy in general and also to exploit more fully alternative sources of energy. This effect was tempered after the first oil price increase by uncertainty as to whether the higher energy prices were going to stick, but evidence suggests there was significantly more response after the 1979–80 increases. As of the late 1980s, it appeared that energy consumption in the industrial countries was over 30 per cent below what it would have been on the basis of pre-1973 trends.

6. The increased relative oil price decreased the rate of growth of potential output of the world economy. The qualitative effects are shown in Figure 20.1. First, some previously installed energy-intensive capital goods must have become uneconomic at the higher oil prices, thus leading to a one-time decline in potential output as shown by the downward step in the growth path. Second, a part of investment was diverted from sectors like manufacturing with a relatively low ICOR to the production of alternative forms of energy or to economizing on energy, which are much more capital-intensive activities. This reduced the increase in output that resulted from a given level of investment and thus the growth rate of potential output, as shown by the shallower slope of the new growth path in Figure 20.1. The growth accountants like Edward Denison reckon that this factor explained a fall of perhaps 0.3 per cent per annum in the rate of growth of United States potential output after the first oil shock, out of a total decline of about 1.5 per cent per annum. In other words, while it would be quite wrong to dismiss the effect of the oil price increase, there were other and more important factors at work in bringing the rapid expansion of the great boom to an end.

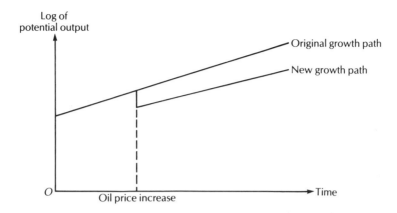

Figure 20.1 Impact of an oil price increase on potential output

One major factor was the approach to technological maturity. By the early 1970s both Western Europe and Japan had largely eliminated the stock of labour in low productivity and subsistence sectors, whose transfer to the modern sector had been at the root of their rapid growth from the end of post-war reconstruction to about 1970. Perhaps the most impressive evidence for believing this to be the major explanation is the fact (documented in Table 20.5) that in the 1970s Japan slipped from being the fastest-growing to the slowest-growing of the capitalist economies of East Asia. It is not easy to think of an explanation that can account so naturally for such a striking change in ranking, except that Japan has closed the technological gap with the West while the rest of the region still has much leeway that it is making up.

A second major factor, which has been much emphasized by Bruno and Sachs, is

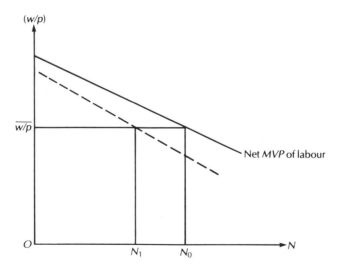

Figure 20.2 Impact of an oil price increase on employment

Table 20.5 Growth rates of GNP/GDP of capitalist East Asia (% per annum)

	1960–70	1970–9
Hong Kong	10.0	9.4
Indonesia	3.9	7.6
Japan	10.5	5.2
Korea	8.6	10.3
Malaysia	6.5	7.9
Philippines	5.1	6.2
Singapore	8.8	8.4
Taiwan	9.2	7.7[1]
Thailand	8.2	7.7

[1] For period 1970 to 1977.
Sources: World Bank, *World Development Report 1981*, app. table 2; used by permission. For Taiwan, Johns Hopkins University Press, *World Tables* (Baltimore, 1980).

real-wage rigidity. The higher oil price decreased the real income available to share between labour and capital: that is, it reduced the net marginal value product (MVP) of labour at any given level of employment, as shown by the leftward shift of the schedule to its dashed position in Figure 20.2. If labour resists a fall in the real wage from its initial value of $(\overline{w/p})$, the effect is to reduce employment from N_0 to N_1. And if governments attempt to expand employment back to N_0 by Keynesian demand expansion, the result is explosive inflation.

Even without the oil price increase, therefore, the 1970s would probably have been a decade of stagflation – of slowing output as opportunities for easy growth were exhausted in the developed countries, of continuing inflation as real-income aspirations remained ahead of the collective possibilities, and of increasing unemployment as governments sought to combat unemployment in the lopsided ideologically fashionable way which excluded any attempt to maintain equilibrium real wages through incomes policy. These problems were accentuated rather than caused by the oil price increase.

The massive current account imbalances superimposed on a stagflationary world economy were, in contrast, a direct result of the oil price increase. Those imbalances provoked fears on two distinct scores.

First, there were renewed worries about a possible inconsistency in current account targets of the same sort that caused concern in the OECD in the 1960s but on a much bigger scale. In place of the division of a collective *surplus* of $5 billion to $10 billion among the OECD countries, the problem was how to divide up a collective *deficit* of $30 billion or $40 billion among the oil importers. There were fears that countries might refuse to accept their fair share of the oil deficit and that the attempt to adjust deficits away more quickly than OPEC was increasing its imports would drive the world into renewed protectionism, competitive devaluation or cumulative deflation. The only one of these that would have cut the OPEC surplus, as opposed to shifting it around, was deflation, but this would have been an extremely costly solution –

elimination of the OPEC surplus of perhaps 0.5 per cent of GWP would have required a cut of perhaps 10 per cent in GWP.[6] Some economists therefore recommended that the IMF should get into the business of developing sensible rules of thumb that would enable it to allocate consistent current account targets to its member countries. As usual, the forces of inertia prevailed, and the facts that the rise in protectionism was limited, that there was no sign of competitive devaluation and that the non-system muddled through were adduced to demonstrate the wrongheadedness of those who called for a more active IMF role.

The second fear was that countries might be unable to finance the current account deficits that they were willing to accept: that is, the fear that the recycling process might break down. This fear reached its peak in the second half of 1974, following the failure of the Herstatt Bank in Germany and of the Franklin National Bank in the United States. The fear was reinforced by the spectre of a major industrial country – Italy – unable to borrow more from the private market and forced to use its gold as collateral to raise a loan from Germany in order to finance its current account deficit. There were subsequent crises of overindebtedness in countries like Peru, Turkey and Zaire, which were overcome after the countries involved adopted severe measures of economic retrenchment under the tutelage of the IMF. There was, however, no general breakdown in the process of recycling in the 1970s. And by 1978 there seemed grounds to hope that the dangers were past: the OPEC surplus had been whittled down, the industrial countries were back in comfortable current account surplus (and with the prospect of a reasonable balance among them) and the LDC deficit was down close to a sustainable level. Then came the Iranian revolution, the consequential cutback in oil supplies, the new oil price increases of 1979–80 and the resulting transfer of a further 2 per cent of GWP from the importers to the exporters of oil. The oil deficit re-emerged and with it new worries as to the sustainability of the recycling process, which on this occasion proved well founded.

Although southern growth held up much better than did northern growth after the first oil shock, it nevertheless declined. This was the first reversal of the acceleration in the trend of LDC growth since the Second World War. It was attributed not just to the drag of high oil prices, but also to the weakening of external demand by the OECD countries.

By 1976, in fact, concern had begun to grow in some OECD countries about the weakness of recovery from the 1975 recession. President Jimmy Carter's administration and the OECD led a call for a co-ordinated economic expansion to get the world economy expanding more rapidly. First the three major countries in strong payments positions (the United States, Japan and Germany) were likened to locomotives that would be able to pull the world out of recession without causing payments problems for each other if they expanded jointly. Then, when a number of other countries were in stronger payments positions, the locomotive approach was supplanted by the convoy approach, under which a convoy of countries was supposed to expand demand simultaneously. The idea was again to relieve countries of the dangers of an isolated expansion, in terms both of bigger current account deficits and of currency depreciation leading to an acceleration of inflation. In the event, Germany and Japan agreed to adopt more expansionary policies only in mid-1978, in the course of a summit conference in Bonn, but by that time the United States was already suffering from a recrudescence of the problems of deficit, depreciation and inflation, which were aggravated by the fact that its previous expansion had been isolated.

The same type of analysis that supported the case for a concerted OECD expansion in 1976–8 suggested that a resumption of northern growth was what was needed to pull the South back on to a higher growth path and reverse the trend towards increasing indebtedness. Some economists, like Nicholas Kaldor, argued that increased northern demand would meet an elastic southern supply of manufactures. Others, like Lance Taylor, view the world economy in structuralist terms, as driven by the interaction between a Keynesian (demand-constrained) North that produces manufactures and a neo-classical (supply constrained) South that produces primary products. Higher northern demand, generated by deficit spending by northern governments or livelier animal spirits on the part of northern entrepreneurs, would raise the demand for (but not the supply of) primary products and so shift income towards the South. Conversely, a northern decision to fight inflation by demand restraint reduces the relative price of the South's output: to the extent that it succeeds in curbing inflation, it does this by squeezing southern incomes and so relieving the inconsistency of northern real-income claims. Not surprisingly, the South tends to wish that the North would find another solution to the problem of reconciling inconsistent claims to real income.

The view that faster growth by one part of the world economy will necessarily have positive spillover effects for other areas is not, however, universally accepted. The most striking alternative hypothesis was one that emerged in 1979, when the oil price was being bid up by the competitive scramble of the oil importers to ensure access to supplies. It was suggested that the supply of energy was so inelastic that world output was effectively limited by an energy constraint, rather than by the level of productive capacity. An expansion of world output would at some point lead to a bidding up of energy prices that would continue until the redistribution of income to the high-saving oil exporters cut back demand. This hypothesis would imply that the oil importers were engaged in a zero-sum game among themselves: higher output by one could be sustained only if output elsewhere fell and so reduced the demand for energy to the available supply. In such a world, developed countries would have no incentive to ease the LDC payments constraint by liberalizing their imports, increasing aid or sustaining the recycling process.

20.5 Payments imbalances in the 1980s

One of the expectations of advocates of floating exchange rates was that these would help to maintain balance of payments equilibrium. Ironically, in the 1980s floating rates helped to generate the largest current account imbalances in history – imbalances even larger than the oil deficits of the 1970s. By 1986 the United States had a current account deficit equal to some 3 per cent of its GNP, for which the principal counterpart surpluses were nearly 5 per cent and around 4 per cent of GNP in Japan and Germany respectively.

The origin of these imbalances is to be found in the contrasting macroeconomic policies pursued. Early in the decade virtually all the industrial countries were principally preoccupied with fighting inflation. If that had the incidental effect of putting pressure on OPEC and reducing the oil price, as it ultimately did, this was regarded as a side-benefit. If it provoked a debt crisis among Third World borrowers, as it also did in due course, that was regarded as unfortunate. But the priority was to fight inflation, and in the age of monetarism the only tool that most people took seriously was monetary restraint.

Where policies came to differ sharply was on the fiscal front. While Europe and Japan had become concerned at the size of the fiscal deficit that had developed in the 1970s, and were therefore embarking on a programme of fiscal consolidation even in the face of recession, the United States administration had been captured by supply-side ideologues who managed to convince themselves that cutting tax rates would actually increase tax revenue and reduce the budget deficit. This did not happen, but the fiscal expansion certainly created a strong Keynesian demand expansion that pulled the United States out of the 1982 recession far more briskly than Europe or even Japan recovered. The cumulative growth over the period 1982–7 was 20 per cent in the United States versus only 12 per cent in OECD Europe.

Such a growth gap could by itself have been expected to produce a sizeable shift in payments balances due to income effects. However, it was mightily reinforced by the appreciation of the dollar, whose real effective exchange rate rose by over 40 per cent between 1980 and its peak in February 1985. The appreciation of the dollar was in turn the result, at least in its initial stages, of the differential fiscal policies being pursued in the United States and the other industrial countries: fiscal profligacy in the United States served to push up the relative interest rate there and thus attract capital inflows that bid up the dollar, at least while confidence lasted. For the last few months of the dollar's appreciation, from mid-1984 to February 1985, the interest differential in favour of the dollar actually fell; that final run-up can be interpreted only as a speculative bubble.

The massive payments imbalances provoked two types of concern. The dominant one was that one day the markets would wake up to appreciate the unsustainability of what was happening, just as they had done in Mexico in 1982, and that confidence in the dollar would as a result collapse. Some economists thought this might happen overnight. Others anticipated a long period during which the dollar would slide down, the Fed would raise interest rates to defend the dollar, but then the J-curve would increase the US deficit, confidence would erode further and the dollar would slide further anyway, leading to a 'hard landing' involving a simultaneous intensification of inflation from the dollar's fall and recession from the need to tighten both monetary and fiscal policy to restore confidence. Since such growth as there was elsewhere in the world at that time was export led, a US recession would translate into a world recession.

The other concern sparked by the US deficit was that it would trigger irresistible protectionist pressures in the US Congress. This indeed seemed to be happening in 1985: by September of that year no fewer than 300 protectionist bills were before the

Congress. The US exporting community had been so decimated by the overvalued dollar that the normal free-trade counterweight to the industrial cripples that lobby for protection had vanished. Even though the deficit could still be financed easily through capital inflows, the US administration decided that it had to act to head off the protectionist assault on the trading system. It convened a meeting at the New York Plaza Hotel in September 1985, where all five major countries (the members of the G–5) found it easy to agree that the dollar was too high and should decline. They encouraged this by their public pronouncements, by (sterilized) intervention in the exchange markets and by modifications to monetary policy, with Japan raising its interest rates and the United States tending to ease.

The dollar did indeed decline in the months that followed, in a series of step-like movements. By early 1987 it had fallen back close to its level before the great appreciation of the early 1980s. Amid signs that the market anticipated further declines and that interest rates were rising while the currency was falling (a classic symptom of eroding confidence), the G–7 announced at a meeting at the Louvre in Paris that exchange rates had moved enough. The Louvre Accord also stated the desirability of fiscal consolidation in the United States and of faster growth in Europe and Japan – a sentiment that was backed up by Japanese fiscal expansion two months later when the yen was threatening to appreciate even more.

After the stock market crash in October 1987 the Federal Reserve loosened monetary policy and the dollar began to depreciate again. The G–7 mounted a formidable bear squeeze in the first days of 1988, which proved highly effective in changing market sentiment and preventing any further fall. This experience compelled a revision of the conventional wisdom of the early 1980s, which held that sterilized intervention was ineffective in influencing exchange rates. Indeed, the dollar tended to become rather too strong for comfort in the following two years.

Although exchange-rate changes are usually a necessary part of an adjustment programme, they are not by themselves generally sufficient (Chapter 12). Indeed, the effect of an exchange-rate change on the balance of payments depends on what *causes* the exchange rate to change. Typical estimates are that a 10 per cent dollar devaluation will improve the US current account by $70 billion if the dollar is devalued because a tighter fiscal policy lowers interest rates, by around $10 billion if the dollar falls because of an exogenous change in portfolio preferences (or sterilized intervention) and by nothing at all if the devaluation is induced by an easier monetary policy (the difference being accounted for by income effects, which go in opposite directions with a fiscal tightening and a monetary easing). Thus most economists regarded the promise of a tighter US fiscal policy as an essential complement to the lower dollar in curbing the US payments deficit.

The US current account deficit peaked in 1987, two years after the dollar had peaked, and then declined to around $100 billion as this goes to press in 1991. This result is more or less what the models predicted, given the boom that developed in Europe and Japan and the modest fiscal improvement and easing of growth in the United States.

A deficit of 2 per cent of GNP is, however, still large. Moreover, the central expectation is that the deficit will grow rather than decline on the basis of the policy stance as it was in the first half of 1990. Three factors underlie this expectation. First, as US debt builds up due to the continuing current account deficit, so does the interest cost of servicing the debt: at a 10 per cent interest rate, this factor is increasing the deficit at about $10 billion each year. Second, there is the 'gap factor': if both imports and exports grow in value in future at the same rate, the difference between them will increase simply because imports are initially larger than exports. For example, if both grow at 10 per cent per annum and the initial difference is $100 billion, the deficit will grow at $10 billion each year because of the gap factor. Third, the dollar has appreciated since the beginning of 1988: this must be expected to worsen the current account in due course unless US growth remains below its potential.

Does a build-up of US external debt of 2 per cent of GNP, and tending to increase again in the future, matter? This remains a controversial issue. Some economists argue that in the brave new world of capital mobility the United States will encounter no problem in financing deficits on this scale indefinitely. Some claim that the capital inflow is a reflection of the high rates of return created by the health of the economy. Others point to expected demographic trends over the next two decades, during which the baby-boom generation will move into the high-savings phase of the life-cycle in the United States, while the retired population builds up in Europe and Japan, thus tending to shift world savings from the Eastern to the Western Hemisphere.

The optimists also point out that the official debt estimates overstate the net external 'debt' of the United States. Despite the official estimate of a net international investment position of −$535 billion at the end of 1988, the United States had a deficit on investment income of only $1 billion in 1989. This is partly because the United States tends to earn a higher rate of return on its assets than it has to pay on its liabilities: most US direct investments abroad have been in place much longer than foreign investments in the United States, and have thus passed the start-up phase when earnings are low, while the US banking sector tends to receive low-yielding foreign deposits and make high-yielding loans (though admittedly the loans to problem debtors have turned out to yield less than expected). But it is also partly because US direct investments have not in general been revalued over time to reflect capital gains.

There is something in these arguments, except perhaps for the second, which would be convincing only if the capital inflow had been financing an investment boom (when in fact investment as a share of GNP was slightly smaller in the 1980s than in the 1970s: the counterpart to the current account deficit was in fact the increased fiscal deficit). Nevertheless, 2 per cent of GNP and rising looks to many to be too high for comfort. If the deficit were maintained at a constant 2 per cent of GNP, then the debt/GNP ratio would approach 29 per cent asymptotically.[7] This is somewhat below the 40 per cent that a common rule of thumb claims to be the maximum safe debt/GNP ratio. But the United States is still a relatively closed economy, with an export/GNP ratio of only 10 per cent. Thus a 29 per cent debt/GNP ratio translates into a 290 per cent debt/export ratio, well above the traditional prudent maximum of 200 per cent. And that assumes, contrary to the projections, that the deficit does not rise above 2 per cent of GNP.

These are presumably among the reasons that contributed to the decision of the Bush administration to make a serious attempt in mid-1990 to reduce the fiscal deficit. Another factor seems to have been pressure from Japan in the 'Structural Impediments Initiative' talks. These started as an attempt to outflank American protectionists who were convinced that the continuing US deficit and Japanese surplus, both multilateral and bilateral, were caused by subtle forms of Japanese protection ('structural impediments'). In the event the United States made a series of proposals for liberalizing Japan's domestic economy, many of which seem unlikely to have much impact on the trade balance but most of which should improve the welfare of the Japanese consumer. Japan countered with a series of proposals directed mainly to US macro policy, including fiscal policy. Both countries ended up by accepting the core of what the other had urged upon it, despite the sensitivity of the issues involved. The success of these talks provides a hopeful precedent for the way in which future international negotiations may overstep the traditional restraints of national sovereignty to a degree that had previously occurred only in the European Community, to the benefit of the citizens of all countries.

While international factors helped to change US policy, the decisive development was doubtless the projections that without policy changes the US budget deficit was set to increase again rather than decrease further. In any event, by June 1990 it had become clear that the Bush administration was intent on reducing the deficit, even at the cost of going back on candidate Bush's pledge not to raise taxes ('read my lips') in 1988. The result is the best hope since President Reagan's tax cuts in 1981 that the US budget will in due course be restored to balance. As the markets come to perceive this, long-term interest rates will fall: it is argued that because of this the short-run impact on income of a credible programme of fiscal restraint may well be positive. A part of the reason is that lower interest rates will depreciate the dollar, improving the current account. If it does, the debt build-up of the United States should be reined in before it results in the sort of catastrophe that afflicted so many LDC debtors in the 1980s.

20.6 Global environmental problems

In 1989 the 'economic summit' of the G–7, held in Paris on the occasion of the two hundredth anniversary of the French Revolution, spent more time discussing global environmental problems than the traditional staples of economic summits like policy co-ordination, exchange rates and the danger of protectionist pressures. It is unlikely to be the last time that meetings of world leaders are dominated by environmental concerns.

The environment first emerged as a widespread source of public concern in the early 1970s. Three types of issue were prominent at that time. The first set were essentially local issues, involving pollution of land, water and air. Even these issues had important cross-border spillover effects in Western Europe, with its small, densely populated countries, but elsewhere they could be adequately tackled by national governments.

The OECD nonetheless came to play a prominent role as a forum for exchanging information and ideas on how best to curb pollution. Being an organization dominated by economists, it became a counterweight to the initial bureaucratic tendency to assume that a government that wanted to cut pollution had to issue a set of administrative edicts telling industry what maximum permissible emissions were going to be. The OECD tended to argue instead for harnessing the price mechanism, by making the polluter pay through emission charges. This allows any given degree of clean-up to be achieved in the most efficient way, since there is an incentive to vary the resources devoted to pollution abatement both within and between firms to where they will be most effective. It also provides a continuing incentive to innovate in producing less polluting processes, which is again absent from a system of administrative ceilings on emissions.[8] Moreover, by setting the emission charge equal to the estimated marginal social damage being caused by pollution, industry is provided with an incentive to devote the optimal volume of resources to pollution abatement. (Those who place a higher value on a clean environment should campaign for higher emission charges, not for administrative regulations rather than emission charges.)

The combination of administrative regulations, emissions charges and high energy prices had a dramatic effect in ameliorating the more visible forms of local pollution over the following years. Chemical plants became less objectionable neighbours, many inland waterways stopped smelling and once again boasted of thriving fish stocks, and the air quality in major cities from London to Tokyo improved beyond recognition. Few people realized just how successful these policies had been until the opening of Eastern Europe in 1989 revealed the ecological catastrophe that had occurred in the absence of such policies.

The second set of issues that emerged in the early 1970s was raised by the 'Club of Rome', whose computer model projected that a relatively early exhaustion of many key natural resources would preclude continuing rapid economic growth. This threat seemed to receive quick confirmation with the quadrupling of the oil price in 1973. Resource depletion is inherently a global issue, since any individual country can compensate for the exhaustion of domestic stocks of a particular resource by importing it from elsewhere, but this is not possible for the closed economy of the earth (the biosphere).

Perception of this threat helped motivate the convening of the 1972 UN Conference on the Environment in Stockholm, which marked the first international recognition that environmental problems had a global dimension. Some developing countries were at that time hostile to international involvement in environmental protection, on the ground that this was a luxury that only rich countries could afford, while they had more urgent priorities ('send us your polluting industries', invited the Brazilian Minister of Industry). Despite such reservations, the conference was instrumental in awakening global consciousness and in creating a small permanent UN specialized agency for promoting continuing negotiations on environmental issues, the UN Environment Programme (UNEP) based in Nairobi.

It now seems clear that depletion of exhaustible resources is not in fact a significant threat to continued growth of the world economy. Supplies of most minerals, and hydrocarbon energy, are vast, while at the moment only a tiny fraction of the energy reaching the earth from the sun is tapped. Scientific ingenuity seems capable of finding substitutes for anything that does run into short supply once the incentive to search is perceived. The doomsday forecasts of the Club of Rome are no longer credible.

The third issue of major concern in the 1970s was the population explosion. The rate of growth of world population is now believed to have peaked in 1968, at about 2.1 per cent per annum. If such a rate of increase were maintained indefinitely, the world's population would multiply by almost eight times in the course of the century, reaching over 30 billion by 2070. Such numbers would clearly guarantee a global crisis – 'standing room only' – in a historically short period of time. Alarm at this prospect contributed to a substantial international effort to promote birth control.

This effort lagged in the 1980s. The major cause was spillover from the emotional anti-abortion campaign in the United States, which caused a cut-off of US funding to all agencies with any association with any form of abortion. But complacency on the population issue was also nurtured by the clear evidence that the world rate of population growth is now slowing, having fallen from its peak of about 2.1 per cent in 1968 to around 1.7 per cent in 1990, as a result of the lower fertility rates that accompany economic development (the 'demographic transition') and the increasing use of contraception. (But the absolute annual increase in the world's population, some 90 million, is still the highest it has ever been.) The UN's population projections now envisage world population stabilizing at about 14 billion in the second half of the next century.

Even if that projection is correct (and long-term population projections have not been noted for their accuracy in the past), there is a question as to whether the world economy will be able to sustain so many people, at least at reasonable living standards. This question is viewed more pessimistically by most biologists than by most economists, because of a basic difference in the paradigm they appeal to. Economists typically incorporate the natural world into their model in the form of a stock of (exhaustible or renewable) resources as a factor of production which yields diminishing returns. Having convinced themselves that depletion of exhaustible resources is not a problem, the only other potential problem is caused by diminishing returns as the labour/resources ratio climbs (and, with luck, that will be offset by technical progress).

The typical biological model is quite different. Think of the ability of a lake to sustain fishermen. The constraint on the fish population is typically the supply of nutrients in the lake, so fishing will – up to a certain point – leave the stock of fish intact; it will remove fish that have already reproduced, and leave the nutrients available to younger fish. But this regenerative feature of natural systems breaks down beyond some threshold. With too many fishermen, the stocks of young fish begin to be caught, reproduction is interfered with, the fishermen intensify their efforts to maintain their catch and the fish population crashes. This sequence has in fact occurred time after time.

The point is not that economists are unaware of this phenomenon. On the contrary, fisheries economists have known about it for years, pointed to it as a classic case of over-exploitation caused by a lack of property rights, and advocated restraints on the fish catch calibrated to limit extraction to the maximum sustainable rate.[9] The point is that economists do not think of increasing human population in a biosphere of constant size as analogous, in the way that biologists do. Perhaps the earth can support a population of 14 billion without a collapse of the biological support system, as most economists implicitly assume. Perhaps it cannot, as many biologists seem to fear. We do not know, and it seems sensible to try not to find out. That is the essence of the case for intensifying the effort to limit population growth. (Estimates suggest that, with universal access to contraception by the end of the 1990s, world population might be stabilized in the vicinity of 9 billion rather than 14 billion.)

Hence, with the controversial exception of population growth, the environmental problems that seemed most threatening in the early 1970s are not a cause of acute concern today. Unfortunately their place has been taken by a series of others: the threat to the ozone layer, global warming, loss of biological diversity, acid rain, loss of topsoil, nuclear safety . . . Note that virtually all of these problems (except perhaps the nuclear one) tend *ceteris paribus* to be magnified at least in proportion to the size of the human population. Note that they are all issues where cross-border spillovers are of critical importance: indeed, the first three are issues of quintessential global concern. Finally, it is interesting to note that the traditional concern with exhaustion of non-renewable resources has given way to concern over the adequacy of what was not traditionally thought of as an economic constraint at all: the ability of the biosphere to absorb waste.[10]

The principal success in dealing with the new issues has so far concerned negotiation of an international agreement to phase out chlorofluorocarbons (CFCs), chemicals with many constructive industrial applications from refrigeration to cleaning computer chips, but with the unfortunate side-effect of destroying the earth's ozone layer, which shields the planet's surface from cancer-causing ultra-violet radiation. The possibility that CFCs might deplete the stratospheric ozone layer was first hypothesized in 1974, some four decades after these seemingly benign chemicals had been invented. US consumers reacted remarkably quickly to the news of what was still an unproven threat: sales of spray aerosols (which were powered by CFCs) had already fallen by two-thirds by 1977, in the absence of government controls (which came the following year).[11]

With a few small exceptions (Canada and Scandinavia), other countries (at the behest of their chemical industries) were slow to follow the US lead. By the early 1980s scientific evidence seemed to suggest that the initial hypotheses had overstated the threat from ozone depletion. However, UNEP had taken up the cause of an international agreement to limit CFC emissions, and in 1982 it initiated negotiations to that end. In 1985 these yielded a Vienna Convention on Protection of the Ozone Layer, whose signatories accepted a general obligation to take 'appropriate measures' to protect the ozone layer as well as mechanisms for co-operation in research, monitoring and data exchange. Weak as these provisions were, they marked the first international effort to counter an environmental threat before it had actually materialized.

In late 1985 British scientists published their surprising discovery of an Antarctic 'ozone hole' larger than the continental United States, in which stratospheric ozone fell each Antarctic spring to more than 40 per cent below the levels recorded in the 1960s. Given the enormous scientific uncertainty that had prevailed until then, this presumably helped invigorate the next stage of international negotiations designed to control and ultimately phase out CFC production. These reached fruition in 1987 in the Montreal Protocol on Substances that Deplete the Ozone Layer, which provided for an immediate freeze on CFCs at 1986 levels and progressive cuts to halve global production by the end of the century. This Protocol entered into force at the beginning of 1989, having been ratified by twenty-nine countries accounting for over 80 per cent of global consumption.

Shortly after the Montreal Protocol had been signed, and long before it had been ratified, hard scientific evidence for the first time confirmed (1) that the layer of stratospheric ozone over major population centres in the Northern Hemisphere had diminished by small but significant amounts; and (2) that CFCs bore responsibility for the ozone hole over Antarctica. New projections suggested that the Montreal Protocol would allow a continuing build-up of chlorine in the stratosphere and hence progressive destruction of the ozone layer. Nothing short of a total phase-out of CFCs (and certain other compounds) would give hope of allowing ozone levels to recover, and even then only over decades. Such a phase-out was in fact agreed in mid-1990, but only after the developed countries had agreed to establish a fund to finance technology transfer to allow developing countries to substitute the alternatives to CFCs that were being developed in the North.

Environmentalists consider action to preserve the ozone layer a case where the benefits of protective action were large and the costs were relatively modest. Prevention of greenhouse warming, which is expected to occur through the accumulation of carbon dioxide (plus other greenhouse gases, including CFCs) in the atmosphere as a result principally of the combustion of carbon-based fuels, is a case in which the benefits of control are uncertain but potentially also large, while the costs will certainly be large. International negotiations on this topic have hardly begun. They are almost certain to be a major area of economic/environmental diplomacy in the 1990s. The scientific evidence is again agonizingly uncertain, just as it was with the ozone layer: we do not know how much CO_2 concentrations will build up, how much global temperatures will rise with a given build-up or how much damage a given temperature rise will do.[12] Indeed, there will probably be some benefits mixed in with the costs, in increasing photosynthesis (and thus crop yields) and in increasing rainfall in some arid parts of the world. Countries which anticipate minimal costs or even net benefits from a CO_2 build-up will obviously be reluctant to accede to an international convention restricting consumption of fossil fuels, and even those that can anticipate heavy costs from CO_2 build-up may regard it as advantageous to free-ride. Some economists believe that because of this free-rider problem the chances of averting continuing rapid CO_2 accumulation are negligible. That is probably a correct assessment if countries are as 'rational' as the consumers featured in economic theory, but as we remark in note 11, many consumers appear to be technically irrational, so perhaps there is hope.

The third global environmental threat that seems likely to feature in international negotiations in the 1990s is the loss of biological diversity. This threat is geographically widespread, including the oceans as well as within nation-states, but because of the incredible richness of life there, it is concentrated particularly in tropical forests. The benefits of preserving biodiversity accrue worldwide, primarily through preservation of a gene-pool which if not destroyed will undoubtedly find many economic applications in the future (the pool is hardly known at the moment). The costs of preservation fall primarily on the (developing) countries where the forests are located, in the form of forgone opportunities for economic exploitation of land currently forested. The host countries have few opportunities to recover benefits from genetic resources residing in the forest, owing to the lack of opportunities for patenting such resources and the difficulty of establishing from where the resources originated.

Given such pay-offs, any effective programme to internalize international spill-overs is virtually bound to involve transfers from developed to developing countries. Suggestions have periodically been advanced for debt forgiveness in exchange for forest conservation, which is a particular form of such transfers, and President Bush's June 1990 proposal that interest on public-sector debt owed to the United States could be paid in local currency which would be devoted to mutually agreed environmental purposes is an application of this idea. The best reason for hoping that progress may be made in this direction is the increasing evidence that the economic benefits of converting tropical forests to agricultural uses are often low or negative even from the narrowest economic perspective.

The question is also likely to be raised before long as to whether the current international regime provides an adequate framework for tackling environmental issues as they arise. So far these have been tackled mainly by the inflexible instruments of formal international agreements requiring parliamentary ratification (like the Law of the Sea, or the Montreal Protocol), supplemented by occasional massive UN conferences (Stockholm 1972, Rio de Janeiro, 1992). The World Bank is now seeking to create a 'Green Fund' which it can use to provide financial support for environmental projects, presumably especially those with important international spillover effects. But there is no regular ongoing international organization, except tiny UNEP, charged with responsibility for monitoring environmental issues. There is no organization charged with regular review of a country's policies, as is done for economic policies in the IMF and OECD. There is no substantial body of international civil servants responsible for monitoring what is happening, trying to anticipate problems before they emerge and empowered to recommend policy adjustments in an ongoing framework. There is no pool of national civil servants who have had the experience of working in such an international organization, either on the staff or as executive directors, and in the process absorbed a transnational perspective. Even if the World Bank gets its Green Fund, the kitty available to internalize international externalities will be trivial relative to the scale of the problem. In short, there seems to be a case either for expanding UNEP or for creating a new international organization.

20.7 Summary

Global economic interdependence has long since reached the point where study of world economic developments is essential to understand the prospects of individual countries. In the 1960s the international community developed efforts to influence the policies adopted by the major countries with a view to improving the performance of the system as a whole. However, the combination of insufficient instruments and overambitious employment targets in some of the central countries of the system led to the outbreak of inflation, which was generalized to the world as a whole by the attempt to preserve a fixed exchange-rate system. The adoption of floating allowed inflation rates to diverge, but it did not eliminate interdependence. The oil price increases magnified the problems of slower growth and stagflation that would in any event have troubled the 1970s, while creating new concerns regarding the proper distribution of payments deficits and the sustainability of the LDCs' debt-led growth.

In due course inflation was defeated by the adoption of stern monetary policies, but at the cost of precipitating the 1980–2 recession. This led to the debt crisis. Recovery from the recession was much faster in the United States than elsewhere, owing to the Keynesian fiscal expansion inadvertently nurtured by the Reagan tax cuts. But this lopsided expansion led to vast payments imbalances which threatened the United States with a 'hard landing'. So far this has been averted, and the willingness of the Bush administration to consider a tax increase raises the hope that the twin deficits may in the end be cured without a crisis.

In the meantime, global environmental problems have forced their way to the top of the international agenda. Agreement to phase out CFCs has already been reached. The next two global issues are likely to be limiting greenhouse warming and preserving biological diversity, both of which raise very difficult questions relating to the distribution of international costs for preventing events whose occurrence would impose potentially large but extremely uncertain damage. To those who believe that all the really interesting economic issues arise on the frontiers between economics and other disciplines, few topics can be more challenging than the need to make the modern world economy sustainable.

20.8 Bibliography

Richard Cooper (1968) wrote the classic work on the logic of policy co-ordination. The outbreak of worldwide inflation was analyzed in Krause and Salant (1977), with Swoboda's chapter providing a good statement of the monetarist interpretation. For the determination of the world money supply under fixed exchange rates, see Swoboda (1978). Analyses of the first oil shock can be found in Fried and Schultze (1975) and Corden (1977), while the Bruno–Sachs thesis regarding the failure of the real wage to adjust is in Bruno and Sachs (1985). On recovery from the 1980–2 recession and the danger of a hard landing, see Marris (1987) and Bryant, Holtham and Hooper (1988).

The doomsday forecasts of the Club of Rome were presented in Meadows *et al.* (1972). See OECD (1979) for an account of the role of the OECD in nurturing emission charges. Mathews (1990) provides a comprehensive survey of global environmental issues, with chapters *inter alia* on population growth, the ozone layer, greenhouse warming, biological diversity and international regime building. Nord-haus (1990) expresses a typical economist's caution in urging avoidance of panic response to the threat of greenhouse warming.

Notes

1. Supported by other German-speakers (including the Dutch, who can all speak German too).
2. The figures cited include an estimate for the increase in OECD income that comes about because of the induced rise in the rest of the world's income, but the figures do not include an estimate for that increase in the rest of the world's income.
3. Assuming, at least, that the targets are consistent.
4. Limited port capacity constituted a real constraint on the expansion of OPEC imports.
5. This neglects two factors: the centrally planned economies (which ran deficits of up to $10 billion per annum) and timing asymmetries. These were large in some years, especially when oil prices rose, since the oil exporters then included the value of their oil exports at the new high prices while the oil importers were still recording in their import statistics the cheap oil that had set to sea some weeks before.
6. In round numbers, oil provided 50 per cent of energy requirements, OPEC provided 60 per cent of the oil and OPEC's surplus was a third of its receipts. Thus, assuming a constant oil price, GWP would have had to fall by some 10 per cent if energy could not be economized.
7. When $\hat{Y}/Y = \hat{D}/D = 0.07$ and $\hat{D}/Y = 0.02$, $D/Y = (\hat{D}/Y)/(\hat{Y}/Y) = 0.02/0.07 = 0.286$.
8. Tradable permits to pollute provide an alternative mechanism that retains the above-mentioned benefits of emissions charges.
9. Strictly speaking, with a positive discount rate the optimal plan will involve initial exploitation somewhat above the maximum steady-state rate.
10. In his classic proof of the existence of general equilibrium, Debreu (1959) postulated the possibility of free disposal, and for years no one questioned the reasonableness of the assumption. (Can equilibrium be proved to exist *without* free disposal? The answer turns out to be yes, provided one permits negative prices for bads – a highly intuitive result.)
11. Repeated cases, over the last twenty years, where consumers have ceased purchasing products that have acquired a reputation for being environmentally harmful, despite the absence of any direct incentive and in the certain knowledge that individual actions are too small to feed back on individual welfare, would seem to pose a fundamental problem for the axiom of a purely self-interested consumer that underlies classical consumer theory. It seems (fortunately) that most of us are technically irrational, i.e. socially responsible.
12. The extent of the damage will depend on the *rate* at which the temperature rises as well as on how much it rises, since a slow increase gives more chance for the natural environment to adjust.

References

Agarwal, M., Askari, H. and Corson, W. (1975) 'A testing of the Ricardian theory of comparative advantage', *Economia Internazionale*, **28**, 341–52.

Alexander, S. S. (1952) 'Effects of a devaluation on a trade balance', *IMF Staff Papers*, April; reprinted in Caves and Johnson (1968).

Amano, A. (1977) 'Specific factors, comparative advantage and international investment', *Economica*, **44**, 131–44.

Aquino, A. (1981) 'Changes over time in the pattern of comparative advantage in manufactures: an empirical analysis of the period 1962–74', *European Economic Review*, **15**, 41–62.

Ashworth, W. (1962) *A Short History of the International Economy Since 1850*, 2nd edn, London: Longman.

Ayres, R. L. (1983) *Banking on the Poor*, Washington: Overseas Development Council.

Bacha, E. L. (1989) 'Debt crisis, net transfers, and the GDP growth rate of the developing countries', a paper presented at a conference at the Getúlio Vargas Foundation, Rio de Janeiro, 7–8 August; forthcoming in R. Dornsbusch and M. H. Simonsen (eds.), *The Economic Reconstruction of Latin America*.

Balassa, B. (1963) 'An empirical demonstration of the classical comparative cost theory', *Review of Economics and Statistics*, **45**, 231–8.

Balassa, B. (1964) 'The purchasing power parity doctrine: a reappraisal', *Journal of Political Economy*, **72**, 584–96.

Balassa, B. (1970) 'Growth strategies in semi-industrial countries', *Quarterly Journal of Economics*, **84**, 24–47.

Balassa, B. (ed.) (1975) *European Economic Integration*, Amsterdam: North Holland.

Balassa, B. (1979) 'The changing pattern of comparative advantage in manufactured goods', *Review of Economics and Statistics*, **61**, 259–66.

Balassa, B. (1980) *The Process of Industrial Development and Alternative Development Strategies*, Princeton Essays in International Finance, no. 141.

Balassa, B. (ed.) (1982) *Development Strategies in Semi-Industrialized Economies*, Baltimore: Johns Hopkins University Press.

Balassa, B. and Williamson, J. (1990) *Adjusting to Success: Balance of payments policy in the East Asian NICs*, revised edn, Washington: Institute for International Economics.

Baldwin, Robert E. (1952) 'The new welfare economics and gains in trade', *Quarterly Journal of Economics*, **66**, 91–101.

Baldwin, Robert E. (1969) 'The case against infant industry protection', *Journal of Political Economy*, **77**, 295–305.

Baldwin, Robert E. (1970) *Non-Tariff Distortions of International Trade*, Washington: Brookings Institution.

Baldwin, Robert E. (1971) 'Determinants of the commodity structure of US trade', *American Economic Review*, **61**, 126–46.

Baldwin Robert E. (1979) *Beyond the Tokyo Round Negotiations*, London: Trade Policy Research Centre.

Baldwin, Robert E. (1984) 'Trade policies in developed countries', in Jones and Kenen (1984).

Baldwin, Robert E. (1985) *The Political Economy of US Import Policy*, Cambridge, Mass.: MIT Press.

Baldwin, Robert E. (1988) *Trade Policy in a Changing World Economy*, London: Wheatsheaf.

Barro, R. J. (1976), 'Rational expectations and the role of monetary policy', *Journal of Monetary Economics*, **2**, 1–32.

Bell, M., Ross-Larson, B. and Westphal, L. (1984) 'Assessing the performance of infant industries', *Journal of Development Economics*, **16**, 101–28.

Bergsten, C. F. and Williamson, J. (1983) 'Exchange rates and trade policy', in W. R. Cline (ed.), *Trade Policy in the 1980s*, Washington: Institute for International Economics.

Bhagwati, J. N. (1956) 'Immizerizing growth: a geometrical note', *Review of Economic Studies*, **25**, 201–5.

Bhagwati, J. N. (1964) 'A survey of the theory of international trade', *Economic Journal*, **74**, 1–84.

Bhagwati, J. N. (1972) 'The United States in the Nixon era: the end of innocence', *Daedalus*.

Bhagwati, J. N. (1979) 'International factor movements and national advantage', *Indian Economic Review*, October.

Bhagwati, J. N. (ed.) (1982) *Import Competition and Response*, Chicago: Chicago University Press.

Bhagwati, J. N. (ed.) (1987) *International Trade: Selected readings*, 2nd edn, Cambridge, Mass.: MIT Press.

Bhagwati, J. N. (1989) 'Is free trade passé after all?', *Weltwirtschaftliches Archiv*, **125**, 17–44.

Bhagwati, J. N. and Bharadwaj, R. (1967) 'Human capital and the pattern of foreign trade: the Indian case', *Indian Economic Review*, **2**, 117–42.

Bhagwati, J. N. and Ramaswami, V. K. (1963) 'Domestic distortions, tariffs and the theory of optimum subsidy', *Journal of Political Economy*, **1**, 44–50.

Blanchard, O. J. (1979) 'Speculative bubbles, crashes and rational expectations', *Economic Letters*, **4**, 387–9.

Blaug, M. (1976) 'Human capital theory: a slightly jaundiced survey', *Journal of Economic Literature*, **14**, 827–55.

Bliss, C. J. (1980) 'Optimal tariffs to raise revenue', in G. A. Hughes and G. M. Heal (eds.), *Public Policy and the Tax System*, London, Allen & Unwin.

Bloomfield, A. T. (1963) *Short-term International Capital Movements under the Pre-1914 Gold Standard*, Princeton Studies in International Finance, no. 11.

Brander, J. A. and Krugman, P. (1983) 'A reciprocal dumping model of international trade', *Journal of International Economics*, **13**, 313–21.

Brander, J. A. and Spencer, B. J. (1984) 'Trade warfare: tariffs and cartels', *Journal of International Economics*, **16**, 227–42.

Branson, W. H. (1968) *Financial Capital Flows in the United States Balance of Payments*, Amsterdam: North Holland.

Braudel, F. (1984) *Civilization and Capitalism: 15th–18th century*, 3 vols., London: Harper & Row; first published in French in 1979.

Brecher, R. A. and Diaz Alejandro, C. (1977) 'Tariffs, foreign capital, and immiserizing growth', *Journal of International Economics*, **14**, 317–22.

Brock, W. A and Magee, S. P. (1978) 'The economics of special interest politics: the case of the tariff', *American Economic Review*, **68**, 246–50.

Bruno, M. (1972) 'Domestic resource cost and effective protection: clarification and synthesis', *Journal of Political Economy*, **80**, 16–33.

Bruno, M. and Sachs, J. G. (1985) *Economics of Worldwide Stagflation*, Cambridge, Mass.: Harvard University Press.

Bryant, R. C., Holtham, G. and Hooper, P. (1988) *External Deficits and the Dollar*, Washington: Brookings Institution.

Cable, V. and Rebelo, I. (1980) 'Britain's pattern of specialisation in manufactured goods with developing countries and trade protection', World Bank Staff Working Paper, no. 425, Washington: World Bank.

Cassell, G. (1922) *Money and Foreign Exchange after 1914*, London: Constable.

Caves, R. E. (1979) 'International cartels and monopolies in international trade', in R. Dornbusch and J. Frenkel (eds.), *International Economic Policy*, Baltimore: Johns Hopkins University Press.

Caves, R. E. and Johnson, H. G. (eds.) (1968) *Readings in International Economics*, Homewood, Ill.: Irwin.

Chacholiades, M. (1970) 'Increasing returns and the theory of comparative advantage', *Southern Economic Journal*, **37**, 157–62.

Chenery, H. B. and Bruno, M. (1962) 'Development alternatives in an open economy: the case of Israel', *Economic Journal*, **72**, 79–103; reprinted with modifications as chapter 8 in H. B. Chenery (1979) *Structural Change and Development Policy*, New York: Oxford University Press.

Chipman, J. S. (1965) 'A survey of the theory of international trade: part 2', *Econometrica*, **33**, 685–760.

Chipman, J. S. (1966) 'A survey of the theory of international trade: part 3', *Econometrica*, **34**, 18–76.

Choksi, A. M. and Papageorgiou, D. (1986) *Economic Liberalization in Developing Countries*, Oxford: Blackwell.

Cline, W. R. (1984) *International Debt: Systemic risk and policy response*, Washington: Institute for International Economics.

Cline, W. R. and Delgado, E. (1978) *Economic Integration in Central America*, Washington, Brookings Institution.

Cohen, B. J. (1981) in association with F. Basagni, *Banks and the Balance of Payments*, Montclair, NJ: Allenheld Osmun.

Committee on the Study of Economic and Monetary Union (1989) *Report on Economic and Monetary Union in the European Community* (Delors Report), Brussels: Office for Official Publications in the European Community.

Cooper, R. N. (1968) *The Economics of Interdependence: Economic policy in the Atlantic community*, New York: McGraw-Hill.

Cooper, R. N. (ed.) (1969) *International Finance: Selected readings*, London: Penguin.

Cooper, R. N. (1971) *Currency Devaluation in Developing Countries*, Princeton Essays in International Finance, no. 86.

Corden, W. M. (1960) 'The geometric representation of policies to attain internal and external balance', *Review of Economic Studies*, October; reprinted in Cooper (1969).

Corden, W. M. (1966) 'The structure of a tariff system and the effective protection rate',

Journal of Political Economy, **74**, 221–37.

Corden, W. M. (1967), 'Monopoly, tariffs and subsidies', *Economica*, **24**, 50–8.

Corden, W. M. (1971) *The Theory of Protection*, Oxford: Clarendon Press.

Corden, W. M. (1974) *Trade Policy and Economic Welfare*, Oxford: Clarendon Press.

Corden, W. M. (1975) 'The costs and consequences of protection: a survey of empirical work', in P. B. Kenen (ed.) *International Trade and Finance: Frontiers for research*, Cambridge: Cambridge University Press.

Corden, W. M. (1977) *Inflation, Exchange Rates, and the World Economy*, Oxford: Oxford University Press.

Corden, W. M. (1984) 'The normative theory of international trade', in Jones and Kenen (1984).

Cox, D. and Harris, R. (1985) 'Trade liberalisation and industrial organisation: some estimates for Canada', *Journal of Political Economy*, **93**, 115–45.

Crafts, N. F. R. (1985) *British Economic Growth During the Industrial Revolution*, Oxford: Clarendon Press.

Crowther, G. (1957) *An Outline of Money*, London: Nelson.

Cuddington, J. and Smith, G. W. (1985) *International Debt and the Developing Countries*, Washington: World Bank.

Curzon, G. (1965) *Multilateral Commercial Diplomacy*, London: Michael Joseph.

Dam, K. W. (1970) *The GATT: Law and international organisation*, Chicago: University of Chicago Press.

Deane, P. and Cole, W. A. (1969) *British Economic Growth, 1688–1959*, Cambridge: Cambridge University Press.

Deardorff, A. V. (1982) 'The general validity of the Heckscher–Ohlin theorem', *American Economic Review*, **72**, 683–94.

Deardorff, A. V. (1984) 'Testing trade theories and predicting trade flows', in Jones and Kenen (1984).

De Grauwe, P. and Vansanten, K. (1990) *Deterministic Chaos in the Foreign Exchange Market*, CEPR Discussion Paper, no. 370.

Debreu, G. (1959) *Theory of Value*, London: Chapman & Hall.

Denison, E. F. (1967) *Why Growth Rates Differ*, Washington: Brookings Institution.

de Soto, H. (1989), *The Other Path: The invisible revolution in the Third World*, London: Tauris.

Diaz Alejandro, C. (1975) 'Trade policies and economic development', in P. B. Kenen (ed.), *International Trade and Finance*, Cambridge: Cambridge University Press.

Diaz Alejandro, C. (1984) 'Latin American debt: I don't think we are in Kansas anymore', *Brookings Papers on Economic Activity*, 2.

Dixit, A. K. (1984) 'International trade policy for oligopolistic industries', *Economic Journal*, **94**, 1–16; reprinted in Bhagwati (1987).

Dixit, A. K. and Norman, V. (1980) *Theory of International Trade*, Cambridge, Cambridge University Press.

Dornbusch, R. (1973) 'Devaluation, money and non-traded goods', *American Economic Review*, **63**, 871–80.

Dornbusch, R. (1976) 'Expectations and exchange rate dynamics', *Journal of Political Economy*, **84**, 1161–76.

Dornbusch, R. (1980) *Open Economy Macroeconomics*, New York: Basic Books.

Eaton, J. and Kierzkowski, H. (1984) 'Oligopolistic competition, product variety and international trade', in H. Kierzkowski (ed.), *Monopolistic Competition and International Trade*, Oxford: Oxford University Press.

Economic Commission for Latin America (1950) *The Economic Development of Latin*

America and its Principal Problems, New York: United Nations Economic Commission for Latin America.

Edgren, G., Faxén, K. O. and Odhner, C. E. (1969) 'Wages, growth and the distribution of income', *Swedish Journal of Economics*, September.

Eichengreen, B. (1990) *Elusive Stability: Essays in the theory of international finance, 1919–39*, Cambridge: Cambridge University Press.

Ellis, H. S. and Metzler, L. A. (eds.) (1949) *Readings in the Theory of International Trade*, Philadelphia: Blakiston.

Ethier, W. J. (1984) 'Higher dimensional issues in trade theory', in Jones and Kenen (1984).

Eulenberg, F. (1929) *Aussenhandel und Aussenhandelspolitik*, Tübingen: Grundriss der Sozial-
ökonomik, VIII, Abteilung.

Falvey, R. E. (1981) 'Commercial policy and intra-industry trade', *Journal of International Economics*, **11**, 495–511.

Feinberg, R. E. (1986) *Between Two Worlds: The World Bank's next decade*, Washington: Overseas Development Council.

Feldstein, M. S. (1988) 'Thinking about international economic coordination', *Journal of Economic Perspectives*, **2**, 3–13.

Ffrench-Davis, R. (ed.) (1983) *Las Relaciones Financieras Externas*, Mexico City: Fondo de Cultura Económica.

Findlay, R. (1981) 'The fundamental determinants of the terms of trade', in S. Grassman and E. Lundberg (eds.), *The World Economic Order: Past and prospects*, London: Macmillan.

Findlay, R. (1984) 'Growth and development in trade models', in Jones and Kenen (1984).

Finger, J. M. (1975) 'Trade overlap and intra-industry trade', *Economic Inquiry*, **13**, 581–9.

Finger, J. M. and Olechowski, A. (1986) *The Uruguay Round: A handbook on the multilateral trade negotations*, Washington: World Bank.

Fischer, S. and Frenkel, J. (1972) 'Investment, the two-sector model, and trade in debt and capital goods', *Journal of International Economics*, **2**, 211–33.

Fleming, J. M. (1962) 'Domestic financial policies under fixed and floating exchange rates', *IMF Staff Papers*, **9**, 369–79.

Fleming, J. M. (1972) *Essays in International Economics*, London: Allen & Unwin.

Ford, A. G. (1962) *The Gold Standard 1880–1916: Britain and Argentina*, Oxford: Clarendon Press.

Frankel, J. A. and Froot, K. A. (1990) 'Chartists, fundamentalists, and trading in the foreign exchange market', *American Economic Review*, **80**, 181–5.

Frenkel, J. A. (1981) 'Flexible exchange rates, prices and the role of "News"', *Journal of Political Economy*, **89**, 665–705.

Frenkel, J. A. (1987) 'The international monetary system: should it be reformed?', *American Economic Review*, **77**, 133–53.

Frenkel, J. A., Gylfason, T. and Helliwell, J. E. (1980) 'Synthesis of monetary and Keynesian approaches to short-run balance-of-payments theory', *Economic Journal*, **90**, 582–92.

Frenkel, J. A. and Johnson, H. G. (eds.) (1976) *The Monetary Approach to the Balance of Payments*, London: Allen & Unwin.

Frenkel, J. A. and Mussa, M. (1985) 'Asset markets, exchange rates and the balance of payments', in Jones and Kenen (1985).

Frey, B. (1984) *International Political Economics*, Oxford: Martin Robertson.

Fried, E. R. and Schultze, C. L. (eds.) (1975) *Higher Oil Prices and the World Economy*, Washington: Brookings Institution.

Friedman, M. (1953) *Essays in Positive Economics*, Chicago: University of Chicago Press.

Friedman, M. (1969) *The Optimum Quantity of Money*, London: Macmillan.

Fukuyama, F. (1989) 'The end of history?', *The Public Interest*, summer.

Gardner, R. N. (1969) *Sterling–Dollar Diplomacy*, 2nd edn, London: McGraw-Hill.

Gerschenkron, A. (1962) *Economic Backwardness in Historical Perspective*, Cambridge, Mass.: Harvard University Press.

Giavazzi, F. and Giovannini, A. (1989a) *Can the EMS be Exported? Lessons from ten years of monetary cooperation in Europe*, CEPR Discussion Paper, no. 285.

Giavazzi, F. and Giovannini, A. (1989b) *Limiting Exchange Rate Flexibility: The European Monetary System*, London: MIT Press.

Giavazzi, F., Micossi, S. and Miller, M. (eds.) (1988) *The European Monetary System*, Cambridge: Cambridge University Press.

Greenaway, D. (1982) 'Identifying the gains from pure intra-industry exchange', *Journal of Economic Studies*, **9**, 40–56.

Greenaway, D. (1983) *International Trade Policy: From tariffs to the new protectionism*, London: Macmillan.

Greenaway, D. (ed.) (1985) *Current Issues in International Trade*, London: Macmillan.

Greenaway, D. (ed.) (1988) *Economic Development and International Trade*, London: Macmillan.

Greenaway, D. and Hindley, B. (1985) *What Britain Pays for Voluntary Export Restraints*, London: Trade Policy Research Centre.

Greenaway, D., Hyclak, T. and Thornton, R. (eds.) (1989) *Economic Aspects of Regional Trading Arrangements*, Brighton: Wheatsheaf.

Greenaway, D. and Milner, C. R. (1986) *The Economics of Intra-Industry Trade*, London: Blackwell.

Greenaway, D. and Milner, C. R. (1987a) 'Intra-industry trade: current perspectives and unresolved issues', *Weltwirtschaftliches Archiv*, **123**, 39–57.

Greenaway, D. and Milner, C. R. (1987b) 'Trade theory and less developed countries' in N. Gemmell (ed.), *Surveys in Development Economics*, Oxford: Blackwell.

Greenaway, D. and Milner, C. R. (1990) 'South–South trade: theory, evidence and policy', *World Bank Research Observer*, **5**, 47–68.

Greenaway, D. and Milner, C. R. (1991) *Trade Policy and Development: A manual and policy analysis*, London: Macmillan.

Greenaway, D. and Nam, C. H. (1988) 'Industrialisation and macroeconomic performance in developing countries under alternative liberalisation scenarios', *Kyklos*, **41**, 419–35.

Gros, D. and Thygesen, N. (1989) *The EMS: Achievements, current issues and directions for the future*, Brussels: Centre for European Policy Studies.

Grubel, H. G. and Lloyd, P. J. (1975) *Intra-Industry Trade*, London: Macmillan.

Gylfason, T. and Risegar, O. (1984) 'Does devaluation improve the current account?', *European Economic Review*, **51**, 129–39.

Haberler, G. (1937) *The Theory of International Trade*, New York: Macmillan.

Haberler, G. (1949) 'The market for foreign exchange and the stability of the balance of payments', *Kyklos*, **3**, 193–218; reprinted in Cooper (1969).

Haberler, G. (1990) 'Strategic trade policy and the new international economics: a critical analysis', in Jones and Krueger (1990).

Halm, G. (1965) *The Band Proposal*, Princeton Special Papers in International Economics, no. 6.

Hamilton, C. (1985) 'Economic aspects of voluntary export restraints', in Greenaway (1985).

Harberger, A. C. (1990) 'Reflections on uniform taxation', in Jones and Krueger (1990).

Harrod, R. F. (1951) *The Life of Jon Maynard Keynes*, London: Macmillan.

Hartwell, R. M. (1971) *The Industrial Revolution and Economic Growth*, London: Methuen.

Havrylyshyn, O. and I. Alikhani (1982) 'Is there cause for export optimism? An enquiry into the existence of a second generation of successful exporters', *Weltwirtschaftliches Archiv*,

118, 651–63.

Heller, H. R. and Rhomberg, R. R. (eds.) (1977) *The Monetary Approach to the Balance of Payments*, Washington: International Monetary Fund.

Helpman, E. (1984) 'Increasing returns, imperfect markets and trade theory', in Jones and Kenen (1984).

Helpman, E. (1990) *Monopolistic Competition in Trade Theory*, Princeton Special Papers in International Finance, no. 16.

Helpman, E. and Krugman, P. (1985) *Market Structure and Foreign Trade*, Brighton: Wheatsheaf.

Helpman, E. and Razin, A. (1978) *A Theory of International Trade under Uncertainty*, New York: Academic Press.

Herin, J., Lindbeck, A. and Myhrman, J. (eds.) (1977) *Flexible Exchange Rates and Stabilization Policy*, Boulder: Westview Press.

Herring, R. J. and Marston, R. C. (1977) *National Monetary Policies and International Financial Markets*, Amsterdam: North Holland.

Hirsch, S. (1975) 'The product cycle model of international trade: a multi-country cross-section analysis', *Oxford Bulletin of Economics and Statistics*, **37**, 305–17.

Hocking, R. (1980) 'Trade in motor cars between major European producers', *Economic Journal*, **90**, 504–19.

Horsefield, J. K. (1969) *The International Monetary Fund 1945–65*, Washington: International Monetary Fund.

Houthakker, H. S. and Magee, S. P. (1969) 'Income and price elasticities in world trade', *Review of Economics and Statistics*, **51**, 111–125.

Hufbauer, G. C. (1966) *Synthetic Materials and the Theory of International Trade*, London: Duckworth.

Hufbauer, G. C. (1970) 'The impact of national characteristics and technology on the commodity composition of trade in manufactured goods' in R. Vernon, (ed.), *The Technology Factor in International Trade*, New York: Columbia University Press.

Hufbauer, G. C. and Chilas, J. G. (1974) 'Specialisation by industrial countries: extent and consequences', in H. Giersch (ed.), *The International Division of Labour: Problems and perspectives*, Tübingen: J. C. B. Mohr.

Hume, D. (1752) 'Of the balance of trade', in *Essays, Moral, Political and Literary*, vol. 1, London: Longmans Green, 1898; reprinted in Cooper (1969).

International Monetary Fund (1987) *Final Report of the Working Party on the Statistical Discrepancy in World Current Account Balances*, Washington: International Monetary Fund.

Isard, P. (1977) 'How far can we push the law of one price?', *American Economic Review*, **68**, 942–8.

Iversen, C. (1936) *Aspects of the Theory of International Capital Movements*, Copenhagen: Levin & Munksgaard.

Johnson, E. and Moggridge, D. (various years) *The Collected Writings of John Maynard Keynes*, 30 vols., London: Macmillan.

Johnson, H. G. (1954) 'Increasing productivity, income–price trends, and the trade balance', *Economic Journal*, **64**, 462–85; reprinted in Johnson (1961).

Johnson, H. G. (1955) 'Economic expansion and international trade', *Manchester School*, **23**, 91–112.

Johnson, H. G. (1956) 'The transfer problem and exchange stability', *Journal of Political Economy*, **64**, 212–25.

Johnson, H. G. (1958) *International Trade and Economic Growth*, London: Unwin.

Johnson, H. G. (1965a) 'The theory of tariff structure, with special reference to world trade and development', in H. G. Johnson and P. B. Kenen (eds.), *Trade and Development*, Geneva: Librairie Droz.

Johnson, H. G. (1965b) 'Optimal trade interventions in the presence of domestic distortions', in R. E. Baldwin (ed.), *Trade, Growth and the Balance of Payments: Essays in honour of Gottfried Haberler*, New York: Rand McNally; reprinted in Bhagwati (1987).

Johnson, H. G. (1967) 'The possibility of income losses from increased efficiency or factor accumulation in the presence of tariffs', *Economic Journal*, **77**, 151–4.

Johnson, H. G. (1971) *Aspects of the Theory of Tariffs*, London: Allen & Unwin.

Jones, E. L. (1981) *The European Miracle*, Cambridge: Cambridge University Press.

Jones, E. L. (1988) *Growth Recurring: Economic change in world history*, Oxford: Clarendon Press.

Jones, K. (1984) 'The political economy of voluntary export restraint agreements', *Kyklos*, **37**, 82–101.

Jones, R. W. (1971) 'A three-factor model in theory, trade and history', in J. N. Bhagwati *et al.* (eds.), *Trade, Balance of Payments and Growth: Essays in honour of C. P. Kindleberger*, Amsterdam: North Holland.

Jones, R. W. (1979) *Essays in Trade Theory*, Amsterdam: North Holland.

Jones, R. W. and Kenen, P. B. (eds.) (1984) *Handbook of International Economics*, vol. 1, Amsterdam: North Holland.

Jones, R. W. and Kenen, P. B. (eds.) (1985) *Handbook of International Economics*, vol. 2, Amsterdam: North Holland.

Jones, R. W. and Krueger, A. O. (eds.) (1990) *The Political Economy of International Trade*, London: Blackwell.

Jones, R. W. and Neary, J. P. (1984) 'The positive theory of international trade', in Jones and Kenen (1984).

Kaletsky, A. (1985) *The Costs of Default*, New York: Priority Press for the Twentieth-Century Fund.

Kenen, P. B. (1989) *International Economics*, Englewood Cliffs, N.J.: Prentice Hall.

Kenen, P. B. (1990) 'Organizing debt relief: the need for a new institution', *Journal of Economic Perspectives*, **4**, 7–18.

Keynes, J. M. (1923) *A Tract on Monetary Reform*, London: Macmillan; reprinted as vol. IV in Johnson and Moggridge (various years).

Keynes, J. M. (1929) 'The German transfer problem', *Economic Journal*, **39**, 1–7; reprinted as vol. XVIII in Johnson and Moggridge (various years).

Keynes, J. M. (1936) *The General Theory of Employment, Interest and Money*, London: Macmillan.

Kierzkowski, H. (1985) 'Models of international trade in differentiated goods', in Greenaway (1985).

Kindleberger, C. P. (1968) *International Economics*, 4th edn, Homewood, Ill.: Irwin.

Kirkpatrick, C. (1987) 'Trade policy and industrialisation in LDCs', in N. Gemmell (ed.), *Surveys in Development Economics*, Oxford: Blackwell.

Kouri, P. J. K. and Porter, M. G. (1974) 'International capital flows and portfolio equilibrium', *Journal of Political Economy*, **82**, 443–67.

Krause, L. B. and Salant, W. (eds.) (1977) *Worldwide Inflation: Theory and recent experience*, Washington: Brookings Institution.

Krauss, M. B. (ed.) (1973) *The Economics of Integration*, London: Allen & Unwin.

Krauss, M. B. (1979) *The New Protectionism, the Welfare State and International Trade*, Oxford: Blackwell.

Kravis, I. B. (1983) *Towards an Explanation of National Price Levels*, Princeton Studies in International Finance, no. 52.

Kravis, I. B. (1984) 'Comparative studies of national incomes and prices', *Journal of Economic Literature*, **22**, 1–39.

Kravis, I. B. and Lipsey, R. E. (1978) 'Price behaviour in the light of balance of payments theories', *Journal of International Economics*, **8**, 193–246.

Krueger, A. O. (1972) 'Evaluating restrictionist trade regimes: theory and measurement', *Journal of Political Economy*, **80**, 48–62.

Krueger, A. O. (1978) *Liberalisation Attempts and Consequences*, Cambridge, Mass.: Ballinger.

Krueger, A. O. (1984) 'Trade policies in developing countries', in Jones and Kenen (1984).

Krugman, P. (1979) 'Increasing returns, monopolistic competition and international trade', *Journal of International Economics*, **9**, 469–79; reprinted in Bhagwati (1987).

Krugman, P. (1980) 'Scale economies, product differentiation and the pattern of trade', *American Economic Review*, **70**, 950–9.

Krugman, P. (1981) 'Intra-industry specialisation and the gains from trade', *Journal of Political Economy*, **89**, 959–73.

Krugman, P. (1985) 'Is the strong dollar sustainable?', in *The US Dollar: Prospects and policy options*, Federal Reserve Bank of Kansas City.

Krugman, P. (ed.) (1986) *Strategic Trade Policy and the New International Economics*, Cambridge, Mass.: MIT Press.

Krugman, P. (1987) 'Is free trade passé?', *Journal of Economic Perspectives*, **1**, 131–44.

Krugman, P. and Taylor, L. (1978) 'Contractionary effects of devaluation', *Journal of International Economics*, **9**, 445–56.

Kuczynski, P.-P. (1988) *Latin American Debt*, London: Johns Hopkins Press for the Twentieth-Century Fund.

Kuznets, S. (1956) 'Quantitative aspects of the economic growth of nations', *Economic Development and Cultural Change*, October.

Lal, D. and Rajapatirana, S. (1987) 'Foreign trade regimes and economic growth in developing countries', *World Bank Research Observer*, **2**, 189–218.

Lancaster, K. (1980) 'Intra-industry trade under perfect monopolistic competition', *Journal of International Economics*, **10**, 151–76.

Landes, D. S. (1990) 'Why are we so rich and they so poor?', *American Economic Review*, **80**, 1–13.

Langhammer, R. J. and Sapir, A. (1987) *Economic Impact of Generalised Tariff Preferences*, London: Trade Policy Research Centre.

Lawrence, C. and Spiller, P. (1983) 'Product diversity, economies of scale and international trade', *Quarterly Journal of Economics*, **98**, 63–83.

Leamer, E. E. (1974) 'The commodity composition of international trade in manufactures: an empirical analysis', *Oxford Economic Papers*, **26**, 351–74.

Leamer, E. E. (1984) *Sources of International Comparative Advantage: Theory and evidence*, Cambridge, Mass.: MIT Press.

Leontief, W. (1953), 'Domestic production and foreign trade: the American capital position re-examined', *Proceedings of the American Philosophical Society*, **97**, 332–49.

Lerner, A. P. (1932) 'The diagrammatical representation of cost conditions in international trade', *Economica*, **12**, 346–56.

Lessard, D. R. (1981) 'Financial mechanisms for international risk sharing: issues and prospects', paper presented to the Second International Conference on Latin American and Caribbean Financial Development, Caraballeda, Venezuela, April.

Lewis, A. W. (1954) 'Economic development with unlimited supplies of labour', *Manchester School of Economic and Social Studies*, **22**, 139–91.

Lewis, W. A. (1978) *The Evolution of the International Economic Order*, Princeton: Princeton

University Press.

Lewis, W. A. (1980) 'The slowing down of the engine of growth', *American Economic Review*, **70**, 555–64.

Linder, S. B. (1961) *An Essay on Trade and Transformation*, London: John Wiley.

Lindert, P. H. (1969) *Key Currencies and Gold, 1900–13*, Princeton Studies in International Finance, no. 24.

Little, I. M. D., Scitovsky, T. and Scott, M. (1970) *Industry and Trade in Some Developing Countries*, Oxford: Oxford University Press.

Lowinger, T. C. (1971) 'The neo-factor proportions theory of international trade: an empirical investigation', *American Economic Review*, **61**, 675–81.

Lucas, R. E. (1981) *Studies in Business Cycle Theory*, London: MIT Press.

Macarro, S. (1964) 'Protection and industrialisation in Latin America', *Economic Bulletin for Latin America*, March.

Macbean, A. J. and Nguyen, D. T. (1988) 'Export instability and growth performance', in Greenaway (1988).

McCloskey, D. N. and Zecher, J. R. (1976) 'How the gold standard really worked', in Frenkel and Johnson (1976).

MacDougall, G. D. A. (1951) 'British and American exports: a study suggested by the theory of comparative costs, part I', *Economic Journal*, **61**, 697–724.

MacDougall, G. D. A. (1952) 'British and American exports: a study suggested by the theory of comparative costs, part II', *Economic Journal*, **62**, 487–521.

MacDougall, G. D. A. (1960) 'The benefits and costs of private investment from abroad', *Economic Record*, March.

Machlup, F. (1939) 'The theory of foreign exchanges', *Economica*, **6**, 375–97; reprinted in Ellis and Metzler (1949).

Machlup, F. (1943) *International Trade and the National Income Multiplier*, Philadelphia: Blakiston.

Machlup, F. (1955) 'Relative prices and aggregate spending in the analysis of devaluation', *American Economic Review*, **65**, 255–78.

Machlup, F. and Malkiel, B. (eds.) (1964) *International Monetary Arrangements: The problem of choice*, Princeton: International Finance Section.

McKenzie, G. W. (1976) *The Economics of the Euro-currency System*, London: Macmillan.

McKinnon, R. I. (1963) 'A theory of optimum currency areas', *American Economic Review*, **53**, 717–25.

McKinnon, R. I. (1964) 'Foreign exchange constraints in economic development and efficient aid allocation', *Economic Journal*, **74**, 388–409.

McKinnon, R. I. (1971) *Monetary Theory and Controlled Flexibility in the Foreign Exchanges*, Princeton Essays in International Finance, no. 84.

McKinnon, R. I. (1977) *The Eurocurrency Market*, Princeton Essays in International Finance, no. 125.

McKinnon, R. I. (1988) 'Monetary and exchange rate policies for international financial stability: a proposal', *Journal of Economic Perspectives*, **2**, 83–103.

Makin, J. H. (1990) 'International imbalance: the role of exchange rates', in R. O'Brien and I. Iversen (eds.), *Finance and the International Economy*, vol. 3, Oxford: Oxford University Press for the AMEX Bank Review.

Malmgren, H. (1977) *International Order for Public Subsidies*, London: Trade Policy Research Centre.

Markowitz, H. (1952) 'Portfolio selection', *Journal of Finance*, **7**, 77–91.

Marris, S. (1987) *Deficits and the Dollar: The world economy at risk*, revised edn, Washington: Institute for International Economics.

Masson, P. R. and Tryon, R. W. (1990) 'Macroeconomic effects of projected population ageing in industrial countries', IMF Working Paper, 90/5.

Mathews, J. T. (1990) *Preserving the Global Environment: The challenge of shared leadershp*, New York: Norton.

Meade, J. E. (1951) *The Theory of International Economic Policy, Vol. I: The balance of payments*, London: Oxford University Press.

Meade, J. E. (1955a) 'The case for variable exchange rates', *Three Banks Review*, September

Meade, J. E. (1955b) *The Theory of Customs Unions*, Amsterdam: North Holland.

Meadows, D. H., Meadows, D. L., Randers, J. and Behrens, W. W. (1972) *The Limits to Growth*, New York: Universe Books.

Meese, R. and Rogoff, K. (1983) 'Empirical exchange rate models of the 1970s: do they fit out of sample?', *Journal of International Economics*, **14**, 3–24.

Meier, G. (1973) *Problems of Trade Policy*, Oxford: Oxford University Press.

Melvin, J. R. (1969) 'Increasing returns to scale as a determinant of trade', *Canadian Journal of Economics and Political Science*, **2**, 389–402.

Melvin, J. R. and Warne, R. D. (1973) 'Monopoly and the theory of international trade', *Journal of International Economics*, **3**, 117–34.

Metzler, L. A. (1942) 'The transfer problem reconsidered', *Journal of Political Economy*, **50**, 397–414.

Metzler, L. A. and Laursen, S. (1950) 'Flexible exchange rates and the theory of employment', *Review of Economics and Statistics*, **32**, 281–99.

Milner, C. R. (1985) 'Empirical analyses of the costs of protection', in Greenaway (1985).

Milner, C. R. (ed.) (1990) *Export Promotion Strategies: Theory and Evidence from Developing Countries*, Brighton: Wheatsheaf.

Mosley, P., Harrigan, J . and Toye, J. (1990) *Aid and Power: The World Bank and policy-based lending*, 2 vols., London: Routledge.

Mueller, D. C. (1979) *Public Choice*, Cambridge: Cambridge University Press.

Mundell, R. A. (1961a) 'Flexible exchange rates and employment policy', *Canadian Journal of Economic and Political Science*, **27**, 509–17.

Mundell, R. A. (1961b) 'A theory of optimum currency areas', *American Economic Review*, **51**, 509–17; reprinted as chapter 12 in Mundell (1968).

Mundell, R. A. (1962) 'The appropriate use of monetary and fiscal policy under fixed exchange rates', *IMF Staff Papers*, March; reprinted as chapter 16 in Mundell (1968).

Mundell, R. A. (1968) *International Economics*, London: Macmillan.

Murray, T. (1977) *Trade Preferences in Developing Countries*, New York: John Wiley.

Murray, T., Schmidt, W. and Walter, I. (1983) 'On the equivalence of import quotas and voluntary export restraints', *Journal of International Economics*, **14**, 191–4.

Musgrave, R. A. (1987) 'Tax reform in developing countries', in Newbery and Stern (1987).

Muth, J. F. (1961) 'Rational expectations and the theory of price movements', *Econometrica*, **29**, 315–35.

Neary, J. P. (1978) 'Short-run capital specificity and the pure theory of international trade', *Economic Journal*, **88**, 488–510; reprinted in Bhagwati (1987).

Neary, J. P. (1982) 'Inter sectoral capital mobility, wage stickiness and the case for adjustment assistance', in Bhagwati (1982).

Neary, J. P. (1985) 'Theory and policy of adjustment in an open economy', in Greenaway (1985).

Newbery, M. G. D. and Stern, N. (eds.) (1987) *Tax Theory for Developing Countries*, Oxford: Oxford University Press.

Newbery, M. G. D. and Stigitz, J. E. (1981) *The Theory of Commodity Price Stabilization*, Oxford: Oxford University Press.

Nordhaus, W. D. (1990) 'Greenhouse economics: count before you leap', *The Economist*, 7 July, 21–4.

Nurkse, R. (1944) *International Currency Experience: Lessons of the inter-war period*, New York: Columbia University Press for the League of Nations.

Nurkse, R. (1959) *Patterns of Trade and Development*, Oxford: Oxford University Press.

OECD (1979) *OECD and the Environment*, Paris: OECD.

Officer, L. H. (1976) 'The purchasing power parity theory of exchange rates', *IMF Staff Papers*, **23**, 1–61.

Ohlin, B. (1929) 'The reparation problem: a discussion', *Economic Journal*, **39**, 172–3.

Ohlin, B. (1933) *International and Inter-regional Trade*, Cambridge, Mass.: Harvard University Press.

Oudiz, G. and Sachs, J. (1984) 'Macroeconomic policies among the industrial countries', *Brookings Papers on Economic Activity*, 1.

Polak, J. J. (1957) 'Monetary analysis of income formation', *IMF Staff Papers*, **4**, 1–50.

Pomery, J. (1984) 'Uncertainty in trade models', in Jones and Kenen (1984).

Pomfret, R. (1979) 'Intra-industry trade in intra-regional and international trade', in H. Giersch (ed.), *On the Economics of Intra-Industry Trade*, Tübingen, J. C. B. Mohr.

Pomfret, R. (1988) *Unequal Trade: The economics of discriminatory international trade policies*, Oxford: Blackwell.

Posner, M. W. (1961) 'International trade and technical change', *Oxford Economic Papers*, **13**, 323–41.

Rhomberg, R. R. (1976) 'Indices of effective exchange rates', *IMF Staff Papers*, March.

Ricardo, D. (1817) *On the Principles of Political Economy and Taxation*, Harmondsworth: Penguin, 1971.

Robinson, J. (1937) 'The foreign exchanges', in J. Robinson, *Essays in the Theory of Employment*, Oxford: Blackwell; reprinted in Ellis and Metzler (1949).

Robson, P. (1987) *The Economics of International Integration*, London: Allen & Unwin.

Rosenstein-Rodan, P. (1943) 'Problems of industrialisation in Eastern and Southeastern Europe', *Economic Journal*, **53**, 202–11.

Rostow, W. W. (1958) *The Stages of Economic Growth: A non-communist manifesto*, Cambridge: Cambridge University Press.

Rybczynski, T. M. (1955) 'Factor endowments and relative commodity prices', *Economica*, **22**, 336–41.

Sachs, J. (1980) 'Wages, flexible exchange rates, and macroeconomic policy', *Quarterly Journal of Economics*, **94**, 731–47.

Sachs, J. (ed.) (1989) *Developing Country Debt and Economic Performance*, Chicago: University of Chicago Press.

Salter, W. E. G. (1959) 'Internal and external balance: the role of price and expenditure effects', *Economic Record*, **35**, 226–38.

Samuelson, P. A. (1948) 'International trade and the equalisation of factor prices', *Economic Journal*, **58**, 163–84.

Samuelson, P. A. (1949) 'International factor-price equalisation once again', *Economic Journal*, **59**, 181–97.

Samuelson, P. A. (1952) 'The transfer problem and transfer costs: the terms of trade when impediments are absent', *Economic Journal*, **62**, 278–304.

Samuelson, P. A. (1971) 'An exact Hume–Ricardo–Marshall model of international trade', *Journal of International Economics*, **1**, 1–18.

Sanyal, K. and Jones, R. W. (1982) 'The theory of trade in middle products', *American Economic Review*, **72**, 16–31.

Sapsford, D. (1988) 'The debate over trends in the terms of trade', in Greenaway (1988).

Sargent, T. and Wallace, N. (1975) 'Rational expectations, the optimal monetary instrument, and the optimal money supply rule', *Journal of Political Economy*, **83**, 241–54.

Shaked, A. and Sutton, J. (1983) 'Natural oligopolies', *Econometrica*, **51**, 1469–83.

Siebert, H. (1989) 'The half and the full debt cycle', *Weltwirtschaftliches Archiv*, **125**, 217–229.

Sinn, S. (1990) *Net External Asset Positions of 145 Countries: Data, estimation and interpretation*, Kiel: Institut für Weltwirtschaft.

Smith, A. (1776) *An Enquiry into the Nature and Causes of the Wealth of Nations*, Harmondsworth: Penguin, 1982.

Solomon, R. (1982) *The International Monetary System: An insider's view*, 2nd edn, London: Harper & Row.

Stern, N. (1962) 'British and American productivity and comparative costs in international trade', *Oxford Economic Papers*, **14**, 275–92.

Stern, N. (1984) 'Optimal taxation and tax policy', *IMF Staff Papers*, **31**, 339–78.

Stern, R. M. (1975) 'Testing trade theories', in P. B. Kenen (ed.), *International Trade and Finance: Frontiers for research*, Cambridge: Cambridge University Press.

Stern R. M. and Maskus, K. F. (1981) 'Determinants of the structure of US foreign trade, 1958–76', *Journal of International Economics*, **11**, 207–24.

Stiglitz, J. E. (ed.) (1966) *The Collected Works of Paul A. Samuelson*, Cambridge, Mass: Harvard University Press.

Stolper, W. F. and Samuelson, P. A (1941) 'Protection and real wages', *Review of Economic Studies*, **9**, 58–73.

Summers, R. and Heston, A. (1988) 'A new set of international comparisons of real product and price level estimates for 130 countries, 1950–1985', *Review of Income and Wealth*, **34**, 1–25.

Swan, T. (1960) 'Economic control in a dependent economy', *Economic Record*, March.

Swoboda, A. K. (1978) 'Gold, dollars, Euro-dollars and the world money stock under fixed exchange rates', *American Economic Review*, **68**, 625–42.

Takacs, W. (1978) 'The non-equivalence of tariffs, import quotas and voluntary export restraints', *Journal of International Economics*, **8**, 565–73.

Tharakan, P. K. M. (1975) 'Empirical analyses of the commodity composition of trade', in Greenaway (1985).

Tobin, J. (1958) 'Liquidity preference as behaviour towards risk', *Review of Economic Studies*, **25**, 65–85.

Tower, E. and Willett, T. D. (1976) *The Theory of Optimum Currency Areas and Exchange Rate Flexibility*, Princeton Special Papers in International Economics, no. 11.

Triffin, R. (1960) *Gold and the Dollar Crisis*, New Haven: Yale University Press.

Triffin, R. (1964) *The Evolution of the International Monetary System: Historical reappraisal and future perspectives*, Princeton Studies in International Finance, no. 12.

Tsiang, S. C. (1961) 'The role of money in trade-balance stability: synthesis of the elasticity and absorption approaches', *American Economic Review*, **51**, 912–36; reprinted in Caves and Johnson (1968) and Cooper (1969).

Tyler, W. G. (1972) 'Trade in manufactures and labour skill content: the Brazilian case', *Economia Internazionale*, **25**, 314–34.

Vanek, J. (1968) 'The factor proportions theory: the n-factor case', *Kyklos*, **4**, 749–56.

Verdoorn, P. J. (1960) 'The intra-block trade of Benelux', in E. A. G. Robinson (ed.), *The Economic Consequences of the Size of Nations*, London: Macmillan.

Vernon, R. (1966) 'International investment and international trade in the product cycle', *Quarterly Journal of Economics*, **80**, 121–5.

Viner, J. (1950) *The Customs Union Issue*, New York: Carnegie Endowment.

Warr, P. G. (1989) 'Export processing zones: the economics of enclave manufacturing', *World*

Bank Research Observer, **4**, 65–88.

Williamson, J. (1977) *The Failure of World Monetary Reform 1971–74*, London: Nelson.

Williamson, J. (1981) *Exchange Rate Rules*, London: Macmillan.

Williamson, J. (1982) 'A survey of the emergent literature on the optimal peg', *Journal of Development Economics*, **11**, 39–61.

Williamson, J. (1985) *The Exchange Rate System*, revised edn, Washington: Institute for International Economics.

Williamson, J. (1989) *Voluntary Approaches to Debt Relief*, revised edn, Washington: Institute for International Economics.

Williamson, J. and Miller, M (1987) *Targets and Indicators: A blueprint for the international coordination of economic policy*, Washington: Institute for International Economics.

Wonnacott, P. and Wonnacott, R. (1967) *Free Trade between the United States and Canada: The potential economic effects*, Cambridge, Mass.: Harvard University Press.

World Bank (1988) *Report on Adjustment Lending*, no. R88–199, Washington: World Bank.

World Product and Income: International comparisons of real gross product (1982) Baltimore: Johns Hopkins University Press for the World Bank.

Wrightsman, D. (1970) 'IS, LM and external equilibrium', *American Economic Review*, **60**, 203–8.

Yeager, L. B. (1976) *International Monetary Relations: Theory, History, and Policy*, 2nd edn, New York: Harper & Row.

Young, A. A. (1928) 'Increasing returns and economic progress', *Economic Journal*, **38**, 527–42.

Notation

The notation used is in most cases standard throughout the book, although it can be seen that a few letters serve double duty, often for closely related concepts. As far as possible symbols have been chosen to conform with customary usage.

A	Absorption
B	Base money
C	Consumption
D	Demand; domestic credit
D_1	Central bank component of domestic credit.
D_2	Commercial bank component of domestic credit
E	Equilibrium
F	Foreign liabilities (usually); foreign assets (on occasion)
G	Government expenditure
H	Money supply
K	Capital stock
L	Labour
M	Importable good; imports
N	Non-traded good
O	Origin
P	Production point
PPP	Purchasing power parity
Q	Quantity
R	Reserves
S	Savings
T	Tax revenue
TB	Trade balance, current account balance
U	Our country, 'us'; unemployment
W	The other (large) country; the rest of the world
X	Exportable good; exports
Y	Output; income, nominal or real, depending on context
c	Marginal propensity to consume

d	Differential
e	Exchange rate (units of domestic currency per unit of foreign exchange)
f	Forward exchange rate
g	Rate of growth; fiscal stimulus
i	Nominal interest rate
m	Marginal propensity to import
n	$1 \ldots n$, the number of something
p	Prices; general price level
q	Quantity
r	Real interest rate
s	Marginal propensity to save
t	Time when subscript; tariff elsewhere
w	Nominal wage rate
y	Output per capita
ε	Elasticity of supply
ζ	Capital inflow/income ratio
η	Elasticity of demand
κ	Money multiplier
λ	Rate of population growth
π	Purchasing power parity, PPP
ρ	Rate of productivity growth
σ	Standard deviation
ϕ	Reserve ratio of commercial banking system
*	Foreign variables (for example, $Y^* =$ income in W)
$\cdot$	Rate of change (for example, $\dot{Y} = dY/dt$)
$\char`^$	Rate of growth (for example, $\hat{Y} = \dot{Y}/Y$)
the dollar:	country W's currency
the peso:	country U's currency

Index